Mathematics

A Revision Course for the Caribbean

Fourth Edition

Full list of books published by Nelson Thornes available on request

Certificate Mathematics

A Revision Course for the Caribbean

Fourth Edition

A. Greer
Formerly Senior Lecturer
Gloucestershire College of Technology
England

and

C. E. Layne
Formerly Principal
Harrison College, Bridgetown, Barbados

First published in 1980 by:
Stanley Thornes (Publishers) Ltd
Second edition 1986
Third edition 1994

This edition published in 2001 by:
Nelson Thornes Ltd
Delta Place
27 Bath Road
CHELTENHAM
GL53 7TH
United Kingdom.

11 / 27 26 25 24 23

A catalogue record of this is available from the British Library.

ISBN 978 0 7487 6304 7

Printed and bound in China by 1010 Printing International Ltd

Preface to the Fourth Edition

This is a revision course in mathematics intended for students studying the General Proficiency Syllabus of the Caribbean Examinations Council (CXC). The contents cover completely all the objectives in the syllabus. In order to help both students and teachers topics belonging to the General Syllabus have been marked † and special topics in the General Syllabus have been marked *. The explanations and examples are designed to help students learn mathematics with understanding and acquire the skills and knowledge necessary for solving problems.

Reference to all the basic aspects of mathematics have been included where this seemed desirable. Because this is a revision book the sections on Arithmetic, Algebra, Geometry, etc. have been dealt with separately.

A very large number of exercises, together with answers, have been included. These have been graded by the letters A, B, C and D. A indicates that the problems are fairly easy and it is expected that nearly all the students will be able to solve these. D indicates that the problems are difficult and only a few students can be expected to solve these.

Paper 1 of the examination consists of objective type questions and, in order that the student is prepared for these in the examination, Self-Tests, in an objective style, have been included at the end of most chapters. In addition two multiple choice tests of 60 items each, similar to CXC Paper 1, have been included. There are also two long answer type tests similar to CXC Paper 2. Past CXC examination papers are readily available throughout the region, and we recommend that these be used with the text for further practice.

In this edition we have included a summary and points to remember at the end of each chapter. These additions will enhance the usefulness of the text for consolidation and revision.

Some recommendations for users of the text

To the students

Remember that maths is a "doing" subject – **"I hear and I forget. I see and I remember. I do and I understand" (Chinese proverb).** You will be able to solve problems in maths by doing the exercises and not by simply reading solutions to the problems. Here then are a few hints to use as you revise:
(i)   Have paper and a pen or pencil available, and as you read through the solutions, perform the steps as they are stated.
(ii) If possible work in small groups and discuss your work and your ideas with members of your group and try to explain your approach.

To the teacher

Remember that mathematics may be viewed as one of the primary vehicles through which the educational system may develop structured thinking in students.
(i)   Encourage students to verbalize the nature of the task at hand in connection with the type of answer expected.
(ii)   Let students communicate, orally and in writing, the connection between the concepts and the vocabulary used.
(iii) Emphasize the need for "reasonableness of answers", whether it refers to the magnitude of a result or to the possibility of it.
(iv)   Encourage co-operative learning groups as a teaching/learning strategy.
(v)   Encourage students to read aloud symbolic notation, expressions and relations.

Some questions which may be used to help students understand and appreciate mathematics

1. Questions that help students make sense of maths.

    Who used a different method and got the same result?

Who got a different answer? Explain how you got it.

2. Questions to help students solve problems.
    What would happen if . . . . ?
    Do you see a pattern being formed?
    Describe it.
    Is there anything you can change that will give a different result?
    Will your method work for different numbers? Why? Why not?

3. Questions and prompts to help students gain confidence.
    Does it make sense to you?
    What would be a more reasonable result?
    How can you check your answer?
    What follows from this?
    Explain your method to the class.
    Would a diagram help you to explain?
    Is there anyone who thinks they can help?

4. Questions and prompts that promote reasoning.
    Will that method always work? How do you know?
    Could you make it easier for us to see?
    Is there a pattern? What is it?
    Can you find a shorter way?
    Are there any special numbers for which this only works?

5. Questions and prompts that help students apply mathematics to other subjects and to everyday life problems.

    Have you solved a problem like this before?
    Can you think of people who use this kind of mathematics?
    Have you ever had to use this in your science or any other class?
    Can you think of any objects that have these shapes?
    Is there any material that will help you to solve this problem?

Questions similar to the above, if well designed, should help students see themselves as problem solvers, and not just doing what someone else directs.

Try to use open-ended questions whenever possible and let them be related to real situations. They should be such that the students are forced to communicate and use their reasoning power.

Creating such problems is not an easy task. It takes time and patience. It is a good idea to work with colleagues.

This strategy should help students improve their understanding and appreciation of maths as well as build confidence and independence as they explain their thinking.

Some techniques for answering questions in the examination

It is important and necessary for you to have a plan when solving problems in mathematics. Here is such a plan.

(i)   First read the question and identify what is being asked.
      What are you required to find or to do? Whatever it is, find it and circle it. This is to ensure that you are solving for what is being asked.
(ii) Secondly, find and underline the information which you are given. Draw a picture or diagram if you can. This will let you know what you have and help you to form an equation if necessary.
(iii) Set up an equation or some system with the given information.
(iv) Is all the information necessary to solve your problem? Choose what you need and don't waste time on what is not required.
(v)   Solve the equation, work the necessary calculations, or draw the necessary figure or graph. Be sure that you are working in the correct units (e.g. you may have to change metres to centimetres, kilograms to grams, etc.).
(vi) Did you answer the question? A common error is failure to answer what is being asked.
(vii) Finally, is your answer reasonable? Check to make sure that you did not give a ridiculous answer.

Hints on answering multiple choice items

(i) Read all the instructions to the paper carefully.
(ii) Starting with the first item, read the question you are about to answer all the way through, including the answer choices. Having read all the answer choices given, make your selection.

(iii) Do not spend too much time on any one item. If you do not know an answer immediately, go on to the next item.

(iv) If you skip an item, be sure that you also skip the corresponding space on your answer sheet. Go through the whole test this way, marking answers to those items you are sure of.

(v) Now return and try those items you couldn't answer the first time. This time, read the answer choices to see if there are any that you can eliminate.

(vi) Having eliminated some choices, guess an answer from those remaining.

(vii) Look for clues to the correct answer. Pay attention to specific words such as *always*, *never*, *none*.

(viii) Work out all calculations as a check on the accuracy of your choice.

How marks are gained or lost in an examination

Contrary to popular belief, marks may be awarded for a question even though the final answer is numerically incorrect. You should therefore get into the habit of showing all your working. When a particular result is required, you must show sufficient working for the examiner to award the method mark.

Some terms used in maths examinations and their meaning

Term	Meaning
Write down or State	No reason or working is required.
Calculate, Find, Show, Solve	You should show on your answer sheet working which will make your method clear.
Hence, Deduce	Make use of what you have previously stated or proved to get the required result.
Draw, Construct	You are required to plot or draw accurately the graph or figure.
Sketch	You should show the general shape of the figure. Accurate measurements are not necessary.
Find the exact value	You should leave your answer as a fraction. Using a calculator or tables should be avoided.

For some further help with your revision, go to the following web site:
http://www.gcse.com/Maths/pre.htm

A. Greer
C.E. Layne

Contents

PREFACE TO THE FOURTH EDITION   v

1   OPERATIONS IN ARITHMETIC   1
Some definitions – commutative law –
associative law – distributive law –
sequence of arithmetical operations –
additive identity – multiplicative
identity – multiplicative property of
zero – closure – division by zero –
factors and multiples – lowest common
multiple – highest common factor –
powers of numbers – sequences –
Chapter 1 summary.

2   FRACTIONS   6
Vulgar fractions – reducing a fraction
to its lowest terms – types of fractions –
lowest common multiple – lowest
common denominator – addition of
fractions – subtraction of fractions –
combined addition and subtraction –
multiplication – cancelling – reciprocal
or multiplication inverse – division of
fractions – operations with fractions –
Chapter 2 summary.

3   THE DECIMAL SYSTEM   14
The decimal system – addition and
subtraction of decimals – multiplication
and division of decimals – long
multiplication – long division –
significant figures – the number of
significant figures in an answer – the
range in which the exact value of a
computation must lie – rough checks
for calculations – fraction to decimal
conversion – conversion of decimals to
fractions – short cuts in calculations –
Chapter 3 summary.

4   CURRENCY   24
The Caribbean system – addition and
subtraction – multiplication and division
– ready reckoners – foreign exchange.

5   RATIO AND PROPORTION   26
Proportional parts – direct proportion –
inverse proportion – Chapter 5
summary.

6   PERCENTAGES   30
Percentage of a quantity – percentage
profit and loss – discount – percentage
change – Chapter 6 summary.

7   AVERAGES   36
Averages – average speed – Chapter 7
summary.

**8   SALARIES, HOUSEHOLD BILLS,
RATES AND TAXES**   39
Payment by the hour – overtime –
commission – salaries – rates –
income tax – sales tax – hire purchase
– bank loans – electricity bills –
Chapter 8 summary.

9   SIMPLE AND COMPOUND INTEREST   47
Simple interest – compound interest –
compound interest tables –
depreciation – Chapter 9 summary.

10   INVESTMENT   53
Shares – stock.

**11   SQUARES, SQUARE ROOTS AND
RECIPROCALS**   56
Squares of numbers – square roots –
the square root of a product – the
square root of a fraction – square roots
using tables – iterative method of
finding a square root – reciprocals of
numbers – use of tables in calculations
– Chapter 11 summary.

**HOW TO ANSWER EXAMINATION
QUESTIONS 1**   62
Examination Type Questions 1.

12   DIRECTED NUMBERS   66
Introduction – positive and negative
numbers – the addition of directed
numbers – the addition of numbers
having different signs – subtraction of
directed numbers – multiplication of
directed numbers – division of directed
numbers – types of numbers –

sequences of numbers – Chapter 12 summary.

13 BASIC ALGEBRA   71
Introduction – use of symbols – substitution – powers – addition of algebraic terms – multiplication and division of algebraic quantities – brackets – operations with numbers – Chapter 13 summary.

14 FACTORISATION   77
Factorising – highest common factor – the product of two binomial expressions – factorising by grouping – factors of quadratic expressions.

15 ALGEBRAIC FUNCTIONS   82
Multiplication and division of fractions – addition and subtraction of fractions – lowest common multiple of algebraic terms – Chapter 15 summary.

16 EQUATIONS AND INEQUATIONS   87
Introduction – inequations – simple equations and inequations – solving simple equations and inequations – making expressions – construction of simple equations – Chapter 16 summary.

17 FORMULAE   95
Evaluating formulae – formulae and equations – transposition of formulae – Chapter 17 summary.

18 SIMULTANEOUS EQUATIONS   101
Elimination method in solving simultaneous equations – problems involving simultaneous equations – Chapter 18 summary.

19 QUADRATIC EQUATIONS   106
Introduction – equations of the type $ax^2 + c = 0$ – solution by factors – completing the square – solving quadratic equations by completing the square – using the formula to solve quadratic equations – equations giving rise to quadratic equations – problems involving quadratic equations – Chapter 19 summary.

20 INDICES AND LOGARITHMS   114
Laws of indices – multiplication – division – powers – negative indices – fractional indices – zero index –

numbers in standard form – logarithms – negative characteristics – anti-logarithms – rules for the use of logarithms: multiplication, division, powers, roots – use of logarithms in evaluating formulae – writing formulae in logarithmic form – solving logarithmic equations – Chapter 20 summary.

HOW TO ANSWER EXAMINATION QUESTIONS 2   122
Examination Type Questions 2.

21 MENSURATION   125
The metric system of length – the metric system of mass – SI units – units of area – areas of plane figures – errors in measurement – calculations involving numbers obtained by measurement – units of volume – units of capacity – the tetrahedron – volumes and surface areas – nets – nets of curved surfaces – time – the clock – Chapter 21 summary.

22 ORTHOGRAPHIC PROJECTION   142
First-angle projection – projection lines – hidden details – two-view drawings – pictorial drawing – plans of houses and buildings – Chapter 22 summary.

23 GRAPHS   153
Axes of reference – scales – coordinates – drawing a graph – graphs of simple equations – graphs of quadratic equations – the axis of symmetry of a parabola – solution of equations – intersecting graphs – graphical solutions of simultaneous equations – Chapter 23 summary.

24 COORDINATE GEOMETRY   165
Rectangular coordinates – the length of a line – the mid-point of a line – linear equations – the equation of a straight line – the meaning of m and c in the equation of a straight line – experimental data – parallel lines – perpendicular lines – Chapter 24 summary.

25 FUNCTIONS AND RELATIONS   173
Relations – functions – function notation – graphs and functions – the reciprocal function – the law of

Contents   xi

natural growth – the graph of x^3 – the graph of x^{-2} – direct variation – inverse variation – inverse functions – using the inverse of a function to solve an equation – composite functions – the inverse of a composite function – Cartesian product – Chapter 25 summary.

26 FURTHER GRAPHICAL WORK   **187**
The gradient of a curve – rates of change – turning points – maximum or minimum value of a quadratic expression – area under a curve – the trapezium rule – average speed – distance–time graphs – velocity – velocity–time graphs – Chapter 26 summary.

27 INEQUALITIES   **204**
Solutions of inequalities – simple inequations – quadratic inequations – graphs of linear inequalities – linear programming – the fundamental theorem of linear programming – Chapter 27 summary.

HOW TO ANSWER EXAMINATION QUESTIONS 3   **213**
Examination Type Questions 3.

28 ANGLES AND STRAIGHT LINES   **219**
Angles – angular measurement – radian measure – relation between radians and degrees – length of an arc of a circle – area of the sector of a circle – types of angles – properties of angles and straight lines – Chapter 28 summary.

29 TRIANGLES   **226**
Types of triangle – angle properties of triangles – standard notation for a triangle – Pythagoras' theorem – properties of the isosceles triangle – congruent triangles – similar triangles – areas of similar triangles – Chapter 29 summary.

30 QUADRILATERALS AND POLYGONS   **244**
Quadrilateral – parallelogram – rectangle – rhombus – square – trapezium – polygons – area of a parallelogram – area of a trapezium – Chapter 30 summary.

31 THE CIRCLE   **253**
Angles in circles – tangent properties of a circle – Chapter 31 summary.

32 GEOMETRIC CONSTRUCTIONS   **262**
Chapter 32 summary.

33 LOCI   **268**
Standard loci – intersecting loci – Chapter 33 summary.

HOW TO ANSWER EXAMINATION QUESTIONS 4   **270**
Examination Type Questions 4.

34 TRIGONOMETRY   **276**
The notation for a right-angled triangle – the trigonometrical ratios – the sine of an angle – decimals of a degree – reading the table of sines of angles – the cosine of an angle – the tangent of an angle – logarithms of the trigonometrical ratios – trigonometrical ratios for $30°$, $60°$ and $45°$ – given one ratio to find the others – complementary angles – the squares of the trigonometrical ratios – angle of elevation – altitude of the sun – angle of depression – bearings – Chapter 34 summary.

35 THE SINE AND COSINE RULES   **293**
Trigonometrical ratios between $0°$ and $360°$ – sine, cosine and tangent curves – the standard notation for a triangle – the solution of triangles – the sine rule – use of the sine rule to find the diameter of the circumscribing circle of a triangle – the cosine rule – area of a triangle – area of a segment of a circle – Chapter 35 summary.

36 SOLID TRIGONOMETRY   **305**
The plane – the angle between a line and a plane – the angle between two planes – Chapter 36 summary.

37 THE SPHERE, LATITUDE AND LONGITUDE   **310**
The earth as a sphere – latitude and longitude – circles of latitude – Chapter 37 summary.

HOW TO ANSWER EXAMINATION QUESTIONS 5   **313**
Examination Type Questions 5.

38 SETS   **317**
Collections – elements – naming sets –
types of sets – membership of a set –
subsets – relations between number
systems – the number of subsets –
equality – the universal set – set builder
notation – Venn diagrams –
complement – intersection – union –
problems with intersections and unions
– the number of elements in a set –
intersection of three sets –
correspondence and equivalence – sets
and logical chains – deduction and
truth – subsets and complements –
intersecting sets – Chapter 38
summary.

39 NUMBER SCALES   **335**
The binary system – conversion from
binary to decimal and vice versa –
addition of binary numbers –
subtraction of binary numbers –
multiplication of binary numbers –
division of binary numbers –
operations with bicimals – other
number scales – conversion from one
base to another – Chapter 39 summary.

40 MATRICES   **341**
Types of matrices – addition and
subtraction of matrices – multiplication
of matrices – matrix notation – equality
of matrices – transposition of matrices
– diagonalising a matrix – inverting a
matrix – solution of simultaneous
equations – Chapter 40 summary.

41 TRANSFORMATIONAL GEOMETRY   **347**
Introduction – translation – properties
of translations – reflection – reflecting
a line – reflecting polygons –
orientation and reflection – symmetric
figures – summary of the properties of
reflections – congruence – rotation –
finding the centre of rotation –
rotational symmetry – properties of
rotations – size transformations –
properties of size transformations –
glide reflections – properties of glide
reflections – shear – properties of a
shear transformation – Chapter 41
summary.

42 VECTORS   **361**
Vector quantities – resultant vectors –

triangle law – equal vectors – inverse
vectors – the sum of two vectors –
subtraction of vectors – multiplying by
a scalar – distributive law for vectors –
the parallelogram of vectors –
application of vectors to geometry –
Chapter 42 summary.

43 APPLICATIONS OF VECTORS   **370**
Vector quantities – velocity vectors –
course and airspeed – track and
groundspeed – wind direction and
speed – drift – the triangle of velocities
– the triangle of velocities applied to
boats – Chapter 43 summary.

**44 VECTORS, MATRICES AND
TRANSFORMATIONS**   **375**
Vectors represented as matrices –
addition of vectors – transformations
and matrices – reflection – obtaining a
matrix to describe a particular
transformation – reflection in the line
$y = -x$ – isometrics – other
transformations – double
transformations – glide reflection –
rotation – inverse transformations –
similarities – stretch – shearing –
Chapter 44 summary.

**HOW TO ANSWER EXAMINATION
QUESTIONS 6**   **388**
Examination Type Questions 6.

45 STATISTICS   **391**
Introduction – the proportionate bar
chart – simple bar charts –
chronological bar charts – pie chart –
raw data – frequency distributions –
grouped distributions – class intervals –
class boundaries – width of a class
interval – discrete and continuous
variables – the histogram – histogram
for a grouped distribution – discrete
distributions – the frequency polygon –
frequency curves – types of frequency
curve – statistical averages – the
arithmetic mean – the mean of a
frequency distribution – the mean of a
grouped distribution – the coded
method of calculating the mean – the
median – cumulative frequency
distributions – the mode – the mode of
a frequency distribution – comparison
of statistical averages – which average

to use – relation between the mean, median and mode – quartiles – measures of dispersion – the range – quartile deviation – the standard deviation – the standard deviation of a frequency distribution – analysis of statistical data – skewed distributions – sampling – the sample size – cluster sampling – Chapter 45 summary.

46 **PROBABILITY** 418
Equiprobable events and favourable outcomes – non-equiprobable events – use of set notation – probability scale – total probability – experimental probability – permutations – permutations of things which are not all different – combinations – probability, permutations and combinations – mutually exclusive events – non-mutually exclusive events – independent events – dependent events – the probability tree – Chapter 46 summary.

HOW TO ANSWER EXAMINATION QUESTIONS 7 431
Examination Type Questions 7.

SPECIMEN EXAMS 434

ANSWERS 453

INDEX 473

Chapter 1 Operations in Arithmetic

SOME DEFINITIONS

The result obtained by adding numbers is called the *sum*. The sum of 4, 6 and 8 is $4 + 6 + 8 = 18$.

The *difference* of two numbers is the larger number minus the smaller number. The difference of 15 and 10 is $15 - 10 = 5$.

The result obtained by multiplying numbers is called the *product*. The product of 8 and 7 is $8 \times 7 = 56$.

The result obtained by division is called the *quotient*. The quotient of $8 \div 4$ is 2.

COMMUTATIVE LAW

(1) For addition the law states that the order in which numbers are added does not affect their sum. Thus

$$4 + 6 + 8 \ = \ 6 + 4 + 8 \ = \ 8 + 4 + 6 \ = \ 18$$

This law may be used

(a) to simplify addition. Thus

$$20 + 72 + 280 \ = \ 20 + 280 + 72 \ = \ 372$$

(b) to check addition. Thus numbers may be added upwards and checked downwards.

add up	check downwards
217 ↑	217 ↓
79	79
386	386
682	682

(2) For multiplication the law states that the order in which we multiply numbers does not affect their product. Thus

$$3 \times 4 \times 6 \ = \ 4 \times 3 \times 6 \ = \ 6 \times 3 \times 4 \ = \ 72$$

This law may be used

(a) to simplify multiplication. Thus

$$4 \times 7 \times 25 \ = \ 4 \times 25 \times 7 \ = \ 100 \times 7 \ = \ 700$$

(b) to check a product by interchanging numbers. Thus

$$
\begin{array}{r}
34 \\
\times\, 89 \\
\hline
306 \\
2720 \\
\hline
3026 \\
\hline
\end{array}
\qquad
\begin{array}{r}
89 \\
\times\, 34 \\
\hline
356 \\
2670 \\
\hline
3026 \\
\hline
\end{array}
$$

The commutative law does not apply to subtraction or division. Thus

$$8 - 4 \text{ is not the same as } 4 - 8$$

$$8 \div 4 \text{ is not the same as } 4 \div 8$$

ASSOCIATIVE LAW

For addition and multiplication the law states that the way in which numbers are added or multiplied in groups of two does not affect their sum or product.

Thus

$$3 + 5 + 7 \ = \ (3 + 5) + 7 \ = \ 8 + 7 \ = \ 15$$
$$= \ 3 + (5 + 7) \ = \ 3 + 12 \ = \ 15$$

Also

$$8 \times 2 \times 5 \ = \ (8 \times 2) \times 5 \ = \ 16 \times 5 \ = \ 80$$
$$= \ 8 \times (2 \times 5) \ = \ 8 \times 10 \ = \ 80$$

DISTRIBUTIVE LAW

$$5 \times (3 + 4) \ = \ 5 \times 3 + 5 \times 4 \ = \ 15 + 20 \ = \ 35$$

$$8 \times (7 - 3) \ = \ 8 \times 7 - 8 \times 3 \ = \ 56 - 24 \ = \ 32$$

These two examples illustrate the distributive law which states that multiplication is distributive over addition for a set of numbers a, b and c if $a(b + c) = ab + ac$.

SEQUENCE OF ARITHMETICAL OPERATIONS

Numbers are often combined in a series of arithmetical operations. When this happens a definite sequence must be observed.

(1) Brackets are used if there is any danger of ambiguity. The contents of the brackets must be evaluated before performing any other operation. Thus

$$2 \times (7 + 4) = 2 \times 11 = 22$$
$$15 - (8 - 3) = 15 - 5 = 10$$

(2) Multiplication and division must be done before addition and subtraction. Thus

$5 \times 8 + 7 = 40 + 7 = 47$ (not 5×15)

$8 \div 4 + 9 = 2 + 9 = 11$ (not $8 \div 13$)

$5 \times 4 - 12 \div 3 + 7 = 20 - 4 + 7 = 27 - 4 = 23$

ADDITIVE IDENTITY

If 0 is added to any number, the sum is the number. Thus

$$562 + 0 = 562 \quad \text{and} \quad 0 + 1982 = 1982$$

Since identically the same number remains when 0 is added to it, 0 is called the *additive identity*.

MULTIPLICATIVE IDENTITY

If any number is multiplied by 1, the product is the number. Thus

$$763 \times 1 = 763 \quad \text{and} \quad 1 \times 1876 = 1876$$

Since identically the same number remains when it is multiplied by 1, 1 is called the *multiplicative identity*.

MULTIPLICATIVE PROPERTY OF ZERO

If any number is multiplied by zero, the result is zero. Thus

$$19 \times 0 = 0 \quad \text{and} \quad 0 \times 237 = 0$$

CLOSURE

If the whole numbers 5 and 7 are added the result is 12. It is true that when any two whole numbers are added the result is *always* a whole number.

Again, if we multiply 6 and 9 the result is 54. If we multiply any two whole numbers together the result is *always* a whole number.

We say that the set of whole numbers is closed under addition and multiplication in accordance with the *law of closure* which states:

A set of numbers is closed under an operation, if when the operation is applied to any two members of the set, the result is a member of the set.

Note that the set of whole numbers is not necessarily closed under division, because, for example, $9 \div 6$ does not result in a whole number.

DIVISION BY ZERO

It is impossible to divide by zero. Hence $\dfrac{4}{0}$ and $\dfrac{127}{0}$ are meaningless operations.

However, if 0 is divided by a number, the result is 0. Thus $\dfrac{0}{17} = 0$ and $\dfrac{0}{249} = 0$.

So far we have used the standard operations of add, subtract, multiply and divide. However if we wished we could make up some operations of our own.

Suppose we have an operation shown by the symbol ‡ which means double the first number and add the second number. Then,

$$3 \ddagger 4 = 2 \times 3 + 4 = 6 + 4 = 10$$
$$5 \ddagger 3 = 2 \times 5 + 3 = 10 + 3 = 13$$

Exercise 1 – *Questions 1–4 and 11–14 type A, remainder B*

Find values for the following:

1) $3 + 5 \times 2$
2) $3 \times 6 - 8$
3) $7 \times 5 - 2 + 4 \times 6$
4) $8 \div 2 + 3$
5) $7 \times 5 - 12 \div 4 + 3$
6) $11 - 9 \div 3 + 7$
7) $3 \times (8 + 7)$
8) $2 + 8 \times (3 + 6)$
9) $17 - 2 \times (5 - 3)$
10) $11 - 12 \div 4 + 3 \times (6 - 2)$

The operation * means divide the first number by 2 and add the second number. Use this operation to work out the following:

11) $2 * 4$ **13)** $8 * 3$

12) $6 * 7$ **14)** $10 * 2$

The operation † means add the first number to 3 times the second number. Use this operation to work out the following:

15) $8 † 2$ **17)** $2 † 5$

16) $9 † 4$ **18)** $4 † 3$

19) Perform the following arithmetic operations as quickly as possible:

(a) $25 + (389 + 275)$ (b) $11 + (182 + 89)$
(c) $5 \times 6 \times 20$ (d) $4 \times 19 \times 25$

20) Find the value of each of the following:

(a) $8000 + 0$ (b) 2000×1
(c) 50×0 (d) $20 \times 30 \times 0$
(e) $0 \times 2 \times 3 \times 5$ (f) $5 \times 4 \times 1$
(g) $10 \times 0 + 8$ (h) $18 \times 1 + 12$
(i) $11 - 12 \times 0 + 3$
(j) $11 - 12 \div 6 + 0 \times (6 + 1)$
(k) $762 \div 0$ (l) $0 \div 21$
(m) $5 \times (8 + 2) + 0 \div 3$
(n) $(7 - 7) \div 8 + 7 \times 2$

FACTORS AND MULTIPLES

If one number divides exactly into a second number the first number is said to be a factor of the second. Thus

$$35 \div 5 = 7 \ldots 5 \text{ is a factor of } 35$$

or $35 = 5 \times 7$ and so is 7.

$240 \div 3 = 80 \ldots$ 3, 80, 8, 30, 10, 24, 12 and
$240 \div 8 = 30$ 20 are all factors of 240
$240 \div 10 = 24$
$240 \div 12 = 20$

$$63 = 3 \times 21 = 7 \times 9$$

63 is said to be a *multiple* of any of the numbers 3, 7, 9 and 21 because each of them divides exactly into 63.

Every number has itself and 1 as factors. If a number has no other factors apart from these, it is said to be a *prime number*. Thus 2, 3, 7, 11, 13, 17 and 19 are all prime numbers.

A factor which is a prime number is called a *prime factor*.

LOWEST COMMON MULTIPLE (L.C.M.)

The L.C.M. of a set of numbers is the *smallest* number into which each of the given numbers

will divide. Thus the L.C.M. of 4, 5 and 10 is 20 because 20 is the smallest number into which the numbers 4, 5 and 10 will divide exactly.

The L.C.M. of a set of numbers can usually be found by inspection, or by the following method:

To find the L.C.M. of two numbers, 8 and 12 say, we reduce $\frac{8}{12}$ to lowest terms, i.e. $\frac{8}{12} = \frac{2}{3}$ and then cross multiply:

L.C.M. of 8 and 12 is 8×3 or $2 \times 12 = 24$.

For three numbers, say 6, 8 and 9
$\frac{6}{8} = \frac{3}{4}$ L.C.M. of 6, 8 = $6 \times 4 = 24$.

Now find L.C.M. of 24 and 9.

HIGHEST COMMON FACTOR (H.C.F.)

The H.C.F. of a set of numbers is the greatest number which is a factor of each of the numbers. Thus 12 is the H.C.F. of 24, 36 and 60. Also 20 is the H.C.F. of 40, 60 and 80.

It can be shown that the H.C.F. of
(a, b) × L.C.M. of (a, b) = ab

POWERS OF NUMBERS

The quantity $2 \times 2 \times 2 \times 2$ is written 2^4 and is called the fourth power of 2. The figure 4, which gives the number of 2s to be multiplied together is called the index (plural: indices).

$$5^6 = 5 \times 5 \times 5 \times 5 \times 5 \times 5 = 15\,625$$

$$7^3 = 7 \times 7 \times 7 = 343$$

Exercise 2 – *Question 7 type A, remainder B*

1) What numbers are factors of:
(a) 24   (b) 56   (c) 42?

2) Which of the following numbers are factors of 12:

2, 3, 4, 5, 6, 12, 18 and 24?

Which of them are multiples of 6?

3) Write down all the multiples of 3 between 10 and 40.

4) Express as a product of prime factors:
(a) 24   (b) 36   (c) 56   (d) 132

5) Write down the two prime numbers next larger than 19.

6) Find the L.C.M. of the following sets of numbers:

(a) 8 and 12   (b) 3, 4 and 5
(c) 2, 6 and 12   (d) 3, 6 and 8
(e) 2, 8 and 10   (f) 20 and 25
(g) 20 and 32   (h) 10, 15 and 40
(i) 12, 42, 60 and 70   (j) 18, 30, 42 and 48

7) Find the values of:

(a) 2^5 (b) 3^4 (c) 5^3
(d) 6^2 (e) 8^3

8) Find the H.C.F. of each of the following sets of numbers:

(a) 8 and 12   (b) 24 and 36
(c) 10, 15 and 30   (d) 26, 39 and 52
(e) 18, 30, 12 and 42
(f) 28, 42, 84, 98 and 112

SEQUENCES

A set of numbers which are connected by some definite law is called a sequence of numbers. Each of the numbers in the sequence is called a term of the sequence. Here are some examples:

1, 3, 4, 7   . . . (each term is obtained by adding 2 to the previous term)

2, 6, 18, 54   . . . (each term is obtained by multiplying the previous term by 3)

EXAMPLE 1

Write down the next two terms of the following sequence:

$$112, 56, 28, . . .$$

The second term is found by dividing the first term by 2 and the third term is found by dividing the second term by 2. Hence:

$$\text{Fourth term} = \frac{28}{2} = 14$$

$$\text{Fifth term} = \frac{14}{2} = 7$$

Exercise 3 – *All type A*

Write down the next two terms of each of the following sequences of numbers:

1) 3, 12, 48, . . .   **4)** 162, 54, 18, . . .

2) 1, 4, 7, 10, . . .   **5)** 6, 12, 24, . . .

3) 5, 11, 17, 23, . . .

SELF-TEST 1

In Questions 1 to 14 state the letter (or letters) corresponding to the correct answer (or answers).

1) $3 + 7 \times 4$ is equal to:

a 31   **b** 40   **c** 84

2) $6 \times 5 - 2 + 4 \times 6$ is equal to:

a 18   **b** 42   **c** 52

3) $7 \times 6 - 12 \div 3 + 1$ is equal to:

a 21   **b** 39   **c** 40

4) $17 - 2 \times (6 - 4)$ is equal to:

a 1   **b** 13   **c** 30

5) $a * b$ means multiply the first number by 5 and subtract the second number multiplied by 3. $6 * 4$ is equal to:

a 2   **b** 6   **c** 18   **d** 26

6) $a \ddagger b$ means 5 times the first number plus 2 times the second number. $3 \ddagger 5$ is equal to:

a 5   **b** 25   **c** 31   **d** 150

7) Which of the following is a prime number?

a 15   **b** 27   **c** 38   **d** 41

8) The product of 9 and 7 is:

a 2   **b** 16   **c** 63   **d** none of these

9) 2, 3 and 5 are the factors of:

a 6   **b** 10   **c** 15   **d** 30

10) 54 is a multiple of:

a 3   **b** 4   **c** 5   **d** none of these

11) The next two numbers in the sequence 5, 4, 6, 5, 7, 6, 8 are:

a 9 and 7   **b** 7 and 6   **c** 9 and 6
d 7 and 9

12) Consider the numbers 11, 21, 31, 77 and 112. Three of these numbers have a common factor. It is:

a 2   **b** 7   **c** 11   **d** 14

13) The L.C.M. of 2, 4, 6 and 5 is:

a 5   **b** 6   **c** 60   **d** 240

14) The H.C.F. of 20, 30 and 60 is:

a 2   **b** 10   **c** 20   **d** 60

CHAPTER 1 SUMMARY

Points to remember

(i)   A *factor* of a number divides exactly into that number.
      e.g. 2, 3 and 5 are factors of 30

(ii) A *multiple* of a number has the number as a factor.
      e.g. 12, 15 and 24 are multiples of 3.

(iii) A *prime number* is a natural number, other than 1, that has only two factors, 1 and itself.
      e.g. 2, 3 and 29 are prime numbers.

(iv) A *natural number* other than 1 that is not a prime number is called a composite number.
      e.g. 4, 6 and 10 are composite numbers.

(v)   The *least common multiple* (L.C.M.) of a set of numbers is the smallest number which is a multiple of all the given numbers.
      e.g. the LCM of 4, 6 and 10 is 60.

(vi) The *highest common factor* (H.C.F.) of a set of numbers is the largest number which is a factor of the given numbers.
      e.g. the HCF of 12, 24 and 30 is 6.

(vii) The *power* (*index*, *exponent*) is a number placed as a superscript to the right of another number or variable to show repeated multiplication.
      e.g. $3 \times 3 \times 3 \times 3 = 3^4$. We read this as "3 to the power of 4".

Chapter 2 **Fractions**

VULGAR FRACTIONS

The circle in Fig. 2.1 has been divided into eight equal parts. Each part is called one-eighth of the circle and is written as $\frac{1}{8}$. The number 8 below the line shows how many equal parts there are and it is called the *denominator*. The number above the line shows how many of the equal parts are taken and it is called the *numerator*. If five of the eight equal parts are taken then we have taken $\frac{5}{8}$ of the circle.

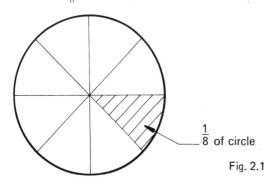

$\frac{1}{8}$ of circle

Fig. 2.1

From what has been said above we see that a fraction is always a part of something. The number below the line (the denominator) gives the fraction its name and tells us the number of equal parts into which the whole has been divided. The top number (the numerator) tells us the number of these equal parts that are to be taken. For example the fraction $\frac{3}{4}$ means that the whole has been divided into four equal parts and that three of these parts are to be taken.

The value of a fraction is unchanged if we multiply or divide both its numerator and denominator by the same amount.

$\frac{3}{5} = \frac{12}{20}$ (by multiplying the numerator (top number) and denominator (bottom number) by 4)

$\frac{2}{7} = \frac{10}{35}$ (by multiplying the numerator and denominator by 5)

$\frac{12}{32} = \frac{3}{8}$ (by dividing the numerator and denominator by 4)

$\frac{16}{64} = \frac{1}{4}$ (by dividing the numerator and denominator by 16)

EXAMPLE 1

Write down the fraction $\frac{2}{7}$ with a denominator (bottom number) of 28.

In order to make the denominator (bottom number) 28, we must multiply the original denominator of 7 by 4 because $7 \times 4 = 28$. Remembering that to leave the value of the fraction unchanged we must multiply both numerator (top number) and denominator (bottom number) by the same amount, then

$$\frac{2}{7} = \frac{2 \times 4}{7 \times 4} = \frac{8}{28}$$

Exercise 4 – *All type A*

Write down the following fractions with the denominator (bottom number) stated:

1) $\frac{3}{4}$ with denominator 28

2) $\frac{3}{5}$ with denominator 20

3) $\frac{5}{6}$ with denominator 30

4) $\frac{1}{9}$ with denominator 63

5) $\frac{2}{3}$ with denominator 12

6) $\frac{1}{6}$ with denominator 24

7) $\frac{3}{8}$ with denominator 64

8) $\frac{5}{7}$ with denominator 35

REDUCING A FRACTION TO ITS LOWEST TERMS

Fractions like $\frac{3}{8}$, $\frac{7}{16}$ and $\frac{3}{52}$ are said to be in their *lowest terms* because it is impossible to find a number which will divide exactly into both the top and bottom numbers. However, fractions like $\frac{9}{18}$, $\frac{8}{12}$ and $\frac{21}{24}$ are not in their lowest terms because they can be reduced further by dividing both the top and bottom numbers by some number which divides exactly into both of them. Thus,

$$\frac{9}{18} = \frac{1}{2} \quad \text{(by dividing both top and bottom by 9)}$$

$$\frac{8}{12} = \frac{2}{3} \quad \text{(by dividing both top and bottom by 4)}$$

$$\frac{21}{24} = \frac{7}{8} \quad \text{(by dividing both top and bottom by 3)}$$

Sometimes we can divide the top and bottom by the same number several times.

EXAMPLE 2

Reduce $\frac{210}{336}$ to its lowest terms.

$$\frac{210}{336} = \frac{105}{168} \quad \text{(by dividing top and bottom by 2)}$$

$$= \frac{35}{56} \quad \text{(by dividing top and bottom by 3)}$$

$$= \frac{5}{8} \quad \text{(by dividing top and bottom by 7)}$$

Hence $\frac{210}{336}$ reduced to its lowest terms is $\frac{5}{8}$.

Exercise 5 – *Questions 1–5 type A, remainder B*

Reduce the following fractions to their lowest terms:

1) $\frac{8}{16}$ 4) $\frac{15}{25}$ 7) $\frac{210}{294}$ 10) $\frac{210}{315}$

2) $\frac{9}{15}$ 5) $\frac{42}{48}$ 8) $\frac{126}{245}$

3) $\frac{8}{64}$ 6) $\frac{180}{240}$ 9) $\frac{132}{198}$

TYPES OF FRACTIONS

If the top number of a fraction is less than its bottom number the fraction is called a *proper fraction*. Thus $\frac{2}{3}$, $\frac{5}{8}$ and $\frac{3}{4}$ are all proper fractions. Note that a proper fraction has a value which is less than 1.

If the top number of a fraction is greater than its bottom number then the fraction is called an *improper fraction* or a *top heavy fraction*. Thus

$\frac{5}{4}$, $\frac{3}{2}$ and $\frac{9}{7}$ are all top heavy, or improper, fractions. Note that all top heavy fractions have a value which is greater than 1.

Every top heavy fraction can be expressed as a whole number and a proper fraction. These are sometimes called *mixed numbers*. Thus $1\frac{1}{2}$, $5\frac{1}{3}$ and $9\frac{3}{4}$ are all mixed numbers. In order to convert a top heavy fraction into a mixed number it must be remembered that

$$\frac{\text{top number}}{\text{bottom number}} = \text{top number} \div \text{bottom number}$$

EXAMPLE 3

Express $\frac{15}{8}$ as a mixed number.

$$\frac{15}{8} = 1\frac{7}{8}$$

(because $15 \div 8 = 1$ and remainder 7)

From Example 3 we see that we convert a top heavy fraction into a mixed number by dividing the bottom number into the top number. Notice that the remainder becomes the top number in the fractional part of the mixed number. To change a mixed number into an improper fraction we multiply the whole number by the bottom number of the fractional part. To this we add the numerator of the fractional part and this sum then becomes the top number of the improper fraction. Its bottom number is the same as the bottom number of the fractional part of the mixed number.

EXAMPLE 4

Express $3\frac{5}{8}$ as a top heavy fraction.

$$3\frac{5}{8} = \frac{(8 \times 3) + 5}{8} = \frac{24 + 5}{8} = \frac{29}{8}$$

Exercise 6 – *All type A*

Express each of the following as a mixed number:

1) $\frac{7}{2}$ 3) $\frac{22}{10}$ 5) $\frac{21}{8}$

2) $\frac{9}{4}$ 4) $\frac{12}{11}$

Express each of the following as top heavy fractions:

6) $2\frac{3}{8}$ 8) $8\frac{2}{3}$ 10) $4\frac{3}{7}$

7) $5\frac{1}{10}$ 9) $6\frac{7}{20}$

LOWEST COMMON MULTIPLE (L.C.M.)

The L.C.M. of a set of numbers has already been explained on page 3.

We often need to work out an L.C.M. when we compare fractions, as we will see in the next section on the lowest common denominator.

Exercise 7 – *Questions 1–7 type A, remainder B*

Find the L.C.M. of the following sets of numbers:

1) 8 and 10   6) 10 and 25
2) 3, 4 and 6   7) 10 and 32
3) 2, 6 and 16   8) 10, 25 and 40
4) 3, 6 and 12   9) 12, 21, 30 and 70
5) 2, 8 and 12   10) 9, 15, 21 and 24

LOWEST COMMON DENOMINATOR

When we wish to compare the values of two or more fractions the easiest way is to express the fractions with the same bottom number. This common denominator is usually the L.C.M. of the denominators of the fractions to be compared and it is called the *lowest common denominator*.

EXAMPLE 5

Arrange the fractions $\frac{3}{4}, \frac{5}{8}, \frac{7}{10}$ and $\frac{11}{20}$ in order of size starting with the smallest.

The lowest common denominator of 4, 8, 10 and 20 is 40. Expressing each of the given fractions with a bottom number of 40 gives:

$$\frac{3}{4} = \frac{3 \times 10}{4 \times 10} = \frac{30}{40} \qquad \frac{5}{8} = \frac{5 \times 5}{8 \times 5} = \frac{25}{40}$$

$$\frac{7}{10} = \frac{7 \times 4}{10 \times 4} = \frac{28}{40} \qquad \frac{11}{20} = \frac{11 \times 2}{20 \times 2} = \frac{22}{40}$$

Therefore the order is:

$$\frac{22}{40}, \frac{25}{40}, \frac{28}{40}, \frac{30}{40} \text{ or } \frac{11}{20}, \frac{5}{8}, \frac{7}{10} \text{ and } \frac{3}{4}$$

Exercise 8 – *All type A*

Arrange the following sets of fractions in order of size, beginning with the smallest:

1) $\frac{1}{2}, \frac{5}{6}, \frac{2}{3}, \frac{7}{12}$ 4) $\frac{3}{4}, \frac{5}{8}, \frac{3}{5}, \frac{13}{20}$

2) $\frac{9}{10}, \frac{3}{4}, \frac{6}{7}, \frac{7}{8}$ 5) $\frac{11}{16}, \frac{7}{10}, \frac{9}{14}, \frac{3}{4}$

3) $\frac{13}{16}, \frac{11}{20}, \frac{7}{10}, \frac{3}{5}$ 6) $\frac{3}{8}, \frac{4}{7}, \frac{5}{9}, \frac{2}{5}$

ADDITION OF FRACTIONS

The steps when adding fractions are as follows:

(1) Find the lowest common denominator of the fractions to be added.

(2) Express each of the fractions with this common denominator.

(3) Add the numerators of the new fractions to give the numerator of the answer. The denominator of the answer is the lowest common denominator found in (1).

EXAMPLE 6

Find the sum of $\frac{2}{7}$ and $\frac{3}{4}$.

First find the lowest common denominator (this is the L.C.M. of 7 and 4).

It is 28. Now express $\frac{2}{7}$ and $\frac{3}{4}$ with a bottom number of 28.

$$\frac{2}{7} = \frac{2 \times 4}{7 \times 4} = \frac{8}{28} \qquad \frac{3}{4} = \frac{3 \times 7}{4 \times 7} = \frac{21}{28}$$

Adding the top numbers of the new fractions:

$$\frac{2}{7} + \frac{3}{4} = \frac{8}{28} + \frac{21}{28} = \frac{29}{28} = 1\frac{1}{28}$$

Another way of setting out the work is as follows:

$$\frac{2}{7} + \frac{3}{4} = \frac{2 \times 4 + 3 \times 7}{28} = \frac{8 + 21}{28} = \frac{29}{28} = 1\frac{1}{28}$$

EXAMPLE 7

Simplify $\frac{3}{4} + \frac{2}{3} + \frac{7}{10}$.

The L.C.M. of the bottom numbers 4, 3 and 10 is 60.

11) $\frac{5}{8} \times \frac{4}{15}$ is equal to one of the following, when the answer is expressed in its lowest terms:

a $\frac{1}{6}$ **b** $\frac{20}{120}$ **c** $\frac{9}{23}$ **d** $\frac{32}{75}$

12) $\frac{3}{4} \div \frac{8}{9}$ is equal to:

a $\frac{2}{3}$ **b** $\frac{24}{36}$ **c** $\frac{27}{32}$ **d** $\frac{3}{2}$

13) $6\frac{4}{9} \div 3\frac{2}{3}$ is equal to:

a $\frac{58}{33}$ **b** $2\frac{2}{3}$ **c** $18\frac{8}{27}$ **d** $\frac{638}{27}$

14) $3 \times \frac{1}{2} - \frac{1}{3}$ is equal to:

a $\frac{1}{2}$ **b** $1\frac{1}{2} - \frac{1}{3}$ **c** $3 \times \frac{1}{2} - 3 \times \frac{1}{3}$

d none of these

15) $\frac{5}{8} + \frac{1}{2} \times \frac{1}{4}$ is equal to:

a $\frac{3}{32}$ **b** $\frac{9}{32}$ **c** $\frac{9}{16}$ **d** $\frac{3}{4}$

CHAPTER 2 SUMMARY

Points to remember

(i) The value of a fraction is unchanged when the numerator and denominator are multiplied or divided by the same number.
e.g. $\frac{a}{b} = \frac{ac}{bc}$

(ii) If the product of two numbers is 1, each is called the *reciprocal* of the other.
e.g. The reciprocal of $\frac{3}{4}$ is $\frac{4}{3}$.

(iii) To divide by a fraction, multiply by its reciprocal.
e.g. $\frac{4}{5} \div \frac{2}{3} = \frac{4}{5} \times \frac{3}{2}$

(iv) A proper fraction is a fraction with the numerator less than the denominator.

(v) An improper fraction is a fraction with the numerator greater than the denominator.

(vi) A mixed number is written with a whole number and a fraction. E.g. $3\frac{5}{8}$.

Chapter 3 The Decimal System

THE DECIMAL SYSTEM

The decimal system is an extension of our ordinary number system. When we write the number 666 we mean $600 + 60 + 6$. Reading from left to right each figure 6 is ten times the value of the next one.

We now have to decide how to deal with fractional quantities, that is, quantities whose values are less than one. If we regard 666.666 as meaning $600 + 60 + 6 + \frac{6}{10} + \frac{6}{100} + \frac{6}{1000}$ then the dot, called the decimal point, separates the whole numbers from the fractional parts. Notice that with the fractional, or decimal parts, e.g. $.666$, each figure 6 is ten times the value of the following one, reading from left to right. Thus $\frac{6}{10}$ is ten times as great as $\frac{6}{100}$, and $\frac{6}{100}$ is ten times as great as $\frac{6}{1000}$ and so on.

Decimals then are fractions which have denominators of 10, 100, 1000 and so on, according to the position of the figure after the decimal point.

If we have to write six hundred and five we write 605; the zero keeps the place for the missing tens. In the same way if we want to write $\frac{3}{10} + \frac{5}{1000}$ we write $.305$; the zero keeps the place for the missing hundredths. Also $\frac{6}{100} + \frac{7}{1000}$ would be written $.067$; the zero in this case keeps the place for the missing tenths.

When there are no whole numbers it is usual to insert a zero in front of the decimal point so that, for instance, $.35$ would be written 0.35.

Exercise 16 – *All type A*

Read off as decimals:

1) $\dfrac{7}{10}$

2) $\dfrac{3}{10} + \dfrac{7}{100}$

3) $\dfrac{5}{10} + \dfrac{8}{100} + \dfrac{9}{1000}$

4) $\dfrac{9}{1000}$

5) $\dfrac{3}{100}$

6) $\dfrac{1}{100} + \dfrac{7}{1000}$

7) $8 + \dfrac{6}{100}$

8) $24 + \dfrac{2}{100} + \dfrac{9}{10\,000}$

9) $50 + \dfrac{8}{1000}$

Read off the following with denominators (bottom numbers) 10, 100, 1000, etc., using mixed numbers where appropriate:

10) 0.2

11) 4.6

12) 3.58

13) 437.25

14) 0.004

15) 0.036

16) 400.029

17) 0.001

18) $0.032\,9$

ADDITION AND SUBTRACTION OF DECIMALS

Adding or subtracting decimals is done in exactly the same way as for whole numbers. Care must be taken, however, to write the decimal points directly underneath one another. This makes sure that all the figures having the same place value fall in the same column.

EXAMPLE 1

Simplify $11.36 + 2.639 + 0.047$.

$$
\begin{array}{r}
11.36 \\
2.639 \\
\underline{0.047} \\
14.046
\end{array}
$$

EXAMPLE 2

Subtract 8.567 from 19.126.

$$
\begin{array}{r}
19.126 \\
\underline{8.567} \\
10.559
\end{array}
$$

Exercise 17 – *All type A*

Write down the values of:

1) $2.375 + 0.625$

2) $4.25 + 7.25$

3) $3.196 + 2.475 + 18.369$

4) $38.267 + 0.049 + 20.3$

5) $27.418 + 0.967 + 25 + 1.467$

6) $12.48 - 8.36$

7) $19.215 - 3.599$

8) $2.237 - 1.898$

9) $0.876 - 0.064$

10) $5.48 - 0.0691$

MULTIPLICATION AND DIVISION OF DECIMALS

One of the advantages of decimals is the ease with which they may be multiplied or divided by 10, 100, 1000, etc.

EXAMPLE 3

Find the value of 1.4×10.

$$1.4 \times 10 = 1 \times 10 + 0.4 \times 10$$
$$= 10 + \frac{4}{10} \times 10 = 10 + 4 = 14$$

EXAMPLE 4

Find the value of 27.532×10.

$$27.532 \times 10 = 27 \times 10 + 0.5 \times 10$$
$$+ 0.03 \times 10 + 0.002 \times 10$$
$$= 270 + \frac{5}{10} \times 10 + \frac{3}{100} \times 10$$
$$+ \frac{2}{1000} \times 10$$
$$= 270 + 5 + \frac{3}{10} + \frac{2}{100}$$
$$= 275.32$$

In both of the above examples you will notice that the figures have not been changed by the multiplication; only the *positions* of the figures have been changed. Thus in Example 3, $1.4 \times 10 = 14$, that is the decimal point has been moved one place to the right. In Example 4, $27.532 \times 10 = 275.32$; again the decimal point has been moved one place to the right.

To multiply by 10, then, is the same as shifting the decimal point one place to the right. In the same way to multiply by 100 is the same as shifting the decimal point two places to the right and so on.

EXAMPLE 5

$17.369 \times 10 = 1736.9$.

The decimal point has been moved two places to the right.

EXAMPLE 6

$0.07895 \times 1000 = 78.95$.

The decimal point has been moved three places to the right.

Exercise 18 – *All type A*

Multiply each of the numbers in Questions 1 to 6 by 10, 100 and 1000.

1) 4.1

2) 2.42

3) 0.046

4) 0.35

5) 0.1486

6) 0.001753

7) 0.4853×100

8) 0.009×1000

9) 170.06×10

10) 0.56396×10000

When dividing by 10 the decimal point is moved one place to the left, by 100, two places to the left and so on. Thus,

$$154.26 \div 10 = 15.426$$

The decimal point has been moved one place to the left.

$$9.432 \div 100 = 0.09432$$

The decimal point has been moved two places to the left.

$$35 \div 1000 = 0.035$$

The decimal point has been moved three places to the left.

In the above examples note carefully that use has been made of zeros following the decimal point to keep the places for the missing tenths.

Exercise 19 – *All type A*

Divide each of the numbers in Questions 1 to 5 by 10, 100 and 1000.

1) 3.6

2) 64.198

3) 0.07

4) 510.4

5) 0.352

6) $5.4 \div 100$

7) $2.05 \div 1000$

8) $0.04 \div 10$

9) $0.008\,6 \div 1000$

10) $627.428 \div 10\,000$

LONG MULTIPLICATION

Consider the following products:

(a) $25 \times 5 = 125$

(b) $25 \times 0.5 = 25 \times \dfrac{5}{10} = \dfrac{25 \times 5}{10} = \dfrac{125}{10} = 12.5$

(c) $2.5 \times 0.5 = \dfrac{25}{10} \times \dfrac{5}{10} = \dfrac{25 \times 5}{10 \times 10} = \dfrac{125}{100} = 1.25$

(d) $2.5 \times 0.05 = \dfrac{25}{10} \times \dfrac{5}{100} = \dfrac{25 \times 5}{10 \times 100}$

$\qquad = \dfrac{125}{1000} = 0.125$

If you study the multiplications in (b), (c) and (d) you will notice that there is a relationship between the number of decimal places in each product and the number of decimal places in the two numbers that are multiplied.

In each case the number of decimal places in the product is equal to the sum of the number of decimal places in the two numbers. Thus in (b) the number 25 contains 0 decimal places, while 0.5 contains one decimal place. The sum of the number of decimal places is $0 + 1 = 1$, which agrees with the number of decimal places in the product of 12.5.

Similarly in (c) the sum of the number of decimal places is $1 + 1 = 2$ which agrees with the number of decimal places in the product of 1.25. In (d) the sum of the number of decimal places is $1 + 2 = 3$ which agrees with the number of decimal places in the product of 0.125.

As a short cut to decimal multiplication, first multiply as you would with whole numbers. Then find the sum of the numbers of decimal places in the two numbers to be multiplied. This sum gives the number of decimal places in the final product.

EXAMPLE 7

Find the value of 36.5×3.504.

First disregard the decimal points and multiply 365 by 3504

```
       365
      3 504
      1 460
    182 500
  1 095 000
  1 278 960
```

Now count up the total number of figures following the decimal points in both numbers (i.e. $1 + 3 = 4$). In the answer to the multiplication (the product), count this total number of figures from the right and insert the decimal point. The product is then 127.896 0 or 127.896 since the zero does not mean anything.

Exercise 20 – *All type A*

Find the values of the following:

1) 25.42×29.23

2) $0.361\,8 \times 2.63$

3) 0.76×0.38

4) 3.025×2.45

5) 0.043×0.032

LONG DIVISION

EXAMPLE 8

Find the value of $19.24 \div 2.6$.

First convert the divisor (2.6) into a whole number by multiplying it by 10. To compensate multiply the dividend (19.24) by 10 also so that we now have $192.4 \div 26$. Now proceed as in ordinary division.

```
26)192.4(7.4
   182      – this line  26 × 7
   104      – 4 brought down from
   104        above. Since 4 lies to
   · · ·      the right of the decimal
              point in the dividend
              insert a decimal point
              in the answer (the
              quotient).
```

Notice how the decimal point in the quotient was obtained. The 4 brought down from the dividend lies to the right of the decimal point. Before bringing this down put a decimal point in the quotient immediately following the 7.

The division in this case is exact (i.e. there is no remainder) and the answer is 7.4. Now let us see what happens when there is a remainder.

EXAMPLE 9

Find the value of $15.187 \div 3.57$.

As before make the divisor into a whole number by multiplying it by 100 so that it becomes 357. To compensate multiply the dividend also by 100 so that it becomes 1518.7. Now divide

```
357)1518.7(4.254 06
    1428          – this line  357 × 4
     907          – 7  brought down
     714            from the dividend.
                    Since it lies to the
                    right of the decimal
                    point insert a
                    decimal point in
                    the quotient.
    1930          – bring down a zero
    1785            as all the figures in
    1450            the dividend have
    1428            been used up.
    2200          – Bring down a zero.
    2142            The divisor will not
      58            go into  220  so
                    place  0  in the
                    quotient and bring
                    down another zero.
```

The answer to 5 decimal places is 4.254 06. This is not the exact answer because there is a remainder. The division can be continued in the way shown to give as many decimal places as desired, or until there is no remainder.

It is important to realise what is meant by an answer given to so many decimal places. It is the number of figures that follow the decimal point which gives the number of decimal places. If the first figure to be discarded is 5 or more then the previous figure is increased by 1. Thus:

$85.768\,4 = 85.8$ correct to 1 decimal place

$= 85.77$ correct to 2 decimal places

$= 85.768$ correct to 3 decimal places

Notice that zeros must be kept:

$0.007\,362 = 0.007$ correct to 3 decimal places

$= 0.01$ correct to 2 decimal places

$7.601 = 7.60$ correct to 2 decimal places

$= 7.6$ correct to 1 decimal place

If an answer is required correct to 3 decimal places the division should be continued to 4 decimal places and the answer corrected to 3 decimal places.

Exercise 21 – *All type B*

Find the value of:

1) $18.89 \div 14.2$ correct to 2 decimal places.

2) $0.039\,6 \div 2.51$ correct to 3 decimal places.

3) $7.21 \div 0.038$ correct to 2 decimal places.

4) $13.059 \div 3.18$ correct to 4 decimal places.

5) $0.1382 \div 0.003\,2$ correct to 1 decimal place.

SIGNIFICANT FIGURES

Instead of using the number of decimal places to express the accuracy of an answer, significant figures can be used. The number 39.38 is correct to 2 decimal places but it is also correct to 4 significant figures since the number contains four figures. The rules regarding significant figures are as follows:

(1) If the first figure to be discarded is 5 or more the previous figure is increased by 1.

$8.192\,5 = 8.193$ correct to 4 significant figures

$= 8.19$ correct to 3 significant figures

$= 8.2$ correct to 2 significant figures

(2) Zeros must be kept to show the position of the decimal point, or to indicate that the zero is a significant figure.

$24\,392 = 24\,390$ correct to 4 significant figures

$= 24\,400$ correct to 3 significant figures

$0.085\,8 = 0.086$ correct to 2 significant figures

$425.804 = 425.80$ correct to 5 significant figures

$= 426$ correct to 3 significant figures

THE NUMBER OF SIGNIFICANT FIGURES IN AN ANSWER

The answer to a calculation should not contain more significant figures than the least number of significant figures used amongst the given numbers.

EXAMPLE 10

Find the value of $7.231 \times 1.24 \times 1.3$, each number being correct to the number of significant figures shown.

$$7.231 \times 1.24 \times 1.3 = 11.656\,372$$

The least number of significant figures amongst the given numbers is 2 (for the number 1.3). Hence the answer should only be stated correct to 2 significant figures.

$$\therefore \qquad 7.231 \times 1.24 \times 1.3 = 12$$
$$\text{correct to 2 significant figures.}$$

THE RANGE IN WHICH THE EXACT VALUE OF A COMPUTATION MUST LIE

Consider the number 8.32 correct to 3 significant figures. The exact value of this number must lie between $8.32 + 0.005$ and $8.32 - 0.005$, that is 8.32 ± 0.005. Now consider the addition of 7.2 and 9.3, both numbers being stated correct to 2 significant figures.

Greatest value	Least value
7.25	7.15
9.35	9.25
16.60	16.40

Hence the correct value of the sum must lie between 16.40 and 16.60. Since $7.2 + 9.3 = 16.50$ we may write the range in which the exact sum must lie as 16.50 ± 0.10.

EXAMPLE 11

Express the range in which the exact value of 5.1×8.3 lies in the form $a \pm b$. Both numbers are correct to 2 significant figures.

Greatest value of product
$$= 5.15 \times 8.35 = 43.00$$

Least value of product
$$= 5.05 \times 8.25 = 41.66$$

Product using given values
$$= 5.1 \times 8.3 = 42.33$$

Hence the range is 42.33 ± 0.67.

EXAMPLE 12

Express the range in which the exact value of $\frac{90}{15}$ must lie in the form $a \pm b$ if both numbers are correct to 2 significant figures.

Greatest value of quotient $= \dfrac{90.5}{14.5} = 6.24$

Least value of quotient $= \dfrac{89.5}{15.5} = 5.77$

Quotient using given values $= \dfrac{90}{15} = 6.0$

Here the range is 6.0 ± 0.23.

(Note that the greatest quotient is the largest value of the top number divided by the smallest value of the bottom number. Similarly, the smallest quotient is the smallest value of the top number divided by the greatest value of the bottom number.)

Exercise 22 – *All type B*

Write down the following numbers correct to the number of significant figures stated:

1) $24.865\,82$ (a) to 6 (b) to 4 (c) to 2

2) $0.008\,357\,1$ (a) to 4 (b) to 3 (c) to 2

3) $4.978\,48$ (a) to 5 (b) to 3 (c) to 1

4) 21.987 to 2

5) 35.603 to 4

6) $28\,387\,617$ (a) to 5 (b) to 2

7) $4.149\,76$ (a) to 5 (b) to 4 (c) to 3

8) $9.204\,8$ to 3

9) Each number in the following questions is correct to the number of significant figures shown. Find the value of each calculation to the correct number of significant figures:

(a) 17.63×20.5 (b) 11.3×3.2

(c) $25.14 \div 0.36$ (d) $11.63 + \dfrac{17.63}{0.273}$

10) Write down, in the form $a \pm b$, the range within which each of the following numbers must lie:

(a) 2.4 (b) 3.16 (c) 18.432

11) Express, in the form $a \pm b$, the range within which the exact value of the following calculations must lie:

(a) $\dfrac{60}{3}$ (b) $\dfrac{1.5}{5}$ (c) 1.6×2.4

(d) 2.34×1.88

ROUGH CHECKS FOR CALCULATIONS

The worst mistake that can be made in a calculation is that of misplacing the decimal point. To place it wrongly, even by one place, makes

Chapter 3   19

the answer ten times too large or ten times too small. To prevent this occurring it is always worth while doing a rough check by using approximate numbers. When doing these rough checks always try to select numbers that are easy to multiply or that will cancel.

EXAMPLE 13

(1) 0.23×0.56.

For a rough check we will take 0.2×0.6.
Product roughly $= 0.2 \times 0.6 = 0.12$.
Correct product $= 0.128\,8$

(The rough check shows that the answer is $0.128\,8$, not 1.288 or $0.012\,88$.)

(2) $173.3 \div 27.8$.

For a rough check we will take $180 \div 30$.
Quotient roughly $= 6$.
Correct quotient $= 6.23$.

(Note the rough check and the correct answer are of the same order.)

(3) $\dfrac{8.198 \times 19.56 \times 30.82 \times 0.198}{6.52 \times 3.58 \times 0.823}$.

Answer roughly $= \dfrac{8 \times 20 \times 30 \times 0.2}{6 \times 4 \times 1} = 40$.

Correct answer $= 50.94$.

(Although there is a big difference between the rough answer and the correct answer, the rough check shows that the answer is 50.94 and not 509.4.)

Exercise 23 – *All type B*

Find rough checks for the following:

1) $223.6 \times 0.004\,8$

2) 32.7×0.259

3) $0.682 \times 0.097 \times 2.38$

4) $78.41 \div 23.78$

5) $0.059 \times 0.002\,68$

6) $33.2 \times 29.6 \times 0.031$

7) $\dfrac{0.728 \times 0.006\,25}{0.028\,1}$

8) $\dfrac{27.5 \times 30.52}{11.3 \times 2.73}$

FRACTION TO DECIMAL CONVERSION

We found, when doing fractions, that the line separating the numerator and the denominator of a fraction takes the place of a division sign. Thus:

$\dfrac{17}{80}$ is the same as $17 \div 80$

Therefore to convert a fraction into a decimal we divide the denominator into the numerator.

EXAMPLE 14

Convert $\dfrac{27}{32}$ to decimals.

$$\frac{27}{32} = 27 \div 32$$

```
32)27.0(0.843 75
   25 6
   ─────
    1 40
    1 28
    ─────
     120
      96
     ─────
     240
     224
     ─────
     160
     160
     ─────
     . . .
```

Therefore $\dfrac{27}{32} = 0.843\,75$.

EXAMPLE 15

Convert $2\dfrac{9}{16}$ into decimals.

When we have a mixed number to convert into decimals we need only deal with the fractional part. Thus to convert $2\frac{9}{16}$ into decimals we only have to deal with $\frac{9}{16}$.

$$\frac{9}{16} = 9 \div 16$$

```
16)9.0(0.562 5
   80
   ────
   1 00
     96
   ────
     40
     31
   ────
     80
     80
     . .
```

The division shows that $\frac{9}{16} = 0.562\,5$ and hence $2\frac{9}{16} = 2.562\,5$.

Sometimes a fraction will not divide out exactly as shown in Example 16.

EXAMPLE 16

Convert $\frac{1}{3}$ to decimals.

$$\frac{1}{3} = 1 \div 3$$

$$
\begin{array}{r}
3)\overline{1.0}\,(0.333 \\
\underline{9} \\
10 \\
\underline{9} \\
10 \\
\underline{9} \\
1
\end{array}
$$

It is clear that all we shall get from the division is a succession of threes.

This is an example of a recurring decimal and in order to prevent endless repetition the result is written $0.\dot{3}$. Therefore $\frac{1}{3} = 0.\dot{3}$

Further examples of recurring decimals are:

$\frac{2}{3} = 0.\dot{6}$ (meaning $0.666\,6 \ldots$ etc.)

$\frac{1}{6} = 0.1\dot{6}$ (meaning $0.166\,6 \ldots$ etc.)

$\frac{5}{11} = 0.\dot{4}\dot{5}$ (meaning $0.454\,545 \ldots$ etc.)

$\frac{3}{7} = 0.\dot{4}28\,57\dot{1}$ (meaning $0.428\,571\,428\,571 \ldots$ etc.)

For all practical purposes we never need recurring decimals; what we need is an answer given to so many significant figures or decimal places. Thus:

$\frac{2}{3} = 0.67$ (correct to 2 decimal places)

$\frac{5}{11} = 0.455$ (correct to 3 significant figures)

Exercise 24 – *Questions 1–6 and 11–16 type A, remainder B*

Convert the following to decimals correcting the answers, where necessary, to 4 decimal places:

1) $\frac{1}{4}$ 3) $\frac{3}{8}$ 5) $\frac{1}{2}$

2) $\frac{3}{4}$ 4) $\frac{11}{16}$ 6) $\frac{2}{3}$

---

7) $\frac{21}{32}$ 9) $1\frac{5}{6}$

8) $\frac{29}{64}$ 10) $2\frac{7}{16}$

Write down the following recurring decimals correct to 3 decimal places:

11) $0.\dot{3}$ 15) $0.3\dot{5}$ 19) $0.\dot{3}2\dot{8}$

12) $0.\dot{7}$ 16) $0.\dot{2}\dot{3}$ 20) $0.\dot{5}67\dot{1}$

13) $0.1\dot{3}$ 17) $0.5\dot{2}$

14) $0.1\dot{8}$ 18) $0.3\dot{8}$

CONVERSION OF DECIMALS TO FRACTIONS

We know that decimals are fractions with denominators 10, 100, 1000, etc. Using this fact we can always convert a decimal to a fraction.

EXAMPLE 17

Convert 0.32 to a fraction.

$$0.32 = \frac{32}{100} = \frac{8}{25}$$

When comparing decimals and fractions it is best to convert the fraction into a decimal.

EXAMPLE 18

Find the difference between $1\frac{3}{16}$ and $1.163\,2$.

$$1\frac{3}{16} = 1.187\,5$$

$$1\frac{3}{16} - 1.163\,2 = 1.187\,5 - 1.163\,2$$

$$= 0.024\,3$$

Exercise 25 – *Questions 1 and 2 type A, remainder B*

Convert the following to fractions in their lowest terms:

1) 0.2   3) 0.312 5   5) 0.007 5

2) 0.45   4) 2.55   6) 2.125

7) What is the difference between 0.281 35 and $\frac{9}{32}$?

8) What is the difference between $\frac{19}{64}$ and 0.295?

SHORT CUTS IN CALCULATIONS

Consider the calculation 24×0.25. If we remember that $0.25 = \frac{1}{4}$, then the calculation becomes $24 \times \frac{1}{4} = 24 \div 4 = 6$. There are many cases where it is easier to divide by a whole number than multiply by a decimal. The following conversions should be remembered:

$0.5 = \frac{1}{2}$	$0.25 = \frac{1}{4}$	$0.125 = \frac{1}{8}$
$0.062\,5 = \frac{1}{16}$	$0.2 = \frac{1}{5}$	$0.\dot{3} = \frac{1}{3}$
$0.1\dot{6} = \frac{1}{6}$	$0.1\dot{1} = \frac{1}{9}$	

EXAMPLE 19

Find $27 \div 0.125$.

Now $0.125 = \frac{1}{8}$. Hence:

$$27 \div 0.125 = 27 \div \frac{1}{8} = 27 \times \frac{8}{1} = 27 \times 8 = 216$$

By observing that certain numbers will cancel, short cuts in calculations it is possible to make.

EXAMPLE 20

Evaluate $125 \times 0.053 \times 16$.

Now $125 = \dfrac{1000}{8}$ and $0.053 = \dfrac{53}{1000}$

Hence:

$$125 \times 0.053 \times 16 = \frac{1000}{8} \times \frac{53}{1000} \times 16$$

$$= 53 \times 2 = 106$$

Some calculations may be simplified by using the distributive law.

EXAMPLE 21

Find the value of $3.2 \times 17 + 3.2 \times 8$.

By the distributive law,

$$3.2 \times 17 + 3.2 \times 8 = 3.2 \times (17 + 8) = 3.2 \times 25$$

$$= 3.2 \times \frac{100}{4} = 0.8 \times 100$$

$$= 80$$

EXAMPLE 22

Evaluate 198×17.

$$198 \times 17 = (200 - 2) \times 17$$

$$= 200 \times 17 - 2 \times 17$$

$$= 3400 - 34$$

$$= 3366$$

EXAMPLE 23

Evaluate 1003×0.9.

$$1003 \times 0.9 = 0.9 \times (1000 + 3)$$

$$= 0.9 \times 1000 + 0.9 \times 3$$

$$= 900 + 2.7 = 902.7$$

Exercise 26 – *All type B*

By using short-cut methods evaluate the following:

1) $0.36 \times 0.3\dot{3}$
2) $36 \times 0.1\dot{1}$
3) 64×0.125
4) $128 \times 0.062\,5$
5) $25 \times 0.61 \times 4$
6) $50 \times 40 \times 0.25$
7) $1.5 \times 11 + 1.5 \times 9$
8) $2.3 \times 19 - 2.3 \times 9$
9) 299×16
10) 99×23
11) 101×182
12) 1003×27

SELF-TEST 3

In Questions 1 to 10 state the letter (or letters) corresponding to the correct answer (or answers).

1) The number $0.028\,57$ correct to 3 places of decimals is:

a 0.028 b 0.028 6 c 0.029 d 0.286

2) The sum of $5\dfrac{1}{100} + \dfrac{7}{1000}$ is:

a 5.0107 b 5.017 c 5.107 d 5.17

3) $13.006\,3 \times 1000$ is equal to:

a 13.063 b 130.063
c 1300.63 d 13 006.3

4) $1.500\,3 \div 100$ is equal to:

a 0.015 003 b 0.150 03
c 0.153 d 1.53

5) $18.2 \times 0.013 \times 5.21$ is equal to:

a 0.123 268 6   **b** 1.232 686

c 12.326 86   **d** 123.268 6

6) The number 158 861 correct to 2 significant figures is:

a 15   **b** 16   **c** 150 000   **d** 160 000

7) The number 0.081 778 correct to 3 significant figures is:

a 0.081   **b** 0.081 7

c 0.081 8   **d** 0.082

8) The number 0.075 538 correct to 2 decimal places is:

a 0.07   **b** 0.075   **c** 0.076   **d** 0.08

9) The number $0.16\dot{}$ correct to 4 significant figures is:

a 0.161 6   **b** 0.166 6

c 0.161 7   **d** 0.166 7

10) $0.017 \div 0.027$ is equal to (correct to 2 significant figures):

a 0.063   **b** 0.63   **c** 6.3   **d** 63

11) 0.72 is equivalent to:

a $\frac{72}{1000}$ **b** $\frac{7}{10}$ **c** $\frac{18}{25}$ **d** $7\frac{1}{5}$

12) The value of $4.7 - 1.9 + 2.1$ is:

a 0.7   **b** 1.7   **c** 4.9   **d** 5.9

13) 0.4×1.4 equals:

a 0.05   **b** 0.56   **c** 5.6

d 56

14) In the number 8.679 2 the value of the digit 7 is:

a $\frac{7}{1000}$ **b** $\frac{7}{100}$ **c** $\frac{7}{10}$ **d** 70

15) Given that $225 \times 35 = 7875$ then 22.5×0.35 is equal to:

a 787.5   **b** 7.875   **c** 0.787 5

d 0.078 75

16) The exact value of 1.2×1.4 must lie within one of the following ranges. Which one?

a 1.5 ± 0.5 **b** 1.6 ± 0.8

c 1.7 ± 0.03 **d** 2.0 ± 0.4

CHAPTER 3 SUMMARY

Points to remember

(i) "Decimal places" refers to the number of digits after the decimal point.
e.g. 73.128 is correct to 3 decimal places.

(ii) "Significant figures" refers to the total number of digits, beginning with a digit other than 0, in the number.
e.g. 83.51 has 4 significant figures.
0.0236 has 3 significant figures: 2, 3 and 6.

(iii) To multiply decimals, multiply as usual. Find the sum of the decimal places in the numbers being multiplied.

Chapter 4 **Currency**

THE CARIBBEAN SYSTEM

In most English-speaking Caribbean territories the dollar is used as the basic unit of currency. The dollar is subdivided into 100 parts, each of which is called a cent, such that

$$100 \text{ cents} = 1 \text{ dollar}$$

The abbreviation c is used for cents and the abbreviation $ for dollars. Amounts will sometimes be expressed in dollars, sometimes in dollars and cents, and sometimes just in cents.

For example:

$$\$4 = \$4.00 = 400\,c$$

$$\$2.15 = 215\,c$$

$$\$0.74 = 74\,c$$

$$\$0.05 = 5\,c$$

ADDITION AND SUBTRACTION

The addition of sums of money is done in the same way as the addition of decimals.

EXAMPLE 1
Add together $3.78, $5.23 and $8.19.

$$
\begin{array}{r}
\$3.78 \\
\$5.23 \\
\underline{\$8.19} \\
\underline{\$17.20}
\end{array}
$$

EXAMPLE 2
Add together 39 c, 84 c and $1.73.

$$
\begin{array}{r}
\$0.39 \\
\$0.84 \\
\underline{\$1.73} \\
\underline{\$2.96}
\end{array}
$$

When amounts are given in cents it is best to write these as dollars. Thus 39 c is written $0.39, etc. The addition is then performed as previously described.

EXAMPLE 3
Subtract $2.36 from $3.08.

$$
\begin{array}{r}
\$3.08 \\
\underline{\$2.36} \\
\underline{\$0.72}
\end{array}
$$

Exercise 27 – *All type A*

1) Express the following amounts as cents:
$0.68, $0.04, $0.63, $0.07.

2) Express the following as cents:
$2.16, $3.59, $17.68.

3) Express the following as dollars:
35 c, 78 c, 6 c, 3 c

4) Express the following as dollars:
246 c, 983 c, 26 532 c

5) Add the following sums of money together:
(a) $2.15, $3.28, $4.63
(b) $8.28, $109.17, $27.98, $70.15
(c) $0.17, $1.63, $1.71, $1.90
(d) 82 c, 71 c, 82 c
(e) 17 c, 27 c, 81 c, 74 c

6) Subtract the following:
(a) $7.60 from $9.84
(b) $3.49 from $11.42
(c) $18.73 from $87.35
(d) $0.54 from $1.32
(e) 54 c from $2.63

MULTIPLICATION AND DIVISION

The multiplication and division of decimal currency are very similar to the methods used with decimal numbers.

EXAMPLE 4
Find the cost of 23 articles if each costs 27 c.

Now $27\,c = \$0.27$

Cost of 23 articles @ $0.27

$$= 23 \times \$0.27 = \$6.21$$

EXAMPLE 5

If 127 articles cost $13.97 find the cost of each article.

Cost of each article

$$= \$13.97 \div 127 = \$0.11 \quad \text{or} \quad 11\,\text{c}$$

READY RECKONERS

Ready reckoners provide a quick way of multiplying decimal sums. Table 4.1 shows an extract from a ready reckoner giving the price of N articles at 27 c each.

Table 4.1

N		N		N		N	
21	5.67	63	17.01	105	28.35	500	135.00
22	5.94	64	17.28	106	28.62	525	141.75
23	6.21	65	17.55	107	28.89	550	148.50
24	6.48	66	17.82	108	29.16	600	162.00
25	6.75	67	18.09	109	29.43	625	168.75
26	7.02	68	18.36	110	29.70	650	175.50
27	7.29	69	18.63	111	29.97	700	189.00
28	7.56	70	18.90	112	30.24	750	202.50
29	7.83	71	19.17	113	30.51	800	216.00
30	8.10	72	19.44	114	30.78	900	243.00

EXAMPLE 6

Use the table above to find the cost of:

(1) 23 articles at 27 c each.
(2) 571 articles at 27 c each.
(3) $6\frac{1}{4}$ m of material at 27 c per metre.
(4) 72.9 kg of foodstuff at 27 c per kilogram.

(1) Directly from the table, the cost is $6.21.

(2) From the table:

$$\begin{array}{l}
\text{cost of } 500 \text{ articles} = \$135.00 \\
\text{cost of } 71 \ \text{ articles} = \$\ \ 19.17 \\
\hline
\text{cost of } 571 \text{ articles} = \$154.17
\end{array}$$

(3) $6\frac{1}{4} = 6.25$. To use the tables we find the cost of 625 m to be $162.00 + $6.75 = $168.75. Hence the

cost of 6.25 m is $\$\dfrac{168.75}{100} = \$1.69$.

(4) The cost of 729 kg @ 27 c per kg is $189.00 + $7.83 = $196.83. Hence the

cost of 72.9 kg is $\$\dfrac{196.83}{10} = \$19.68$.

Exercise 28 – *All type B*

1) Find the cost of 12 articles costing 15 c each.

2) Find the cost of 85 articles costing 7 c each.

3) How much do 43 articles @ 39 c each cost?

4) What is the cost of 24 articles costing $7.03 each?

5) If 12 identical articles cost $1.56, how much does each cost?

6) If 241 identical articles cost $50.61, how much does each cost?

7) If 5000 articles cost $6550, find the cost of each article.

8) If 125 articles cost $271.25, what is the cost of each article?

Use Table 4.1 above to find the cost of:

9) 23 articles @ 27 c each.

10) 64 articles @ 27 c each.

11) 828 articles @ 27 c each.

12) 672 articles @ 27 c each.

FOREIGN EXCHANGE

Every country has its own monetary system. If there is to be trade and travel between any two countries there must be a rate at which the money of one country can be converted into money of the other country. This rate is called the rate of exchange.

EXCHANGE RATES, JANUARY 2001

Country	Monetary unit	Exchange rate
Barbados	100 cents = 1 dollar	BDS $1.98 = US $1
Belize	100 cents = 1 dollar	BEL $1.98 = US $1
Canada	100 cents = 1 dollar	CAN $1.53 = US $1
east Caribbean	100 cents = 1 dollar	EC $2.68 = US $1
Guyana	100 cents = 1 dollar	GUY $167.8 = US $1
Jamaica	100 cents = 1 dollar	JA $44.92 = US $1
Martinique	100 centimes = 1 franc	F4.80 = US $1
Trinidad & Tobago	100 cents = 1 dollar	TT $6.21 = US $1
United Kingdom	100 pence = 1 pound	£0.68 = US $1

EXAMPLE 7

If BDS $1.98 = US $1 find, to the nearest cent, the value in Barbados money of US $1200.

Since   US $1   = BDS $1.98

US $1200 = BDS $(1.98 × 1200)

= BDS $2376

EXAMPLE 8

A British tourist changes traveller's cheques for £75 into Jamaican money. The exchange rates

are £0.70 = US $1 and JA $44.92 = US $1.
How much Jamaican money does he receive?

Since

$$£0.70 = US \$1$$

$$£1 = \$\frac{1}{0.70} = US \$1.43$$

$$£75 = US \$(75 \times 1.43)$$

$$= US \$107$$

Since

$$US \$1 = JA \$44.92$$

$$US \$107 = JA \$(107 \times 44.92)$$

$$= JA \$4806.44$$

Hence the tourist receives JA $4806.44 for £75.

Exercise 29 – *Questions 1–5 type A,
remainder B*

Where necessary give answers correct to 2
decimal places.

Using the exchange rates previously given find:

1) The number of Barbados dollars equivalent to US $60.

2) The number of east Caribbean dollars equivalent to US $85.

3) The number of US dollars equivalent to GUY $850.

4) The number of US dollars equivalent to BEL $920.

5) The number of Barbados dollars equivalent to JA $920.

6) The number of Trinidad and Tobago dollars equivalent to CAN $200.

7) The number of east Caribbean dollars equivalent to £50.

8) A holidaymaker from the U.K. changes a traveller's cheque for £100 into Barbados dollars at £0.35 = BDS $1. He spends BDS $250 and changes the remainder into pounds at a rate of £0.33 = BDS $1. Find the amount he receives.

9) A Canadian tourist changes CAN $500 into Barbados dollars at a rate of CAN $0.67 = BDS $1. She spends, in Barbados, BDS $400. She then travels to Jamaica where she changes her Barbados money into Jamaican money, the exchange being JA $22.46 = BDS $1.

(a) How much Barbados money does she receive?

(b) How much Jamaican money does she get?
(c) She spends JA $200 and changes the remainder into Canadian money at a rate of CAN $0.034 = JA $1. How much Canadian money does she get?

SELF-TEST 4

1) The cost of 4 articles at 72 c each is:

a $2.88   **b** $2.89   **c** $2.90
d $2.92

2) The cost of $2\frac{1}{2}$ kg of tomatoes at 36 c per kg is:

a 72 c   **b** 84 c   **c** 86 c
d 90 c

3) The cost of 2 metres of material at $1.20 per metre and 3 metres at $1.50 per metre is:

a $2.70   **b** $6.60   **c** $6.90
d $7.10

4) The cost of 2000 articles at 25 c each is:

a $50   **b** $500   **c** $2500
d $5000

5) The change from $1 after buying 18 buttons at 2 c each is:

a 35 c   **b** 52 c   **c** 55 c
d 64 c

6) The cost of 200 articles at 3 c each is:

a $3   **b** $6   **c** $30
d $60

7) In Holland there are 100 cents in a florin. There are 5 florins to 4 Barbados dollars. How many Barbados cents is a 25 cent coin worth?

a 10   **b** 20   **c** 25   **d** 50

8) The ratio of the shares of two partners A and B in the profits of a business is 5:3.

(a) How much will B receive when the profit is $1200?

   a $300   **b** $360
   c $450   **d** $720

(b) How much will A receive when B receives $480?

   a $216   **b** $288
   c $300   **d** $800

9) Change £150 into Barbados dollars when the exchange rate is £0.25 = BDS $1.

a 75   **b** 125   **c** 300   **d** 600

Chapter 5 Ratio and Proportion

A ratio is a comparison between two similar quantities. If the length of a certain ship is 120 metres and a model of it is 1 metre long then the length of the model is $\frac{1}{120}$ of the length of the ship. In making the model the dimensions of the ship are all reduced in the ratio of 1 to 120. The ratio 1 to 120 is usually written $1:120$.

As indicated above a ratio may be expressed as a fraction and all ratios may be looked upon as fractions. Thus the ratio $2:5 = \frac{2}{5}$. The two terms of a ratio may be multiplied or divided without altering the value of the ratio. Hence $6:36 = 1:6 = \frac{1}{6}$. Again, $1:5 = 0.20$.

Before a ratio can be stated the units must be the same. We can state the ratio between 7 cents and $2 provided both sums of money are brought to the same units. Thus if we convert $2 to 200 c the ratio between the two amounts of money is $7:200$.

EXAMPLE 1
Express the ratio 20 c to $4 in its simplest form.

$$\$4 = 4 \times 100\,c = 400\,c$$

$$20:400 = \frac{20}{400} = \frac{1}{20}$$

$$\therefore \qquad 20\,c:\$4 = 1:20$$

EXAMPLE 2
Express the ratio $4:\frac{1}{4}$ in its lowest terms.

$$4:\frac{1}{4} = 4 \div \frac{1}{4} = 4 \times \frac{1}{4} = \frac{16}{1}$$

$$4:\frac{1}{4} = 16:1$$

EXAMPLE 3
Two lengths are in the ratio $8:5$. If the first length is 120 metres, what is the second length?

The second length $= \frac{5}{8}$ of the first length $= \frac{5}{8} \times 120 = 75$ metres.

EXAMPLE 4
Two amounts of money are in the ratio of $12:7$. If the second amountr is $21 what is the first amount?

$$\text{First amount} = \frac{12}{7} \times \$21 = \$36$$

Exercise 30 – *Questions 1–7 type A, remainder B*

Express the following ratios as fractions in their lowest terms:

1) $8:3$ 4) $9:15$

2) $4:6$ 5) $8:12$

3) $12:4$

6) Express the ratio of 30 c to $2 as a fraction in its lowest terms.

7) Express the ratio $5:80\,c$ as a fraction in its lowest terms.

8) Two lengths are in the ratio $7:5$. If the first length is 210 metres, what is the second length?

9) Two amounts of money are in the ratio $8:5$. If the second amount is $120, what is the first amount?

10) Express $3:\frac{1}{2}$ in its lowest terms.

PROPORTIONAL PARTS

The diagram (Fig. 5.1) shows a line AB whose length is 16 centimetres divided into two parts in the ratio $3:5$. As can be seen in the diagram the line has been divided into a total of 8 parts. The length AC contains 3 parts and the length BC contains 5 parts. Each part is $\frac{16}{8} = 2$ centimetres long; hence AC is $3 \times 2 = 6$ centimetres long and BC is $5 \times 2 = 10$ centimetres long. We could tackle this problem in this way:

Total number of parts $= 3 + 5 = 8$ parts.

Length of each part $= \dfrac{16}{8} = 2$ centimetres.

Length of AC $= 3 \times 2 = 6$ centimetres.

Length of BC $= 5 \times 2 = 10$ centimetres.

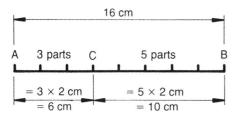

Fig. 5.1

EXAMPLE 5

Divide $1100 into two parts in the ratio $7 : 3$.

Total number of parts $= 7 + 3 = 10$

Amount of each part $= \dfrac{1100}{10} = \$110$

Amount of first part $= 7 \times 110 = \$770$

Amount of second part $= 3 \times 110 = \$330$

EXAMPLE 6

An aircraft carries 2880 litres of fuel distributed in three tanks in the ratio $3 : 5 : 4$. Find the quantity in each tank.

Total number of parts $= 3 + 5 + 4 = 12$

Amount of each part $= \dfrac{2880}{12} = 240$ litres

Amount of 3 parts $= 3 \times 240 = 720$ litres

Amount of 4 parts $= 4 \times 240 = 960$ litres

Amount of 5 parts $= 5 \times 240 = 1200$ litres

The three tanks contain 720, 1200 and 960 litres

Exercise 31 – *Questions 1–3 type A, remainder B*

1) Divide $800 in the ratio $5 : 3$.

2) Divide $80 in the ratio $4 : 1$.

3) Divide $120 in the ratio $5 : 4 : 3$.

4) A sum of money is divided into two parts in the ratio $5 : 7$. If the smaller amount is $200, find the larger amount.

5) An alloy consists of copper, zinc and tin in the ratios $2 : 3 : 5$. Find the amount of each metal in 75 kilograms of the alloy.

6) A line is to be divided into three parts in the ratios $2 : 7 : 11$. If the line is 840 millimetres long, calculate the length of each part.

7) Two villages have populations of 336 and 240 respectively. The two villages are to share a grant of $10 728 in proportion to their populations. Calculate how much each village receives.

8) Four friends contribute sums of money to a charitable organisation in the ratio of $2 : 4 : 5 : 7$. If the largest amount contributed is $1.40, calculate the total amount contributed by the four people.

DIRECT PROPORTION

Two quantities are said to vary directly, or be in direct proportion, if they increase or decrease at the same rate. Thus the quantity of petrol used and the distance travelled by a motor car are in direct proportion. Again if we buy potatoes at 80 cents for 2 kilograms then we expect to pay 160 cents for 4 kilograms and 40 cents for 1 kilogram. That is, if we double the amount bought then we double the cost; if we halve the amount bought we halve the cost.

In solving problems on direct proportion we can use either the unitary method or the fractional method. They are illustrated in Example 7.

EXAMPLE 7

If 25 kilograms of butter cost $37.50, how much do 8 kilograms cost?

(1) Using the unitary method:

25 kilograms cost $37.50

1 kilogram costs $\dfrac{\$37.50}{25} = \$1.50$

8 kilograms cost $\$1.50 \times 8 = \$12.00$

(2) Using the fractional method:

Cost of 8 kilograms

$$= \dfrac{8}{25} \times \$37.50 = \dfrac{8 \times 37.50}{25}$$

$$= \$12.00$$

EXAMPLE 8

A recipe for Boeuf Stroganoff quotes the following amounts to serve four people: 450 grams of rump steak, 3 tablespoons flour, 4 tablespoons butter, 50 grams of onion, 75 grams of mushrooms, 140 grams of sour cream.
What amounts should be used for six people?

The quantities required and the number of people are in direct proportion. Hence the amounts must be increased in the ratio of $6:4$ or $3:2$.

Amount of rump steak

$$= \frac{3}{2} \times 450 = 675 \text{ grams}$$

Amount of flour $= \frac{3}{2} \times 3 = 4\frac{1}{2}$ tablespoons

Amount of butter $= \frac{3}{2} \times 4 = 6$ tablespoons

Amount of onion $= \frac{3}{2} \times 50 = 75$ grams

Amount of mushrooms

$$= \frac{3}{2} \times 75 = 112\frac{1}{2} \text{ grams}$$

Amount of sour cream

$$= \frac{3}{2} \times 140 = 210 \text{ grams}$$

Exercise 32 – *All type A*

1) If 7 kilograms of bananas cost $8.40, how much do 12 kilograms cost?

2) If 74 exercise books cost $44.40, how much do 53 cost?

3) If 40 articles cost $35.20, how much does 1 article cost? What is the cost of 55 articles?

4) Eggs cost $7.20 per dozen. How much will 25 eggs cost?

5) A car travels 205 kilometres on 20 litres of petrol. How much petrol is needed for a journey of 340 kilometres?

6) The ingredients for a cake which will serve 12 people are as follows: 55 grams of butter, 110 grams of caster sugar, 6 egg yolks, 120 grams plain flour and 3 tablespoons of milk. What quantities are needed to serve 4 people?

7) If 9 metres of carpet cost $135, how much will 96 metres cost?

8) A train travels 200 kilometres in 4 hours. How long will it take to complete a journal of 350 kilometres?

INVERSE PROPORTION

Suppose that 8 men working on a certain job take 10 days to complete it. If we double the number of men then we should halve the time taken. If we halve the number of men then the job will probably take twice as long. This is an example of inverse proportion.

EXAMPLE 9

20 men working in a factory produce 3000 articles in 12 working days. How long will it take 15 men to produce the 3000 articles?

The number of men is reduced in the ratio $\frac{15}{20} = \frac{3}{4}$.

Since this is an example of inverse proportion the number of days required must be increased in the ratio $\frac{4}{3}$.

Number of days required $= \frac{4}{3} \times 12 = 16$ days.

Exercise 33 – *All type A*

1) A farmer employs 12 men to harvest his crops. They take 9 days to do the job. If he had employed 8 men how long would it have taken them?

2) 10 men produce 500 articles in 5 working days. How long would it take 15 men to produce the same amount?

3) Two gear wheels mesh together. One has 40 teeth and the other has 25 teeth. If the larger wheel makes 100 revolutions per minute how many revolutions per minute does the smaller wheel make?

4) A bag contains sweets. When divided amongst 8 children each child receives 9 sweets. If the sweets were divided amongst 12 children how many sweets would each receive?

5) 4 men can do a piece of work in 30 hours. How many men would be required to do the work in 6 hours?

SELF-TEST 5

1) In Holland there are 100 cents in a florin. There are 5 florins to 4 Barbados dollars. How many Barbados cents is a 25 cent coin worth?

a 10   **b** 20   **c** 25   **d** 50

2) The ratio of A's share to B's share in the profits of a business is $5:4$. If the total profit is $450 then A's share is:

a $90   **b** $200   **c** $225   **d** $250

3) If $120 is divided in the ratio 2 to 3 then the smaller share is:

a $40   **b** $48   **c** $60   **d** $72

4) The ratio of the shares of two partners A and B in the profits of a business is $5:3$.

(a) How much will B receive when the profit is $1200?

a $300   **b** $360   **c** $450   **d** $720

(b) How much will A receive when B receives $480?

a $216   **b** $288   **c** $300   **d** $800

5) A car does 12 kilometres per litre of petrol. How many complete litres of petrol will be needed to be sure of completing a journey of 100 kilometres?

a 8   **b** 9   **c** 12   **d** 1200

6) If two men can paint a fence in 6 hours, how many hours will it take three men to paint it, assuming they all work at the same rate?

a 3   **b** 4   **c** 9   **d** 12

7) Change £150 into Barbados dollars when the exchange rate is £0.25 = BDS$1.

a 75   **b** 125   **c** 300   **d** 600

8) Divide $1200 in the ratio $5:3$.

a $240 and $960   **b** $800 and $400
c $1050 and $150   **d** $750 and $450

CHAPTER 5 SUMMARY

Points to remember

(i) Ratio is a comparison of two numbers by division.
The ratio of a to b, written $a:b$, is the number represented by a/b, where $b \neq 0$. e.g Mike is 150 cm tall, and Jane is 120 cm tall. The ratio of Mike's height to Jane's is $150:120 = 5:4$.

(ii) A proportion is a number sentence that states that two ratios are equal.

If two ratios $a:b$ and $c:d$ are equal, we can represent them in a proportion $a/b = c/d$, then $ad = bc$.

(iii) Direct proportion—if 2 numbers are in direct proportion then "one number"= a constant × "other number".

(iv) Inverse proportion—if two numbers are in inverse proportion then "one number"= a constant ÷ "other number".

Chapter 6 **Percentages**

When comparing fractions it is often convenient to express them with a denominator of a hundred. Thus:

$$\frac{1}{2} = \frac{50}{100}$$

$$\frac{2}{5} = \frac{40}{100}$$

Fractions with a denominator of 100 are called *percentages*. Thus:

$$\frac{1}{4} = \frac{25}{100} = 25 \text{ per cent}$$

$$\frac{3}{10} = \frac{30}{100} = 30 \text{ per cent}$$

The sign % is usually used instead of the words per cent.

To convert a fraction into a percentage we multiply it by 100.

EXAMPLE 1

$$\frac{3}{4} = \frac{3}{4} \times 100\% = 75\%$$

$$\frac{17}{20} = \frac{17}{20} \times 100\% = 85\%$$

Exercise 34 – *All type A*

Convert the following fractions to percentages:

1) $\frac{7}{10}$ 4) $\frac{4}{5}$ 7) $\frac{18}{75}$

2) $\frac{11}{20}$ 5) $\frac{31}{50}$ 8) $\frac{19}{20}$

3) $\frac{9}{25}$ 6) $\frac{1}{4}$

Decimal numbers may be converted into percentages by using the same rule. Thus:

$$0.3 = \frac{3}{10} = \frac{3}{10} \times 100\% = 30\%$$

The same result is obtained if we omit the intermediate step of turning 0.3 into a vulgar fraction and just multiply 0.3 by 100. Thus:

$$0.3 = 0.3 \times 100\% = 30\%$$

EXAMPLE 2

$$0.56 = 0.56 \times 100\% = 56\%$$

$$0.683 = 0.683 \times 100\% = 68.3\%$$

Exercise 35 – *All type A*

Convert the following decimal numbers into percentages:

1) 0.7 4) 0.813 7) 0.819

2) 0.73 5) 0.927 8) 0.02

3) 0.68 6) 0.333

To convert a percentage into a fraction we divide by 100.

EXAMPLE 3

$$45\% = \frac{45}{100}$$

As a decimal this is 0.45.

$$3.9\% = \frac{3.9}{100} = \frac{39}{1000}$$

As a decimal this is 0.039.

Note that all we have done to change a percentage into a decimal is to move the decimal point 2 places to the left.

Exercise 36 – *All type A*

Convert the following percentages into decimal fractions:

1) 32% 5) 31.5% 9) 3.95%

2) 78% 6) 48.2% 10) 20.1%

3) 6% 7) 2.5%

4) 24% 8) 1.25%

PERCENTAGE OF A QUANTITY

It is easy to find the percentage of a quantity if we first express the percentage as a fraction.

EXAMPLE 4

(1) What is 10% of 40?

Expressing 10% as a fraction it is $\frac{10}{100}$ and the problem then becomes: what is $\frac{10}{100}$ of 40?

$$10\% \text{ of } 40 = \frac{10}{100} \times 40 = 4$$

(2) What is 25% of $50?

$$25\% \text{ of } \$50 = \frac{25}{100} \times \$50 = \$12.50$$

(3) 22% of a certain length is 55 cm. What is the complete length?

We have that 22% of the length = 55 cm.

$$1\% \text{ of the length} = \frac{55}{22} \text{ cm} = 2.5 \text{ cm}$$

Now the complete length will be 100%, hence:

Complete length = 100×2.5 cm = 250 cm.

Alternatively

$$22\% \text{ of the length} = 55 \text{ cm}$$

$$\text{Complete length} = \frac{100}{22} \times 55$$

$$= \frac{100 \times 55}{22} = 250 \text{ cm}$$

(4) What percentage is 51 of 350? Give the answer correct to 3 significant figures.

$$\text{Percentage} = \frac{51}{350} \times 100$$

$$= \frac{51 \times 100}{350} = 14.6\%$$

Exercise 37 – *Questions 1–6 type A, remainder B*

Where necessary give the answer correct to 3 significant figures.

1) What is:
(a) 20% of 50
(b) 30% of 80
(c) 5% of 120
(d) 12% of 20
(e) 20.3% of 105
(f) 3.7% of 68?

2) What percentage is:
(a) 25 of 200
(b) 30 of 150
(c) 24 of 150
(d) 29 of 178
(e) 15 of 33?

3) A girl scores 36 marks out of 60 in an examination. What is her percentage mark? If the percentage needed to pass the examination is 45% how many marks are needed to pass?

4) If 20% of a length is 23 cm what is the complete length?

5) Given that 13.3 cm is 15% of a certain length, what is the complete length?

6) What is:
(a) 9% of $80
(b) 12% of $110
(c) 75% of $250?

7) Express the following statements in the form of a percentage:
(a) 3 eggs are bad in a box containing 144 eggs.
(b) In a school of 650 pupils, 20 are absent.
(c) In a school of 980 pupils, 860 eat lunch at school.

8) In a certain territory the average number of children eating lunches at school was 11 248, which represents 74% of the total number of children attending school. Calculate the total number of children attending school in that territory.

9) 23% of a consignment of bananas is bad. There are 34.5 kg of bad bananas. How many kilograms were there in the consignment?

10) A retailer accepts a consignment of 5000 ballpoint pens. He finds that 12% are faulty. How many faulty pens were there?

PERCENTAGE PROFIT AND LOSS

When a dealer buys or sells goods, the cost price is the price at which he buys the goods and the selling price is the price at which he sells the goods. If the selling price is greater than the cost price then a profit is made. The amount of profit is the difference between the selling price and the cost price. That is:

$$\text{Profit} = \text{selling price} - \text{cost price}$$

The profit per cent is always calculated on the cost price. That is:

$$\text{Profit \%} = \frac{\text{selling price} - \text{cost price}}{\text{cost price}} \times 100\%$$

If a loss is made the cost price is greater than the selling price. The loss is the difference between the cost price and the selling price. That is:

$$\text{Loss} = \text{cost price} - \text{selling price}$$

$$\text{Loss \%} = \frac{\text{cost price} - \text{selling price}}{\text{cost price}} \times 100\%$$

EXAMPLE 5

(1) A shopkeeper buys an article for $5.00 and sells it for $6.00. What is his profit per cent?

We are given:

$$\text{cost price} = \$5 \quad \text{and} \quad \text{selling price} = \$6$$

$$\text{Profit \%} = \frac{6-5}{5} \times 100\%$$

$$= \frac{1}{5} \times 100\% = 20\%$$

(2) A dealer buys 20 articles at a total cost of $5. He sells them for 30 c each. What is his profit per cent?

Since $5 = 500 c,

$$\text{cost price per article} = \frac{500}{20} = 25\,c$$

$$\text{Profit \%} = \frac{30-25}{25} \times 100\%$$

$$= \frac{5}{25} \times 100\% = 20\%$$

(3) A man buys a car for $6000 and sells it for $4000. Calculate his percentage loss.

$$\text{Loss} = \text{cost price} - \text{selling price}$$

$$= \$6000 - \$4000 = \$2000$$

$$\text{Loss \%} = \frac{2000}{6000} \times 100\% = 33\tfrac{1}{3}\%$$

Exercise 38 – *Questions 1–4 type A,
remainder type B*

1) A shopkeeper buys an article for 80 c and sells it for $1. Calculate the percentage profit.

2) Calculate the profit per cent when:
(a) Cost price is $1.50 and selling price is $1.80.
(b) Cost price is 30 c and selling price is 35 c.

3) Calculate the loss per cent when:
(a) Cost price is 75 c and selling price is 65 c.
(b) Cost price is $6.53 and selling price is $5.88.

4) The price of gas has increased from $0.56 to $0.62 per litre. What is the percentage increase in the price of gas?

5) A greengrocer buys a box of 200 oranges for $25. He sells them for 15 c each. Calculate his percentage profit.

6) A dealer buys 100 similar articles for $60 and sells them for 80 c each. Find his profit per cent.

7) A retailer buys 30 articles at 8 c each. Three are damaged and unsaleable but he sells the others at 10 c each. What is the profit per cent?

8) A car is bought for $8500 and sold for $7000. What is the loss per cent?

DISCOUNT

When a customer buys an article from a retailer for cash he will often ask the retailer for a *discount*. This discount, which is usually a percentage of the selling price, is the amount which the retailer will take off his selling price, thus reducing his profit.

EXAMPLE 6

A record player is offered for sale at $1800. A customer is offered a 10% discount for cash. How much does the customer actually pay?

$$\text{Discount} = 10\% \text{ of } \$1800$$

$$= \frac{10}{100} \times \$1800 = \$180$$

Amount paid by customer

$$= \$1800 - \$180 = \$1620$$

(*Alternatively*: since only 90% of the selling price is paid,

Amount customer pays

$$= 90\% \text{ of } \$1800 = \frac{90}{100} \times \$1800 = \$1620)$$

Sometimes discounts are quoted as so much in the dollar, for instance 5 c in the \$1. If we remember that 5 c in the \$1 is the same as 5% then the calculation of discounts is the same as that shown in Example 6.

EXAMPLE 7

How much will a girl pay for goods priced at \$12.50 if a discount of 8 c in the \$1 is offered for cash?

8 c in \$1 is the same as 8%.

$$\text{Discount} = \frac{8}{100} \times \$12.50 = \$1.00$$

Amount paid by the girl

$$= \$12.50 - \$1.00 = \$11.50$$

EXAMPLE 8

A dealer buys a table for \$50. It is marked for sale at \$80 but the dealer offers a discount of 10% for cash. What percentage profit does the dealer make on a cash sale?

$$\text{Cash price} = 90\% \text{ of } \$80 = \frac{9\cancel{0}}{1\cancel{00}} \times \frac{8\cancel{0}}{1} = \$72$$

$$\text{Profit \%} = \frac{72 - 50}{50} \times \frac{100}{1}\%$$

$$= \frac{22}{\cancel{50}} \times \frac{\cancel{100}^2}{1}\% = 44\%$$

Exercise 39 – *All type A*

1) A chair marked for sale at \$56 is sold for cash at a discount of 10%. What price did the customer pay?

2) A tailor charges \$360 for a suit of clothes but allows a discount of 5% for cash. What is the cash price?

3) A grocer offers a discount of $2\frac{1}{2}\%$ to his customers provided their bills are paid within one week. If a bill of \$7.20 is paid within one week, how much discount will the grocer allow?

4) A shop offers a discount of 5 c in the \$1. How much discount will be allowed on a washing machine costing \$1700?

5) A furniture store offers a discount of 7 c in the \$1 for cash sales. A customer buys a three piece suite priced at \$2280. How much will she actually pay?

6) A coat was bought by a retailer for \$200. It was marked for sale at \$300 but the retailer offers a discount of 20% for cash. Find the retailer's percentage profit on a cash sale.

7) During a sale a shopkeeper offers a discount of 25% on household goods. A vacuum cleaner is marked at \$300.

(a) Calculate the discounted price of the cleaner.
(b) If the shopkeeper paid \$200 for the cleaner, calculate his percentage profit on the sale.

PERCENTAGE CHANGE

An increase of 5% in a number means that the number has been increased by $\frac{5}{100}$ of itself.

Thus if the number is represented by 100, the increase is 5 and the new number is 105. The ratio of the new number to the old number is 105 : 100.

EXAMPLE 9

(1) An increase of 10% in salaries makes the wage bill for a factory \$55 000.
(a) What was the wage bill before the increase?
(b) What is the amount of the increase?

(a) If 100% represents the wage bill before the increase, then 110% represents the wage bill after the increase.

$$\therefore \quad \text{Wage bill before the increase}$$

$$= \frac{100}{110} \times \$55\,000 = \$50\,000$$

(b) The amount of the increase

$$= 10\% \text{ of } 50\,000$$

$$= \frac{10}{100} \times 50\,000 = \$5000$$

(2) By selling an article for $4.23 a dealer makes a profit of $12\frac{1}{2}\%$ on his cost price. What is his profit?

If 100% represents the cost price then $112\frac{1}{2}\%$ represents the selling price

$$\therefore \text{ Cost price } = \frac{100}{112\frac{1}{2}} \times \$4.23 = \frac{200}{225} \times \$4.23$$

$$= \$3.76$$

$$\text{Profit } = \text{ selling price } - \text{ cost price}$$

$$= \$4.23 - \$3.76 = \$0.47$$

A decrease of 5% in a number means that if the original number is represented by 100 then the decrease is 5 and the new number is 95. The ratio of the new number to the old number is $95 : 100$.

EXAMPLE 10

An article was sold for $30, which was a loss on the cost price of 10%. What was the cost price?

If 100% represents the cost price then 90% represents the selling price.

$$\therefore \quad \text{Cost price } = \$\frac{100}{90} \times 30 = \$33.33$$

Exercise 40 – *All type B*

1) Calculate the selling price when:

(a) Cost price is $5.00 and profit per cent is 20%.

(b) Cost price is $3.75 and profit per cent is 16%.

2) Calculate the cost price when:

(a) Selling price is $20.00 and profit is 25%.
(b) Selling price is 63 c and profit is $12\frac{1}{2}\%$.

3) By selling an article for $10.80 a shopkeeper makes a profit of 8%. What should be the selling price for a profit of 20%?

4) (a) An article can be bought from a shopkeeper for a single cash payment of $74 or by 18 monthly instalments of $4.30. Calculate the extra cost of paying by instalments.
(b) By selling for $74 the shopkeeper made a profit of 25%. Find how much he paid for the article.

5) A shopkeeper marks an article to allow himself 25% profit on the cost price. If he sells it for $80 how much was the cost price?

6) If 8% of a sum of money is $2.40 find $9\frac{1}{2}\%$ of the sum.

7) The duty on an article is 20% of its value. If the duty is 60 c, find the value of the article.

8) When a sum of money is decreased by 10% it becomes $18. What was the original sum?

9) A man sells a car for $4250, losing 15% of what he paid for the car. How much did the car cost him?

10) Equipment belonging to a firm is valued at $60 000. Each year 10% of the value of the equipment is written off for depreciation. Find the value of the equipment at the end of two years.

SELF-TEST 6

In Questions 1 to 15 state the letter (or letters) corresponding to the correct answer (or answers).

1) 35% is not the same as:

a $\dfrac{35}{100}$ **b** $\dfrac{7}{20}$ **c** 0.35 **d** $\dfrac{35}{10}$

2) $\dfrac{11}{25}$ is the same as:

a 4.4% **b** 25% **c** 44% **d** 440%

3) 30% of a certain length is 600 mm. The complete length is:

a 2 mm **b** 20 mm **c** 200 mm
d 2000 mm

4) $\frac{9}{10}$ as a percentage is:

a 0.9% **b** 9% **c** 90% **a** 99%

5) The word *discount* means:

a Money put down on an article bought on hire purchase.

b Money taken out of your wage.
c Money taken off the price of an article.
d Money owed to someone.

6) $\frac{3}{40}$ as a percentage is:

a 3%   **b** $7\frac{1}{2}$%   **c** 40%   **d** 75%   **e** 97%

7) A boy scored 70% in a test. If the maximum mark was 40, then the boy's mark was:

a 4   **b** 10   **c** 28   **d** 30

8) During a sale, a shop reduced the price of everything by 10%. What was the sale price of an article originally priced at $4.30?

a $0.43   **b** $3.40   **c** $3.87   **d** $3.97

9) For his holidays a man put aside 10% of his $175 weekly wage for 40 weeks in the year. How much did he save for his holiday?

a $175   **b** $350   **c** $525   **d** $700

10) A special offer of 2 c off the normal selling price of 25 c for an article is made. What percentage reduction does this represent?

a 2%   **b** 4%   **c** 8%   **d** 25%

11) In a sale, a discount of 10 c in the $1 is allowed off all marked prices. The price of an article is marked at $16.50. For how much can the article be bought in the sale?

a $1.65   **b** $14.85   **c** $16.00   **d** $18.15

12) A girl bought a record for $6 and sold it for $4.80.

(a) Her loss, as a percentage of the cost price, is:

   a 20%   **b** 24%   **c** 30%   **d** 60%

(b) For what price should she have sold the record to make a profit of 20% on her cost price of $6?

   a $5.20   **b** $6.10   **c** $6.40   **d** $7.20

(c) The shopkeeper from whom she bought the record made a profit of 50% on his cost price. How much did the record cost him?

   a $2.40   **b** $4.00   **c** $6.40
   d $7.00

13) When a dealer sells an article for $50 he makes a profit of 25%. The price he paid for the article is:

a $20   **b** $37.50   **c** $40   **d** $40.50

14) A dealer buys 40 articles at a total cost of $10. He sells them at 30 c each. His percentage profit is:

a $16\frac{2}{3}$%   **b** 20%   **c** 25%   **d** 30%

15) An article was sold for $60 which was a loss on the cost price of 10%. The cost price was therefore:

a $54   **b** $66   **c** $66.67   **d** $70.50

CHAPTER 6 SUMMARY

Points to remember

(i)   To change decimals to percentages
      (a) move the decimal point two places to the right
      (b) insert a percentage sign.
(ii) To change a fraction to a percentage
      (a) change the fraction to a decimal
      (b) change the decimal to a percentage.
(iii) To change percentages to decimals
      (a) remove the percentage sign
      (b) move the decimal point two places to the left. (It may be necessary to add zeros.)
(iv) To change percentages to fractions
      (a) remove the percentage sign
      (b) write the number obtained over 100.
(v)   To find a given percentage of a number
      (a) write the percentage as a fraction
      (b) multiply the number by this fraction.

(vi)   To find the percentage profit or loss
       (a) find the profit or loss
       (b) express the profit or loss as a percentage of the cost.
(vii) To find the *selling price* when the *cost price* and percentage profit (loss) are given
       (a) add to (subtract from) 100% the percentage profit (loss)
       (b) find this percentage of the cost price.
(viii) To find the cost price when selling price and profit (loss) percentage are given
       (a) add to (subtract from) 100% the percentage profit (loss)
       (b) divide the selling price by this percentage.

Chapter 7 Averages

AVERAGES

One way to find the "average" of a set of quantities is to add together and divide by the number of quantities in the set. Thus,

$$\text{Average} = \frac{\text{sum of the quantities}}{\text{number of quantities}}$$

EXAMPLE 1

(1) A boy makes the following scores at cricket: 8, 20, 3, 0, 5, 9, 15 and 12. What is his average score?

Average score

$$= \frac{8 + 20 + 3 + 0 + 5 + 9 + 15 + 12}{8}$$

$$= \frac{72}{8} = 9$$

(2) The oranges in a box have a mass of 4680 gm. If the average mass of an orange is 97.5 gm find the number of oranges in the box.

Total mass = average mass of an orange

× number of oranges in the box

∴ Number of oranges in the box $= \dfrac{4680}{97.5} = 48$

(3) Find the average age of a team of boys given that four of them are each 15 years 4 months old and the other three boys are each 14 years 9 months old.

Total age of 4 boys

at 15 years 4 months = 61 years 4 months

Total age of 3 boys

at 14 years 9 months = 44 years 3 months

Total age of 7 boys   = 105 years 7 months

$$\text{Average age} = \frac{105 \text{ years } 7 \text{ months}}{7}$$

$$= 15 \text{ years } 1 \text{ month}$$

(4) The average age of the teachers in a school is 39 years and their total age is 1170 years, whereas the pupils, whose average age is 14 years, have a total age of 6580 years. Find the average age of all the people in the school.

The first step is to find the number of teachers:

Number of teachers

$$= \frac{\text{total age of the teachers}}{\text{average age of the teachers}}$$

$$= \frac{1170}{39} = 30$$

We now find the number of pupils:

$$\text{Number of pupils} = \frac{6580}{14} = 470$$

We can now find the average age of all the people in the school:

Total age of all the people in the school

$$= (1170 + 6580) \text{ years} = 7750 \text{ years}$$

Total number of people in the school

$$= 30 + 470 = 500$$

Average age of all the people in the school

$$= \frac{7750}{500} \text{ years} = 15.5 \text{ years}$$

Exercise 41 – *Questions 1–4 type A, 5–10 type B, remainder C*

1) Find the average of the following readings: 22.3 mm, 22.5 mm, 22.6 mm, 21.8 mm and 22.0 mm.

2) Find the average mass of 22 boxes if 9 have a mass of 12 kg each, 8 have a mass of $12\frac{1}{2}$ kg each and 5 have a mass of $11\frac{3}{4}$ kg each.

3) 4 kg of apples costing 80 c per kg are mixed with 8 kg costing 56 c per kg. What is the average price per kg?

Chapter 7   37

4) 30 litres of petrol costing $1.92 per litre is mixed with 40 litres costing $1.68 per litre. Find the average price of the mixture.

5) The average of nine numbers is 72 and the average of four of them is 40. What is the average of the other five?

6) The oranges in a box have a mass of 240 kg. If the average mass of an orange is 120 g find the number of oranges in the box.

7) Find the average age of a team of boys if 5 of them are each 15 years old and 6 of them are 14 years 1 month old.

8) A grocer sells 40 tins of soup at $2.40 per tin, 50 at 90 c per tin and 60 tins at $3 per tin. Find the average price per tin.

9) The average mark of 24 candidates taking an examination is 42. Find what the average mark would have been if one candidate, who scored 88, had been absent.

10) The average of three numbers is 58. The average of two of them is 49. Find the third number.

11) In a school, three classes took the same examination. Class A contained 30 pupils and the average mark for the class was 66. Class B contained 22 pupils and their average mark was 54. Class C contained 20 pupils. The average obtained by all pupils together was 61.5. Calculate the average

AVERAGE SPEED

The average speed is defined as total distance travelled divided by the total time taken. The unit of speed depends on the unit of distance and the unit of time. For instance, if the distance travelled is in kilometres (km) and the time taken is in hours (h) then the speed will be stated in kilometres per hour (km/h). If the distance is given in metres (m) and the time in seconds (s) then the speed is in metres per second (m/s).

EXAMPLE 2

(1) A car travels a total distance of 200 km in 4 hours. What is its average speed?

$$\text{Average speed} = \frac{\text{distance travelled}}{\text{time taken}} = \frac{200}{4} \text{km/h}$$

$$= 50 \text{ km/h}$$

(2) A car travels 30 km at 30 km/h and 30 km at 40 km/h. Find its average speed.

Time taken to travel 30 km at 30 km/h

$$= \frac{30}{30} \text{ hours} = 1 \text{ hour}$$

Time taken to travel 30 km at 40 km/h

$$= \frac{30}{40} \text{ hours} = 0.75 \text{ hour}$$

Total distance travelled = (30 + 30) km = 60 km.
Total time taken = (1 + 0.75) hours = 1.75 hour.

$$\therefore \quad \text{Average speed} = \frac{60}{1.75} \text{ km/h} = 34.3 \text{ km/h}$$

(3) A train travels for 4 hours at an average speed of 64 km/h. For the first 2 hours its average speed is 50 km/h. What is its average speed for the last 2 hours?

Total distance travelled in 4 hours

= average speed × time taken = (64 × 4) km

= 256 km

Distance travelled in first two hours

= (50 × 2) km = 100 km

∴ Distance travelled in last two hours

= (256 − 100) km = 156 km

Average speed for the last two hours

$$= \frac{\text{distance travelled}}{\text{time taken}} = \frac{156}{2} \text{ km/h} = 78 \text{ km/h}$$

Exercise 42 – *Questions 1–3 type A, remainder B*

1) A train travels 300 km in 4 hours. What is its average speed?

2) A car travels 200 km at an average speed of 50 km/h. How long does it take?

3) If a car travels for 5 hours at an average speed of 70 km/h how far has it gone?

4) For the first $1\frac{1}{2}$ hours of a 91 km journey the average speed was 30 km/h. If the average speed for the remainder of the journey was 23 km/h, calculate the average speed for the entire journey.

5) A motorist travelling at a steady speed of 90 km/h covers a section of motorway in 25 minutes. After a speed limit is imposed he finds that, when travelling at the maximum speed allowed he takes 5 minutes longer than before to cover the same section. Calculate the speed limit.

6) In winter, in Canada, a train travels between two towns 264 km apart at an average speed of 72 km/h. In summer the journey takes 22 minutes less than in the winter. Find the average speed in summer.

7) A train travels between two towns 135 km apart in $4\frac{1}{2}$ hours. If on the return journey the average speed is reduced by 3 km/h, calculate the time taken for the return journey.

8) A car travels 272 km at an average speed of 32 km/h. On the return journey the average speed is increased to 48 km/h. Calulate the average speed over the whole journey.

SELF-TEST 7

In the following questions state the letter (or letters) corresponding to the correct answer (or answers).

1) The average of 11.2, 11.3, 11.5, 11.1 and 11.2 is:

a 11.22   **b** 11.26   **c** 11.3   **d** 11.4

2) The average weight of two adults in a family is 81 kg and the average weight of the three children in the family is 23 kg. The average weight of the whole family is:

a 20.8 kg   **b** 45.3 kg   **c** 46.2 kg
d 52.0 kg

3) 50 litres of oil costing 8 c per litre is mixed with 70 litres of oil costing 9 c per litre. The average price per litre of the mixture is about:

a 8.5 c   **b** 8.6 c   **c** 9.6 c   **d** 10.8 c

4) A grocer sells 20 tins of soup at 50 c per tin, 30 at 80 c per tin and 40 at 70 c per tin. The average price per tin of the soup is:

a 60 c   **b** 66.7 c   **c** 68.9 c   **d** 75 c

5) The average of three numbers is 116. The average of two of them is 98. The third number is:

a 18   **b** 107   **c** 110   **d** 152

6) An aeroplane flies non-stop for $2\frac{1}{4}$ hours and travels 1620 km. Its average speed in km/h is:

a 364.5   **b** 720   **c** 800   **d** 3645

7) A car travels 50 km at 50 km/h and 70 km at 70 km/h. Its average speed is:

a 58 km/h   **b** 60 km/h   **c** 62 km/h
d 65 km/h

8) A car travels for 3 hours at a speed of 45 km/h and for 4 hours at a speed of 50 km/h. It has therefore travelled a distance of:

a 27.5 km   **b** 95 km   **c** 335 km
d 353 km

9) A car travels 540 km at an average speed of 30 km/h. On the return journey the average speed is doubled to 60 km/h. The average speed over the entire journey is:

a 45 km/h   **b** 42 km/h   **c** 40 km/h
d 35 km/h.

10) A car travels between two towns 270 km apart in 9 hours. On the return journey the speed is increased by 10 km/h. The time taken for the return journey is:

a $2\frac{7}{10}$ hours   **b** $4\frac{1}{2}$ hours   **c** $6\frac{1}{2}$ hours
d $6\frac{3}{4}$ hours.

CHAPTER 7 SUMMARY

Points to remember

"Average" used in a popular sense means a general type or that which is ordinary or common. The most widely used average is really the arithmetic mean. When used in this sense the average value of a set of numbers may be calculated as "the sum of the values" divided by the "number of members in the set".

The average speed = total distance ÷ total time.

Chapter 8 **Salaries, Household Bills, Rates and Taxes**

Everyone who works for an employer receives a wage or salary in return for their labours. However, the payment can be made in several different ways.

PAYMENT BY THE HOUR

Many people who work in factories, in the transport industry and in the building and construction industry are paid a certain amount of money for each hour that they work. Most employees work a basic week of so many hours and it is this basic week which fixes the hourly (or basic) rate of wages. The basic rate and the basic week are usually fixed by negotiation between the employer and the trade union which represents the workers.

EXAMPLE 1

A man works a basic week of 38 hours and his basic rate is $3.75 per hour. Calculate his total wage for the week.

$$38 \text{ hours at } \$3.75 \text{ per hour}$$
$$= 38 \times \$3.75 = \$142.50$$

Hence the total wage for the week is $142.50.

EXAMPLE 2

A factory worker is paid $156 for a basic week of 40 hours. What is his hourly rate?

$$\text{Hourly rate} = \frac{\$156}{40} = \$3.90$$

Exercise 43 – *All type A*

Calculate the total pay in each of the following cases:

1) Basic rate = $4.80 per hour.
   Basic week = 42 hours.

2) Basic rate = $3.45 per hour.
   Basic week = 39 hours.

3) Basic rate = $4.68 per hour.
   Basic week = 37 hours.

4) Basic rate = $4.14 per hour.
   Basic week = 40 hours.

Calculate the hourly rate in each of the following cases:

5) Basic week = 42 hours.
   Weekly wage = $141.12.

6) Basic week = 39 hours.
   Weekly wage = $175.50.

7) Basic week = 40 hours.
   Weekly wage = $96.00.

8) Basic week = 44 hours.
   Weekly wage = $121.44.

OVERTIME

Hourly paid workers are usually paid extra money for working more hours than the basic week demands. These extra hours of work are called *overtime*.

Overtime is usually paid at one of the following rates:

(1) Time and a quarter – $1\frac{1}{4}$ times the basic rate.
(2) Time and a half – $1\frac{1}{2}$ times the basic rate.
(3) Double time – twice the basic rate.

EXAMPLE 3

A girl working in a shop is paid a basic rate of $4.32 per hour. Find the rates of pay for overtime in the following cases: (1) time and a quarter; (2) time and a half; (3) double time.

(1) Overtime rate at time and a quarter
$$= 1\frac{1}{4} \times \$4.23$$
$$= 1.25 \times \$4.32 = \$5.40$$

(2) Overtime rate at time and a half
$$= 1\frac{1}{2} \times \$4.32$$
$$= 1.5 \times \$4.32 = \$6.48$$

(3) Overtime rate at double time
$$= 2 \times \$4.32 = \$8.64$$

EXAMPLE 4

John Smith works a 42 hour week for which he is paid a basic wage of $113.40. He works 6 hours overtime at time and a half and 4 hours overtime at double time. Calculate his gross wage for the week.

$$\text{Basic hourly rate} = \frac{\$113.40}{42} = \$2.70$$

Overtime rate at time and a half
$$= 1\tfrac{1}{2} \times \$2.70 = \$4.05$$

Overtime rate at double time
$$= 2 \times \$2.70 = \$5.40$$

Gross wage
$$= \$113.40 + 6 \times \$4.05 + 4 \times \$5.40$$
$$= \$113.40 + \$24.30 + \$21.60 = \$159.30$$

Exercise 44 – *All type B*

1) A secretary works a 46 hour week for which she is paid $182.16. She works 4 hours overtime which is paid for at time and a quarter. How much did she earn that week?

2) Tom Brown works 54 hours in a certain week. His basic week is 42 hours for which he is paid $151.12. His overtime rate is time and a half. Calculate his gross wage for the week.

3) In an engineering firm employees work a basic week of 38 hours. Any overtime worked from Monday to Friday is paid for at time and a quarter. Overtime worked on Saturday is paid for at time and a half whilst on sunday it is paid for at double time. If the basic rate is $3.72 per hour find the wages of a man who worked 6 hours overtime from Monday to Friday, 4 hours overtime on Saturday and 7 hours overtime on sunday.

4) A man's basic wage for a 38 hour week is $159.60. In a certain week he earned $191.10 by working overtime. If he worked 5 hours overtime what is the overtime rate?

5) A man's basic hourly rate is $8.64. Overtime is paid for at time and a quarter. If the basic week is 40 hours, how many hours of overtime must be worked in order to earn $410.40 for the week?

6) A man is paid a basic hourly rate of $4.80 for a 40 hour week. On weekdays he is paid at time and a half for overtime. If his wage for a certain week was $278.40, how many hours of overtime did he work?

COMMISSION

Shop assistants, salesmen and representatives are sometimes paid *commission* on top of their basic wage. This commission is usually a small percentage of the total value of the goods they have sold.

EXAMPLE 5

A salesman is paid a commission of $2\tfrac{1}{2}\%$ on the value of the goods he has sold. Calculate the amount of his commission if he sells goods to the value of $4100 during a certain week.

$$\text{Commission} = 2\tfrac{1}{2}\% \text{ of } \$4100$$
$$= \frac{2.5}{100} \times \$4100 = \$102.50$$

EXAMPLE 6

A shop assistant is paid a basic wage of $132 per week. In addition she is paid a commission of 2% of the value of the goods that she sells. During a certain week she sells goods worth $2040. How much does she earn in the week?

$$\text{Commission} = 2\% \text{ of } \$2040$$
$$= \frac{2}{100} \times \$2040 = \$40.80$$

Total wages for the week
$$= \$132 + \$40.80 = \$172.80$$

Exercise 45 – *All type B*

1) A salesman sells $650 of goods during a week. If he is paid a commission of 2% how much commission will he be paid?

2) Calculate the commission due to a car salesman if he sells a car for $8850 and his commission is 3%.

3) A sales assistant is paid a basic wage of $150 per week. In addition she is paid a commission of $2\frac{1}{2}\%$ on the value of the goods she sells. How much commission will she be paid on sales amounting to $2850 and what are her earnings for that week?

4) An agent selling agricultural machinery is paid a basic wage of $300 per week. In addition he is paid a commission of 3% of his sales. In one week he made sales totalling $9750. How much are his gross wages?

SALARIES

People like teachers, civil servants, secretaries and company managers are paid a definite amount for one year's work. It is unusual for them to be paid overtime, commission or a bonus. The annual salary is usually divided into twelve equal parts which are paid to the employee at the end of each month.

EXAMPLE 7

A teacher is employed at an annual salary of $18 000. How much is he paid monthly?

    Monthly salary $= \$18\,000 \div 12 = \$1500$

Exercise 46 – *All type A*

Calculate the monthly payment for each of the following annual salaries:

1) $4050   **3)** $11 568   **5)** $5076
2) $6780   **4)** $7488

RATES

Every property in a town or city is given a *rateable value* which is fixed by the valuation department. This rateable value depends upon the size, condition and position of the property.

The rates of a town or village are levied at so much in the $1 of rateable value, for instance, $0.85 in the $1. The money brought in by the rates is used to pay for such things as education, police, libraries, etc.

EXAMPLE 8

The rateable value of a house is $120. If the rates are 75c in the $1, how much must the owner pay in rates per annum?

Rates payable per annum
$$= 120 \times \$0.75 = \$90$$

EXAMPLE 9

A householder pays $90 in rates on property which has a rateable value of $150. What is the local rate?

    For a rateable value of $150 rates paid are $90.

    For a rateable value of $1 rates paid are
$$\$\frac{90}{150} = \$0.60.$$

Hence the rates are levied at $0.60 in the $1.

EXAMPLE 10

What rate should be charged to raise $4 510 000 from a total rateable value of $8 200 000?

Rates chargeable in the $1
$$= \frac{4\,510\,000}{8\,200\,000} = 0.55.$$

Hence the rates should be $0.55 in the $1.

EXAMPLE 11

The cost of highways and bridges in a town is equivalent to a rate of 9.28 c in the $1. If the rateable value of all the property in the town is $15 400 000 find how much money is available for spending on highways and bridges during the financial year.

    Amount available
$$= 9.28 \times 15\,400\,000\,c$$
$$= \$\frac{9.28 \times 15\,400\,000}{100} = \$1\,429\,120$$

Exercise 47 – *All type A*

1) The rateable value of a house is $90. Calculate the rates payable by a householder when the rates are $0.70 in the $1.

2) A householder pays $90 in rates when the rate levied is $0.75 in the $1. What is the rateable value of the house?

3) A house is assessed at a rateable value of $45. The owner pays $40.50 in rates for the year. What is the rate in the $1?

4) What rate should be charged if the need is to raise $100 000 from a total rateable value of $320 000?

5) Calculate the total income from the rates of a town of rateable value $2 150 000 when the rates are 54 c in the $1.

6) A town of rateable value $772 000 needs to raise $70 400 from the rates. What local rate should be charged?

7) The rateable value of all the property in a city is $8 500 000. What is the product of a rate of 80 c in the $1?

8) The rateable value for all the property in a city is $8 796 000. How much must the rates be if the total expenses for the city for a year are $4 837 800?

9) The total rateable value for all the property in a city is $850 000. Calculate the total cost of public libraries if a rate of 4.6 c in the $1 must be levied for the purpose.

10) The expenditure of a town is $900 000 and its rates are 87 c in the $1. The cost of libraries is $30 000. What rate in the $1 is needed for the upkeep of the libraries?

INCOME TAX

Taxes are levied by the Inland Revenue in order to produce income to pay for the Civil Service, the NHS and other expenditures. The largest producer of revenue is *income tax*.

Every person who has an income above a certain minimum amount has to pay income tax to the Government. Tax is not paid on the whole income. Certain allowances are made as follows:

(1) an allowance, the amount of which varies according to whether the taxpayer is a single person or a married man,

(2) allowances for children, dependent relatives, etc.,

(3) allowances for superannuation contributions, mortgage interest, etc.,

(4) an allowance for the premiums on whole life and endowment insurance policies.

The residue of the income left after the allowances have been deducted is called the *taxable income*. The following example shows the method used in calculating income tax.

EXAMPLE 12

A man's salary is $5500 per year. His taxable

income is found by deducting the following from his salary:

(1) A married man's allowance of $2000.

(2) A children's allowance of $400.

(3) National Insurance $150.

(4) Life assurance $360.

He then pays tax at the standard rate of 35%. Calculate his taxable income and the amount he has to pay in income tax.

To find the taxable income deduct the following from the salary of $5500.

Married man's allowance	= $2000
Children's allowance	= $400
National Insurance	= $150
Life assurance	= $360
Total allowance	$2910

Taxable income
$$= \$5500 - \$2910 = \$2590$$

Total tax payable
$$= 35\% \text{ of } \$2590 = \$906.50$$

SALES TAX

Many Caribbean territories have a sales tax, which is a tax on goods purchased.

EXAMPLE 13

A lady buys a table which is priced at $800 plus sales tax. How much will she pay for the table if the rate of tax is 10%?

$$\text{Sales tax} = 10\% \text{ of } \$800 = \frac{10}{100} \times \$800 = \$80$$

$$\text{Total cost of table} = \$800 + \$80 = \$880$$

EXAMPLE 14

A person buys a washing machine for $990, the price including a sales tax of 10%. What is the price of the machine exclusive of sales tax?

Let 100% be the price exclusive of sales tax
Then

110% is the price inclusive of sales tax

110% represents $900

100% represents $\frac{100}{110} \times \$990 = \$900$

Hence the price exclusive of sales tax is $900.

Exercise 48 – *All type A*

Use the following allowances for the questions in this exercise:

(1) Single person's allowance $1200
(2) Married man's allowance $2000
(3) Child under 11 years old $300
(4) Child 11–16 years old $400
(5) Child over 16 if in full-time
         education $500
(6) Dependent relative $240
(7) National Insurance $150

1) A man's taxable income is $1200. If tax is paid at 6% find the amount paid in income tax.

2) When income tax is levied at 7.5% a man pays $60 in income tax. What is his taxable income?

3) Calculate the amount a single man, with no allowances except his single person's allowance, will pay in income tax when this is levied at 20%, if he earns $7800 per annum.

4) A maried man with two children under 11 years old earns $16 000 per annum. If he has no other allowances find the amount of tax he will pay when income tax is levied at 35%.

5) A married man with one child aged 15 years and a second aged 10 years earns $15 000 per annum. He has a dependent relative whom he helps to support. If he also gets an allowance of $150 for National Insurance calculate the amount he pays in income tax per annun when this is levied at 30%.

6) A man buys a vacuum cleaner, at a price, exclusive of sales tax, of $300. If sales tax of 10% is charged, how much did the man pay?

7) A chair is priced at $110 inclusive of 10% sales tax. What is the price exclusive of sales tax?

8) A set of saucepans is priced at $112.20 inclusive of 10% sales tax. How much are they exclusive of sales tax?

HIRE PURCHASE

When we purchase goods and pay for them by instalments we are said to have purchased them on hire purchase. Usually the purchaser pays a deposit and the balance of the purchase price plus interest is repaid in a number of instalments.

EXAMPLE 15

A woman buys a suite of furniture for $1920. A deposit of 25% is paid and interest at 12% per annum is charged on the outstanding balance.

The balance is paid in 12 monthly instalments. Calculate how much each instalment will be.

Price of suite = $1920

Less deposit = $480 (25% of $1920)

Outstanding balance
   = $1920 − $480 = $1440

Plus interest at 12% on balance for 1 year
   = 12% of $1440 = $172.80

Total amount to be repaid
   = $1440 + $172.80 = $1612.80

Amount of each instalment

$$= \frac{\$1612.80}{12} = \$134.40$$

In Example 15, 12% would only be the true rate of interest if all of the outstanding balance was paid at the end of the year. However as each instalment is paid the amount outstanding is reduced and hence a larger proportion of each successive payment is interest. The true rate of interest is much higher than 12%; it is, in fact, about 22%.

EXAMPLE 16

A woman buys a radio for $80 and pays a deposit of 20% on the purchase price. The outstanding balance plus interest at 10% on this balance for the whole period of repayment is to be repaid in four quarterly instalments. What is the true rate of interest?

Outstanding balance = $80 − 20% of $80
                            = $80 − $16 = $64

Interest at 10% for 1 year = 10% of $64
                                  = $6.40

Total to be repaid = $64 + $6.40 = $70.40

Amount of each instalment = $70.40 ÷ 4
                                  = $17.60

$64 is the balance outstanding for 3 months

$48 is the balance outstanding for the next 3 months

$32 is the balance outstanding for the next
  3 months

$16 is the balance outstanding for the final
  3 months

Average amount of loan for the entire year

$$= \$\frac{64 + 48 + 32 + 16}{4} = \$40$$

If $6.40 is the interest paid on a loan of $40 the
true rate of interest may be found from the
simple interest formula

$$R = \frac{100I}{PT} = \frac{100 \times 6.40}{40 \times 1} = 16\%$$

Note that in calculating the outstanding balance
we have said that the interest payable is $1.60
every 3 months. Thus the amount actually paid
off the balance is $17.60 − $1.60 = $16. The
method of Example 16 is called the *average loan
method*.

BANK LOANS

Many people take out personal loans from a
bank. The bank will calculate the interest for the
whole period of the loan and the loan plus the
interest is usually repaid in equal monthly
payments.

EXAMPLE 17

A man borrows $3000 from his bank. The bank
charges 18% interest for the whole period of
the loan. If the repayments are in 12 equal
monthly instalments calculate the amount of
each payment.

Interest = 18% of $3000 = $540

Total amount to be repaid

    = $3000 + $540 = $3540

Amount of each instalment

$$= \$\frac{3540}{12} = \$295$$

Exercise 49

1) A man buys a television set for $960. He
pays a deposit of $150 and he is to pay the
outstanding balanced plus interest in 12
equal monthly instalments. If the interest is
charged at 10% on the outstanding balance
for the full period of the loan calculate the
amount of the instalment.

2) A woman buys a suite of furniture for
$960. A deposit of 20% is paid and interest
at 12% per annum is charged on the
outstanding balance for the full period of the
loan. The balance is to be paid in 4 quarterly
payments. How much is each payment?

3) A vacuum cleaner is bought for $1050
and a deposit of $300 is paid. The out-
standing balance plus interest at 10% on
this balance for the whole period of the
repayment is to be paid in 4 quarterly
instalments. How much is each quarterly
payment?

4) A radio is priced as $252. It can be
purchased on hire purchase by paying a
deposit of $63 and 12 monthly instalments
of $17.64. What rate of interest is being
charged on the outstanding balance for the
whole period of the loan?

5) A man borrows $2500 from a bank at
15% interest over the whole period of the
loan. If the loan plus interest is to be repaid
in 12 equal monthly instalments calculate
the amount of the instalments to the nearest
$1.

6) A suite of furniture is priced at $1440.
Hire purchase terms are available which are:
deposit 25% and 18 equal instalments of
$70.80. Calculate the total hire purchase
price and find the difference between the
cash price and the hire purchase price.

7) An article of furniture can be purchased
for $80 cash or by hire purchase. When
purchased on the instalment system nine
monthly repayments are required in which
case interest at 18% per annum for nine
months is added to the cash price. Calculate
the amount of each instalment.

8) A bank lends a man $2500. They charge
interest at 12% per annum which is added
to the amount of the loan. If the loan is
repaid in 24 monthly instalments calculate
the amount of each instalment.

9) A woman buys a chest of drawers priced at
$100. She pays no deposit but agrees to repay
the $100 plus interest at 20% over the entire
period of the loan. If she pays two equal
instalments find the amount of each instalment and calculate the true rate of interest.

10) A lady buys a suite of furniture for $2560. She pays a deposit of $320. Interest at 24% per annum is to be paid on the outstanding balance for the full period of the agreement. If the balance is to be paid in four equal quarterly payments, find the true rate of interest.

ELECTRICITY BILLS

Electricity is charged for according to the number of kilowatt-hours (abbreviation: kWh) used. A typical tariff is as follows:

Fixed charge	$3 per month
First 50 kWh	11 c per kWh
Next 250 kWh	9 c per kWh
All over 300 kWh	7 c per kWh
Discount	10% for payment within 15 days of issue of the bill

EXAMPLE 18

A householder uses 460 kWh of electricity in a quarter (three months). What will be the amount of the bill? If the bill is paid within 15 days how much will be paid?

Fixed charge $= 3 \times \$3 = \$9$

First 50 kWh @ 11 c per kWh
$$= 50 \times 11c = \$5.50$$

Next 250 kWh @ 9 c per kWh
$$= 250 \times 9c = \$22.50$$

Next 160 kWh @ 7 c per kWh
$$= 160 \times 7c = \$11.20$$

Total cost $= \$9 + \$5.50 + \$22.50 + \$11.20$
$$= \$48.20$$

Discount $= 10\%$ of $\$48.20 = \$4.82$

Amount paid $= \$48.20 - \$4.82 = \$43.38$

Exercise 50 – *All type A*

1) A householder pays for all the electricity he uses at 10 c per kWh. If he uses 520 kWh in a quarter, what will be his quarterly bill?

2) In a certain area electricity is charged for at a fixed rate of 8 c for every kWh used. If a householder receives a bill for $33.60, how many kWh has he used?

3) A householder receives an electricity bill for $30 and he used 250 kWh. If the electricity is charged for at so much per kWh find the cost per kWh.

4) In a certain territory a householder pays for his electricity as follows: a fixed charge of $7 plus 13 c per kWh for each of the kWh used. Find his bill if he uses 370 kWh.

5) In one of the Caribbean territories, electricity is charged for as follows:

Fixed charge	$4 per month
First 50 kWh	12 c per kWh
Next 200 kWh	10 c per kWh
All over 250 kWh	8 c per kWh

A discount of 10% is allowed on all bills paid within 14 days.
A householder uses 560 kWh of electricity in 3 months. How much will he pay if the bill is paid within 14 days?

SELF-TEST 8

In Questions 1 to 10 state the letter (or letters) corresponding to the correct answer (or answers).

1) A man's basic wage for a 35 hour week is $136.50. His overtime rate is 60 c per hour more than his basic rate. If he works 6 hours of overtime in a certain week his wage for that week will be:

a $137.10   **b** $140.10   **c** $157.50
d $163.50

2) Office workers asked for a rise of 12% but were granted only 5% which brought their weekly wage up to $134.40. If the 12% rise had been granted their weekly wage would have been:

a $322   **b** $288.40   **c** $148.40
d $143.36

3) A man's basic pay for a 40 hour week is $160. Overtime is paid for at 25% above the basic rate. In a certain week he worked overtime and his total wage was $200.

The total number of hours worked is:

a 40   **b** 48   **c** 50   **d** 65

4) A householder is charged for his electricity as follows:
Fixed charge $10 per quarter, 11 c for the first 50 kWh, 10 c for the next 250 kWh and 8 c for all kWh over 300. If a quarterly bill amounted to $16.30, the number of kWh used was:

a 58   **b** 63   **c** 158   **d** 258

5) A householder pays for his electricity by means of a fixed charge of $9 plus 11 c for each unit of electricity used. If he used 45 kWh of electricity his bill was:

a $4.95   **b** $9   **c** $9.11   **d** $13.95

6) The rateable value of a house is $150. If the rates are 80 c in the $1 the rates payable are:

a $120   **b** $148.20   **c** $150.80   **d** $151

7) The cost of highways in a town is equivalent to a rate of 6.2 c in the $1. If the rateable value of all the property in the town is $3 500 000 then the cost of highways is:

a $37 313.43   **b** $217 000   **c** $564 516.12   **d** $3 283 000

8) The expenditure of a town is $300 000 and its rates are 75 c in the $1. The cost of the library is $20 000. The rate needed for the upkeep of the library is:

a 3 c in the $1   **b** 5 c in the $1   **c** 15 c in the $1   **d** 25 c in the $1

9) When income tax was levied at 5% a man paid $90 in income tax. His taxable income was therefore:

a $450   **b** $945   **c** $1710   **d** $1800

CHAPTER 8 SUMMARY

Points to remember

(i)   To calculate sales tax
    (a) Write the percentage as a fraction or a decimal.
    (b) Multiply the price by the fraction or decimal.

(ii) To find the amount of income tax to be paid
    (a) Add the allowances.
    (b) Subtract the total allowance from the total salary.
    (c) Multiply the rate of interest by the remainder.

(iii) To calculate the hire purchase instalment
    (a) Subtract the deposit from the hire purchase cost of the article. This is the outstanding balance.
    (b) Divide this balance by the number of months or weeks.

(iv) To calculate the amount of commission
    (a) Write the rate of commission as a decimal or a fraction.
    (b) Multiply the amount of sales by this decimal or fraction.

Chapter 9 Simple and Compound Interest

SIMPLE INTEREST

Interest is the profit return on investment. If money is invested then interest is paid to the investor. If money is borrowed then the person who borrows the money will have to pay interest to the lender. The money which is invested or lent is called the *principal*. The percentage return is called the *rate per cent*. Thus interest at a rate of 12% means that the interest on a principal of $100 will be $12 per annum. The total formed by adding the interest is called the *amount*. The amount is therefore the total sum of money that remains invested after a period of time.

With simple interest the principal always stays the same no matter how many years the investment (or the loan) lasts.

EXAMPLE 1

How much interest does a man pay if he borrows $400 for one year at an interest rate of 12%?

$$\text{Interest} = 12\% \text{ of } \$400$$

$$= \frac{12}{100} \times \$400 = \$48$$

If money is borrowed for two years the amount of interest payable will be doubled; for three years three times as much interest is payable; and so on.

The interest payable (or earned) depends upon:

(1) The amount borrowed or lent, i.e. the *principal*.

(2) The rate of interest charged, i.e. the *rate %*.

(3) The period of the loan, i.e. the *time* (in years).

To calculate the *simple interest* use the formula below:

$$I = \frac{PRT}{100}$$

where P stands for the principal
R stands for the rate per cent
T stands for the time in years

This formula can be transposed to give:

$$T = \frac{100I}{PR}$$

$$R = \frac{100I}{PT}$$

$$P = \frac{100I}{RT}$$

EXAMPLE 2

Find the simple interest on $500 borrowed for 4 years at 11% per annum.

Here we have $P = 500$, $R = 11$ and $T = 4$. Substituting these values in the simple interest formula gives:

$$I = \frac{500 \times 11 \times 4}{100} = 220$$

Thus the simple interest is $220.

EXAMPLE 3

$700 is invested at 4% per annum. How long will it take for the amount to reach $784?

The interest $= \$784 - \$700 = \$84.$

We therefore have $I = 84$, $R = 4$ and $P = 700$ and we have to find T. Substituting these values in the simple interest formula gives:

$$T = \frac{100 \times 84}{700 \times 4} = 3$$

Hence the time taken is 3 years.

Simple interest tables (see page 48) are sometimes used to find the amount of interest due at the end of a given period of time. The table shows the appreciation (the increase in value) of $1. For instance:

$1 invested for 8 years at 11% per annum will become $1.88.

$1 invested for 15 years at 8% per annum will become $2.20.

EXAMPLE 4

Using the simple interest tables calculate the simple interest earned by $850 invested for 9 years at 10% per annum.

From the simple interest table, in 9 years at 10% p.a. $1 becomes $1.90. To find the amount accruing from $850 multiply 1.90 by $850.

Amount accruing
$$= 1.90 \times \$850 = \$1615$$

Interest earned
$$= \$1615 - \$850 = \$765.$$

Exercise 51 – *Questions 1–8 type A, remainder type B*

1) Find the simple interest on $700 invested for 3 years at 6% per annum.

2) Find the simple interest on $500 invested for 6 months at 8% per annum.

3) In what length of time will $500 be the interest on $2500 which is invested at 5% per annum?

4) In what length of time will $16 be the simple interest on $480 invested at 8% per annum?

5) In what length of time will $75 be the simple interest on $500 invested at 6% per annum?

6) The interest on $600 invested for 5 years is $210. What is the rate per cent?

7) The interest on $200 invested for 4 months is $6. What is the rate per cent?

8) What principal is needed so that the interest will be $48 if it is invested at 3% per annum for 5 years?

9) Which receives the more interest per annum: $150 invested at 4% or $180 invested at $3\frac{1}{2}$%? What is the annual difference?

10) A man invests $700 at 6% per annum and $300 at 8% per annum. What is his total annual interest on these investments?

11) A man deposited $350 in a bank and $14 interest was added at the end of the first year. The whole amount was left in the bank for a second year at the same rate of interest. Find the amount of interest on the $364 paid in the second year.

12) Using Table 9.1 calculate the simple interest earned in each of the following cases:

(a) $350 invested at 6% p.a. for 9 years.
(b) $500 invested at 11% p.a. for 5 years.
(c) $2500 invested at 8% p.a. for 16 years.
(d) $7000 invested at 13% p.a. for 11 years.
(e) $900 invested at 9% p.a. for 21 years.

TABLE 9.1 SIMPLE INTEREST

Appreciation of $1 for periods from 1 year to 25 years

Year	5%	6%	7%	8%	9%	10%	11%	12%	13%	14%
1	1.050	1.060	1.070	1.080	1.090	1.100	1.110	1.120	1.130	1.140
2	1.100	1.120	1.140	1.160	1.180	1.200	1.220	1.240	1.260	1.280
3	1.150	1.180	1.210	1.240	1.270	1.300	1.330	1.360	1.390	1.420
4	1.200	1.240	1.280	1.320	1.360	1.400	1.440	1.480	1.520	1.560
5	1.250	1.300	1.350	1.400	1.450	1.500	1.550	1.600	1.650	1.700
6	1.300	1.360	1.420	1.480	1.540	1.600	1.660	1.720	1.780	1.840
7	1.350	1.420	1.490	1.560	1.630	1.700	1.770	1.840	1.910	1.980
8	1.400	1.480	1.560	1.640	1.720	1.800	1.880	1.960	2.040	2.120
9	1.450	1.540	1.630	1.720	1.810	1.900	1.990	2.080	2.170	2.260
10	1.500	1.600	1.700	1.800	1.900	2.000	2.100	2.200	2.300	2.400
11	1.550	1.660	1.770	1.880	1.990	2.100	2.210	2.320	2.430	2.540
12	1.600	1.720	1.840	1.960	2.080	2.200	2.320	2.440	2.560	2.680
13	1.650	1.780	1.910	2.040	2.170	2.300	2.430	2.560	2.690	2.820
14	1.700	1.840	1.980	2.120	2.260	2.400	2.540	2.680	2.820	2.960
15	1.750	1.900	2.050	2.200	2.350	2.500	2.650	2.800	2.950	3.100
16	1.800	1.960	2.120	2.280	2.440	2.600	2.760	2.920	3.080	3.240
17	1.850	2.020	2.190	2.360	2.530	2.700	2.870	3.040	3.210	3.380
18	1.900	2.080	2.260	2.440	2.620	2.800	2.980	3.160	3.340	3.520
19	1.950	2.140	2.330	2.520	2.710	2.900	3.090	3.280	3.470	3.660
20	2.000	2.200	2.400	2.600	2.800	3.000	3.200	3.400	3.600	3.800
21	2.050	2.260	2.470	2.680	2.890	3.100	3.310	3.520	3.730	3.940
22	2.100	2.320	2.540	2.760	2.980	3.200	3.420	3.640	3.860	4.080
23	2.150	2.380	2.610	2.840	3.070	3.300	3.530	3.760	3.990	4.220
24	2.200	2.440	2.680	2.920	3.160	3.400	3.640	3.880	4.120	4.360
25	2.250	2.500	2.750	3.000	3.250	3.500	3.750	4.000	4.250	4.500

COMPOUND INTEREST

Compound interest is different from simple interest in that the interest which is added to the principal also attracts interest. If money is invested at compound interest, the interest due at the end of each year is added to the principal for the next year.

EXAMPLE 5

Find the amount of money gained from an investment of $800 for 3 years at 10% per annum compound interest.

Interest of $800 for 1 year at 10%
$$= 10\% \text{ of } \$800 = \$80$$

Add this interest to the original principal of $800.

New principal = $880.

Interest on $880 for 1 year at 10%
$$= 10\% \text{ of } \$880 = \$88$$

Add this interest to the principal of $880.

New principal = $968.

Interest on $968 for 1 year at 10%
$$= 10\% \text{ of } \$968 = \$96.80$$

Amount accruing at the end of 3 years
$$= \$968 + \$96.80 = \$1064.80$$

Although all problems on compound interest can be worked out by the method of Example 5, the work is tedious and time consuming, particularly if the period is lengthy. Here is a formula which will allow you to calculate the compound interest:

$$A = P\left(1 + \frac{R}{100}\right)^n$$

where A stands for the amount of money accruing after n years
P stands for the principal
R stands for the rate per cent per annum

n stands for the number of years for which the money is invested

You will have to make use of logarithms or a calculator when using this formula.

EXAMPLE 6

Calculate the interest earned on $750 invested at 12% per annum for 8 years.

Here we have $P = \$750$, $R = 12\%$ and $n = 8$ years. Substituting these values in the compound interest formula we have

$$A = 750 \times \left(1 + \frac{12}{100}\right)^8 = 750 \times (1.12)^8$$

We can use logarithms (see Chapter 20).

number	log
1.12	0.049 2
	× 8
	0.393 6
750	2.875 1
	3.268 7

Antilog of 3.268 7 = 1857.

A calculator may be used to do the above calculation. Indeed, we recommend that calculators should be used responsibly to enrich students' learning of mathematics.

Hence the amount accruing after 8 years is $1857.

The interest earned is $1857 − $750 = $1107.

COMPOUND INTEREST TABLES

In business, compound interest tables are used to find the amount of interest due at the end of a given period of time. Part of such a table is shown below (Table 9.2).

TABLE 9.2 COMPOUND INTEREST
Appreciation of $1 from 1 year to 10 years

Year	5%	6%	7%	8%	9%	10%	11%	12%	13%	14%
1	1.050	1.060	1.070	1.080	1.090	1.100	1.110	1.120	1.130	1.140
2	1.103	1.124	1.145	1.166	1.188	1.210	1.232	1.254	1.277	1.300
3	1.158	1.191	1.225	1.260	1.295	1.331	1.368	1.405	1.443	1.482
4	1.216	1.262	1.311	1.360	1.412	1.464	1.518	1.574	1.603	1.689
5	1.276	1.338	1.403	1.469	1.539	1.611	1.685	1.762	1.842	1.925
6	1.340	1.419	1.501	1.587	1.677	1.772	1.870	1.974	2.082	2.195
7	1.407	1.504	1.606	1.714	1.828	1.949	2.076	2.211	2.353	2.502
8	1.477	1.594	1.718	1.851	1.993	2.144	2.304	2.476	2.658	2.853
9	1.551	1.689	1.838	1.999	2.172	2.358	2.558	2.773	3.004	3.252
10	1.629	1.791	1.967	2.159	2.367	2.594	2.839	3.106	3.395	3.707

The table shows the appreciation (the increase in value) of $1. For instance, $1 invested for 5 years at 9% interest will become $1.539. Example 7 shows how the table is used in compound interest calculations.

EXAMPLE 7

Using the compound interest table find the amount of compound interest earned by $750 invested for 6 years at 5% per annum.

From the table in 6 years at 5%, $1 becomes $1.340.

To find the amount accruing from $750 we multiply 1.340 by $750.

Amount accruing

$$= 1.340 \times \$750 = \$1005$$

Interest earned

$$= \$1005 - \$750 = \$255$$

DEPRECIATION

A business will own a number of assets such as machinery, typewriters, motor transport, etc. These assets reduce in value, i.e. *depreciate*, all the time. Each year the depreciation has to be calculated and charged as a business expense. A number of ways exist for calculating the depreciation. The commonest way is to use the reducing balance method in which the depreciation is calculated as a percentage of the book value of the assets at the beginning of the year.

EXAMPLE 8

A small business buys a centre lathe costing $2000. It decides to calculate the depreciation each year as 20% of its value at the beginning of the year. Calculate the book value after three complete years.

Cost of lathe

$$= \$2000$$

Depreciation first year (20%)

$$= \$400 \ (20\% \text{ of } \$2000)$$

Book value at start of second year

$$= \$1600$$

Depreciation second year (20%)

$$= \$320 \ (20\% \text{ of } \$1600)$$

Book value at start of third year

$$= \$1280$$

Depreciation third year (20%)

$$= \$256 \ (20\% \text{ of } \$1280)$$

Book value at end of third year

$$= \$1024$$

Hence the lathe is reckoned to be worth $1024 at the end of the third year.

Although all problems with the reducing balance method of depreciation can be worked out by using the method of Example 8, it is much quicker to use the depreciation formula, which is very similar to the compound interest formula. It is:

$$A = P\left(1 - \frac{R}{100}\right)^n$$

where A stands for the book value after
           n years
           P stands for the initial cost of the asset
           R stands for the rate of depreciation
           n stands for the number of years

EXAMPLE 9

A business buys new machinery costing $12 000. It decides to calculate the depreciation each year at 25% of its value at the beginning of the year. Calculate the book value at the end of 4 years.

We are given that $P = 12\,000$, $R = 25$ and $n = 4$. Substituting these values in the formula we have

$$A = 12\,000 \times \left(1 - \frac{25}{100}\right)^4$$

$$= 12\,000 \times 0.75^4$$

We must use logarithms (see Chapter 20) for this calculation.

number	log
0.75^4	$\bar{1}.875\,1$
	$\times 4$
	$\bar{1}.500\,4$
$12\,000$	$4.079\,2$
	$3.579\,6$

The antilog of $3.579\,6$ is 3798 and hence the book value of the machinery at the end of 4 years is £3798.

Exercise 52 – *All type B*

Use the compound interest formula and the log tables or a calculator to calculate the compound interest earned in each of the following:

1) $250 invested for 5 years at 8% per annum

2) $400 invested for 7 years at 9% per annum

3) $1200 invested for 12 years at 10% per annum

4) $2500 invested for 15 years at 11% per annum

5) $5000 invested for 6 years at 7% per annum

6) How much interest is earned when $800 is invested at 9% per annum simple interest for 6 years? How much would have been earned if the money had been invested at compound interest?

7) A man borrowed $1200 for 8 years at 11% compound interest. How much will he have to repay?

8) Find to the nearest dollar the amount accruing when $970 is invested for 10 years at 12% compound interest

Using the compound interest table calculate the compound interest earned in each of the following:

9) $350 invested for 6 years at 7% per annum

10) $500 invested for 5 years at 11% per annum

11) $2500 invested at 5% per annum for 10 years

12) $7000 invested for 7 years at 13% per annum

13) $900 invested for 10 years at 9% per annum

14) A firm buys office machinery at a cost of $15 000. It is decided to calculate the depreciation each year as 15% of the book value at the beginning of the year. Calculate the book value at the end of 5 years

15) The value of a machine depreciates each year by 12% of its value at the beginning of the year. If it cost $8000 when new calculate its value at the end of 7 years

16) It is estimated that a machine costing $20 000 has a life of 10 years. It is decided to calculate the depreciation each year as $12\frac{1}{2}$% of the book value at the beginning of the year.

Find the value of the machine at the end of the 10 years

17) A machine which cost $5500 depreciates by 15% of the reducing balance. How much is the machine worth at the end of 5 years?

18) A lorry cost $24 000 when new. 20% is written off its book value at the end of each year. Find its book value after 8 years.

SELF-TEST 9

In Questions 1 to 10 state the letter (or letters) corresponding to the correct answer (or answers).

1) The simple interest on $500 for 4 years at 7% per annum is:

a $20   **b** $140   **c** $1400   **d** $14 000

2) The simple interest on $800 invested at 8% per annum for 6 months is:

a $32   **b** $48   **c** $60   **d** $64

3) The simple interest on $800 invested for 5 years was $240. The rate of interest per annum was therefore:

a 3%   **b** 5%   **c** 6%   **d** 7%

4) The simple interest on $800 invested at 5% per annum over a number of years amounted to $160. The cash was therefore invested for:

a 4 years   **b** 5 years   **c** 6 years
d 7 years

5) The simple interest on $400 invested for 4 months was $12. The rate of interest per annum is:

a 4.8%   **b** 7%   **c** 9%   **d** 36%

6) A man invests $700 at 5% per annum and $300 at 6% per annum. The entire investment has an interest rate of:

a $5\frac{1}{2}$%   **b** 5.3%   **c** 11%   **d** 53%

7) A man invests $9000 at 10% per annum and $1000 at 8% per annum. His interest rate on the complete investment is:

a 2%   **b** 9.8%   **c** 10%   **d** 18%

8) What sum of money must be invested to give $30 simple interest if the rate is 6% per annum and the time is 2 years?

a $250   **b** $300   **c** $360   **d** $400

9) A sum of money is invested at 8% per annum for 4 years and the simple interest is $160. The amount of money invested is:

a $320   **b** $500   **c** $640   **d** $1280

10) A sum of money was invested at 5% per annum for 4 years. The total amount lying to the credit of the investor at the end of the 4 years was $600. The amount originally invested was:

a $800   **b** $600   **c** $500   **d** $400

11) $500 invested at 10% compound interest for 2 years becomes:

a $600   **b** $605   **c** $665.50   **d** $700

12) The value of a machine depreciates each year by 15% of its value at the beginning of the year. If it costs $16 000 when new its value at the end of 3 years is about:

a $13 000   **b** $11 500   **c** $9800
d $8800

CHAPTER 9 SUMMARY

Points to remember

(i) *Simple interest* = principal × rate per period × no. of periods.

(ii) To calculate the *compound interest*
   (a) Find the total number of periods, n, required for the interest to be charged.
   i.e. no. of years × no. of periods per year.
   (b) Find the rate percent interest per period, r%

i.e. annual rate % ÷ no. of periods per year.

The amount, A, for a principal, P, is given by

$$A = P(1 + r/100)^n.$$

For a depreciation,
$A = P(1 - r/100)^n.$

Chapter 10 Investment

SHARES

Many people at some time or another will have money to invest. It could be deposited in a bank, a building society or in the National Savings Bank where it will earn a fixed rate of interest. It could also be invested in a company by buying some of its shares.

Companies obtain their capital by the issue of shares to the public. Shares have a nominal value of 25 c, $1, $5, etc., which cannot be divided into fractional amounts. If the company does well the price of the shares will appreciate to a value above the nominal price. On the other hand if the company does badly the price will fall below the nominal value. Shares can be bought and sold through the Stock Exchange. Companies issue different kinds of shares, two of the most important kinds being:

Preference shares, which carry a fixed rate of interest. The holders of these shares have first call on any profits the company may make in order that payments due to them can be made.

Ordinary shares, the dividends on which vary according to the amount of profit that the company makes. The directors of the company decide what dividend shall be paid.

The dividends payable on the shares are a percentage of the nominal value of the shares.

EXAMPLE 1
A man buys 200 Emperor 25 c shares at 44 c. How much does he pay for the shares?

25 c is the nominal value of the shares.

44 c is the price he actually pays for the shares.

$$\text{Amount paid} = 200 \times 44 \text{ c}$$
$$= 8800 \text{ c} = \$88$$

EXAMPLE 2
Tom Jones sells 500 Tuxo $5 shares at $4. How much does he get?

$5 is the nominal value of the shares.

$4 is the price at which he sells the shares.

$$\text{Amount received} = 500 \times \$4 = \$2000$$

EXAMPLE 3
A man owns 300 Ludo shares. The company declares a dividend of 32 c per share. How much does he get in dividends?

$$\text{Amount payable} = 300 \times 32 \text{ c}$$
$$= 9600 \text{ c} = \$96$$

EXAMPLE 4
A man holds 600 Snake 50 c shares which he bought for 35 c. The declared dividend is 8% of the nominal value of the shares. How much does he get in dividends and what is the yield per cent on his investment?

Dividend per share
$$= 8\% \text{ of } 50 \text{ c} = 4 \text{ c}$$

Amount obtained in dividends
$$= 600 \times 4 \text{ c} = 2400 \text{ c} = \$24$$

Yield per cent
$$= \frac{\text{dividend per share}}{\text{price paid per share}} \times 100$$
$$= \frac{4}{35} \times 100 = 11.4\%$$

EXAMPLE 5
The paid up capital of a company consists of 50 000 6% preference shares of $1 each and 200 000 ordinary shares of 50 c each. The profits available for distribution are $11 973. What dividend can be paid to the ordinary shareholders? What is the dividend per cent?

Preference dividend
$$= 6\% \text{ of } \$50\,000 = \$3000$$

Amount of profit remaining
$$= \$11\,973 - \$3000 = \$8973$$

Dividend per share

$$= \frac{8973}{200\,000} = \$0.0448 \text{ or } 4.48\,c$$

Dividend per cent

$$= \frac{4.48}{50} \times 100 = 8.96\%$$

Exercise 53 – *All type C*

1) Find the cost of the following shares:

(a) 400 Oak $2 shares at 314 c
(b) 900 Staite 50 c shares at 39 c
(c) 280 Mako 25 c shares at 59 c

2) Find the amount raised by selling the following shares:

(a) 180 Kneck 80 c shares at 97 c
(b) 350 Truck $5 shares at 87 c
(c) 490 Mill 50 c shares at 117 c

3) Calculate the dividend received from the following investments:

(a) 300 Proof shares; dividend is 8 c per share
(b) 450 Shock shares; dividend is 18 c per share
(c) 750 Stairways shares; dividend is 85 c per share

4) Calculate the amount of dividend received from the following investments:

(a) 300 Well 75 c shares; declared dividend is 10%
(b) 500 Toomet $5 shares; declared dividend is 5%
(c) 1200 Boom 50 c shares; declared dividend is 16%

5) Calculate the yield per cent on the following investments:

(a) 200 Salto $3 shares bought at 250 c; declared dividend is 9%
(b) 500 Melting 40 c shares bought at 85 c; declared dividend is 5%
(c) 85 Penn $2 shares bought at 98 c; declared dividend is 3%

6) Calculate the yearly income from 500 Imperial $2 shares at 150 c when a dividend of 8% is declared. What is the yield per cent on the money invested?

7) Find the cost income and yield per cent from 900 $1 shares at 82 c when a dividend of 7% is declared.

8) 500 Flag 25 c shares are sold for $160. What is the cash value of each share?

9) How much profit does a man make when he sells 900 Emblem $3 shares for 390 c, having bought them for 265 c?

10) The paid up capital of a company consists of 100 000 8% preference shares of $2 each and 250 000 ordinary shares of $1 each. The profits available for distribution are $27 000. What is the dividend per cent that can be paid to the ordinary shareholders?

11) The issued capital of a company is 200 000 8% preference $1 shares, 150 000 6% $2 preference shares and 500 000 ordinary 25 c shares. If the profit available for distribution to the shareholders is $92 000, what dividend per cent is payable to the ordinary shareholders?

12) The paid up capital of a company consists of 90 000 7% preference $1 shares and 110 000 ordinary 50 c shares. If a dividend of 10% is declared, what is the profit of the company?

STOCK

Stock is issued by governments when they need cash. This stock is issued at a fixed rate of interest and it can be redeemed after a certain number of years. Stock is always issued in $100 units but an investor need not necessarily buy whole units of stock. The price of stock varies in the same way as does the price of shares.

If you look in the financial section of your newspaper you will see statements like this:

Treasury 5% 1986–89 52

This means that $100 worth of Treasury Stock, paying 5% interest and redeemable between 1986 and 1989, can be bought for $52.

EXAMPLE 6

How much 9% Treasury Stock at 70 can be bought for $280? How much in dividends are payable and what is the yield per cent?

$70 buys $100 stock

$280 buys $$\frac{100}{70} \times 280 = \$400$$ stock

Interest payable

$$= 9\% \text{ of } \$400 = \$36$$

Yield per cent

$$= \frac{\text{interest payable}}{\text{amount paid for stock}} \times 100$$

$$= \frac{36}{280} \times 100 = 12.86\%$$

Exercise 54 – *All type A*

1) Calculate the amount of stock that can be bought in each case:

(a) $300 invested in 5% stock at 75
(b) $250 invested in stock at 69
(c) $700 invested in stock at 120

2) Calculate the amount of interest received each year from the following:

(a) $800 stock at $3\frac{1}{2}\%$
(b) $1200 stock at 5%
(c) $500 stock at 4%

3) Calculate the amount of 6% stock that can be bought for $600 if the price is 88. What is the interest earned per annum and what is the yield per cent?

4) How much does it cost to buy $300 of stock at 80?

5) What are the proceeds from selling $400 of 3% stock at 75?

6) A man sells $800 worth of Argentine stock at 30 and buys US 8% stock at 110. How much US stock does he buy?

SELF-TEST 10

In each of the following state the letter (or letters) corresponding to the correct answer (or answers).

1) A man buys 500 Empress 50 c shares at 40 c. He therefore pays for the shares:

a $40   **b** $50   **c** $200   **d** $250

2) A person sells 400 Tuxedo $2 shares for 150 c. He gets:

a $60   **b** $80   **c** $600   **d** $800

3) A man holds 500 Ladder 80 c shares which he bought for 70 c. The declared dividend is 8%. He therefore receives:

a $28   **b** $32   **c** $40   **d** $56

4) A person holds 800 Persona 50 c shares which he bought for 75 c. The declared dividend is 10%. The yield per cent on the shares is:

a $6\frac{2}{3}\%$ **b** $7\frac{1}{2}\%$ **c** 10%   **d** 15%

5) How much 8% stock at 75 c can be bought for $150?

a $75   **b** $150   **c** $200   **d** $1200

6) Calculate the interest received per annum from $800 stock at 5%.

a $40   **b** $50   **c** $400   **d** $500

7) A man sells $600 Canadian stock at 50 and buys US stock at 40. How much US stock does he buy?

a $400   **b** $600   **c** $750   **d** $1200

Chapter 11 Squares, Square Roots and Reciprocals

SQUARES OF NUMBERS

When a number is multiplied by itself the result is called the square of the number. The square of 9 is $9 \times 9 = 81$. Instead of writing 9×9 it is usual to write 9^2 which is read as the square of 9. Thus

$$(12)^2 = 12 \times 12 = 144$$

$$(1.3)^2 = 1.3 \times 1.3 = 1.69$$

The square of any number can be found by multiplication but a great deal of time and effort is saved by using three-figure printed tables.

Although the tables only give the squares of numbers from 1 to 10 they can be used to find the squares of numbers outside this range. The method is shown in the following examples .

EXAMPLE 1

Find $(168)^2$.

$$(168)^2 = 168 \times 168$$

$$= 1.68 \times 100 \times 1.68 \times 100$$

$$= (1.68)^2 \times (100)^2$$

From the table of squares,

$$(1.68)^2 = 2.82$$

Hence

$$(1.68)^2 = 2.82 \times (100)^2$$

$$= 28\,200$$

EXAMPLE 2

Find $(0.238)^2$.

$$(0.238)^2 = 2.38 \times \frac{1}{10} \times 2.38 \times \frac{1}{10}$$

$$= (2.38)^2 \times \frac{1}{100} = (2.38)^2 \div 100$$

From the tables $(2.38)^2 = 5.66$

Hence $(0.238)^2 = 5.66 \div 100$

$$= 0.0566$$

EXAMPLE 3

Find the value of $\left(\dfrac{0.9}{0.15}\right)^2$.

$$\left(\frac{0.9}{0.15}\right)^2 = 6^2 = 36$$

Exercise 55 – *Questions 1–12 type A, remainder B*

Find the square of the following numbers.

1) 1.5	**11)** 23
2) 2.1	**12)** 40.6
3) 8.6	**13)** 3090
4) 3.15	**14)** 112
5) 7.68	**15)** 98.1
6) 5.23	**16)** 0.019
7) 4.26	**17)** 0.729
8) 7.91	**18)** 0.004 21
9) 8.01	**19)** 0.283
10) 8.70	**20)** 0.000 578

21) Find the value of $(3.14)^2$ correct to 2 places of decimals.

22) Find the values of:

(a) $\left(\dfrac{0.75}{0.15}\right)^2$ (b) $\left(\dfrac{0.8}{0.2}\right)^2$

(c) $\left(\dfrac{0.25}{2}\right)^2$ (d) $\left(\dfrac{0.36}{6}\right)^2$

SQUARE ROOTS

The square root of a number is the number whose square equals the given number. Thus since $5^2 = 25$, the square root of $25 = 5$. The sign $\sqrt{}$ is used to denote the positive square root and hence we write $\sqrt{25} = 5$.

Similarly, since $9^2 = 81$, $\sqrt{81} = 9$.

THE SQUARE ROOT OF A PRODUCT

The square root of a product is the product of the square roots. For example

$$\sqrt{4 \times 9} = \sqrt{4} \times \sqrt{9} = 2 \times 3 = 6$$

Also, $\sqrt{25 \times 16 \times 49}$

$$= \sqrt{25} \times \sqrt{16} \times \sqrt{49}$$

$$= 5 \times 4 \times 7 = 140$$

Exercise 56 – *All type A*

Find the values of the following:

1) $\sqrt{4 \times 25}$ 5) $\sqrt{16 \times 25 \times 36}$

2) $\sqrt{9 \times 25}$ 6) $\sqrt{4 \times 9 \times 25}$

3) $\sqrt{49 \times 49}$ 7) $\sqrt{36 \times 49 \times 64}$

4) $\sqrt{16 \times 36}$ 8) $\sqrt{4 \times 16 \times 25 \times 49 \times 81}$

THE SQUARE ROOT OF A FRACTION

To find the square root of a fraction, find the square roots of the numerator and denominator separately as shown in Example 4.

EXAMPLE 4

Find the square root of $\frac{16}{25}$.

$$\sqrt{\frac{16}{25}} = \frac{\sqrt{16}}{\sqrt{25}} = \frac{4}{5}$$

If the numbers under a square root sign are connected by a plus or a minus sign then we cannot find the square root by the methods used for products and quotients. We cannot say that $\sqrt{9 + 16} = \sqrt{9} + \sqrt{16} = 3 + 4 = 7$. We must add before finding the square root. Thus:

$$\sqrt{9 + 16} = \sqrt{25} = 5$$

and $$\sqrt{25 - 9} = \sqrt{16} = 4$$

Exercise 57 – *Questions 1–5 type A, remainder B*

Find the square roots of the following:

1) $\frac{4}{9}$ 2) $\frac{9}{16}$

3) $\frac{25}{49}$ 10) $\frac{10}{360}$

4) $\frac{36}{81}$ 11) $25 + 144$

5) $\frac{81}{100}$ 12) $169 - 25$

6) $\frac{12}{27}$ 13) $25 - 16$

7) $\frac{100}{256}$ 14) $43 + 38$

8) $\frac{125}{245}$ 15) $65 - 29$

9) $\frac{48}{75}$

SQUARE ROOTS USING TABLES

The square root of a number can usually be found with sufficient accuracy by using the printed tables of square roots. There are two of these tables. One gives the square roots of numbers 1 to 10 and the other gives the square roots of numbers from 10 to 100. The reason for having two tables is as follows:

$$\sqrt{2.5} = 1.58$$

$$\sqrt{25} = 5$$

Thus there are two square roots for the same figures, depending upon the position of the decimal point. Square root tables are used in the same way as the table of squares.

EXAMPLE 5

(1) $\sqrt{2.74} = 1.66$ (directly from the tables from 1 to 10).

(2) $\sqrt{92.6} = 9.62$ (directly from the tables from 10 to 100).

(3) To find $\sqrt{836}$.

To decide where to position the decimal point in the first place, mark off the figures in pairs to the *left* of the decimal point. Each pair of figures is called a *period*. Thus 836 becomes 8'36.

Hence we place the decimal point after 8 and write

$$\sqrt{836} = \sqrt{8.36 \times 100} = \sqrt{8.36} \times \sqrt{100}$$

Using the table of square roots from 1 to 10 we look up $\sqrt{8.36}$ and find that its value is 2.89.

$$\therefore \qquad \sqrt{836} = 2.89 \times \sqrt{100}$$

$$= 2.89 \times 10 = 28.9$$

(4) To find $\sqrt{173\,000}$.

Marking off in periods $173\,000$ becomes $17'30'00$. The first period is 17 so we write $173\,000 = 17.3 \times 10\,000$

$$\sqrt{173\,000} = \sqrt{17.3} \times \sqrt{10\,000}$$

$$= 4.16 \times 100 = 416$$

(5) To find $\sqrt{0.000\,094\,3}$.

In the case of numbers less than 1 mark off the periods to the right of the decimal point. $0.000\,094\,3$ becomes $0.00'00'94'3$. Apart from the zero pairs the first period is 94 so we

write $\quad 0.000\,094\,3 = 94.3 \times \dfrac{1}{1\,000\,000}$

$$\therefore \qquad \sqrt{0.000\,094\,3} = \frac{\sqrt{94.3}}{\sqrt{1\,000\,000}}$$

$$= \frac{9.71}{1000} = 0.009\,71$$

(6) To find $\sqrt{0.073\,6}$.

Marking off in periods to the right of the decimal point $0.073\,6$ becomes $07'36'$. Since the first period is 07 we write

$0.0736 = 7.36 \times \dfrac{1}{100}$

$$\therefore \qquad \sqrt{0.073\,6} = \frac{\sqrt{7.36}}{\sqrt{100}} = \frac{2.71}{10} = 0.271$$

Exercise 58 – *Questions 1–12 type A, remainder B*

Find the square roots of the following numbers:

1) 3.4   6) 3.01
2) 8.19   7) 35
3) 5.26   8) 89.2
4) 9.23   9) 53.1
5) 7.01   10) 82.9

11) 79.2   18) 893 000 000
12) 50.1   19) 0.153 7
13) 900   20) 0.001 69
14) 725   21) 0.039 4
15) 7140   22) 0.000 783
16) 89 000   23) 0.001 97
17) 3940

ITERATIVE METHOD OF FINDING A SQUARE ROOT

If a calculating machine with a square root key is not available the square root of a real number may be found by using the following iterative formula:

$$x_{n+1} = \left(\frac{a}{x_n} + x_n \right) \div 2$$

where a is the number whose square root is to be found.

EXAMPLE 6

Using an iterative method find $\sqrt{9.61}$.

Now $\sqrt{9.61} \simeq 3$, so we use $x_0 = 3$.

$$x_1 = \left(\frac{9.61}{3} + 3 \right) \div 2 = 3.102$$

Now $(3.102)^2 = 9.622$, hence x_1 is a near approximation to $\sqrt{9.61}$. Continuing:

$$x_2 = \left(\frac{9.61}{3.102} + 3.102 \right) \div 2 = 3.100$$

Now $(3.100)^2 = 9.61$ exactly.

Hence $\qquad\qquad \sqrt{9.61} = 3.100$

EXAMPLE 7

Using an iterative method find $\sqrt{28.72}$.

Now $\sqrt{28.72} \simeq 5$.

$$x_1 = \left(\frac{28.72}{5} + 5 \right) \div 2 = 5.372$$

$$x_2 = \left(\frac{28.72}{5.372} + 5.372 \right) \div 2 = 5.359$$

$$x_3 = \left(\frac{28.72}{5.359} + 5.359 \right) \div 2 = 5.359$$

x_3 is the value of $\sqrt{28.72}$ correct to 4 significant figures, since $x_2 = x_3$ to 4 significant figures.

Exercise 59 – *All type B*

Using two iterations find the following square roots:

1) $\sqrt{1.72}$ 3) $\sqrt{8.61}$ 5) $\sqrt{76.22}$

2) $\sqrt{3.84}$ 4) $\sqrt{12.61}$ 6) $\sqrt{90.41}$

A calculator may be used to find the square roots.

RECIPROCALS OF NUMBERS

The reciprocal of a number is $\dfrac{1}{\text{number}}$.

Thus the reciprocal of $5 = \dfrac{1}{5}$

and the reciprocal of 21.3 is $\dfrac{1}{21.3}$.

The table of reciprocals of numbers is used in much the same way as the table of squares of numbers, except that the proportional parts are subtracted and not added. It gives the reciprocals of numbers from 1 to 10 in decimal form.

From the tables:

the reciprocal of $6 = 0.167$

the reciprocal of $3.15 = 0.317$

The method of finding the reciprocals of numbers less than 1 or greater than 10 is shown in Example 8.

EXAMPLE 8

(1) To find the reciprocal of 639

$$\frac{1}{639} = \frac{1}{6.39} \times \frac{1}{100}$$

From the table of reciprocals we find that the reciprocal of 6.39 is 0.156

$$\frac{1}{639} = 0.156 \times \frac{1}{100}$$

$$= \frac{0.156}{100} = 0.001\,56$$

(2) To find the reciprocal of 0.039 8

$$\frac{1}{0.039\,8} = \frac{1}{3.98} \times \frac{100}{1}$$

From the table of reciprocals we find the reciprocal of 3.98 to be 0.251.

$$\frac{1}{0.039\,8} = 0.251 \times 100 = 25.1$$

Exercise 60 – *Questions 1–5 type A, remainder B*

Find the reciprocals of the following numbers:

1) 3.4   9) 900

2) 8.19   10) 7140

3) 5.26   11) 0.153

4) 9.23   12) 0.001 69

5) 7.01   13) 0.039 4

6) 35   14) 0.000 783

7) 89.2   15) 0.001 97

8) 53.1

USE OF TABLES IN CALCULATIONS

Calculations may often be speeded up by making use of the tables of squares, square roots and reciprocals.

EXAMPLE 9

Find the value of $\sqrt{(8.13)^2 + (12.3)^2}$.

By using the table of squares

$$\sqrt{(8.13)^2 + (12.3)^2}$$
$$= \sqrt{66.1 + 151}$$

By using the table of square roots

$$= \sqrt{217} = 14.7$$

EXAMPLE 10

Find the value of

$$\frac{1}{\sqrt{7.51}} + \frac{1}{(3.62)^2}.$$

By using the square and square root tables

$$\frac{1}{\sqrt{7.51}} + \frac{1}{(3.62)^2}$$

$$= \frac{1}{2.74} + \frac{1}{13.1}$$

By using the reciprocal table

$$= 0.365 + 0.076$$

$$= 0.441$$

Exercise 61 – *Questions 1–6 type B,*
remainder C

Find the values of:

1) $\dfrac{1}{(15.2)^2}$

2) $\dfrac{1}{(0.137)^2}$

3) $\dfrac{1}{(250)^2}$

4) $\dfrac{1}{\sqrt{8.41}}$

5) $\dfrac{1}{\sqrt{18.7}}$

6) $\dfrac{1}{\sqrt{0.0179}}$

7) $\dfrac{1}{(30.1)^2 + (8.29)^2}$

8) $\dfrac{1}{(11.2)^2 + (8.18)^2}$

9) $\sqrt{(2.65)^2 + (5.16)^2}$

10) $\sqrt{(11.1)^2 - (5.23)^2}$

11) $\dfrac{1}{8.2} + \dfrac{1}{9.9}$

12) $\dfrac{1}{0.732} - \dfrac{1}{0.981}$

13) $\dfrac{1}{\sqrt{7.51}} + \dfrac{1}{(8.21)^2} + \dfrac{1}{0.0749}$

14) $\dfrac{1}{71.3} + \dfrac{1}{\sqrt{863}} + \dfrac{1}{(7.58)^2}$

15) Given that $\dfrac{1}{18.27} = 0.0547345$ correct to 6 significant figures find the reciprocal of 3.654 correct to 5 significant figures.

SELF-TEST 11

In the following questions state the letter (or letters) corresponding to the correct answer (or answers). Do not use a calculator or tables.

1) 80^2 is equal to:

  a 6.4   **b** 64   **c** 640   **d** 6400

2) 700^2 is equal to:

  a 490 000   **b** 49 000   **c** 4900   **d** 490

3) 0.8^2 is equal to:

  a 6.4   **b** 0.64   **c** 0.064   **d** 0.0064

4) 0.09^2 is equal to:

  a 0.00081   **b** 0.0081   **c** 0.081   **d** 0.81

5) $\sqrt{0.25}$ is equal to:

  a 0.5   **b** 0.158   **c** 0.05   **d** 0.005

6) $\sqrt{0.036}$ is equal to:

  a 0.6   **b** 0.190   **c** 0.06   **d** 0.0190

7) $\sqrt{0.0049}$ is equal to:

  a 0.7   **b** 0.221   **c** 0.07   **d** 0.0221

8) $\sqrt{1690}$ is equal to:

  a 13   **b** 41.1   **c** 130   **d** 411

9) $\sqrt{810}$ is equal to:

  a 9   **b** 28.5   **c** 90   **d** 285

10) $\sqrt{12\,100}$ is equal to:

  a 110   **b** 348   **c** 1100   **d** 3480

11) $\dfrac{1}{12.5}$ is equal to:

  a 8   **b** 0.8   **c** 0.08   **d** 0.008

12) $\dfrac{1}{0.25}$ is equal to:

  a 0.4   **b** 4   **c** 40   **d** 400

13) $\dfrac{1}{0.020}$ is equal to:

  a 0.5   **b** 5   **c** 50   **d** 500

14) $\dfrac{1}{250}$ is equal to:

  a 0.4   **b** 0.04   **c** 0.004   **d** 0.0004

15) $18.3^2 - 8.3^2$ is equal to:

  a 266   **b** 100   **c** 26.6   **d** 10

16) If $h = \dfrac{1}{u} + \dfrac{1}{v}$ then when $u = 37.17$ and $v = 1.47$ the value of h is:

  a 0.945   **b** 0.707   **c** 0.0945   **d** 0.0707

17) If $p = b\sqrt{\dfrac{c}{q}}$ when $b = 12$, $c = 4$ and $q = 16$ then p is equal to:

  a 6   **b** 7.59   **c** 60   **d** 75.9

18) An approximate value of $\sqrt{2562.8}$ is:

  a 16.2   **b** 50.6   **c** 162   **d** 520

19) $\dfrac{1}{0.312}$ is equal to:

  a 0.0321   **b** 0.321   **c** 3.21   **d** 321

20) $(30.1)^2 + \dfrac{1}{0.047}$ is equal to:

  a 92.7   **b** 111   **c** 927   **d** 1110

CHAPTER 11 SUMMARY

Points to remember

(i)   We say that 7 is a square root of 49, since $7 \times 7 = 49$. We also write $7^2 = 49$.

Now $(-7) \times (-7) = 49$ also.
We call 7 "the principal square root of 49", and we write $\sqrt{49} = 7$.
$\sqrt{49}$ denotes a positive number.
We may write $-\sqrt{49} = -7$.

(ii) If the product of two numbers is 1, then each number is the reciprocal of the other.
e.g. $\frac{3}{4} \times \frac{4}{3} = 1$. We say then $\frac{3}{4}$ is the reciprocal of $\frac{4}{3}$, and $\frac{4}{3}$ is the reciprocal of $\frac{3}{4}$.

How to Answer Examination Questions 1

1) (a) Express $\dfrac{132}{150}$ as a percentage.

(b) Calculate $7\frac{1}{2}\%$ of \$160.

(c) Find the average of five numbers if one of them is 11 and the average of the other four numbers is 6.

(a) $\dfrac{132}{150} = \dfrac{132}{150} \times \dfrac{100}{1}\% = 88\%$

(b) $7\frac{1}{2}\%$ of \$160 $= 0.075 \times \$160 = \$12$

(c) Total of the numbers $= 11 + 4 \times 6$

$\qquad\qquad\qquad\quad = 35$

Average of the five numbers $= \dfrac{35}{5} = 7$

2) In a school the ratio of the number of pupils to the number of teachers is $18.2 : 1$.

(a) Assuming that there is a whole number of teachers and a whole number of pupils, find the smallest possible number of pupils in the school.

(b) If the number of teachers and pupils together is 960, find the number of teachers.

(a) Reducing the given ratio to its lowest terms we have:

$18.2 : 1 = 91 : 5$

Hence the smallest number of pupils is 91.

(b) The smallest number of teachers and pupils must be $91 + 5 = 96$.
So if the number of teachers and pupils together is 960, the number of teachers is
$\dfrac{960}{96} \times 5 = 10 \times 5 = 50$.

3) (a) Find the number of years for which \$120 must be invested at 7.50% per annum simple interest to amount to \$174.

(b) Calculate the compound interest on \$1500 at 5% per annum for 2 years.

(a) Interest $= \$174 - \$120 = \$54$

$$I = \dfrac{PRT}{100}$$

or $T = \dfrac{100I}{PR} = \dfrac{100 \times 54}{120 \times 7.5} = 6$ years

So the money must be invested for 6 years.

(b) Interest on first year $= 5\%$ of \$1500

$\qquad\qquad\qquad\qquad\qquad = \$75$

Amount at end of first year $= \$1575$

Interest on second year $= 5\%$ of \$1575

$\qquad\qquad\qquad\qquad\qquad = \$78.75$

Compound interest $= \$75 + \$78.75$

$\qquad\qquad\qquad\qquad = \$153.75$

4) A company which produces paving slabs uses 1 tonne of granite to produce 18 paving slabs. The costs to the company in 1999 were divided between the cost of granite, cost of labour and costs of overheads in the proportions $7 : 5 : 2$. In that year 5000 tonnes of granite were bought at \$10.50 per tonne and the paving slabs were sold at \$1.26 each.

(a) Calculate the company's total costs for 1993 and the percentage of profit made.

(b) In 2000 the company bought the same quantity of granite. The labour costs rose by 40% but the other costs remained unchanged. Calculate the selling price of each paving slab if the percentage profit made by the company remained the same in 1994 as in 1993. State the answer to the nearest cent.

(a) Cost of granite represented by 7 units
$= 5000 \times \$10.50 = \$52\,500$

Total costs represented by 14 units
$= \dfrac{14}{7} \times \$52\,500 = \$105\,000$

Number of paving slabs made
$= 18 \times 5000 = 90\,000$

Income from selling paving slabs
$= 90\,000 \times \$1.26 = \$113\,400$

Profit made $= \$113\,400 - \$105\,000$

$\qquad\qquad\quad = \$8400$

Percentage profit $= \dfrac{8400}{105\,000} \times 100 = 8\%$

Labour costs in 1993 $= \dfrac{5}{14} \times \$105\,000$

$= \$37\,500$

(b) Labour costs in 1994 $= \dfrac{140}{100} \times \$37\,500$

$= 1.4 \times \$37\,500$

$= \$52\,500$

Total costs in 1994

$= \$105\,000 +$ increase in labour costs

$= \$105\,000 + (\$52\,500 - \$37\,500)$

$= \$105\,000 + \$15\,000$

$= \$120\,000$

Selling price of paving slabs

$\dfrac{108}{100} \times \$120\,000$

$= 1.08 \times \$120\,000$

$= \$129\,600$

Price per paving slab

$= \$\dfrac{129\,600}{90\,000}$

$= \$1.44$

5) A shopkeeper purchased 1020 articles for $3570 and planned to sell the articles at a profit of 20%. He sold 700 of the articles at the planned selling price and then, in a sale, reduced the price by 10% and sold a further 170 articles. Later, in order to get the rest off his hands he sold the remainder at a greatly reduced price. When he had sold all the articles he found that he had made a total profit of $282.60. Calculate:

(a) the cost price per article to the shopkeeper.
(b) the planned selling price per article set by the shopkeeper.
(c) the sale price per article.
(d) the greatly reduced price of each article.
(e) his overall percentage profit, giving the answer correct to one place of decimals.

(a) Cost price per article $= \dfrac{\$3570}{1020} = \$3.50$

(b) Planned selling price $= \dfrac{120}{100} \times \$3.50$

$= \$4.20$

(c) Sale price per article $= \dfrac{90}{100} \times \$4.20$

$= \$3.78$

(d) Income from planned selling price

$= 700 \times \$4.20 = \$2940.00$

Income from sale

$= 170 \times \$3.78 = \$642.60$

Total income from planned selling price and sale

$= \$(2940.00 + 642.60) = \$3582.60$

Total overall income

$= \$(3570 + 282.60) = \$3852.60$

Income from greatly reduced price

$= \$(3852.60 - 3582.60) = \$270.00$

Number sold at greatly reduced price

$= 1020 - 700 - 170 = 150$

Greatly reduced price per article

$= \dfrac{\$270}{150} = \$1.80$

(e) Total overall profit $= \$282.60$

Overall percentage profit

$= \dfrac{282.60}{3570} \times 100 = 7.9\%$

EXAMINATION TYPE QUESTIONS 1

This exercise is divided into two sections, A and B. The questions in Section A are intended to be done very quickly, but those in Section B should take about 20 minutes each to complete. All the questions are of the type found in CXC examination papers.

Section A

1) (a) Calculate the mean (average) of the numbers 438, 440, 442 and 444.
   (b) A greyhound runs 800 metres in 50 seconds. Calculate its average speed in kilometres per hour.
   (c) In an election where there were only two candidates, 27 180 votes were cast and the winner's majority was 3558. Find how many votes the loser received.

2) (a) A scale model of an aircraft is made to a scale of 1 : 78. If the wing span of the model is 35 cm, find the wing span of the actual aircraft.

(b) Find the difference between the simple and the compound interest on $1250 for 2 years at 8% per annum.

(c) An agent buys 3600 articles for $2000. He sells 3060 of them at a profit of 30% and the remainder at a loss of 10%. Find his profit and express it as a percentage of his outlay.

3) (a) Find 5% of $260.

(b) Round off 0.049 49:
   (i) Correct to three significant figures.
   (ii) Correct to three decimal places.

4) (a) The value of a car, after each year's use, decreases by a fixed percentage of its value at the beginning of that year. If a car costs $25 600 when new and its value after one year was $20 800 by what percentage has the value decreased? Calculate its value after a further year's use.

(b) After prices have risen by 8% the new price of an article is $70.47. Calculate the original price.

(c) Articles are purchased at $5.00 per 100 and sold at 7 cents each. Calculate the profit as a percentage of the purchase price.

5) (a) Next year a man will receive a 12% wage increase and his weekly wage will then be $241.92. What is his present weekly wage?

(b) A car journey takes 3 hours at an average speed of 60 kilometres per hour. How long will it take if the average speed is reduced to 40 kilometres per hour?

(c) Given that Sales Tax on goods supplied is 8% of their value, calculate the Sales Tax on goods valued at $64.

6) (a) A car travels 20 km at an average speed of 48 kilometres an hour and then for a further 15 minutes at an average speed of 40 kilometres an hour. Calculate the average speed for the entire journey.

(b) The mean of five numbers is 15 and the mean of a further eight numbers is 2. Calculate the mean of all thirteen numbers.

(c) The number of people working for a company at the end of 1999 was 1210. This was an increase of 10% on the number working for the company at the beginning of 1974. How many people worked for the company at the beginning of 1974?

7) (a) A car is travelling at a uniform speed of 90 kilometres an hour. Calculate the time, in seconds, it takes to travel 600 m.

(b) $979 is to be divided into three parts in the proportions $1 : \frac{1}{2} : \frac{1}{3}$. Calculate the value of the smallest part.

(c) By selling a chair for $10.35 a shopkeeper makes a profit of 15% on his cost price. Calculate his profit.

8) (a) A man left $\frac{3}{8}$ of his money to his wife and half the remainder to his son. The rest was divided equally amongst his five daughters. Find what fraction of the money each daughter received.

(b) By selling an article for $18 a shopkeeper makes a profit of 44% on the cost price. At what price must it be sold in order to make a profit of 40%?

(c) On a bus journey of 117 km, the average speed for the first 27 km was 45 kilometres per hour and for the rest of the journey the average speed was 37.5 kilometres per hour. Calculate the uniform speed at which the bus would have to travel in order to cover the whole distance in the same total time.

Section B

9) A man wishes to make a journey from his home to a meeting near to a town A and finds that the journey will consist of three parts:

(i) A car journey of 48 km from his home to the nearest bus station, which he hopes to cover in 45 minutes.

(ii) A journey on the 9.10 a.m. bus from this station to town A, a distance of 315 km, over which the bus normally averages 90 kilometres per hour.

(iii) A 24 minute taxi ride from the bus station at A to his meeting place, over which he hopes to average 40 kilometres per hour.

Neglecting the time taken changing from car to bus and bus to taxi, calculate:

(a) the average speed of his car.
(b) the time at which the bus would normally arrive at A.
(c) the distance between the bus station at A and the meeting place.
(d) the average speed over the journey from home to the meeting place, giving your answer to the nearest whole number.

All went according to plan on the actual journey except for the fact that the bus had to reduce speed to an average of 18 kilometres per hour for 10 minutes before picking up speed again. Assuming that the bus averages 90 kilometres per hour over the rest of its journey, calculate by how many minutes the bus was late.

10) In 1973 the cost of building a garage was divided between materials, labour and overheads in the ratio 10 : 13 : 2 and the garage cost $2400. Calculate the respective costs of materials, labour and overheads. In 1974 the cost of materials rose by 10%, the cost of labour by 15% and the costs of overheads by 15%. Calculate the percentage increase in the cost of the garage. What percentage of this increase is due to the increase in the cost of labour?

11) In 1999, A, B and C started a business in which their investments were in the proportion 4 : 7 : 9. They agreed to distribute the profits in proportion to their investments. Calculate the amount A received if $23 000 profit was made. In 2000 and thenceforward, they agreed to accept salaries from the profit before it was shared and then distribute the balance in proportion to their investments. The salaries were to be $4000, $3000 and $2500 respectively. The profit in 1970 was again $23 000. Calculate:

(a) the total amount each person received in 1970.
(b) the percentage gain in A's return from the business in 1970 compared with 1969 correct to one decimal place. In 1971 B received $6500. Calculate the total profit for that year before any salaries were paid.

12) The first $5000 of a sum of money is taxed at 30% and the remainder, if any, is taxed at 40%. Calculate:

(a) the tax on $6805.
(b) the sum on which the tax is $1110.
(c) the sum on which the tax is $1710.

Chapter 12 **Directed Numbers**

INTRODUCTION

Directed numbers are numbers which have either a plus or a minus sign attached to them such as $+7$ and -5. In this chapter we will study the rules for the addition, subtraction, multiplication and division of directed numbers.

POSITIVE AND NEGATIVE NUMBERS

Fig. 12.1 shows part of a Celsius thermometer. The freezing point of water is $0°\text{C}$ (nought $°$ Celsius). Temperatures above freezing point may be read off the scale directly and so may those below freezing. We now have to decide on a method for showing whether a temperature is above or below zero. We may say that a temperature is $6°$ above zero or $5°$ below zero but these statements are not compact enough for calculations. Therefore we say that a temperature of $+6°$ is a temperature which is $6°$ above zero and a temperature of $5°$ below zero would be written $-5°$. We have thus used the signs $+$ and $-$ to indicate a change of direction.

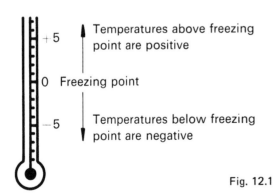

Fig. 12.1

Again if starting from a given point, distances measured to the right are regarded as being positive and distances measured to the left are regarded as being negative. As stated in the introduction, numbers which have a sign attached to them are called directed numbers.

Thus $+7$ is a positive number and -7 is a negative number.

THE ADDITION OF DIRECTED NUMBERS

In Fig. 12.2 a movement from left to right (i.e. in the direction 0A) is regarded as positive, whilst a movement from right to left (i.e. in the direction 0B) is regarded as negative.

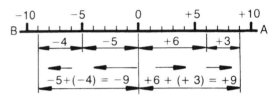

Fig. 12.2

To find the value of $+6+(+3)$

Measure 6 units to the right of 0 (Fig. 12.2) and then measure a further 3 units to the right. The final position is 9 units to the right of 0. Hence,

$$+6+(+3) = +9$$

To find the value of $-5+(-4)$

Again in Fig. 12.2, measure 5 units to the left of 0 since -5 is the opposite of $+5$. Then measure a further 4 units to the left. The final position is 9 units to the left of 0. Hence,

$$-5+(-4) = -9$$

From these results we obtain the rule:

To add several numbers together whose signs are the same add the numbers together. The sign of the sum is the same as the sign of each of the numbers.

To simplify the writing used when adding directed numbers the brackets may be omitted and the $+$ sign may also be omitted when it means "add". When the first number is positive it is usual to omit its $+$ sign.

1) $+5+(+9) = +14$.

More often this is written $5+9 = 14$.

2) $-7 + (-9) = -16$.

More often this is written $-7 - 9 = -16$.

3) $-7 - 6 - 4 = -17$.

Exercise 62 – *All type A*

Find the values of the following:

1) $+8 + 7$ 5) $-9 - 6 - 5 - 4$

2) $-7 - 5$ 6) $3 + 6 + 8 + 9$

3) $-15 - 17$ 7) $-2 - 5 - 8 - 3$

4) $8 + 6$ 8) $9 + 6 + 5 + 3$

THE ADDITION OF NUMBERS HAVING DIFFERENT SIGNS

To find the value of $-4 + 11$

Measure 4 units to the left of 0 (Fig. 12.3) and from this point measure 11 units to the right. The final position is 7 units to the right of 0. Hence,

$$-4 + 11 = 7$$

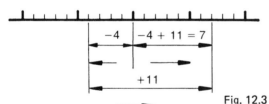

Fig. 12.3

To find the value of $8 - 15$

Measure 8 units to the right of 0 (Fig. 12.4) and from this point measure 15 units to the left. The final position is 7 units to the left of 0. Hence,

$$8 - 15 = -7$$

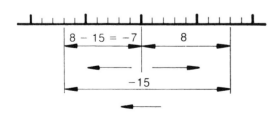

Fig. 12.4

From these results we obtain the rule:

To add two numbers together whose signs are different, subtract the numerically smaller from the larger. The sign of the result will be the same as the sign of the numerically larger number.

EXAMPLE 1

(1) $-12 + 6 = -6$

(2) $11 - 16 = -5$

If two numbers are numerically equal but have different signs we get an important result.

Consider $-7 + 7$.

Measuring 7 units to the left (to represent -7) and from this point, measuring 7 units to the right (to represent $+7$), the final position is 0.

Hence $-7 + 7 = 0$

and similarly $-15 + 15 = 0$

We have the following rule: The result of adding two numbers which are numerically equal but have different signs is 0.

When the sum of two numbers is 0, each is called the *additive inverse* of the other. Hence:

the additive inverse of -7 is $+7$

the additive inverse of $+15$ is -15

When dealing with several numbers having mixed signs add the positive and negative numbers together separately. The set of numbers is then reduced to two numbers, one positive and the other negative, which are added in the way shown above.

EXAMPLE 2

$$-16 + 11 - 7 + 3 + 8$$
$$= -23 + 22 = -1$$

Exercise 63 – *All type A*

Find the values of the following:

1) $6 - 11$ 5) $-8 + 9 - 2$

2) $7 - 16$ 6) $15 - 7 - 8$

3) $-5 + 10$ 7) $23 - 21 - 8 + 2$

4) $12 - 7$ 8) $-7 + 11 - 9 - 3 + 15$

SUBTRACTION OF DIRECTED NUMBERS

To find the value of $-4 - (+7)$

To represent $+7$ we measure 7 units to the right of 0 (Fig. 12.5). Therefore to represent $-(+7)$ we must reverse direction and measure 7 units to the left of 0 and hence $-(+7)$ is the same as -7. Hence,

$$-4 - (+7) = -4 - 7 = -11$$

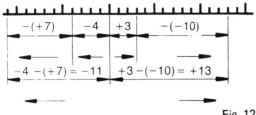

Fig. 12.5

To find the value of $+3 - (-10)$

To represent -10 we measure 10 units to the left of 0 (Fig. 12.5). Therefore to represent $-(-10)$ we measure 10 units to the right of 0 and hence $-(-10)$ is the same as $+10$. Hence,

$$+3 - (-10) = 3 + 10 = 13$$

The rule is:

To subtract a directed number change its sign and add the resulting number.

EXAMPLE 3

(1) $-10 - (-6) = -10 + 6 = -4$

(2) $7 - (+8) = 7 - 8 = -1$

(3) $8 - (-3) = 8 + 3 = 11$

Exercise 64 – *All type A*

Find the values of the following:

1) $8 - (+6)$ 5) $-4 - (-5)$

2) $-5 - (-8)$ 6) $-2 - (+3)$

3) $8 - (-6)$ 7) $-10 - (-5)$

4) $-3 - (-7)$ 8) $7 - (-9)$

MULTIPLICATION OF DIRECTED NUMBERS

Now $5 + 5 + 5 = 15$

That is, $3 \times 5 = 15$

Thus two positive numbers multiplied together give a positive product.

Now $(-5) + (-5) + (-5) = -15$

That is, $3 \times (-5) = -15$

Thus a positive number multiplied by a negative number gives a negative product.

Suppose now that we wish to find the value of $(-3) \times (-5)$.

$$-5 + 5 = 0$$
$$(-3) \times 0 = 0$$
$$(-3) \times (-5 + 5) = 0$$
$$(-3) \times (-5) + (-3) \times (5)$$
$$= (-3) \times (-5) - 15 = 0$$

Since $+15 - 15 = 0$
$$(-3) \times (-5) = +15$$

Thus a negative number multiplied by a negative number gives a positive product.

We may summarize the above results as follows:

$$(+) \times (+) = (+) \qquad (-) \times (+) = (-)$$
$$(+) \times (-) = (-) \qquad (-) \times (-) = (+)$$

and the rule is:

The product of two numbers with like signs is positive whilst the product of two numbers with unlike signs is negative.

EXAMPLE 4

(1) $7 \times 4 = 28$

(2) $7 \times (-4) = -28$

(3) $(-7) \times 4 = -28$

(4) $(-7) \times (-4) = 28$

Exercise 65 – *All type A*

Find the values of the following:

1) $7 \times (-6)$ 5) $(-2) \times (-4) \times (-6)$

2) $(-6) \times 7$ 6) $(-2)^2$

3) 7×6 7) $3 \times (-4) \times (-2) \times 5$

4) $(-7) \times (-6)$ 8) $(-3)^2$

DIVISION OF DIRECTED NUMBERS

The rules for division must be very similar to those used for multiplication, since if

$3 \times (-5) = -15$,   then

$$\frac{-15}{3} = -5. \quad \text{Also} \quad \frac{-15}{-5} = 3.$$

The rule is:

When dividing, numbers with like signs give a positive quotient and numbers with unlike signs give a negative quotient.

The rule may be summarised as follows:

$$(+) \div (+) = (+) \qquad (+) \div (-) = (-)$$
$$(-) \div (+) = (-) \qquad (-) \div (-) = (+)$$

EXAMPLE 5

(1) $\dfrac{20}{4} = 5$ (3) $\dfrac{-20}{4} = -5$

(2) $\dfrac{20}{-4} = -5$ (4) $\dfrac{-20}{-4} = 5$

(5) $\dfrac{(-9) \times (-4) \times 5}{3 \times (-2)} = \dfrac{36 \times 5}{-6} = \dfrac{180}{-6} = -30$

Exercise 66 – *Questions 1–9 type A, remainder type B*

1) $6 \div (-2)$ 8) $(-3) \div 3$

2) $(-6) \div 2$ 9) $8 \div (-4)$

3) $(-6) \div (-2)$ 10) $\dfrac{(-6) \times 4}{(-2)}$

4) $6 \div 2$ 11) $\dfrac{(-8)}{(1-4) \times (-2)}$

5) $(-10) \div 5$ 12) $\dfrac{(-3) \times (-4) \times (-2)}{3 \times 4}$

6) $1 \div (-1)$ 13) $\dfrac{4 \times (-6) \times (-8)}{(1-3) \times (-2) \times (-4)}$

7) $(-4) \div (-2)$ 14) $\dfrac{5 \times (-3) \times 6}{(10) \times 3}$

TYPES OF NUMBERS

Natural numbers are the numbers 1, 2, 3, . . . , etc.

Whole numbers are the numbers 0, 1, 2, 3, . . . , etc.

Integers are whole numbers but they include zero and negative numbers. Thus, -15, -8, 0, 2 and 137 are all integers.

Rational numbers are numbers which can be expressed as vulgar fractions. Thus 0.625 is a rational number because it can be written $\frac{5}{8}$. Recurring decimals are all rational because they can be converted into fractions. Thus:

$$0.\dot{1} = \frac{1}{9}$$

$$0.0\dot{1} = \frac{1}{99}$$

$$0.\dot{7}\dot{3} = \frac{73}{99}$$

$$0.00\dot{7}\dot{3} = \frac{73}{9900}$$

$$0.\dot{6}4\dot{7} = \frac{647}{999} \text{ etc.}$$

Irrational numbers cannot be expressed as a fraction. Consider $\sqrt{2}$. Since $1 \times 1 = 1$ and $2 \times 2 = 4$ the value of $\sqrt{2}$ lies between 1 and 2. Some fractions are very close to the exact value of $\sqrt{2}$, for instance:

$$\frac{7}{5} \times \frac{7}{5} = \frac{49}{25} = 1.96$$

$$\frac{71}{50} \times \frac{71}{50} = \frac{5041}{2500} = 2.016\,4$$

$$\frac{707}{500} \times \frac{707}{500} = \frac{499\,849}{250\,000} = 1.999\,396$$

However, it is impossible to find a fraction, which when multiplied by itself gives exactly 2. Hence $\sqrt{2}$ is an irrational number. Similarly $\sqrt{3}$, $\sqrt{5}$ and $\sqrt{7}$ are all irrational numbers. Not all square roots are irrational numbers. For instance $\sqrt{9}$ is not irrational because it equals 3. $\sqrt{2.25} = 1.5$ and hence $\sqrt{2.25}$ is rational because $1.5 = \frac{3}{2}$.

Imaginary numbers. Numbers like $\sqrt{-1}$, $\sqrt{-4}$, $\sqrt{-11}$, etc. have no real meaning. $1 \times 1 = 1$ and $(-1) \times (-1) = 1$ and hence it is impossible to find the value of $\sqrt{-1}$. Similarly, it is not possible to find $\sqrt{-4}$ or the square root of any negative number. The square root of a negative number is said to be an imaginary number. Numbers which are not imaginary are said to be *real*. Thus $\sqrt{16} = 4$ and $\sqrt{1.849\,6} = 1.36$ are *real rational numbers*. A number like $\sqrt{13}$ is called a *real irrational number*.

1) Which of the following are positive integers?

5, -8, $\frac{2}{3}$, $1\frac{1}{2}$, 2.75 and 198.

2) Which of the following are negative integers?

$8\frac{1}{2}$, -9, 7, $-\frac{1}{3}$ and $-4\frac{3}{4}$.

3) Which of the following are rational and which are irrational?

1.57, $\frac{1}{4}$, -5.625, $\sqrt{9}$, $\sqrt{15}$, 6.76 and $-3\frac{1}{2}$.

4) Which of the following are real numbers?

9.5782, -7.38, $\sqrt{8}$, $\sqrt{-4}$, $7\frac{2}{3}$ and $\sqrt{-5}$.

SEQUENCES OF NUMBERS

A set of numbers connected by some definite law is called a *sequence*. Some examples are:

3, 1, -1, -3 (each number is 2 less than the preceding number)

1, 4, 9, 16 (squares of successive integers: $1^2 = 1$, $2^2 = 4$, etc.)

2, 1, $\frac{1}{2}$, $\frac{1}{4}$ (each number is $\frac{1}{2}$ of the preceding number).

Write down the next two terms of each of the following sequences:

1) 1, 4, 7, 10 . . .

2) 5, 11, 17, 23, . . .

3) 2, 0, -2, -4, . . .

4) -5, -3, -1, 1, . . .

5) $\frac{3}{4}$, $\frac{1}{4}$, $\frac{1}{12}$, $\frac{1}{36}$, . . .

6) 16, 25, 36, 49, . . .

7) 2, -2, 2, -2, . . .

8) 1.2, 1.44, 1.728, . . .

9) 3, -1.5, 0.75, -0.375, . . .

10) 1.1, -1.21, 1.331, . . .

SELF-TEST 12

In the following questions state the letter (or letters) corresponding to the correct answer (or answers).

1) $(-2) \times (-3)$ is equal to:

a -6 **b** -5 **c** $+5$ **d** $+6$

2) The value of $(+4)(-2) - (-2)$ is:

a -6 **b** -4 **c** $+4$ **d** $+6$

3) The value of $(-3)^2$ is:

a -9 **b** -6 **c** $+6$ **d** $+9$

4) $(-4) \times (-3)$ is equal to:

a -7 **b** $+7$ **c** -12 **d** $+12$

5) The value of $-6 - (-6)$ is:

a -12 **b** 0   **c** 12   **d** 36

6) Which of the following is a rational number?

a $\sqrt{2}$ **b** $\sqrt{3}$ **c** $\sqrt{4}$ **d** $\sqrt{6}$

7) The next number in the series 3, -1, $\frac{1}{3}$, $-\frac{1}{9}$ is:

a $-\frac{2}{9}$ **b** $-\frac{1}{27}$ **c** $\frac{1}{27}$ **d** $\frac{2}{9}$

8) One of the following is an irrational number. Which?

a $\sqrt{-5}$ **b** $\sqrt{-6}$ **c** $\sqrt{5}$ **d** $\sqrt{9}$

CHAPTER 12 SUMMARY

Points to remember

(i)   On a number line, the number to the right is always larger than those on its left.

(ii) When adding two numbers with the same sign, add the numbers and keep that same sign.

(iii) When adding two numbers with different signs, subtract the numbers and keep the sign of the one with the larger magnitude.

(iv) When subtracting two numbers, change the sign of the number being subtracted and use the addition rule, e.g.
$10 - 3 = 10 + (-3) = 7$
$-13 - (-4) = -13 + 4 = -9$.

(v)   When multiplying or dividing directed numbers, remember
(a) an odd number of negative numbers produces a negative answer.
e.g. $(-4)(2)(-3)(-5) = -120$
(b) an even number of negative numbers produces a positive answer.
e.g. $(-8)(4)(-2) = 64$.

Chapter 13 **Basic Algebra**

INTRODUCTION

The methods of algebra are an extension of those used in arithmetic. In algebra we use letters and symbols as well as numbers to represent quantities. When we write that a sum of money is $50 we are making a *particular statement* but if we write that a sum of money is $P we are making a *general statement*. This general statement will cover any number we care to substitute for P.

USE OF SYMBOLS

The following examples will show how verbal statements can be translated into algebraic symbols. Notice that we can choose any symbol we like to represent the quantities concerned.

(1) The sum of two numbers.
  Let the two numbers be x and y.
  Sum of the two numbers $= x + y$.

(2) Three times a number.
  Let the number be N.
  Three times the number $= 3 \times N$
  $\qquad\qquad\qquad\qquad\quad = 3N$.

(3) One number divided by another number.
  Let one number be a and the other number be b.
  One number divided by another number
  $= \dfrac{a}{b}$.

(4) Five times the product of two numbers.
  Let the two numbers be m and n.
  5 times the product of the two numbers
  $= 5 \times m \times n$, written $5mn$.

Exercise 69 – *All type A*

Translate the following into algebraic symbols:

1) Seven times a number, x.

2) Four times a number x minus three.

3) Five times a number x plus a second number, y.

4) The sum of two numbers x and y divided by a third number, z.

---

5) Half of a number, x.

6) Eight times the product of three numbers, x, y and z.

7) The product of two numbers x and y divided by a third number, z.

8) Three times a number, x, minus four times a second number, y.

SUBSTITUTION

The process of finding the numerical value of an algebraic expression for given values of the symbols that appear in it is called *substitution*.

EXAMPLE 1

If $x = 3$, $y = 4$ and $z = 5$ find the values of:

(a) $2y + 4$ \qquad (b) $3y + 5z$

(c) $8 - x$ \qquad (d) $\dfrac{y}{x}$

(e) $\dfrac{3y + 2z}{x + z}$.

Note that multiplication signs are often missed out when writing algebraic expressions so that, for instance, $2y$ means $2 \times y$. These missed multiplication signs must reappear when the numbers are substituted for the symbols.

(a) $2y + 4 = 2 \times 4 + 4 = 8 + 4 = 12$

(b) $3y + 5z = 3 \times 4 + 5 \times 5$
  $\qquad\qquad\quad = 12 + 25 = 37$

(c) $8 - x = 8 - 3 = 5$

(d) $\dfrac{y}{x} = \dfrac{4}{3} = 1\dfrac{1}{3}$

(e) $\dfrac{3y + 2z}{x + z} = \dfrac{3 \times 4 + 2 \times 5}{3 + 5}$
  $\qquad\qquad\quad = \dfrac{12 + 10}{8} = \dfrac{22}{8} = 2\dfrac{3}{4}$

Exercise 70 – *All type A*

If $a=2$, $b=3$ and $c=5$ find the values of the following:

1) $a+7$
2) $c-2$
3) $6-b$
4) $6b$
5) $9c$
6) ab
7) $3bc$
8) abc
9) $5c-2$
10) $4c+6b$
11) $8c-7$
12) $a+2b+5c$
13) $8c-4b$
14) $14 \div a$
15) $\dfrac{ab}{8}$
16) $\dfrac{abc}{6}$
17) $\dfrac{2c}{a}$
18) $\dfrac{5a+9b+8c}{a+b+c}$

POWERS

The quantity $a \times a \times a$ or aaa is usually written as a^3. a^3 is called the third power of a. The number 3 which indicates the number of threes to be multiplied together is called the *index* (plural: *indices*).

$$2^4 = 2 \times 2 \times 2 \times 2 = 16$$
$$y^5 = y \times y \times y \times y \times y$$

EXAMPLE 2
Find the value of b^3 when $b=5$.
$$b^3 = 5^3 = 5 \times 5 \times 5 = 125$$

When dealing with expressions like $8mn^4$ note that it is only the symbol n which is raised to the fourth power. Thus:
$$8mn^4 = 8 \times m \times n \times n \times n \times n$$

EXAMPLE 3
Find the value of $7p^2q^3$ when $p=5$ and $q=4$.
$$7p^2q^3 = 7 \times 5^2 \times 4^3 = 7 \times 25 \times 64$$
$$= 11\,200$$

Exercise 71 – *All type A*

If $a=2$, $b=3$ and $c=4$ find the values of the following:

1) a^2
2) b^4
3) ab^3
4) $2a^2c$
5) ab^2c^3
6) $5a^2+6b^2$
7) a^2+c^2
8) $7b^3c^2$
9) $\dfrac{3a^4}{c^2}$
10) $\dfrac{c^5}{ab^3}$

ADDITION OF ALGEBRAIC TERMS

Like terms are numerical multiples of the same algebraic quantity. Thus:
$$7x, \; 5x \text{ and } -3x$$
are three like terms.

An expression consisting of like terms can be reduced to a single term by adding the numerical coefficients together. Thus:
$$7x-5x+3x = (7-5+3)x = 5x$$
$$3b^2+7b^2 = (3+7)b^2 = 10b^2$$
$$-3y-5y = (-3-5)y = -8y$$
$$q-3q = (1-3)q = -2q$$

Note that by the commutative law of addition,
$$5x+3x+15x = 15x+5x+3x = 23x$$
i.e. the order in which we add algebraic terms is unimportant.

Only like terms can be added or subtracted. Thus $7a+3b-2c$ is an expression containing three unlike terms and it cannot be simplified any further. Similarly with $8a^2b+7ab^3+6a^2b^2$ which are all unlike terms.

It is possible to have several sets of like terms in an expression and each set can then be simplified:
$$8x+3y-4z-5x+7z-2y+2z$$
$$= (8-5)x+(3-2)y+(-4+7+2)z$$
$$= 3x+y+5z$$

MULTIPLICATION AND DIVISION OF ALGEBRAIC QUANTITIES

The rules are exactly the same as those used with directed numbers:
$$(+x)(+y) = +(xy) = +xy = xy$$
$$5x \times 3y = 5 \times 3 \times x \times y = 15xy$$

$$(x)(-y) = -(xy) = -xy$$

$$(2x)(-3y) = -(2x)(3y) = -6xy$$

$$(-4x)(2y) = -(4x)(2y) = -8xy$$

$$(-3x)(-2y) = +(3x)(2y) = 6xy$$

Note that by the commutative law of multiplication,

$$3x \times 2y = 2y \times 3x = 6xy$$

i.e. the order in which we multiply algebraic terms is unimportant.

$$\frac{+x}{+y} = +\frac{x}{y} = \frac{x}{y}$$

$$\frac{-3x}{2y} = -\frac{3x}{2y}$$

$$\frac{-5x}{-6y} = +\frac{5x}{6y} = \frac{5x}{6y}$$

$$\frac{4x}{-3y} = -\frac{4x}{3y}$$

When *multiplying* expressions containing the same symbols, indices are used:

$$m \times m = m^2$$

$$3m \times 5m = 3 \times m \times 5 \times m = 15m^2$$

$$(-m) \times m^2 = (-m) \times m \times m = -m^3$$

$$5m^2n \times 3mn^3$$

$$= 5 \times m \times m \times n \times 3 \times m \times n \times n \times n$$

$$= 5 \times 3 \times m \times m \times m \times n \times n \times n \times n$$

$$= 15m^3n^4$$

$$3mn \times (-2n^2)$$

$$= 3 \times m \times n \times (-2) \times n \times n = -6mn^3$$

When *dividing* algebraic expressions, cancellation between numerator and denominator is often possible. Cancelling is equivalent to dividing both numerator and denominator by the same quantity:

$$\frac{pq}{p} = \frac{\cancel{p} \times q}{\cancel{p}} = q$$

$$\frac{3p^2q}{6pq^2} = \frac{3 \times \cancel{p} \times p \times \cancel{q}}{6 \times \cancel{p} \times \cancel{q} \times q} = \frac{3p}{6q} = \frac{p}{2q}$$

$$\frac{18x^2y^2z}{6xyz} = \frac{18 \times \cancel{x} \times x \times y \times \cancel{y} \times \cancel{z}}{6 \times \cancel{x} \times \cancel{y} \times \cancel{z}} = 3xy$$

Exercise 72 – *All type A*

Simplify the following:

1) $7x + 11x$
2) $7x - 5x$
3) $3x - 6x$
4) $-2x - 4x$
5) $-8x + 3x$
6) $-2x + 7x$
7) $8a - 6a - 7a$
8) $5m + 13m - 6m$
9) $6b^2 - 4b^2 + 3b^2$
10) $6ab - 3ab - 2ab$
11) $14xy + 5xy - 7xy + 2xy$
12) $-5x + 7x - 3x - 2x$
13) $-4x^2 - 3x^2 + 2x^2 - x^2$
14) $3x - 2y + 4z - 2x - 3y + 5z$ $+6x + 2y - 3z$
15) $3a^2b + 2ab^3 + 4a^2b^2 - 5ab^3$ $+11b^4 + 6a^2b$
16) $1.2x^3 - 3.4x^2 + 2.6x + 3.7x^2$ $+3.6x - 2.8$
17) $pq + 2.1qr - 2.2rq + 8qp$
18) $2.6a^2b^2 - 3.4b^3 - 2.7a^3 - 3a^2b^2$ $-2.1b^3 + 1.5a^3$
19) $2x \times 5y$
20) $3a \times 4b$
21) $3 \times 4m$
22) $\frac{1}{4}q \times 16p$
23) $x \times (-y)$
24) $(-3a) \times (-2b)$
25) $8m \times (-3n)$
26) $(-4a) \times 3b$
27) $8p \times (-q) \times (-3r)$
28) $3a \times (-4b) \times (-c) \times 5d$
29) $12x \div 6$
30) $4a \div (-7b)$
31) $(-5a) \div 8b$
32) $(-3a) \div (-3b)$

33) $4a \div 2b$

34) $4ab \div 2a$

35) $12x^2yz^2 \div 4xz^2$

36) $(-12a^2b) \div 6a$

37) $8a^2bc^2 \div 4ac^2$

38) $7a^2b^2 \div 3ab$

39) $a \times a$

40) $b \times (-b)$

41) $(-m) \times m$

42) $(-p) \times (-p)$

43) $3a \times 2a$

44) $5X \times X$

45) $5q \times (-3q)$

46) $3m \times (-3m)$

47) $(-3pq) \times (-3q)$

48) $8mn \times (-3m^2n^3)$

49) $7ab \times (-3a^2)$

50) $2q^3r^4 \times 5qr^2$

51) $(-3m) \times 2n \times (-5p)$

52) $5a^2 \times (-3b) \times 5ab$

53) $m^2n \times (-mn) \times 5m^2n^2$

BRACKETS

Brackets are used for convenience in grouping terms together. The *distributive law* states that if a, b and c are real numbers, then $a(b+c) = ab + ac$. Hence, when removing brackets *each term* within the bracket is multiplied by the quantity outside the bracket:

$$3(x+y) = 3x + 3y$$
$$5(2x+3y) = 5 \times 2x + 5 \times 3y = 10x + 15y$$
$$4(a-2b) = 4 \times a - 4 \times 2b = 4a - 8b$$
$$m(a+b) = ma + mb$$
$$3x(2p+3q) = 3x \times 2p + 3x \times 3q = 6px + 9qx$$
$$4a(2a+b) = 4a \times 2a + 4a \times b = 8a^2 + 4ab$$

When a bracket has a minus sign in front of it, the signs of all the terms inside the bracket are changed when the bracket is removed. The reason for this rule may be seen from the following examples:

$$-3(2x-5y) = (-3) \times 2x + (-3) \times (-5y)$$
$$= -6x + 15y$$
$$-(m+n) = -m-n$$
$$-(p-q) = -p+q$$
$$-2(p+3q) = -2p-6q$$

When simplifying expressions containing brackets first remove the brackets and then add the like terms together:

$$(3x+7y) - (4x+3y) = 3x + 7y - 4x - 3y$$
$$= -x + 4y$$
$$3(2x+3y) - (x+5y) = 6x + 9y - x - 5y$$
$$= 5x + 4y$$
$$x(a+b) - x(a+3b) = ax + bx - ax - 3bx$$
$$= -2bx$$
$$2(5a+3b) + 3(a-2b) = 10a + 6b + 3a - 6b$$
$$= 13a$$

Exercise 73 – *Questions 1–20 type A, remainder B*

Remove the brackets in the following:

1) $3(x+4)$

2) $2(a+b)$

3) $3(3x+2y)$

4) $\frac{1}{2}(x-1)$

5) $5(2p-3q)$

6) $7(a-3m)$

7) $-(a+b)$

8) $-(a-2b)$

9) $-(3p-3q)$

10) $-(7m-6)$

11) $-4(x+3)$

12) $-2(2x-5)$

13) $-5(4-3x)$

14) $2k(k-5)$

15) $-3y(3x+4)$

16) $a(p-q-r)$

17) $4xy(ab-ac+d)$

18) $3x^2(x^2-2xy+y^2)$

19) $-7P(2P^2-P+1)$

20) $-2m(-1+3m-2n)$

Remove the brackets and simplify:

21) $3(x+1) + 2(x+4)$

22) $5(2a+4) - 3(4a+2)$

23) $3(x+4) - (2x+5)$

24) $4(1-2x) - 3(3x-4)$

25) $5(2x-y) - 3(x+2y)$

26) $\frac{1}{2}(y-1) + \frac{1}{3}(2y-3)$

27) $-(4a+5b-3c) - 2(2a+3b-4c)$

28) $2x(x-5) - x(x-2) - 3x(x-5)$

29) $3(a-b) - 2(2a-3b) + 4(a-3b)$

30) $3x(x^2 + 7x - 1) - 2x(2x^2 + 3) - 3(x^2 + 5)$

OPERATIONS WITH NUMBERS

Given any two numbers, there are various ways of operating on them apart from the familiar operations of adding, subtracting, dividing and multiplying. The method is shown in Examples 1 and 2.

EXAMPLE 4

If $a * b$ means $\sqrt{ab}$ find the value of $4 * 9$.

Here we have $a = 4$ and $b = 9$.

Hence $\qquad 4 * 9 = \sqrt{4 \times 9} = 6$

EXAMPLE 5

If $a * b$ means $\frac{1}{2}(2a - b)$ find the value of $5 * 2$.

Here $a = 5$ and $b = 2$.

Hence $\quad 5 * 2 = \frac{1}{2}(2 \times 5 - 2)$

$\qquad = \frac{1}{2}(10 - 2) = \frac{1}{2} \times 8 = 4$

Exercise 74 – *All type B*

1) If $a * b$ means $2a + b$ find the value of $3 * 1$.

2) If $x * y$ means $3x - 2y$ find the value of $2 * 5$.

3) If $a * b$ means $\frac{1}{4}(a - b)$ find the value of $5 * 3$.

4) If $a * b$ means $(a + b)^2$ find the value of $2 * 3$.

5) If $x * y$ means $\sqrt{xy}$ find the value of $9 * 16$.

6) If $a * b$ means $\sqrt{a^2 - b^2}$ find the value of $5 * 3$.

7) If $p * q$ means $\frac{1}{2}(p^2 + q^3)$ find the value of $4 * 2$.

8) If $a * b$ means $(a - b^2)^2$ find the value of $3 * (-2)$.

9) If $a * b$ means $(a^3 + b)^2$ find the value of $(-5) * 3$.

10) If $m * n$ means $m^2 - 2mn + n^3$ find the value of $2 * 3$.

SELF-TEST 13

In Questions 1 to 38 the answer is either 'true' or 'false', state which.

1) The sum of two numbers can be represented by the expression $a + b$.

2) The expression $a - b$ represents the difference of two numbers a and b.

3) The product of 8 and x is $8 + x$.

4) 3 times a number minus 7 can be written as $3x - 7$.

5) Two numbers added together minus a third number and the result divided by a fourth number may be written as $(a + b - c) \div d$.

6) The value of $3a + 7$ when $a = 5$ is 36.

7) The value of $8x - 3$ when $x = 3$ is 21.

8) The value of $3b - 2c$ when $b = 4$ and $c = 3$ is 6.

9) The value of $8ab \div 3c$ when $a = 6$, $b = 4$ and $c = 2$ is 32.

10) The quantity $a \times a \times a \times a$ is written a^3.

11) The quantity $y \times y \times y$ is written y^3.

12) $a^3 b^2$ is equal to $a \times a \times a \times b \times b$.

13) The value of a^4 when $a = 3$ is 81.

14) When $x = 2$, $y = 3$ and $z = 4$ the value of $2x^2 y^3 z$ is 258.

15) $5x + 8x$ is equal to $13x^2$.

16) $3x + 6x$ is equal to $9x$.

17) $8x - 5x$ is equal to 3.

18) $7x - 2x$ is equal to $5x$.

19) $15xy + 7xy - 3xy - 2xy$ is equal to $17xy$.

20) $8a \times 5a$ is equal to $40a$.

21) $9x \times 5x$ is equal to $45x^2$.

22) $(-5x) \times (-8x) \times 3x$ is equal to $120x^3$.

23) $a^2 b$ is the same as ba^2.

24) $5x^3 y^2 z$ is the same as $5y^2 zx^3$.

25) $8a^3 b^2 c^4$ and $16a^3 b^3 c^3$ are like terms.

26) $6x^2 \div (-3x)$ is equal to $3x$.

27) $(-5pq^2) \times (-8p^2q)$ is equal to $40p^3q^3$.

28) $a^2b^2 \times (-a^2b^2) \times 5a^2b^2$ is equal to $5a^2b^2$.

29) $3(2x+7)$ is equal to $6x+7$.

30) $5(3x+4)$ is equal to $15x+20$.

31) $4(x+8)$ is equal to $4x+32$.

32) $-(3x+5y)$ is equal to $-3x+5y$.

33) $-(2a+3b)$ is equal to $-2a-3b$.

34) $4x(3x-2xy)$ is equal to $12x^2-8x^2y$.

35) $-8a(a-3b)$ is equal to $-8a^2-24ab$.

36) $3(x-y)-5(2x-3y)$ is equal to $12y-7x$.

37) $2x(x-2)-3x(x^2-5)$ is equal to $-3x^3+2x^2-19x$.

38) $3a(2a^2+3a-1)-2a(3a^2+3)$ is equal to $9a^2+3a$.

CHAPTER 13 SUMMARY

Points to remember

(i)   When combining several operations, perform operations within brackets first. If there are no brackets, do all multiplication and division first in order from left to right. Then all addition and subtraction in the same order.

(ii) When multiplying powers of the same base, add their powers. E.g.
$2x^5 \times 7x^3 = 14x^8$.

(iii) When dividing powers of the same base, subtract their powers. E.g.
$24x^5 \div 4x^3 = 6x^2$.

(iv) A quantity outside a bracket multiplies each term within the bracket. E.g.
$a(b+c) = ab+ac$.

Chapter 14 **Factorisation**

FACTORISING

The expression $3x + 3y$ has the number 3 common to both terms. By the distributive law $3x + 3y = 3(x + y)$; 3 and $(x + y)$ are said to be *the factors of* $3x + 3y$.

To factorise $2x + 6$ we note that 2 is common to both terms. We place 2 outside the bracket. To find the terms inside the bracket divide each of the terms making up the expression by 2. Thus:

$$2x + 6 = 2(x + 3)$$

$$5x^2 - 10x = 5x(x - 2)$$

Exercise 75 – *All type B*

Factorise the following:

1) $4x + 4y$	6) $3y - 9y^2$
2) $5x - 10$	7) $ab^3 - ab$
3) $4x - 6xy$	8) $3x^2 - 6x$
4) $mx - my$	9) $7a - 14b$
5) $5a - 10b + 15c$	10) $36a^2 - 9a$

†HIGHEST COMMON FACTOR (H.C.F.)

The H.C.F. of a set of algebraic expressions is the highest expression which is a factor of each of the given expressions. To find the H.C.F. we therefore select the lowest power of each of the quantities which occur, as a factor, in *all* of the expressions and multiply them together. The method is shown in the following examples.

EXAMPLE 1

(1) Find the H.C.F. of ab^2c^2, $a^2b^3c^3$, $a^2b^4c^4$.

Each expression contains the quantities a, b and c. To find the H.C.F. choose the *lowest* power of each of the quantities which occur in the three expressions and multiply them together. The lowest power of a is a, the lowest power of b is b^2 and the lowest power of c is c^2. Thus:

$$\text{H.C.F.} = ab^2c^2$$

(2) Find the H.C.F. of x^2y^3, $x^3y^2z^2$, xy^2z^3.

We notice that only x and y appear in all three expressions. The quantity z appears in only two of the expressions and cannot therefore appear in the H.C.F. To find the H.C.F. choose the lowest powers of x and y which occur in the three expressions and multiply them together. Thus:

$$\text{H.C.F.} = xy^2$$

(3) Find the H.C.F. of $3m^2np^3$, $6m^3n^2p^2$, $24m^3p^4$.

Dealing with the numerical coefficients 3, 6 and 24 we note that 3 is a factor of each of them. The quantities m and p occur in all three expressions, their lowest powers being m^2 and p^2. Hence:

$$\text{H.C.F.} = 3m^2p^2$$

More difficult algebraic expressions may be factorised by finding the H.C.F. of all the terms making up the expression.

EXAMPLE 2

Find the factors of $m^2n - 2mn^2$.

The H.C.F. of m^2n and $2mn^2$ is mn.

$$\therefore \ m^2n - 2mn^2 = mn(m - 2n)$$

$$\left(\text{since} \quad \frac{m^2n}{mn} = m \quad \text{and} \quad \frac{2mn^2}{mn} = 2n \right).$$

EXAMPLE 3

Find the factors of $3x^4y + 9x^3y^2 - 6x^2y^3$.

The H.C.F. of $3x^4y$, $9x^3y^2$ and $6x^2y^3$ is $3x^2y$.

$$\therefore \ 3x^4y + 9x^3y^2 - 6x^2y^3$$
$$= 3x^2y(x^2 + 3xy - 2y^2)$$

$$\left(\text{since} \quad \frac{3x^4y}{3x^2y} = x^2, \quad \frac{9x^3y^2}{3x^2y} = 3xy \right.$$

$$\left. \text{and} \quad \frac{6x^2y^3}{3x^2y} = 2y^2 \right).$$

EXAMPLE 4

Find the factors of $\dfrac{ac}{x}+\dfrac{bc}{x^2}-\dfrac{cd}{x^3}$.

The H.C.F. of $\dfrac{ac}{x}$, $\dfrac{bc}{x^2}$ and $\dfrac{cd}{x^3}$ is $\dfrac{c}{x}$

$$\therefore \quad \frac{ac}{x}+\frac{bc}{x^2}-\frac{cd}{x^3} = \frac{c}{x}\left(a+\frac{b}{x}-\frac{d}{x^2}\right)$$

$$\left(\text{since} \quad \frac{ac}{x}\div\frac{c}{x}=a, \quad \frac{bc}{x^2}\div\frac{c}{x}=\frac{b}{x}\right.$$

$$\left.\text{and} \quad \frac{cd}{x^3}\div\frac{c}{x}=\frac{d}{x^2}\right).$$

Exercise 76 – *Questions 1–12 type B, remainder C*

Find the H.C.F. of the following:

1) p^3q^2, p^2q^3, p^2q

2) $a^2b^3c^3, a^3b^3, ab^2c^2$

3) $3mn^2, 6mnp, 12m^2np^2$

4) $2ab, 5b, 7ab^2$

5) $3x^2yz, 12x^2yz, 6xy^2z^3, 3xyz^2$

Factorise the following:

6) $x^2y^2-axy+bxy^2$

7) $5x^3-10x^2y+15xy^2$

8) $9x^3y-6x^2y^2+3xy^5$

9) $\dfrac{x}{3}-\dfrac{y}{6}+\dfrac{z}{9}$

10) $I_0+I_0\alpha t$

11) $2a^2-3ab$

12) x^3-x^2+7x

13) $\dfrac{m^2}{pn}-\dfrac{m^3}{pn^2}+\dfrac{m^4}{p^2n^2}$

14) $\dfrac{x^2y}{2a}-\dfrac{2xy^2}{5a^2}+\dfrac{xy^3}{a^3}$

15) $\dfrac{l^2m^2}{15}-\dfrac{l^2m}{20}+\dfrac{l^3m^2}{10}$

16) $\dfrac{a^3}{2x^3}-\dfrac{a^2b}{4x^4}-\dfrac{a^2c}{6x^3}$

†THE PRODUCT OF TWO BINOMIAL EXPRESSIONS

A binomial expression consists of *two terms*. Thus $3x+5$, $a+b$, $2x+3y$ and $4p-q$ are all binomial expressions.

To find the product of $(a+b)(c+d)$ consider the diagram (Fig. 14.1).

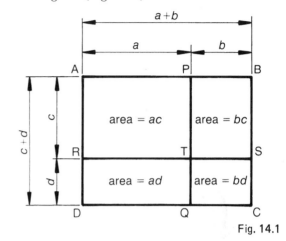

Fig. 14.1

In Fig. 14.1 the rectangular area ABCD is made up as follows:

$$\text{ABCD} = \text{APTR}+\text{TQDR}+\text{PBST}+\text{STQC}$$

i.e. $(a+b)(c+d)=ac+ad+bc+bd$

It will be noticed that the expression on the right hand side is obtained by multiplying each term in the one bracket by each term in the *other* bracket. The process is illustrated below where each pair of terms connected by a line are multiplied together.

$$\overbrace{(a+b)(c+d)} = ac+ad+bc+bd$$

$$(3x+2)(x+4) = (3x)(x)+(3x)(4)$$
$$+(2)(x)+(2)(4)$$
$$= 3x^2+12x+2x+8$$
$$= 3x^2+14x+8$$

$$(2p-3)(3p-4) = (2p)(3p)+(2p)(-4)$$
$$+(-3)(3p)+(-3)(-4)$$
$$= 6p^2-8p-9p+12$$
$$= 6p^2-17p+12$$

Exercise 77 – *All type B*

Remove the brackets from the following:

1) $(x+1)(x+3)$ 6) $(x-2)(x-3)$

2) $(2x+5)(x+3)$ 7) $(4x-1)(2x-3)$

3) $(5x-2)(2x+4)$ 8) $(x-1)(x+1)$

4) $(a+3)(a-6)$ 9) $(2x-3)(2x+3)$

5) $(3x+1)(2x-5)$ 10) $(x-4)(2x+5)$

FACTORISING BY GROUPING

To factorise the expression $ax + ay + bx + by$ first group the terms in pairs so that each pair of terms has a common factor. Thus:

$$ax + ay + bx + by = (ax + ay) + (bx + by)$$
$$= a(x + y) + b(x + y)$$

Now notice that in the two terms $a(x+y)$ and $b(x+y)$, $(x+y)$ is a common factor. Hence,

$$a(x + y) + b(x + y) = (x + y)(a + b)$$
$$\therefore \ ax + ay + bx + by = (x + y)(a + b)$$

Similarly,

$$np + mp - qn - qm = (np + mp) - (qn + qm)$$
$$= p(n + m) - q(n + m)$$
$$= (n + m)(p - q)$$

Exercise 78 – *All type C*

Factorise the following:

1) $ax + by + bx + ay$

2) $mp + np - mq - nq$

3) $a^2c^2 + acd + acd + d^2$

4) $2pr - 4ps + qr - 2qs$

5) $4ax + 6ay - 4bx - 6by$

6) $ab(x^2 + y^2) - cd(x^2 + y^2)$

7) $mn(3x - 1) - pq(3x - 1)$

8) $k^2l^2 - mnl - k^2l + mn$

†FACTORS OF QUADRATIC EXPRESSIONS

A quadratic expression is an expression in which the highest power of the symbol used is 2. Thus:

$$x^2 - 5x + 7 \ \text{ and } \ 3a^2 + 2a - 5$$

are both quadratic expressions.

(a) Factorising when the coefficient of the squared term is 1.

$$(x + 3)(x + 2) = x^2 + 5x + 6$$

Note that the factors of 6 are 3 and 2. The coefficient of x is 5 which equals the factors of 6 added together (i.e. $3 + 2 = 5$). This example gives a clue as to how we factorise quadratic expressions.

EXAMPLE 5

(1) Factorise $x^2 + 7x + 12$.

We see that $12 = 4 \times 3$ and that $7 = 4 + 3$.

Hence $(x^2 + 7x + 12) = (x + 4)(x + 3)$

(2) Factorise $x^2 - 2x - 3$.

We see that $-3 = (-3) \times 1$ and that $-3 + 1 = -2$.

Hence $x^2 - 2x - 3 = (x - 3)(x + 1)$

(b) Factorising where the coefficient of the squared term is not 1. In case (a) above the clue to factorising the quadratic expression was to find two numbers whose product was the constant term and whose sum the coefficient of x.

For example in $x^2 + 7x + 12$ we need two numbers whose product is 12 and sum 7. These two numbers are 4 and 3.

Now write $x^2 + 7x + 12$
$$= x^2 + 4x + 3x + 12$$
$$= x(x + 4) + 3(x + 4)$$
$$= (x + 4)(x + 3).$$

This technique is also useful when factorising $ax^2 + bx + c$, and $a \neq 1$.

It can be proved that $ax^2 + bx + c$ can be factorised if we can find two integers whose product is ac and sum b.

Consider the expression $12x^2 + 11x - 15$.
$a = 12$, $b = 11$, $c = -15$.
$ac = (12) \times (-15) = -180$

By factorising 180 as $2^2 \times 3^2 \times 5$ it is now easily seen that the two integers whose product is -180 and whose sum is 11 are 20 and -9.

We conclude that $12x^2 + 11x - 15$ can be factorised.

Since $11x = 20x - 9x$,
$12x^2 + 11x - 15$
$$= 12x^2 + 20x - 9x - 15$$
$$= 4x(3x + 5) - 3(3x + 5)$$
$$= (3x + 5)(4x - 3)$$

This method follows naturally from factorising by grouping and is not a trial and error method.

Hence

$$12x^2 + 11x - 15 = (3x + 5)(4x - 3)$$

Exercise 79 – *Questions 1–8 type C,*
remainder D

Factorise the following quadratic expressions:

1) $x^2 - 5x + 6$ 9) $2x^2 - 7x + 5$

2) $x^2 + 6x + 8$ 10) $2x^2 + 13x + 15$

3) $x^2 - 7x + 10$ 11) $3x^2 + x - 2$

4) $x^2 - 11x + 30$ 12) $3x^2 - 8x - 28$

5) $x^2 - x - 2$ 13) $2x^2 - 5x - 3$

6) $x^2 - 2x - 15$ 14) $10x^2 + 19x - 15$

7) $x^2 + 2x - 8$ 15) $6x^2 + x - 35$

8) $x^2 + x - 12$

(c) Where the factors form a perfect square.

$$(a+b)^2 = (a+b)(a+b)$$
$$= a^2 + ab + ab + b^2$$
$$= a^2 + 2ab + b^2$$
$$(a-b)^2 = (a-b)(a-b)$$
$$= a^2 - ab - ab + b^2$$
$$= a^2 - 2ab + b^2$$

The square of a binomial expression therefore consists of:

$$(\text{first term})^2 + 2 \times (\text{first term})$$
$$\times (\text{second term}) + (\text{last term})^2$$

EXAMPLE 6

(1) Factorise $9a^2 + 12ab + 4b^2$.

$$9a^2 = (3a)^2 \qquad 4b^2 = (2b)^2$$
$$2 \times 3a \times 2b = 12ab$$
$$\therefore \; 9a^2 + 12ab + 4b^2 = (3a + 2b)^2$$

(2) Factorise $16x^2 - 40x + 25$.

$$16x^2 = (4x)^2 \qquad 25 = 5^2$$
$$2 \times 4x \times 5 = 40x$$
$$\therefore \; 16x^2 - 40x + 25 = (4x - 5)^2$$

(d) Where the factors form the difference of two squares.

$$(a+b)(a-b) = a^2 + ab - ab - b^2$$
$$= a^2 - b^2$$

Hence the factors of $a^2 - b^2$ are the sum and difference of the square roots of each of the squares.

EXAMPLE 7

(1) Factorise $x^2 - 1$.

$$x^2 = (x)^2 \quad \text{and} \quad 1 = (1)^2$$

Hence $x^2 - 1 = (x + 1)(x - 1)$.

(2) Factorise $9x^2 - 16$.

$$9x^2 = (3x)^2 \quad \text{and} \quad 16 = 4^2$$

Hence $9x^2 - 16 = (3x + 4)(3x - 4)$.

Exercise 80 – *Questions 11–17, type B*
remainder C

Factorise the following:

1) $x^2 + 2x + 1$ 6) $x^2 - 4x + 4$

2) $x^2 - 2x + 1$ 7) $4x^2 - 1$

3) $x^2 + 4x + 4$ 8) $a^2 - b^2$

4) $9x^2 + 6x + 1$ 9) $1 - x^2$

5) $25x^2 - 20x + 4$ 10) $121x^2 - 64$

In Questions 11 to 17 complete the bracket which has been left blank.

11) $x^2 - x - 6 = (x + 2)(\quad)$

12) $x^2 - 12x + 35 = (x - 5)(\quad)$

13) $6x^2 + 31x + 40 = (3x + 8)(\quad)$

14) $10x^2 - 31x + 15 = (2x - 5)(\quad)$

15) $x^2 + 2x + 1 = (\quad)^2$

16) $x^2 - 2x + 1 = (\quad)^2$

17) $9p^2 - 25 = (3p + 5)(\quad)$

SELF-TEST 14

In Questions 1 to 30 the answer is either 'true' or 'false', state which.

1) The H.C.F. of a^2bc^3 and ab^2 is ab.

2) The H.C.F. of x^2y^3z and x^2yz^2 is $x^2y^3z^2$.

3) The H.C.F. of $a^3b^2c^2$, $a^2b^3c^3$ and ab^4c^4 is ab^2c^2.

4) The factors of $a^2x^3 + bx^2$ are $x^2(a^2x + b)$.

5) The factors of $3a^3y + 6a^2x + 9a^4z$ are $3a(a^2y + 2ax + 3a^3z)$.

6) The factors of $\dfrac{bz}{y} - \dfrac{cz}{y^2} + \dfrac{dz}{y^3}$ are

$$\frac{z}{y}\left(b - \frac{c}{y} + \frac{d}{y^2}\right).$$

7) One factor of $a^2b^3 - a^3b^4 + ab^2$ is $(ab - a^2b^2 + 1)$. The other factor is ab^2.

8) $(2p + 5)(3p - 7)$ is equal to $6p^2 + 29p - 35$.

9) $(3x + 7)(2x - 7)$ is equal to $6x^2 - 7x + 49$.

10) $(5x + 2)(3x - 8)$ is equal to $15x^2 - 34x - 16$.

11) $(2x + 3)^2$ is equal to $4x^2 + 6x + 9$.

12) $(3x + 5)^2$ is equal to $9x^2 + 30x + 25$.

13) $(7x - 2)^2$ is equal to $49^2 - 28x - 4$.

14) $(3x - 4)^2$ is equal to $9x^2 - 24x + 16$.

15) $(2x - 3)(2x + 3)$ is equal to $4x^2 - 9$.

16) $(5x - 2)(5x + 2)$ is equal to $25x^2 + 4$.

17) $x^2 + 5x + 6$ is equal to $(x + 3)(x + 2)$.

18) $x^2 - 8x + 15$ is equal to $(x + 3)(x + 5)$.

19) $x^2 - 9x + 14$ is equal to $(x - 2)(x - 7)$.

20) $x^2 - 2x - 15$ is equal to $(x + 3)(x - 5)$.

21) $x^2 + 2x - 35$ is equal to $(x - 5)(x + 7)$.

22) $9x^2 - 3x - 12$ is equal to $(3x + 4)(3x - 3)$.

23) $8x^2 - 10x - 25$ is equal to $(2x - 5)(4x + 5)$.

24) $25x^2 + 10x - 3$ is equal to $(5x - 1)(5x + 3)$.

25) $(3x + 2)^2$ is equal to $9x^2 + 12x + 4$.

26) $4x^2 - 12x + 9$ is equal to $(2x - 3)^2$.

27) $25x^2 - 10x - 1$ is equal to $(5x - 1)^2$.

28) $49x^2 + 70x + 25$ is equal to $(7x + 5)^2$.

29) $4x^2 - 25$ is equal to $(2x + 5)(2x - 5)$.

30) $9x^2 - 49$ is equal to $(3x - 7)(3x + 7)$.

Chapter 15 **Algebraic Functions**

†MULTIPLICATION AND DIVISION OF FRACTIONS

As with ordinary arithmetic fractions, numerators can be multiplied together, as can denominators, in order to form a single fraction. Thus:

$$\frac{a}{b} \times \frac{c}{d} = \frac{a \times c}{b \times d} = \frac{ac}{bd}$$

and

$$\frac{3x}{2y} \times \frac{p}{4q} \times \frac{r^2}{s} = \frac{3x \times p \times r^2}{2y \times 4q \times s} = \frac{3xpr^2}{8yqs}$$

Factors which are common to both numerator and denominator may be *cancelled*. It is important to realise that this cancelling means dividing the numerator and denominator by the same quantity. For instance,

$$\frac{8ab}{3mn} \times \frac{9n^2m}{4ab^2}$$

$$= \frac{\overset{2}{\cancel{8}} \times \cancel{a} \times \cancel{b} \times \overset{3}{\cancel{9}} \times \cancel{n} \times n \times \cancel{m}}{\cancel{3} \times \cancel{m} \times \cancel{n} \times \cancel{4} \times \cancel{a} \times \cancel{b} \times b} = \frac{6n}{b}$$

and

$$\frac{7ab}{8mn^2} \times \frac{3m^2n^3}{2ab^3} \times \frac{16an}{63bm}$$

$$= \frac{\cancel{7} \times \cancel{a} \times \cancel{b} \times \cancel{3} \times \cancel{m} \times \cancel{m} \times \cancel{n} \times \cancel{n} \times n \times \cancel{16} \times a \times n}{\cancel{8} \times \cancel{m} \times \cancel{n} \times \cancel{n} \times \cancel{2} \times \cancel{a} \times b \times b \times b \times \underset{3}{\cancel{63}} \times \cancel{b} \times \cancel{m}}$$

$$= \frac{an^2}{3b^3}$$

To divide by a fraction invert it and then multiply.

EXAMPLE 1

Simplify $\dfrac{ax^2}{by} \div \dfrac{a^2}{b^2y^2}$.

$$\frac{ax^2}{by} \div \frac{a^2}{b^2y^2} = \frac{ax^2}{by} \times \frac{b^2y^2}{a^2} = \frac{bx^2y}{a}$$

Exercise 81 – *All type B*

Simplify the following:

1) $\dfrac{a}{bc^2} \times \dfrac{b^2c}{a}$

2) $\dfrac{3pq}{r} \times \dfrac{qs}{2t} \times \dfrac{3rs}{pq^2}$

3) $\dfrac{2z^2y}{3ac^2} \times \dfrac{6a^2}{5zy^2} \times \dfrac{10c^3}{3y^2}$

4) $\dfrac{3pq}{5rs} \div \dfrac{p^2}{15s^2}$

5) $\dfrac{6ab}{5cd} \div \dfrac{4a^2}{7bd}$

†Before attempting to simplify, factorise where this is possible and then cancel factors which are common to both numerator and denominator. Remember that the contents of a bracket may be regarded as a single term. Hence the expressions $(x - y)$, $(b + c)$ and $(x - 3)$ may be regarded as single terms.

†EXAMPLE 2

(1) Simplify $\dfrac{x^2 - x}{x - 1}$.

$$x^2 - x = x(x - 1)$$

Hence, $\dfrac{x^2 - x}{x - 1} = \dfrac{x(x - 1)}{(x - 1)} = x$

(2) Simplify $\dfrac{3x - 12}{4x^2 - 8} \times \dfrac{2x^2 - 4}{9x - 36}$.

Factorising where this is possible:

$$\frac{3x - 12}{4x^2 - 8} \times \frac{2x^2 - 4}{9x - 36}$$

$$= \frac{3(x - 4)}{4(x^2 - 2)} \times \frac{2(x^2 - 2)}{9(x - 4)} = \frac{1}{6}$$

(3) Simplify $\dfrac{3xy - 6x + y - 2}{y^2 - 4}$.

Now,

$$3xy - 6x + y - 2 = (3xy - 6x) + (y - 2)$$
$$= 3x(y - 2) + (y - 2)$$
$$= (y - 2)(3x + 1)$$

also $y^2 - 4 = (y + 2)(y - 2)$.

$$\therefore \quad \frac{3xy - 6x + y - 2}{y^2 - 4} = \frac{(y-2)(3x+1)}{(y+2)(y-2)}$$

$$= \frac{3x+1}{y+2}$$

(4) Simplify $\dfrac{4x^2 - 9}{4x^2 + 12x + 9}$.

Now $\quad 4x^2 - 9 = (2x+3)(2x-3)$,

and $\quad 4x^2 + 12x + 9 = (2x+3)^2$.

$$\therefore \frac{4x^2 - 9}{4x^2 + 12x + 9} = \frac{(2x+3)(2x-3)}{(2x+3)^2} = \frac{2x-3}{2x+3}$$

†**Exercise 82** *Questions 1 and 2 type B,*
remainder C

Simplify the following:

1) $\dfrac{3x - 6}{5x - 10}$

2) $\dfrac{4m - 2}{3m^2 - 15} \times \dfrac{5m^2 - 25}{8m - 4}$

3) $\dfrac{2az + 6bz}{6az + 3bz} \times \dfrac{8a + 4b}{az + bz} \times \dfrac{2az + 4bz}{3a + 9b}$

4) $\dfrac{2m - 5}{3m + 2} \div \dfrac{4m^2 - 10m}{9m^2 + 6m}$

5) $\dfrac{3x + 3y}{2x^2 + 4xy} \div \dfrac{6x + 6y}{4x}$

6) $\left(\dfrac{3x + 6}{2x + 6} \times \dfrac{5x}{3x^2 + 6x} \right) \div \dfrac{2x + 8}{x^2 + 3x}$

7) $\dfrac{a^2 - b^2}{a + b}$

8) $\dfrac{3a - 2b}{9a^2 - 12ab + 4b^2}$

9) $\dfrac{3x + 2}{12x^2 + 23x + 10}$

10) $\dfrac{4x + 7}{8x^2 + 2x - 21}$

11) $\dfrac{2x - 1}{2x^2 + 5x - 3}$

12) $\dfrac{a^2 - b^2 + 2a + 2b}{a - b + 2}$

13) $\dfrac{2a^3 - 18ax^2}{2a + 6x}$

14) $\dfrac{(2x - y)^2 + 3a(2x - y)}{3a - y + 2x}$

ADDITION AND SUBTRACTION OF FRACTIONS

The method for algebraic fractions is the same as for arithmetical fractions, that is:

(1) Find the L.C.M. of the denominators.

(2) Express each fraction with the common denominators.

(3) Add or subtract the fractions.

EXAMPLE 3

(1) Simplify $\dfrac{a}{2} + \dfrac{b}{3} - \dfrac{c}{4}$.

The L.C.M. of 2, 3 and 4 is 12.

$$\frac{a}{2} + \frac{b}{3} - \frac{c}{4} = \frac{6a}{12} + \frac{4b}{12} - \frac{3c}{12}$$

$$= \frac{6a + 4b - 3c}{12}$$

(2) Simplify $\dfrac{2}{x} + \dfrac{3}{2x} + \dfrac{4}{3x}$.

The L.C.M. of x, $2x$ and $3x$ is $6x$.

$$\frac{2}{x} + \frac{3}{2x} + \frac{4}{3x} = \frac{12 + 9 + 8}{6x} = \frac{29}{6x}$$

The sign in front of a fraction applies to the fraction as a whole. The line which separates the numerator and denominator acts as a bracket.

EXAMPLE 4

Simplify $\dfrac{m}{12} + \dfrac{2m + n}{4} - \dfrac{m - 2n}{3}$.

The L.C.M. of 12, 4 and 3 is 12.

$$\therefore \quad \frac{m}{12} + \frac{2m + n}{4} - \frac{m - 2n}{3}$$

$$= \frac{m + 3(2m + n) - 4(m - 2n)}{12}$$

$$= \frac{m + 6m + 3n - 4m + 8n}{12}$$

$$= \frac{3m + 11n}{12}$$

Exercise 83 – *All type B*

Simplify the following:

1) $\dfrac{x}{3} + \dfrac{x}{4} + \dfrac{x}{5}$ 3) $\dfrac{2}{q} - \dfrac{3}{2q}$

2) $\dfrac{5a}{12} - \dfrac{7a}{18}$ 4) $\dfrac{3}{y} - \dfrac{5}{3y} + \dfrac{4}{5y}$

5) $\dfrac{3}{5p} - \dfrac{2}{3q}$

10) $\dfrac{3a + 5b}{4} - \dfrac{a - 3b}{2}$

6) $\dfrac{3x}{2y} - \dfrac{5y}{6x}$

11) $\dfrac{3m - 5n}{6} - \dfrac{3m - 7n}{2}$

7) $3x - \dfrac{4y}{5z}$

12) $\dfrac{x - 2}{4} + \dfrac{2}{5}$

8) $1 - \dfrac{2x}{5} + \dfrac{x}{8}$

13) $\dfrac{x - 5}{3} - \dfrac{x - 2}{4}$

9) $3m - \dfrac{2m + n}{7}$

14) $\dfrac{3x - 5}{10} + \dfrac{2x - 3}{15}$

†LOWEST COMMON MULTIPLE (L.C.M.) OF ALGEBRAIC TERMS

In arithmetic the L.C.M. of two or more given numbers is the smallest number into which the given numbers will divide.

EXAMPLE 5

Find the L.C.M. of 12, 40 and 45.

$$12 = 2^2 \times 3; \quad 40 = 2^3 \times 5; \quad 45 = 3^2 \times 5$$

$$\text{L.C.M.} = 2^3 \times 3^2 \times 5 = 360$$

(Note that in finding the L.C.M. we have selected the highest power of each of the prime factors which occur in any of the given *numbers*.)

To find the L.C.M. of a set of algebraic expressions we select the highest power of each factor which occurs in any of the *expressions*.

EXAMPLE 6

(1) Find the L.C.M. of $a^3 b^2$, abc^3, $ab^3 c$.

The highest powers of a, b and c which occur in any of the given expressions are a^3, b^3 and c^3.

$$\therefore \qquad \text{L.C.M.} = a^3 b^3 c^3$$

(2) Find the L.C.M. of $5a^4 b^4$, $10a^2 b^3$, $6a^4 b$.

The L.C.M. of the numerical coefficients 5, 10 and 6 is 30. The highest powers of a and b which occur are a^4 and b^4. Hence:

$$\text{L.C.M.} = 30a^4 b^4$$

(3) Find the L.C.M. of $(x + 4)^2$, $(x + 4)(x + 1)$.

Since the contents of a bracket may be regarded as a single symbol,

$$\text{L.C.M.} = (x + 4)^2 (x + 1)$$

(4) Find the L.C.M. of $(a + b)$, $(a^2 - b^2)$.

We note that $a^2 - b^2$ factorises to give $(a + b)(a - b)$.

$$\therefore \qquad \text{L.C.M.} = (a + b)(a - b)$$

If the denominators factorise then this must be done before attempting to find the L.C.M. of the denominators.

†EXAMPLE 7

(1) Express as a single fraction in its lowest terms:

$$\frac{1}{x - 1} + \frac{2x}{1 - x^2}$$

Now $1 - x^2 = (1 + x)(1 - x)$.

We can rewrite $\dfrac{1}{x - 1}$ as

$$\frac{(-1) \times 1}{(-1) \times (x - 1)} = -\frac{1}{1 - x}$$

$$\therefore \quad \frac{1}{x - 1} + \frac{2x}{1 - x^2} = -\frac{1}{1 - x} + \frac{2x}{(1 + x)(1 - x)}$$

The L.C.M. of $(1 - x)$ and $(1 + x)(1 - x)$ is $(1 + x)(1 - x)$.

$$\therefore \quad \frac{-1}{1 - x} + \frac{2x}{(1 + x)(1 - x)} = \frac{-1(1 + x) + 2x}{(1 + x)(1 - x)}$$

$$= \frac{-1 - x + 2x}{(1 + x)(1 - x)}$$

$$= \frac{x - 1}{(1 + x)(1 - x)}$$

$$= -\frac{1}{1 + x}$$

(2) Simplify $\dfrac{2x}{x^2 + x - 6} + \dfrac{1}{x - 2}$.

$$\frac{2x}{x^2 + x - 6} + \frac{1}{x - 2} = \frac{2x}{(x + 3)(x - 2)} + \frac{1}{x - 2}$$

$$= \frac{2x + (x + 3)}{(x + 3)(x - 2)}$$

$$= \frac{3x + 3}{(x + 3)(x - 2)}$$

$$= \frac{3(x + 1)}{(x + 3)(x - 2)}$$

†Exercise 84 – *Questions 1–4 type A, 5 and 6 type B, remainder C*

Find the L.C.M. of the following:

1)   4, 12x

2) $3x, 6y$

3) $2ab, 4a, 6b$

4) ab, bc, ac

5) $3m^2pq, 9mp^2q, 12mpq, 3mn^2$

6) $5a^2b^3, 10ab^4, 2a^2b^3$

7) $(m-n)^2, (m-n)$

8) $(x+3)^2, (x+3), (x+1)$

9) $(x-1), (x^2-1)$

10) $(9a^2-b^2), (3a+b), (3a-b)$

Simplify the following:

11) $\dfrac{4}{x-5} - \dfrac{15}{x(x-5)} - \dfrac{3}{x}$

12) $\dfrac{3}{2x-1} - \dfrac{2x}{4x^2-1}$

13) $\dfrac{5x}{x^2-x-6} - \dfrac{2}{x+2}$

14) $\dfrac{7}{x^2+3x-10} - \dfrac{2}{x^2+5x} - \dfrac{2}{x^2-2x}$

15) $\dfrac{x+2}{x+3} - \dfrac{x-2}{x-3}$

16) $\dfrac{3x}{x^2-y^2} - \dfrac{x+3}{(x+y)^2}$

SELF-TEST 15

In the questions below state the letter (or letters) corresponding to the correct answer (or answers).

1) $\dfrac{a^2-a}{a-1}$ is equal to:

a a **b** a^2-1 **c** a^2 **d** $1-a^2$

2) $\dfrac{2x-6}{4x^2-8x} \times \dfrac{3x^2-6x}{4x-16}$ is equal to:

a $\dfrac{3x-9}{8x-32}$ **b** $\dfrac{1}{4}$ **c** $\dfrac{3(x-3)}{8(x-4)}$ **d** 0

3) $\dfrac{9x^2-25}{9x^2-9x-10}$ is equal to:

a $\dfrac{1-5x}{1-9x}$ **b** $\dfrac{3x+5}{3x+2}$ **c** $\dfrac{5}{2}$ **d** 2

4) $\left(\dfrac{6y+12}{4y+12} \times \dfrac{5y}{3y^2+6y}\right) \div \dfrac{4y+16}{2y^2+6y}$ is equal to:

a $\dfrac{5y}{4y+16}$ **b** $\dfrac{1}{4}$ **c** $\dfrac{75}{(3y+2)(2y+3)}$

d $\dfrac{5y}{4(y+4)}$

5) The L.C.M. of a^4b^3, ab^2c^4 and ab^3c^3 is:

a abc **b** ab^2 **c** $a^4b^3c^4$ **d** $a^6b^8c^7$

6) The L.C.M. of $(x+3)^2, (x+2)(x+3)$ and $(x+2)^2$ is:

a $(x+3)^3(x+2)^3$ **b** $(x+3)^2(x+2)^2$ **c** $(x+2)(x+3)$ **d** $x+5$

7) The L.C.M. of $a^2+2ab+b^2$ and a^2-b^2 is:

a $2a^2b^2$ **b** $(a^2-b^2)(a^2+2ab+b^2)$ **c** $2a^3b^3$ **d** $(a-b)(a+b)^2$

8) $\dfrac{6m-2n}{2}$ is equal to:

a $\dfrac{3m-2n}{2}$ **b** $6m-n$ **c** $3m-2n$

d $3m-n$

9) $t - \dfrac{3-t}{2} + \dfrac{3+t}{2}$ is equal to:

a t **b** $2t$ **c** $3+2t$ **d** $4t$

10) $\dfrac{x}{x^2-1} - \dfrac{2x}{x-1}$ is equal to:

a $\dfrac{1-2x}{x-1}$ **b** $\dfrac{x(3-2x)}{x^2-1}$

c $\dfrac{x(2x+1)}{1-x^2}$ **d** $\dfrac{1}{x-1}+2$

11) $\dfrac{3x-7}{3} - \dfrac{2x-5}{2}$ is equal to:

a -12 **b** -2 **c** $\dfrac{1}{6}$ **d** $-\dfrac{29}{6}$

12) $\dfrac{5x-10}{5} - \dfrac{3x-6}{3}$ is equal to:

a 0 **b** -4 **c** $2x-4$ **d** $2x$

CHAPTER 15 SUMMARY

Points to remember

(i) Factorize before multiplying or dividing polynomial expressions.

(ii) To find the L.C.M. of two or more algebraic expressions:
  (a) Factor each expression completely.
  (b) Take each factor the greatest number of times it occurs in any one expression.
  (c) Find the product of all these different factors.
  This product is the L.C.M. of the given expressions.

(iii) To add or subtract polynomial expressions with different denominators, rewrite each as an equivalent expression in which the denominator is the L.C.M. of the denominators. Add or subtract the resulting numerators and place the result over the L.C.M. previously obtained.

(iv) To reduce a fraction to its lowest terms
  (a) Express both numerator and denominator as products of their factors.
  (b) Cancel all the factors common to both the numerator and denominator. The result is the fraction in its lowest terms.

Chapter 16 **Equations and Inequations**

INTRODUCTION

Fig. 16.1 shows a pair of scales which are in balance. That is each scale pan contains exactly the same number of kilograms. Therefore

$$x + 2 = 7$$

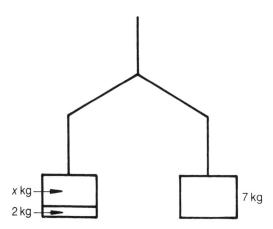

Fig. 16.1

This is an example of an equation. To solve the equation we have to find a value for x such that the scales remain in balance. Now the only way to keep the scales in balance is to add or subtract the same amount from each pan. If we take 2 kg from the left hand pan then we are left with x kg in this pan, but we must also take 2 kg from the right hand pan to maintain balance. That is,

$$x + 2 - 2 = 7 - 2$$
$$x = 5$$

Therefore x kg is 5 kg.

We now take a second example as shown in Fig. 16.2. In the left hand pan we have three packets exactly the same, whilst in the right hand pan there is 6 kg. How many kilograms are there in each packet?

If we let there be x kg in each packet then there are $3x$ kg in the three packets. Therefore we have the equation:

$$3x = 6$$

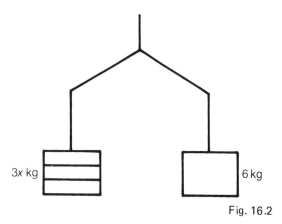

Fig. 16.2

We can maintain the balance of the scales if we multiply or divide the quantities in each scale by the same amount. In our equation if we divide each side by three we have

$$\frac{3x}{3} = \frac{6}{3}$$

Cancelling the threes on the left hand side we have

$$x = 2$$

and hence each packet contains 2 kg.

From these two examples we can say:

(1) An equation expresses balance between two sets of quantities.

(2) We can add or subtract the same amount from each side of the equation without destroying the balance.

(3) We can multiply or divide each side of the equation by the same amount without destroying the balance.

INEQUATIONS

The examples above showed scales which were in balance. If, on the other hand, the scales are not in balance, one side would contain a greater number of kilograms than the other. For example, if 3 kg were added to the scale pan on the right in Fig. 16.1, we would have the situation shown in Fig. 16.3.

In this case the number of kilograms in the scale pan on the left is less than the number of kilograms on the right. That is,

$$x + 2 \text{ is less than } 10$$

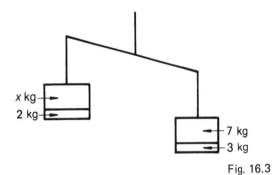

Fig. 16.3

This is an example of an inequation. The method of solving inequations is similar to that used for equations but the equality sign, $=$, is replaced by one of the following inequality signs:

$<$ meaning less than (e.g. $2 < 4$)

$>$ meaning greater than (e.g. $6 > 3$)

$\leqslant$ meaning less than or equal to

$\geqslant$ meaning greater than or equal to

Returning to our example we find that

$$x + 2 < 10$$

$\therefore$ $x < 8$

The following must be remembered when solving inequations.

$\qquad 4 > 2 \qquad$ (4 is greater than 2)

but

$\qquad -4 < -2 \qquad$ (-4 is less than -2)

$\qquad 6 < 15 \qquad$ (6 is less than 15)

but

$\qquad -6 > -15 \quad$ (-6 is greater than -15)

It follows from this pattern that

if $-x > -7$

then $x < 7$

If $-x > 5$

then $x < -5$

The general rule is:

If the signs on both sides of an inequation are changed, then the inequality sign must be reversed.

SIMPLE EQUATIONS AND INEQUATIONS

Simple equations and inequations contain only the first power of the unknown quantity. Thus

$$7t - 5 = 4t + 7$$

$$\frac{5x}{3} = \frac{2x + 5}{2}$$

are both examples of simple equations. After an equation is solved, the solution should be checked by substituting the result in each side of the equation separately. If each side of the equation then has the same value the solution is correct.

Examples of simple inequations are

$$7x - 3 < 5x + 11$$

$$\frac{4x}{3} > \frac{2x - 3}{2}$$

SOLVING SIMPLE EQUATIONS AND INEQUATIONS

Equations and inequations requiring multiplication and division.

EXAMPLE 1

(1) Solve the equation $\dfrac{x}{6} = 3$.

Multiplying each side by 6, we get

$$\frac{x}{6} \times 6 = 3 \times 6$$

$$x = 18$$

Check: When $x = 18$, L.H.S. $= \dfrac{18}{6} = 3$

$$\text{R.H.S.} = 3$$

Hence the solution is correct.

(2) Solve the inequation $5x > 10$.

Dividing each side by 5, we get

$$\frac{5x}{5} > \frac{10}{5}$$

$$x > 2$$

The solution may be written using set notation (see page 276). The solution set is $\{x : x > 2\}$.

We are saying that the inequation $5x > 10$ is true, not for a single value of x but for a set of different values. Unlike in an equation, it is not uncommon to have more than one value satisfying an inequation.

In the equation $5x > 10,$ there is no limit to the values of x which will satisfy the inequation.

Checking some of these values we have:

When $x = 3,$ L.H.S. $= 5 \times 3 = 15$
$$\text{R.H.S.} = 10$$

Since $15 > 10,$ $x = 3$ is a solution.

When $x = 4,$ L.H.S. $= 5 \times 4 = 20$
$$\text{R.H.S.} = 10$$

Since $20 > 10,$ $x = 4$ is a solution.

It is clear that any value of x greater than 2 will satisfy the inequation.

Equations and inequations requiring addition and subtraction.

EXAMPLE 2
(1) Solve $x - 4 = 8.$

If we add 4 to each side, we get:

$$x - 4 + 4 = 8 + 4$$
$$x = 12$$

The operation of adding 4 to each side is the same as transferring -4 to the R.H.S. but in so doing the sign is changed from a minus to a plus. Thus,

$$x - 4 = 8$$
$$x = 8 + 4$$
$$x = 12$$

Check: When $x = 12,$ L.H.S. $= 12 - 4 = 8$
$$\text{R.H.S.} = 8$$

Hence the solution is correct.

(2) Solve $x + 5 < 20.$

If we subtract 5 from each side, we get

$$x + 5 - 5 < 20 - 5$$
$$x < 15$$

Alternatively moving $+5$ to the R.H.S.

$$x < 20 - 5$$
$$x < 15$$

Check: When $x = 14,$ L.H.S. $= 14 + 5 = 19$
$$\text{R.H.S.} = 20$$

Since $19 < 20,$ $x = 14$ is a solution.

When $x = 13,$ L.H.S. $= 13 + 5 = 18$
$$\text{R.H.S.} = 20$$

Since $18 < 20,$ $x = 13$ is a solution.

It is clear that any value of x less than 15 is a solution.

Hence the solution set is $\{x : x < 15\}.$

Equations and inequations containing the unknown quantity on both sides

In equations and inequations of this kind group all the terms containing the unknown quantity on one side of the equation and the remaining terms on the other side.

EXAMPLE 3
(1) Solve $7x + 3 = 5x + 17.$

Transferring $5x$ to the L.H.S. and $+3$ to the R.H.S.

$$7x - 5x = 17 - 3$$
$$2x = 14$$
$$x = \frac{14}{2}$$
$$x = 7$$

Check: When $x = 7,$
$$\text{L.H.S.} = 7 \times 7 + 3 = 52$$
$$\text{R.H.S.} = 5 \times 7 + 17 = 52$$

Hence the solution is correct.

(2) Solve $3x - 2 \leqslant 5x + 6.$
$$3x - 5x \leqslant 6 + 2$$
$$-2x \leqslant 8$$
$$-x \leqslant 4$$
$$x \geqslant -4$$

Note the change in the inequality sign $\leqslant$ to $\geqslant$ as the signs on both sides of the inequation are changed.

Check: When $x = -4,$
$$\text{L.H.S.} = 3 \times (-4) - 2 = -14$$
$$\text{R.H.S.} = 5 \times (-4) + 6 = -14$$

Since $-14 = -14,$ L.H.S. $=$ R.H.S. and -4 satisfies the equation $3x - 2 = 5x + 6.$

When $x = -3,$
$$\text{L.H.S.} = 3 \times (-3) - 2 = -11$$

R.H.S. $= 5 \times (-3) + 6 = -9$

Since $-11 < -9$, L.H.S. $<$ R.H.S.

Hence $x = -3$ satisfies the inequation $3x - 2 < 5x + 6$.

Clearly $x \geqslant -4$ satisfies $3x - 2 \leqslant 5x + 6$.

Hence the solution set is $\{x : x \geqslant -4\}$.

Equations and inequations containing brackets

When an equation or an inequation contains brackets remove these first and then solve as shown previously.

EXAMPLE 4

(1) Solve $2(3x + 7) = 16$.

Remove the bracket,

$$6x + 14 = 16$$
$$6x = 16 - 14$$
$$6x = 2$$
$$x = \frac{2}{6}$$
$$x = \frac{1}{3}$$

Check: When $x = \frac{1}{3}$,

$$\text{L.H.S.} = 2 \times \left(3 \times \frac{1}{3} + 7\right) = 2 \times (1 + 7)$$
$$= 2 \times 8 = 16$$
$$\text{R.H.S.} = 16$$

Hence the solution is correct.

(2) Solve $3(x + 4) - 5(x - 1) \leqslant 19$.

Remove the brackets,

$$3x + 12 - 5x + 5 \leqslant 19$$
$$-2x + 17 \leqslant 19$$
$$-2x \leqslant 19 - 17$$
$$-2x \leqslant 2$$
$$-1x \leqslant 1$$
$$x \geqslant -1$$

Check: When $x = -1$,
$$\text{L.H.S.} = 3(-1 + 4) - 5(-1 - 1)$$
$$= 9 + 10 = 19$$
$$\text{R.H.S.} = 19$$

Since L.H.S. $=$ R.H.S., -1 satisfies $3(x + 4) - 5(x - 1) = 19$.

When $x = 0$, L.H.S. $= 3(0 + 4) - 5(0 - 1)$
$$= 17.$$

Since $17 < 19$, L.H.S. $<$ R.H.S. and $x = 0$ is a solution.

Clearly, $x \geqslant -1$ satisfies $3(x + 4) - 5(x - 1) \leqslant 19$.

Hence the solution set is $\{x : x \geqslant -1\}$.

Equations and inequations containing fractions

When an equation or inequation contains fractions, multiply each term of the equation by the L.C.M. of the denominators.

EXAMPLE 5

(1) Solve $\dfrac{x}{4} + \dfrac{3}{5} = \dfrac{3x}{2} - 2$.

The L.C.M. of the denominators 2, 4 and 5 is 20.

Multiplying each term by 20 gives,

$$\frac{x}{4} \times 20 + \frac{3}{5} \times 20 = \frac{3x}{2} \times 20 - 2 \times 20$$
$$5x + 12 = 30x - 40$$
$$5x - 30x = -40 - 12$$
$$-25x = -52$$
$$x = \frac{-52}{-25}$$
$$\therefore \qquad x = \frac{52}{25}$$

The solution may be verified by the check method shown in the previous examples.

(2) Solve the inequation

$$\frac{x - 4}{3} - \frac{2x - 1}{2} \geqslant 4.$$

In solving equations and inequations of this type remember that the line separating the numerator and denominator acts as a bracket. The L.C.M. of the denominators 3 and 2 is 6. Multiplying each term of the equation by 6,

$$\frac{x - 4}{3} \times 6 - \frac{2x - 1}{2} \times 6 \geqslant 4 \times 6$$
$$2(x - 4) - 3(2x - 1) \geqslant 24$$
$$2x - 8 - 6x + 3 \geqslant 24$$

$$-4x - 5 \geqslant 24$$
$$-4x \geqslant 24 + 5$$
$$-4x \geqslant 29$$
$$-x \geqslant \frac{29}{4}$$
$$x \leqslant -\frac{29}{4}.$$

The solution set is $\{x : x \leqslant -\frac{29}{4}\}$.

Exercise 85 – *Questions 1–19 type A, remainder B*

Solve the equations and inequations:

1) $x + 2 = 7$

2) $t - 4 < 3$

3) $2q = 4$

4) $x - 8 > 12$

5) $q + 5 = 2$

6) $3x = 9$

7) $\frac{y}{2} = 3$

8) $\frac{m}{3} < 4$

9) $2x + 5 = 9$

10) $5x - 3 > 12$

11) $6p - 7 = 17$

12) $3x + 4 > -2$

13) $7x + 12 = 5$

14) $6x - 3x + 2x = 20$

15) $14 - 3x = 8$

16) $5x - 10 = 3x + 2$

17) $6m + 11 = 25 - m$

18) $3x - 22 < 8x + 18$

19) $0.3d = 1.8$

20) $1.2x - 0.8 = 0.8x + 1.2$

21) $2(x + 1) = 8$

22) $5(m - 2) \geqslant 15$

23) $3(x - 1) - 4(2x + 3) \leqslant 14$

24) $5(x + 2) - 3(x - 5) = 29$

25) $3x \leqslant 5(9 - x)$

26) $4(x - 5) = 7 - 5(3 - 2x)$

27) $\frac{x}{5} - \frac{x}{3} = 2$

28) $\frac{x}{3} + \frac{x}{4} + \frac{x}{5} = \frac{5}{6}$

29) $\frac{m}{2} + \frac{m}{3} + 3 \geqslant 2 + \frac{m}{6}$

30) $3x + \frac{3}{4} = 2 + \frac{2x}{3}$

31) $\frac{3}{m} = 3$

32) $\frac{5}{x} = 2$

33) $\frac{4}{t} < \frac{2}{3}$

34) $\frac{7}{x} = \frac{5}{3}$

35) $\frac{4}{7}y - \frac{3}{5}y \geqslant 2$

36) $\frac{1}{3x} + \frac{1}{4x} = \frac{7}{20}$

37) $\frac{x+3}{4} - \frac{x-3}{5} = 2$

38) $\frac{2x}{15} - \frac{x-6}{12} - \frac{3x}{20} = \frac{3}{2}$

39) $\frac{2m-3}{4} = \frac{4-5m}{3}$

40) $\frac{3-y}{4} = \frac{y}{3}$

MAKING EXPRESSIONS

It is important to be able to translate information into symbols thus making up algebraic expressions. The following examples will illustrate how this is done.

EXAMPLE 6

(1) Find an expression which will give the total mass of a box containing x articles if the box has a mass of 7 kg and each article has a mass of 1.5 kg.

The total mass of x articles is $1.5x$ kg

$\therefore$ Total mass of the box of articles is $(1.5x + 7)$ kg

(2) If x bananas can be bought for 6 cents write down the cost of y bananas.

If x bananas cost 6 cents then 1 banana costs $\frac{6}{x}$ cents.

Hence y bananas cost $\frac{6}{x} \times y = \frac{6y}{x}$ cents.

Exercise 86 – *Questions 1 and 2 type A, remainder B*

1) A boy is x years old now. How old was he 5 years ago?

2) Find the total cost of 3 pencils at a cents each and 8 pens at b cents each.

3) A man works x hours per weekday except Saturday when he works y hours. If he works z hours on sunday how many hours does he work per week?

4) What is the perimeter of a rectangle l mm long and b mm wide?

5) A man A has $\$a$ and a man B has $\$b$. If A gives B $\$x$ how much will each have?

6) How many minutes are there between x minutes to 10 o'clock and 12 o'clock?

7) Find in dollars the total cost of a gramophone costing $\$Y$ and n records costing X cents each.

8) m articles are bought for x cents. Find the cost in dollars of buying n articles at the same rate.

9) In one innings a batsman hit a sixes, b fours and c singles. How many runs did he score?

10) A factory employs M men, N boys and P women. If a man earns $\$x$ per week, a boy $\$y$ per week and a women $\$z$ per week, what is the total wage bill per week?

CONSTRUCTION OF SIMPLE EQUATIONS

It often happens that we are confronted with mathematical problems that are difficult or impossible to solve by arithmetical methods. We then represent the quantity that has to be found by a symbol. Then by constructing an equation which conforms to the data of the problem we can solve it to give us the value of the unknown quantity. Both sides of the equation must be in the same units.

EXAMPLE 7

(1) The perimeter of a rectangle is 56 cm. If one of the two adjacent sides is 4 cm longer than the other, find the dimensions of the rectangle.

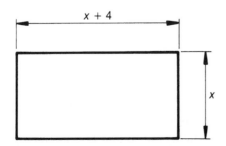

Fig. 16.4

As shown in Fig. 16.4:

Let $\qquad x$ cm $=$ length of the shorter side

Then $\quad (x+4)$ cm $=$ length of the longer side

$$\text{Total perimeter} = x + (x+4) + x + (x+4)$$
$$= (4x+8)\,\text{cm}$$

But the total perimeter $= 56$ cm.

$\therefore \qquad\qquad 4x + 8 = 56$

$\qquad\qquad\qquad 4x = 48$

$\qquad\qquad\qquad x = 12$

Hence the shorter side is 12 cm long and the longer side is $12 + 4 = 16$ cm long.

(2) 20 articles are to be bought. Some cost $\$2$ each whilst the others cost $\$3$ each. If less than $\$52$ must be spent, what is the least number of $\$2$ articles that can be bought?

Let x be the number of articles bought at $\$2$.

Then $(20 - x)$ articles are bought at $\$3$ each.

$$\text{Total amount spent} = \$[2x + 3(20 - x)]$$
$$= \$(60 - x)$$

But the total amount spent is less than $\$52$

$\therefore \qquad\qquad 60 - x < 52$

$\qquad\qquad\qquad -x < -8$

$\qquad\qquad\qquad x > 8$

Hence the least number of $\$2$ articles that can be bought is 9.

Exercise 87 – *All type B*

1) I think of a number. If I subtract 8 from it and multiply this difference by 3 the result is 21. What is the number I thought of?

2) 15 articles are bought. Some cost 5 c each and the remainder cost 8 c each. If the total amount spent is 90c, how many of each are bought?

3) A room is 3 m longer than its width. If its perimeter must not exceed 126 m, what is the greatest width the room may have?

4) 18 books are to be bought for a library. Some cost $\$2$ each and the remainder cost $\$2.50$ each. What is the greatest number of books which can be bought at $\$2.50$ each if the total cost must be less than $\$40$?

5) Find the number, which when added to the numerator and denominator of the fraction $\frac{3}{5}$ gives a new fraction which is equal to $\frac{4}{5}$.

6) Find three consecutive whole numbers whose sum is 48.

7) \$380 is divided between A and B. If A receives \$144 more than B, how much does each receive?

8) The sum of two whole numbers is 9. If 5 times the first number minus 4 times the second number is less than 9, what is the least value of the second number?

9) The sides of a triangle are x cm, $(x-4)$ cm and $(x+2)$ cm long respectively. If its perimeter is 46 cm, find the length of each side.

10) The three angles of a triangle are $(x-20)°$, $50°$ and $(2x+30)°$. Find the magnitude of each angle, given that the sum of the angles of a triangle is $180°$.

SELF-TEST 16

In Questions 1 to 25 the answer is either 'true' or 'false'.

1) If $\frac{x}{7}=3$ then $x=21$.

2) If $\frac{x}{5}=10$ then $x=2$.

3) If $\frac{x}{4}<16$ then $x<64$.

4) If $5x>20$ then $x>4$.

5) If $3x=6$ then $x=18$.

6) If $x-5=10$ then $x=5$.

7) If $x+8\geqslant16$ then $x\leqslant2$.

8) If $x+7=14$ then $x=21$.

9) If $x+3\geqslant6$ then $x\geqslant3$.

10) If $x-7=14$ then $x=21$.

11) If $3x+5>2x+10$ then $x>5$.

12) If $2x+4=x+8$ then $x=4$.

13) If $5x-2=3x-8$ then $x=-6$.

14) If $3x-8=2-2x$ then $x=10$.

15) If $2(3x+5)=18$ then $x=1$.

16) If $2(x+4)-5(x-7)<7$ then $x>12$.

17) If $6y=10(8-y)$ then $y=15$.

18) If $\frac{5}{y}=10$ then $y=2$.

19) If $\frac{8}{y}=4$ then $y=2$.

20) If $\frac{x}{3}+\frac{x}{4}>\frac{2x}{5}-11$ then $x>60$.

21) If $\frac{x}{2}-1=\frac{x}{3}-\frac{1}{2}$ then $x=3$.

22) If $\frac{3}{x+5}=\frac{4}{x-2}$ then $x=26$.

23) If $\frac{3}{x-6}=\frac{2}{x-4}$ then $x=-2$.

24) If $\frac{x-4}{2}-\frac{x-3}{3}=4$ then $x=10$.

25) If $\frac{2x-3}{2}-\frac{x-6}{5}=3$ then $x=3$.

In Questions 26 to 38 state the letter (or letters) corresponding to the correct answer (or answers).

26) If $3(2x-5)-2(x-3)=3$ then x is equal to:

a $\frac{5}{4}$ **b** $\frac{11}{4}$ **c** 3   **d** 6

27) If $2(x+6)-3(x-4)=1$ then x is equal to:

a -7 **b** 17   **c** 23   **d** 25

28) If $\frac{x-5}{3}=\frac{x+2}{2}$ then x is equal to:

a -16 **b** -7 **c** 7   **d** 16

29) If $3(x-2)-5(x-7)=12$ then x is equal to:

a $-8\frac{1}{2}$ **b** -7 **c** 0   **d** $8\frac{1}{2}$

30) If $\frac{3-2y}{4}=\frac{2y}{6}$ then y is equal to:

a -3 **b** $\frac{9}{10}$ **c** 1   **d** 3

31) The cost of electricity is obtained as follows: A fixed charge of \$$a$, rent of a meter \$$b$ and a charge of c cents for each unit of electricity supplied. The total cost of using n units of electricity is therefore:

a $\$(a+b+nc)$ **b** $\$(100(a+b)+nc)$

c $[100(a+b)+nc]$ cents

d $\$\left(\dfrac{a+b+nc}{100}\right)$

32) At a factory p men earn an average wage of $\$a$, q women earn an average wage of $\$b$ and r youths earn an average wage of $\$c$. The average wage for all these employees is

a $\$(a+b+c)$ **b** $\$\left(\dfrac{a}{p}+\dfrac{b}{q}+\dfrac{c}{r}\right)$

c $\$\dfrac{(ap+bq+cr)}{a+b+c}$ **d** $\$\left(\dfrac{ap+bq+cr}{p+q+r}\right)$

33) A dealer ordered N tools from a manufacturer. The manufacturer can produce p tools per day but $x\%$ of these are faulty and unfit for sale. The number of days it takes the manufacturer to complete the order is:

a $\dfrac{N}{p(100-x)}$ **b** $\dfrac{100N}{p(100-x)}$

b $\dfrac{N}{p(1-x)}$ **d** $\dfrac{p(100-x)}{N}$

34) A shopkeeper pays $\$c$ for $x\,$kg of bananas. He sells them for b cents per kg. His percentage profit is therefore:

a $\dfrac{bx-c}{c}$ **b** $\dfrac{bx-100c}{100c}$

c $\dfrac{100(bx-c)}{c}$ **d** $\dfrac{bx-100c}{c}$

35) A man walked for t hours at $v\,$km per hour and then cycled a distance of $x\,$km at $c\,$km per hour. His average speed for the whole journey was:

a $\dfrac{vt+x}{t+x}$ **b** $\dfrac{vt+x}{t}$ **c** $\dfrac{c(vt+x)}{c+x}$ **d** $\dfrac{vt+x}{t+\dfrac{x}{c}}$

36) The cost of hiring a bus is $\$60$. If nine of the seats are unoccupied the cost per person is $\$1$ more than each person would have to pay if all the seats were full. If n is the number of seats in the bus then:

a $\dfrac{60}{n}-\dfrac{60}{n-9}=1$ **b** $\dfrac{60}{n-9}-\dfrac{60}{n}=1$

c $\dfrac{60}{n}=n$ **d** $\dfrac{60}{n-9}=n$

37) At the beginning of term a student bought x books at a total cost of $\$22$. A few days later he bought three more books than the previous week, for a further expenditure of $\$4$. He found that this purchase had reduced the average cost per book by 20 cents. An equation from which x can be found is:

a $\dfrac{26}{x}=20$ **b** $\dfrac{26}{x+3}=0.20$

c $\dfrac{22}{x}-\dfrac{26}{x+3}=0.20$ **d** $\dfrac{26}{x+3}-\dfrac{22}{x}=0.20$

38) The smallest of three consecutive even numbers is m. Twice the square of the largest is greater than the sum of the squares of the other two numbers by 244. Hence:

a $2(m+2)^2 > (m+1)^2 + m^2 + 244$

b $2(m+2)^2 - (m+1)^2 + m^2 = 244$

c $2(m+4)^2 = (m+2)^2 + m^2 + 244$

d $2(m+4)^2 - (m+2)^2 + m^2 > 244$

CHAPTER 16 SUMMARY

Points to remember

(i)   To solve word problems:
  (a) Read the problem carefully and draw a diagram if necessary.
  (b) Represent the variable to be found by a letter.
  (c) Write the condition stated in the problem by an equation or inequation.
  (d) Solve the equation or inequation.
  (e) Check the solution by substituting the value you found for the variable in the equation you had written.

Chapter 17 **Formulae**

†**EVALUATING FORMULAE**

A formula is an equation which *describes the relationship* between two or more quantities. The statement that $E = IR$ is a formula for E in terms of I and R. The value of E may be found by simple arithmetic after substituting the given values of I and R.

EXAMPLE 1

If $E = IR$ find the value of E when $I = 6$ and $R = 4$.

Substituting the given values of I and R and remembering that multiplication signs are omitted in formulae, we have:

$$E = IR = 6 \times 4 = 24$$

EXAMPLE 2

The formula for the surface area of a sphere is $A = 4\pi r^2$ where $\pi = 3.142$ and r is the radius of the sphere. Find the surface area of a sphere whose radius is 8.

Substituting the given values

$$A = 4 \times 3.142 \times 8^2 = 804.4$$

Exercise 88 – *All type B*

1) If $v = u + at$ find v when $u = 5$, $a = 3$ and $t = 4$.

2) If $P = \dfrac{RT}{V}$ find P when $R = 48$, $T = 20$ and $V = 6$.

3) If $C = \pi D$ find C when $\pi = 3.142$ and $D = 6$.

4) If $I = \dfrac{PRT}{100}$ find I when $P = 700$, $R = 12$ and $T = 3$.

5) If $P = \dfrac{1}{n}$ find P when $n = 5$.

6) If $K = \dfrac{WV^2}{2g}$ find K when $W = 64$, $V = 20$ and $g = 32$.

7) If $A = \frac{1}{2}BH$ find A when $B = 6$ and $H = 7$.

8) If $S = 90(n - 4)$ find S when $n = 6$.

9) If $P = 3r^4$ find P when $r = 5$.

10) If $y = \dfrac{3t}{c}$ find y when $t = 12$ and $c = 6$.

†**FORMULAE AND EQUATIONS**

Suppose that we are given the formula $M = \dfrac{P}{Q}$ and that we have to find the value of Q given the values of M and P. We can do this by substituting the given values and solving the resulting equation for Q.

EXAMPLE 3

Find Q from the equation $M = \dfrac{P}{Q}$ if $M = 3$ and $P = 6$.

Substituting the given values we have:

$$3 = \frac{6}{Q}$$

$$3Q = 6 \quad \text{(multiplying each side by } Q\text{)}$$

$$Q = 2 \quad \text{(dividing each side by 3)}$$

EXAMPLE 4

Find T from the formula $D = \dfrac{T + 2}{P}$ when $D = 5$ and $P = 3$.

Substituting the given values we have

$$5 = \frac{T + 2}{3}$$

$$15 = T + 2 \quad \text{(multiplying each side by 3)}$$

$$13 = T \quad \text{(subtracting 2 from each side)}$$

Hence $T = 13$.

Exercise 89 – *All type B*

1) Find n from the formula $P = \dfrac{1}{n}$ when $P = 2$.

2) Find R from the formula $E = IR$ when $E = 20$ and $I = 4$.

3) Find B from the formula $A = BH$ when $A = 12$ and $H = 4$.

4) Find c from the formula $H = abc$ when $H = 40$, $a = 2$ and $b = 5$.

5) Find P from the formula $I = \dfrac{PRT}{100}$ when $I = 20$, $R = 5$ and $T = 4$.

6) Find D from the formula $C = \pi D$ when $\pi = 3.142$ and $C = 27$.

7) Find r from the formula $A = \pi r l$ when $\pi = 3.142$, $A = 96$ and $l = 12$.

8) Find W from the formula $K = Wa + b$ when $K = 30$, $b = 6$ and $a = 4$.

†TRANSPOSITION OF FORMULAE

Consider, again, the formula $M = \dfrac{P}{Q}$. M is called the *subject* of the formula. We may be given several corresponding values of M and Q and we want to find the corresponding values of P. We could, of course, find these by using the methods shown in Examples 3 and 4 but considerable time and effort would be spent in solving the resulting equations. Much of this time and effort would be saved if we could express the formula with P as the subject, because then we need only substitute the given values of M and Q in the rearranged formula.

The process of rearranging a formula so that one of the other symbols becomes the subject is called *transposing the formula*. The rules used in transposition are the same as those used in solving equations. The methods used are as follows:

Symbols connected as a product

EXAMPLE 5

(1) Transpose the formula $F = ma$ to make a the subject.

Divide both sides by m, then:

$$\frac{F}{m} = \frac{ma}{m}$$

$$\frac{F}{m} = a$$

or
$$a = \frac{F}{m}$$

(2) Make h the subject of the formula $V = \pi r^2 h$.

Divide both sides by πr^2, then:

$$\frac{V}{\pi r^2} = \frac{\pi r^2 h}{\pi r^2}$$

$$\frac{V}{\pi r^2} = h$$

or
$$h = \frac{V}{\pi r^2}$$

Symbols connected as a quotient

EXAMPLE 6

(1) Transpose $x = \dfrac{y}{b}$ for y.

Multiply both sides by b, then:

$$x \times b = \frac{y}{b} \times b$$

$$bx = y$$

or
$$y = bx$$

(2) Transpose $M^3 = \dfrac{3x^2 w}{p}$ for p.

Multiply both sides by p, then:

$$M^3 p = 3x^2 w$$

Divide both sides by M^3, then:

$$\frac{M^3 p}{M^3} = \frac{3x^2 w}{M^3}$$

$$p = \frac{3x^2 w}{M^3}$$

Symbols connected by a plus or minus sign

Remember that when a term is transferred from one side of a formula to the other its sign is changed.

EXAMPLE 7

(1) Transpose $\ x = 3y + 5\ $ for y.

Subtract 5 from both sides of the equation,

$$x - 5 \ = \ 3y$$

Divide both sides by 3,

$$\frac{x-5}{3} \ = \ y$$

or

$$y \ = \ \frac{x-5}{3}$$

(2) Transpose $\ w = H + Cr\ $ for r.

Subtract H from both sides, then:

$$w - H \ = \ Cr$$

Divide both sides by C,

$$\frac{w-H}{C} \ = \ r$$

or

$$r \ = \ \frac{w-H}{C}$$

Formulae containing brackets

EXAMPLE 8

(1) Transpose $\ y = a + \dfrac{x}{b}\ $ for x.

Subtract a from both sides, then:

$$y - a \ = \ \frac{x}{b}$$

Multiply both sides by b,

$$b(y-a) \ = \ x$$

or

$$x \ = \ b(y-a)$$

(2) Transpose $\ l = a + (n-1)d\ $ for n.

Subtract a from both sides, then:

$$l - a \ = \ (n-1)d$$

Divide both sides by d,

$$\frac{l-a}{d} \ = \ n - 1$$

Add 1 to each side,

$$\frac{l-a}{d} + 1 \ = \ n$$

or

$$n \ = \ \frac{l-a}{d} + 1$$

(3) Transpose $\ y = \dfrac{ab}{a-b}\ $ for a.

Multiply both sides by $\ a - b$,

$$y(a-b) \ = \ ab$$

Remove the brackets as a is on both sides,

$$ay - yb \ = \ ab$$

Group the terms containing a on the L.H.S. and other terms on the R.H.S.

$$ay - ab \ = \ yb$$

Factorise the L.H.S.

$$a(y-b) \ = \ yb$$

Divide both sides by $\ y - b$,

$$a \ = \ \frac{yb}{y-b}$$

(4) Transpose $\ Q = \dfrac{w(H-h)}{T-t}\ $ for t.

Multiply both sides by $\ (T-t)$,

$$Q(T-t) \ = \ w(H-h)$$

Divide both sides by Q,

$$T - t \ = \ \frac{w(H-h)}{Q}$$

Take t to the R.H.S. so that it becomes positive and take $\dfrac{w(H-h)}{Q}$ to the L.H.S.

$$T - \frac{w(H-h)}{Q} \ = \ t$$

or

$$t = T - \frac{w(H-h)}{Q}$$

Formulae containing roots

In tackling formulae containing square roots it must be remembered that when a term containing a root is squared, all that happens is that the root sign disappears. Thus,

$$(\sqrt{H})^2 \ = \ H$$

$$(\sqrt{gh})^2 \ = \ gh$$

EXAMPLE 9

(1) Transpose $\ d = \sqrt{2hr}\ $ for r.

Square both sides,

$$d^2 \ = \ (\sqrt{2hr})^2$$

$$d^2 \ = \ 2hr$$

Divide both sides by $2h$,

$$\frac{d^2}{2h} = r$$

or

$$r = \frac{d^2}{2h}$$

(2) Transpose $d = \sqrt{\dfrac{b(x-b)}{c}}$ for x.

Square both sides,

$$d^2 = \frac{b(x-b)}{c}$$

Multiply both sides by c,

$$cd^2 = b(x-b)$$

Divide both sides by b,

$$\frac{cd^2}{b} = x - b$$

Add b to both sides,

$$\frac{cd^2}{b} + b = x$$

or

$$x = \frac{cd^2}{b} + b$$

(3) Transpose $y = \dfrac{3t}{\sqrt{c}}$ for c.

Multiply both sides by $\sqrt{c}$,

$$y\sqrt{c} = 3t$$

Divide both sides by y,

$$\sqrt{c} = \frac{3t}{y}$$

Square both sides

$$c = \left(\frac{3t}{y}\right)^2$$

or

$$c = \frac{3t}{y} \times \frac{3t}{y} = \frac{9t^2}{y^2}$$

Exercise 90 – *Questions 1–12 and 15–18 type B, 13, 14, 19–28, 33, 34 type C, remainder D*

Transpose the following:

1) $C = \pi d$ for d
2) $S = \pi dn$ for d

3) $PV = c$ for V
4) $A = \pi rl$ for l
5) $v^2 = 2gh$ for h
6) $I = PRT$ for R
7) $x = \dfrac{a}{y}$ for y
8) $I = \dfrac{E}{R}$ for R
9) $x = \dfrac{u}{a}$ for u
10) $P = \dfrac{RT}{V}$ for T
11) $d = \dfrac{0.866}{N}$ for N
12) $S = \dfrac{ts}{T}$ for t
13) $H = \dfrac{PLAN}{33\,000}$ for L
14) $V = \dfrac{\pi d^2 h}{4}$ for h
15) $p = P - 14.7$ for P
16) $v = u + at$ for t
17) $n = p + cr$ for r
18) $y = ax + b$ for x
19) $y = \dfrac{x}{5} + 17$ for x
20) $H = S + qL$ for q
21) $a = b - cx$ for x
22) $D = B - 1.28d$ for d
23) $V = \dfrac{2R}{R-r}$ for r
24) $C = \dfrac{E}{R+r}$ for E
25) $S = \pi r(r + h)$ for h
26) $H = wS(T - t)$ for T
27) $C = \dfrac{N-n}{2p}$ for N
28) $T = \dfrac{12(D-d)}{L}$ for d
29) $V = \dfrac{2R}{R-r}$ for R

30) $P = \dfrac{S(C - F)}{C}$ for C

31) $V = \sqrt{2gh}$ for h

32) $w = k\sqrt{d}$ for d

33) $t = 2\pi\sqrt{\dfrac{l}{g}}$ for l

34) $t = 2\pi\sqrt{\dfrac{W}{gf}}$ for f

35) $P - mg = \dfrac{mv^2}{r}$ for m

36) $Z = \sqrt{\dfrac{x}{x + y}}$ for x

37) $k = \dfrac{3n + 2}{n + 1}$ for n

38) $a = \dfrac{3}{4t + 5}$ for t

39) $v^2 = 2k\left(\dfrac{1}{x} - \dfrac{1}{a}\right)$ for x

40) $d = \dfrac{2(S - an)}{n(n - l)}$ for a

41) $c = 2\sqrt{2hr - h^2}$ for r

42) $x = \dfrac{dh}{D - d}$ for d

43) $\dfrac{D}{d} = \sqrt{\dfrac{f + p}{f - p}}$ for f

SELF-TEST 17

In the following questions state the letter (or letters) corresponding to the correct answer (or answers).

1) The value of $\dfrac{ab - c^2}{a^2 - bc}$ when $a = 2$, $b = -2$ and $c = -3$ is:

a -6.5 b -2.5 c 2.5 d 6.5

2) The value of $x^2 + y^2 + z^2 - 3yz$ when $x = -2$, $y = 3$ and $z = -4$ is:

a -47 b -7 c 25 d 65

3) The value of $(2a - 5b)^2 + 8ab$ when $a = 3$ and $b = -2$ is:

a -32 b 16 c 208 d 304

4) The value of $\dfrac{x}{y^2} - \dfrac{y}{z^2} - \dfrac{z}{x^2}$ when $x = -2$, $y = 3$ and $z = -4$ is:

a $-\dfrac{203}{144}$ b $-\dfrac{148}{244}$ c $\dfrac{85}{144}$ d $\dfrac{139}{144}$

5) The value of $ab(b - 2c) - 3abc$ when $a = 3$, $b = -4$ and $c = 1$ is:

a -60 b -36 c 60 d 108

6) If $v = u - at$ then t is equal to:

a $\dfrac{v - u}{a}$ b $\dfrac{u - v}{a}$ c $\dfrac{-v}{au}$ d $\dfrac{u}{av}$

7) If $a = b + t\sqrt{x}$ then x is equal to:

a $\dfrac{(a - b)^2}{t}$ b $\dfrac{t}{(a - b)^2}$ c $\dfrac{t^2}{(a - b)^2}$

d $\dfrac{(a - b)^2}{t^2}$

8) If $x = 2y - \dfrac{w}{v}$ then v is equal to:

a $\dfrac{w}{2y - x}$ b $\dfrac{2y - x}{w}$ c $\dfrac{w}{x - 2y}$

d $\dfrac{-w}{2y - x}$

9) If $y = \dfrac{1 - t^2}{1 + t^2}$ then t is equal to:

a $\left(\dfrac{1 - y}{y + 1}\right)^2$ b $\sqrt{\dfrac{1 - y}{y + 1}}$ c $\sqrt{\dfrac{1 - y}{2}}$

d $\dfrac{(1 - y)^2}{4}$

10) If $F = \dfrac{W(v - u)}{gt}$ then u is equal to:

a $v - \dfrac{WF}{gt}$ b $\dfrac{Fgt}{W} - v$

c $v - \dfrac{Fgt}{W}$ d $Fgt - Wv$

11) If $y = \dfrac{1 - 3x}{1 + 5x}$ then x is equal to:

a $\dfrac{1 - y}{8}$ b $\dfrac{1 - y}{2}$ c $\dfrac{1 - y}{5y + 3}$ d $\dfrac{1 - y}{5y - 3}$

12) If $A = 2\pi R(R + H)$ then H is equal to:

a $A - 2\pi R^2$ b $\dfrac{A}{2\pi R} - R$

c $A - 2\pi R - R$ d $\dfrac{A + 2\pi R^2}{2\pi R}$

13) If $S = 90(2n - 4)$ then n is equal to:

a $\dfrac{S}{180} + 4$ **b** $\dfrac{S}{180} - 2$ **c** $\dfrac{S}{180} + 2$

d $\dfrac{S - 360}{180}$

14) If $k = \dfrac{3n + 2}{n + 1}$ then n is equal to:

a $\dfrac{2 - k}{k - 3}$ **b** $\dfrac{k + 2}{3 + k}$ **c** $\dfrac{1}{k - 3}$ **d** $\dfrac{1}{3 - k}$

15) If $T = 2\pi\sqrt{\dfrac{R - H}{g}}$ then R is equal to:

a $\dfrac{T^2}{2\pi} + \dfrac{H}{g}$ **b** $\dfrac{gT^2}{2\pi} + H$

c $\dfrac{gT^2 + 2\pi H}{2\pi}$ **d** $\dfrac{gT^2}{4\pi^2} + H$

16) If $K = \dfrac{Wv^2}{2g}$ then v is equal to:

a $\sqrt{\dfrac{K}{2g} - W}$ **b** $\sqrt{2Kg - W}$

c $\sqrt{\dfrac{2Kg}{W}}$ **d** $\sqrt{2KgW}$

17) If $H = wS(T - t)$ then t is equal to:

a $\dfrac{H}{wS} - T$ **b** $\dfrac{H - wST}{wS}$ **c** $\dfrac{T - H}{wS}$

d $\dfrac{wST - H}{wS}$

18) If $y = \dfrac{ab}{a - b}$ then b is equal to:

a $\dfrac{ya}{a + 1}$ **b** $\dfrac{ya}{a - 1}$ **c** $\dfrac{ya}{a + y}$ **d** $\dfrac{ya}{a - y}$

19) If $a = \sqrt{\dfrac{b}{b + c}}$ then b is equal to:

a $\dfrac{a^2 c}{1 + a^2}$ **b** $\dfrac{a^2 c}{1 - a^2}$ **c** $\dfrac{c}{1 + a^2}$ **d** $\dfrac{c}{1 - a^2}$

20) If $x = \sqrt{\dfrac{a^2 - b^2}{ay}}$ then b is equal to:

a $a - x^2 ay$ **b** $\sqrt{x^2 ay - a^2}$

c $\sqrt{a^2 + x^2 ay}$ **d** $\sqrt{a(a - x^2 y)}$

CHAPTER 17 SUMMARY

Points to remember

The rules for transposing in a formula are the same as those used in solving equations.

(i) The same quantity may be added or subtracted from both sides of the formula. This is commonly referred to as "moving a quantity from one side to the other and changing the sign".

(ii) Both sides of the equation may be multiplied or divided by the same quantity (except 0).

(iii) Both sides of the equation may be raised to the same power or the same root may be taken of both sides
e.g. $\sqrt{A} = B \Rightarrow A = B^2$.

The Golden Rule is, "Perform exactly the same operation on both sides of an equation".

Chapter 18 **Simultaneous Equations**

Consider the two equations:

$$2x + 3y = 13 \qquad [1]$$

$$3x + 2y = 12 \qquad [2]$$

Each equation contains the unknown quantities x and y. The solutions of the equations are the values of x and y which satisfy both equations. Equations such as these are called *simultaneous equations*.

ELIMINATION METHOD IN SOLVING SIMULTANEOUS EQUATIONS

The method will be shown by considering the following examples.

EXAMPLE 1

(1) Solve the equations

$$3x + 4y = 11 \qquad [1]$$

$$x + 7y = 15 \qquad [2]$$

If we multiply equation [2] by 3 we shall have the same coefficient of x in both equations:

$$3x + 21y = 45 \qquad [3]$$

We can now eliminate x by subtracting equation [1] from equation [3]

$$3x + 21y = 45 \qquad [3]$$

$$3x + 4y = 11 \qquad [1]$$

$$17y = 34$$

$$y = 2$$

To find x we substitute for $y = 2$ in either of the original equations. Thus, substituting for $y = 2$ in equation [1].

$$3x + 4 \times 2 = 11$$

$$3x + 8 = 11$$

$$3x = 11 - 8$$

$$3x = 3$$

$$x = 1$$

Hence the solutions are

$$x = 1 \quad \text{and} \quad y = 2$$

To check these values substitute them in equation [2]. There is no point in substituting them in equation [1] because this was used in finding the value of x. Thus,

$$\text{L.H.S.} = 1 + 7 \times 2 = 15 = \text{R.H.S.}$$

Hence the solutions are correct since the L.H.S. and R.H.S. are equal.

(2) Solve the equations

$$5x + 3y = 29 \qquad [1]$$

$$4x + 7y = 37 \qquad [2]$$

The same coefficient of x can be obtained in both equations if equation [1] is multiplied by 4 (the coefficient of x in equation [2]) and equation [2] is multiplied by 5 (the coefficient of x in equation [1]).

Multiplying equation [1] by 4 we have

$$20x + 12y = 116 \qquad [3]$$

Multiplying equation [2] by 5 we have

$$20x + 35y = 185 \qquad [4]$$

Subtracting equation [3] from equation [4] we have

$$23y = 69$$

$$y = 3$$

Substituting for $y = 3$ in equation [1] we have

$$5x + 3 \times 3 = 29$$

$$5x + 9 = 29$$

$$5x = 20$$

$$x = 4$$

Hence the solutions are:

$$y = 3 \quad \text{and} \quad x = 4$$

Check in equation [2],

$$\text{L.H.S.} = 4 \times 4 + 7 \times 3$$

$$= 16 + 21 = 37 = \text{R.H.S.}$$

(3) Solve the equations:

$$7x + 4y = 41 \qquad [1]$$

$$4x - 2y = 2 \qquad [2]$$

In these equations it is easier to eliminate y because the same coefficient of y can be obtained in both equations by multiplying equation [2] by 2.

Multiplying equation [2] by 2, we have

$$8x - 4y = 4 \qquad [3]$$

Adding equations [1] and [3], we have

$$15x = 45$$

$$x = 3$$

Substituting for $x = 3$ in equation [1], we have

$$7 \times 3 + 4y = 41$$

$$21 + 4y = 41$$

$$4y = 20$$

$$y = 5$$

Hence the solutions are:

$$x = 3 \quad \text{and} \quad y = 5$$

Check in equation [2],

$$\text{L.H.S.} = 4 \times 3 - 2 \times 5$$

$$= 12 - 10 = 2 = \text{R.H.S.}$$

(4) Solve the equations

$$\frac{2x}{3} - \frac{y}{4} = \frac{7}{12} \qquad [1]$$

$$\frac{3x}{4} - \frac{2y}{5} = \frac{3}{10} \qquad [2]$$

It is best to clear each equation of fractions before attempting to solve.

In equation [1] the L.C.M. of the denominators is 12. Hence by multiplying equation [1] by 12, we have

$$8x - 3y = 7 \qquad [3]$$

In equation [2] the L.C.M. of the denominators is 20. Hence by multiplying equation [2] by 20, we have

$$15x - 8y = 6 \qquad [4]$$

We now proceed in the usual way. Multiplying equation [3] by 8, we have

$$64x - 24y = 56 \qquad [5]$$

Multiplying equation [4] by 3, we have

$$45x - 24y = 18 \qquad [6]$$

Subtracting equation [6] from equation [5], we have

$$19x = 38$$

$$x = 2$$

Substituting for $x = 2$ in equation [3], we have

$$16 - 3y = 7$$

$$-3y = -9$$

$$y = 3$$

Since equation [3] came from equation [1] we must do the check in equation [2].

$$\text{L.H.S.} = \frac{3 \times 2}{4} - \frac{2 \times 3}{5} = \frac{6}{4} - \frac{6}{5}$$

$$= \frac{30 - 24}{20} = \frac{6}{20} = \frac{3}{10} = \text{R.H.S.}$$

Exercise 91 – *Questions 1–5 type B, remainder C*

Solve the following equations for x and y and check the solutions:

1) $3x + 2y = 7$
   $x + y = 3$

2) $4x - 3y = 1$
   $x + 3y = 19$

3) $x + 3y = 7$
   $2x - 2y = 6$

4) $7x - 4y = 37$
   $6x + 3y = 51$

5) $4x - 6y = -2.5$
   $7x - 5y = -0.25$

6) $\dfrac{x}{2} + \dfrac{y}{3} = \dfrac{13}{6}$

$\dfrac{2x}{7} - \dfrac{y}{4} = \dfrac{5}{14}$

7) $\dfrac{x}{8} - y = -\dfrac{5}{2}$

$3x + \dfrac{y}{3} = 13$

8) $\dfrac{x-2}{3} + \dfrac{y-1}{4} = \dfrac{13}{12}$

$\dfrac{2-x}{2} + \dfrac{3+y}{3} = \dfrac{11}{6}$

9) $\dfrac{x}{3} - \dfrac{y}{2} + 1 = 0$

$6x + y + 8 = 0$

10) $3x - 4y = 5$

$2x - 5y = 8$

11) $x - y = 3$

$\dfrac{x}{5} - \dfrac{y}{7} = \dfrac{27}{35}$

12) $3x + 4y = 0$

$2x - 2y = 7$

PROBLEMS INVOLVING SIMULTANEOUS EQUATIONS

In problems which involve two unknowns it is first necessary to form two separate equations from the data. The equations may then be solved as shown previously.

EXAMPLE 2

(1) A bill for $74 was paid with $5 and $1 notes, a total of 50 notes being used. Find how many $5 notes were used.

Let x be the number of $5 notes and y be the number of $1 notes. Then

$$x + y = 50 \qquad [1]$$

The total value of x $5 notes is $5x$ and the value of y $1 notes is y. Hence the total value of x $5 notes and y $1 notes is $(5x + y)$ and this must equal $74. Hence

$$5x + y = 74 \qquad [2]$$

Subtracting equation [1] from equation [2],

$$4x = 24$$
$$x = 6$$

Therefore six $5 notes were used.

(2) Find two numbers such that their sum is 108 and their difference is 54.

Let x and y be the two numbers.

Then their sum is $x + y$ and their difference is $x - y$. Hence,

$$x + y = 108 \qquad [1]$$
$$x - y = 54 \qquad [2]$$

adding equations [1] and [2],

$$2x = 162$$
$$x = 81$$

Substituting for x in [1],

$$81 + y = 108$$
$$y = 108 - 81$$
$$y = 27$$

(3) A foreman and 7 men together earn $1560 per week whilst 2 foremen and 17 men together earn $3660 per week. Find the weekly wages of a foreman.

Let a foreman earn x per week and a man earn y per week.

$$\therefore \qquad x + 7y = 1560 \qquad [1]$$
$$2x + 17y = 3660 \qquad [2]$$

Multiplying equation [1] by 2, we have

$$2x + 14y = 3120 \qquad [3]$$

Subtracting equation [3] from equation [2] we have

$$3y = 540$$
$$y = 180$$

Substituting for $y = 180$ in equation [1], we have

$$x + 7 \times 180 = 1560$$
$$x + 1260 = 1560$$
$$x = 300$$

Hence a foreman earns $300 per week.

Exercise 92 – *Questions 1 and 2 type B,*
3–8 type C, remainder D

1) Find two numbers such that their sum is 27 and their difference is 3.

2) A bill for $123 was paid with $5 and $1 notes, a total of 59 notes being used. Find how many $5 notes were used.

3) $x is invested at 6% and $y is invested at 8%. The annual income from these investments is $23.20. If $x had been invested at 8% and $y at 6% the annual income would have been $21.60. Find x and y.

4) An alloy containing 8 cm³ of copper and 7 cm³ of tin has a mass of 121 g. A second alloy contains 9 cm³ of copper and 11 cm³ of tin and has a mass of 158 g. Find the densities of copper and tin in g/cm³.

5) A motorist travels x km at 40 km/h and y km at 50 km/h. The total time taken is $2\frac{1}{2}$ hours. If the time taken to travel $6x$ km at 30 km/h and $4y$ km at 50 km/h is 14 hours find x and y.

6) 500 tickets were sold for a concert, some at 40 c each and the remainder at 25 c each. The money received for the dearer tickets was $70 more than for the cheaper tickets. Find the number of dearer tickets which were sold.

7) The ages of A and B are in the ratio 4 : 3. In eight years time the ratio of their ages will be 9 : 7. Find their present ages. If n years ago, A was three times as old as B, find the value of n.

8) The organisers of a charity concert sold tickets at two different prices. If they had sold 112 of the dearer tickets and 60 of the cheaper ones they would have received $45.60 but if they had sold 96 of the dearer tickets and 120 of the cheaper ones they would have received $52.80. Find the price of the dearer tickets.

9) Two numbers are in the ratio 5 : 7. When 15 is added to each the ratio changes to 5 : 6. Calculate the two numbers.

10) A man bought a number of 3 c stamps and also sufficient 4 c stamps to make his total expenditure 120 c. If, instead of the 3 c stamps, he had bought three times as many 2 c stamps he would have needed 9 fewer 4 c stamps than before for his expenditure to be 120 c. Find how many 3 c stamps he bought.

SELF-TEST 18

In the following questions state the letter (or letters) which correspond to the correct answer (or answers).

1) In the simultaneous equations:

$$2x + 3y = 17$$

$$3x + 4y = 24$$

x is equal to 4. Hence the value of y is:

a 3   **b** 4   **c** $\dfrac{25}{3}$ **d** 75

2) In the simultaneous equations:

$$2x - 3y = -16$$

$$5y - 3x = 25$$

x is equal to -5. Hence the value of y is:

a -2 **b** 0   **c** 2   **d** $\dfrac{26}{3}$

3) By eliminating x from the simultaneous equations:

$$2x - 5y = 8$$

$$2x - 3y = -7$$

we obtain the equation below:

a $-8y = 1$ **b** $-2y = 15$
c $-8y = 15$ **d** $-2y = 1$

4) By eliminating y from the simultaneous equations:

$$3x - 4y = -10$$

$$x + 4y = 8$$

we obtain the equation below:

a $2x = -18$ **b** $4x = -18$
c $2x = -2$ **d** $4x = -2$

5) By eliminating x from the simultaneous equations:

$$3x + 5y = 2$$

$$x + 3y = 7$$

we obtain the equation below:

a $4y = -19$ **b** $8y = 9$

c $4y = 19$ **d** $4y = 5$

6) By eliminating y from the simultaneous equations:

$$2x - 4y = 3$$
$$3x + 8y = 7$$

we obtain the equation below:

a $7x = 13$ **b** $x = -1$

c $x = 1$ **d** $7x = 10$

7) The solutions to the simultaneous equations:

$$2x - 5y = 3$$
$$x - 3y = 1 \quad \text{are:}$$

a $x = 4, y = 1$ **b** $y = 4, x = 1$

c $y = 4, x = 13$ **d** $x = 4, y = 3$

8) The solutions to the simultaneous equations:

$$3x - 2y = 5$$
$$4x - y = 10 \quad \text{are:}$$

a $x = -3, y = 22$ **b** $x = -3, y = -22$

c $x = 3, y = 2$ **d** $x = 3, y = -2$

9) Two numbers, x and y, are such that their sum is 18 and their difference is 12. The equations below will allow x and y to be found:

a $x + y = 18$ **b** $x + y = 18$
   $y - x = 12$ $x - y = 12$

c $x - y = 18$ **d** $y - x = 18$
   $x + y = 12$ $x + y = 12$

10) A bill for $40 is paid by means of $5 and $10 notes. Seven notes were used in all. If x is the number of $5 notes used and y is the number of $10 notes used then:

a $x + y = 7$ **b** $x + y = 7$
   $x + 2y = 40$ $5x + 10y = 40$

c $x - y = 7$ **d** $x - y = 7$
   $x + y = 40$ $5x + 10y = 40$

11) A motorist travels x km at 50 km/h and y km at 60 km/h. The total time taken is 5 hours. If his average speed is 56 km/h then:

a $50x + 60y = 5$ **b** $6x + 5y = 1500$
   $x + y = 280$ $x + y = 280$

c $\dfrac{x}{50} + \dfrac{y}{60} = 5$ **d** $50x + 60y = 5$
                                                $x + y = 280$
   $\dfrac{x+y}{5} = 56$

12) 300 tickets were sold for a school concert, some at 20 c each and the remainder at 30 c each. The cash received for the cheaper tickets was $10 more than that received for the dearer tickets. Therefore:

a $x + y = 300$ **b** $x + y = 300$
   $20x - 30y = 10$ $20x - 30y = 1000$

c $x + y = 300$ **d** $x + y = 300$
   $2x - 3y = 100$ $2x + 3y = 1$

CHAPTER 18 SUMMARY

Points to remember

To eliminate by addition or subtraction

(i)   If necessary, multiply through the equations by the smallest number that will make the coefficients of the variable to be eliminated equal.

(ii) If the signs of these coefficients are different, add the corresponding members of the two equations.

(iii) If the signs are the same, subtract the corresponding members.

Chapter 19 Quadratic Equations

An equation of the type $ax^2 + bx + c = 0$ is called a *quadratic equation*. The constants a, b and c can have any numerical values. Thus:

$$x^2 - 36 = 0$$

in which $a = 1$, $b = 0$ $c = -36$.

$$5x^2 + 7x + 8 = 0$$

in which $a = 5$, $b = 7$ and $c = 8$.

$$2.5x^2 - 3.1x - 2 = 0$$

in which $a = 2.5$, $b = -3.1$ and $c = -2$.

These are all examples of quadratic equations. A quadratic equation may contain only the square of the unknown quantity, as in the first of the above equations, or it may contain both the square and the first power as in the remaining two equations.

†EQUATIONS OF THE TYPE $ax^2 + c = 0$

When $b = 0$, the standard quadratic equation $ax^2 + bx + c = 0$ becomes $ax^2 + c = 0$. The methods of solving such equations are shown in the examples which follow.

EXAMPLE 1

(1) Solve the equation $x^2 - 16 = 0$.

Since $$x^2 - 16 = 0$$

$$x^2 = 16$$

Taking the square root of both sides we have

$$x = \pm\sqrt{16}$$

and $$x = \pm 4$$

It is necessary to insert the double sign before the value obtained for x since $+4$ and -4 when squared both give 16. This means that there are two solutions which will satisfy the given equation. The solution $x = \pm 4$ means that either $x = +4$ or $x = -4$.

The solution to a quadratic equation always consists of a pair of numbers (i.e. there are always two solutions although it is possible for both solutions to have the same numerical value).

(2) Solve the equation $2x^2 - 12 = 0$.

Since $$2x^2 - 12 = 0$$

$$2x^2 = 12$$

$$x^2 = 6$$

$$x = \pm\sqrt{6}$$

and $$x = \pm 2.45$$

(by using the square root tables to find $\sqrt{6}$).

(3) Solve the equation $2x^2 + 18 = 0$.

Since $$2x^2 + 18 = 0$$

$$2x^2 = -18$$

$$x^2 = -9$$

and $$x = \pm\sqrt{-9}$$

The square root of a negative quantity has no arithmetic meaning and it is called an imaginary number. The reason is as follows:

$$(-3)^2 = 9 \qquad (+3)^2 = 9$$

$$\therefore \qquad \sqrt{9} = \pm 3$$

Hence it is not possible to give a meaning to $\sqrt{-9}$. The equation $2x^2 + 18 = 0$ is said, therefore, to have imaginary roots.

†SOLUTION BY FACTORS

If the product of two factors is zero, then one factor or the other factor must be zero or they may both be zero. Thus if $ab = 0$, then either $a = 0$ or $b = 0$ or both $a = 0$ and $b = 0$.

We make use of this fact in solving quadratic equations.

EXAMPLE 2

(1) Solve the equation

$$(2x + 3)(x - 5) = 0$$

Since the product of the two factors $(2x+3)$ and $(x-5)$ is zero then,

either $\qquad 2x+3 = 0$ giving $x = -\dfrac{3}{2}$

or $\qquad\qquad x-5 = 0$ giving $x = 5$

The solutions are $\quad x = -\frac{3}{2}$ or $\quad x = 5$.

(2) Solve the equation $\quad x^2 - 5x + 6 = 0$.

Factorising gives $\quad (x-3)(x-2) = 0$ so that

either $\qquad x-3 = 0$ giving $x = 3$

or $\qquad\quad x-2 = 0$ giving $x = 2$

The solutions are $\quad x = 3$ or $\quad x = 2$.

(3) Solve the equation $\quad 6x^2 + x - 15 = 0$.

Factorising gives $\quad (2x-3)(3x+5) = 0$ so that

either $\qquad 2x-3 = 0$ giving $x = \dfrac{3}{2}$

or $\qquad\quad 3x+5 = 0$ giving $x = -\dfrac{5}{3}$

The solutions are $\quad x = \dfrac{3}{2}$ or $\quad x = -\dfrac{5}{3}$.

(4) Solve the equation $\quad x^2 - 5x = 0$.

Factorising gives $\quad x(x-5) = 0$ so that

either $\qquad\qquad x = 0$

or $\qquad\quad x-5 = 0$ giving $x = 5$

The solutions are $\quad x = 0$ and $\quad x = 5$ (note that it is incorrect to say that the solution is $x = 5$. The solution $\quad x = 0$ must be stated also).

Exercise 93 – *All type C*

Solve the following quadratic equations:

1) $x^2 - 25 = 0$ 4) $3x^2 - 48 = 0$

2) $x^2 - 8 = 0$ 5) $5x^2 - 80 = 0$

3) $x^2 - 16 = 0$ 6) $7x^2 - 21 = 0$

7) $(x-5)(x-2) = 0$

8) $(3x-4)(x+3) = 0$

9) $x(x+7) = 0$

10) $3x(2x-5) = 0$

11) $m^2 + 4m - 32 = 0$ 16) $14q^2 = 29q - 12$

12) $x^2 + 9x + 20 = 0$ 17) $9x + 28 = 9x^2$

13) $m^2 = 6m - 9$ 18) $x^2 - 3x = 0$

14) $x^2 + x - 72 = 0$ 19) $y^2 + 8y = 0$

15) $3x^2 - 7x + 2 = 0$ 20) $4a^2 - 4a - 3 = 0$

SHORT CUT

If $\quad ax^2 + bx + c = ax^2 + px + qx + c$

where $\quad p + q = b$ and $\quad pq = ac$

The roots of $\quad ax^2 + bx + c = 0$

are $\quad \dfrac{-p}{a}, \dfrac{-q}{a}$

e.g. $\quad 2x^2 - 5x - 3 = 2x^2 - 6x + x - 3$

$\therefore$ roots of $\quad 2x^2 - 5x - 3 = 0$ are $\dfrac{6}{2}$ and $\dfrac{-1}{2}$

†COMPLETING THE SQUARE

It will be recalled that

$$(x+h)^2 = x^2 + 2hx + h^2$$

The quadratic expression $x^2 + 2hx + h^2$ is said to be a *perfect square*. To factorise it we note that the last term (it is h^2) is (half the coefficient of x)^2, i.e.

$$\left(\tfrac{1}{2} \times 2h\right)^2 = h^2$$

To factorise $x^2 + 8x + 16$ we note that

$$\left(\tfrac{1}{2} \text{ coefficient of } x\right)^2 = \left(\tfrac{1}{2} \times 8\right)^2 = 4^2 = 16$$

Since this equals the last term,

$$x^2 + 8x + 16 = (x+4)^2$$

Similarly, because

$$(x-h)^2 = x^2 - 2hx + h^2$$

$$x^2 - 6x + 9 = (x-3)^2$$

Many quadratic expressions do not form a perfect square. For such expressions, it is often useful to complete the square so that

$$ax^2 + bx + c = a(x+h)^2 + k$$

The problem is to find the numerical values of h and k.

EXAMPLE 3

Write $3x^2 + 8x + 5$ in the form $a(x+h)^2 + k$.

$$3x^2 + 8x + 5 = 3(x^2 + \tfrac{8}{3}x) + 5$$

Adding (half the coefficient of x)^2 to the

expression in the bracket, we have

$3x^2 + 8x + 5$

$$= 3[x^2 + \tfrac{8}{3}x + (\tfrac{4}{3})^2] + 5 - (\tfrac{4}{3})^2 \times 3$$

$$= 3(x + \tfrac{4}{3})^2 - \tfrac{1}{3}$$

EXAMPLE 4

Write $-5x^2 + 6x + 2$ in the form $k - a(x + h)^2$.

$-5x^2 + 6x + 2$

$$= 2 - 5(x^2 - \tfrac{6}{5}x)$$

$$= 2 - 5[x^2 - \tfrac{6}{5}x + (\tfrac{3}{5})^2] + (\tfrac{3}{5})^2 \times 5$$

$$= \tfrac{19}{5} - 5(x - \tfrac{3}{5})^2$$

Exercise 94 – *Questions 1–4 type A,*
5–8 type C, remainder D

Factorise the following:

1) $x^2 + 4x + 4$ 3) $4x^2 - 12x + 9$

2) $9x^2 + 12x + 4$ 4) $25x^2 - 10x + 1$

Express each of the following in the form $a(x + h)^2 + k$ or $k - a(x + h)^2$.

5) $x^2 + 4x + 3$ 10) $3x^2 + 4x - 5$

6) $x^2 + 6x - 2$ 11) $10x^2 - 20x + 9$

7) $x^2 - 8x + 3$ 12) $-x^2 + 4x - 2$

8) $x^2 - 8x - 2$ 13) $-2x^2 + 4x + 7$

9) $4x^2 + 8x + 1$ 14) $-4x^2 + 2x + 3$

---

†SOLVING QUADRATIC EQUATIONS BY COMPLETING THE SQUARE

Any quadratic equation may be solved by completing the square as shown in Examples 3 and 4.

EXAMPLE 5

Solve the equation $4x^2 - 8x + 1 = 0$.

Completing the square of $4x^2 - 8x + 1$, we have

$4(x - 1)^2 - 3 = 0$

$$4(x - 1)^2 = 3$$

$$(x - 1)^2 = \frac{3}{4}$$

$$x - 1 = \pm\sqrt{\frac{3}{4}} = \pm\frac{\sqrt{3}}{2} = \pm 0.866$$

$$x = 1 \pm 0.866 = 1.8666 \text{ or } 0.134$$

EXAMPLE 6

Solve the equation $-3x^2 + 6x + 5 = 0$.

Multiplying through by -1, we have

$$3x^2 - 6x - 5 = 0$$

On completing the square of $3x^2 - 6x - 5$, we have

$$3(x - 1)^2 - 8 = 0$$

$$(x - 1)^2 = \frac{8}{3}$$

$$x - 1 = \pm\sqrt{\frac{8}{3}} = \pm 1.633$$

$$x = 1 \pm 1.633$$

$$= 2.633 \text{ or } -0.633$$

†USING THE FORMULA TO SOLVE QUADRATIC EQUATIONS

Although any quadratic equation may be solved by completing the square, it is useful to derive a formula for solving such equations.

$$ax^2 + bx + c = 0 \quad \therefore \ ax^2 + bx = -c$$

Multiply by $4a$

$$\therefore \qquad 4a^2x^2 + 4abx = -4ac$$

Completing the square

$$4a^2x^2 + 4abx + b^2 = b^2 - 4ac$$

$$\therefore \qquad (2ax + b)^2 = b^2 - 4ac$$

$$\therefore \qquad 2ax + b = \pm\sqrt{b^2 - 4ac}$$

$$2ax = -b \pm\sqrt{b^2 - 4ac}$$

$$x = \frac{-b \pm\sqrt{b^2 - 4ac}}{2a}$$

This equation is called the quadratic formula. Note that the whole of the numerator, including $-b$, is divided by $2a$. The formula is used when factorisation is not possible, although it may be used to solve any quadratic equation.

EXAMPLE 7

(1) Solve the equation

$$3x^2 - 8x + 2 = 0$$

Comparing with $ax^2 + bx + c = 0$ we have $a = 3$, $b = -8$ and $c = 2$. Substituting these values in the formula gives

$$x = \frac{-(-8) \pm \sqrt{(-8)^2 - 4 \times 3 \times 2}}{2 \times 3}$$

$$= \frac{8 \pm \sqrt{64 - 24}}{6}$$

$$= \frac{8 \pm \sqrt{40}}{6}$$

$$= \frac{8 \pm 6.325}{6}$$

Either

$$x = \frac{8 + 6.325}{6} \quad \text{or} \quad \frac{8 - 6.325}{6}$$

$$= \frac{14.325}{6} \quad \text{or} \quad \frac{1.675}{6}$$

$$= 2.39 \quad \text{or} \quad 0.28$$

(2) Solve the equation

$$-2x^2 + 3x + 7 = 0$$

Where the coefficient of x^2 is negative it is best to make it positive by multiplying both sides of the equation by (-1). This is equivalent to changing the sign of each of the terms. Thus,

$$2x^2 - 3x - 7 = 0$$

This gives $a = 2$, $b = -3$ and $c = -7$.

$$x = \frac{-(-3) \pm \sqrt{(-3)^2 - 4 \times 2 \times (-7)}}{2 \times 2}$$

$$= \frac{3 \pm \sqrt{9 + 56}}{4}$$

$$= \frac{3 \pm \sqrt{65}}{4}$$

$$= \frac{3 \pm 8.063}{4}$$

Either

$$x = \frac{11.063}{4} \quad \text{or} \quad x = \frac{-5.063}{4}$$

$$= 2.766 \quad \text{or} \quad -1.266$$

Exercise 95 – *Questions 1–6 type B, remainder C*

Solve the following equations:

1) $4x^2 - 3x - 2 = 0$

2) $x^2 - x - 1 = 0$

3) $3x^2 + 7x - 5 = 0$

4) $7x^2 + 8x - 2 = 0$

5) $5x^2 - 4x - 1 = 0$

6) $2x^2 - 7x = 3$

7) $x(x + 4) + 2x(x + 3) = 5$

8) $5x(x + 1) - 2x(2x - 1) = 20$

9) $x(x + 5) = 66$

10) $(2x - 3)^2 = 13$

†EQUATIONS GIVING RISE TO QUADRATIC EQUATIONS

EXAMPLE 8

(1) Solve the simultaneous equations:

$$3x - y = 4 \qquad [1]$$

$$x^2 - 3xy + 8 = 0 \qquad [2]$$

From equation [1],

$$y = 3x - 4$$

Substituting for y in equation [2] gives

$$x^2 - 3x(3x - 4) + 8 = 0$$

$$x^2 - 9x^2 + 12x + 8 = 0$$

$$-8x^2 + 12x + 8 = 0$$

$$8x^2 - 12x - 8 = 0$$

Dividing throughout by 4 gives

$$2x^2 - 3x - 2 = 0$$

$$(2x + 1)(x - 2) = 0$$

Either $2x + 1 = 0$ giving $x = -\frac{1}{2}$

or $x - 2 = 0$ giving $x = 2$

when $x = -\frac{1}{2}$, $y = 3 \times \left(-\frac{1}{2}\right) - 4 = -5\frac{1}{2}$

when $x = 2$, $y = 3 \times 2 - 4 = 2$.

Thus the solutions are:

$$x = -\frac{1}{2}, \quad y = -5\frac{1}{2} \quad \text{or} \quad x = 2, \quad y = 2$$

(2) Solve the simultaneous equations:

$$x - 6y - 5 = 0 \qquad [1]$$

$$xy - 6 = 0 \qquad [2]$$

From equation [1],

$$x = 6y + 5$$

Substituting for x in equation [2] gives

$$(6y + 5)y - 6 = 0$$

$$6y^2 + 5y - 6 = 0$$

$$(3y - 2)(2y + 3) = 0$$

Either $3y - 2 = 0$ giving $y = \dfrac{2}{3}$

or $2y + 3 = 0$ giving $y = -\dfrac{3}{2}$

When $y = \dfrac{2}{3}$, $x = 6 \times \dfrac{2}{3} + 5 = 9$

When $y = -\dfrac{3}{2}$, $x = 6 \times \left(-\dfrac{3}{2}\right) + 5 = -4$

Thus the solutions are:

$$x = 9, \quad y = \dfrac{2}{3} \quad \text{or} \quad x = -4, \quad y = -\dfrac{3}{2}$$

Exercise 96 – *All type D*

Solve the following simultaneous equations:

1) $x + y = 3$
  $xy = 2$

2) $x - y = 3$
  $xy + 10x + y = 150$

3) $x^2 + y^2 - 6x + 5y = 21$
  $x + y = 9$

4) $x + y = 12$
  $2x^2 + 3y^2 = 7xy$

5) $2x^2 - 3y^2 = 20$
  $2x + y = 6$

6) $x^2 + y^2 = 34$
  $x + 2y = 13$

7) $3x + 2y = 13$
  $xy = 2$

8) $-3x + y + 15 = 0$
  $2x^2 + 4x + y = 0$

PROBLEMS INVOLVING QUADRATIC EQUATIONS

EXAMPLE 9

(1) The area of a rectangle is 6 square metres. If the length is 1 metre longer than the width find the dimensions of the rectangle.

Let x metres be the width of the rectangle.

Then the length of the rectangle is $(x + 1)$ metres. Since the area is length × breadth, then

$$x(x + 1) = 6$$

$$x^2 + x - 6 = 0$$

$$(x + 3)(x - 2) = 0$$

so either $x + 3 = 0$ giving $x = -3$

or $x - 2 = 0$ giving $x = 2$

The solution cannot be negative and hence $x = 2$. Hence the width is 2 metres and the length is $(2 + 1) = 3$ metres.

(2) Two square rooms have a total floor area of 208 square metres. One room is 4 metres longer each way than the other. Find the floor dimensions of each room.

Let the smaller room have sides of x metres. The area of this room is then x^2 square metres.

The larger room will then have sides of $(x + 4)$ metres and its floor area is $(x + 4)(x + 4) = (x + 4)^2$ square metres.

Hence $x^2 + (x + 4)^2 = 208$

$$x^2 + x^2 + 8x + 16 = 208$$

$$2x^2 + 8x - 192 = 0$$

Dividing through by 2, we have

$$x^2 + 4x - 96 = 0$$

$$(x + 12)(x - 8) = 0$$

so either $x + 12 = 0$ giving $x = -12$

or $x - 8 = 0$ giving $x = 8$

The negative value of x is not possible hence $x = 8$.

The floor dimensions of the two rooms are 8 metres by 8 metres and 12 metres by 12 metres.

(3) A rectangular room is 4 metres wider than it is high and it is 8 metres longer than it is wide. The total area of the walls is 512 square metres. Find the width of the room.

Let the height of the room be x metres.

Then the width of the room is $(x + 4)$ metres and the length of the room is $x + 4 + 8 = (x + 12)$ metres.

These dimensions are shown in Fig. 19.1.

The total wall area is $2x(x+12)+2x(x+4)$.

Hence $2x(x+12)+2x(x+4)=512$

Divide both sides of the equation by 2,

$$x(x+12)+x(x+4)=256$$

$$x^2+12x+x^2+4x=256$$

$$2x^2+16x=256$$

Divide both sides of the equation by 2 again,

$$x^2+8x=128$$

$$x^2+8x-128=0$$

$$(x+16)(x-8)=0$$

Either $x+16=0$ giving $x=-16$

or $x-8=0$ giving $x=8$

Thus the height of the room is 8 metres. Its width is $(x+4)=8+4=12$ metres.

(4) The smallest of three consecutive positive numbers is m. Three times the square of the largest is greater than the sum of the squares of the other two numbers by 67. Find m.

The three numbers are m, $m+1$ and $m+2$.

Three times the square of the larger number is $3(m+2)^2$.

The sum of the squares of the other two numbers is $m^2+(m+1)^2$.

$\therefore$ $3(m+2)^2-[m^2+(m+1)^2]=67$

$3(m^2+4m+4)-[m^2+m^2+2m+1]=67$

$3m^2+12m+12-[2m^2+2m+1]=67$

$3m^2+12m+12-2m^2-2m-1=67$

$m^2+10m+11=67$

$m^2+10m-56=0$

$(m-4)(m+14)=0$

either $m-4=0$ giving $m=4$

or $m+14=0$ giving $m=-14$

Since m must be positive its value is 4.

Exercise 97 – *Questions 1–8 type C, remainder D*

1) Find the number which when added to its square gives a total of 42.

2) A rectangle is 72 square metres in area and its perimeter is 34 metres. Find its length and breadth.

3) Two squares have a total area of 274 square centimetres and the sum of their perimeters is 88 centimetres. Find the side of the larger square.

4) The area of a rectangle is 4 square metres and its length is 3 metres longer than its width. Find the dimensions of the rectangle.

5) Part of a garden consists of a square lawn with a path 1.5 metres wide around its perimeter. If the lawn area is two-thirds of the total area find the length of a side of the lawn.

6) The largest of three consecutive positive numbers is n. The square of this number exceeds the sum of the other two numbers by 38. Find the three numbers.

7) The length of a rectangle exceeds its breadth by 4 centimetres. If the length were halved and the breadth decreased by 5 cm the area would be decreased by 55 square centimetres. Find the length of the rectangle.

8) In a certain fraction the denominator is greater than the numerator by 3. If 2 is added to both the numerator and denominator, the fraction is increased by $\frac{6}{35}$. Find the fraction.

9) A piece of wire which is 18 metres long is cut into two parts. The first part is bent to form the four sides of a square. The second part is bent to form the four sides of a rectangle. The breadth of the rectangle is 1 metre and its length is x metres. If the sum of the areas of the square and rectangle is A square metres show that:

$$A=16-3x+\frac{x^2}{4}$$

If $A=9$, calculate the value of x.

10) One side of a rectangle is d cm long. The other side is 2 cm shorter. The side of a square is 2 cm shorter still. The sum of the areas of the square and rectangle is 148 square centimetres. Find an equation for d and solve it.

SELF-TEST 19

In the following questions state the letter (or letters) corresponding to the correct answer (or answers).

1) If $(2x - 3)(3x + 4) = 0$ then x is equal to:

a $-\dfrac{3}{2}$ or $\dfrac{4}{3}$ **b** $-\dfrac{2}{3}$ or $\dfrac{3}{4}$

c $\dfrac{2}{3}$ or $-\dfrac{3}{4}$ **d** $\dfrac{3}{2}$ or $-\dfrac{4}{3}$

2) If $(5x + 2)(3x - 2) = 0$ then x is equal to:

a $-\dfrac{2}{5}$ or $\dfrac{2}{3}$ **b** $-\dfrac{2}{5}$ or $-\dfrac{2}{3}$

c $\dfrac{5}{2}$ or $-\dfrac{3}{2}$ **d** $\dfrac{2}{5}$ or $-\dfrac{2}{3}$

3) If $(2x + 5)(4x - 7) = 0$ then x is equal to:

a $-\dfrac{2}{5}$ or $\dfrac{4}{7}$ **b** $-\dfrac{5}{2}$ or $\dfrac{7}{4}$

c $-\dfrac{5}{2}$ or $-\dfrac{7}{4}$ **d** $\dfrac{2}{5}$ or $-\dfrac{4}{7}$

4) If $x(2x - 5) = 0$ then x is equal to:

a $-\dfrac{5}{2}$ **b** $\dfrac{5}{2}$

c 0 or $\dfrac{5}{2}$ **d** 0 or $-\dfrac{5}{2}$

5) If $x^2 - 25 = 0$ then x is equal to:
a 0 **b** 5 **c** ± 5

6) If $3x^2 - 27 = 0$ then x is equal to:
a 3 **b** ± 3 **c** 9

7) If $x^2 - 5x - 2 = 0$ then x is equal to:

a $\dfrac{-5 \pm \sqrt{33}}{2}$ **b** $\dfrac{5 \pm \sqrt{33}}{2}$

c $\dfrac{-5 \pm \sqrt{17}}{2}$ **d** $\dfrac{5 \pm \sqrt{17}}{2}$

8) If $3x^2 + 2x - 3 = 0$ then x is equal to:

a $\dfrac{2 \pm \sqrt{40}}{6}$ **b** $\dfrac{-2 \pm \sqrt{40}}{6}$

c $\dfrac{2 \pm \sqrt{32}}{6}$ **d** $\dfrac{-2 \pm \sqrt{36}}{6}$

9) If $x^2 + 9x + 7 = 0$ then x is equal to:

a $\dfrac{9 \pm \sqrt{109}}{2}$ **b** $\dfrac{9 \pm \sqrt{53}}{2}$

c $\dfrac{-9 \pm \sqrt{109}}{2}$ **d** $\dfrac{-9 \pm \sqrt{53}}{2}$

10) If $x^2 - 7x + 3 = 0$ then x is equal to:

a $\dfrac{7 \pm \sqrt{37}}{2}$ **b** $\dfrac{7 \pm \sqrt{61}}{2}$

c $\dfrac{-7 \pm \sqrt{37}}{2}$ **d** $\dfrac{-7 \pm \sqrt{61}}{2}$

11) If $\dfrac{3}{x - 3} - \dfrac{2}{x - 1} = 5$ then:

a $5x^2 - 21x + 24 = 0$
b $5x^2 - 21x + 12 = 0$
c $x - 14 = 0$ **d** $x - 2 = 0$

12) If $\dfrac{2}{x + 1} - 3 = \dfrac{1}{x - 2}$ then:

a $3x^2 + 2x + 11 = 0$
b $-3x^2 - 2x - 11 = 0$
c $3x^2 - 4x - 1 = 0$
d $-3x^2 + 4x + 1 = 0$

CHAPTER 19 SUMMARY

Points to remember

(i)   To solve quadratic equations by
      factoring
   (a) First transpose, if necessary, all
        terms to the left side of the
        equation.
   (b) Factorize the expression on the left
        side.
   (c) Set each factor containing the
        variable equal to zero.
   (d) Solve these equations.

(e) Check, by substituting the value
     obtained for the unknown in the
     original equation.

(ii) To solve a quadratic equation using a
      formula
      The general form of a quadratic
      equation is $ax^2 + bx + c = 0$.
      The solution is

$$x = \{-b \pm \sqrt{(b^2 - 4ac)}\}/2a.$$

Chapter 20 Indices and Logarithms

LAWS OF INDICES

The laws of indices are as shown below.

MULTIPLICATION

When multiplying powers of the same quantity together *add* the indices.

$$x^6 \times x^7 = x^{6+7} = x^{13}$$
$$y^2 \times y^3 \times y^4 \times y^5 = y^{2+3+4+5} = y^{14}$$

DIVISION

When dividing powers of the same quantity *subtract* the index of the denominator (bottom part) from the index of the numerator (top part).

$$\frac{x^5}{x^2} = x^{5-2} = x^3$$

$$\frac{a^3 \times a^4 \times a^8}{a^5 \times a^7} = \frac{a^{3+4+8}}{a^{5+7}}$$

$$= \frac{a^{15}}{a^{12}} = a^{15-12} = a^3$$

$$\frac{3y^2 \times 2y^5 \times 5y^4}{6y^3 \times 4y^4} = \frac{30y^{2+5+4}}{24y^{3+4}}$$

$$= \frac{30y^{11}}{24y^7} = \frac{5y^{11-7}}{4} = \frac{5y^4}{4}$$

POWERS

When raising the power of a quantity to a power *multiply* the indices together.

$$(3x)^3 = 3^{1\times3} \times x^{1\times3} = 3^3 x^3 = 27x^3$$
$$(a^2 b^3 c^4)^2 = a^{2\times2} b^{3\times2} c^{4\times2} = a^4 b^6 c^8$$
$$\left(\frac{3m^3}{5n^2}\right)^2 = \frac{3^2 m^{3\times2}}{5^2 n^{2\times2}} = \frac{9m^6}{25n^4}$$

†NEGATIVE INDICES

A negative index indicates the reciprocal of the quantity.

$$a^{-1} = \frac{1}{a}$$

$$5x^{-3} = \frac{5}{x^3}$$

$$a^2 b^{-2} c^{-3} = \frac{a^2}{b^2 c^3}$$

†FRACTIONAL INDICES

The numerator of a fractional index indicates the power to which the quantity must be raised; the denominator indicates the root which is to be taken.

$$x^{\frac{2}{3}} = \sqrt[3]{x^2}$$

$$ab^{\frac{3}{4}} = a \times \sqrt[4]{b^3}$$

$$a^{\frac{1}{2}} = \sqrt{a}$$

(Note that for square roots the number indicating the root is usually omitted.)

$$\sqrt{64a^6} = (64a^6)^{\frac{1}{2}} = (8^2 a^6)^{\frac{1}{2}}$$

$$= 8^{2\times\frac{1}{2}} a^{6\times\frac{1}{2}} = 8a^3$$

†ZERO INDEX

Any quantity raised to the power of zero is equal to 1.

$$a^0 = 1$$

$$\left(\frac{x}{y}\right)^0 = 1$$

EXAMPLE 1

(1) $\left(\dfrac{1}{3}\right)^{-4} = \dfrac{1^{-4}}{3^{-4}} = \dfrac{3^4}{1^4} = 81$

(2) $4^{\frac{5}{2}} = (2^2)^{\frac{5}{2}} = 2^{\frac{2}{1}\times\frac{5}{2}}$

$= 2^5 = 32$

(3) $\sqrt{9x^2} = (3^2 x^2)^{\frac{1}{2}} = 3^{\frac{2}{1}\times\frac{1}{2}} x^{\frac{2}{1}\times\frac{1}{2}}$

$= 3^1 x^1 = 3x$

EXAMPLE 2

If $3^{p+4} = 9^{p-2}$ find the value of p.

$$3^{p+4} = (3^2)^{p-2}$$

$$3^{p+4} = 3^{2p-4}$$

Since $(p+4)$ and $(2p-4)$ are both powers of 3, they must be equal.

$$\therefore \qquad p+4 = 2p-4$$

$$p = 8$$

Exercise 98 – *Questions 1–7 type A, 8–15 type B, remainder C*

Simplify the following:

1) $3^5 \times 3^2 \times 3^7$

2) $b^2 \times b^4 \times b^5 \times b^8$

3) $\dfrac{5^7}{5^2}$

4) $\dfrac{2^3 \times 2^4 \times 2^7}{2^2 \times 2^5}$

5) $(7^2)^3$

6) $(3x^2y^3)^4$

7) $(a^2b^3c)^5$

8) $\left(\dfrac{5a^3}{2b^2}\right)^7$

† 9) Find the values of: 10^{-1}, 2^{-5}, 3^{-4} and 5^{-2}.

†10) Find the values of: $4^{\frac{1}{2}}$, $8^{\frac{1}{3}}$, $32^{\frac{1}{5}}$.

11) Express as powers of 3: 9^2, 27^4, 81^3.

†12) Express as powers of x: $\sqrt[3]{x}$, $\sqrt[5]{x^3}$, $\sqrt[7]{x^4}$.

†13) Find the value of: $32^{\frac{1}{5}} \times 25^{\frac{1}{2}} \times 27^{\frac{1}{3}}$.

†14) Find the values of: $(\frac{1}{5})^0$, $125^{-\frac{1}{3}}$, $(1\,000\,000)^{\frac{1}{3}}$.

†15) Find the value of $\sqrt{\dfrac{p}{q}}$ when $p=64^{\frac{2}{3}}$ and $q=3^{-2}$.

†16) If $3^m = 9$, find m.

†17) If $2^{x+1} = 4^x$ find x.

†18) If $5^{2x+3} = 125^{x+5}$, find x.

†19) Find the value of p for which $3^{2p-1} = 243$.

†20) Find the value of x if $(2^{2x})(4^{x+1}) = 64$.

NUMBERS IN STANDARD FORM

A number expressed in the form $A \times 10^n$, where A is a number between 1 and 10 and n is an integer is said to be in standard form.

EXAMPLE 3

$$50\,000 = 5 \times 10\,000 = 5 \times 10^4$$

$$0.003 = \frac{3}{1000} = \frac{3}{10^3} = 3 \times 10^{-3}$$

Exercise 99 – *All type B*

Express each of the following in standard form:

1) 8000

2) 92 500

3) 893

4) 5 600 000

5) 0.035

6) 0.7

7) 0.000 365

8) 0.007 12

LOGARITHMS

Any positive number can be expressed as a power of 10. For instance:

$$1000 = 10^3$$

$$74 = 10^{1.869}$$

These powers of 10 are called *logarithms to the base 10*.

That is:

$$\text{number} = 10^{\text{logarithm}}$$

Log tables give the logarithms of numbers between 1 and 10.

Thus $\qquad \log 5.17 = 0.713$

To find the logarithms of numbers outside this range we make use of numbers in standard form and the multiplication law of indices. For example:

$$324 = 3.24 \times 10^2$$

$$\log 3.24 = 0.511$$

$$324 = 10^{0.511} \times 10^2$$

$$= 10^{2.511}$$

$\therefore \qquad \log 324 = 2.511$

A logarithm therefore consists of two parts:

(1) A whole number part called the *characteristic*.

(2) A decimal part called the *mantissa* which is found directly from the log tables.

For a number, 10 or greater, the characteristic is found by subtracting 1 from the number of figures to the left of the decimal point in the given number.

In the number 825 the characteristic is 2.

$$\therefore \qquad \log 825 \ = \ 2.916$$

In the number 18 600 the characteristic is 4.

$$\therefore \qquad \log 18\,600 \ = \ 4.270$$

NEGATIVE CHARACTERISTICS

$$0.632 \ = \ 6.32 \times 10^{-1}$$

$$\log 6.32 \ = \ 0.801$$

$$0.632 \ = \ 10^{0.801} \times 10^{-1}$$

$$= \ 10^{-1+0.801}$$

The characteristic is therefore -1 and the mantissa is 0.801. However writing $-1 + 0.801$ for the logarithm of 0.632 would be awkward and we therefore write:

$$\log 0.632 \ = \ \bar{1}.801$$

Note that the minus sign has been written above the characteristic but must be clearly understood that

$$\bar{2}.735 \ = \ -2 + 0.735$$

and $\qquad \bar{4}.067 \ = \ -4 + 0.067$

All numbers between 0 and 1 have negative characteristics which are found by adding 1 to the number of zeros following the decimal point.

In the number 0.073 58 the characteristic is $\bar{2}$.

$$\therefore \qquad \log 0.073\,5 \ = \ \bar{2}.866$$

In the number 0.000 612 the characteristic is $\bar{4}$.

$$\therefore \qquad \log 0.000\,612 \ = \ \bar{4}.787$$

ANTI-LOGARITHMS

Tables of *antilogs* contain the numbers which correspond to the given logarithms. In using these tables remember that only the decimal part of the log is used.

EXAMPLE 4

(1) To find the number whose log is 2.531. Using the mantissa .531, we find 340 as the number corresponding. Since the characteristic is 2 the number must be 340.
(Note that $\log 340 = 2.531$.)

(2) To find the number whose log is $\bar{3}.617$. Using the mantissa .617 we find 414 as the number corresponding. Since the characteristic is $\bar{3}$ the number must be 0.004 14.
(Note that $\log 0.004\,14 = \bar{3}.617$.)

Exercise 100 – *All type A*

Write down the logarithms of the following numbers:

1) 7.26	**7)** 70.0
2) 8.19	**8)** 176 000
3) 63.2	**9)** 0.178
4) 716	**10)** 0.006 34
5) 1820	**11)** 0.068 9
6) 78 600	**12)** 0.000 718

Write down the antilogs of the following:

13) 2.61	**17)** $\bar{1}.23$
14) 1.73	**18)** $\bar{2}.60$
15) 0.62	**19)** $\bar{4}.63$
16) 3.10	**20)** $\bar{3}.55$

RULES FOR THE USE OF LOGARITHMS

MULTIPLICATION

Find the logs of the numbers and *add* them together. The antilog of the sum gives the required answer.

EXAMPLE 5

$19.6 \times 0.067\,3 \times 0.918$

	number	logarithm
	19.6	1.292
	0.067 3	$\bar{2}.828$
	0.918	$\bar{1}.963$
Answer =	1.21	0.083

Chapter 20 117

DIVISION

Find the log of each number. Then *subtract* the log of the denominator (bottom number) from the log of the numerator (top number).

EXAMPLE 6

$$\frac{17.6}{0.0386}$$

number	logarithm
17.6	1.246
0.0386	$\bar{2}$.587

Answer = 456   2.659

EXAMPLE 7

$$\frac{0.617 \times 20.3}{136 \times 0.0927}$$

In problems where there is multiplication and division a table layout like the one below is helpful.

Numerator		Denominator	
number	logarithm	number	logarithm
0.617	$\bar{1}$.790	136	2.134
20.3	1.307	0.0927	$\bar{2}$.967
numerator	1.097	denominator	1.101
denominator	1.101		

Answer = 0.991 $\bar{1}$.996

POWERS

Find the log of the number and *multiply* it by the index denoting the power.

EXAMPLE 8

$$(0.317)^3$$

$$\log(0.317)^3 = 3 \times \log 0.317$$
$$= 3 \times \bar{1}.501 = \bar{2}.503$$

By finding the antilog of $\bar{2}$.503

$$(0.317)^3 = 0.0318$$

EXAMPLE 9

$$\frac{(0.763)^4 \times 18.2}{0.916}$$

The table layout shown below is helpful when powers or roots form part of the calculation.

number	operator	logarithm
$(0.763)^4$	$4 \times \bar{1}.883$	$\bar{1}.532$
18.2		1.260
		0.792
0.916		$\bar{1}.962$
Answer = 6.76		0.830

ROOTS

Find the logarithm of the number and *divide* it by the number denoting the root.

EXAMPLE 10

$$\sqrt[3]{18.1}$$

$$\log 18.1 = 1.258$$
$$\log \sqrt[3]{18.1} = \frac{1.258}{3}$$
$$= 0.419$$
$$\therefore \quad \sqrt[3]{18.1} = 2.62$$

Exercise 101 – *All type C*

Use logs to find the values of:

1) 37.1×9.23
2) $11.1 \times 1.78 \times 28.4$
3) 158×0.778
4) 0.0873×0.118
5) $\dfrac{186}{27.9}$
6) $\dfrac{0.917}{0.0348}$
7) $\dfrac{2.41}{0.00613}$
8) $\dfrac{0.158}{29.4}$
9) $\dfrac{178 \times 0.00634}{11.4 \times 0.736}$
10) $\dfrac{7650 \times 0.000116}{178 \times 26.4}$
11) $(9.76)^4$
12) $(27.1)^3$
13) $(0.563)^3$

14) $(0.013\,2)^2$ **17)** $\dfrac{463\,0 \times (0.618)^3}{19.1 \times (2.48)^2}$

15) $(0.299)^2 \times 17.6$ **18)** $\sqrt[3]{17.6}$

16) $\dfrac{(0.516)^2}{0.063\,1}$ **19)** $\sqrt[4]{1.28}$

     20) $\sqrt[5]{618.2}$

†USE OF LOGARITHMS IN EVALUATING FORMULAE

EXAMPLE 11

(1) A positive number is given by the formula

$$y = \frac{3t}{\sqrt{c}}$$

(i) Use tables to calculate y when $t = 7.32$ and $c = 205$.

(ii) If t may take any value from 5 to 8 (inclusive) and c may take any value from 100 to 225 (inclusive), calculate the greatest possible value of y.

(i) Substituting the given values $t = 7.32$ and $c = 205$ gives

$$y = \frac{3 \times 7.32}{\sqrt{205}} = \frac{21.96}{14.3}$$

by using the square root tables.

Using the log tables and stating 21.96 to 3 significant figures gives

number	log
22.0	1.342
14.3	1.155
Answer = 1.54	0.187

Hence $y = 1.54$

(ii) The greatest possible value of y will occur when t has its greatest possible value and c has its least possible value. Hence, when $t = 8$ and $c = 100$,

$$y = \frac{3 \times 8}{\sqrt{100}} = \frac{24}{10} = 2.4$$

(2) Calculate the value of y from the formula

$$y^3 = \frac{ab}{a - b}$$

when $a = 1.64$ and $b = 1.02$.

Since

$$y^3 = \frac{ab}{a - b}$$

$$y = \sqrt[3]{\frac{ab}{a - b}}$$

Substituting the given values $a = 1.64$ and $b = 1.02$ gives

$$y = \frac{1.64 \times 1.02}{1.64 - 1.02} = \frac{1.64 \times 1.02}{0.62}$$

Using the log tables we have

number	log
1.64	0.215
1.02	0.009
1.64 × 1.02	0.224
0.62	$\bar{1}.792$
1.64 × 1.02 ÷ 0.62	0.432
	÷3
Answer = 1.39	0.144

Hence $y = 1.39$

(Note that we can only use logs when numbers are to be multiplied or divided. They must never be used when numbers are to be added or subtracted.)

Calculations similar to the above may be done using calculators.

†WRITING FORMULAE IN LOGARITHMIC FORM

When working with formulae it is often useful to write the equation connecting the quantities in logarithmic form.

The rules governing logarithms are:
(i) $\log ab = \log a + \log b$

(ii) $\log \dfrac{a}{b} = \log a - \log b$

(iii) $\log x^n = n \log x$.

EXAMPLE 12

(1) Write the equation $P = \dfrac{RT}{V}$ in logarithmic form.

We are given that $P = R \times T \div V$

$\therefore \qquad \log P = \log R + \log T - \log V$

Note that multiplication signs become plus signs and division signs become minus signs.

(2) Write the equation $t = 2\pi \sqrt{\dfrac{W}{gf}}$ in logarithmic form.

Writing the equation in index form it becomes:

$$t = 2\pi\left(\frac{W}{gf}\right)^{1/2} = \frac{2\pi W^{1/2}}{g^{1/2}f^{1/2}}$$

$$= 2\pi W^{1/2}g^{-1/2}f^{-1/2}$$

$$\therefore \quad \log t$$
$$= \log 2 + \log \pi + \tfrac{1}{2}\log W - \tfrac{1}{2}\log g - \tfrac{1}{2}\log f$$

(3) Express as a formula without logarithms:

$$\log y = 3 - n\log x$$

The expressions on the R.H.S. must all be made logarithms and since $\log 1000 = 3$,

$$\log y = \log 1000 - n\log x$$

$$\therefore \quad y = \frac{1000}{x^n}$$

†SOLVING LOGARITHMIC EQUATIONS

The methods are shown in the following examples.

EXAMPLE 13

(1) If $\log x^2 - \log 10 = 1$ find x.

Now $\log x^2 = 2\log x$ and $\log 10 = 1$

$$\therefore \qquad 2\log x - 1 = 1$$
$$\therefore \qquad 2\log x = 2$$
$$\therefore \qquad \log x = 1$$
$$\therefore \qquad x = 10^1$$

Since the anti-log of 1 is 10,

$$x = 10$$

(2) If $VT^n = C$ find the value of n when $V = 12$, $T = 3$ and $C = 108$.

Substituting the given values in the equation gives

$$12 \times 3^n = 108$$

Taking logs of both sides

$$\log 12 + n\log 3 = \log 108$$

Since $\log 12 = 1.079$, $\log 3 = 0.477$
and $\log 108 = 2.033$ we have

$$1.079 + 0.477n = 2.033$$
$$\therefore \qquad 0.477n = 0.954$$
$$\therefore \qquad n = \frac{0.954}{0.477}$$
$$\therefore \qquad n = 2$$

Alternatively:

Since $\qquad 12 \times 3^n = 108$

$$3^n = 9 = 3^2 \quad \therefore \ n = 2$$

1) Evaluate the formula $1.73 \times \sqrt[3]{d^2}$ when $d = 2.8$.

2) Find D from the formula $D = 1.2 \times \sqrt{dL}$ when $d = 12$ and $L = 0.756$.

3) Find the value of the expression:
$$0.25 \times (d - 0.5)^2 \times \sqrt{S}$$
when $d = 4.33$ and $S = 5.12$.

4) Find the value of the expression:
$$\frac{p_1v_1 - p_2v_2}{c - 1}$$
when $v_1 = 28.6$, $v_2 = 32.2$, $p_1 = 18.5$, $p_2 = 13.5$ and $c = 1.42$.

5) Find P from the formula:
$$P = \sqrt{\frac{x^2 - y^2}{2xy}}$$
when $x = 15.5$ and $y = 3.4$.

6) If $A = PV^n$ find A when $P = 0.931$, $V = 1.68$ and $n = \tfrac{1}{2}$.

7) Calculate M from the formula:
$$M^3 = \frac{3x^2w}{p}$$
when $x = 2.35$, $w = 1.66$ and $p = 2.31$.

8) Given that $x = \dfrac{dh}{D - d}$ find x when $d = 0.638$, $h = 0.516$ and $D = 0.721$.

9) Find the value of R from the equation:
$$R = k\sqrt{\frac{P}{H^2}}$$
when $k = 65.2$, $P = 681$ and $H = 22.7$.

10) Transpose the formula:
$$y = \frac{Wl^3}{48EI}$$
to make I the subject and find its value when $y = 0.346$, $W = 10\,300$, $l = 122$ and $E = 30 \times 10^6$.

11) If $N = 10^x$ find N when x is:
(a) 3   (b) $\tfrac{1}{2}$ (c) $\tfrac{1}{5}$

12) Solve the following equations for x:
(a) $10^{2x} = 320$ (b) $3^{3x} = 9$
(c) $5 \times 2^x = 100$ (d) $\log x^2 = 4$
(e) $2\log x + 3 = 1$

13) If $pv^n = C$ find n when $p = 80$, $v = 3.1$ and $C = 329$.

14) If $\log x^4 - \log 100 = 1$ find x.

15) Find x if

$$\log x^2 = \log \sqrt{16} - \log 2 + \log 3^2.$$

SELF-TEST 20

State the letter (or letters) corresponding to the correct answer (or answers) to all questions.

1) If $2^x = 32$ then x is equal to:

a $\dfrac{1}{5}$ **b** 5   **c** $\sqrt{32}$ **d** 16

2) The product of 2.5×10^4 and 8×10^{-5} is:

a 1.8   **b** 2.0   **c** 5.5   **d** 105

3) $(x^{1/2})^3 \times \sqrt{x^9}$ is equal to:

a $x^{9/2}$ **b** $x^{11/2}$ **c** x^6 **d** x^9

4) The cube root of 3.600 is:

a 0.153   **b** 0.330   **c** 1.53   **d** 3.30

5) $(8x^3)^{-1/3}$ is equal to:

a $\dfrac{1}{2x}$ **b** $\dfrac{8}{x}$ **c** $2x$ **d** $8x$

6) $(3x^3)^2$ is equal to:

a $3x^5$ **b** $9x^5$ **c** $3x^6$ **d** $9x^6$

7) $\sqrt{9p^4} \div \dfrac{1}{2}p^2$ is equal to:

a 3   **b** 6   **c** $3p^4$ **d** $6p^4$

8) 0.097 63 in standard form is:

a 9.763×10^{-2} **b** 97.63×10^{-3}
c 9.763×10^2 **d** 97.63×10^3

9) If $a = 1.2 \times 10^7$ and $b = 3.2 \times 10^6$ then $\sqrt{a^2 + b^2}$ is equal to:

a 1.24×10^6 **b** 1.24×10^7
c 2.09×10^6 **d** 2.09×10^7

10) If $\sqrt{3} = 1.732$ correct to three decimal places then $\sqrt{27}$, correct to two decimal places, is equal to:

a 2.99   **b** 5.19   **c** 5.20   **d** 8.98

11) The cube root of 27×10^{-6} is:

a 3×10^{-3} **b** 5.20×10^{-3}
c 3×10^{-2} **d** 5.20×10^{-2}

12) $(5 \times 7^3) \times (3 \times 7^5)$ is equal to:

a 8×7^8 **b** 15×7^8 **c** 8×7^{15}
d 15×7^{15}

13) $\sqrt{16a^4b^{16}}$ is equal to:

a $8a^2b^4$ **b** $4a^2b^4$ **c** $4a^2b^8$ **d** $8a^2b^8$

14) If $\log y = -2$ then y is equal to:

a -100 **b** -0.01 **c** 0.01   **d** 0.1

15) The largest of the numbers $\dfrac{1}{7}$, 1.3×10^{-1}, 0.12 and 1.4×10^{-2} is:

a 1.3×10^{-1} **b** 0.12   **c** $\dfrac{1}{7}$
d 1.4×10^{-2}

16) The value of $32^{-3/5}$ is:

a -19.2 **b** $\dfrac{1}{8}$ **c** 8   **d** -19.2

17) In standard form $\dfrac{5 \times 10^{-6}}{0.001}$ is equal to:

a 5×10^{-9} **b** 5×10^{-4} **c** 5×10^{-3}
d 5×10^{-2}

18) The value of $\left(\dfrac{1}{9}\right)^{-1/2}$ is:

a -9 **b** $-\dfrac{1}{3}$ **c** $-\dfrac{1}{18}$ **d** 3

19) $8 \times 10^{-3} \times 1.25 \times 10^4$ is equal to:

a 1   **b** 2   **c** 10   **d** 100

20) The value of $10^{1.324}$ is:

a 0.1324   **b** 2.11   **c** 13.24   **d** 21.1

21) The value of $10^{0.301} \times 10^{0.477}$ is:

a 0.778   **b** 6   **c** 7.78   **d** 60

22) The value of $(10^{1.431})^{1/3}$ is:

a 0.477   **b** 3   **c** 4.77   **d** 30

CHAPTER 20 SUMMARY**

Points to remember

(i) The product of two or more powers of the same base is the power of that base that has an index or exponent, equal to the sum of the indices or exponents of the given powers.
e.g. $y^5 \times y^4 = y^{5+4} = y^9$.

(ii) The quotient of two powers of the same base is the power of that base that has an index or exponent, equal to the difference of the indices or exponents of the given powers.
e.g. $a^7 \div a^3 = a^{7-3} = a^4$.

(iii) $(a^x)^y = a^{xy}$. E.g. $(3^2)^4 = 3^{2\times4} = 3^8$.

(iv) For any number x, except 0, $x^0 = 1$.

(v) $x^{-n} = 1/x^n$.

(vi) The characteristic of the logarithm of a number greater than 1 is positive, and its numerical value is 1 less than the number of digits to the left of the decimal point.

(vii) The characteristic of a number between 0 and 1 is negative, and its numerical value is 1 more than the number of zeros between the decimal point and the first digit other than 0.
E.g. the characteristic of 0.079 is -2.

(viii) To multiply numbers using logs: find the log of each number and add them. Find the antilogarithm of this sum.

(ix) To divide numbers using logs: find the log of each number, and subtract the log of the divisor from the log of the dividend. Find the antilogarithm of the result.

(x) To raise a number to a given exponent (index): multiply the log of the number by the exponent and find the antilog of the result.

(xi) To find the root of a number: divide the log of the number by the index of the root, and find the antilog of this quotient.

How to Answer Examination Questions 2

1) Solve the following equations for x:

(a) $4(x-3)^2 = 9(x-3)$

(b) $5^{2x} = 125^{x-4}$

(c) $\log x^3 - \log 1000 = 1$ correct to 4 s.f.

(a) $4(x-3)^2 = 9(x-3)$

$$4(x-3)^2 - 9(x-3) = 0$$

$$(x-3)(4(x-3)-9) = 0$$

$$(x-3)(4x-12-9) = 0$$

$$(x-3)(4x-21) = 0$$

Either $x-3 = 0$, so $x = 3$

or $\qquad 4x - 21 = 0$

$$4x = 21$$

$$x = \tfrac{21}{4} = 5\tfrac{1}{4}$$

(b) $5^{2x} = 125^{x-4}$

First notice that $125 = 5^3$

$125^{x-4} = (5^3)^{x-4} = 5^{3(x-4)}$

So $5^{2x} = 5^{3(x-4)}$

Since both sides of the equation contain powers of 5, the two indices must be equal.

$\therefore \qquad 2x = 3(x-4)$

$$2x = 3x - 12$$

$$2x - 3x = -12$$

$$-x = -12$$

$$x = 12$$

(c) $\log x^3 - \log 1000 = 1$

Since $\log 1000 = 3$ and $\log x^3 = 3\log x$,

$3\log x - 3 = 1$

$3\log x = 1 + 3$

$3\log x = 4$

$\log x = \tfrac{4}{3}$

$\log x = 1.3333$

Using a calculator,

$x = 21.54$ correct to 4 s.f.

2) (a) Factorise each of the following:

(i) $9 - (x-y)^2$

(ii) $(2a^2 - ab - b) + 2a + b$

(b) Solve for x:

$$\frac{x}{2} - 4 = \frac{x}{6} + 8$$

(c) Solve the simultaneous equations for p and q:

$$p + q = 5$$

$$pq = 6$$

(a) (i) $9 - (x-y)^2$

$$= (3 + x - y)(3 - (x - y))$$

$$= (3 + x - y)(3 - x + y)$$

(ii) $(2a^2 - ab - b^2) + 2a + b$

$$= (2a + b)(a - b) + (2a + b)$$

$$= (2a + b)(a - b + 1)$$

(b) $\dfrac{x}{2} - 4 = \dfrac{x}{6} + 8$

The L.C.M. of the denominators is 6, so multiplying each term by 6, gives

$$3x - 24 = x + 48$$

$$3x - x = 48 + 24$$

$$2x = 72$$

$$x = \frac{72}{2}$$

$$x = 36$$

(c) $p + q = 5$ $\qquad\qquad$ [1]

$pq = 6$ $\qquad\qquad$ [2]

From equation [2],

$$p = \frac{6}{q}$$

Substituting for p in [1],

$$\frac{6}{q} + q = 5$$

Multiplying each term by q gives,

$$6 + q^2 = 5q$$

$$q^2 - 5q + 6 = 0$$

which is a quadratic equation.

Factorising the L.H.S.,

$$(q - 3)(q - 2) = 0$$

Either $q - 3 = 0$, giving $q = 3$

or $q - 2 = 0$, giving $q = 2$

When $q = 3$, $p = \dfrac{6}{3} = 2$

When $q = 2$, $p = \dfrac{6}{2} = 3$

3) (a) Make into a single fraction, in its lowest terms,

$$\frac{2x}{x^2 - 1} - \frac{x}{x + 1}$$

(b) Solve the following inequation:

$$4x - 3 \leqslant 6x + 7$$

(c) Make R the subject of the formula $I = \dfrac{PRT}{100}$ and find its value when $I = 105$, $P = 3000$ and $T = 5$.

(d) (i) Find the value of $16^{\frac{1}{4}} \times 64^{\frac{1}{3}} \times 25^{\frac{1}{2}}$

    (ii) Find the value of: $(\frac{1}{4})^0$, $27^{-\frac{1}{3}}$ and $(10\,000)^{\frac{1}{2}}$.

(a) The L.C.M. of the denominators is $(x^2 - 1)$ because $x^2 - 1 = (x + 1)(x - 1)$.

$$\therefore \quad \frac{2x}{x^2 - 1} - \frac{x}{(x + 1)} = \frac{2x}{(x - 1)(x + 1)}$$

$$- \frac{x}{(x + 1)}$$

$$= \frac{2x - x(x - 1)}{(x - 1)(x + 1)}$$

$$= \frac{2x - x^2 + x}{(x - 1)(x + 1)}$$

$$= \frac{3x - x^2}{(x - 1)(x + 1)}$$

(b)

$$4x - 3 \leqslant 6x + 7$$

$$4x - 6x \leqslant 7 + 3$$

$$-2x \leqslant 10$$

$$-x \leqslant 5$$

$$x \geqslant -5$$

(c) $I = \dfrac{PRT}{100}$

Multiplying both sides by 100,

$$100I = PRT$$

Dividing both sides by PT

$$\frac{100I}{PT} = R \quad \text{or} \quad R = \frac{100I}{PT}$$

When $I = 105$, $P = 3000$ and $T = 5$,

$$R = \frac{100 \times 105}{3000 \times 5} = 0.7$$

(d) (i) $16^{\frac{1}{4}} \times 64^{\frac{1}{3}} \times 25^{\frac{1}{2}} = (2^4)^{\frac{1}{4}} \times (4^3)^{\frac{1}{3}} \times (5^2)^{\frac{1}{2}}$

$$= 2 \times 4 \times 5 = 40$$

(ii) $(\frac{1}{4})^0 = 1$

$$27^{-\frac{1}{3}} = \left(\frac{1}{27}\right)^{\frac{1}{3}} = \left(\frac{1}{3^3}\right)^{\frac{1}{3}}$$

$$= \frac{1}{3^{3 \times \frac{1}{3}}} = \frac{1}{3^1} = \frac{1}{3}$$

$$(10\,000)^{\frac{1}{2}} = (10^4)^{\frac{1}{2}} = 10^{4 \times \frac{1}{2}}$$

$$= 10^2 \quad = 100$$

EXAMINATION TYPE QUESTIONS 2

This exercise is divided into two sections A and B. The questions in Section A are intended to be done very quickly, but those in Section B should take about 20 minutes each to complete. All the questions are of the type found in CXC examination papers.

Section A

1) (a) Factorise completely:
    (i) $3x^2 + 12$
    (ii) $3x^2 + 12x$
    (iii) $3x^2 + 12x + 9$

    (b) Solve the following equations for x:
    (i) $x^2 + 4x = 0$
    (ii) $x^2 - 4 = 0$

2) (a) Given the formula $y = mx + c$, obtain a formula for x in terms of y, m and c.

    (b) The real numbers x and y are related by

$$y = \tfrac{2}{3}(x - 18)$$

    (i) Find the value of y when $x = 6$.
    (ii) Find the value of x when $y = 6$.

3) (a) Solve the simultaneous equations

$$3x + 2y = 4$$
$$x + 2y = 0$$

(b) Write down the expansion of $(x+y)^2$.
Given that $x^2 + y^2 = 37$ and $x + y = 7$, find the value of xy.

4) (a) If x is a real number, find correct to 2 decimal places, the positive value of x which satisfies the equation $2x^2 - x - 4 = 0$.

(b) State the two possible values of x for which $x^2 - 5x - 6 = 0$.

5) (a) Calculate the value of $(y + y^{-\frac{1}{2}}) \div y^{\frac{1}{3}}$ when $y = 64$.

(b) Find the value of p which satisfies the equation:

$$2^{p+3} = 4^p.$$

6) (a) (i) Find the quotient of
$2x^3 - 9x^2 + 10x - 3 \div (x - 3)$

(ii) Factorise completely
$2x^3 - 9x^2 + 10x - 3$

(b) Factorise $(3x + 4)^2 - 9$.

(c) Factorise completely $27 - 3x^2$.

(d) Factorise $x^2 - 7x + 10$.

7) (a) Factorise $12 - x - 6x^2$.

(b) Hence solve the equation
$12 - x - 6x^2 = 0$.

8) (a) Make x the subject of the formula

$$y = \frac{p + x}{1 - px}$$

(b) Simplify $\dfrac{4x + 6}{4x^2 - 9}$

(c) Without using tables or a calculator, evaluate:
(i) $\left(\frac{8}{27}\right)^{-\frac{1}{3}}$ (ii) $\sqrt[3]{0.027}$ (iii) $16^{\frac{3}{4}}$

9) (a) Make into a single fraction:

$$\frac{5}{x^2 - 1} - \frac{2}{(x - 1)^2}$$

(b) Solve the equation
$\frac{1}{5}(x - 2) - \frac{1}{7}(x + 3) = 1$

(c) Solve the simultaneous equations

$$3p - 4q = 11$$
$$5p + 9q = -13.$$

10) Solve the simultaneous equations:

$$xy = 42$$
$$x - 4y = 17.$$

Section B

11) In a factory, x metal hooks and $(x + 4)$ plastic hooks are produced every minute.

(a) Write down expressions for the times, in seconds, to produce one metal hook and one plastic hook respectively.

(b) If a metal hook takes $1\frac{1}{4}$ seconds longer to produce than a plastic hook, form an equation in x and solve it.

(c) Calculate the total number of hooks produced altogether in 8 minutes.

12) In the following questions, $a = \dfrac{1}{x - 1}$ and $b = \dfrac{1}{2x + 3}$.

(a) Find the value of $3a + b$ when $x = 4$.

(b) Use a calculator to find $\sqrt[3]{5a}$ when $x = 7.911$.

(c) Express $a - 2b$ in terms of x as a single fraction in its simplest terms.

(d) When $a + b = \frac{1}{6}$, prove that x satisfies the equation
$2x^2 - 17x - 15 = 0$.

(e) Solve this equation for x, giving the roots correct to one decimal place.

13) When the price of admission to a discotheque rises by \$5, the takings rise from \$3750 to \$4000 but the attendance drops by 50. Given that the new price of admission is \$$x$, obtain expressions in terms of x for:
(a) the old price of admission,
(b) the old attendance,
(c) the new attendance.
Hence obtain an equation in x and solve it.

14) Given that $\dfrac{6 - 3y}{2y + 1} = x$
(a) Find y in terms of x.
(b) Express $2x + 3$ as a single fraction in terms of y.
(c) Calculate the values of y for which $x = 2y$.

15) (a) If $\log_{10} 2 = 0.301\,03$ and $\log_{10} 3 = 0.477\,12$ find, correct to 5 decimal places:
(i) $\log_{10} 6$ (ii) $\log_{10} 9$ (iii) $\log_{10} 1.5$
(b) Without using tables or a calculator, find the value of x if $2^x = 4^{x-4}$.

Chapter 21 **Mensuration**

THE METRIC SYSTEM OF LENGTH

The metric system is essentially a decimal system. The standard unit of length is the metre but for some purposes the metre is too large a unit and it is therefore split up into smaller units as follows:

$$1 \text{ metre (m)} = 10 \text{ decimetres (dm)}$$
$$= 100 \text{ centimetres (cm)}$$
$$= 1000 \text{ millimetres (mm)}$$

When dealing with large distances the metre is too small a unit and large distances are measured in kilometres.

$$1 \text{ kilometre (km)} = 1000 \text{ metres}$$

Since the metric system is essentially a decimal system we can easily convert from one unit to another by simply moving the decimal point the required number of places.

EXAMPLE 1

Convert 3.792 m into centimetres.

$$1 \text{ m} = 100 \text{ cm}$$
$$3.792 \text{ m} = 100 \times 3.792 \text{ cm}$$
$$= 379.2 \text{ cm}$$

EXAMPLE 2

Convert 98 375 mm into metres.

$$1000 \text{ mm} = 1 \text{ m}$$
$$1 \text{ mm} = \frac{1}{1000} \text{ m}$$
$$98\,375 \text{ mm} = \frac{98\,375}{1000} \text{ m} = 98.375 \text{ m}$$

Sometimes you may have difficulty in deciding whether to multiply or divide when converting from one unit to another. If you remember that when converting to a smaller unit you multiply and when converting to a larger unit you divide, this difficulty will disappear.

THE METRIC SYSTEM OF MASS

The standard unit of mass is the kilogram, which is suitable for most purposes connected with weights and measures. However for some purposes the kilogram is too large a unit and the gram is then used. For very small masses the milligram is used.

$$1 \text{ kilogram (kg)} = 1000 \text{ gram (g)}$$
$$1 \text{ gram} = 1000 \text{ milligrams (mg)}$$

For very large masses the tonne is used, such that

$$1 \text{ tonne} = 1000 \text{ kg}$$

EXAMPLE 3

Convert 5397 mg into grams

$$1000 \text{ mg} = 1 \text{ g}$$
$$1 \text{ mg} = \frac{1}{1000} \text{ g}$$
$$5397 \text{ mg} = \frac{5397}{1000} \text{ g} = 5.397 \text{ g}$$

EXAMPLE 4

Convert 2.56 kg into grams.

$$1 \text{ kg} = 1000 \text{ g}$$
$$2.56 \text{ kg} = 1000 \times 2.56 \text{ g} = 2560 \text{ g}$$

EXAMPLE 5

Convert 5.4 tonnes into kilograms.

$$5.4 \text{ tonnes} = 5.4 \times 1000 \text{ kg}$$
$$= 5400 \text{ kg}$$

Exercise 103 – *All type A*

1) Convert to metres:

(a) 5.63 km   (b) 0.68 km
(c) 17.698 km   (d) 592 cm
(e) 68 cm   (f) 6895 mm
(g) 73 mm   (h) 4597 cm
(i) 798 mm   (j) 5 mm

2) Convert to kilometres:

(a) 9753 m   (b) 259 m
(c) 58 m   (d) 2985 cm
(e) 790 685 mm

3) Convert to centimetres:

(a) 4.68 m   (b) 0.782 m
(c) 5.16 km   (d) 3897 mm
(e) 88 mm

4) Convert to millimetres:

(a) 1.234 m   (b) 0.58 km
(c) 25.8 cm   (d) 389 cm
(e) 0.052 m

5) Convert to kilograms:

(a) 530 g   (b) 35 000 g
(c) 2473 mg   (d) 597 600 mg

6) Convert into grams:

(a) 56 000 mg   (b) 96 mg
(c) 8.63 kg   (d) 0.081 kg
(e) 584 mg

7) Convert 18 200 kg into tonnes.

8) Convert 19.4 tonnes into kilograms.

SI UNITS

The Systeme International d'Unites (the international system of units) is essentially a metric system. It is based upon six fundamental units which are:

     Length – the metre (abbreviation m)
     Mass – the kilogram (kg)
     Time – the second (s)
     Electric current – the ampère (A)
     Luminous intensity – the candela (cd)
     Temperature – the Kelvin (K)

For many applications some of the above units are too small or too large and hence multiples and sub-multiples are often needed. These multiples and sub-multiples are given special names.

Where possible, multiples and sub-multiples should be of the form 10^{3n} where n is an integer. Thus 5000 metres should be written as 5 kilometres and not as 50 hectometres. Double prefixes are not permitted in the SI system. For example 1000 km cannot be written as 1 kkm but only as 1 Mm. Again, 0.000 006 km cannot be written as 6 μkm but only as 6 mm.

EXAMPLE 6

(1) Express 203 560 kg as the highest multiple possible.

$$203\,560\,\text{kg} = 203\,560 \times 10^3 \text{ gram}$$
$$= 203.560 \times 10^3 \times 10^3 \text{ gram}$$
$$= 203.560 \times 10^6 \text{ gram}$$
$$= 203.560\,\text{Mg}$$

(It is usually better to use 203.560 Mg rather than 0.203 560 Gg.) Note that 203.560 Mg is also written 203.560 tonnes.

(2) A measurement is taken as 0.000 000 082 m. Express this measurement as a standard sub-multiple of a metre.

MULTIPLICATION FACTOR	PREFIX	SYMBOL
1 000 000 000 000	10^{12} tera	T
1 000 000 000	10^{9} giga	G
1 000 000	10^{6} mega	M
1 000	10^{3} kilo	k
100	10^{2} hecto	h
10	10^{1} deca	da
0.1	10^{-1} deci	d
0.01	10^{-2} centi	c
0.001	10^{-3} milli	m
0.000 001	10^{-6} micro	μ
0.000 000 001	10^{-9} nano	n
0.000 000 000 001	10^{-12} pico	p
0.000 000 000 000 001	10^{-15} femto	f
0.000 000 000 000 000 001	10^{-18} atto	a

$$0.000\,000\,082\,\text{m} = \frac{82}{1\,000\,000\,000}\,\text{m}$$
$$= \frac{82}{10^9}\,\text{m} = 82 \times 10^{-9}\,\text{m}$$
$$= 82\,\text{nm}$$

(It is better to use 82 nm rather than 0.082 pm).

Exercise 104 – *All type A*

Express each of the following as a standard multiple or sub-multiple.

1) 8000 m   **6)** 0.000 001 3 m

2) 15 000 kg   **7)** 0.028 kg

3) 3800 km   **8)** 0.000 36 km

4) 1 891 000 kg   **9)** 0.000 064 kg

5) 0.007 m   **10)** 0.003 6 A

Express each of the following in the form $A \times 10^n$ where A is a number between 1 and 10 and n is an integer.

11) 53 km

12) 18 kg

13) 3.563 Mg

14) 18.76 Gg

15) 70 mm

16) 78 mg

17) 358 pm

18) 18.2 μm

19) 270.6 Tm

20) 253 μg

UNITS OF AREA

The area of a plane figure is measured by seeing how many square units it contains. 1 square metre (abbreviation: m^2) is the area contained in a square whose side is 1 metre. Similarly 1 square centimetre (abbreviation: cm^2) is the area contained in a square having a side of 1 cm.

EXAMPLE 7

(1) Figure 21.1 shows the cross-section of a girder. Find its area in square centimetres. The section may be split up into two rectangles and a parallelogram as shown

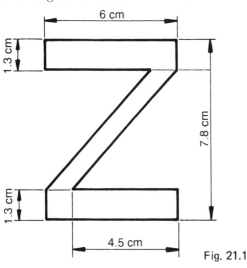

Fig. 21.1

$$\text{Area of rectangle} = 6 \times 1.3$$
$$= 7.8\,\text{cm}^2$$
$$\text{Area of parallelogram} = 1.5 \times 5.2$$
$$= 7.8\,\text{cm}^2$$
$$\text{Area of section} = 7.8 + 7.8 + 7.8$$
$$= 23.4\,\text{cm}^2$$

(2) A quadrilateral has the dimensions shown in Fig. 21.2. Find its area.

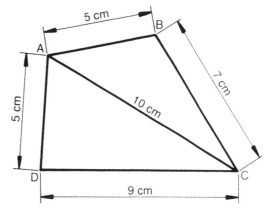

Fig. 21.2

The quadrilateral is made up of the triangles ABC and ACD.

To find the area of $\triangle ABC$,

$$s = \frac{5 + 7 + 10}{2} = 11$$

Area of $\triangle ABC$

$$= \sqrt{s(s-a)(s-b)(s-c)}$$
$$= \sqrt{11 \times (11-5) \times (11-7) \times (11-10)}$$
$$= \sqrt{11 \times 6 \times 4 \times 1}$$
$$= \sqrt{264} = 16.25\,\text{cm}^2$$

To find the area of $\triangle ACD$,

$$s = \frac{5 + 9 + 10}{2} = 12$$

Area of $\triangle ACD$

$$= \sqrt{s(s-a)(s-b)(s-c)}$$
$$= \sqrt{12 \times (12-5) \times (12-9) \times (12-10)}$$
$$= \sqrt{12 \times 7 \times 3 \times 2}$$
$$= \sqrt{504} = 22.45\,\text{cm}^2$$

$\therefore$ area of quadrilateral

$$= \text{area of } \triangle ABC + \text{area of } \triangle ACD$$
$$= 16.25 + 22.45 = 38.70\,\text{cm}^2$$

AREAS OF PLANE FIGURES

The following table gives the areas and perimeters of some simple geometrical shapes.

Figure	Diagram	Formulae
Rectangle		Area $= l \times b$ Perimeter $= 2l + 2b$
Parallelogram		Area $= b \times h$
Triangle		Area $= \frac{1}{2} \times b \times h$ Area $= \sqrt{s(s-a)(s-b)(s-c)}$ where $\quad s = \dfrac{a+b+c}{2}$
Trapezium		Area $= \frac{1}{2} \times h \times (a+b)$
Circle		Area $= \pi r^2$ Circumference $= 2\pi r$ ($\pi = 3.142$ or $\frac{22}{7}$)
Sector of a circle		Area $= \pi r^2 \times \dfrac{\theta}{360}$ Length of arc $= 2\pi r \times \dfrac{\theta}{360}$
Quadrilateral		Area $=$ $\frac{1}{2}AC \times BD \times \sin\theta$

(3) The cross-section of a block of metal is shown in Fig. 21.3. Find its area.

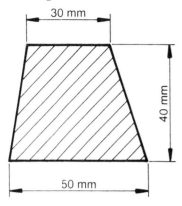

Fig. 21.3

$$\text{Area of trapezium} = \tfrac{1}{2} \times 40 \times (30 + 50)$$

$$= \tfrac{1}{2} \times 40 \times 80$$

$$= 1600 \, \text{mm}^2$$

(4) A hollow shaft has an outside diameter of 3.25 cm and an inside diameter of 2.5 cm. Calculate the cross-sectional area of the shaft (Fig. 21.4).

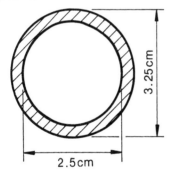

Fig. 21.4

Area of cross-section

= area of outside circle − area of inside circle

$$= \pi \times 1.625^2 - \pi \times 1.25^2$$

$$= \pi(1.625^2 - 1.25^2)$$

$$= 3.142 \times (2.641 - 1.563)$$

$$= 3.142 \times 1.078$$

$$= 3.387 \, \text{cm}^2$$

(5) Calculate:
(a) the length of the arc of a circle whose radius is 8 m and which subtends an angle of 60° at the centre, and

(b) the area of the sector so formed.

$$\text{Length of arc} = 2\pi r \times \frac{\theta°}{360°}$$

$$= 2 \times \pi \times 8 \times \frac{60°}{360°}$$

$$= 8.37 \, \text{m}$$

$$\text{Area of sector} = \pi r^2 \times \frac{\theta°}{360°}$$

$$= \pi \times 8^2 \times \frac{60°}{360°}$$

$$= 33.5 \, \text{m}^2$$

ERRORS IN MEASUREMENT

If we measure the length of a metal bar and state the measurement to be 123.42 mm to the nearest $\frac{1}{100}$ mm we mean that the true length of the bar is greater than 123.415 mm and less than 123.425 mm. If it were less than 123.415 we would state the measurement as 123.41 mm; if it were greater than 123.425 the measurement would be stated as 123.43 mm. This means that the greatest error in the measurement is 0.005 mm too large or too small. We may say, then, that the measurement is 123.42 ± 0.005 mm meaning that

greatest possible measurement

$$= 123.42 + 0.00\dot{5} = 123.425 \, \text{mm}$$

least possible measurement

$$= 123.42 - 0.005 = 123.415 \, \text{mm}$$

This does not mean that the error is bound to be as great as 0.005 mm – it may be considerably less; but it cannot possibly be any more.

CALCULATIONS INVOLVING NUMBERS OBTAINED BY MEASUREMENT

To illustrate what happens when numbers obtained by actual measurement are used in calculations, consider the following examples.

EXAMPLE 8
(1) The lengths of three bars are measured to an accuracy of $\frac{1}{10}$ mm and the lengths are found to be 24.7 mm, 35.2 mm and 61.8 mm. Find the total length of the three bars.

Greatest possible dimensions
$$24.6 + 0.05 = 24.75$$
$$35.2 + 0.05 = 35.25$$
$$61.8 + 0.05 = 61.85$$
$$\overline{121.85}$$

Least possible dimensions
$$24.7 - 0.05 = 24.65$$
$$35.2 - 0.05 = 35.15$$
$$61.8 - 0.05 = 61.75$$
$$\overline{121.55}$$

The sum of the lengths therefore lies somewhere between 121.55 mm and 121.85 mm. If we simply add $24.7 + 35.2 + 61.8$ we get 121.7. We see that the final figure 7 is worthless and we can only quote the answer as 122 mm, correct to 3 significant figures.

(2) The dimensions of a rectangular plate were measured and found to be 2.16 m and 3.28 m correct to 3 significant figures. What is the area of the plate?

Apparent area of the plate

$$= 2.16 \times 3.28 = 7.0848 \, \text{m}^2$$

Greatest possible area

$$= 2.165 \times 3.285 = 7.112\,025 \, \text{m}^2$$

Least possible area

$$= 2.155 \times 3.275 = 7.057\,625 \, \text{m}^2$$

We see that it is not possible to state the area of the plate more accurately than $7.1 \, \text{m}^2$ correct to 2 significant figures.

Generally the answer should not contain more significant figures than the least number of significant figures given amongst the numbers used.

Exercise 105 – *All type B*

1) The area of a rectangle is $220 \, \text{mm}^2$. If its width is 25 mm find its length.

2) A sheet metal plate has a length of 147.5 mm and a width of 86.5 mm. Find its area in m^2.

3) Find the areas of the sections shown in Fig. 21.5 (to the nearest mm^2).

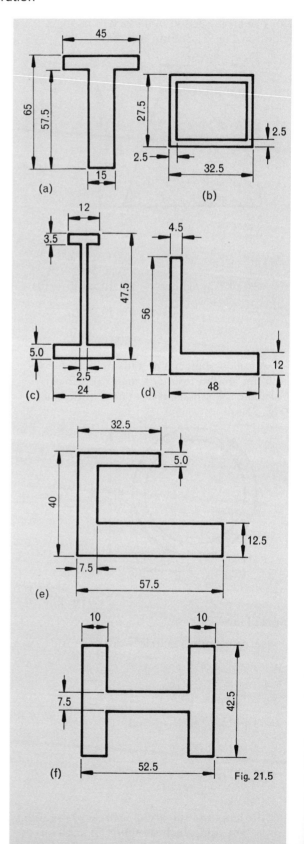

Fig. 21.5

4) Find the area of a triangle whose base is 7.5 cm and whose altitude is 5.9 cm.

5) A triangle has sides 4 cm, 7 cm and 9 cm long. What is its area?

6) A triangle has sides 37 mm, 52 mm and 63 mm long. What is its area in cm^2?

7) Find the area of the shape shown in Fig. 21.6.

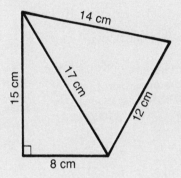

Fig. 21.6

8) Find the areas of the quadrilateral shown in Fig. 21.7.

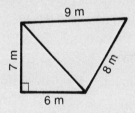

Fig. 21.7

9) What is the area of a parallelogram whose base is 7 cm long and whose vertical height is 4 cm?

10) Determine the length of the side of a square whose area is equal to that of a parallelogram with a base of 3 m and a vertical height of 1.5 m.

11) Find the area of a trapezium whose parallel sides are 75 mm and 82 mm long respectively and whose vertical height is 39 mm.

12) The parallel sides of a trapezium are 12 cm and 16 cm long. If its area is $200\,cm^2$, what is its altitude?

13) Find the areas of the shaded portions in each of the diagrams of Fig. 21.8.

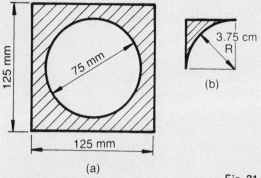

(a)

(b)

Fig. 21.8

14) Find the circumference of circles whose radii are:

(a) 3.5 mm   (b) 13.8 m   (c) 4.2 cm

15) Find the diameter of circles whose circumferences are:

(a) 34.4 mm   (b) 18.54 cm
(c) 195.2 m

16) A ring has an outside diameter of 3.85 cm and an inside diameter of 2.63 cm. Calculate its area.

17) A hollow shaft has a cross-sectional area of $8.68\,cm^2$. If its inside diameter is 0.75 cm, calculate its outside diameter.

18) Find the area of the plate shown in Fig. 21.9.

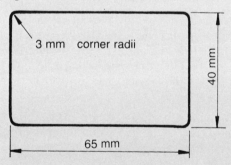

Fig. 21.9

19) How many revolutions will a wheel make in travelling 2 km if its diameter is 700 mm?

20) If r is the radius and θ is the angle subtended at the centre by an arc find the length of arc when:

(a) $r = 2$ cm, $\theta = 30°$
†(b) $r = 3.4$ cm, $\theta = 38°40'$.

21) If l is the length of an arc, r is the radius and θ is the angle subtended by the arc, find θ when:

(a) $l = 9.4\,\text{cm}$, $r = 4.5\,\text{cm}$
(b) $l = 14\,\text{mm}$, $r = 79\,\text{mm}$

22) If an arc 7 cm long subtends an angle of 45° at the centre what is the radius of the circle?

23) Find the areas of the following sectors of circles:

(a) radius 3 m, angle of sector 60°.
†(b) radius 2.7 cm, angle of sector 79°45′.
†(c) radius 7.8 cm, angle of sector 143°42′.

24) Calculate the area of the cross-section shown in Fig. 21.10.

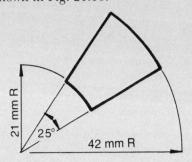

Fig. 21.10

25) The following measurements are correct to the nearest 0.01 mm. Write down the greatest and least possible measurements.

(a) 32.15 mm   (b) 3.58 mm
(b) 5.00 mm   (d) 14.20 mm

26) 5 lengths of wood are measured correct to the nearest 0.1 cm. Their lengths were: 19.5, 43.2, 16.1, 8.2 and 67.9 cm. Write down the total length of the 5 pieces of wood stating the answer to an appropriate degree of accuracy.

27) The side of a square plate is measured as 25 mm correct to the nearest millimetre. Find the greatest and least possible areas of the plate.

28) The sides of a rectangle are measured as 214 mm and 371 mm correct to the nearest millimetre. Find the area of the rectangle stating the answer to an appropriate number of significant figures.

UNITS OF VOLUME

The volume of a solid figure is measured by seeing how many cubic units it contains. A cubic metre is the volume inside a cube which has a side of 1 metre. Similarly a cubic centimetre is the volume inside a cube which has a side of 1 centimetre. The standard

abbreviations for units of volume are:

cubic metre m^3

cubic centimetre cm^3

cubic millimetre mm^3

EXAMPLE 9

(1) How many cubic centimetres are contained in 1 cubic metre?

$$1\,\text{m} = 10^2\,\text{cm}$$

$$1\,\text{m}^3 = (10^2\,\text{cm})^3 = 10^6\,\text{cm}^3$$

$$= 1\,000\,000\,\text{cm}^3$$

(2) A tank contains 84 000 000 cubic millimetres of liquid. How many cubic metres does it contain?

$$1\,\text{mm} = 10^{-3}\,\text{m}$$

$$1\,\text{mm}^3 = (10^{-3}\,\text{m})^3 = 10^{-9}\,\text{m}^3$$

$$84\,000\,000\,\text{mm}^3 = 84\,000\,000 \times 10^{-9}\,\text{m}^3$$

$$= 8.4 \times 10^7 \times 10^{-9}\,\text{m}^3$$

$$= 8.4 \times 10^{-2}\,\text{m}^3$$

$$= \frac{8.4}{10^2} = 0.084\,\text{m}^3$$

UNITS OF CAPACITY

The capacity of a container is usually measured in litres (ℓ), such that

$$1\,\text{litre} = 1000\,\text{cm}^3$$

EXAMPLE 10

A tank contains 30 000 litres of liquid. How many cubic metres does it contain?

$$30\,000\,\text{litres} = 30\,000 \times 1\,000\,\text{cm}^3$$

$$= 3 \times 10^7\,\text{cm}^3$$

$$1\,\text{cm} = 10^{-2}\,\text{cm}$$

$$1\,\text{cm}^3 = (10^{-2}\,\text{m})^3 = 10^{-6}\,\text{m}^3$$

$$\therefore \quad 3 \times 10^7\,\text{cm}^3 = 3 \times 10^7 \times 10^{-6}\,\text{m}^3$$

$$= 3 \times 10 = 30\,\text{m}^3$$

Exercise 106 – *All type B*

Convert the following volumes into the units stated:

1) $5\,\text{m}^3$ into cm^3.

2) $0.08 \, \text{m}^3$ into mm^3.

3) $18 \, \text{m}^3$ into mm^3.

4) $830\,000 \, \text{cm}^3$ into m^3.

5) $850\,000 \, \text{mm}^3$ into m^3.

6) $78\,500 \, \text{cm}^3$ into m^3.

7) A tank contains 5000 litres of petrol. How many cubic metres of petrol does it contain?

8) A small vessel contains $2500 \, \text{mm}^3$ of oil. How many litres does it contain?

9) A tank holds, when full, $827 \, \text{m}^3$ of water. How many litres does it hold?

10) A container holds $8275 \, \text{cm}^3$ when full. How many litres does it hold?

EXAMPLE 11

A steel section has the cross-section shown in Fig. 21.11. If it is $9 \, \text{m}$ long calculate its volume and total surface area.

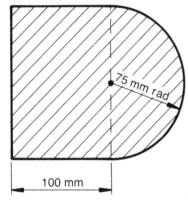

Fig. 21.11

To find the volume:

Area of cross-section

$$= \tfrac{1}{2} \times \pi \times 75^2 + 100 \times 150$$

$$= 23\,831 \, \text{mm}^2$$

$$= \frac{23\,831}{(1000)^2} = 0.023\,831 \, \text{m}^2$$

Volume of solid

$$= 0.023\,831 \times 9$$

$$= 0.214\,5 \, \text{m}^3$$

To find the surface area:

Perimeter of cross-section

$$= \pi \times 75 + 2 \times 100 + 150$$

$$= 585.5 \, \text{mm}$$

$$= \frac{585.5}{1000} = 0.585\,5 \, \text{m}$$

Lateral surface area

$$= 0.585\,5 \times 9 = 5.270 \, \text{m}^2$$

Surface area of ends

$$= 2 \times 0.024 = 0.048 \, \text{m}^2$$

Total surface area

$$= 5.270 + 0.048$$

$$= 5.318 \, \text{m}^2$$

THE TETRAHEDRON

A tetrahedron is a pyramid which has a triangular base (Fig. 21.12). Hence it possesses four triangular faces.

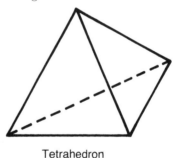

Tetrahedron   Fig. 21.12

EXAMPLE 12

A tetrahedron has a base with sides $8 \, \text{cm}$, $7 \, \text{cm}$ and $9 \, \text{cm}$ long respectively. Its altitude is $5 \, \text{cm}$. Calculate its volume.

Using the formula

$$A = \sqrt{s(s-a)(s-b)(s-c)}$$

to find the area of the base, we have

$$a = 8 \, \text{cm}, \quad b = 7 \, \text{cm} \quad \text{and} \quad c = 9 \, \text{cm}$$

$$s = \frac{a+b+c}{2} = \frac{8+7+9}{2} = 12 \, \text{cm}$$

$$A = \sqrt{12 \times (12-8) \times (12-7) \times (12-9)}$$

$$= \sqrt{12 \times 4 \times 5 \times 3} = 26.83 \, \text{cm}^2$$

The volume of the tetrahedron is:

$$V = \tfrac{1}{3}AH = \tfrac{1}{3} \times 26.83 \times 5 = 44.72 \, \text{cm}^3$$

VOLUMES AND SURFACE AREAS

The following table gives volumes and surface areas of some simple solids.

Figure	Volume	Surface Area
Any solid having a uniform cross-section	Cross-sectional area × length of solid	Curved surface + ends, i.e. (perimeter of cross-section × length of solid) + (total area of ends)
Cylinder	$\pi r^2 h$	$2\pi r(h + r)$
Cone	$\frac{1}{3}\pi r^2 h$ (h is the vertical height)	$\pi r l$ (l is the slant height)
Frustum of a cone	$\frac{1}{3}\pi h(R^2 + Rr + r^2)$ Curved surface area (h is the vertical height)	$= \pi l(R + r)$ Total surface area $= \pi l(R + r) + \pi R^2 + \pi r^2$ (l is the slant height)
Sphere	$\frac{4}{3}\pi r^3$	$4\pi r^2$
Pyramid	$\frac{1}{3}Ah$	Sum of the areas of the triangles forming the sides plus the area of the base

area of base = A

Exercise 107 – *Questions 1–7 type B,*
remainder C

1) A steel ingot whose volume is $2\,m^3$ is rolled into a plate $15\,mm$ thick and $1.75\,m$ wide. Calculate the length of the plate in m.

2) A block of lead $1.5\,m \times 1\,m \times 0.75\,m$ is hammered out to make a square sheet $10\,mm$ thick. What are the dimensions of the square?

3) Calculate the volume of a metal tube whose bore is $50\,mm$ and whose thickness is $8\,mm$ if it is $6\,m$ long.

4) The volume of a small cylinder is $180\,cm^3$. If the radius of the cross-section is $25\,mm$ find its height.

5) A steel ingot is in the shape of a cylinder $1.5\,m$ diameter and $3.5\,m$ long. How many metres of square bar of $50\,mm$ side can be rolled from it?

6) A cone has a diameter of $70\,mm$ and a height of $100\,mm$. What is its volume?

7) Calculate the diameter of a cylinder whose height is the same as its diameter and whose volume is $220\,cm^3$.

8) An ingot whose volume is $2\,m^3$ is to be made into ball bearings whose diameters are $12\,mm$. Assuming 20% of the metal in the ingot is wasted, how many ball bearings will be produced from the ingot (to the nearest thousand)?

9) The washer shown in Fig. 21.13 has a square of side l cut out of it. If its thickness is t find an expression for the volume, V, of the washer. Hence find the volume of a washer when $D = 6\,cm$, $t = 0.2\,cm$ and $l = 4\,cm$.

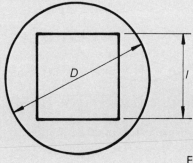

Fig. 21.13

10) A water tank with vertical sides has a horizontal base in the shape of a rectangle with semi-circular ends as illustrated in Fig. 21.14. The total inside length of the tank is $7\,m$, its width $4\,m$ and its height $2\,m$.

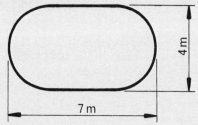

Fig. 21.14

Calculate:
(a) the surface area of the vertical walls of the tank in m^2,
(b) the area of the base in m^2,
(c) the number of litres of water in the tank when the depth of water is $1.56\,m$.

11) A tank $1\,m$ long and $60\,cm$ wide, internally, contains water to a certain depth. An empty tank $40\,cm$ long, $30\,cm$ wide and $25\,cm$ deep, internally, is filled with water from the first tank. If the depth of water in the first tank is now $35\,cm$, what was the depth at first?

12) Figure 21.15 represents a bird cage in the form of a cylinder surmounted by a cone. The diameter of the cylinder is $35\,cm$ and its height is $25\,cm$. The total volume of the bird cage is $31\,178\,cm^3$. Calculate:
(a) the total height of the bird cage,
(b) the surface area of the cover for the cage (except the base).

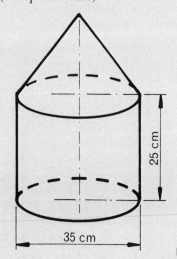

Fig. 21.15

13) A solid iron cone is 12 cm in height and the radius of the circular base is 4 cm. It is placed on its base in a cylindrical vessel of internal radius 5 cm. Water is poured into the cylinder until the depth of water is 16 cm. The cone is then removed. Find by how much the water level falls.

14) A rolling mill produces steel sheet 1.2 m wide and 3 mm thick. If the length of sheeting produced per hour is 2 km and the steel has a density of 7.75 grams per cubic centimetre, find in kilograms the mass of steel produced per hour.

15) A measuring jar is in the form of a vertical cylinder which is graduated so that the volume of liquid in the jar can be read directly in cubic centimetres. The internal radius of the jar is 2.4 cm. Find to the nearest millimetre the distance between the two marks labelled 200 cm³ and 300 cm³. When the jar is partly full of water, a steel sphere of radius 1.8 cm is lowered into the jar and completely immersed in the water without causing the water to overflow. Find in millimetres the distance the water level rises in the jar.

16) A cylindrical tank, open at the top, is made of metal 75 mm thick. The internal radius of the tank is 1.2 m and the internal depth of the tank is 1.9 m. The tank stands with its plane base horizontal. Calculate:
(a) the number of litres of liquid in the tank when it is $\frac{4}{5}$ full,
(b) the area of the external curved surface of the tank,
(c) the area of the plane surface of metal at the base of the tank.

17) A cylindrical can whose height is equal to its diameter has a capacity of 9 litres. Find the height of the can. If the diameter is halved and the height altered so that the can still has a capacity of 9 litres, find the ratio of the original curved surface area to the final curved surface area.

18) A cheese is made in the form of a cylinder of radius 21 cm and height 45 cm. The slice shown in Fig. 21.16 (where AB is 13.5 cm and lies along the axis of the cylinder and where ∠XAY = 30°) has a mass of 1.3 kg. Calculate the mass of the whole cheese in kg.

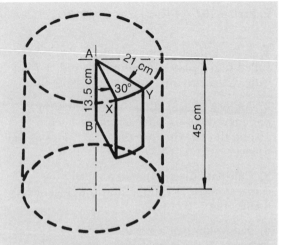

Fig. 21.16

19) The diagram (Fig. 21.17) shows a section through a chemical flask consisting of a spherical body of internal radius r cm with a cylindrical neck of internal radius $\frac{1}{6}r$ cm and a length r cm. Show that when filled to the brim the flask will hold approximately $\frac{77r^3}{18}$ cm³. (The volumes enclosed by the sphere and cylinder overlap – between the dotted lines – but this fact may be ignored.)

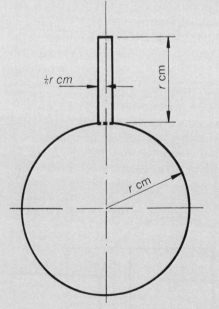

Fig. 21.17

20) A cylindrical can is filled with water. It has a capacity of 300 cm³ and is 6.5 cm high. Calculate its radius. The water is now poured into another container which has a square horizontal base of side 8 cm and vertical sides. Calculate the depth of water in this container. Calculate also the area of this container which is in contact with the water.

21) A pyramid has a rectangular base 8 cm long and 5 cm wide. Its altitude is 7 cm. Calculate the volume of the pyramid.

22) A piece of steel is in the form of a tetrahedron whose base is a right-angled triangle. The sides forming the right angle are 5 cm and 6 cm long, respectively. If the height of the tetrahedron is 7 cm, calculate its volume. If the tetrahedron is melted down, calculate the length of bar of diameter 20 mm that can be made from it, assuming no waste.

NETS

Suppose that we have to make a cube out of thin sheet metal. We need a pattern giving us the shape of the metal needed to make the cube. As shown in Fig. 21.18, the pattern consists of six squares. The shape which can be folded to make a cube is called the *net* of the cube. (Engineers call the net the *development*.)

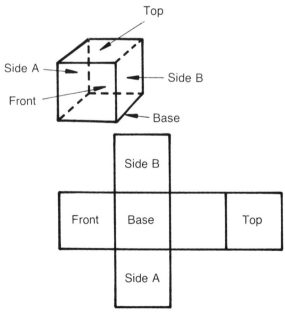

Fig. 21.18

It is possible for there to be more than one net for a solid object. For instance, the cube in

Fig. 21.18 can be made from the net shown in Fig. 21.19.

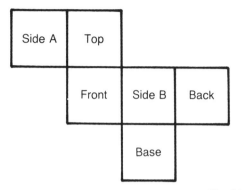

Fig. 21.19

EXAMPLE 13

Sketch the net of the triangular prism shown in Fig. 21.20. As can be seen from Fig. 21.21, the net consists of three rectangles representing the base and the two sides and two triangles representing the two ends.

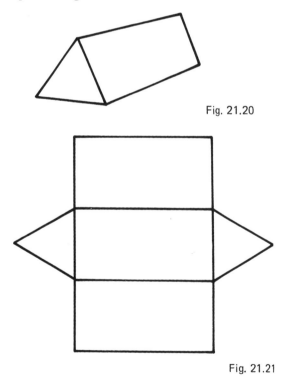

Fig. 21.20

Fig. 21.21

NETS OF CURVED SURFACES

The net for a cylinder without a top and bottom is shown in Fig. 21.22. The length of the net is equal to the circumference of the cylinder.

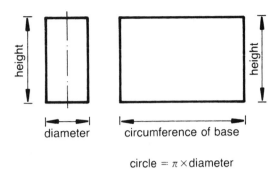

circle = $\pi \times$ diameter

Fig. 21.22

EXAMPLE 14

Draw the net for the cone shown in Fig. 21.23.

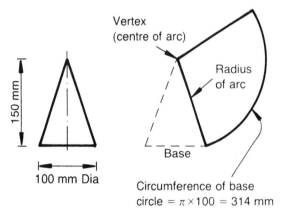

circle = $\pi \times 100$ = 314 mm

Fig. 21.23

The net is in the form of a sector of a circle. Note that the arms of the sector are equal to the slant height of the cone and that the length of the arc is equal to the circumference of the base circle of the cone.

Exercise 108 – *All type B*

Sketch the nets for the following solids:

1) A cuboid 8 cm long, 3 cm wide and 4 cm high.

2) A triangular prism whose ends are right-angled triangles of base 3 cm and height 4 cm and whose length is 6 cm.

3) A pyramid with a square base of side 5 cm and a height (altitude) of 8 cm.

4) A cube with an edge of 4 cm.

5) A cylinder with a height of 5 cm and a diameter of 3 cm.

6) A cone with a vertical height of 8 cm and a base diameter of 7 cm.

7) The diagrams (Fig. 21.24) show the nets of various solids. Name each solid.

(a)

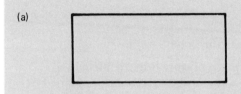

(b)

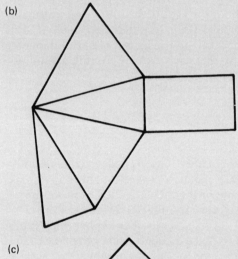

(c)

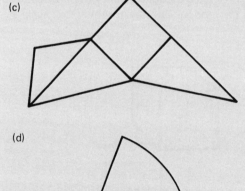

(d)

Fig. 21.24

TIME

The units of time are the second, minute, hour and day.

60 seconds (s)   = 1 minute (min)

60 minutes (min) = 1 hour (h)

24 hours (h)   = 1 day (d)

The symbols in brackets give the standard abbreviations for each of the units of time.

THE CLOCK

A standard clock face is marked off in hours from 1 to 12 (Fig. 21.25). However, since 1 day equals 24 hours we need a method of finding out if a stated time is between 12 midnight and 12 noon, or between 12 noon and 12 midnight. Traditionally times between 12 midnight and 12 noon were called a.m. (e.g. 9.15 a.m.) and times between 12 noon and 12 midnight were called p.m. (e.g. 9.30 p.m.). A second way is to use a 24 hour clock, see Fig. 21.26. Times between 12 midnight and 12 noon are given the times 00 hours to 12 hours and times between 12 noon and 12 midnight take the times 12 hours to 24 hours. Thus 3.30 a.m. is written 03 30 and 3.30 p.m. is written as 15 30.

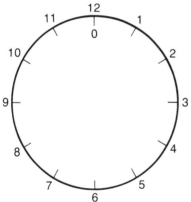

Fig. 21.25

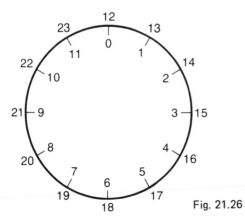

Fig. 21.26

EXAMPLE 15

Find the length of time, in hours, between:

(1) 2.15 a.m. and 7.30 p.m.,
(2) 04 25 and 17 12.

(1) The easiest way is to use the 24 hour clock so that 7.30 p.m. becomes 19 30. The problem then becomes

$$19.30 - 2.15 = 17 \text{ hours and } 15 \text{ minutes}$$
$$= 17\tfrac{1}{4} \text{ hours}$$

(2) The problem is

$$17\ 12 - 04\ 25 = 12 \text{ hours and } 47 \text{ minutes}$$

Exercise 109 – *All type A*

Find the length of time in hours and minutes between the following times:

1) 0.36 a.m. and 9.27 a.m.

2) 2.15 p.m. and 8.38 p.m.

3) 1.36 a.m. and 12.00 noon.

4) 3.35 a.m. and 7.29 a.m.

5) 11.34 p.m. and 7.19 a.m.

6) 5.36 p.m. and 11.16 a.m.

7) 6.28 a.m. and 1.15 p.m.

8) 00 49 hours and 12 36 hours.

9) 17 45 hours and 01 16 hours.

10) 02 42 hours and 14 48 hours.

SELF-TEST 21

1) How many square metres are there in $30\,000\,\text{cm}^2$?

a $3\,\text{m}^2$ b $30\,\text{m}^2$ c $300\,\text{m}^2$
d $3000\,\text{m}^2$

2) How many cm^2 are there in $5\,\text{m}^2$?

a $50\,\text{cm}^2$ b $500\,\text{cm}^2$ c $5000\,\text{cm}^2$
d $50\,000\,\text{cm}^2$

3) How many cm^2 are there in $2000\,\text{mm}^2$?

a $0.2\,\text{cm}^2$ b $2\,\text{cm}^2$ c $20\,\text{cm}^2$
d $200\,\text{cm}^2$

4) How many m^2 are there in $600\,000\,\text{mm}^2$?

a $6000\,\text{m}^2$ b $600\,\text{m}^2$ c $6\,\text{m}^2$
d $0.6\,\text{m}^2$

5) How many mm^2 are there in $0.3\,m^2$?

a $30\,mm^2$ **b** $300\,mm^2$
c $30\,000\,mm^2$ **d** $300\,000\,mm^2$

6) How many m^2 are there in $20\,km^2$?

a $2000\,m^2$ **b** $20\,000\,m^2$
c $200\,000\,m^2$ **d** $20\,000\,000\,m^2$

7) A rectangular plot of ground is $4\,km$ long and $8\,km$ wide. Its area is therefore:

a $0.32\,Mm^2$ **b** $32\,km^2$ **c** $32\,mm^2$
d $32\,000\,m^2$

8) A triangle has an altitude of $100\,mm$ and a base of $50\,mm$. Its area is:

a $250\,m^2$ **b** $50\,cm^2$ **c** $2500\,mm^2$
d $5000\,mm^2$

9) A parallelogram has a base $10\,cm$ long and a vertical height of $5\,cm$. Its area is:

a $25\,cm^2$ **b** $50\,cm^2$ **c** $2500\,mm^2$
d $5000\,mm^2$

10) A trapezium has parallel sides whose lengths are $18\,cm$ and $22\,cm$. The distance between the parallel sides is $10\,cm$. Hence the area of the trapezium is:

a $200\,cm^2$ **b** $400\,cm^2$ **c** $495\,cm^2$
d $3960\,cm^2$

11) The area of a circle of radius r is given by the formula:

a $2\pi r^2$ **b** $2\pi r$ **c** πr^2 **d** πr

12) The circumference of a circle of radius r and diameter d is given by the formula:

a πr^2 **b** $2\pi r$ **c** πr **d** πd

13) A ring has an outside diameter of $8\,cm$ and an inside diameter of $4\,cm$. Its area is therefore:

a $\pi(8^2-4^2)\,cm^2$ **b** $8\pi-4\pi\,cm^2$
c $\pi(8+4)(8-4)\,cm^2$ **d** $\pi(4^2-2^2)\,cm^2$

14) A wheel has a diameter of $70\,cm$. The number of revolutions it will make in travelling $55\,km$ is:

a $50\,000$ **b** $25\,000$ **c** 5000 **d** 2500

15) An arc of a circle is $22\,cm$ and the radius of the circle is $140\,cm$. The angle subtended by the arc is:

a $9°$ **b** $18°$ **c** $90°$ **d** $180°$

16) A sector of a circle subtends an angle of $120°$. If the radius of the circle is $42\,cm$ then the area of the sector is:

a $44\,cm^2$ **b** $88\,cm^2$ **c** $132\,cm^2$
d $1848\,cm^2$

17) A tank has a volume of $8\,m^3$. Hence the volume of the tank is also:

a $800\,cm^3$ **b** $8000\,cm^3$ **c** $80\,000\,cm^3$
d $8\,000\,000\,cm^3$

18) A solid has a volume of $200\,000\,mm^3$. Hence the volume of the solid is also:

a $20\,cm^3$ **b** $200\,cm^3$ **c** $2000\,cm^3$
d $20\,000\,cm^3$

19) The capacity of a container is 50 litres. Hence its capacity is also:

a $50\,000\,cm^3$ **b** $5000\,cm^3$ **c** $0.5\,m^3$
d $0.05\,m^3$

20) The area of the curved surface of a cylinder of radius r and height h is:

a $2\pi rh$ **b** $2\pi r^2h$ **c** πrh **d** πr^2h

21) The volume of a cylinder of radius r and height h is:

a $2\pi rh$ **b** $2\pi r^2h$ **c** πrh **d** πr^2h

22) The total surface area of a closed cylinder whose radius is r and whose height is h is:

a $\pi rh + 2\pi r^2$ **b** $\pi r(h+2r)$
c $2\pi rh + \pi r^2$ **d** $2\pi r(h+r)$

23) A small cylindrical container has a diameter of $280\,mm$ and a height of $50\,mm$. It will hold:

a $3.08\,\ell$ **b** $6.16\,\ell$ **c** $30.8\,\ell$ **d** $61.6\,\ell$

CHAPTER 21 SUMMARY

Points to remember

(i)	Quantity	Base unit	Symbol	(ii)	Prefixes	Number of base units	Symbol
	Length	metre	m				
	Mass	gram	g		mega	1 000 000	M
	Capacity	litre	ℓ		kilo	1000	k
	Temperature	degree Celsius	°C		hecto	100	h
	Area	metre squared	m^2		deca	10	da
	Volume	metre cubed	m^3				
					deci	0.1	d
					centi	0.01	c
					milli	0.001	m

Chapter 22 **Orthographic Projection**

The diagram (Fig. 22.1) is very easy to understand but it shows only three sides of the object out of a possible six. To overcome this disadvantage a system of drawing known as orthographic projection has been developed. In this system a full view of each side of the object is shown in turn. Usually, three of these views are sufficient to show the details of the object. There are two versions of orthographic projection. They are first-angle and third-angle projection. Only first-angle projection will be dealt with in this book.

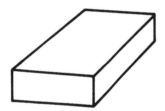

Fig. 22.1

FIRST-ANGLE PROJECTION

Fig. 22.2 shows a pictorial drawing of a wooden block. To represent this object in *first-angle projection* we look at the front of the block in the direction indicated by the arrow **B**. The view we see is called the elevation (Fig. 22.3).

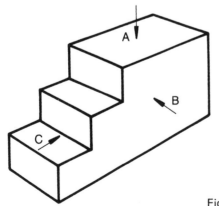

Fig. 22.2

Next we look at the object in the direction of the arrow **A**. This view is called the plan view and as shown in Fig. 22.3 the plan view is drawn directly underneath the elevation. Finally, to complete the projection, we look at the object in the direction of the arrow **C**. The view we see is called the end view or the end elevation. This is drawn in line with the elevation and the plan view as shown by the faint projection lines.

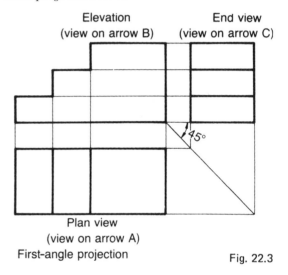

Elevation (view on arrow B)   End view (view on arrow C)

45°

Plan view (view on arrow A)

First-angle projection

Fig. 22.3

PROJECTION LINES

These are used when drawing in orthographic projection to make sure that the views are correctly positioned. In Fig. 22.3 the faint projections are shown and these allow the plan, elevation and end view to line up properly.

HIDDEN DETAILS

These are shown by dotted lines. In drawing the object shown in Fig. 22.4 we cannot see the face **AB** when looking at the top of the object. This face is represented by the dotted lines in the plan view (Fig. 22.5).

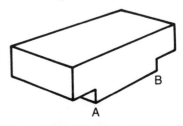

Fig. 22.4

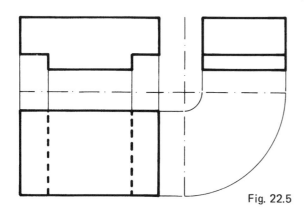

Fig. 22.5

TWO-VIEW DRAWINGS

Sometimes two views are enough to represent an object fully. The pipe and flange shown in Fig. 22.6 may be fully represented by an elevation and plan as shown in Fig. 22.7.

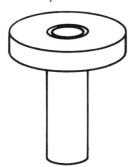

Fig. 22.6

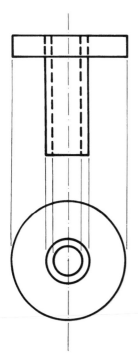

Fig. 22.7

Exercise 110 – *All type B*

1) Make three-view freehand drawings of each of the objects shown in Figs. 22.8, 22.9, 22.10, 22.11 and 22.12.

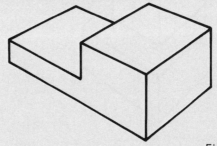

Fig. 22.8

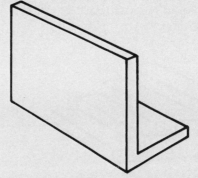

Fig. 22.9

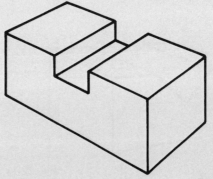

Fig. 22.10

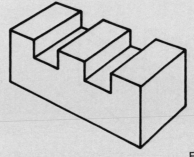

Fig. 22.11

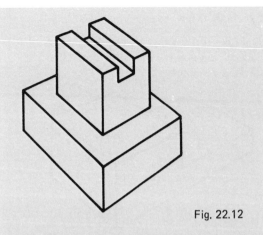

Fig. 22.12

2) Make three-view sketches of each of the articles shown in Figs. 22.13, 22.14, 22.15, 22.16, 22.17 and 22.18.

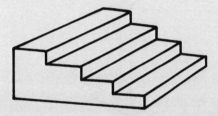

Fig. 22.13

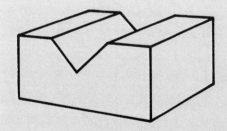

Fig. 22.14

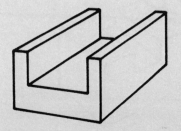

Fig. 22.15

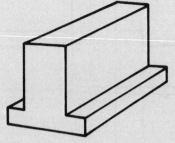

Fig. 22.16

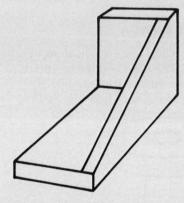

Fig. 22.17

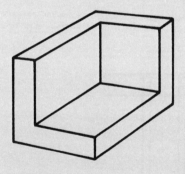

Fig. 22.18

3) Make three-view sketches of each of the articles shown in Figs. 22.19, 22.20, 22.21, 22.22, 22.23 and 22.24.

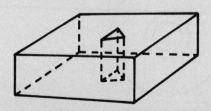

Fig. 22.19

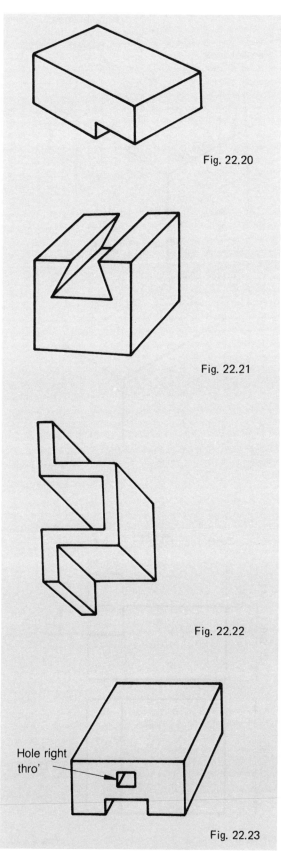

Fig. 22.20

Fig. 22.21

Fig. 22.22

Hole right thro'

Fig. 22.23

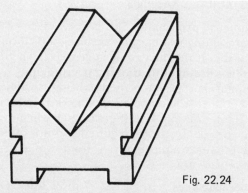

Fig. 22.24

4) Sketch two-view drawings of each of the objects shown in Figs. 22.25 and 22.26.

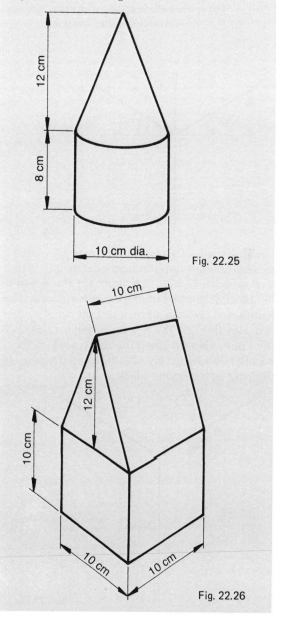

12 cm

8 cm

10 cm dia.

Fig. 22.25

10 cm

12 cm

10 cm

10 cm

10 cm

Fig. 22.26

PICTORIAL DRAWING

Isometric projection. This is a way of representing an object by means of a pictorial drawing. It resembles a perspective sketch but it is often drawn using drawing instruments. Isometric projection is used only to provide a pictorial view of an object. It is never used for a working drawing. It is of great value when sketches of objects are required and it is often used to make a pictorial view from two- and three-view drawings.

Isometric axes.   In Fig. 22.27 three lines OX, OY and OZ have been drawn which make equal angles with each other. One of the lines is made vertical. These three lines are called the *isometric axes* and they form the basis for isometric drawing.

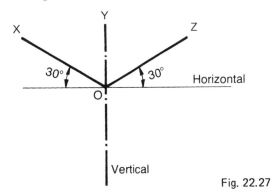

Fig. 22.27

Vertical edges of an object will be represented by vertical lines in the isometric drawing. When a rectangular object is being drawn the depth of the block is marked off on the vertical axis. The length and breadth are marked off on the other two axes (Fig. 22.28). For rectangular objects all the lines either lie along the three axes or are parallel with them. Fig. 22.29 shows two ways of drawing a rectangular block.

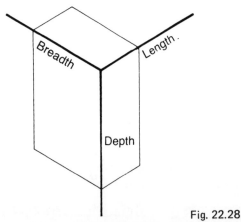

Fig. 22.28

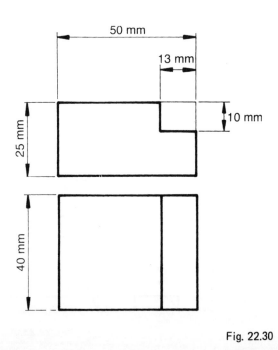

Fig. 22.29

Fig. 22.30

Fig. 22.30 shows a three-view drawing of a metal block. To make an isometric drawing of this, first draw the rectangular shape without the step. The step can then be drawn by the aid of the faint lines shown in Fig. 22.31. The last step in making the drawing is to line in the heavy lines and it is these which make the drawing clear.

Fig. 22.33

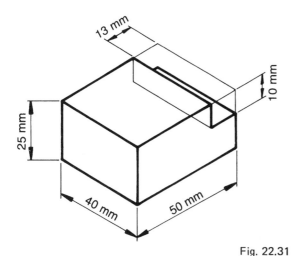

Fig. 22.31

Fig. 22.34 shows the method of making an isometric drawing of a cylinder. The rectangular shape shown by the faint lines is needed to obtain the circular shape of the ends of the cylinder.

Isometric representation of circles. Circles and parts of circles are usually drawn free-hand in isometric drawings. Most people find this difficult. Fig. 22.32 will give the clue necessary to overcome this difficulty. Fig. 22.32(a) shows a true circle inscribed in a square. At the points marked × the circumference of the circle and the sides of the square appear to touch. This must be the same in the pictorial view shown in Fig. 22.32(b). Fig. 22.33 shows a cube with a circle inscribed on each of its faces. Here again the circumference of the circles and the edges of the cube touch at the centre-lines of each of the faces.

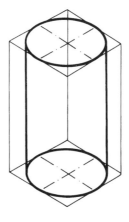

Fig. 22.34

Fig. 22.35 shows a two-view drawing of a metal block. The faint lines on the isometric drawing show how the circular shape is obtained.

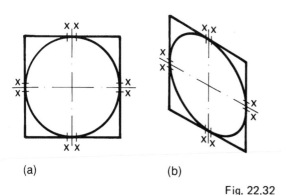

(a)　　　(b)

Fig. 22.32

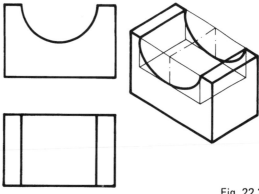

Fig. 22.35

Oblique projection. This is another way of representing objects pictorially. Fig. 22.36 shows the axes used. The axis AO is horizontal whilst axis BO is vertical. The axis OC is drawn at 45° to the axis AO produced. Measurements made along AO and BO (or parallel to them) are made full size. Those made along OC (or parallel to it) are generally made half size. Fig. 22.37 shows a 26 mm cube drawn in oblique projection. The lengths OA and OB are both made 26 mm but the length OC is made 13 mm.

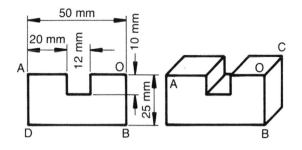

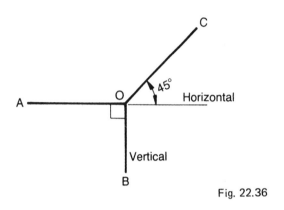

Fig. 22.36

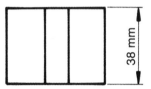

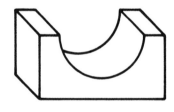

Fig. 22.38

When the circles have to be drawn it is often easier to make an oblique drawing than an isometric drawing. Figs. 22.39 and 22.40 are examples. It will be noticed that the circles are drawn as true circles at the front of the drawings.

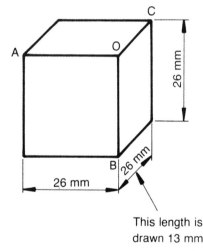

This length is drawn 13 mm

Fig. 22.37

Fig. 22.39

Fig. 22.38 shows a three-view drawing of a metal block. To make the oblique projection first draw the three axes OA, OB and OC. *The front face of the block in the oblique drawing is the same as the front elevation.* Thus in the diagram the front face of the block is drawn using the axes OA and OB. The length OC is made 19 mm (that is half of 38 mm). The diagram shows how the rest of the block is completed.

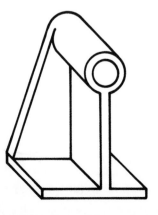

Fig. 22.40

Exercise 111 – *All type B*

1) Make isometric drawings of the objects shown in Figs. 22.41, 22.42 and 22.43.

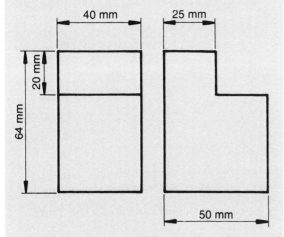

Fig. 22.41

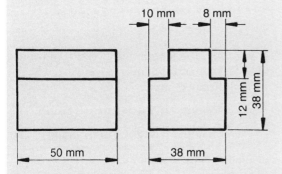

Fig. 22.42

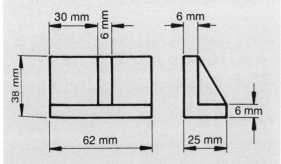

Fig. 22.43

2) Make oblique drawings of the objects shown in Figs. 22.41, 22.42 and 22.43.

3) Make pictorial drawings of the articles shown in Figs. 22.44, 22.45 and 22.46 (a) in isometric projection; (b) in oblique projection.

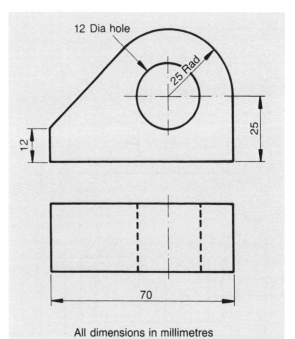

All dimensions in millimetres

Fig. 22.44

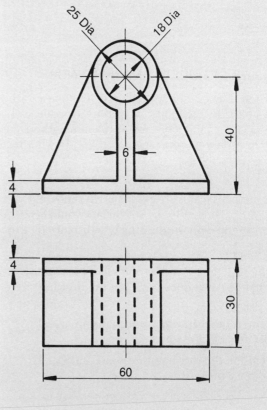

All dimensions in millimetres

Fig. 22.45

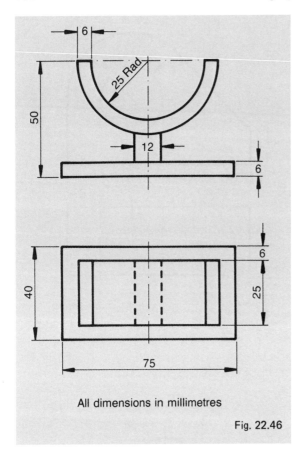

All dimensions in millimetres

Fig. 22.46

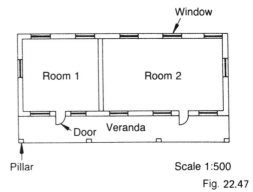

Scale 1:500

Fig. 22.47

PLANS OF HOUSES AND BUILDINGS

When drawings of large objects like houses are to be made, they must be drawn to a scale such as $1 \text{ cm} = 5 \text{ m}$. This means that a length of 20 m would be represented on the drawing by a length of $\dfrac{20}{5} = 4 \text{ cm}$.

Sometimes scales are expressed as ratios, e.g. $1 : 500$. Thus a distance of 500 m would be represented on the drawing by a distance of 1 m.

EXAMPLE 1

The scale of a drawing of a school is $250 : 1$. What distance does 3 cm on the drawing represent?

1 cm on the drawing represents an actual distance of 250 cm

3 cm on the drawing represents an actual distance of

$$3 \times 250 \text{ cm} = 750 \text{ cm} = 7.50 \text{ m}$$

Fig. 22.47 represents part of a bungalow. Note the way in which the doors and windows have been represented.

EXAMPLE 2

In Fig. 22.47, find:

(1) the length of the veranda,

(2) the area of each of the two rooms shown.

(1) By scaling, the veranda is 6.7 cm long.

1 cm on the drawing represents

$$500 \text{ cm} = 5 \text{ m}$$

$\therefore$ 6.7 cm on the drawing represents

$$6.7 \times 5 \text{ m} = 33.5 \text{ m}$$

(2) By scaling, the length and breadth of room 1 is 2.4 cm and 2.2 cm respectively. The actual distances are:

$$\text{length} = 2.4 \times 5 \text{ m} = 12 \text{ m}$$
$$\text{breadth} = 2.2 \times 5 \text{ m} = 11 \text{ m}$$

Hence the area of room 1 is

$$\text{area} = 12 \text{ m} \times 11 \text{ m} = 132 \text{ m}^2$$

By scaling the dimensions of room 2 are $3.8 \text{ cm} \times 2.2 \text{ cm}$. The actual dimensions are:

$$\text{length} = 3.8 \times 5 \text{ m} = 19 \text{ m}$$
$$\text{breadth} = 2.2 \times 5 \text{ m} = 11 \text{ m}$$
$$\text{area} = 19 \text{ m} \times 11 \text{ m} = 209 \text{ m}^2$$

Exercise 112 – *All type B*

1) Fig. 22.48 shows the plan of a garage. What is its inside area?

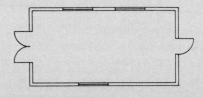

Scale 1:500

Fig. 22.48

2) Fig. 22.49 shows the plan of part of a school.

(a) How many doors are shown?

(b) How many windows are there in the three rooms?

(c) How many windows are there in the outside wall of the corridor?

(d) Calculate the areas of each of the three rooms.

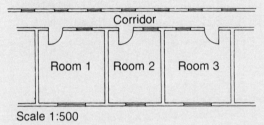

Scale 1:500

Fig. 22.49

3) Fig. 22.50 is a plan of two laboratories and their associated store room.

(a) What is the length of the veranda?

(b) What are the inside dimensions of the store room?

(c) What is the area of Lab. 1?

(d) What is the area of Lab. 2?

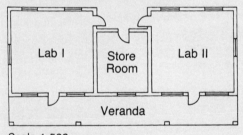

Scale 1:500

Fig. 22.50

4) Fig. 22.51 shows the plan view of a bungalow. Copy and complete the following table.

Name of room	Length (m)	Breadth (m)	Area (m²)
Lounge			
Dining room			
Bedroom 1			
Bedroom 2			
W.C.			
Bathroom			

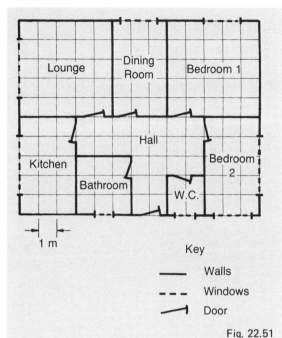

1 m

Key

——— Walls

- - - Windows

⌐| Door

Fig. 22.51

5) In Fig. 22.51, what is the area of the hall?

6) Fig. 22.52 represents the plan of the main footings for a house (shown shaded). The footings are 2 m deep. How many cubic metres of soil have to be excavated for the footings?

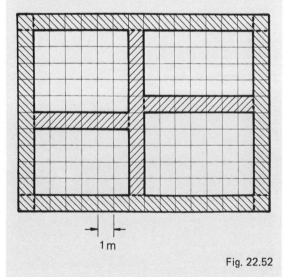

1 m

Fig. 22.52

CHAPTER 22 SUMMARY

Points to remember

(i)   A plane is a flat surface on which a line will lie in any position.

(ii) Orthographic projection is based on mutually perpendicular projection planes, and projectors which are perpendicular to these projection planes.

(iii) Projection planes are plane surfaces onto which a point or object in space is projected.

(iv) A *plan* or *top view* (*horizontal projection*) is a view in which the lines of sight of an observer are vertical.

(v)   An *elevation view* is a view in which the line of sight of the observer is level or horizontal.

(vi) In all elevation views the horizontal projection plane always appears as an edge.

Chapter 23 Graphs

In newspapers, business reports and government publications use is made of pictorial illustrations to present and compare quantities of the same kind. These diagrams help the reader to understand what deductions can be drawn from the quantities represented in the diagrams. The most common form of diagram is the *graph*.

AXES OF REFERENCE

To plot a graph we take two lines at right angles to each other (Fig. 23.1). These lines are called the axes of reference. Their intersection, the point O, is called the origin. Note that the origin is sometimes denoted by the capital letter O (short for *origin*) and sometimes by a zero, 0 (which is a short way of showing that the value at that point is zero on both axes).

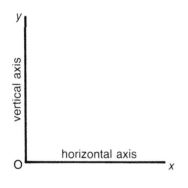

Fig. 23.1

SCALES

The number of units represented by a unit length along an axis is called the *scale*. For instance 1 cm could represent 2 units. The scales need not be the same on both axes.

The most useful scales are 1 cm to 1, 2, 5 and 10 units. Some multiples of these are also satisfactory. For instance, 1 cm to 20, 50 and 100 units.

COORDINATES

Coordinates are used to mark the points of a graph. In Fig. 23.2 values of x are to be plotted against values of y. The point P has been plotted so that $x = 8$ and $y = 10$. The values of 8 and 10 are said to be the rectangular coordinates of the point P. We then say that P is the point $(8, 10)$.

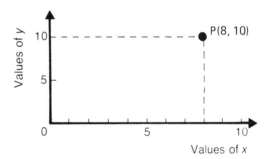

Fig. 23.2

DRAWING A GRAPH

Every graph shows a relation between two sets of numbers. The table below gives corresponding values of x and y.

x	0	2	4	6	8
y	0	4	16	36	64

To plot the graph we first draw the two axes of reference. Values of x are always plotted along the horizontal axis and values of y along the vertical axis. We next choose suitable scales. In Fig. 23.3 we have chosen 1 cm = 2 units along the horizontal axis and 1 cm = 10 units along the vertical axis. On plotting the graph we see that it is a smooth curve which passes through all the plotted points.

When a graph is either a straight line or a smooth curve we can use the graph to deduce corresponding values of x and y between those given in the table.

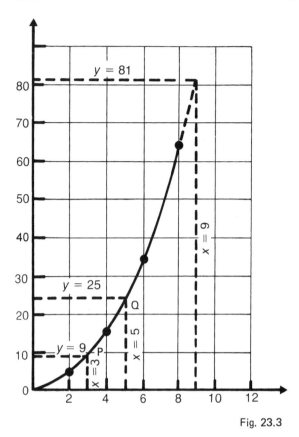

Fig. 23.3

To find the value of y corresponding to $x = 3$, find 3 on the horizontal axis and draw a vertical line to meet the graph at point P (Fig. 23.3). From P draw a horizontal line to meet the vertical axis and read off the value which is 9. Thus when $x = 3$, $y = 9$.

To find the value of x corresponding to $y = 25$ find 25 on the vertical axis and draw a horizontal line to meet the graph at point Q. From Q draw a vertical line to meet the horizontal axis and read off this value which is 5. Thus when $y = 25$, $x = 5$.

Using a curve in this way to find values which are not given in the table is called *interpolation*. If we extend the curve so that it follows the general trend we can estimate values of x and y which lie *just beyond* the range of the given values. Thus in Fig. 23.3 by extending the curve we can find the probable value of y when $x = 9$. This is found to be 81. Finding a probable value in this way is called *extrapolation*.

An extrapolated value can usually be relied upon, but in certain cases it may contain a substantial amount of error. Extrapolated values must therefore be used with care.

It must be clearly understood that interpolation can only be used if the graph is a smooth curve or a straight line. It is no use applying interpolation in the graph of the next example.

EXAMPLE 1

The table below gives the temperature at 12.00 noon on seven successive days. Plot a graph to illustrate this information.

Day June	1	2	3	4	5	6	7
Temp (°C)	20	24	20	22	26	19	20.5

As before we draw two axes at right angles to each other, indicating the day on the horizontal axis. Since the temperatures range from 19°C to 26°C we can make 18°C (say) our starting point on the vertical axis. This will allow us to use a larger scale on that axis, which makes for greater accuracy in plotting the graph.

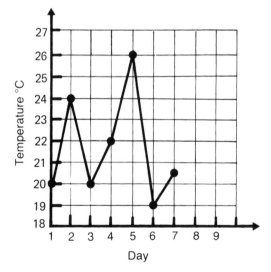

Fig. 23.4

On plotting the points (Fig. 23.4) we see that it is impossible to join the points by means of a smooth curve. The best we can do is to join the points by means of a series of straight lines. The rise and fall of temperatures do not follow any mathematical law and the graph shows this by means of the erratic line obtained. However the graph does present in pictorial form the variations in temperature and at a glance we can see that the 1st, 3rd and 6th June were cooler days whilst the 2nd and 5th were warm days.

Exercise 113 — *All type A*

1) The table below gives particulars of the amount of steel delivered to a factory during successive weeks. Plot a graph to show this with the week number on the horizontal axis.

Week number	1	2	3
Amount delivered (kg)	25 000	65 000	80 000

Week number	4	5
Amount delivered (kg)	30 000	50 000

2) The table below gives corresponding values of x and y. Plot a graph and from it estimate the value of y when $x = 1.5$ and the value of x when $y = 30$.

x	0	1	2	3	4	5
y	3	5	11	21	35	63

3) The areas of circles for various diameters is shown in the table below. Plot a graph with diameter on the horizontal axis and from it estimate the area of a circle whose diameter is 18 cm.

Diameter (cm)	5	10	15	20	25
Area (cm^2)	19.6	78.5	176.7	314.2	490.9

4) The values in the table below are corresponding values of two quantities i and v.

v	15	25	35	50	70
i	1.1	2.0	2.5	3.2	3.9

Plot a graph with i horizontal and find v when $i = 3.0$.

5) An electric train starts from A and travels to its next stop 6 km from A. The following readings were taken of the time since leaving A (in minutes) and the distance from A (in km).

Time	$\frac{1}{2}$	1	$1\frac{1}{2}$	2	$2\frac{1}{2}$	3
Distance	0.10	0.34	0.8	1.46	2.46	3.50

Time	$3\frac{1}{2}$	4	$4\frac{1}{2}$	5	$5\frac{1}{2}$	6
Distance	4.34	5.0	5.44	5.74	5.92	6

Draw a graph of these values taking time horizontally. From the graph estimate the time taken to travel 2 km from A.

GRAPHS OF SIMPLE EQUATIONS

Consider the equation:
$$y = 2x + 5$$
We can give x any value we please and so calculate a corresponding value of y. Thus,

when $x = 0$ $y = 2 \times 0 + 5 = 5$

when $x = 1$ $y = 2 \times 1 + 5 = 7$

when $x = 2$ $y = 2 \times 2 + 5 = 9$ and so on.

The value of y therefore depends on the value allocated to x. We therefore call y the *dependent variable*. Since we can give x any value we please, we call x the *independent variable*. It is usual to mark the values of the independent variable along the horizontal axis and this axis is frequently called the x-axis. The values of the dependent variable are then marked off along the vertical axis, which is often called the y-axis.

In plotting graphs representing equations we may have to include coordinates which are positive and negative. To represent these on a graph we make use of the number scales used in directed numbers (Fig. 23.5).

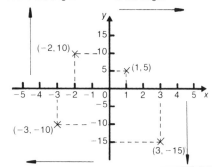

Positive values of y are measured upwards above the origin.

Positive values of x are measured to the right of the origin.

Negative values of x are measured to the left of the origin.

Negative values of y are measured downwards below the origin.

Fig. 23.5

EXAMPLE 2

(1) Draw the graph of $y = 2x - 5$ for values of x between -3 and 4.

Having decided on some values for x we calculate the corresponding values for y by substituting in the given equation. Thus,

when $x = -3$,

$$y = 2 \times (-3) - 5 = -6 - 5 = -11$$

For convenience the calculations are tabulated as shown below.

x	-3	-2	-1	0
$2x$	-6	-4	-2	0
-5	-5	-5	-5	-5
$y = 2x - 5$	-11	-9	-7	-5

x	1	2	3	4
$2x$	2	4	6	8
-5	-5	-5	-5	-5
$y = 2x - 5$	-3	-1	1	3

A graph may now be plotted using these values of x and y (Fig. 23.6). The graph is a straight line.

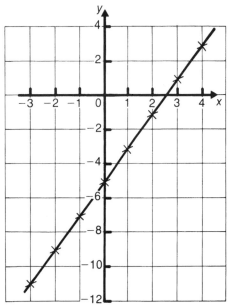

Fig. **23.6**

Equations of the type $y = 2x - 5$, where the highest powers of the variables x and y is the first are called equations of the *first degree*. All equations of this type give graphs which are straight lines and hence they are often called *linear equations*. In order to draw graphs of linear equations we need only take two points.

It is safer, however, to take three points, the third point acting as a check on the other two.

(2) By means of a graph show the relationship between x and y in the equation $y = 5x + 3$. Plot the graph between $x = -3$ and $x = 3$.

Since this is a linear equation we need only take three points.

x	-3	0	$+3$
$y = 5x + 3$	-12	3	$+18$

The graph is shown in Fig. 23.7.

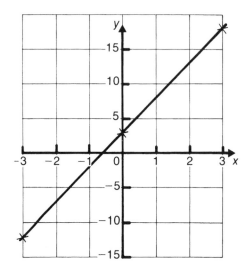

Fig. **23.7**

Exercise 114

Draw graphs of the following simple equations:

1) $y = x + 2$ taking values of x between -3 and 2.

2) $y = 2x + 5$ taking values of x between -4 and 4.

3) $y = 3x - 4$ taking values of x between -4 and 3.

4) $y = 5 - 4x$ taking values of x between -2 and 4.

GRAPHS OF QUADRATIC EQUATIONS

The expression $ax^2 + bx + c$ where a, b and c are constants is called a *quadratic expression* in x. We call $y = ax^2 + bx + c$ a *quadratic equation* and when this is plotted it always gives a smooth curve known as a *parabola*.

EXAMPLE 3

Plot the graph of $y = 3x^2 + 10x - 8$
between $x = -6$ and $x = 4$.

A table may be drawn up as follows giving
values of y for chosen values of x.

x	-6	-5	-4	-3	-2	-1
$3x^2$	108	75	48	27	12	3
$10x$	-60	-50	-40	-30	-20	-10
-8	-8	-8	-8	-8	-8	-8
y	40	17	0	-11	-16	-15

x	0	1	2	3	4
$3x^2$	0	3	12	27	48
$10x$	0	10	20	30	40
-8	-8	-8	-8	-8	-8
y	-8	5	24	49	80

The graph is shown in Fig. 23.8 and it is a
smooth curve. Equations which are non-linear
always give a graph which is a smooth curve.

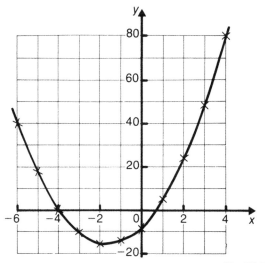

Fig. 23.8

THE AXIS OF SYMMETRY OF A PARABOLA

Fig. 23.9 shows the graph of
$y = ax^2 + bx + c$. The curve is symmetrical
about the line $x = -\dfrac{b}{2a}$ which is the axis of
symmetry. By using the axis of symmetry we can
often reduce the amount of work in drawing up
a table of values for a quadratic function.

EXAMPLE 4

Plot the graph of $y = x^2 - 4x + 3$ between
$x = -2$ and $x = 6$.

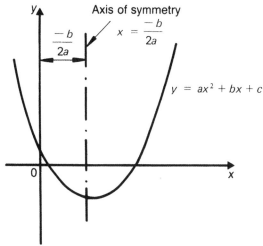

Fig. 23.9

The axis of symmetry is $x = -\dfrac{(-4)}{2} = 2$.

Hence in drawing up the table of corresponding
values of x and y we choose values of x so
that they are symmetrical about the line
$x = 2$. The graph is drawn in Fig. 23.10.

x	-2	-1	0	1	2	3	4	5	6
x^4	4	1	0	1	4				
$-4x$	8	4	0	-4	-8				
3	3	3	3	3	3				
y	15	8	3	0	-1	0	3	8	15

Note that, for example, the point $(5, 8)$ is the
image of the point $(-1, 8)$ when it is reflected
in the line $x = 2$ (see Chapter 41), and
similarly for the points $(-2, 15)$ and $(6, 15)$,
$(0, 3)$ and $(4, 3)$, $(1, 0)$ and $(3, 0)$.

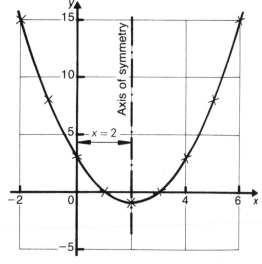

Fig. 23.10

SOLUTION OF EQUATIONS

An equation may be solved by means of a graph. The following example shows the method.

EXAMPLE 5

(1) Plot the graph of $y = 6x^2 - 7x - 5$ between $x = -2$ and $x = 3$. Hence solve the equation $6x^2 - 7x - 5 = 0$.

A table is drawn up as follows.

x	-2	-1	0	1	2	3
y	33	8	-5	-6	5	28

The curve is shown in Fig. 23.11. To solve the equation $6x^2 - 7x - 5 = 0$ we have to find the values of x when $y = 0$. That is, we have to find the values of x where the graph cuts the x-axis. These are points A and B in Fig. 23.11 and hence the solutions are:

$$x = -0.5 \quad \text{or} \quad x = 1.67$$

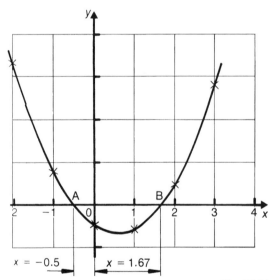

Fig. 23.11

(2) Plot the graph of $y = 2x^2 - x - 6$ and hence solve the following equations:

(a) $2x^2 - x - 6 = 0$

(b) $2x^2 - x - 4 = 0$

(c) $2x^2 - x - 9 = 0$.

Take values of x between -4 and 6.

To plot $y = 2x^2 - x - 6$ draw up table values as shown below:

x	-4	-3	-2	-1	0
y	30	15	4	-3	-6

x	1	2	3	4	5	6
y	-5	0	9	22	39	60

(a) The graph is plotted as shown in Fig. 23.12. The curve cuts the x-axis, i.e. where $y = 0$, at the points where $x = -1.5$ and $x = 2$. Hence the solutions of the equation $2x^2 - x - 6 = 0$ are

$$x = -1.5 \quad \text{or} \quad x = 2$$

(b) The equation $2x^2 - x - 4 = 0$ may be written in the form

$$2x^2 - x - 6 = -2$$

Hence if we find the values of x when $y = -2$ we shall obtain the solutions required. These are where the line $y = -2$ cuts the curve (see Fig. 23.12). The solutions are therefore

$$x = -1.18 \quad \text{or} \quad 1.69$$

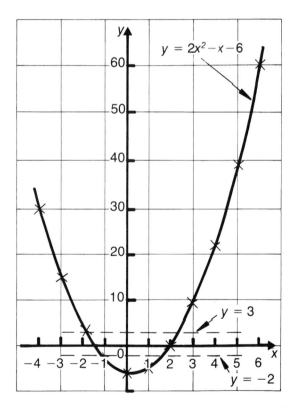

Fig. 23.12

(c) The equation $2x^2 - x - 9 = 0$ may be written in the form

$$2x^2 - x - 6 = 3$$

Hence by drawing the line $y = 3$ and finding where it cuts the curve we shall obtain the solutions. They are

$$x = -1.89 \quad \text{or} \quad 2.36$$

Exercise 115 – *Questions 1–5 type A,*
6–9 type B, remainder type C

Plot the graphs of the following equations:

1) $y = 2x^2 - 7x - 5$ between $x = -4$ and $x = 12$.

2) $y = x^2 - 4x + 4$ between $x = -3$ and $x = 3$.

3) $y = 6x^2 - 11x - 35$ between $x = -3$ and $x = 5$.

4) $y = 3x^2 - 5$ between $x = -2$ and $x = 4$.

5) $y = 1 + 3x - x^2$ between $x = -2$ and $x = 3$.

By plotting suitable graphs solve the following equations:

6) $x^2 - 7x + 12 = 0$ (take values of x between 0 and 6).

7) $x^2 + 16 = 8x$ (take values of x between 1 and 7).

8) $x^2 - 9 = 0$ (take values of x between -4 and 4).

9) $3x^2 + 5x = 60$ (take values of x between 0 and 4).

10) Plot the graph of $y = x^2 + 7x + 3$ taking values of x between -12 and 2. Hence solve the equations:

(a) $x^2 + 7x + 3 = 0$ (b) $x^2 + 7x - 2 = 0$
(c) $x^2 + 7x + 6 = 0$

11) Draw the graph of $y = 1 - 2x - 3x^2$ between $x = -4$ and $x = 4$. Hence solve the equations:

(a) $1 - 2x - 3x^2 = 0$
(b) $3 - 2x - 3x^2 = 0$
(c) $9x^2 + 6x = 6$

12) Draw the graph of $y = x^2 - 9$ taking values of x between -5 and 5. Hence solve the equations:

(a) $x^2 - 9 = 0$ (b) $x^2 - 5 = 0$
(c) $x^2 + 6 = 0$

INTERSECTING GRAPHS

Equations may also be solved graphically by using intersecting graphs. The method is shown in the following example.

EXAMPLE 6

Plot the graph of $y = 2x^2$ and use it to solve the equation $2x^2 - 3x - 2 = 0$. Take values of x between -2 and 4.

The equation $2x^2 - 3x - 2 = 0$ can be solved graphically by the method used in earlier examples, but the alternative method shown here is often preferable. The equation $2x^2 - 3x - 2 = 0$ may be written in the form $2x^2 = 3x + 2$. We now plot on the same axes and to the same scales the graphs

$$y = 2x^2 \quad \text{and} \quad y = 3x + 2$$

x	-2	-1	0	1	2	3	4
$y = 2x^2$	8	2	0	2	8	18	32
$y = 3x + 2$	-4		2				14

Note that to plot $y = 3x + 2$ we need only three points since this is a linear equation. The graphs are shown plotted in Fig. 23.13.

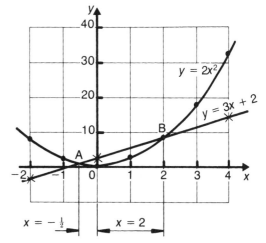

Fig. 23.13

At the points of intersection of the curve and the line (points A and B in Fig. 23.13) the y value of $2x^2$ is the same as the y value of $3x + 2$. Therefore at these points the equation $2x^2 = 3x + 2$ is satisfied. The required values of x may now be found by inspection of the graph. They are at A, where $x = -\frac{1}{2}$ and at B, where $x = 2$. The required solutions are therefore $x = -\frac{1}{2}$ or $x = 2$.

GRAPHICAL SOLUTIONS OF SIMULTANEOUS EQUATIONS

The method is shown in the following examples.

EXAMPLE 7

(1) Solve graphically

$$y - 2x = 2 \qquad [1]$$

$$3y + x = 20 \qquad [2]$$

Equation [1] may be written as:

$$y = 2 + 2x$$

Equation [2] may be written as:

$$y = \frac{20 - x}{3}$$

Drawing up the following table we can plot the two equations on the *same axes*.

x	-3	0	3
$y = 2 + 2x$	-4	2	8
$y = \dfrac{20 - x}{3}$	7.7	6.7	5.7

The solutions of the equations are the coordinates of the point where the two lines cross (that is, point P in Fig. 23.14). The coordinates of P are $x = 2$ and $y = 6$. Hence the solutions of the given equations are

$$x = 2 \quad \text{and} \quad y = 6$$

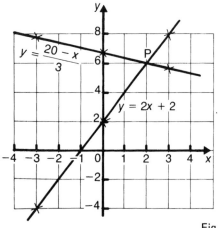

Fig. 23.14

(2) Draw the graph of $y = (3 + 2x)(3 - x)$ for values of x from $-1\frac{1}{2}$ to 3. On the same axes, and with the same scales, draw the graph of $3y = 2x + 14$. From your graphs determine the values of x for which $3(3 + 2x)(3 - x) = 2x + 14$.

To plot the graph of $y = (3 + 2x)(3 - x)$ we draw up the following table.

x	$-1\frac{1}{2}$	-1	$-\frac{1}{2}$	0
$y = (3 + 2x)(3 - x)$	0	4	7	9

x	$\frac{1}{2}$	1	$1\frac{1}{2}$	2	$2\frac{1}{2}$	3
$y = (3 + 2x)(3 - x)$	10	10	9	7	4	0

The equation $3y = 2x + 14$ may be rewritten as

$$y = \frac{2x + 14}{3}$$

To draw this graph we need only take three points since it is a linear equation

x	-1	1	3
$y = \dfrac{2x + 14}{3}$	4	$5\frac{1}{3}$	$6\frac{2}{3}$

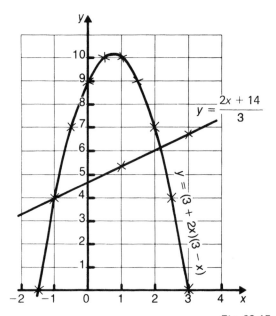

Fig. 23.15

The graphs are shown in Fig. 23.15. Since the equation $3(3 + 2x)(3 - x) = 2x + 14$ may be rewritten to give

$$(3 + 2x)(3 - x) = \frac{2x + 14}{3}$$

the coordinates where the curve and the line intersect give the solutions, which are:

$$x = -1 \quad \text{and} \quad x = 2.17$$

Exercise 116 – *All type B*

1) Plot the graph of $y = 3x^2$ taking values of x between -3 and 4. Hence solve the following equations:

(a) $3x^2 = 4$ (b) $3x^2 - 2x - 3 = 0$
(c) $3x^2 - 7x = 0$

2) Plot the graph of $y = x^2 + 8x - 2$ taking values of x between -12 and 2. On the same axes, and to the same scale, plot the graph of $y = 2x - 1$. Hence find the values of x which satisfy the equation $x^2 + 8x - 2 = 2x - 1$.

Solve graphically the following simultaneous equations:

3) $2x - 3y = 5$; $x - 2y = 2$

4) $7x - 4y = 37$; $6x + 3y = 51$

5) $\dfrac{x}{2} + \dfrac{y}{3} = \dfrac{13}{6}$; $\dfrac{2x}{7} - \dfrac{y}{4} = \dfrac{5}{14}$

6) If $y = x^2(15 - 2x)$ construct a table of values of y for values of x from -1 to $1\frac{1}{2}$ at half-unit intervals. Hence draw the graph of this function. Using the same axes and scales draw the straight line $y = 10x + 10$. Write down and simplify an equation which is satisfied by the values of x where the two graphs intersect. From your graph find the approximate value of the roots of this equation.

7) Write down the three values missing from the following table which gives values of $2x^3 + x + 3$ for values of x from -2 to 2.

x	-2.0	-1.5	-1.0	-0.5
$2x^3 + x + 3$	-15.0	-5.25		2.25

x	0	0.5	1.0	1.5	2.0
$2x^3 + x + 3$		3.75	6.0		21.0

Using the same axes draw the graphs of $y = 2x^3 + x + 3$ and $y = 9x + 3$. Use your graphs to write down:

(a) the range of values of x for which $2x^3 + x + 3$ is less than $9x + 3$;

(b) the solution of the equation $2x^3 + x + 3 = 5$. Write down and simplify the equation which is satisfied by the values of x at the points of intersection of the two graphs.

8) Write down the three values missing from the following table which gives values, correct to two decimal places, of $6 - \dfrac{10}{2x + 1}$ for values of x from 0.25 to 5.

x	0.25	0.5	1	1.5
$6 - \dfrac{10}{2x+1}$	-0.67	1.00	2.67	3.50

x	2	3	3.5	4	4.5	5
$6 - \dfrac{10}{2x+1}$		4.57		4.89		5.09

Using the same axes draw the graphs of $y = 6 - \dfrac{10}{2x + 1}$ and $y = x + 1$. Use your graphs to solve the equation $2x^2 - 9x + 5 = 0$.

9) If $y = \dfrac{x + 10}{x + 1}$ construct a table of values of y when $x = 0, 1, 2, 3, 4, 5$. Draw the graph of this function and also using the same axes and scales draw the graph of $y = x - 1$. Write down, and simplify, an equation which is satisfied by the values of x where the graphs intersect. From your graphs find the approximate value of the positive root of this equation.

10) Calculate the values of $\dfrac{x^2}{4} + \dfrac{24}{x} - 12$ which are omitted from the table below.

x	2	2.5	3	3.5	4
$\dfrac{x^2}{4} + \dfrac{24}{x} - 12$		-0.84		-2.08	

x	4.5	5	5.5	6
$\dfrac{x^2}{4} + \dfrac{24}{x} - 12$	-1.60	-0.95	-0.07	1.00

Draw the graph of $y = \dfrac{x^2}{4} + \dfrac{24}{x} - 12$ from $x = 2$ to $x = 6$. Using the same scales and axes draw the graph of $y = \dfrac{x}{3} - 2$. Write down, but do not simplify, an equation which is satisfied by the values of x where the graphs intersect. From your graphs find approximate values for the two roots of this equation.

SELF-TEST 23

In Questions 1 to 20 the answer is either "true" or "false".

1) The intersection of the two axes of reference, used when plotting a graph, is called the origin.

2) When a graph is a straight line it means that there is a definite law connecting the two quantities which are plotted.

3) When a graph is a smooth curve it means that there is not a definite law connecting the two quantities which are plotted.

4) Interpolation means using a graph to find values which are not given in the table from which the graph is drawn.

5) In order to extrapolate the graph is extended just beyond the range of the values from which the graph was plotted.

6) The coordinates of the point shown in Fig. 23.16 are $(3, 5)$.

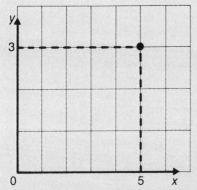

Fig. 23.16

7) The coordinates of the point shown in Fig. 23.17 are $(2, 3)$.

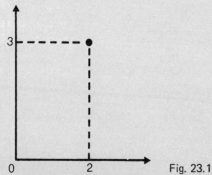

Fig. 23.17

8) When the coordinates of a point are stated as $(3, 6)$ it means that $x = 3$ and $y = 6$.

9) When the coordinates of a point are stated as $(-2, 4)$ it means that $y = -2$ when $x = 4$.

10) The equation $y = 3x + 7$ will give a graph which is not a straight line.

11) The equation $y = 3 - 5x$ will give a graph which is a straight line.

12) The equation $p = \dfrac{5}{q}$ will give a graph which is a straight line.

13) The equation $y = 8 - \dfrac{3}{x}$ will give a graph which is a straight line.

14) The equation $y = 3 + x^2$ will give a graph which is a curve.

15) The equation $y = 3 - 2x^3$ will give a graph which is a curve.

16) When the graph of $y = 5x^2 + 7x + 8$ is drawn, values of y are usually plotted on the vertical axis.

17) When the graph of $M = q^2 + 3$ is drawn, values of q are usually plotted on the vertical axis.

18) When $r = 3s + 7$, r is called the independent variable.

19) When $q = 7p - 8$, p is called the independent variable.

20) When $V = 8r^3$, V is called the dependent variable.

In Questions 21 to 25 state the letter (or letters) which correspond to the correct answer (or answers).

21) The graph of $y = 3 + 2x$ will look like one of the following diagrams (Fig. 23.18).

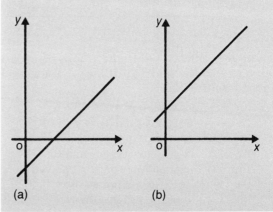

(a)   (b)

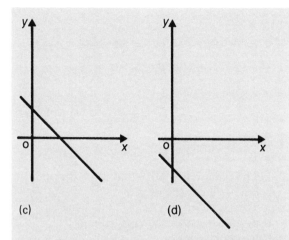

(c)   (d)

Fig. 23.18

22) The graph of $y = 5 - 3x$ will look like one of the following diagrams (Fig. 23.19).

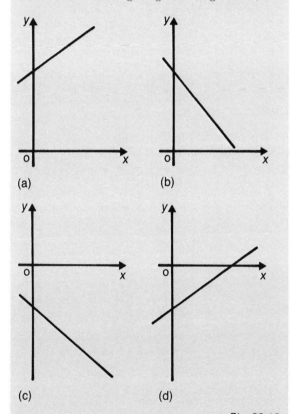

(a)   (b)

(c)   (d)

Fig. 23.19

23) Fig. 23.20 shows the graphs of $y = 3x - 2$ and $y = 8 - 2x$, plotted on the same axes. What are the solutions of the simultaneous equations $3x - y = 2$ and $2x + y = 8$?

a They cannot be found from the graphs,
b $x = 2$ and $y = 4$,

c $x = 4$ and $y = 2$,
d $x = 4$ and $y = -2$.

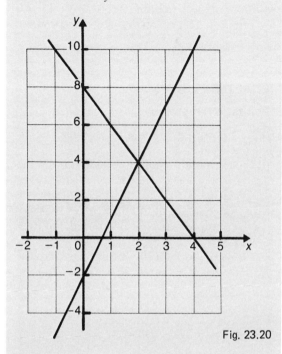

Fig. 23.20

24) Fig. 23.21 shows the graphs of $y = x^2 - 3x + 2$ and $y = 3x + 6$, plotted on the same axes. The solutions of the equation $x^2 - 6x - 4 = 0$ are

a 2 and 6
b -0.6 and 6.6
c 4.2 and 25.8
d -0.6 and 6.6 and 4.2 and 25.8

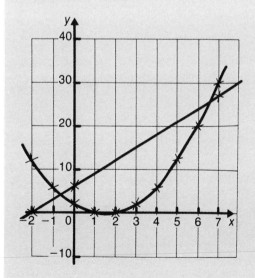

Fig. 23.21

25) You are given the graph of $y = 2x^2 + x - 15$. From the graph the solutions of the equation $2x^2 - 11x + 15 = 0$ are required. Hence, on the same axes, you would plot:

a $y = 30 - 12x$ **b** $y = 10x - 30$

c $y = 12x - 30$ **d** $y = 10x + 30$

CHAPTER 23 SUMMARY

Points to remember

(i)   A linear equation has a straight line as its graph.

(ii) A linear equation may be written in the form $y = mx + c$, where m and c are constants.

(iii) An equation of the form $y = k$ has as its graph a straight line parallel to the x-axis.

(iv) An equation of the form $x = c$ has as its graph a straight line parallel to the y-axis.

(v)   The equation $y = ax$ has as its graph a line through the origin.

(vi) The equation $y = ax^2 + bx + c$ has as its graph a smooth curve called a parabola.

(vii) To solve $ax^2 + bx + c = 0$, graphically
(a) Draw the graph for $y = ax^2 + bx + c$
(b) Find the values of x at which the graph cuts the x-axis.

Chapter 24 **Coordinate Geometry**

†RECTANGULAR COORDINATES

It has been shown on page 153 that a point can be positioned by means of rectangular coordinates. Thus in Fig. 24.1 the point P has the coordinates $x = 3$ and $y = 5$. We say that P is the point $(3, 5)$. Similarly Q is the point $(-2, -4)$.

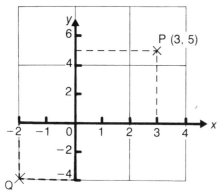

Fig. 24.1

EXAMPLE 1

Plot the points A$(3, 4)$, B$(5, 4)$, C$(6, 2)$ and D$(2, 2)$. Join up the points in alphabetical order to form the quadrilateral ABCD.

(a) Name the quadrilateral.
(b) Find its area.

The points are plotted in Fig. 24.2 and the quadrilateral is seen to be a trapezium.

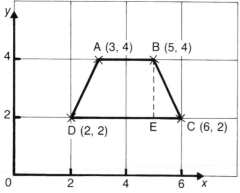

Fig. 24.2

To find its area we need to know the lengths of the two parallel sides and the distance between them. From the diagram:

$$AB = 5 - 3 = 2 \text{ units}$$
$$DC = 6 - 2 = 4 \text{ units}$$
$$BE = 4 - 2 = 2 \text{ units}$$

Here,

$$\text{Area} = \tfrac{1}{2}(AB + BC) \times BE$$
$$= \tfrac{1}{2} \times (2 + 4) \times 2$$
$$= \tfrac{1}{2} \times 6 \times 2 = 6 \text{ square units}$$

Exercise 117 – *All type B*

In each of the following problems, plot the given points. Join them up in alphabetical order and name the resulting figure. Find the area of each (in square units).

1) P$(3, 2)$, Q$(6, 2)$ and R$(6, 8)$.

2) A$(2, 3)$, B$(8, 3)$, C$(8, 8)$ and D$(2, 8)$.

3) E$(2, 5)$, F$(6, 5)$, G$(7, 10)$ and H$(3, 10)$.

4) W$(-2, 2)$, X$(3, 2)$, Y$(2, 4)$ and Z$(-1, 4)$.

5) A$(-3, -2)$, B$(2, 1)$ and C$(2, -2)$.

†THE LENGTH OF A LINE

Given the coordinates of its end points, the length of a line can be found by Pythagoras' theorem as shown in Example 2.

EXAMPLE 2

A is the point $(3, 5)$ and B is the point $(6, 3)$. Find the length of AB.

The line is drawn in Fig. 24.3. Constructing the right-angled triangle ABC we see that C has the coordinates $(3, 3)$. Hence

$$AC = (5 - 3) \text{ units} = 2 \text{ units}$$

and $BC = (6 - 3) \text{ units} = 3 \text{ units}$

Applying Pythagoras' theorem we have

$$AB^2 = AC^2 + BC^2 = 2^2 + 3^2 = 4 + 9 = 13$$

$$AB = \sqrt{13} = 3.606 \text{ units}$$

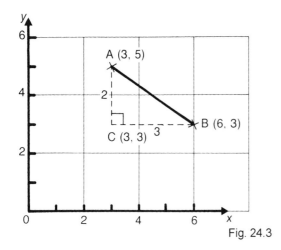

Fig. 24.3

†THE MID-POINT OF A LINE

EXAMPLE 3

A is the point $(4, 2)$ and B is the point $(12, 4)$. Find the coordinates of the mid-point of the line AB.

The line AB is drawn in Fig. 24.4. C is the mid-point of the line. From the construction shown:

x coordinate of C $= \frac{1}{2}(12 + 4) = \frac{1}{2} \times 16 = 8$

y coordinate of C $= \frac{1}{2}(2 + 4) = \frac{1}{2} \times 6 = 3$

Hence C is the point $(8, 3)$.

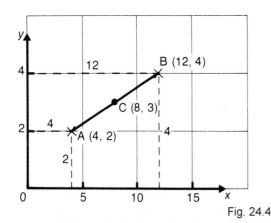

Fig. 24.4

Exercise 118 – *All type B*

Find the lengths of the lines AB in Questions 1 to 5.

1) $A(3, 5)$, $B(6, 8)$.

2) $A(1, 6)$, $B(3, 9)$.

3) $A(-1, 5)$, $B(4, 9)$.

4) $A(-2, -5)$, $B(3, -8)$.

5) $A(7, -2)$, $B(9, -6)$.

Find the coordinates of the mid-points of the following lines AB.

6) $A(3, 7)$, $B(0, 4)$.

7) $A(-3, 5)$, $B(-1, 8)$.

8) $A(0, 3)$, $B(5, 9)$.

LINEAR EQUATIONS

It was shown on page 156 that every simple equation gives a graph which is a straight line. Hence these equations are also called *linear equations*. Thus

$$y = 3x + 7$$

$$y = 4x - 5$$

$$y = 6 - 2x$$

$$2x + 3y = 5$$

are all linear equations.

†THE EQUATION OF A STRAIGHT LINE

Every linear equation may be written in the standard form:

$$y = mx + c$$

Hence $y = 2x - 5$ is in the standard form with $m = 2$ and $c = -5$.

The equation $y = 4 - 3x$ is in standard form if we rearrange it to give $y = -3x + 4$ so that we see $m = -3$ and $c = 4$.

The equation

$$4x + 5y = 6$$

may be rearranged to give

$$5y = -4x + 6$$

i.e.

$$y = -\frac{4}{5}x + \frac{6}{5}$$

Hence $m = -\frac{4}{5}$ and $c = \frac{6}{5}$.

†THE MEANING OF m AND c IN THE EQUATION OF A STRAIGHT LINE

The point B is any point on the straight line shown in Fig. 24.5 and it has the coordinates x and y. Point A is where the line cuts the y-axis and it has coordinates $x = 0$ and $y = c$.

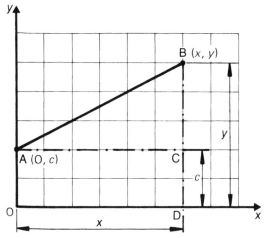

Fig. 24.5

$\dfrac{BC}{AC}$ is called the gradient of the line

Now

$$BC = \frac{BC}{AC} \times AC = AC \times \text{gradient of the line}$$

$$y = BC + CD = BC + AO$$

$$= AC \times \text{gradient of the line} + AO$$

$$= x \times \text{gradient of the line} + c$$

But $y = mx + c$.

Hence it can be seen that:

$$m = \text{gradient of the line}$$

$$c = \text{intercept on the } y\text{-axis}$$

Figure 24.6 shows the difference between *positive* and *negative* gradients.

(When the angle between the line and the positive direction of Ox is *acute* the gradient is *positive*. When the angle is *obtuse* the gradient is *negative*.)

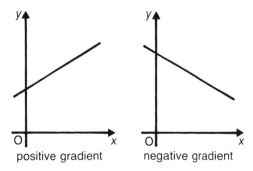

positive gradient   negative gradient

Fig. 24.6

EXAMPLE 4

(1) Find the equation of the straight line shown in Fig. 24.7.

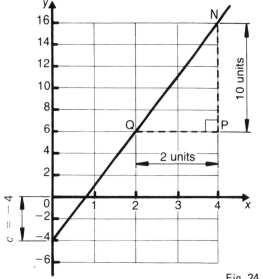

Fig. 24.7

Since the origin is at the intersection of the axes, c is the intercept on the y-axis. From Fig. 24.7 it will be seen that $c = -4$. We now have to find m. Since this is the gradient of the line we draw $\triangle$ QNP making the sides reasonably long since a small triangle will give very inaccurate results. Using the scales of x and y we see that QP = 2 units and PN = 10 units.

$$\therefore \quad m = \frac{NP}{QP} = \frac{10}{2} = 5$$

∴ The standard equation of a straight line $y = mx + c$ becomes $y = 5x - 4$.

(2) Find the values of m and c if the straight line $y = mx + c$ passes through the point $(-1, 3)$ and has a gradient of 6.

Since the gradient is 6 we have $m = 6$

$$\therefore \qquad\qquad y = 6x + c$$

Since the line passes through the point $(-1, 3)$ we have $y = 3$ when $x = -1$. By substitution,

$$3 = 6 \times (-1) + c$$

$$3 = -6 + c$$

$$\therefore \qquad c = 9$$

Hence $y = 6x + 9$.

(3) Find the equation of the straight line shown in Fig. 24.8.

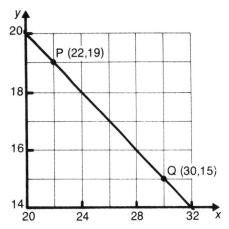

Fig. 24.8

It will seem from Fig. 24.8 that the *origin is not at the intersection of the axes*. In order to determine the law of the straight line we use two simultaneous equations as follows: Choose two convenient points P and Q and find their coordinates (these two points should be as far apart as possible to get maximum accuracy). If a point lies on a line then the x and y values of that point must satisfy the equation:

$$y = mx + c$$

at point P, $x = 22$ and $y = 19$

$$\therefore \qquad 19 = 22m + c \qquad [1]$$

at point Q, $x = 30$ and $y = 15$

$$15 = 30m + c \qquad [2]$$

Subtracting equation [2] from equation [1], we have

$$4 = -8m$$

$$\therefore \qquad m = \frac{4}{-8}$$

$$m = -0.5$$

Substituting $m = -0.5$ in equation [1], we have

$$19 = 22 \times (-0.5) + c$$

$$19 = -11 + c$$

$$c = 30$$

Thus the equation of the line shown in Fig. 25.8 is

$$y = -0.5x + 30$$

(4) Find the values of m and c if the straight line $y = mx + c$ passes through the points $(3, 4)$ and $(7, 10)$.

$$y = mx + c$$

The first point has coordinates $x = 3$, $y = 4$. Hence

$$4 = 3m + c \qquad [1]$$

The second point has coordinates $x = 7$, $y = 10$. Hence

$$10 = 7m + c \qquad [2]$$

Subtracting equation [1] from equation [2], we have

$$6 = 4m$$

$$\therefore \qquad m = 1.5$$

Substituting for $m = 1.5$ in equation [1], we have

$$4 = 4.5 + c$$

$$\therefore \qquad c = -0.5$$

The equation of the straight line is

$$y = 1.5x - 0.5$$

†EXPERIMENTAL DATA

One of the most important applications of the straight-line equation is the determination of an equation connecting two quantities when values have been obtained from an experiment.

EXAMPLE 5

In an experiment carried out with a lifting machine the effort E and the load W were found to have the values given in the table below:

W (kg)	15	25	40	50	60
E (kg)	2.75	3.80	5.75	7.00	8.20

Plot these results and obtain the equation connecting E and W which is thought to be of the type $E = aW + b$.

If E and W are connected by an equation of the type $E = aW + b$ then the graph must be a straight line. Note that when plotting the graph, W is the independent variable and must be plotted on the horizontal axis. E is the dependent variable and must be plotted on the vertical axis.

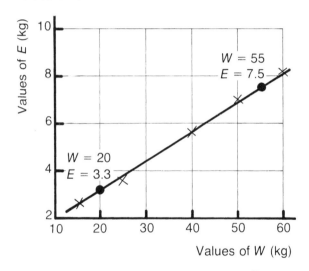

Fig. 24.9

On plotting the points (Fig. 24.9) it will be noticed that they deviate only slightly from a straight line. Since the data are experimental we must expect errors in measurement and observation and hence slight deviations from a straight line must be expected. Although the straight line will not pass through some of the points, an attempt must be made to ensure an even spread of the points above and below the line.

To determine the equation we choose two points which lie on the straight line. Do not use any of the experimental results from the table unless they happen to lie exactly on the line. Choose the points as far apart as is convenient because this will help the accuracy of your result.

The point $W = 55$, $E = 7.5$ lies on the line. Hence

$$7.5 = 55a + b \qquad [1]$$

The point $W = 20$, $E = 3.3$ also lies on the line. Hence

$$3.3 = 20a + b \qquad [2]$$

Subtracting equation [2] from equation [1], we have

$$4.2 = 35a$$
$$a = 0.12$$

Substituting for $a = 0.12$ in equation [2], we have

$$3.3 = 20 \times 0.12 + b$$
$$b = 0.9$$

The required equation connecting E and W is therefore

$$E = 0.12W + 0.9$$

Exercise 119 – *Questions 1–6 type A, 7–11 type B, remainder C*

The following equations represent straight lines. State in each case the gradient of the line and the intercept on the y-axis.

1) $y = x + 3$ **3)** $y = -5x - 2$

2) $y = -3x + 4$ **4)** $y = 4x - 3$

5) Find the values of m and c if the straight line $y = mx + c$ passes through the point $(-2, 5)$ and has a gradient of 4.

6) Find the values of m and c if the straight line $y = mx + c$ passes through the point $(3, 4)$ and the intercept on the y-axis is -2.

In the following find the values of m and c if the straight line $y = mx + c$ passes through the given points:

7) $(-2, -3)$ and $(3, 7)$

8) $(1, 1)$ and $(2, 4)$

9) $(-2, 1)$ and $(3, -9)$

10) $(-3, 13)$ and $(1, 1)$

11) $(2, 17)$ and $(4, 27)$

12) The following table gives values of x and y which are connected by an equation of the type $y = ax + b$. Plot the graph and from it find the values of a and b.

x	2	4	6	8	10	12
y	10	16	22	28	34	40

13) The following observed values of P and Q are supposed to be related by the linear equation $P = aQ + b$, but there are experimental errors. Find by plotting the graph the most probable values of a and b.

Q	2.5	3.5	4.4	5.8
P	13.6	17.6	22.2	28.0

Q	7.5	9.6	12.0	15.1
P	35.5	47.4	56.1	74.6

14) In an experiment carried out with a machine the effort E and the load W were found to have the values given in the table below. The equation connecting E and W is thought to be of the type $E = aW + b$. By plotting the graph check if this is so and hence find a and b.

W (kg)	10	30	50	60	80	100
E (kg)	8.9	19.1	29	33	45	54

15) A test on a metal filament lamp gave the following values of resistance (R ohms) at various voltages (V volts).

V	62	75	89	100	120
R	100	117	135	149	175

These results are expected to agree with an equation of the type $R = mV + c$ where m and c are constants. Test this by drawing the graph and find suitable values for m and c.

16) During an experiment to verify Ohm's Law the following results were obtained.

E (volts)	0	1.0	2.0	2.5	3.7
I (amperes)	0	0.24	0.5	0.63	0.92

E (volts)	4.1	5.9	6.8	8.0
I (amperes)	1.05	1.48	1.70	2.05

Plot these values with I horizontal and find the equation connecting E and I.

†PARALLEL LINES

Two lines are parallel if their gradients are the same.

It was previously shown that the general equation of a straight line is

$$y = mx + c$$

where m is the gradient of the line and c is the intercept on the y-axis.

EXAMPLE 6

Show that the straight lines $2y + 4x = 7$ and $3y + 6x = 2$ are parallel.

If
$$2y + 4x = 7$$

then
$$y = 3\tfrac{1}{2} - 2x$$

If
$$3y + 6x = 2$$

then
$$y = \tfrac{2}{3} - 2x$$

For each line the gradient is -2 and hence the two straight lines are parallel.

†PERPENDICULAR LINES

Two lines are perpendicular if the product of their gradients is -1.

EXAMPLE 7

Show that the lines $y - 3x = 2$ and $3y + x = 10$ are perpendicular.

When
$$y - 3x = 2$$
$$y = 3x + 2 \qquad [1]$$

When
$$3y + x = 10$$
$$y = -\frac{1}{3}x + \frac{10}{3} \qquad [2]$$

The gradient for line [1] is 3 and the gradient for line [2] is $-\tfrac{1}{3}$. The product of these two gradients is $3 \times (-\tfrac{1}{3}) = -1$ and hence the two lines are perpendicular.

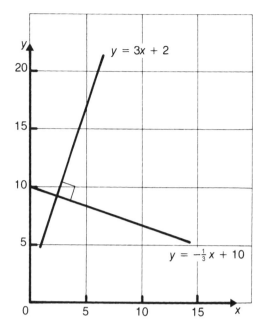

Fig. 24.10

The two lines are shown plotted in Fig. 24.10. Note that the scales on both axes are the same and the lines are clearly perpendicular to each other. If the scales are different on the two axes, the lines will not look as though they are perpendicular.

Exercise 120 – *All type B*

State if the following lines are:

a   parallel,
b   perpendicular to each other, or
c   neither parallel nor perpendicular to each other.

1) $y = 5x - 3$ and $y = 7 + 5x$.

2) $y = 2x - 5$ and $y = 5 - \frac{1}{2}x$.

3) $y = 3x + 1$ and $y = 2x + 1$.

4) $3y + 6x = 2$ and $5y + 10x = 8$.

5) $2y + x = 7$ and $3y - 2x = 7$.

6) $3y + 2x = 5$ and $2y - 3x = 5$.

7) $4y + x = 4$ and $2y - x = 8$.

SELF-TEST 24

1) When the points A(1, 2), B(4, 2), C(5, 4) and D(2, 4) are joined in alphabetical order they form which figure?

a square   b rectangle

c parallelogram   d trapezium

2) A is the point (1, 3) and B is the point (4, 7). What is the length of the straight line AB?

a 5 units   b 10 units   c 15 units

d 25 units

3) A(5, 2) and B(9, 6) are joined by a straight line. What are the rectangular coordinates of the mid-point of AB?

a (7, 4)   b (14, 8)   c (8, 14)   d (4, 7)

4) Which of the following is a linear equation?

a $y = 3 + \frac{5}{x}$ b $y = x^2 + 3$

c $y = 3 - 8x$ d $y = 3\sqrt{x} + 7$

5) One of the following diagrams (Fig. 24.11) represents the graph of the equation $y = 5x - 2$. Which?

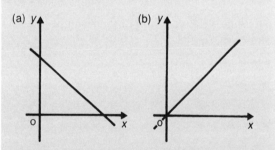
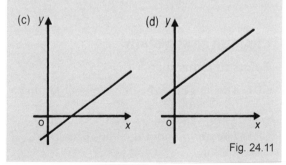

Fig. 24.11

6) Which one of the diagrams in Fig. 24.12 represents the graph of $y = 5 - 2x$?

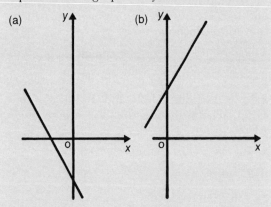

(a)   (b)   (c)   (d)

Fig. 24.12

7) What is the equation of the straight line shown in Fig. 24.13?

a $y = x + 2$

b $y = 2x + 1$

c $y = 4x + 6$

d $y = 6x + 4$

8) Four pairs of lines are given below. Which pair is perpendicular to each other?

a $y = 3x + 2$
$y = -3x - 2$

b $y = 4x + 1$
$y = \frac{1}{4}x + 1$

c $y = 2 - 3x$
$y = -\frac{1}{2} - 3x$

d $y = 2x + 3$
$y = 4 - \frac{1}{2}x$

9) In Question 8, which pair of lines is parallel?

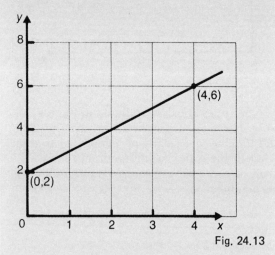

Fig. 24.13

10) Which of the following points is *not* on the straight line whose equation is $y = 3 - 2x$?

a $(0, 3)$ **b** $(-1, 5)$ **c** $(1.5, 0)$

d $(2, 1)$

CHAPTER 24 SUMMARY

Points to remember

(i) The length of the line segment joining (x_1, y_1) and (x_2, y_2) is $\sqrt{\{(x_1 - x_2)^2 + (y_1 - y_2)^2\}}$.

(ii) The midpoint of the line segment joining (x_1, y_1) and (x_2, y_2) is $((x_1 + x_2)/2, (y_1 + y_2)/2)$.

(iii) The equation of the line through (h, k) with gradient m is $y - k = m(x - h)$.

(iv) The lines $y = m_1 x + c$ and $y = m_2 x + k$ are
(a) parallel if $m_1 = m_2$.
(b) perpendicular if $m_1 m_2 = -1$.

(v) Any line parallel to $ax + by = c$ is of the form $ax + by = k$.

(vi) A line perpendicular to $ax + by = c$ is of the form $bx - ay = k$.

Chapter 25 **Functions and Relations**

RELATIONS

A relation is a set of ordered pairs. Thus the set

$$\{(0,0), (4,2), (8,4), (10,5), (16,8)\}$$

is a relation.

The *domain* of the relation is the set of first elements of the ordered pairs whilst the *range* is the second elements of the ordered pairs. Thus for the above set of ordered pairs the domain is $\{0,4,8,10,16\}$. The range is $\{0,2,4,5,8\}$.

The relation may be shown in the form of a diagram (Fig. 25.1). The values of the domain and range connected by the arrowed lines constitute ordered pairs. The relation may also be shown in the form of a graph (Fig. 25.2).

Note that the range is taken on the vertical axis whilst the domain is taken on the horizontal axis.

Fig. 25.3 shows a relationship between the domain X and the range Y. X and Y are related by the relationship $x \rightarrow 3x + 2$ which reads 'x is mapped onto $3x + 2$'. The elements in Y are obtained by substituting the values in X into the expression $3x + 2$. Thus, when

$$x = 0: \quad 3x + 2 = 3 \times 0 + 2 = 2$$

$$x = 1: \quad 3x + 2 = 3 \times 1 + 2 = 5$$

$$x = 2: \quad 3x + 2 = 3 \times 2 + 2 = 8$$

and so on.

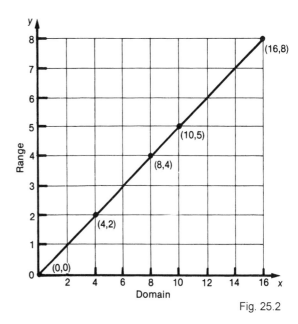

Fig. 25.2

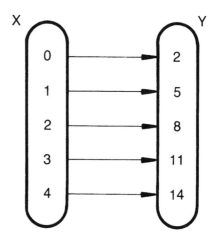

Fig. 25.3

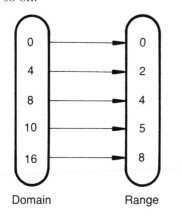

Domain   Range   Fig. 25.1

Exercise 121 – *All type A*

1) Copy and complete Fig. 25.4 if the relation is:

(a) $x \rightarrow 2x + 4$ (b) $x \rightarrow 6x$

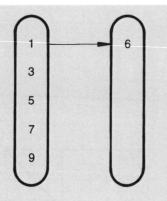

Fig. 25.4

2) For the relation $x \to x^2$:

(a) what is 3 mapped onto?
(b) what is 6 mapped onto?

3) Fig. 25.5 shows a relationship between A and B.

(a) What number should be in the position marked *?
(b) Give the relationship between an element, x, in A and the corresponding element in B.

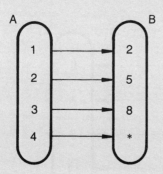

Fig. 25.5

4) With 2, 3, 4 and 5 as domain draw a mapping diagram for:

(a) $x \to 4 - 2x$ (b) $x \to 2^x$

5) Fig. 25.6 shows a relationship between the domain X and the range Y. Find:

(a) The relationship between an element x in X and the corresponding element in Y.
(b) The numbers marked *.

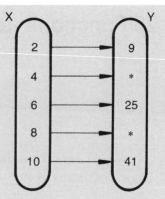

Fig. 25.6

6) If a relation from X to Y is defined by $y = x^2 - 3x + 2$ (i.e. $x \to x^2 - 3x + 2$) complete the mapping diagram shown in Fig. 25.7.

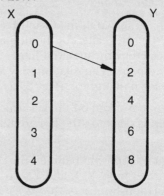

Fig. 25.7

7) State the relationship that gives the mapping shown in Fig. 25.8.

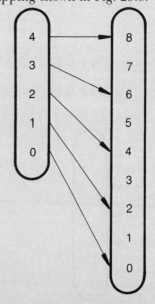

Fig. 25.8

FUNCTIONS

A function is a relation in which each element in the domain is paired with one and only one element in the range. Thus the relations depicted in Figs. 25.1 and 25.3 are functions. Because each arrowed line from the elements of the domain arrives at a different element of the range the function is called a *one to one mapping*.

Now look at the mapping diagram shown in Fig. 25.9. Only one arrowed line leaves each of the elements in the domain and hence the relation is a function. The fact that there is more than one arrow arriving at one of the elements in the range (i.e. at the element 2) is immaterial. It is the 'one arrow leaving each element of the domain' which is the criterion of a function. Such a diagram represents a *many to one mapping*.

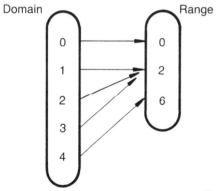

Fig. 25.9

The relation 'is a factor of' shown in Fig. 25.10 is *not a function* because two arrows leave one of the elements in the domain (i.e. from the element 2).

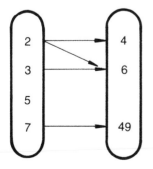

Fig. 25.10

If a relation is not a function a vertical line will pass through the graph of two ordered pairs (Fig. 25.11).

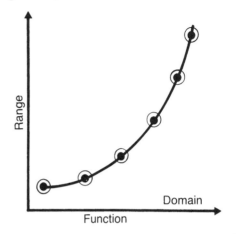

Function

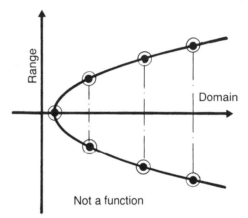

Not a function

Fig. 25.11

FUNCTION NOTATION

Consider the relation $x \rightarrow 2x + 5$ with domain $\{0, 1, 2, 3\}$. The range is found by substituting each element of the domain into $2x + 5$. Thus when:

$$x = 0 \quad 2x + 5 = (2 \times 0) + 5 = 5$$

$$x = 1 \quad 2x + 5 = (2 \times 1) + 5 = 7$$

$$x = 2 \quad 2x + 5 = (2 \times 2) + 5 = 9$$

$$x = 3 \quad 2x + 5 = (2 \times 3) + 5 = 11$$

Hence the range is the set $\{5, 7, 9, 11\}$.

The relation $x \rightarrow 2x + 5$ is a function and we therefore write $f: x \rightarrow 2x + 5$ which is read as 'the function of x is $2x + 5$'.

Instead of writing a function $f: x \rightarrow 2x + 5$ we often write $f(x) = 2x + 5$. Thus if

$y = 3x^2 - 2x + 5$, $y = f(x) = 3x^2 - 2x + 5$
or $f: x \to 3x^2 - 2x + 5$.   The symbols $F, g,$
h and ϕ are also used to represent functions
and we may have

$$n = F(m)$$

n being the range and m the domain.

$$p = g(r)$$

p being the range and r the domain.

$$s = h(t)$$

s being the range and t the domain.

$$X = \phi(u)$$

X being the range and u the domain.

Note that $f(x)$ does not mean f
multiplied by x but is simply shorthand for the
phrase 'a function of x'.

EXAMPLE 1

If $f(x) = x^2 + 7x - 5$ find the values of
$f(2)$ and $f(-1)$.

To find $f(2)$ substitute $x = 2$ into the
expression $x^2 + 7x - 5$. Thus:

$$f(2) = 2^2 + 7 \times 2 - 5$$
$$= 4 + 14 - 5 = 13$$
$$f(-1) = (-1)^2 + 7 \times (-1) - 5$$
$$= 1 - 7 - 5 = -11$$

EXAMPLE 2

If $g: x \to 4x - 1$,   find the values of $g(3)$
and $g(-2)$.

$$g(3) = 4 \times 3 - 1 = 12 - 1 = 11$$
$$g(-2) = 4 \times (-2) - 1 = -8 - 1 = -9$$

GRAPHS AND FUNCTIONS

Functions may be represented as graphs just as
were relations.

EXAMPLE 3

Plot the graph of $f(x) = 3x^2 + 10x - 8$
between $x = -6$ and $x = 4$.

A table may be drawn up as follows giving
corresponding values of y for chosen values
of x.

x	−6	−5	−4	−3	−2	−1
$3x^2$	108	75	48	27	12	3
$10x$	−60	−50	−40	−30	−20	−10
−8	−8	−8	−8	−8	−8	−8
$f(x)$	40	17	0	−11	−16	−15

x	0	1	2	3	4
$3x^2$	0	3	12	27	48
$10x$	0	10	20	30	40
−8	−8	−8	−8	−8	−8
$f(x)$	−8	5	24	49	80

The graph is shown in Fig. 25.12 and it is a
smooth curve. Equations that are non-linear
always give a graph which is a smooth curve.

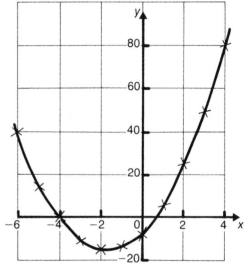

Fig. 25.12

Exercise 122 – *All type B*

1) If $f(x) = 3x^2 - 5x + 2$ find:

(a) $f(2)$ (b) $f(0)$
(c) $f(-3)$ (d) $f(\frac{1}{2})$.

2) If $f(v) = 8v - 7$ find:
(a) $f(3)$ (b) $f(-2)$ (c) $f(0)$.

3) If $M = \phi(p) = 3p^2 - 2p$ find:

(a) $\phi(1)$ (b) $\phi(3)$ (c) $\phi(0)$
(d) $\phi(-1)$ (e) $\phi(-3)$.

4) $F(h) = h^3 - 3h + 1$.   Find $F(1)$, $F(4)$ and
$F(-2)$.

5) If $f: x \to \frac{1}{2}(4x + 1)$ find the values of
$f(3)$ and $f(-2)$.

6) $g: t \rightarrow \frac{1}{4}(1 - 5t)$.   Find the values of $g(-1), g(0)$ and $g(3)$.

7) State which of the graphs in Fig. 25.13 represents a function.

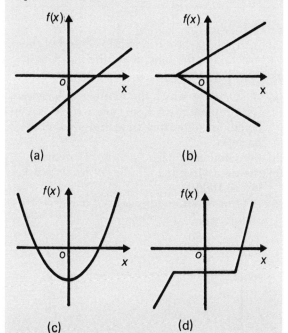

(a)

(b)

(c)

(d)

(e)

Fig. 25.13

8) Draw graphs of the following functions:

(a) $f(x) = 5 - 4x$ taking values of x between -2 and 4.
(b) $f(x) = 2x^2 - 7x - 5$ between $x = -4$ and $x = 12$.
(c) $f(x) = x^2 - 4x + 4$ between $x = -3$ and $x = 3$.

THE RECIPROCAL FUNCTION

The reciprocal of x is $\frac{1}{x}$. The function

$f: x \rightarrow \frac{k}{x}$ is called the reciprocal function since

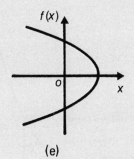

the values of range are k times the reciprocal of the domain (k being a constant).

EXAMPLE 4

Draw the graph of $y = \frac{4}{x}$ for values of x between -4 and 4.

x	-4	-3	-2	-1	1	2	3	4
y	-1	$-1\frac{1}{3}$	-2	-4	4	2	$1\frac{1}{3}$	1

Note that the reciprocal of a negative number is a negative number, whilst the reciprocal of a positive number is a positive number. It is impossible to find a value for the reciprocal of zero (i.e. we cannot divide by zero) and, as shown in Fig. 25.14, the graph consists of two separate branches. The negative branch is the image of the positive branch reflected in the origin. The curve is also symmetrical about the line $y = -x$.

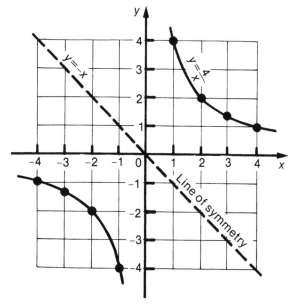

Fig. 25.14

THE LAW OF NATURAL GROWTH

Suppose the sum of $2000 is invested at 10% per annum compound interest.

To find the amount accruing after n years the formula below is used:

$$A_n = 2000\left(1 + \frac{10}{100}\right)^n = 2000 \times 1.1^n$$

That is after 1 year $A_1 = 2000 \times 1.1^1 = 2200$
after 2 years $A_2 = 2000 \times 1.1^2 = 2420$
after 3 years $A_3 = 2000 \times 1.1^3 = 2662$

and so on.

The graph depicting the growth of the money invested is shown in Fig. 25.15. It can be seen that the curve rises as the number of years increase. Curves like this depict the law of natural growth. There are very many examples of natural growth such as population growth, multiplication of bacteria, etc. Expressed mathematically, the exponential or growth function is

$$f : x \to kn^x$$

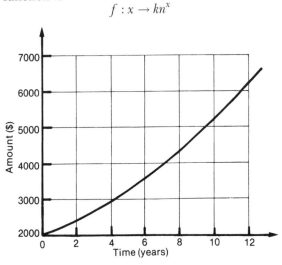

Fig. 25.15

EXAMPLE 5

The population of a certain country appears to be increasing at a rate of 3% per annum. If its population is 8 million in 2001, estimate its population in the year 2023, assuming that the law of natural growth applies and that the rate of increase of 3% per annum is maintained.

We have

$$P = kR^n = 8 \times 1.03^n$$

where P is the population after n years. Hence after 22 years

$$P = 8 \times 1.03^{22} = 15.5 \text{ million}$$

That is, by the year 2000, the population will very nearly double.

Number	Operation	Log
8		0.903
1.03^{22}	22×0.013	1.286
15.5		1.189

EXAMPLE 6

A type of bacterium is checked regularly and recorded in the table below.

Number of bacteria (thousands)	3	6	12	24	48	96	192	384
Time (hours)	0	1	2	3	4	5	6	7

Plot a graph to show the multiplication of the bacteria taking the time along the horizontal axis. Find

(a) the factor by which the number of bacteria is multiplied every hour, and write down an equation connecting time and number of bacteria;

(b) the number of bacteria after $2\frac{1}{2}$ hours;

(c) the time when the number of bacteria will be $150\,000$;

(d) the time when the number of bacteria should reach $500\,000$.

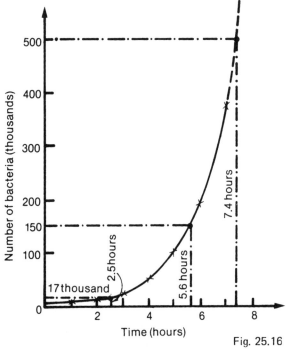

Fig. 25.16

The graph is shown in Fig. 25.16 and it is seen to be a growth curve.

(a) The multiplication factor is 2 because, from the table, we see that every hour the number of bacteria doubles. The equation connecting time $(T$ hours$)$ and number of bacteria (N) is

$$N = 3000 \times 2^T$$

(b) From the graph the number of bacteria after $2\frac{1}{2}$ hours is found to be 6400.

(c) From the graph the time when the number of bacteria will reach 150 000 is 5.6 hours.

(d) By extending the curve, the estimated time when the number of bacteria will reach 500 000, is 7.4 hours.

†THE GRAPH OF x^3

The graph of $y = x^3$ is shown in Fig. 25.17 and the negative part will be seen to be the image of the positive part reflected in the origin.

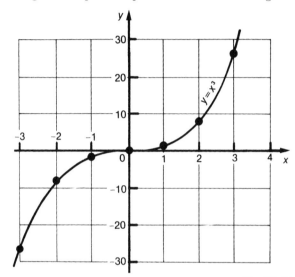

Fig. 25.17

x	−3	−2	−1	0	1	2	3
$y = x^3$	−27	−8	−1	0	1	8	27

†THE GRAPH OF x^{-2}

The graph of $y = \dfrac{1}{x^2}$ or $y = x^{-2}$ is

shown in Fig. 25.18 and it is seen to be symmetrical about the y-axis (i.e. about the line $x = 0$).

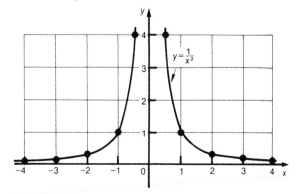

Fig. 25.18

x	−4	−3	−2	−1	$-\frac{1}{2}$
$y = \dfrac{1}{x^2}$	0.06	0.11	0.25	1	4

x	0	$\frac{1}{2}$	1	2	3	4
$y = \dfrac{1}{x^2}$	−	4	1	0.25	0.11	0.06

DIRECT VARIATION

The statement that y is proportional to x (often written $y \propto x$) means that the graph of y against x is a straight line passing through the origin (Fig. 25.19). We may write

$$y = kx$$

where k is called the constant of proportionality. The ratio of y to x is equal to k and y is said to *vary directly* as x. Hence direct variation means that if x is doubled, then y is also doubled. If x is halved then y is halved, and so on.

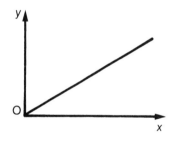

Fig. 25.19

Some examples of direct variation are:

(a) The circumference of a circle is directly proportional to its diameter. ($c = \pi d$, π being the constant of proportionality.)

(b) The volume of a cylinder of given radius is directly proportional to its height. ($V = \pi r^2 h$, πr^2 being the constant of proportionality.)

EXAMPLE 7

If x is directly proportional to x and $y = 2$ when $x = 5$, find the value of y when $x = 6$.

Since $y \propto x$ then $y = kx$.

We are given that when $y = 2$, $x = 5$.

Hence,

$$2 = k \times 5 \quad \text{or} \quad k = \frac{2}{5}$$

$$\therefore \qquad y = \frac{2}{5}x$$

when $x = 6$,

$$y = \frac{2}{5} \times 6 = \frac{12}{5}$$

If y is proportional to x^2 then $y = kx^2$.
If we plot values of y against x we get a curve
(Fig. 25.20), but if we plot y against x^2
(Fig. 25.21) we get a straight line passing
through the origin.

x	0	1	2	3
$y = 3x^2$	0	3	12	27

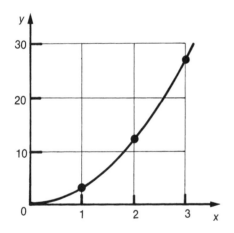

Fig. 25.20

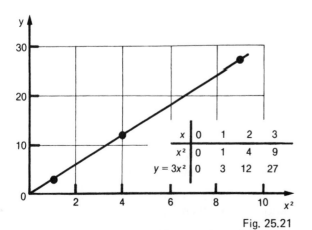

x	0	1	2	3
x^2	0	1	4	9
$y = 3x^2$	0	3	12	27

Fig. 25.21

EXAMPLE 8

The surface area of a sphere, A square
millimetres, varies directly as the square of its
radius, r millimetres. If the surface area of a
sphere of 2 mm radius is 50.25 mm^2 find the
surface area of a sphere whose radius is 4 mm.

Since $A \propto r^2$ then $A = kr^2$.

We are given that $A = 50.24$ when $r = 2$.
Hence

$$50.24 = k \times 2^2 \quad \text{or} \quad k = \frac{50.24}{2^2} = 12.56$$

$$\therefore \qquad A = 12.56r^2$$

when $r = 4$,

$$A = 12.56 \times 4^2 = 200.96 \, \text{mm}^2$$

INVERSE VARIATION

If y is inversely proportional to x, then

$$y = \frac{k}{x}$$

This is the reciprocal function discussed on
page 177 where it was shown that the graph of
this function has two branches. However, if we
plot y against $\frac{1}{x}$ we obtain a straight line as
shown in Fig. 25.22, which shows the graph of
$y = \frac{4}{x}$.

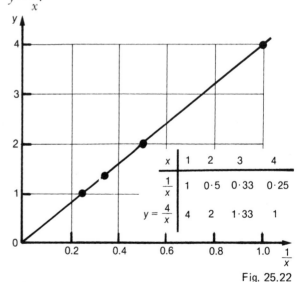

x	1	2	3	4
$\frac{1}{x}$	1	0·5	0·33	0·25
$y = \frac{4}{x}$	4	2	1·33	1

Fig. 25.22

EXAMPLE 9

If S varies inversely as P and $S = 4$ when
$P = 3$, find the value of P when $S = 16$.

We are given that

$$S = \frac{k}{P}$$

When $S = 4$, $P = 3$. Hence

$$4 = \frac{k}{3}$$

$$k = 4 \times 3 = 12$$

$$\therefore \qquad S = \frac{12}{P}$$

When $S = 16$,

$$16 = \frac{12}{P}$$

$$P = \frac{12}{16} = \frac{3}{4}$$

Exercise 123 – *Questions 1–6 type B,*
remainder C

1) Express the following with an equal sign and a constant:

(a) y varies directly as x^2.
(b) U varies directly as the square root of V.
(c) S varies inversely as T^3.
(d) h varies inversely as the cube root of m.

2) If $y = 2$ when $x = 4$ write down the value of y when $x = 9$ for the following:

(a) y varies directly as the square of x.
(b) y varies inversely as the square root of x.
(c) y varies inversely as x.

3) If S varies inversely as T^3 and $S = 54$ when $T = 3$ find the value of T when $S = 16$.

4) If U varies directly as $\sqrt{V}$ and $U = 2$ when $V = 9$ find the value of V when $U = 4$.

5) The surface area of a sphere, $V \, \text{mm}^2$, varies directly as the square of its diameter, $d \, \text{mm}$. If the surface area is to be doubled, by what ratio must the diameter be altered?

6) Draw graphs of the following functions:

(a) $x \rightarrow \dfrac{5}{x}$ for values of x between -5 and 5.
(b) $x \rightarrow 3x^{-2}$ for values of x between -2 and 2.
(c) $x \rightarrow 10x^3$ for values of x between -3 and 3.

7) The table below gives the population (in millions) of a country during the years stated:

Year	1920	1940	1960	1970	1980	1990
Population (millions)	1.50	1.78	2.11	2.30	2.51	2.74

(a) Draw a graph of this information taking the year as the domain.
(b) Write down the factor by which the population increases in each 10 year period.
(c) From the answer to part (b) write down the equation connecting the year and the population.
(d) Use the answer to part (c) to estimate the population in the year 2020 assuming that the rate of increase remains the same.
(e) From your graph obtain the population in 1950.

8) A bacteria multiplies according to the equation $N = 2^T$ where N is the number of bacteria after a time T hours.

(a) Make a table showing the number of bacteria at 1, 2, 3, 4 and 5 hours.
(b) Draw a graph of the equation $N = 2^T$ and use your graph to estimate the number of bacteria after $2\frac{1}{2}$ hours.

9) The population of a Caribbean territory is increasing at 4% per annum. In 1995 the population was 2 000 000. Estimate the population in 2015.

10) The figures below show how $5000 appreciates over a period of years.

Years	2	5	7	10	15
Amount	6050	8050	9745	12 970	20 900

(a) Draw a graph taking years as the domain.
(b) What is the rate of interest per annum?
(c) What is the amount after 8 years?
(d) What is the number of years for the amount to reach $15 000?

†INVERSE FUNCTIONS

Consider the relation

$$F = \{(1,3), (2,6), (3,4), (4,12)\}$$

Interchanging the domain and the range we obtain the relation

$$G = \{(3,1), (6,2), (4,3), (12,4)\}$$

F and G are *inverse relations*. G is the inverse of F and it is denoted by the symbol F^{-1}, read as 'the inverse of F' or 'F inverse'. We may write

$$F = G^{-1}$$

because F is the inverse of G.

The inverse of a relation F is defined as follows:

F^{-1}, *the inverse of the relation* F, *is a relation obtained by interchanging the components of each ordered pair in* F.

Consider the function $f: x \to 3x + 1$ in which the set of ordered pairs in f is

$$\{(-1, -2), (0, 1), (1, 4), (2, 7)\}$$

Interchanging the components of each ordered pair in f we have

$$f^{-1} = \{(-2, -1), (1, 0), (4, 1), (7, 2)\}$$

If we write the defining equation of f as

$$y = 3x + 1$$

then the defining equation for f^{-1} is found by interchanging x and y. That is,

$$x = 3y + 1$$

Transposing this equation to make y the subject, we have

$$y = \frac{x - 1}{3}$$

Using the notation corresponding to

$$f: x \to 3x + 1, \quad \text{we have} \quad f^{-1}: x \to \frac{x - 1}{3}.$$

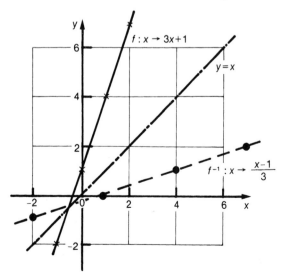

Fig. 25.23

In Fig. 25.23 the graphs of $f: x \to 3x + 1$ and $f^{-1}: x \to \frac{x - 1}{3}$ have been plotted. We see that f^{-1} is the image of f in the mirror line $y = x$. The graph of a function and its inverse are symmetric with respect to the line $y = x$.

In general, if a function is a one to one mapping then its inverse will also be a function. However, if a function is a one to many mapping its inverse will, generally speaking, not be a function.

EXAMPLE 10

If $g = \{(-2, 4), (-1, 1), (0, 0), (1, 1), (2, 4)\}$ show that g^{-1} is not a function.

$$g^{-1} = \{(4, -2), (1, -1), (0, 0), (1, 1), (4, 2)\}$$

g is a function with a one to many mapping but g^{-1} is not a function because the ordered pairs $(4, -2)$ and $(4, 2)$ have the same first element.

EXAMPLE 11

If f is a function defined by $f(x) = \dfrac{3x - 5}{x + 2}$

(a) find the value of $f(3)$,
(b) write down the real number which cannot be in the domain of f,
(c) find an expression for f^{-1},
(d) find the value of $f^{-1}(2)$.

(a) $f(3) = \dfrac{(3 \times 3) - 5}{3 + 2} = \dfrac{4}{5}$.

(b) Because it is impossible to divide by zero,

$$x + 2 \neq 0$$

Hence -2 cannot be in the domain of f.

(c) Writing the defining equation for f as

$$y = \frac{3x - 5}{x + 2}$$

the defining equation for f^{-1} is

$$x = \frac{3y - 5}{y + 2}$$

We now transpose this equation to make y the subject, and we find that

$$y = \frac{2x + 5}{3 - x}$$

$$\therefore \quad f^{-1}(x) = \frac{2x + 5}{3 - x}$$

(d) $$f^{-1}(2) = \frac{(2 \times 2) + 5}{3 - 2} = 9$$

USING THE INVERSE OF A FUNCTION TO SOLVE AN EQUATION

The inverse of a function may be used to solve an equation. The method is shown in Example 12.

EXAMPLE 12

Find the inverse of $f(x) = \dfrac{4x+5}{x+2}$ and hence solve the equation $\dfrac{4x+5}{x+2} = 3$.

Writing the defining equation for f as

$$y = \frac{4x+5}{x+2}$$

gives us the defining equation for f^{-1}:

$$x = \frac{4y+5}{y+2}$$

Transposing this equation to make y the subject, we have

$$y = \frac{5-2x}{x-4}$$

$$f^{-1}(x) = \frac{5-2x}{x-4}$$

The solution of the given equation is found by finding the value of $f^{-1}(3)$.

$$f^{-1}(3) = \frac{5-(2\times3)}{3-4} = 1$$

Hence the solution of the given equation is $x = 1$.

†COMPOSITE FUNCTIONS

Suppose $f: x \to 2x-1$ and $g: x \to 3x+2$

then $\qquad gf: x \to 3(2x-1)+2$

or $\qquad gf: x \to 6x-1$

Note that gf means do f first and then g.

Composite functions are seldom commutative, that is,

$$gf \neq fg$$

For the above,

$$fg: x \to 2(3x+2)-1$$

or $\quad fg: x \to 6x+3 = 3(2x+1)$

Hence $\qquad\qquad gf \neq fg$

EXAMPLE 13

If $f: x \to 2x+5$, $g: x \to \frac{1}{2}x$ and $h: x \to 3x-1$ find:

(a) $fg(2)$ (b) $gf(-1)$ (c) $fgh(3)$
(d) $ghf(-2)$.

(a) $fg: x \to 2(\frac{1}{2}x)+5 = x+5$
$$fg(2) = 2+5 = 7$$

(b) $gf: x \to \frac{1}{2}(2x+5) = x+\frac{5}{2}$
$$gf(-1) = -1+\frac{5}{2} = \frac{3}{2}$$

(c) $fgh: x \to 2[\frac{1}{2}(3x-1)]+5 = 3x+4$
$$fgh(3) = 3\times3+4 = 13$$

(d) $ghf: x \to \frac{1}{2}[3(2x+5)-1] = 3x+7$
$$ghf(-2) = 3\times(-2)+7 = 1$$

†THE INVERSE OF A COMPOSITE FUNCTION

If $f: x \to 3x-5$ and $g: x \to 2x+1$

then $\quad gf: x \to 2(3x-5)+1 = 6x-9$
$$(gf)^{-1}: x \to \frac{1}{6}(x+9)$$

Now $f^{-1}: x \to \frac{1}{3}(x+5)$ and $g^{-1}: x \to \frac{1}{2}(x-1)$

$$f^{-1}g^{-1}: x \to \frac{1}{3}[\frac{1}{2}(x-1)]+\frac{5}{3} = \frac{1}{6}(x-1)+\frac{5}{3}$$
$$= \frac{1}{6}x-\frac{1}{6}+\frac{5}{3} = \frac{1}{6}x+\frac{9}{6} = \frac{1}{6}(x+9)$$

Hence $\quad (gf)^{-1} = f^{-1}g^{-1}$.

Using this relationship often simplifies the work in finding the inverse of a composite function.

EXAMPLE 14

If $f: x \to 7x+2$ and $g: x \to 2x-1$ find $(gf)^{-1}$.

Now $f^{-1}: x \to \frac{1}{7}(x-2)$ and $g^{-1}: x \to \frac{1}{2}(x+1)$

$$(gf)^{-1} = f^{-1}g^{-1}: x \to \frac{1}{7}[\frac{1}{2}(x+1)]-\frac{2}{7}$$
$$= \frac{1}{14}(x+1)-\frac{2}{7}$$
$$= \frac{1}{14}x+\frac{1}{14}-\frac{2}{7}$$
$$= \frac{1}{14}(x-3)$$

†Exercise 124 – *All type C*

Find the inverse functions for the following:

1) $f: x \to 3x$

2) $f: x \to 2x-3$

3) $f : x \rightarrow \dfrac{x-3}{2}$

4) $f : x \rightarrow 3(2x-5)$

5) $f : x \rightarrow \dfrac{2x-5}{x+2}$

6) If $f : x \rightarrow 2(3x-1)$ find:
(a) $f^{-1}(-2)$ (b) $f^{-1}(3)$.

7) If $f : x \rightarrow \dfrac{x-4}{3-x}$ find:

(a) $f^{-1}(2)$ (b) $f^{-1}(-1)$

8) If $f : x \rightarrow 4x-7$ find $f^{-1}(3)$ and $f^{-1}(-2)$.

9) If $f : x \rightarrow 2x-5$, $g : x \rightarrow 3x+1$ and $h : x \rightarrow 4x$, find:

(a) $fg(2)$ (b) $gf(2)$ (c) $fgh(-1)$
(d) $ghf(-3)$ (e) $hgf(2)$.

10) If $f : x \rightarrow 5x-1$ and $g : x \rightarrow 3x+2$, find $(fg)^{-1}(x)$ and $(gf)^{-1}(x)$.

11) By finding the inverse of $f(x) = \dfrac{x+3}{x-5}$,

solve the equation $\dfrac{x+3}{x-5} = 2$.

12) By finding the inverse of $f(x) = \dfrac{3x+1}{4x-3}$,

solve the equation $\dfrac{3x+1}{4x-3} = 5$.

†CARTESIAN PRODUCT

A Cartesian product set is a set consisting of ordered pairs of numbers. These are obtained by taking the first number of each ordered pair from the first of two given sets and the second number from the other set.

If $A = \{1, 2, 3, 4\}$ and $B = \{5, 7, 9\}$ then the following sets of Cartesian products may be obtained:

$A \times B = \{(1,5), (1,7), (1,9), (2,5), (2,7),$
$\qquad (2,9), (3,5), (3,7), (3,9), (4,5),$
$\qquad (4,7), (4,9)\}$

$B \times A = \{(5,1), (5,2), (5,3), (5,4), (7,1),$
$\qquad (7,2), (7,3), (7,4), (9,1), (9,2),$
$\qquad (9,3), (9,4)\}$

Note that for $A \times B$ the first number in each ordered pair is taken from A and the second

from B. In the case of $B \times A$ the first number is taken from B and the second from A.

$A \times B$ is read 'A cross B' whilst $B \times A$ is read 'B cross A'. Note that $A \times B$ is not the same as $B \times A$. That is

$$A \times B \neq B \times A$$

(i.e. $A \times B$ and $B \times A$ are non-commutative).

Cartesian product sets can be obtained by taking both numbers in each ordered pair from a single set. Thus if $A = \{2, 4, 6\}$

$A \times A = \{(2,2), (2,4), (2,6), (4,2), (4,4),$
$\qquad (4,6, (6,2), (6,4), (6,6)\}$

The number of ordered pairs in a Cartesian product set is equal to the product of the numbers of members in each of the sets from which the numbers were chosen. Thus if the number of members in set A is $n(A)$ and the number of members in set B is $n(B)$, then the number of members in A cross B is

$$n(A \times B) = n(A) \times n(B)$$

From the definition of a Cartesian product set the domain of $A \times B$ is set A and the range of $A \times B$ is set B. Hence in plotting a graph of a Cartesian product set $A \times B$, the numbers in set A are plotted along the horizontal axis and

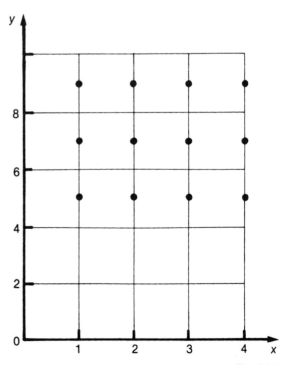

Fig. 25.24

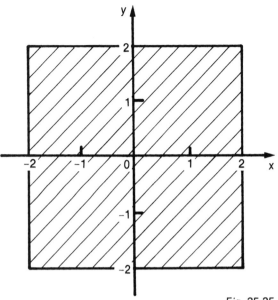

Fig. 25.25

the numbers in set B are plotted along the vertical axis. Fig. 25.24 shows the graph of $A \times B$ where $A = \{1, 2, 3, 4\}$ and $B = \{5, 7, 9\}$.

The shaded region in Fig. 25.25 is the graph of $A \times A$ where $A = \{x : -2 \leqslant x \leqslant 2, x \in R\}$ and $R = \{\text{real numbers}\}$. Here x is any real number between and including -2 and 2. Note that the graph therefore consists of the sides of the square as well as its interior.

Tree diagrams are useful in obtaining the ordered pairs of a Cartesian product set. Thus if $A = \{2, 4, 6\}$ and $B = \{1, 3, 5\}$ the tree diagram would look like Fig. 25.26.

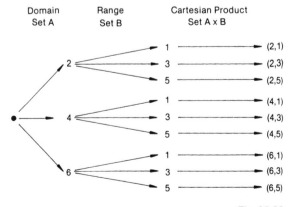

Fig. 25.26

EXAMPLE 15

If $A = \{4, 5, 6\}$ and $B = \{2, 3\}$ list the ordered pairs in each of the following:

(a) $A \times B$ (b) $B \times A$ (c) $A \times A$ (d) $B \times B$.

(a) $A \times B = \{(4, 2), (4, 3), (5, 2), (5, 3),$
$\qquad\qquad (6, 2), (6, 3)\}$

(b) $B \times A = \{(2, 4), (2, 5), (2, 6), (3, 4),$
$\qquad\qquad (3, 5), (3, 6)\}$

(c) $A \times A = \{(4, 4), (4, 5), (4, 6), (5, 4), (5, 5),$
$\qquad\qquad (5, 6), (6, 4), (6, 5), (6, 6)\}$

(d) $B \times B = \{(2, 2), (2, 3), (3, 2), (3, 3)\}$

Exercise 125 – *All type B*

1) State the domain and range of the following Cartesian products:

(a) $\{(2, 10), (2, 15), (4, 10), (4, 15),$
$\quad (8, 10), (8, 15)\}$
(b) $\{(1, 5), (1, 7), (1, 9), (2, 5), (2, 7), (2, 9)\}$

2) If $M = \{2, 5, 7\}$ and $N = \{3, 8\}$, list the ordered pairs in each of the following Cartesian products:

(a) $M \times M$ (b) $N \times N$ (c) $M \times N$
(d) $N \times M$.

3) If $S = \{-4, -2, 0, 1, 2\}$ and $T = \{x : -4 \leqslant x \leqslant 2, x \in R\}$ where $R = \{\text{real numbers}\}$ plot the graphs of:

(a) $S \times S$ (b) $T \times T$.

4) If a set A has 5 elements and a set B has 3 elements, write down the number of elements in the Cartesian products:

(a) $A \times A$ (b) $A \times B$ (c) $B \times A$
(d) $B \times B$.

5) If $P = \{2, 4, 5\}$ and $Q = \{3, 7\}$ plot the graphs of:

(a) $P \times Q$ (b) $P \times P$ (c) $Q \times P$
(d) $Q \times Q$.

CHAPTER 25 SUMMARY

Points to remember

(i)   A *relation* is a set of ordered pairs.
      E.g. $\{(2,4),(3,5),(4,6),(5,7)\}$.

(ii) The set of first elements is called the
      domain. The domain of the above is
      $\{2,3,4,5\}$.

(iii) The set of second elements is called the
      range. The range of the above is
      $\{4,5,6,7\}$.

(iv) We may write (i) as $f(x) = x + 2$ or
      $f : x \rightarrow x + 2$.

(v)   If a function f maps x from the domain
      to y in the range, then the function
      which maps y back to x is called the
      inverse function.

(vi) To find the inverse of a given function,
      interchange the elements of the domain
      and range.

(vii) The inverse of $f(x)$ is written $f^{-1}(x)$.

(viii) If 'y varies directly as x' or 'y is
      proportional to x', we write '$y = kx$',
      where k is a constant.

(ix) If 'y varies inversely as x', then '$y = k/x$'.

(x)   Given two functions f and g, the
      composite function (fg) is found as
      follows:
      (a) Find $g(x)$
      (b) Find the image of $g(x)$ under f,
          i.e. $f[g(x)]$.

Chapter 26 **Further Graphical Work**

†THE GRADIENT OF A CURVE

Consider the graph $y = x^2$, part of which is shown in Fig. 26.1. As the values of x increase so do the values of y, but they do not increase at the same rate. A glance at the portion of the curve shown in Fig. 26.1 shows that the values of y increase faster when x is large because the gradient of the curve is increasing.

To find the rate of change of y with respect to x at a particular point we need to find the gradient of the curve at that point. If we draw a tangent to the curve at the point, the gradient of the tangent will be the same as the gradient of the curve.

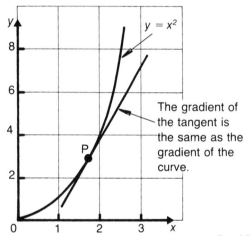

The gradient of the tangent is the same as the gradient of the curve.

Fig. 26.1

EXAMPLE 1

EXAMPLE 1

(1) Draw the curve of $y = x^2$ and find the gradient of the curve at the points where $x = 2$ and $x = -2$.

To draw the curve the table below is drawn up

x	−3	−2	−1	0	1	2	3
$y = x^2$	9	4	1	0	1	4	9

The point where $x = 2$ is the point $(2, 4)$. We draw a tangent at this point as shown in

Fig. 26.2. Then by constructing a right-angled triangle the gradient is found to be $\dfrac{4}{1} = 4$.

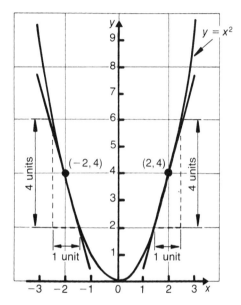

Fig. 26.2

This gradient is positive since the tangent slopes upwards from left to right.

A positive value of the gradient indicates that y is increasing as x increases.

The point where $x = -2$ is the point $(-2, 4)$.

By drawing the tangent at this point and constructing a right-angled triangle as shown in Fig. 26.2, the gradient is found to be

$$\frac{-4}{1} = -4$$

The gradient is negative because the tangent slopes downwards from left to right.

A negative value of the gradient indicates that y is decreasing as x increases.

(2) Draw the graph of $y = x^2 - 3x + 7$ between $x = -4$ and $x = 4$ and hence find the gradients of the curve at the points $x = -3$ and $x = 2$.

To plot the curve draw up the following table.

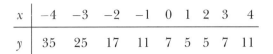

x	−4	−3	−2	−1	0	1	2	3	4
y	35	25	17	11	7	5	5	7	11

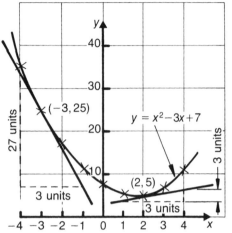

Fig. 26.3

At the point where $x = -3$, $y = 25$.

At the point $(-3, 25)$ draw a tangent to the curve as shown in Fig. 26.3. The gradient is found by drawing a right-angled triangle (which should be as large as possible for accuracy) as shown and measuring its height and base. Hence

gradient at the point

$$(-3, 25) = -\frac{27}{3} = -9$$

at the point where $x = 2$, $y = 5$. Hence by drawing a tangent and a right-angled triangle at the point $(2, 5)$,

$$\text{gradient at point } (2, 5) = \frac{3}{3} = 1$$

(3) Draw the graph of $y = x^2 + 3x - 2$ taking values of x between $x = -1$ and $x = 4$. Hence find the value of $y = x^2 + 3x - 2$ where the gradient of the curve is 7.

To plot the curve the following table is drawn up

x	−1	0	1	2	3	4
y	−4	−2	2	8	16	26

The curve is shown in Fig. 26.4.

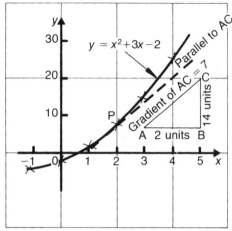

Fig. 26.4

To obtain a line whose gradient is 7 we draw the $\triangle ABC$ making (for convenience) $AB = 2$ units to the scale on the x-axis and $BC = 14$ units to the scale on the y-axis. Hence:

$$\text{gradient of AC} = \frac{BC}{AB} = \frac{14}{2} = 7$$

Using set-squares we draw a tangent to the curve so that the tangent is parallel to AC. As can be seen this tangent touches the curve at the point P where $x = 2$. Hence the gradient of the curve is 7 at the point where $x = 2$.

Exercise 126 – *All type C*

1) Draw the graph of $y = 3x^2 + 7x + 3$ and find the gradient of the curve at the points where $x = -2$ and $x = 2$.

2) Draw the graph of $y = 2x^2 - 5$ for values of x between −2 and 3. Find the gradient of the curve at the points where $x = -1$ and $x = 2$.

3) Draw the curve of $y = x^2 - 3x + 2$ from $x = 2.5$ to $x = 3.5$ and find its gradient at the point where $x = 3$.

4) For what values of x is the gradient of the curve $y = \frac{x^3}{3} + \frac{x^2}{2} - 33x + 7$ equal to 3? In drawing the curve take values of x between −8 and 6.

5) If $y = (1 + x)(5 - 2x)$ copy and complete the table below

x	−2	−1½	−1	0	½	1	1½	2	3
y	−9			0	5		6	5	3	−4

Hence draw the graph of $y = (1 + x)(5 - 2x)$. Find the value of x at which the gradient of the curve is -2.

6) If $y = x^2 - 5x + 4$ find by plotting the curve between $x = 4$ and $x = 12$ the value of x at which the gradient of the curve is 11.

RATES OF CHANGE

There are many applications for rates of change, for example the decay rate of a radioactive substance, the rate of increase of the population of a country, etc.

EXAMPLE 2

The number of a type of bacterium is checked regularly and recorded in the table below:

Number of bacteria (thousands)	5.0	20.8	29.0	77.0	171	302
Time (hours)	1.0	2.5	3.0	5.0	7.5	10.0

Draw a graph of this information with time marked on the horizontal axis. Hence find the rate of increase of the bacteria after
(a) 4 hours   (b) 8 hours

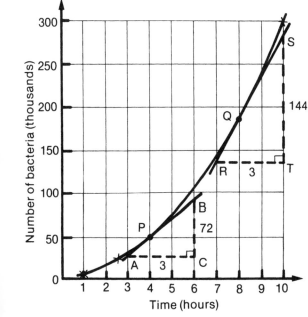

Fig. 26.5

The graph is drawn in Fig. 26.5 and it is seen to be a smooth curve.

(a) To find the rate of increase of the bacteria after 4 hours we draw a tangent to the curve at P and we find its gradient by drawing the right-angled triangle ABC.

$$\text{Rate of increase} = \frac{BC}{AC} = \frac{72}{3} = 24$$

Therefore at a time of 4 hours the bacteria is increasing at a rate of 24 000 per hour.

(b) To find the rate of increase of the bacteria after 8 hours a tangent to the curve is drawn at Q. Using the right-angled triangle RST, we have

$$\text{gradient} = \frac{144}{3} = 48$$

Therefore at a time of 8 hours the bacteria is increasing at a rate of 48 000 per hour.

EXAMPLE 3

The table below shows how the mass of a radioactive material varies with time.

Time (seconds)	0	1	2	3	4	5
Mass (grams)	1	0.5	0.25	0.125	0.063	0.032

Taking time on the horizontal axis, plot a graph of this information and from it determine the rate of decay after 2.5 seconds.

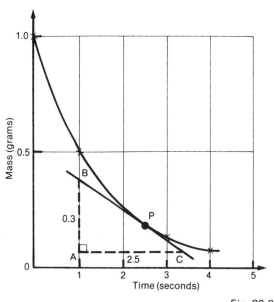

Fig. 26.6

The graph is shown in Fig. 26.6 which shows that the mass is decreasing with time. To determine the rate of decrease of mass with time (i.e. the decay rate) we draw a tangent to the curve at P. Drawing the right-angled triangle ABC,

$$\text{gradient at P} = \frac{AB}{AC} = \frac{0.3}{2.5} = 0.12$$

Hence the rate of decay after 2.5 seconds is 0.12 gram per second.

Exercise 127 – *All type C*

1) A particular bacterial growth, checked at regular intervals, showed the following figures:

Number of bacteria (thousands)	2.75	9.50	20.8	36.5
Time (minutes)	15	30	45	60

Number of bacteria (thousands)	49.5	64.5	100
Time (minutes)	70	80	100

Plot a graph of this information with time on the horizontal axis. From your graph determine the rate of increase of the bacteria:

(a) after 40 minutes,   (b) after 75 minutes.

2) The table below shows corresponding values of pressure, p, in millimetres and the volume, v cubic metres, of a given mass of gas at constant temperature.

p	90	110	130	150	170	190
v	16.7	13.6	11.5	9.95	8.82	7.89

Taking p on the horizontal axis plot a graph of this data and from it find the rate of change of v with respect to p, when $p = 140$ mm.

3) The way in which a radioactive substance decays with time is shown in the table below:

Time (seconds)	0	1	2	3	4
Mass (grams)	1	0.37	0.14	0.05	0.02

Taking time on the horizontal axis plot a graph of this data and from it determine the rate of decay after 2.5 seconds.

4) The table below shows how the population increased over a period of 50 years.

Number of years	0	10	20	30	40	50
Population (millions)	3	3.6	4.5	5.4	6.6	8.07

Taking time on the horizontal axis plot a graph of this information. Hence find the rate of population growth after:

(a) 15 years   (b) 45 years

5) The table below shows how barometric pressure varied with time.

Time (hours)	6	8	10	12
Pressure (mm of mercury)	751.5	753.2	754.7	755.3

Time (hours)	14	16	18
Pressure (mm of mercury)	755.9	755.5	755.2

Taking time on the horizontal axis plot a graph of pressure against time. From it find the rate of change of pressure at:

(a) 9 hours   (b) 15 hours.

†TURNING POINTS

At the points P and Q (Fig. 26.7) the tangent to the curve is parallel to the x-axis. The points P and Q are called *turning points*. The turning point at P is called a *maximum* turning point and the turning point at Q is called a *minimum* turning point. It will be seen from Fig. 26.7 that the value of y at P is not the greatest value of y nor is the value of y at Q the least. The terms maximum and minimum values apply only to the values of y near the turning points and not to the values of y in general.

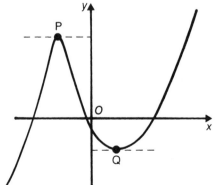

Fig. 26.7

EXAMPLE 4

(1) Plot the graph of $y = x^3 - 5x^2 + 2x + 8$ for values of x between -2 and 6. Hence find the maximum and minimum values of y.

To plot the graph we draw up a table in the usual way.

x	-2	-1	0	1
$y = x^3 - 5x^2 + 2x + 8$	-24	0	8	6

x	2	3	4	5	6
$y = x^3 - 5x^2 + 2x + 8$	0	-4	0	18	56

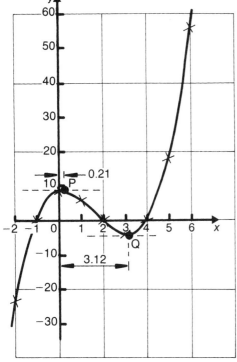

Fig. 26.8

The graph is shown in Fig. 26.8. The maximum value occurs at the point P where the tangent to the curve is parallel to the x-axis. The minimum value occurs at the point Q where again the tangent to the curve is parallel to the x-axis. From the graph the maximum value of y is 8.21 and the minimum value of y is -4.06.

Notice that the value of y at P is not the greatest value of y nor is the value of y at Q the least. However, the values of y at P and Q are called the maximum and minimum values of y respectively.

(2) A small box is to be made from a rectangular sheet of metal 36 cm by 24 cm. Equal squares of side x cm are cut from each of the corners and the box is then made by folding up the sides. Prove that the volume V of the box is given by the expression $V = x(36 - 2x)(24 - 2x)$. Find the value of x so that the volume may be

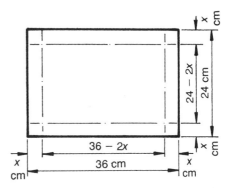

Fig. 26.9

a maximum and find this maximum volume. Referring to Fig. 26.9 we see that after the box has been formed

$$\text{its length} = 36 - 2x$$
$$\text{its breadth} = 24 - 2x$$
$$\text{its height} = x$$

The volume of the box is

$$V = \text{length} \times \text{breadth} \times \text{height}$$
$$\therefore \quad V = x(36 - 2x)(24 - 2x)$$

We now have to plot a graph of this equation and so we draw up the table below:

x	1	2	3	4
$36 - 2x$	34	32	30	28
$24 - 2x$	22	20	18	16
V	748	1280	1620	1792

x	5	6	7	8
$36 - 2x$	26	24	22	20
$24 - 2x$	14	12	20	8
V	1820	1728	1540	1280

The graph is shown in Fig. 26.10 and it can be seen that the maximum volume is 1825 cm^3, which occurs when $x = 4.71 \text{ cm}$.

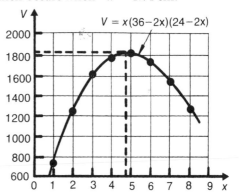

Fig. 26.10

Exercise 128 – *Questions 1–3 type B,*
remainder C

1) Find the minimum value of the curve
$y = 3x^2 + 2x - 3$. Plot the graph for values
of x between -2 and 3.

2) Find the maximum value of the curve
$y = -x^2 + 5x + 7$. Plot the graph for values
of x between -2 and 4.

3) Plot the graph of $y = x^3 - 9x^2 + 15x + 2$
taking values of x from 0 to 7. Hence find
the maximum and minimum values of y.

4) Draw the graph of $y = x^2 - 3x$ from
$x = -1$ to $x = 4$ and use your graph to
find:
(a) the least value of y,
(b) the two solutions of the equation
    $x^2 - 3x = 1$,
(c) the two solutions of the equation
    $x^2 - 2x - 1 = 0$.

5) Draw the graph of $y = (x - 1)(4 - x)$ for
values of x from 0 to 5. From your graph
find the greatest value of $(x - 1)(4 - x)$.

6) Write down the three values missing from
the following table which gives values of
$\frac{1}{2}(3x^2 - 5x - 1)$ for values of x from -2
to 3.

x	-2	-1.5	-1	-0.5
$\frac{1}{2}(3x^2 - 5x - 1)$	10.50	6.63		1.13

x	0	0.5	1
$\frac{1}{2}(3x^2 - 5x - 1)$		-1.38	-1.50

x	1.5	2	2.5	3.0
$\frac{1}{2}(3x^2 - 5x - 1)$	-0.88		2.63	5.50

Draw the graph of $y = \frac{1}{2}(3x^2 - 5x - 1)$ and
from it find the minimum value of
$\frac{1}{2}(3x^2 - 5x - 1)$ and the value of x at which
it occurs.

7) A piece of sheet metal $20\,\text{cm} \times 12\,\text{cm}$ is
used to make an open box. To do this,
squares of side x cm are cut from the
corners and the sides and ends folded over.
Show that the volume of the box is
$$V = x(20 - 2x)(12 - 2x)$$
By taking values of x from 1 cm to 5 cm in
0.5 cm steps, plot a graph of V against x
and find the value of x which gives a
maximum volume. What is the maximum
volume of the box?

8) An open tank which has a square base of
x metres has to hold 200 cubic metres of
liquid when full. Show that the height of the
tank is $\dfrac{200}{x^2}$ and hence prove that the
surface area of the tank is given by
$A = \left(x^2 + \dfrac{800}{x}\right)$ square metres. By plotting a
graph of A against x find the dimensions
of the tank so that the surface area is a
minimum. (Take values of x from 3 to 9.)

9) A rectangular parcel of length x metres,
width k metres and height k metres is to
be sent through the post. The sum of the
length and four times the width is to be
exactly 2 metres. Show that the volume of
the parcel is
$$V = \frac{x}{16}(2 - x)^2$$
Draw a graph of V against x for values of x
from 0.3 to 1 in steps of 0.1 and hence find
the dimensions of the parcel which has the
greatest possible volume.

10) A farmer uses 100 m of hurdles to make
a rectangular cattle pen. If he makes a pen of
length x metres show that the area enclosed
is $(50x - x^2)$ square metres. Draw the graph
of $y = 50x - x^2$ for values of x between 0
and 50 and use your graph to find:
(a) the greatest possible area that can be
    enclosed,
(b) the dimensions of the pen when the area
    enclosed is 450 square metres.

MAXIMUM OR MINIMUM VALUE OF A QUADRATIC EXPRESSION

If the squared term in the quadratic expression
$ax^2 + bx + c$ is positive, then the graph of
$y = ax^2 + bx + c$ is similar to Fig. 26.11.

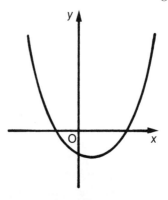

Fig. 26.11

The expression $ax^2 + bx + c$ has a minimum value as shown in the diagram. Although the minimum value can be found by drawing a graph it can also be found by completing the square.

Since, on completing the square, $y = ax^2 + bx + c$, which may be written as

$$y = a(x+h)^2 + k$$

the minimum value of y occurs when

$$(x+h) = 0$$

i.e. when $\qquad x = -h$

and its value is

$$y = k$$

EXAMPLE 5

Find the minimum value of $\quad y = 4x^2 + 8x + 1$ and the value of x where it occurs.

Completing the square of $4x^2 + 8x + 1$, we have

$$y = 4(x^2 + 2x) + 1$$
$$= 4(x^2 + 2x + 1) - 4 + 1$$
$$\therefore \qquad y = 4(x+1)^2 - 3$$

The minimum value of y occurs when

$$x + 1 = 0$$

i.e. when $\qquad x = -1$

and the minimum value is

$$y = -3$$

When the squared term of a quadratic expression is negative then the graph of $y = -ax^2 + bx + c$ is similar to Fig. 26.12.

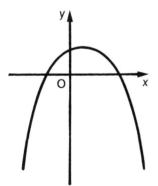

Fig. 26.12

Since, on completing the square,

$$y = k - a(x+h)^2$$

the maximum value of y occurs when

$$x + h = 0$$

i.e. when $\qquad x = -h$

and its value is

$$y = k$$

EXAMPLE 6

Find the maximum value of the quadratic expression $\quad y = -2x^2 + 4x + 7 \quad$ and the value of x where it occurs.

$$y = 7 - 2(x^2 - 2x)$$
$$= 7 - 2(x^2 - 2x + 1) + 2$$
$$\therefore \qquad y = 9 - 2(x-1)^2$$

The maximum value of y occurs when

$$x - 1 = 0$$

i.e. when $\qquad x = 1$

and its value is

$$y = 9$$

Exercise 129 – *Questions 1–2 type C, remainder D*

Find, by completing the square, the maximum or minimum value of each of the following quadratic expressions and the value of x where it occurs.

1) $x^2 + 2x - 3$ 4) $4x^2 - 8x - 1$

2) $-x^2 + 4x + 7$ 5) $-3x^2 + 9x - 2$

3) $2x^2 - 4x + 5$ 6) $-2x^2 - 8x + 7$

AREA UNDER A CURVE

The area under a graph may be found by one of several approximate methods. The simplest method is by counting the squares on the graph paper. Although it is a simple method it gives results which are as accurate as those obtained by more complicated methods.

EXAMPLE 7

Plot the graph of the function $y = 2x^2 - 7x + 8$ for values of x between 0 and 8. Hence, by counting squares find the area under the curve between $x = 2$ and $x = 6$.

x	0	1	2	3	4	5	6	7	8
y	8	3	2	5	12	23	38	57	80

The graph is drawn in Fig. 26.13. On the horizontal axis a scale of length of 1 large square = 2 units

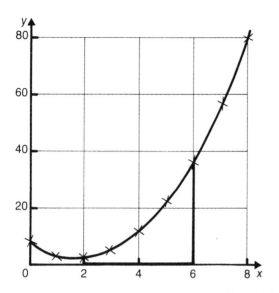

Fig. 26.13

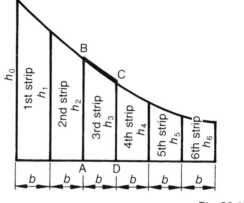

Fig. 26.15

has been used and on the vertical axis the scale is length of 1 large square = 20 units. Hence, on the horizontal axis length of 1 small square = $\frac{2}{10}$ = 0.2 units and on the vertical axis length of 1 small square = $\frac{20}{10}$ = 2 units. Therefore, 1 small square represents an area = 0.2 × 2 = 0.4 square units (Fig. 26.14).

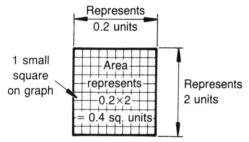

Fig. 26.14

To find the area between the graph, the x-axis and the lines $x = 2$ and $x = 6$ we count up the number of small squares in this region, judgement being exercised in the case of parts of small squares. The number of small squares is found to be about 145. Hence

$$\text{area required} = 145 \times 0.4$$

$$= 58 \text{ square units}$$

(The exact area is $58\frac{2}{3}$ square units. Hence the method of counting squares is a very accurate method.)

THE TRAPEZIUM RULE

This is the second method for finding the area under a curve. In order to find the area shown

in Fig. 26.15 we divide the area up into a number of equal strips each of width b.

Consider the third strip. If we join BC then ABCD is a trapezium and its area is $b \times \frac{1}{2}(\text{AB} + \text{CD})$ which very nearly equals the area of the strip.

If the ordinates at the extremes of the strips are $h_0, h_1, h_2, \ldots$ etc., then the area of the first strip is

$$A_1 = b \times \tfrac{1}{2}(h_0 + h_1) = \tfrac{1}{2}bh_0 + \tfrac{1}{2}bh_1$$

The area of the second strip is

$$A_2 = b \times \tfrac{1}{2}(h_1 + h_2) = \tfrac{1}{2}bh_1 + \tfrac{1}{2}bh_2$$

The area of the third strip is

$$A_3 = b \times \tfrac{1}{2}(h_2 + h_3) = \tfrac{1}{2}bh_2 + \tfrac{1}{2}bh_3$$

and so on.

The total area is:

$$\begin{aligned} A &= A_1 + A_2 + A_3 + \ldots \\ &= \tfrac{1}{2}bh_0 + \tfrac{1}{2}bh_1 + \tfrac{1}{2}bh_1 \\ &\quad + \tfrac{1}{2}bh_2 + \tfrac{1}{2}bh_2 + \tfrac{1}{2}bh_3 + \ldots \\ &= \tfrac{1}{2}bh_0 + bh_1 + bh_2 + \ldots \\ &= b(\tfrac{1}{2}h_0 + h_1 + h_2 + \ldots) \\ &= \text{width of strips} \times (\tfrac{1}{2}\text{the} \\ &\quad \text{sum of first and last ordinates} \\ &\quad + \text{sum of remaining ordinates}) \end{aligned}$$

This is known as the *trapezium rule*.

EXAMPLE 8

Find the area required in Example 7 using the trapezium rule.

Using the values of y given in the table of Example 7 we have:

$$\text{Area} = 1 \times [\tfrac{1}{2}(2 + 38) + 5 + 12 + 23]$$

$$= 60 \text{ square units}$$

This compares very well with the exact area of $58\frac{2}{3}$. A more accurate estimate may be obtained by taking more strips.

Exercise 130 – *All type C*

Find the areas under the following curves by (a) counting squares; (b) using the trapezium rule:

1) Between the curve $y = x^3$, the x-axis and the lines $x = 5$ and $x = 3$.

2) Between the curve $y = 3 + 2x + 3x^2$, the x-axis and the lines $x = 1$ and $x = 2$.

3) Between the curve $y = x^2(2x - 1)$, the x-axis and the lines $x = 1$ and $x = 2$.

4) Between the curve $y = (x + 1)^2$, the x-axis and the lines $x = 1$ and $x = 3$.

5) Between the curve $y = 5x - x^3$, the x-axis and the lines $x = 1$ and $x = 2$.

AVERAGE SPEED

In Chapter 7 it was shown that

$$\text{Average speed} = \frac{\text{distance travelled}}{\text{time taken}}$$

If the distance is measured in metres and the time in seconds, then the speed is measured in metres per second (m/s). Similarly, if the distance is measured in kilometres and the time in hours, then the speed is measured in kilometres per hour (km/h).

EXAMPLE 9

(1) A car travels a distance of 100 km in 2 hours. What is the average speed?

$$\text{Average speed} = \frac{100 \text{ km}}{2 \text{ h}} = 50 \text{ km/h}$$

(2) A body travels a distance of 80 metres in 4 seconds. What is its average speed?

$$\text{Average speed} = \frac{80 \text{ m}}{4 \text{ s}} = 20 \text{ m/s}$$

DISTANCE–TIME GRAPHS

Because

$$\text{distance} = \text{speed} \times \text{time}$$

then if the speed is constant the distance travelled is proportional to time and a graph of distance against time will be a straight line passing through the origin. The gradient of this graph will represent the speed.

EXAMPLE 10

A man travels a distance of 120 km in 2 hours by car. He then cycles 20 km in $1\frac{1}{2}$ hours and finally walks a distance of 8 km in 1 hour, all at constant speed. Draw a graph to illustrate this journey and from it find the average speed for the entire journey.

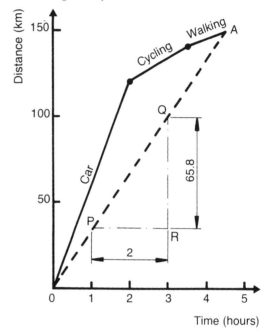

Fig. 26.16

The graph is drawn in Fig. 26.16 and it consists of three straight lines. The average speed is found by drawing the straight line OA and finding its gradient.

To find the gradient of OA we draw the right-angled triangle PQR, which, for accuracy, should be as large as possible.

$$\text{Gradient of OA} = \frac{\text{QR}}{\text{PR}} = \frac{65.8}{2} = 32.9$$

Hence average speed = 32.9 km/h.

If the speed is not constant the distance–time graph will be a curve.

EXAMPLE 11

The table shown overleaf gives the distance travelled, s metres, of a vehicle after a time of t seconds.

t	0	1	2	3	4
s	0	1	8	27	64

Draw a smooth curve to show how s varies with t and use the graph to find the speed after 2.5 seconds.

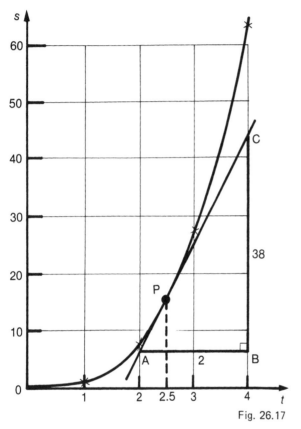

Fig. 26.17

The graph is drawn in Fig. 26.17. To find the speed after 2.5 seconds draw a tangent to the curve at the point P and find its gradient. This is done by drawing the right-angled triangle ABC. The gradient is $\dfrac{38}{2} = 19$. Hence the speed after 2.5 seconds is 19 m/s.

Exercise 131 – *All type B*

1) A vehicle travels 300 km in 5 hours. Calculate its average speed.

2) A car travels 400 km at an average speed of 80 km/h. How long does the journey take?

3) A train travels for 5 hours at an average speed of 60 km/h. How far has it travelled?

4) A vehicle travels a distance of 250 km in a time of 5 hours. Draw a distance–time graph to depict the journey and from it find the average speed of the vehicle.

5) A car travels a distance of 120 km in 3 hours. It then changes speed and travels a further distance of 80 km in $2\frac{1}{2}$ hours. Assuming that the two speeds are constant draw a distance–time graph. From the graph find the average speed of the journey.

6) A girl cycles a distance of 20 km in 100 minutes. She then rests for 20 minutes and then cycles a further 10 km which takes her 50 minutes. Draw a distance–time graph to represent the journey and from it find the average speed for the entire journey.

7) A man travels a distance of 90 km by car which takes him $1\frac{1}{2}$ hours. He then cycles 18 km in a time of $1\frac{1}{2}$ hours. He then rests for 15 minutes before continuing on foot, walking 8 km in 2 hours. By drawing a distance–time graph find his average speed for the entire journey assuming that he travels at constant speed for each of the three parts of the journey.

8) The following table gives the distance, s metres, travelled after a time of t seconds.

t	0	2	4	6	8
s	0	16	128	432	1024

Draw a graph to show how s varies with t and use your graph to find the speed after 5 seconds.

9) A body moves a distance of s metres in t seconds so that $s = t^3 - 3t^2 + 8$.

(a) Draw a graph to show how s varies with t for values of t between 1 second and 6 seconds.

(b) Find the speed of the body at the end of 4 seconds.

10) A body moves s metres in t seconds where $s = \dfrac{1}{t^2}$. By drawing a suitable graph find the speed of the body after 3 seconds.

11) The table below shows how the distance travelled by a body (s metres) varies with the time (t seconds).

t	0	1	2	3	4	5
s	0	1	16	63	160	325

Draw a graph of this information and hence find the speed of the body after 3 seconds.

VELOCITY

Velocity is speed in a given direction, e.g. 50 km/h due north.

VELOCITY–TIME GRAPHS

If a velocity–time graph is drawn (Fig. 26.18), the area under the graph gives the distance travelled. The gradient of the curve gives the acceleration since acceleration is rate of change of velocity. If the velocity is measured in metres per second (m/s), the acceleration will be measured in metres per second per second (m/s^2).

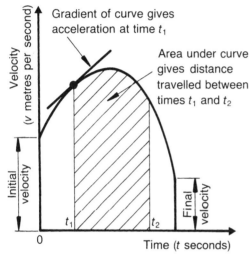

Fig. 26.18

If the acceleration is constant the velocity–time graph will be a straight line (Fig. 26.19). When the velocity is increasing the graph has a positive gradient (i.e. it slopes upwards to the right). If the velocity is decreasing (i.e. there is deceleration, sometimes called retardation) the graph has a negative gradient (i.e. it slopes downwards to the right).

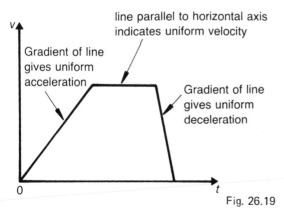

Fig. 26.19

EXAMPLE 12

A car, starting from rest, attains a velocity of 20 m/s after 5 seconds. It continues at this speed for 15 seconds and then slows down and comes to rest in a further 8 seconds. If the acceleration and retardation are constant, draw a velocity–time graph and from it, find:

(a) The acceleration of the car.
(b) The retardation of the car.
(c) The distance travelled in the total time of 28 seconds.

The velocity–time graph is drawn in Fig. 26.20.

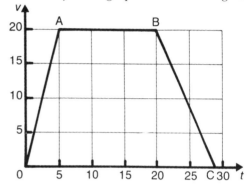

Fig. 26.20

(a) The acceleration is given by the gradient of the line OA.

$$\text{Acceleration} = \frac{20}{5} = 4\,m/s^2$$

(b) The retardation is given by the gradient of the line BC.

$$\text{Retardation} = \frac{20}{8} = 2.5\,m/s^2$$

(c) The distance travelled in the 28 seconds the car was travelling is given by the area of the trapezium OABC.

$$\text{Distance travelled} = 20 \times \tfrac{1}{2} \times (15 + 28)$$
$$= 20 \times \tfrac{1}{2} \times 43$$
$$= 430\,m$$

EXAMPLE 13

The table below gives the speed of a car, v metres per second, after a time of t seconds.

t	0	5	10	15	20	25
v	0	2.4	5.0	7.5	9.5	10.2

t	30	35	40	45	50	55
v	9.2	5.2	2.7	2.3	2.7	3.5

Draw a smooth curve to show how v varies with t. Use the graph:

(a) to find the speed of the car after 47 seconds,
(b) to find the times when the speed is 4 m/s,
(c) to find the acceleration after 15 seconds,
(d) to find the retardation after 35 seconds.

The graph is drawn in Fig. 26.21.

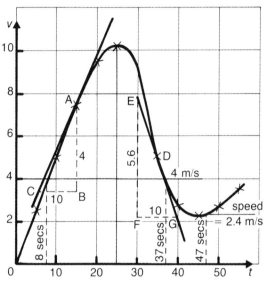

Fig. 26.21

(a) The speed after 47 seconds is read directly from the graph and it is found to be 2.4 m/s.

(b) The times when the speed is 4 m/s are also read directly from the graph and they are found to be 8 seconds and 37 seconds.

(c) To find the acceleration at a time of 15 seconds, draw a tangent to the curve at the point A and find its gradient by constructing the right-angled triangle ABC.

The gradient $= \dfrac{4}{10} = 0.4$. Hence the acceleration is 0.4 m/s^2.

(d) To find the retardation at a time 35 seconds draw a tangent to the curve at the point D. Then by constructing the right-angled triangle EFG,

retardation $= \dfrac{5.6}{10} = 0.56$ m/s^2. Note that the car is slowing down at this time and hence retardation occurs. This is also shown by the negative gradient of the tangent at the point D.

Exercise 132 – *Question 1–6 type B, remainder C*

1) Figure 26.22 shows a number of velocity–time diagrams. In each case state the distance travelled.

(a)

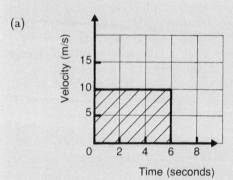

(b)

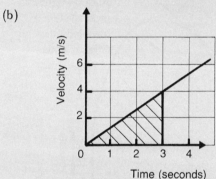

(c)

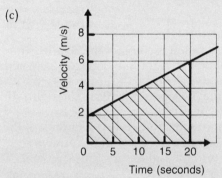

(d)

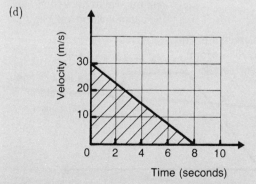

(e)

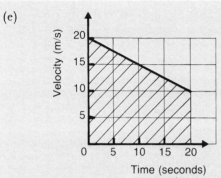

Fig. 26.22

2) Fig. 26.23 shows some velocity–time graphs. For each write down the acceleration or retardation.

(a)

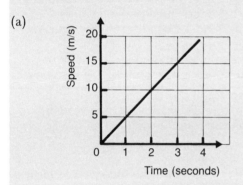

(b)

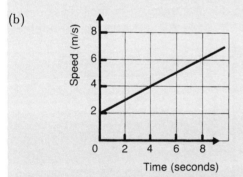

(c)

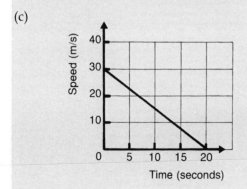

(d)

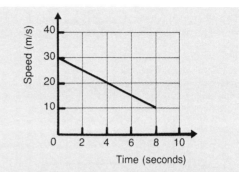

Fig. 26.23

3) Figure 26.24 shows the velocity–time graph for a vehicle travelling at a constant speed of 10 m/s. Find the total distance travelled in 15 s.

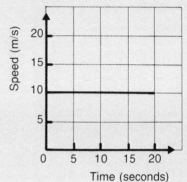

Fig. 26.24

4) The velocity–time graph shown in Fig. 26.25 shows a car travelling with constant acceleration.

(a) What is the acceleration?
(b) What is the initial speed?
(c) What is the distance travelled in the first 30 seconds?

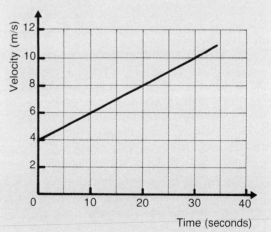

Fig. 26.25

5) From the velocity–time graph of

Fig. 26.26, find:

(a) the acceleration,
(b) the retardation,
(c) the initial speed,
(d) the distance travelled in the first 20 seconds.

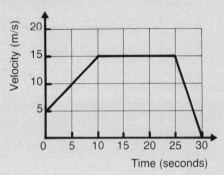

Fig. 26.26

6) Figure 26.27 shows a velocity–time diagram. Find:

(a) the acceleration after 5 seconds,
(b) the acceleration after 18 seconds,
(c) the acceleration after 40 seconds,
(d) the maximum speed reached,
(e) the total distance travelled in the first 50 seconds.

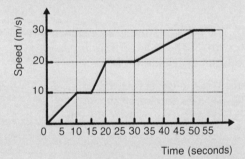

Fig. 26.27

7) A vehicle starting from rest attains a velocity of 16 m/s after it has been travelling for 8 seconds with uniform acceleration. It continues at this speed for 15 seconds and then it slows down, with uniform retardation, until it finally comes to rest in a further 10 seconds.

(a) Draw the velocity–time graph.
(b) Determine the acceleration of the vehicle.
(c) What is the retardation?
(d) From the diagram, find the distance travelled during the 33 seconds represented on the graph.

8) A car has an initial velocity of 5 m/s. It then accelerates uniformly for 6 seconds at $\frac{1}{2}$ m/s^2. It then proceeds at this speed for a further 25 seconds.

(a) Draw a velocity–time graph from this information.
(b) Calculate the distance travelled by the car in 31 seconds.

9) The speed of a body, v metres per second, at various times, t seconds, is shown in the following table:

t	0	1	2	3	4	5	6	7	8
v	0	1	2	6	12	20	30	42	56

(a) Draw a graph showing how v varies with t. Horizontally take 1 cm to represent 1 second and vertically take 1 cm to represent 10 m/s.
(b) From the graph find the acceleration after times (i) 2 seconds, (ii) 6 seconds.

10) The graph, Fig. 26.28, shows how the speed of a vehicle varies over a period of 20 seconds. From the graph, find:

(a) the acceleration of the vehicle at a time of 4 seconds,
(b) the time at which the speed of the car is decreasing at the greatest rate,
(c) the distance travelled by the vehicle in the 20 seconds represented on the graph.

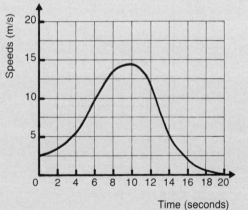

Fig. 26.28

SELF-TEST 26

1) In the curve (Fig. 26.29), the gradient of the curve at the point where $x = -2$ is

a -6 **b** $-\dfrac{1}{6}$ **c** $\dfrac{1}{6}$ **d** 6

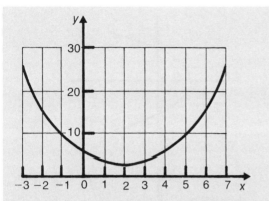

Fig. 26.29

2) In the curve (Fig. 26.29) the gradient of the curve at the point where $x = 3$ is

a -2 **b** $-\dfrac{1}{2}$ **c** $\dfrac{1}{2}$ **d** 2

3) The value of the function shown in Fig. 26.30 at the minimum turning point is
a -2 **b** 2 **c** 25 **d** 30

4) The value of the function shown in Fig. 26.30 at the minimum turning point is
a -3 **b** -1 **c** 10 **d** 20

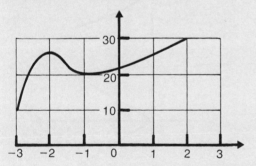

Fig. 26.30

5) Fig. 26.31 shows a velocity–time graph for a vehicle. The acceleration of the vehicle is

a 1 m/s^2 **b** 2 m/s^2 **c** 10 m/s^2
d 175 m/s^2

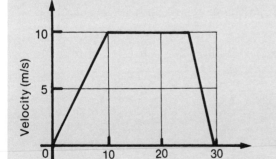

Fig. 26.31

6) In Fig. 26.31 the distance travelled in the 30 seconds shown is

a 75 m **b** 100 m **c** 225 m **d** 300 m

7) In Fig. 26.32, the initial velocity is

a 5 m/s **b** 10 m/s **c** 20 m/s **d** 30 m/s

8) In Fig. 26.32 the retardation is

a $\dfrac{1}{3} \text{ m/s}^2$ **b** 1 m/s^2 **c** $1\dfrac{1}{3} \text{ m/s}^2$
d 3 m/s^2

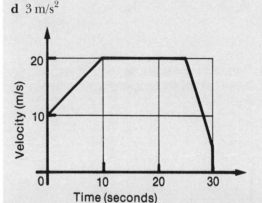

Fig. 26.32

9) All the points on the line PQ (Fig. 26.33) satisfy a certain relation. What is this relation?

a $y = x$ **b** $y = -3$ **c** $y = x + 3$
d $y = x - 3$

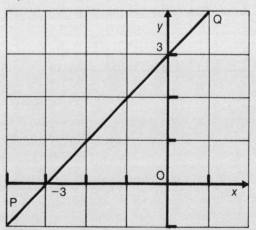

Fig. 26.33

10) What is the relation illustrated in Fig. 26.34?

a $x \to x + 1$ **b** $x \to x + 4$ **c** $x \to x + 3$
d $x \to 2x + 1$

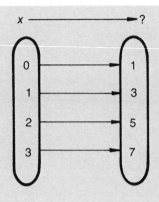

Fig. 26.34

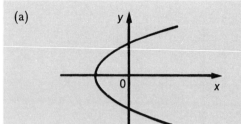

(a)

11) Which of the functions on the set $\{1,2,3,4\}$ does the graph (Fig. 26.35) represent?

a $f(x) = 2x + 2$　　**b** $f(x) = 2x - 2$
c $f(x) = \frac{1}{2}x + 2$　　**d** $f(x) = \frac{1}{2}x - 2$

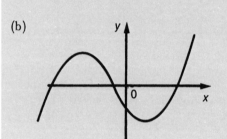

(b)

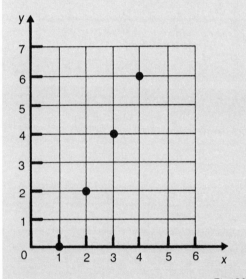

Fig. 26.35

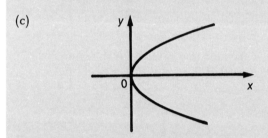

(c)

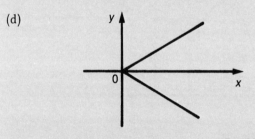

(d)

Fig. 26.36

12) Given that $f: x \to \dfrac{3}{x}$ for the domain $\{x: x \text{ is a real number and } x \neq 0\}$, what is the value of $f(-3)$?

a -1　　**b** 0　　**c** 1　　**d** 6

13) $f: x \to (x-1)(x-3)$ is defined on the domain $\{0,1,2,3\}$. What is 2 mapped onto?

a -1　　**b** 1　　**c** 5　　**d** 15

14) Which one of the graphs in Fig. 26.36 represents a function?

15) What is f^{-1} given that $f: x \to \dfrac{2x+7}{3x-5}$?

a $(7 + 5x)(3x - 2)$　　**b** $(7 - 5x)(3x - 2)$

c $\dfrac{7 + 5x}{3x - 2}$　　**d** $\dfrac{7 - 5x}{3x - 2}$

16) Two numbers x and y are inversely proportional to each other. If y is doubled then x:

a is doubled   **b** is halved   **c** has 2 added
d has 2 subtracted

17) Which one of the diagrams (Fig. 26.37) represents the function $x \to 2^x$?

(a)

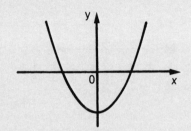

(b)

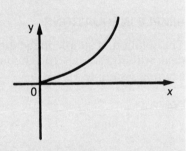

(c)

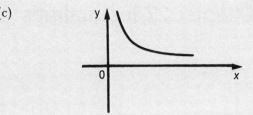

(d)

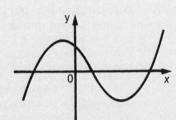

Fig. 26.37

18) If $f: x \to 3x + 2$ and $g: x \to 2x - 7$ then $gf(x)$ is equal to:

a $(2x - 7)(3x + 2)$ **b** $2(3x + 2) - 7$

c $\dfrac{3x + 2}{2x - 7}$ **d** $3(2x - 7) + 2$

CHAPTER 26 SUMMARY

Points to remember

(i) To find the gradient of a tangent line to a curve:
  (a) Draw a right-angled triangle with the tangent line as hypotenuse and the other sides parallel to 0x and 0y, respectively.
  (b) The vertical length divided by the horizontal length of the triangle is a measure of the gradient.

(ii) The gradient of a curve at a given point is the gradient of the tangent line at that point.

(iii) *Maximum* and *minimum* points are points at which the gradient is 0.

(iv) The trapezium rule: if ordinates $y_0, y_1, \ldots y_n$ are drawn at equal distances h along the x-axis to the given curve, the area enclosed by the x-axis, the curve and the ordinates y_0 and y_n is given by $h/2[y_0 + y_n + 2(y_1 + y_2 + \ldots + y_{n-1})]$.

(v) Average speed = total distance/total time.

(vi) In a distance–time graph, the speed at any time is the gradient of the curve at that time.

(vii) In a velocity–time graph,
  (a) the distance travelled in any interval = area under the curve in the interval,
  (b) the acceleration at any time is the gradient of the curve at that time.

Chapter 27 **Inequalities**

An *inequality* is a statement that one number or quantity is greater than a second number or quantity.

If we want to say that n is greater than 5 we write,

$$n > 5$$

Similarly, if x is less than 3 we write,

$$x < 3$$

If x is greater than or equal to 7 we write,

$$x \geqslant 7$$

Similarly, if y is less than or equal to 2 we write,

$$y \leqslant 2$$

Note that the arrow always points to the smaller quantity.

SOLUTIONS OF INEQUALITIES

If $x < 4$, what values of x could there be for the inequality to be true? There are very many different values which will make it true. Some of these are 3, 0, $-1\frac{1}{2}$, -3, but there are very many values all of which are less than 4. However if x has to be a positive whole number then only 1, 2 and 3 are possible solutions.

The solution to an inequality like $x < 4$ can be shown on a number line (Fig. 27.1). The empty circle at the end of the arrowed line shows that $x = 4$ is not included as a possible value of x.

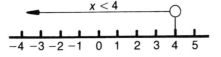

Fig. 27.1

Figure 27.2 shows the solution for $x \geqslant -2$. The solid circle at the end of the arrowed line shows that -2 is included as a possible value for x.

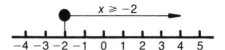

Fig. 27.2

SIMPLE INEQUATIONS

The solution of simple inequations has been dealt with in Chapter 16. The method is shown again in Example 1.

EXAMPLE 1

Solve the inequality $7x + 4 \geqslant 3x + 12$.

$$7x + 4 \geqslant 3x + 12$$

$$7x - 3x \geqslant 12 - 4$$

$$4x \geqslant 8$$

$$x \geqslant 2$$

The process is similar to solving a simple equation and the solution can be shown on a number line (Fig. 27.3).

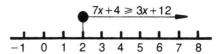

Fig. 27.3

EXAMPLE 2

If x has to be one of the numbers 0, 1, 2, 3, 4, 5 or 6, find the solution for $x < 5$ and $x \geqslant 3$.

Fig. 27.4

Since x has to be one of the numbers 0, 1, 2, 3, 4, 5 or 6, then if $x \geqslant 3$, x must be 3, 4, 5 or 6, and if $x < 5$, x must be 0, 1, 2, 3 or 4. Hence the solution would be the common points 3 and 4. These are indicated on the number line as shown in Fig. 27.4.

EXAMPLE 3

If x must be a whole number between 0 and 10 inclusive find the solution for the pair of inequalities $x \leqslant 2$ and $x \geqslant 5$.

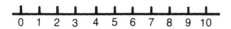

Fig. 27.5

Since if $x \leqslant 2$, x must be 2, 1, 0, and if $x \geqslant 5$, x must be 5, 6, 7, ..., then there are no common points. Hence there are no numbers which make both given equalities true. On the number line there will be no points indicated (Fig. 27.5).

Exercise 133 – *All type B*

Solve the following inequalities and represent the solutions on number lines:

1) $2x > 4$ 4) $3x - 4 \leqslant 8$

2) $x - 4 > 3$ 5) $6x + 4 \leqslant 25 - x$

3) $x + 5 > 7$ 6) $3x + 22 \geqslant 8x - 18$

Use number lines to find solutions for the following pairs of inequalities. In each case x must be one of the numbers 0, 1, 2, 3, 4, 5, 6, 7 and 8.

7) $x < 3$ and $x > 1$

8) $x < 0$ and $x > 6$

9) $x > 3$ and $x < 8$

10) $x \geqslant 0$ and $x \leqslant 7$

QUADRATIC INEQUATIONS

$$2x^2 + 3x - 20 \leqslant 0$$

is an example of a quadratic inequation. To solve it we first solve the equation

$$2x^2 + 3x - 20 = 0$$

$$(2x - 5)(x + 4) = 0$$

$$x = 2.5 \quad \text{or} \quad -4$$

Sketching the graph of $y = 2x^2 + 3x - 20$ (Fig. 27.6) we see that the function $2x^2 + 3x - 20$ is less than or equal to zero when x lies between -4 and 2.5. We may write the solution set $\{x: -4 \leqslant x \leqslant 2.5\}$.

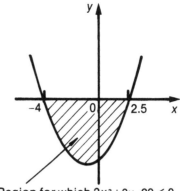

Region for which $2x^2 + 3x - 20 \leqslant 0$

Fig. 27.6

EXAMPLE 4

Solve the quadratic inequation,
$x^2 - 2x - 15 \geqslant 0$.

Solving the equation

$$x^2 - 2x - 15 = 0$$

$$(x + 3)(x - 5) = 0$$

$$x = -3 \quad \text{or} \quad 5$$

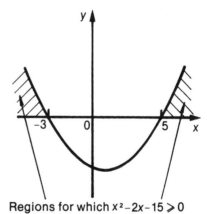

Regions for which $x^2 - 2x - 15 \geqslant 0$

Fig. 27.7

On sketching the graph (Fig. 27.7), we see that the function $x^2 - 2x - 15$ is greater than or equal to zero when $x \leqslant -3$ or when $x \geqslant 5$. Hence the solution set is $\{x: -3 < x < 5\}'$. The solution may also be represented on a number line as shown in Fig. 27.8.

Fig. 27.8

Alternative method

$$x^2 - 2x - 5 \geqslant 0 \qquad \therefore (x+3)(x-5) \geqslant 0$$

∴ Either (i) $(x+3) \geqslant 0$ and $(x-5) \geqslant 0$
or   (ii) $(x+3) \leqslant 0$ and $(x-5) \leqslant 0$

From (i) $x \geqslant -3$ and $x \geqslant 5$ ∴ $x \geqslant 5$
From (ii) $x \leqslant -3$ and $x \leqslant 5$ ∴ $x \leqslant -3$
It follows that x may take any value except those between -3 and 5.

∴   The solution set is $\{x: -3 < x < 5\}'$.

EXAMPLE 5

The length of a room is 1 metre longer than its width. If its area is not to exceed 6 square metres, what is the greatest length that the room may have?

Let x metres be the length of the room, then the width is $(x - 1)$ metres.

The area is $x(x - 1)$ square metres.

∴ $x(x - 1) \leqslant 6$

$$x^2 - x - 6 \leqslant 6$$

Solving the equation

$$x^2 - x - 6 = 0$$

$$(x - 3)(x + 2) = 0$$

$$x = 3 \quad \text{or} \quad -2$$

Hence the length of the room must not exceed 3 metres.

Exercise 134

Solve the following quadratic inequations and represent the solutions on number lines.

1) $x^2 + 2x - 8 \geqslant 0$

2) $x^2 + 8x + 15 \geqslant 0$

3) $x^2 - 5x + 6 \geqslant 0$

4) $3x^2 + 5x - 2 \geqslant 0$

5) $2x^2 - 7x + 4 \geqslant 0$

6) A rectangular room is 12 m wider than it is high and it is 24 m longer than it is wide. The total area of the walls is not to exceed 1024 m². Find the greatest width that the room can have.

7) The length of a rectangle is 6 cm longer than its width. Its area must not exceed 16 cm². What is the greatest length that the rectangle can have?

8) A garden consists of a square lawn with a path 2 m wide around its perimeter. If the lawn area is not to exceed four-ninths of the total area find the greatest length of the side of the lawn.

GRAPHS OF LINEAR INEQUALITIES

EXAMPLE 6

(1) Illustrate on a graph the solution of the inequality $3y + 6x < 8$.

First express the inequality in the form

$$3y < 8 - 6x$$

$$y < \frac{8}{3} - 2x$$

Next draw the graph of $y = \frac{8}{3} - 2x$ as shown in Fig. 27.9. The solution of the inequality $y < \frac{8}{3} - 2x$ is the shaded portion below the straight line representing the equation $y = \frac{8}{3} - 2x$. Since the solution does not include points on the line $y = \frac{8}{3} - 2x$, this is shown dotted.

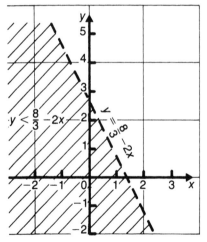

Fig. 27.9

(2) Show graphically the solution of the inequality $y \geqslant 4x - 1$.

The solution is the shaded portion of Fig. 27.10 which lies above the straight line representing the equation $y = 4x - 1$. Since the solution includes all the points lying on the line $y = 4x - 1$, this is shown by a full line.

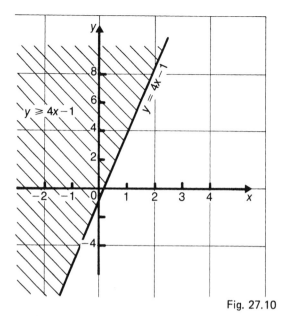

Fig. 27.10

(3) Show graphically the solution of the inequality $x \geqslant 4$.

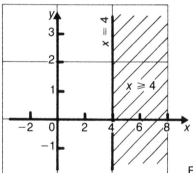

Fig. 27.11

The graph of the straight line $x = 4$ is parallel to the y-axis and 4 units from it (Fig. 27.11). The solution is given by the shaded part of the diagram.

(4) Illustrate on a graph the inequality $y < 2$.

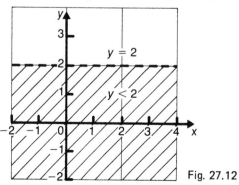

Fig. 27.12

The graph of the straight line $y = 2$ is parallel to the x-axis and 2 units above it (Fig. 27.12). The solution is shown by the shaded portion of the diagram.

Exercise 135 – *All type B*

Illustrate graphically the solutions for the following inequalities:

1) $x > 2$
2) $x \leqslant 3$
3) $x \geqslant -2$
4) $y > 0$
5) $y \leqslant 4$
6) $y \geqslant 1$
7) $y > 2$
8) $x + y \geqslant 2$
9) $y < 3x + 4$
10) $y + x - 1 < 0$
11) $3x + 2y - 5 \geqslant 0$
12) $4x + 2y + 6 \geqslant 0$

When several inequalities are plotted simultaneously on the same axes, their common solution is shown by the overlapping of the different shaded areas. The common area is usually a triangle, a quadrilateral or some kind of polygon.

EXAMPLE 7

Shade the region $y \geqslant 2x$, $y \leqslant 4$, $4x + 3y \geqslant 12$.

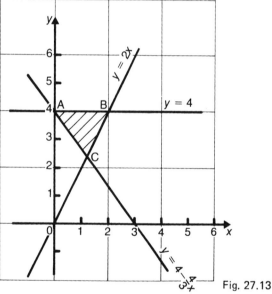

Fig. 27.13

In Fig. 27.13, the lines $y = 2x$, $y = 4$ and $y = 4 - \frac{4}{3}x$ have been drawn on the same axes. The region which contains the common solution is $\triangle ABC$, which has been shaded in the diagram.

EXAMPLE 8

If $y < 2x$, $4x + 3y < 12$, $y > 0$ and $x > 0$ and if x and y are both integers, find the two possible values of $(x + y)$.

In Fig. 27.14, the solution is contained in the shaded triangle. Since x and y are both integers (i.e. whole numbers), only the points P and Q meet the given conditions.

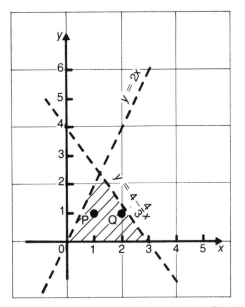

Fig. 27.14

At P,
$$x = 1 \quad \text{and} \quad y = 1$$
$$\therefore \qquad x + y = 1 + 1 = 2$$

At Q,
$$x = 2 \quad \text{and} \quad y = 1$$
$$\therefore \qquad x + y = 2 + 1 = 3$$

Exercise 136 – *All type C*

Shade the following regions:

1) $x \geqslant 0, \quad y \geqslant 0, \quad x + y \geqslant 10$

2) $x \geqslant 0, \quad y \geqslant 0, \quad 2x + 3y \leqslant 12,$
$5x + 2y \leqslant 20$

3) $x \geqslant 2, \quad y \geqslant 1, \quad x + y \leqslant 6, \quad x \leqslant 4,$
$y \leqslant 3$

4) $y \geqslant 4, \quad x \leqslant 3, \quad y \leqslant 2x$

5) $y \leqslant 3, \quad x \geqslant 0, \quad y + 2x \leqslant 5,$
$y - x \geqslant 0$

6) Draw the graph of $y = x^2 - 5x + 4$ for values of x from -1 to 6. On the same axes draw the line $y = 4$. Use these graphs to find the range of values for which $x^2 - 5x + 4 < 4$.

LINEAR PROGRAMMING

Linear programming is a useful application of systems of linear inequalities. Similar systems are used in business management in many industries, where there is a need to determine maximum profits or to find minimum costs or overhead expenses.

THE FUNDAMENTAL THEOREM OF LINEAR PROGRAMMING

A system of linear inequalities, such as that given in Example 9, when plotted on graph paper gives a region which is either a triangle, a quadrilateral or a polygon of some sort. When this happens the system of inequalities is called a *polygonal convex set*. The maximum or minimum value occurs at a vertex of the polygon or at all points along one of its sides.

EXAMPLE 9

Draw the graph of the solution set
$$x \geqslant 0$$
$$y \geqslant 0$$
$$x + 2y \leqslant 15$$

Hence find the maximum value of $3x + y$ for the system.

The solution set is given in the shaded area of Fig. 27.15 and the boundaries of $\triangle OAB$.

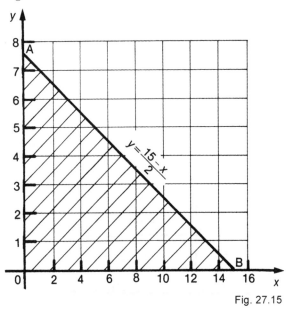

Fig. 27.15

The maximum value of $3x + y$ lies at one of the vertices of OAB, i.e. at either O, A or B.

At O, $x = 0$ and $y = 0$.
Hence $3x + y = 0$

At A, $x = 0$ and $y = 7.5$
Hence $3x + y = 7.5$

At B, $x = 15$ and $y = 0$.

Hence $3x + y = 45$.

Therefore the maximum value of $3x + y$ is 45.

EXAMPLE 10

Draw the graph of the solution set

$$x \geqslant 10$$

$$y \geqslant 5$$

$$4y + 3x \leqslant 120$$

$$y \geqslant 3x - 45$$

Hence find the maximum and minimum values of $3x + 2y - 3$.

The solution set is given by the shaded area shown in Fig. 27.16 and the boundaries of the quadrilateral ABCD.

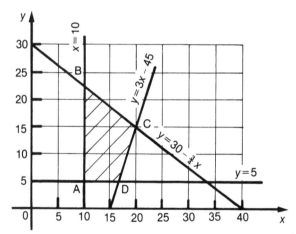

Fig. 27.16

The maximum and minimum values of $3x + 2y - 3$ occur at one of the vertices of ABCD.

At A $(10, 5)$, $3x + 2y - 3 = 37$

At B $(10, 25)$, $3x + 2y - 3 = 77$

At C $(20, 15)$, $3x + 2y - 3 = 87$

At D $\left(\frac{50}{3}, 5\right)$, $3x + 2y - 3 = 57$

Therefore the maximum value of $3x + 2y - 3$ is 87 and its minimum value is 37.

EXAMPLE 11

A shopper wants to buy oranges at 15 c each and grapefruits at 20 c each. She must buy at least one grapefruit and one orange and her basket can hold no more than 5 fruits. If the shopkeeper makes 4c profit on each orange and 6c profit on each grapefruit:

(a) write down three inequalities to represent the conditions given above;

(b) draw graphs on the same axes to show these conditions;

(c) find how many oranges and how many grapefruits the shopper buys if the shopkeeper is to realise the maximum profit;

(d) what is the greatest profit?

Let x = the number of oranges bought

and y = the number of grapefruits bought.

Then, $x \geqslant 1$, $y \geqslant 1$, $x + y \leqslant 5$.

The graphs are shown in Fig. 27.17. To find the greatest profit we have to find the maximum value of $4x + 6y$. This occurs at one of the vertices of $\triangle ABC$.

At A $(1, 1)$, $4x + 6y = 10$

At B $(1, 4)$, $4x + 6y = 28$

At C $(4, 1)$, $4x + 6y = 22$

Hence, for a maximum profit, the shopper must buy 1 orange and 4 grapefruits.

The maximum profit to the shopkeeper is then 28 c.

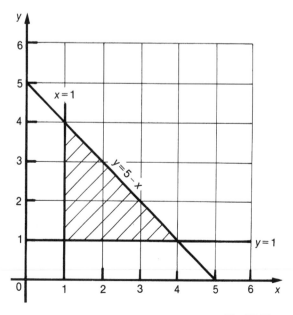

Fig. 27.17

Exercise 137

1) Find the maximum value of $3x - y + 2$ over the polygonal convex set shown in Fig. 27.18.

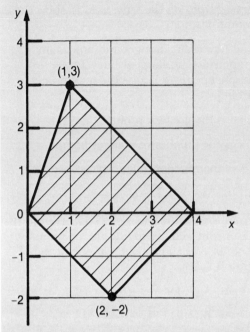

Fig. 27.18

2) Draw the graph of the solution set which satisfies the following inequalities: $x \geqslant 0$, $y \geqslant 0$, $x + y \leqslant 5$ and $y \leqslant -2x + 8$. Find the maximum and minimum values of $4x + y - 5$ for the system.

3) A supermarket sells two kinds of washing powder, Sure-clean and Quick-wash. At least 3 times as much Sure-clean is sold as Quick-wash. The supermarket has, at most, $1800\,\text{cm}^2$ of shelf space for washing powder. A box of Sure-clean requires $25\,\text{cm}^2$ of shelf space and a box of Quick-wash requires $15\,\text{cm}^2$. The profit per box is $8\,\text{c}$ for Sure-clean and $12\,\text{c}$ for Quick-wash. How many boxes of each kind of powder should be stocked for the greatest profit to be made? What is the greatest profit?

4) A radio shop stocks two types of radio, Type P and Type Q. It can sell at least 3 times as many of Type P as Type Q but there is only room to store 32 radios in all. It costs $1 per month to store Type P and $4 per month to store Type Q and the total cost of storage must not exceed $80 per month. If a profit of $20 is made on Type P and a profit of $50 on Type Q, how many of each type should be stored in order that the greatest profit will be made? What is the greatest profit?

5) Part of a farm is to be planted with sugar cane and part with sweet potatoes, observing the following restrictions:

	Sugar cane	Sweet potatoes	Max. total
Labour per hectare (days)	4	3	32
Cost of labour per hectare ($)	1	2	18
Cost of fertiliser per hectare ($)	4	1	24

On graph paper illustrate the above table and from your graph find:

(a) The greatest numbers of hectares of sugar cane and sweet potatoes that can be planted.

(b) The area of each crop that should be planted to give a maximum profit if sugar cane gives a profit of $8 per hectare and sweet potatoes $4 per hectare.

(c) The maximum profit.

6) Make a sketch of Fig. 27.19 and shade the region which represents the solution set for the following inequalities: $x \geqslant 0$, $y \geqslant 0$, $y \leqslant x + 1$ and $x + y \leqslant 5$. Calculate the coordinates of the points A, B and C and hence find the maximum value of $2x + 3y$.

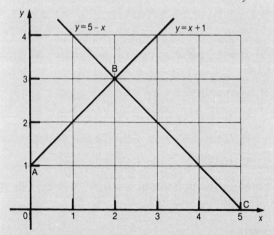

Fig. 27.19

7) A mail order firm has to transport 900 parcels using a lorry which takes 150 at a time and a van which takes 80 a time. The cost of each journey is $5 for the lorry and $4 for the van. If the total cost must be less than $44 and the van must make more journeys than the lorry, how many trips should each make to keep the cost to a minimum? What is the minimum cost?

8) The two positive numbers x and y are such that $A = \{(x,y): 2y - x \leqslant 14\}$, $B = \{(x,y): y + 2x \geqslant 12\}$ and $C = \{(x,y): y \geqslant 3x - 13\}$.

(a) Draw a graph to illustrate the solution set.
(b) If x and y are further defined as being whole numbers how many possible values are there for (x,y)?
(c) What is the maximum value of $x + y$?
(d) What is the minimum value of $x + y$?

9) A shop sells tins of ham at $4 each and tins of beef at $3.20 each. A customer decides that she will buy at least one tin of each but she cannot carry more than 6 tins altogether and she must not spend more than $20.

(a) Draw graphs on the same axes to represent these conditions.
(b) If the shopkeeper makes a profit of $1.60 on a tin of ham and $0.80 on a tin of beef find how many tins of each the customer buys if the shopkeeper obtains the greatest amount of profit.
(c) Calculate this greatest profit.

10) The owner of a business plans to buy two types of machine, Type A and Type B. Type A needs $4\,\text{m}^2$ of floor space and Type B needs $5\,\text{m}^2$. There is $55\,\text{m}^2$ of floor space available. Type A costs $120 each and Type B costs $240 each and up to $2880 can be spent. If at least 5 of Type A and at least 2 of Type B must be bought find the maximum number of machines that can be bought.

SELF-TEST 27

1) x has to be a whole number such that $0 \leqslant x \leqslant 10$. The solution for $x < 4$ and $x \geqslant 7$ is:

a 5   **b** 7   **c** 5, 6 or 7   **d** no solution

2) x has to be a whole number such that $0 \leqslant x \leqslant 6$. The solution for $x < 5$ and $x \geqslant 3$ is $x =$

a 4   **b** 3, 4   **c** 4, 5   **d** 3, 4, 5

3) The shaded portion of Fig. 27.20 represents the solution of the inequality:

a $y \leqslant 6 - \frac{4}{3}x$ **b** $y < 6 - \frac{4}{3}x$
c $y \geqslant 6 - \frac{4}{3}x$ **d** $y > 6 - \frac{4}{3}x$

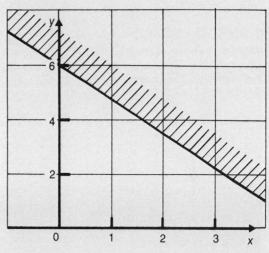

Fig. 27.20

4) The shaded region of Fig. 27.21 represents the solution of the inequalities:

a $y > x + 2$, $y > 2$, $0 < x < 3$
b $y \geqslant x + 2$, $y \geqslant 2$, $0 \leqslant x \leqslant 3$
c $y \leqslant x + 2$, $y \geqslant 2$, $0 \leqslant x \leqslant 3$
d $y < x + 2$, $y > 2$, $0 < x < 3$

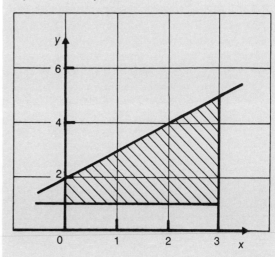

Fig. 27.21

5) The solution of the inequalities $y > 2$, $y < x + 3$, $0 \leqslant x < 4$ is represented by one of the shaded regions in Fig. 27.22. Which one?

6) For which of the following ordered pairs does $3x + 2y$ have a maximum value?

a $(0, 6)$ **b** $(3, 2)$ **c** $(4, 1)$ **d** $(5, -2)$

7) For which of the following ordered pairs does $5x - 2y + 3$ have a minimum value?

a $(2, 3)$ **b** $(4, 4)$ **c** $(3, 5)$ **d** $(1, 3)$

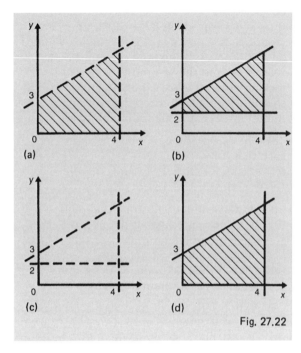

(a)   (b)   (c)   (d)

Fig. 27.22

CHAPTER 27 SUMMARY

Points to remember

(i) When multiplying or dividing by a negative number, the inequality sign is reversed. E.g. $-2x > -10 \Rightarrow x < 5$.

(ii) Linear inequalities, e.g. $2x - y + 4 > 0$. A line divides the plane into two half planes.

(iii) To determine the half plane for the inequality in (ii)

(a) Draw the graph of the line $2x - y + 4 = 0$.

(b) Find the sign of $2x - y + 4$ at a convenient point, e.g. $(0, 0)$. At $(0, 0)$ $2x - y + 4 = 4 > 0$. Hence $2x - y + 4 > 0$ on the side of the line which contains $(0, 0)$. Hence the half plane containing $(0, 0)$ represents the given inequality.

How to Answer Examination Questions 3

1) Fig. E3.1 shows a wedge with measurements as indicated.
CE is perpendicular to the base ABEF.
Calculate:
(a) The length of BC.
(b) The total surface area of the wedge.
(c) The volume of the wedge.
(d) The weight of the wedge, in kilograms, if the material weighs $6.7 \, \text{g/cm}^3$.

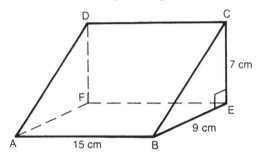

Fig. E3.1

(a) Using Pythagoras' Theorem,

$$BC^2 = BE^2 + CE^2$$

$$= 9^2 + 7^2$$

$$= 81 + 49$$

$$= 130$$

$$BC = \sqrt{130} = 11.40 \, \text{cm}$$

(b) Perimeter of triangle CEB

$$= (7 + 9 + 11.40) \, \text{cm} = 27.40 \, \text{cm}$$

Total surface area of wedge

$$= (27.40 \times 15 + 2(\tfrac{1}{2} \times 7 \times 9)) \, \text{cm}^2$$

$$= (411 + 63) \, \text{cm}^2$$

$$= 474 \, \text{cm}^2$$

(c) Area of triangle CEB $= (\tfrac{1}{2} \times 7 \times 9) \, \text{cm}^2$

$$= 31.5 \, \text{cm}^2$$

Volume of wedge $= (15 \times 31.5) \, \text{cm}^3$

$$= 472.5 \, \text{cm}^3$$

(d) Weight of wedge $= (472.5 \times 6.7) \, \text{g}$

$$= 3166 \, \text{g}$$

$$= 3.166 \, \text{kg}$$

2) The diagram (Fig. E3.2) shows the end view of a metal block which has a uniform cross-section. The block is 90 mm long and has a weight of 2.898 kg.

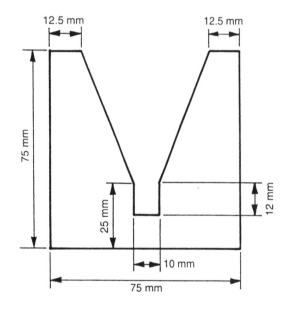

Fig. E3.2

(a) Calculate the area of the cross-section of the block in square centimetres.

(b) Find the volume of the block in cubic centimetres.

(c) Hence find the weight of 1 cubic centimetre of the metal from which the block is made, giving your answer correct to 3 s.f.

(a) To determine the area of the cross-section, it is split up into sections as shown in Fig. E3.3 and the dimensions converted to centimetres.

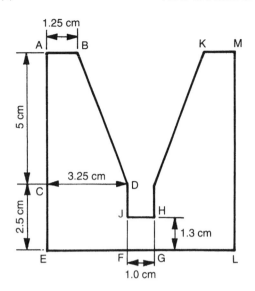

1.25 cm

5 cm

2.5 cm

3.25 cm

1.3 cm

1.0 cm

Fig. E3.3

For the trapezium ABDC,   AB = 1.25 cm,
CD = $\frac{1}{2}(7.5 - 1.0)$ cm = 3.25 cm   and
AC = 5 cm.

Area of ABDC = $\frac{1}{2}(1.25 + 3.25) \times 5$

               = 2.25×5 = 11.25 cm^2

Area of rectangle CDFE = 3.25×2.5

               = 8.125 cm^2

Area of rectangle FGHJ = 1.3×1

               = 1.3 cm^2

Total area of cross-section

  = $2 \times (11.25 + 8.125) + 1.3$

  = 40.05 cm^2

Alternatively,

Cross-sectional area = AELM − BDJHGK

Area of AELM = $(7.5)^2$ = 56.25 cm^2

Area of BDJHGK = $\frac{1}{2}(5 + 1) \times 5 + 1 \times 1.2$

               = 16.2 cm^2

Cross-sectional area = $56.25 - 16.2$

               = 40.05 cm^2

(b) Volume of block = 40.05×9

               = 360.45 cm^3

(c) Weight per cubic centimetre = $\dfrac{2898}{360.45}$

               = 8.04 g/cm^3

3) (a) Given that $f(x) = x - 4 + \dfrac{3}{x}$,   copy and
   complete the following table:

x	0.5	1.0	1.5	2.0
$f(x)$	2.5			−0.5

x	2.5	3.0	4.0	5.0
$f(x)$	−0.3		0.75	

(b) Plot the graph of $f(x) = x - 4 + \dfrac{3}{x}$
    for the domain $0.5 \leqslant x \leqslant 5$ using a
    scale of 2 cm to 1 unit on the x-axis
    and 4 cm to 1 unit on the other axis.

(c) Use your graph to solve the equation:

$$x - 4 + \frac{3}{x} = 1$$

(d) Find the gradient of the curve at the
    point where $x = 2$.

(a)

x	0.5	1.0	1.5	2.0
$f(x)$	2.5	0.0	−0.5	−0.5

x	2.5	3.0	4.0	5.0
$f(x)$	−0.3	0.0	0.75	1.6

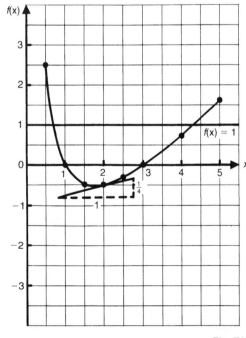

Fig. E3.4

(b) The graph is shown plotted in Fig. E3.4.

(c) From the graph the solution of the equation
$x - 4 + \frac{3}{x} = 1$ is $x = 0.70$ or 4.30.

(d) In Fig. E3.4, a tangent to the curve has been drawn at the point where $x = 2$ and the gradient is $\frac{1}{4}$.

4) The curve $y = ax^2 + bx - 6$ cuts the x-axis at the points $A(1,0)$ and $B(3,0)$.
(a) Determine the values of a and b.
(b) Draw the curve for $0 \leqslant x \leqslant 4$.
(c) By drawing suitable tangents, find the gradients of the curve at the points A and B.
(d) Determine the maximum value of the curve and the coordinates of the point at which it occurs.
(e) Use the trapezium rule to estimate the area bounded by the curve between A and B and the x-axis.

(a) At point A, $x = 1, y = 0$ ∴ $a + b = 6$ [1]

At point B, $x = 3, y = 0$ ∴ $9a + 3b = 6$ [2]

Multiplying equation [1] by 3 gives,
$$3a + 3b = 18 \qquad [3]$$

Subtracting equation [3] from equation [2] gives,
$$6a = -12$$
$$a = -2$$

Substituting for a in equation [1] gives,
$$-2 + b = 6$$
$$b = 6 + 2$$
$$b = 8$$

(b) Hence the function is $y = -2x^2 + 8x - 6$. To plot the graph the following table is drawn up

x	0	0.5	1.0	1.5	2.0
y	−6	−2.5	0.0	1.5	2.0

x	2.5	3.0	3.5	4.0
y	1.5	0.0	−2.5	−6.0

The graph is drawn in Fig. E3.5.

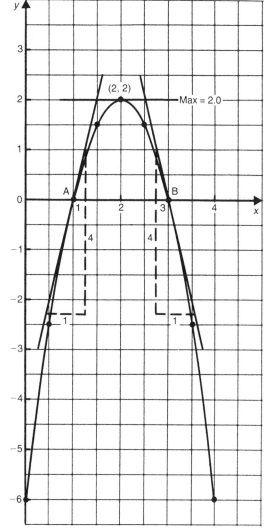
Fig. E3.5

(c) In the diagram, tangents to the curve have been drawn at the points A and B. The gradient of the curve is the same as the gradient of the tangent.

Hence at A, the gradient of the curve is 4. and at B, the gradient of the curve is −4.

(d) The maximum value of the function occurs when the gradient to the curve is parallel to the x-axis. From the diagram, the maximum is 2.0 and it occurs at the point where $x = 2.0$.

(e) Using $h = 0.5$, $x_0 = 1$, $x_1 = 1.5$, $x_2 = 2$, $x_3 = 2.5$, $x_4 = 3$; $y_0 = 0$, $y_1 = 1.5$, $y_2 = 2$, $y_3 = 1.5$, $y_4 = 0$

Area $= 0.5(\frac{1}{2} \times (0 + 0) + 1.5 + 2 + 1.5)$
$= 2.5$ square units

5) The polygon shown in Fig. E3.6 has been obtained by removing the triangle QRT from the rectangle PQRS. The angle $QTR = 90°$ and $QT = TR$. Given that $PQ = 18\,cm$ and $PS = 3x\,cm$, show that the area A, in square centimetres, is given by the formula

$$A = 54x - \frac{9x^2}{4}$$

(a) Calculate A when $x = 7$.

(b) Copy and complete the following table:

x	5	7	9	11	13	15	17
A	214		304		322		268

(c) Draw the graph of $A = 54x - \dfrac{9x^2}{4}$ for values of x between 5 and 25, using a scale of 2 cm to 5 units on the x-axis and 2 cm to 50 units on the other axis.

(d) Use your graph to find the maximum value of A and state the value of x at which it occurs.

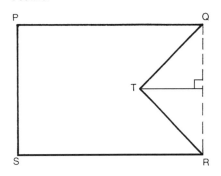

P Q

T

S R

Fig. E3.6

In the triangle QTR, TU is drawn perpendicular to QR. Since $QT = TR$, and $QTR = 90°$, $TU = QU = \dfrac{3x}{2}$.

$\therefore$ Area of QTR $= TU \times QU = \dfrac{3x}{2} \times \dfrac{3x}{2}$

$$= \frac{9x^2}{4}\,cm^2$$

Area of rectangle PQRS $= 18 \times 3x$

$$= 54x\,cm^2$$

Area of polygon PQTRS $=$ area PQRS $-$ area QTR

$\therefore$ $A = 54x - \dfrac{9x^2}{4}$

(a) When $x = 7$, $A = 54 \times 7 - \dfrac{9 \times 49}{4}$

$$= 378 - 110.25$$

$$= 267.75\,cm^2$$

(b)

x	5	7	9	11	13	15	17
A	214	268	304	322	322	304	268

(c) The graph is drawn in Fig. E3.7.

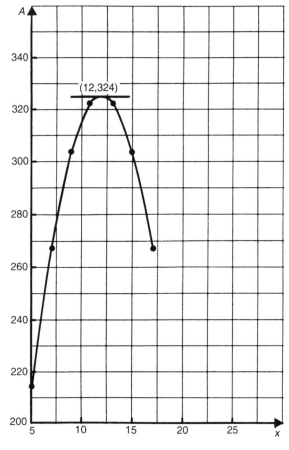

Fig. E3.7

(d) The maximum value of A occurs where the tangent to the curve is parallel to the x-axis. As shown in the diagram, the maximum value of A is $324\,cm$ and it occurs when $x = 12$.

EXAMINATION TYPE QUESTIONS 3

This exercise is divided into two sections, A and B. The questions in Section A are intended to be done very quickly, but those in Section B should take about 20 minutes each to complete. All the questions are of the type found in CXC examination papers.

Section A

1) A rectangular tank open at the top and constructed of thin sheet metal is $90\,cm$ high. Its base measures $104\,cm$ by $85\,cm$. Assuming that there is no overlap at the edges, calculate:
   (a) The area, in square centimetres, of sheet metal used in its construction.
   (b) The capacity of the tank, in litres, expressed to the nearest litre.

2) A pile of 500 sheets of paper is $4\,cm$ thick. Calculate the thickness, in millimetres, of each sheet of paper. (Give your answer in standard form, i.e. in the form $A \times 10^n$ where A is a number between 1 and 10 and n is an integer.)

3) The volume of a cube is $1200\,cm^3$. Calculate the length of one side.

4) A model aircraft, similar to the full-sized version, is made to a scale of 1 in 20. The model has a tail $0.15\,m$ high, a wing area of $0.28\,m^2$ and a cabin volume of $0.016\,m^3$. Calculate the corresponding figures for the full-sized aircraft.

5) The graph of $y = mx + c$ passes through the points $A(0, 4)$ and $B(-2, 2)$. Find the values of c and m and find the value of y when $x = 3$.

6) A rectangular sheet of metal is L metres long, W metres wide and T millimetres thick. If the sheet has a weight of M kilograms, derive a formula for M given that the material weighs D grams per cubic centimetre.

7) Two similar polygons have areas of $160\,cm^2$ and $360\,cm^2$ respectively. The shortest side of the larger polygon is $18\,cm$. Calculate the length of the shortest side of the smaller polygon.

8) A prism has a cross-sectional area of $12\,cm^2$ and is made of material which weighs 3.52 grams per cubic centimetre. Calculate the weight of a 1 metre length of such a prism.

9) Given that y is inversely proportional to x^2 and $y = 9$ when $x = 2$, calculate the value of y when $x = 3$.

10) The diameter of a cylindrical garden roller is $0.77\,m$.
    (a) Calculate the number of complete revolutions it makes in rolling a stretch of ground $84.7\,m$ long.
    (b) If the roller is $1.33\,m$ wide, find the area of ground rolled for every 100 revolutions. (Take $\pi = \frac{22}{7}$)

Section B

11) (a) Draw a graph of the curve $y = x^2 - 3$ for values of x in the range $-3 \leqslant x \leqslant 3$, including the points for which $x = -2.5$ and $x = 2.5$.
    (b) Use your graph to estimate the range of values for which $x^2 - 3 \leqslant 4$, indicating clearly on your graph the limits of the range.
    (c) By drawing a certain straight line on the same axes and to the same scales as your graph of $y = x^2 - 3$, estimate those values of x for which $x^2 - x - 3 = 0$.
    (d) Use your results in (b) and (c) to estimate the range of values for which the inequalities $x^2 - 7 \leqslant 0$ and $x^2 - x - 3 \leqslant 0$, hold simultaneously.

12) (a) Write $5x^2 + 8x + 3$ in the form $a(x + h)^2 + k$.
    (b) Hence deduce the minimum value of $5x^2 + 8x + 3$.
    (c) Write $-3x^2 + 5x + 2$ in the form $k - a(x + h)^2$.
    (d) Hence find the maximum value of $-3x^2 + 5x + 2$.

13) (a) Write down the factors of $x^2 - 9y^2$. Hence, or otherwise, solve the simultaneous equations:
$$x^2 - 9y^2 = 15 \qquad [1]$$
$$x - 3y = 5 \qquad [2]$$
    (b) When a current passes through a wire, the rate at which heat is produced, W watts, is directly proportional to the square of the voltage, V volts, and inversely proportional to the length of the wire, L centimetres. Express W in terms of V, L and a constant of variation, k.

Hence calculate:
(i)   the value of k given that
      $W = 800$ when $V = 200$
      and $L = 40$.
(ii) the value of L given that
      $W = 800$ when $V = 240$.
(iii) the value of V given that
      $W = 800$ when $L = 48.4$.

14) An isosceles triangle ABC has a perimeter of 24 cm. The sides AB and AC have the same lengths and the length of BC is $2x$ centimetres. Show that the area of the triangle is $2x\sqrt{36 - 6x}$ square centimetres. Draw a graph of the function $f: x \rightarrow 2x\sqrt{36 - 6x}$ for $0 \leqslant x \leqslant 6$. Use a scale of 2 cm to 1 unit on the x-axis and 2 cm to 5 units on the other axis. Use your graph to estimate the greatest possible area for this triangle.

15) A machine was tested in a laboratory to find the effort, P newtons, to lift a weight of M kilograms. The following results were obtained:

M	1	3	4	5	7	8
P	7.0	12.7	15.5	18.2	23.5	26.5

(a) Plot these points on a graph and show that M and P could be connected by an equation of the form:
$$P = aM + b$$
where a and b are constants. Use your graph to estimate values of a and b. (Scales: take 2 cm to represent 1 kg on the M-axis and 2 cm to represent 2 newtons on the P-axis.)

(b) In a second machine P and M are connected by the formula:
$$P = 0.6M + 12$$
Choose any three suitable values of M and calculate corresponding values of P. Use the axes and scales of your first graph to draw a further graph which shows the relationship between M and P for the second machine.

(c) Use your graphs to find which machine requires the greatest effort to lift a load of 6 kg and by how much.

Chapter 28 **Angles and Straight Lines**

ANGLES

When two lines meet at a point they form an angle. The size of the angle depends only upon the amount of opening between the lines. It does not depend upon the lengths of the lines forming the angle. In Fig. 28.1 the angle A is larger than the angle B despite the fact that the lengths of the arms are shorter.

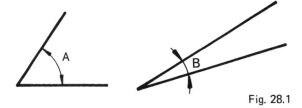

Fig. 28.1

ANGULAR MEASUREMENT

An angle or the measure of an angle may be looked upon as the amount of rotation or turning. In Fig. 28.2 the line OA has been turned about O until it takes up the position OB. The angle through which the line has turned is the amount of opening between the lines OA and OB.

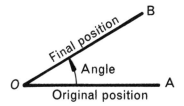

Fig. 28.2

When writing angles we write seventy degrees as $70°$. The small $°$ at the right hand corner of the figure replaces the word degrees. Thus $87°$ reads 87 degrees.

If the line OA is rotated until it returns to its original position it will have described one revolution. Hence we can measure an angle as a fraction of a revolution. Figure 28.3 shows a circle divided up into 36 equal parts. The first division is split up into 10 equal parts so that

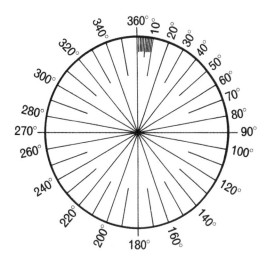

Fig. 28.3

each small division is $\frac{1}{360}$ of a complete revolution. We call this division a *degree*.

$$1 \text{ degree} = \frac{1}{360} \text{ of a revolution}$$

$$360 \text{ degrees} = 1 \text{ revolution}$$

The right angle is $\frac{1}{4}$ of a revolution and hence it contains $\frac{1}{4}$ of $360° = 90°$. Two right angles contain $180°$ and three right angles contain $270°$.

EXAMPLE 1
Find the angle in degrees corresponding to $\frac{1}{8}$ of a revolution.

$$1 \text{ revolution} = 360°$$

$$\tfrac{1}{8} \text{ revolution} = \tfrac{1}{8} \times 360° = 45°$$

EXAMPLE 2
Find the angle in degrees corresponding to 0.6 of a revolution.

$$1 \text{ revolution} = 360°$$

$$0.6 \text{ revolution} = 0.6 \times 360° = 216°$$

For some purposes the degree is too large a unit and it is sub-divided into minutes and seconds so that:

$$60 \text{ seconds } = 1 \text{ minute}$$

$$60 \text{ minutes } = 1 \text{ degree}$$

$$360 \text{ degrees } = 1 \text{ revolution}$$

An angle of 25 degrees 7 minutes 30 seconds is written $25°7'30''$.

EXAMPLE 3

(1) Add together $22°35'$ and $49°42'$.

$$\begin{array}{r} 22°35' \\ 49°42' \\ \hline 72°17' \end{array}$$

The minutes 35 and 42 add up to 77 minutes which is $1°17'$. The 17 is written in the minutes column and $1°$ carried over to the degrees column. The degrees 22, 49 and 1 add up to 72 degrees.

(2) Subtract $17°49'$ from $39°27'$.

$$\begin{array}{r} 39°27' \\ 17°49' \\ \hline 21°38' \end{array}$$

We cannot subtract $49'$ from $27'$ so we exchange $1°$ from the $39°$ making it $38°$. The $27'$ now becomes $27' + 60' = 87'$. Subtracting $49'$ from $87'$ gives $38'$ which is written in the minutes column. The degree column is now $38° - 17° = 21°$.

Exercise 138 – *All type A*

1) How many degrees are there in $1\frac{1}{2}$ right angles?

2) How many degrees are there in $\frac{3}{5}$ of a right angle?

3) How many degrees are there in $\frac{2}{3}$ of a right angle?

4) How many degrees are there in 0.7 of a right angle?

5) $\frac{1}{20}$ revolution.

6) $\frac{3}{8}$ revolution.

7) $\frac{4}{5}$ revolution.

8) 0.8 revolution.

9) 0.3 revolution.

10) 0.25 revolution.

Add together the following angles:

11) $11°8'$ and $17°29'$.

12) $25°38'$ and $43°45'$.

13) $8°38'49''$ and $5°43'45''$.

14) $27°4'52''$ and $35°43'19''$.

15) $72°15'4''$, $89°27'38''$ and $17°28'43''$.

Subtract the following angles:

16) $8°2'$ from $29°5'$.

17) $17°28'$ from $40°16'$.

18) $0°7'15''$ from $6°2'5''$.

19) $48°19'21''$ from $85°17'32''$.

†RADIAN MEASURE

We have seen that an angle is measured in degrees. There is however a second way of measuring an angle. In this second system the unit is known as the *radian*. Referring to Fig. 28.4

$$\text{angle in radians } = \frac{\text{length of arc}}{\text{radius of circle}}$$

$$\theta \text{ radians } = \frac{l}{r}$$

$$l = r\theta$$

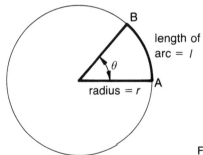

Fig. 28.4

RELATION BETWEEN RADIANS AND DEGREES

If we make the arc AB (Fig. 28.4) equal to a semi-circle then,

$$\text{length of arc } = \pi r$$

$$\text{angle in radians } = \frac{\pi r}{r} = \pi$$

But the angle at the centre subtended by a semi-circle is $180°$ and hence

$$\pi \text{ radians} = 180°$$

$$1 \text{ radian} = \frac{180°}{\pi} = 57.3°$$

It is worth remembering that

$$\theta° = \frac{\pi\theta}{180} \text{ radians}$$

$$60° = \frac{\pi}{3} \text{ radians}$$

$$45° = \frac{\pi}{4} \text{ radians}$$

$$90° = \frac{\pi}{2} \text{ radians}$$

$$30° = \frac{\pi}{6} \text{ radians}$$

EXAMPLE 4

(1) Find the angle in radians subtended by an arc $12.9\,\text{cm}$ long whose radius is $4.6\,\text{cm}$.

$$\text{Angle in radians} = \frac{\text{length of arc}}{\text{radius of circle}}$$

$$= \frac{12.9}{4.6} \text{ radians}$$

$$= 2.804 \text{ radians}$$

(2) Express an angle of 1.26 radians in degrees and minutes.

$$\text{Angle in degrees}$$

$$= \frac{180 \times \text{angle in radians}}{\pi}$$

$$= \frac{180 \times 1.26°}{\pi} = 72.18°$$

Now

$$0.18° = 0.18 \times 60 \text{ minutes} = 11 \text{ minutes}$$

$$\text{Angle} = 72°11'$$

(3) Express an angle of $104°$ in radians.

$$\text{Angle in radians}$$

$$= \frac{\pi \times \text{angle in degrees}}{180}$$

$$= \frac{\pi \times 104}{180} \text{ radians}$$

$$= 1.815 \text{ radians}$$

†LENGTH OF AN ARC OF A CIRCLE

If the angle θ (Fig. 28.5) is measured in radians and l is the length of the arc, then

$$l = r\theta$$

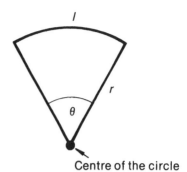

Centre of the circle

Fig. 28.5

EXAMPLE 5

An arc of a circle whose radius is $8\,\text{cm}$ subtends an angle of 1.3 radians at the centre. Calculate the length of the arc.

We are given $r = 8$ and $\theta = 1.3$.

$$\therefore \qquad l = r\theta = 8 \times 1.3 = 10.4$$

The length of the arc is $10.4\,\text{cm}$.

†AREA OF THE SECTOR OF A CIRCLE

It can be shown that the area of the sector of the circle shown in Fig. 28.5 is

$$A = \tfrac{1}{2}r^2\theta$$

because θ is measured in radians.

EXAMPLE 6

Find the area of a sector of a circle if its radius is $12\,\text{cm}$ and the angle subtended at the centre is 0.7 radian.

We are given $r = 12$ and $\theta = 0.7$.

$$\therefore \quad \text{Area, } A = \tfrac{1}{2}r^2\theta = \tfrac{1}{2} \times 12^2 \times 0.7 = 50.4\,\text{cm}^2$$

Exercise 139 – *All type B*

1) Find the angle in radians subtended by the following arcs:

(a) arc $= 10.9\,\text{cm}$, radius $= 3.4\,\text{cm}$
(b) arc $= 7.2\,\text{m}$, radius $= 2.3\,\text{m}$

2) Express the following angles in degrees and minutes:

(a) 5 radians
(b) 1.73 radians
(c) 0.159 radians

3) Express the following angles in radians:

(a) $83°$

(b) $189°$

(c) $295°$

(d) $5.21°$

4) Calculate the lengths of the following arcs:

(a) Angle at centre $= 0.25$ radian,
     radius of circle $= 15$ cm

(b) Angle at centre $= \pi$ radians,
     radius of circle $= 5$ cm

(c) Angle at centre $= \dfrac{3\pi}{4}$ radians,
     radius of circle $= 10$ cm

5) Find the areas of the following sectors of a circle:

(a) Angle at centre $= 0.3$ radian,
     radius of circle $= 4$ cm

(b) Angle at centre $= 1.8$ radians,
     radius of circle $= 7$ cm

(c) Angle at centre $= \dfrac{\pi}{3}$ radians,
     radius of circle $= 10$ cm

TYPES OF ANGLES

An *acute angle* (Fig. 28.6) is less than $90°$.

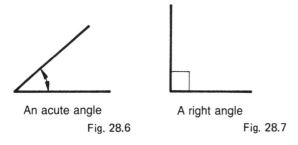

An acute angle

Fig. 28.6

A right angle

Fig. 28.7

A *right angle* (Fig. 28.7) is equal to $90°$.

A *reflex angle* (Fig. 28.8) is greater than $180°$.

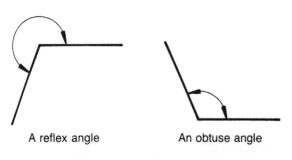

A reflex angle

Fig. 28.8

An obtuse angle

Fig. 28.9

An *obtuse angle* (Fig. 28.9) lies between $90°$ and $180°$.

Complementary angles are angles whose sum is $90°$.

Supplementary angles are angles whose sum is $180°$.

PROPERTIES OF ANGLES AND STRAIGHT LINES

(1) *The total angle on a straight line is* $180°$ (Fig. 28.10). The angles A and B are called adjacent angles. They are also supplementary.

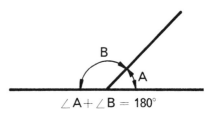

$$\angle A + \angle B = 180°$$

Fig. 28.10

(2) *When two straight lines intersect the opposite angles are equal* (Fig. 28.11). The angles A and C are called vertically opposite angles. Similarly the angles B and D are also vertically opposite angles.

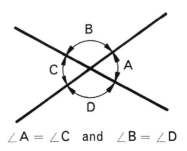

$$\angle A = \angle C \quad \text{and} \quad \angle B = \angle D$$

Fig. 28.11

(3) *When two parallel lines are cut by a transversal* (Fig. 28.12).

(a) The corresponding angles are
    equal $a = l; \quad b = m; \quad c = p; \quad d = q.$

(b) The alternate angles are equal $d = m;$
    $c = l.$

(c) The interior angles are supplementary
    $d + l = 180°; \quad c + m = 180°.$

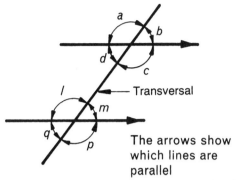

The arrows show which lines are parallel

Fig. 28.12

Conversely if two straight lines are cut by a transversal the lines are parallel if any *one* of the following is true:

(a) Two corresponding angles are equal.
(b) Two alternate angles are equal.
(c) Two interior angles are supplementary.

EXAMPLE 7

(1) Find the angle A shown in Fig. 28.13.

$\angle B = 180° - 138° = 42°$
                                   (angles on a straight line)

$\angle B = \angle A$ (corresponding angles)

$\angle A = 42°$

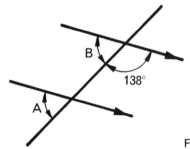

Fig. 28.13

(2) In Fig. 28.14 the line BF bisects $\angle ABC$. Find the value of the angle α.

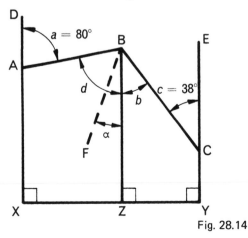

Fig. 28.14

The lines AX, BZ and EY are all parallel because they lie at right angles to the line XY.

$$c = b \quad \text{(alternate angles: BZ} \parallel \text{EY)}$$

$$b = 38° \quad \text{(since   } c = 38°\text{)}$$

$$a = d \quad \text{(alternate angles: XD} \parallel \text{BZ)}$$

$$d = 80° \quad \text{(since   } a = 80°\text{)}$$

$$\angle ABC = b + d = 80° + 38° = 118°$$

$$\angle FBC = 118° \div 2 = 59° \quad \text{(since BF}$$

$$\text{bisects   } \angle ABC\text{)}$$

$$b + \alpha = 59°$$

$$38° + \alpha = 59°$$

$$\alpha = 59° - 38° = 21°$$

Exercise 140 – *All type A*

1) Find x in Fig. 28.15.

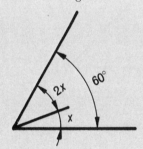

Fig. 28.15

2) Find A in Fig. 28.16.

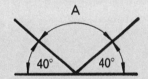

Fig. 28.16

3) Find x in Fig. 28.17.

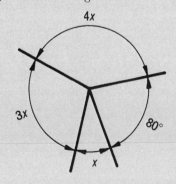

Fig. 28.17

4) In Fig. 28.18 find *a*, *b*, *c* and *d*.

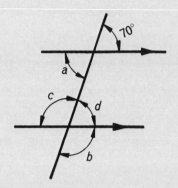

Fig. 28.18

5) Find the angle *x* in Fig. 28.19.

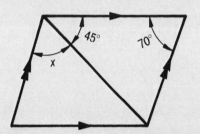

Fig. 28.19

6) Find *x* in Fig. 20.20.

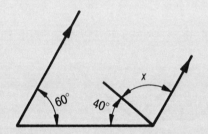

Fig. 28.20

7) A reflex angle is:

a less than 90°   **b** greater than 90°

c greater than 180°   **d** equal to 180°

8) Angles whose sum is 180° are called:

a complementary angles

b alternate angles

c supplementary angles

d corresponding angles

9) In Fig. 28.21 find A.

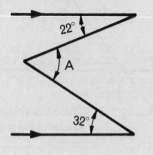

Fig. 28.21

10) In Fig. 28.22, AB is parallel to ED. Find the angle *x*.

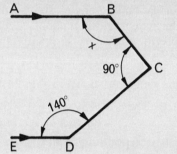

Fig. 28.22

11) Find A in Fig. 28.23.

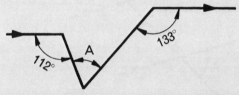

Fig. 28.23

12) In Fig. 28.24 the lines AB, CD and EF are parallel. Find the values of *x* and *y*.

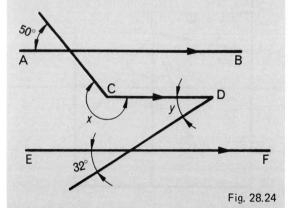

Fig. 28.24

13) In Fig. 28.25:

a $q = p + r$ **b** $p + q + r = 360°$

c $q = r - p$ **d** $q = 360 - p - r$

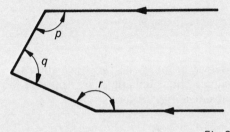

Fig. 28.25

SELF-TEST 28

In the following state the letter (or letters) corresponding to the correct answer (or answers).

1) The angle shown in Fig. 28.26 is

a acute   **b** right   **c** reflex   **d** obtuse

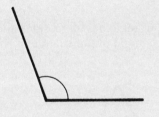

Fig. 28.26

2) The angle a shown in Fig. 28.27 is equal to:

a 120°   **b** 60°   **c** neither of these

3) The angle b shown in Fig. 28.27 is equal to:

a 120°   **b** 60°   **c** neither of these

4) The angle c shown in Fig. 28.27 is equal to:

a 120°   **b** 60°   **c** neither of these

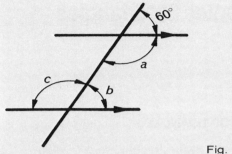

Fig. 28.27

5) In Fig. 28.28:

a $a = d$ **b** $a = e$

c $e = b$ **d** $a = b$

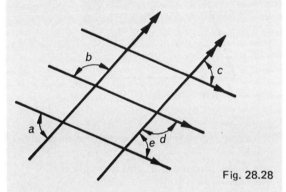

Fig. 28.28

6) In Fig. 28.29:

a $x = y$ **b** $x = 180°$

c $x = y - 180°$ **d** $x + y = 180°$

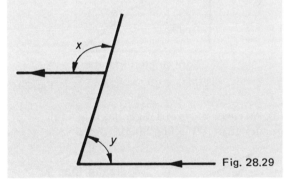

Fig. 28.29

CHAPTER 28 SUMMARY

Points to remember

(i) A radian is the measure of an angle at the centre of a circle, radius r, subtended by an arc of length r.

(ii) π radians = 180°.

(iii) The length s of an arc of a circle radius r subtending an angle of θ radians at the centre is given by $s = r\theta$.

(iv) The area of a sector = $\frac{1}{2}r^2\theta$. (θ is measured in radians.)

(v) Angle properties and straight lines – see page 222–223.

Chapter 29 **Triangles**

TYPES OF TRIANGLE

(1) An *acute-angled* triangle has all its angles less than 90° (Fig. 29.1).

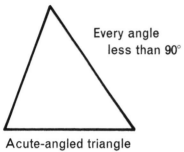

Every angle less than 90°

Acute-angled triangle

Fig. 29.1

(2) A *right-angled* triangle has one of its angles equal to 90°. The side opposite to the right angle is the longest side and it is called the hypotenuse (Fig. 29.2).

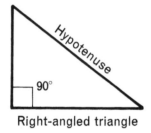

Right-angled triangle

Fig. 29.2

(3) An *obtuse-angled* triangle has one angle greater than 90° (Fig. 29.3).

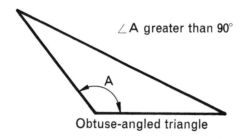

∠A greater than 90°

Obtuse-angled triangle

Fig. 29.3

(4) A *scalene* triangle has all three sides of different length.

(5) An *isosceles* triangle has two sides and two angles equal. The equal angles lie opposite to the equal sides (Fig. 29.4).

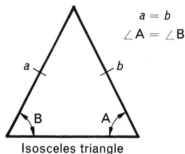

$a = b$

$\angle A = \angle B$

Isosceles triangle

Fig. 29.4

(6) An *equilateral* triangle has all its sides and angles equal. Each angle of the triangle is 60° (Fig. 29.5).

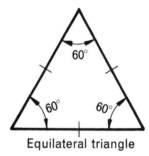

Equilateral triangle

Fig. 29.5

ANGLE PROPERTIES OF TRIANGLES

(1) *The sum of the angles of a triangle is equal to 180°* (Fig. 29.6).

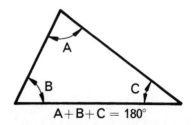

$A + B + C = 180°$

Fig. 29.6

(2) *In every triangle the greatest angle is opposite to the longest side. The smallest angle is opposite to the shortest side.* In every triangle the sum of the lengths of any two sides is always greater than the length of the third side (Fig. 29.7).

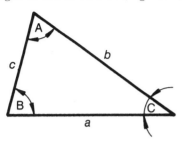

Fig. 29.7

a is the longest side since it lies opposite to the greatest angle A. *c* is the shortest side since it lies opposite to the smallest angle C. *a + b* is greater than *c*, *a + c* is greater than *b* and *b + c* is greater than *a*.

(3) *When the side of a triangle is produced the exterior angle so formed is equal to the sum of the opposite interior angles* (Fig. 29.8).

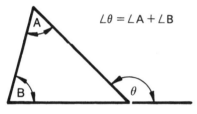

$\angle \theta = \angle A + \angle B$

Fig. 29.8

EXAMPLE 1

In Fig. 29.9, find the angles x and y.

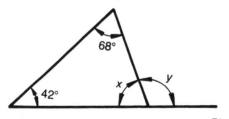

Fig. 29.9

Since the three angles of a triangle add up to 180°,

$$x + 42 + 68 = 180$$

$$x = 180 - 42 - 68 = 70$$

Hence the angle x is 70°.

The exterior angle of a triangle is equal to the sum of the opposite interior angles. Hence:

$$y = 42 + 68 = 110$$

Therefore the angle y is 110°.

Exercise 141 – *All type A*

Find the angles x and y shown in Figs. 29.10.

1)

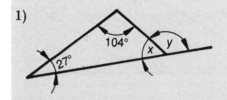

2)

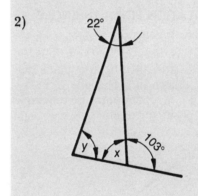

3)

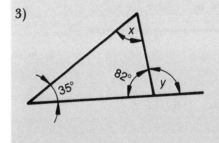

4)

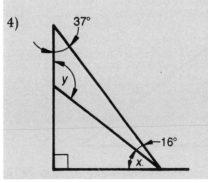

5)
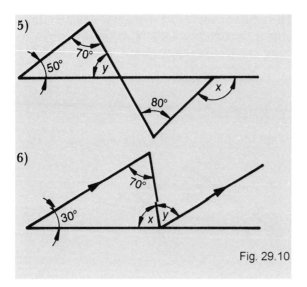

6)

Fig. 29.10

STANDARD NOTATION FOR A TRIANGLE

Figure 29.11 shows the *standard notation for a triangle*. The three vertices are marked A, B and C. The angles are called by the same letter as the vertices (see diagram). The side a lies opposite the angle A, b lies opposite the angle B and c lies opposite the angle C.

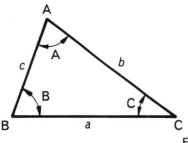

Fig. 29.11

PYTHAGORAS' THEOREM

In any right-angled triangle the square on the hypotenuse is equal to the sum of the squares on the other two sides. In the diagram (Fig. 29.12),

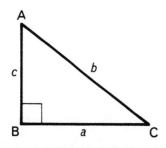

Fig. 29.12

$$AC^2 = AB^2 + BC^2$$

or

$$b^2 = a^2 + c^2$$

The hypotenuse is the longest side and it always lies opposite to the right angle. Thus in Fig. 29.12 the side b is the hypotenuse since it lies opposite the right angle at B. It is worth remembering that triangles with sides of 3, 4, 5; 5, 12, 13; 7, 24, 25 or multiples of these are right-angled triangles.

EXAMPLE 2

(1) In $\triangle$ ABC, $\angle$ B $= 90°$, $a = 4.2$ cm and $c = 3.7$ cm. Find b (Fig. 29.13).

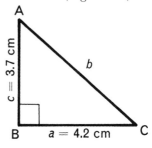

Fig. 29.13

By Pythagoras' Theorem,

$$b^2 = a^2 + c^2$$
$$b^2 = 4.2^2 + 3.7^2$$
$$= 17.64 + 13.69$$
$$= 31.33$$
$$b = \sqrt{31.33} = 5.598 \text{ cm}$$

(2) In $\triangle$ ABC, $\angle$ A $= 90°$, $a = 6.4$ cm and $b = 5.2$ cm. Find c (Fig. 29.14).

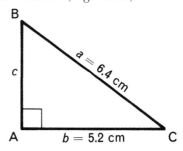

Fig. 29.14

$$a^2 = b^2 + c^2$$
$$c^2 = a^2 - b^2 = 6.4^2 - 5.2^2$$
$$= 40.96 - 27.04 = 13.92$$
$$c = \sqrt{13.92} = 3.731 \text{ cm}$$

PROPERTIES OF THE ISOSCELES TRIANGLE

The most important properties of an isosceles triangle are that the perpendicular dropped from the apex to the unequal side:

(1) Bisects the unequal side. Thus in Fig. 29.15, BD = CD.

(2) Bisects the apex angle. Thus in Fig. 29.15, angle BAD = angle CAD.

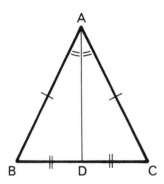

Fig. 29.15

EXAMPLE 3

An isosceles triangle has equal sides 6 cm long and a base 4 cm long.

(a) Find the altitude of the triangle.
(b) Calculate the area of the triangle.

(a) The triangle is shown in Fig. 29.16. The altitude AD is perpendicular to the base and hence it bisects the base.

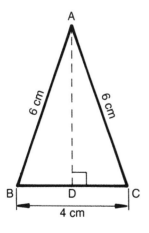

Fig. 29.16

In triangle ABD, by Pythagoras' Theorem,

$$AD^2 = AB^2 - BD^2 = 6^2 - 2^2 = 32$$

$$AD = \sqrt{32} = 5.66$$

Hence the altitude of the triangle is 5.66 cm.

(b) Area of triangle

$$= \tfrac{1}{2} \times \text{base} \times \text{altitude}$$

$$= \tfrac{1}{2} \times 4 \times 5.66 = 11.32 \, \text{cm}^2$$

Exercise 142 – *All type B*

1) Find the side a in Fig. 29.17.

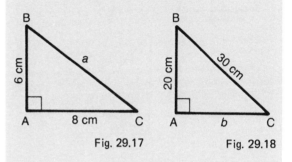

Fig. 29.17   Fig. 29.18

2) Find the side b in Fig. 29.18.

3) Find the side c in Fig. 29.19.

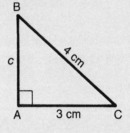

Fig. 29.19

4) Find the sides marked x in Fig. 29.20.

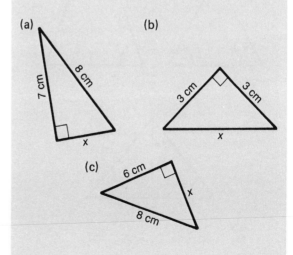

Fig. 29.20

5) Find the altitudes of the triangles shown in Fig. 29.21. All the triangles are isosceles.

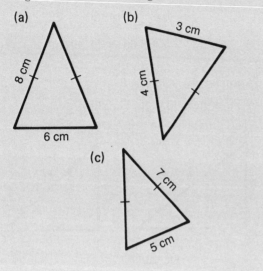

Fig. 29.21

6) Find the angles marked θ for each of the isosceles triangles in Fig. 29.22.

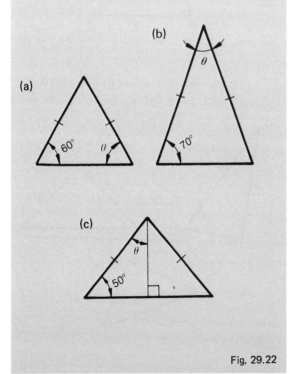

Fig. 29.22

7) Find the angles marked $x, y,$ and z in Fig. 29.23.

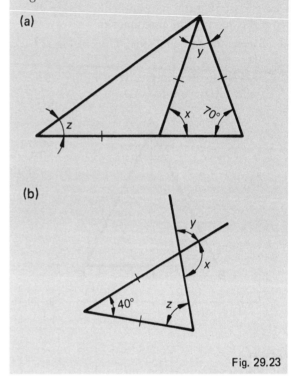

Fig. 29.23

CONGRUENT TRIANGLES

Two triangles are said to be congruent if they are equal in every respect. Thus in Fig. 29.24 the triangles ABC and XYZ are congruent because:

$$AC = XZ \qquad \angle B = \angle Y$$
$$AB = XY \quad \text{and} \quad \angle C = \angle Z$$
$$BC = YZ \qquad \angle A = \angle X$$

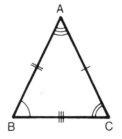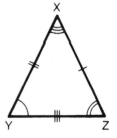

Fig. 29.24

Note that the angles which are equal lie opposite to the corresponding sides.

If two triangles are congruent they will also be equal in area. The notation used to express the fact that $\triangle ABC$ is congruent to $\triangle XYZ$ is $\triangle ABC \equiv \triangle XYZ$.

For two triangles to be congruent the six elements of one triangle (three sides and three angles) must be equal to the six elements of the second triangle. However to prove that two triangles are congruent it is not necessary to prove all six equalities. Any of the following are sufficient to prove that two triangles are congruent:

(1) *One side and two angles in one triangle equal to one side and two similarly located angles in the second triangle* (Fig. 29.25).

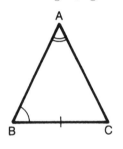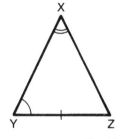

Fig. 29.25

(2) *Two sides and the angle between them in one triangle equal to two sides and the angle between them in the second triangle* (Fig. 29.26).

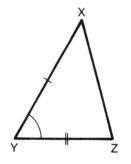

Fig. 29.26

(3) *Three sides of one triangle equal to three sides of the other triangle* (Fig. 29.27).

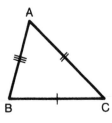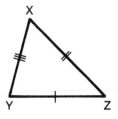

Fig. 29.27

(4) *In right-angled triangles if the hypotenuses are equal and one other side in each triangle are also equal* (Fig. 29.28).

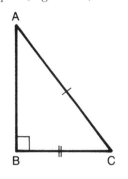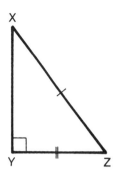

Fig. 29.28

Note that three equal angles are not sufficient to prove congruency and neither are two sides and a non-included angle. An included angle is an angle between the two equal sides of the triangles (e.g. $\angle ABC$ and $\angle XYZ$ in Fig. 29.27 and $\angle ACB$ and $\angle XZY$ in Fig. 29.28).

EXAMPLE 4
(1) The mid-points of the sides MP and ST of $\triangle LMP$ and $\triangle RST$ are X and Y respectively. If $LM = RS$, $MP = ST$ and $LX = RY$ show that $\triangle LMP \equiv \triangle RST$.

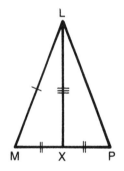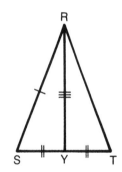

Fig. 29.29

Referring to Fig. 29.29:

$\triangle LMX \equiv \triangle RSY$ (condition (3) above)

therefore $\angle M = \angle S$

In $\triangle$s LMP and RST

$LM = RS$; $MP = ST$; $\angle M = \angle S$.

That is, two sides and the included angle in $\triangle LMP$ equal the two sides and the included angle in $\triangle RST$. Hence $\triangle LMP \equiv \triangle RST$.

(2) The diagonals of the quadrilateral XYZW intersect at O. Given that OX = OW and OY = OZ show that XY = WZ.

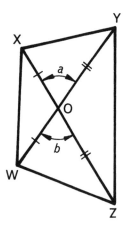

Fig. 29.30

Referring to Fig. 29.30:

In △s XOY and WOZ

OX = OW   and   OY = OZ   (given)

$a = b$ (vertically opposite angles)

Hence the two sides and the included angle in △XOY equal two sides and the included angle in △WOZ. Hence △XOY ≡ △WOZ.

Therefore   XY = WZ

Exercise 143 – *All type B*

1) In Fig. 29.31 state the letter corresponding to those triangles which are definitely congruent.

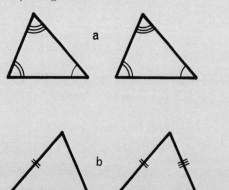

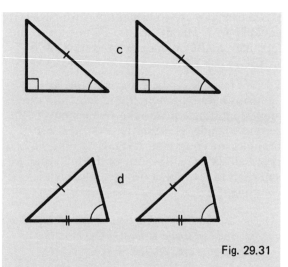

Fig. 29.31

2) In Fig. 29.32 state the letter corresponding to those triangles which are definitely congruent.

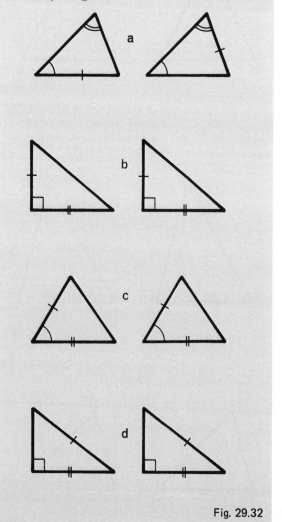

Fig. 29.32

3) In Fig. 29.33 find the lengths of RQ and SX. The diagram is not drawn to scale. What is the magnitude of ∠SXP?

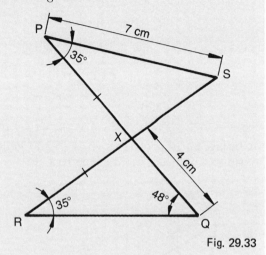

Fig. 29.33

4) In Fig. 29.34 find the length of PY.

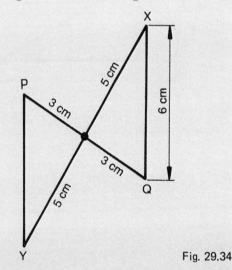

Fig. 29.34

5) In Fig. 29.35 AB is parallel to DC and each is 4 cm long. If AD = 5 cm, find the length of BC. If ∠DAC = 42°, find ∠BCA.

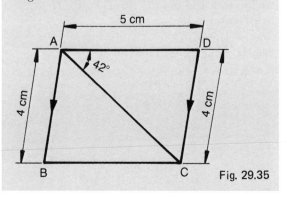

Fig. 29.35

6) In Fig. 29.36 name all the triangles which are congruent. G is the mid-point of DE, H is the mid-point of DF and J is the mid-point of EF.

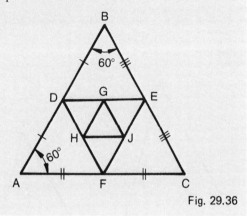

Fig. 29.36

SIMILAR TRIANGLES

Triangles that are equi-angular are called *similar triangles*. Thus in Fig. 34.37 if:

$$\angle A = \angle X, \quad \angle B = \angle Y \quad \text{and} \quad \angle C = \angle Z$$

the triangles ABC and ZYX are similar. In similar triangles the ratios of corresponding sides are equal. Thus for the triangles shown in Fig. 29.37,

$$\frac{a}{x} = \frac{b}{y} = \frac{c}{z} = \frac{H}{h}$$

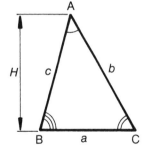 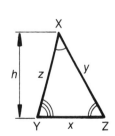

Fig. 29.37

Note that by corresponding sides we mean the sides opposite to the equal angles. It helps in solving problems on similar triangles if we write the two triangles with the equal angles under each other. Thus in △s ABC and XYZ if
∠A = ∠X, ∠B = ∠Y and ∠C = ∠Z

we write $\qquad \dfrac{\text{ABC}}{\text{XYZ}}$

The equations connecting the sides of the triangles are then easily obtained by writing any two letters in the first triangle over any two corresponding letters in the second triangle. Thus,

$$\frac{AB}{XY} = \frac{AC}{XZ} = \frac{BC}{YZ}$$

In Fig. 29.38 to prove $\triangle ABC$ is similar to $\triangle XYZ$ it is sufficient to prove any one of the following:

Fig. 29.38

(1) *Two angles in $\triangle ABC$ are equal to two angles in $\triangle XYZ$.* For instance, the triangles are similar if $\angle A = \angle X$ and $\angle B = \angle Y$, since it follows that $\angle C = \angle Z$.

(2) *The three sides of $\triangle ABC$ are proportional to the corresponding sides of $\triangle XYZ$.* Thus $\triangle ABC$ is similar to $\triangle XYZ$ if,

$$\frac{AB}{XY} = \frac{AC}{XZ} = \frac{BC}{YZ}$$

(3) *Two sides in $\triangle ABC$ are proportional to two sides in $\triangle XYZ$ and the angles included between these sides in each triangle are equal.* Thus $\triangle ABC$ is similar to $\triangle XYZ$ if,

$$\frac{AB}{XY} = \frac{AC}{XZ} \quad \text{and} \quad \angle A = \angle X$$

EXAMPLE 5

(1) In Fig. 29.39 find the dimension marked x.

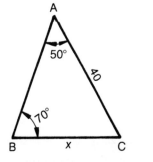
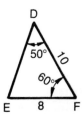

Fig. 29.39

In $\triangle ABC$, angle

$$C = 180° - 50° - 70° = 60°$$

In $\triangle DEF$, angle

$$E = 180° - 50° - 60° = 70°$$

therefore $\triangle ABC$ and $\triangle DEF$ are similar.

$$\frac{40}{10} = \frac{x}{8} \quad \text{or} \quad 320 = 10x$$

$$x = \frac{320}{10} = 32$$

(2) In Fig. 29.40 prove that $\triangle$s PTS and PQR are similar and calculate the length of TS.

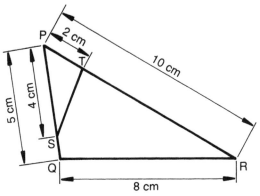

Fig. 29.40

In $\triangle$s PTS and PQR

$$\frac{PS}{PR} = \frac{4}{10} = 0.4$$

$$\frac{PT}{PQ} = \frac{2}{5} = 0.4$$

therefore

$$\frac{PS}{PR} = \frac{PT}{PQ}$$

Also $\angle P$ is common to both triangles and it is the included angle between PS and PT in $\triangle PTS$ and PR and PQ in $\triangle PQR$. Hence $\triangle$s PTS and PQR are similar.

Writing $\dfrac{\triangle PTS}{\triangle PQR}$ we see that

$$\frac{TS}{QR} = \frac{PT}{PQ}$$

$$\frac{TS}{8} = \frac{2}{5}$$

$$TS = \frac{2 \times 8}{5} = 3.2 \text{ cm}$$

Exercise 144 – *Questions 1–4 type B,*
remainder C

1) Figure 29.41 shows a large number of
triangles. Write down the letters representing
triangles which are similar. You should be
able to find five sets of similar triangles.

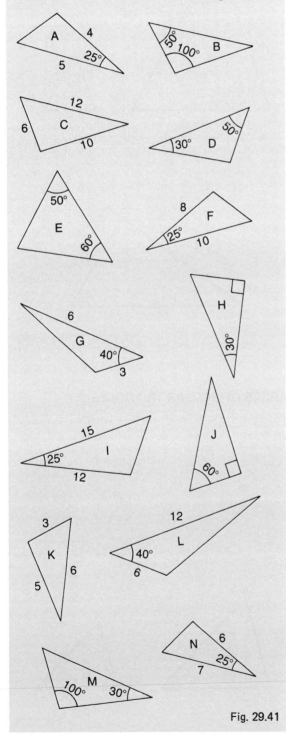

Fig. 29.41

2) The triangles shown in Fig. 29.42 are:

a congruent   **b** similar   **c** neither of these

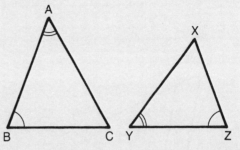

Fig. 29.42

3) If the triangles ABC and XYZ shown in
Fig. 29.42 are similar then:

a $\dfrac{AC}{XY} = \dfrac{XZ}{BC}$ **b** $\dfrac{AC}{XY} = \dfrac{BC}{XZ}$

c $\dfrac{BC}{AB} = \dfrac{YZ}{XZ}$ **d** $\dfrac{BC}{AB} = \dfrac{XZ}{YZ}$

4) In Fig. 29.43 if $\dfrac{AB}{XY} = \dfrac{AC}{XZ}$ and

$\angle B = \angle Y$ then

I $\dfrac{AB}{XY} = \dfrac{BC}{YZ}$ **II** $\angle A = \angle X$ **III** $\angle C = \angle Z$

Which of the above is necessarily correct?

a **I** only   **b** **II** and **III** only
c **III** only   **d** **I**, **II** and **III**

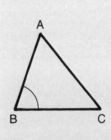
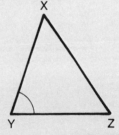

Fig. 29.43

5) In Fig. 29.44, $\angle A = \angle X$ and
$\angle B = \angle Y$. Hence:

a $XY = 6\frac{7}{8}$ cm   **b** $XY = 17\frac{3}{5}$ cm
c $YZ = 7\frac{1}{2}$ cm   **d** $YZ = 19\frac{1}{5}$ cm

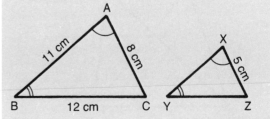

Fig. 29.44

6) In Fig. 29.45,   PS = 8 cm   and
QS = 2 cm.   Hence $\dfrac{ST}{QR}$ is equal to:

a $\dfrac{1}{4}$ **b** $\dfrac{4}{5}$ **c** $\dfrac{5}{4}$ **d** $\dfrac{4}{1}$

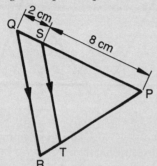

Fig. 29.45

7) In Fig. 29.46, XY is parallel to BC and
AB is parallel to YZ. Hence:
a $\angle B = \angle Z$
b $\triangle$s ABC and YZC are similar
c $\dfrac{YZ}{ZC} = \dfrac{AC}{BC}$ **d** $\dfrac{ZC}{AC} = \dfrac{YZ}{AB}$

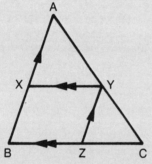

Fig. 29.46

8) In Fig. 29.47, AB is parallel to DC and
AB = 3 cm   and   DC = 5 cm. Hence
$\dfrac{XD}{XB}$ is equal to:

a $\dfrac{3}{5}$ **b** $\dfrac{5}{8}$ **c** $\dfrac{5}{3}$ **d** none of these

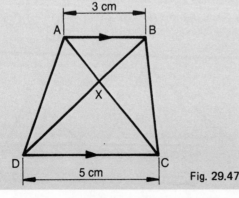

Fig. 29.47

9) In Fig. 29.48 find BC, AB and DE if
possible.

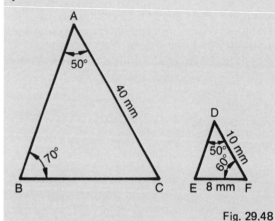

Fig. 29.48

10) In Fig. 29.49, find EC and AB.

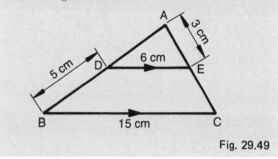

Fig. 29.49

AREAS OF SIMILAR TRIANGLES

*The ratio of the areas of similar triangles is equal to
the ratio of the squares on corresponding sides.*

If in Fig. 29.50 $\triangle$s ABC and XYZ are similar
then,

$$\frac{\text{area of } \triangle ABC}{\text{area of } \triangle XYZ} = \frac{AB^2}{XY^2} = \frac{AC^2}{XZ^2}$$

$$= \frac{BC^2}{YZ^2} = \frac{AD^2}{WX^2}$$

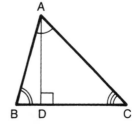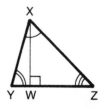

Fig. 29.50

EXAMPLE 6

Find the area of triangle XYZ given that the area of triangle ABC is $12\,\text{cm}^2$ (see Fig. 29.51).

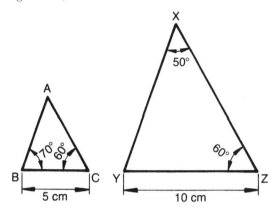

Fig. 29.51

In triangle XYZ, $\angle Y = 70°$ and in triangle ABC, $\angle A = 50°$. Hence the two triangles are similar because they are equi-angular. BC and YZ correspond; hence

$$\frac{\text{Area of } \triangle XYZ}{\text{Area of } \triangle ABC} = \frac{YZ^2}{BC^2}$$

$$\frac{\text{Area of } \triangle XYZ}{12} = \frac{10^2}{5^2} = \frac{100}{25} = 4$$

$$\text{Area of } \triangle XYZ = 4 \times 12 = 48\,\text{cm}^2$$

Exercise 145 – *All type C*

1) In Fig. 29.52, the triangles ABC and EFG are similar. If the area of $\triangle ABC$ is $8\,\text{cm}^2$, calculate the area of $\triangle EFG$.

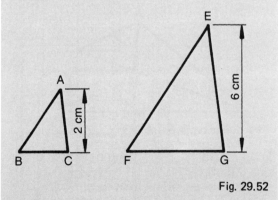

Fig. 29.52

2) In Fig. 29.53, the area of triangle XYZ is $9\,\text{cm}^2$. What is the area of $\triangle ABC$?

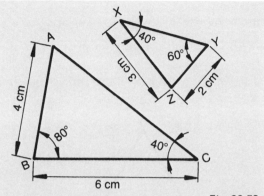

Fig. 29.53

3) In Fig. 29.53 if the area of $\triangle XYZ$ is $10\,\text{cm}^2$ then the area of $\triangle ABC$ is:
a impossible to find from the given information
b $40\,\text{cm}^2$ **c** $80\,\text{cm}^2$ **d** $160\,\text{cm}^2$

4) In Fig. 29.54, $\triangle$s ABC and DEF are similar triangles. If the area of $\triangle ABC$ is $27\,\text{cm}^2$ then the area of $\triangle DEF$ is:
a $4\,\text{cm}^2$ **b** $6.7\,\text{cm}^2$ **c** $13.5\,\text{cm}^2$
d none of these

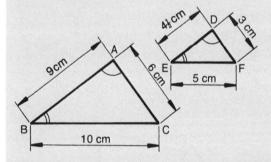

Fig. 29.54

5) In Fig. 29.55, $\angle A = \angle X$ and $\angle B = \angle Y$. $\triangle ABC$ has an area of $36\,\text{cm}^2$ and $\triangle XYZ$ has an area of $4\,\text{cm}^2$. If $AB = 4\,\text{cm}$ then XY is equal to:
a $\frac{4}{9}\,\text{cm}$ **b** $\frac{3}{4}\,\text{cm}$ **c** $\frac{4}{3}\,\text{cm}$ **d** $\frac{9}{4}\,\text{cm}$

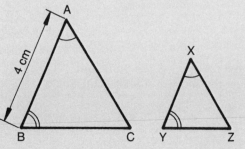

Fig. 29.55

6) In Fig. 29.56, $\dfrac{AX}{XB} = \dfrac{2}{1}$. The area of $\triangle ABC$ is $36\,cm^2$. Hence the area of XYCB is:

a $12\,cm^2$ **b** $18\,cm^2$ **c** $20\,cm^2$
d $16\,cm^2$

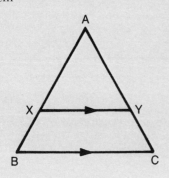

Fig. 29.56

Exercise 146 (Miscellaneous) – *Questions 1, 2, 4, 6, 7 type B, 3, 5, 8 type C, remainder D*

1) In Fig. 29.57, AB = AC and BCF is a straight line. $\angle BAC = 70°$, $\angle CED = 68°$ and $\angle ECF = 81°$. Prove that two of the sides of $\triangle CDE$ are equal.

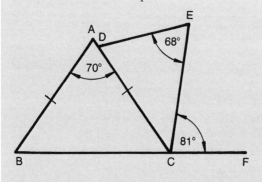

Fig. 29.57

2) In $\triangle ABC$, $\angle A$ is obtuse and $\angle C = 45°$. Name the shortest side of the triangle.

3) In Fig. 29.58, UWR is a straight line. RS = RW, ST = SW, WT = WU and $\angle R = \angle TSW = x°$. Prove that WS bisects $\angle RWT$ and $\angle TWU = x°$.

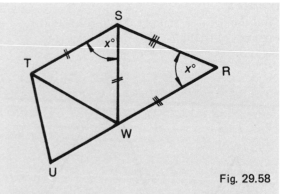

Fig. 29.58

4) In $\triangle ABC$, the sides AB and AC are equal. The side CA is produced to D and $\angle BAD = 148°$. Calculate $\angle ABC$.

5) The mid-points of the sides MP and ST of $\triangle LMP$ and $\triangle RST$ are X and Y respectively. If LM = RS, MP = ST and LX = RY prove that $\triangle LMP \equiv \triangle RST$.

6) Two similar triangles have areas of $27\,cm^2$ and $48\,cm^2$. Find the ratio of the lengths of a pair of corresponding sides of the two triangles.

7) In $\triangle ABC$, AN is the perpendicular from A to BC. If BN = 9 cm, CN = 16 cm and AN = 12 cm, prove $\angle BAC = 90°$.

8) In Fig. 29.59, ABCD is a quadrilateral in which $\dfrac{AB}{AD} = \dfrac{5}{3}$. AX bisects $\angle BAD$ and XY is parallel to BC. Calculate the ratio $\dfrac{XY}{BC}$.

$\left(\text{Hint: } \dfrac{AB}{AD} = \dfrac{BX}{XD}.\right)$ Also find

$\dfrac{\text{area } \triangle AXD}{\text{area } \triangle ABD}$ and $\dfrac{\text{area } \triangle DXY}{\text{area } \triangle DBC}$.

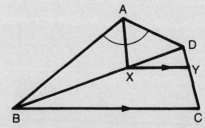

Fig. 29.59

9) In Fig. 29.60, F is the mid-point of the side AB of $\triangle ABC$ and FE is parallel to BC. If AC = 12 cm, BD = 8 cm and DC = 2 cm, calculate:

(a) the lengths FE and CX;
(b) the ratio of the areas of $\triangle$s XCD and XEF.

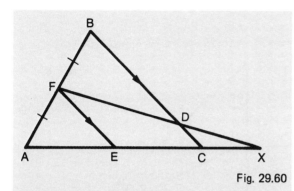

Fig. 29.60

10) BM and CN are altitudes of $\triangle$ABC and BN = CM. Prove that:

(a) $\triangle$BCN ≡ $\triangle$BCM;

(b) AB = AC.

11) PQR is a triangle in which PQ = 5 cm, QR = 8 cm and RP = 10 cm. S and T are points on PQ and PR respectively such that PS = 4 cm and PT = 2 cm. Prove that $\triangle$s PTS and PQR are similar and calculate the length of ST.

12) PQR is a triangle in which $\angle$PRQ = 62°. S is a point on QR between Q and R such that SP = SR and $\angle$QPS = 27°. Calculate $\angle$PRQ and hence prove that SR is greater than QS.

13) In $\triangle$ABC, the perpendicular from A to BC meets BC at D and the perpendicular from D to AB meets AB at E. Given that BD = 4 cm, DC = 6 cm and the area of $\triangle$ABC is 15 cm², prove that AD = 3 cm and calculate AE.

14) In $\triangle$ABC, D is the mid-point of BC and E is the mid-point of CA. The lines AD and BE meet at G. Prove that:

(a) $\triangle$s ABG and DEG are similar;

(b) $\triangle$s AGE and BGD are equal in area.

15) In $\triangle$PQR, the line ST is drawn parallel to QR meeting PQ at S and PR at T such that PS = 3SQ. Calculate $\dfrac{ST}{QR}$. Given that the area of $\triangle$TQS is 3 cm², calculate:

(a) the area of $\triangle$PST;

(b) the area of $\triangle$TQR.

16) A line cuts three parallel lines at A, B and C such that AB = BC. Another line cuts the parallel lines at P, Q and R. Draw lines through P and Q parallel to AC and use congruent triangles to prove that PQ = QR.

SELF-TEST 29

State the letter (or letters) corresponding to the correct answer (or answers).

1) The triangle shown in Fig. 29.61 is:

a acute-angled   **b** obtuse-angled

c scalene   **d** isosceles

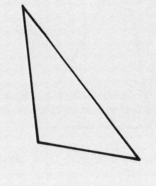

Fig. 29.61

2) In Fig. 29.62, $\angle$B is equal to:

a 40°   **b** 50°   **c** 80°   **d** 90°

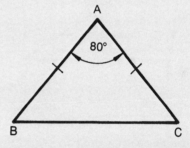

Fig. 29.62

3) In Fig. 29.63, $\angle$A is equal to:

a 20°   **b** 40°   **c** 60°   **d** 80°

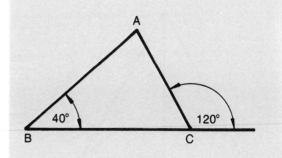

Fig. 29.63

4) In Fig. 29.64, x is equal to:

a $60°$ **b** $70°$ **c** $80°$ **d** $140°$

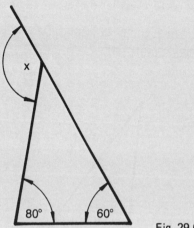

Fig. 29.64

5) In Fig. 29.65 the largest angle of the triangle is:

a $\angle A$ **b** $\angle B$ **c** $\angle C$

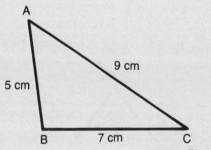

Fig. 29.65

6) A triangle is stated to have sides whose lengths are $5\,\text{cm}$, $8\,\text{cm}$ and $14\,\text{cm}$.

a It is possible to draw the triangle.

b It is impossible to draw the triangle.

7) In Fig. 29.66 which one of the following is not true?

a $\angle BAD = \angle DAC$ **b** $\angle ABD = \angle ACD$

c $BD = DC$ **d** $AD = BD$

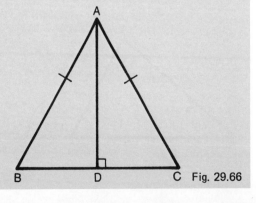

Fig. 29.66

8) In Fig. 29.67, x is equal to:

a $48°$ **b** $25°$ **c** $17°$ **d** $8°30'$

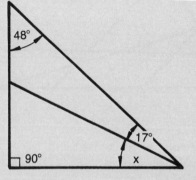

Fig. 29.67

9) In Fig. 29.68, q is equal to:

a $100°$ **b** $80°$ **c** $60°$ **d** $40°$

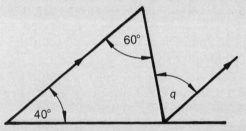

Fig. 29.68

10) Two angles of a triangle are $(2x - 40)°$ and $(3x + 10)°$. The third angle is therefore:

a $(210 - 5x)°$ **b** $(230 + x)°$

c $(220 - 5x)°$

11) The three angles of a triangle are $(2x + 20)°$, $(3x + 20)°$ and $(x + 20)°$. The value of x is:

a $60°$ **b** $40°$ **c** $20°$ **d** $10°$

12) In Fig. 29.69, $AD = BC$ and $AC = DB$. Hence:

a $\angle DAC = \angle DBC$ **b** $\angle ADB = \angle DBC$

c $\angle ADC = \angle BCD$ **d** $\angle ADC = \angle BDC$

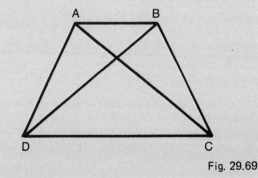

Fig. 29.69

13) In Fig. 29.70 △DEC is equilateral and ABCD is a square. ∠DEA is therefore:

a 15°   **b** 20°   **c** 30°   **d** 45°

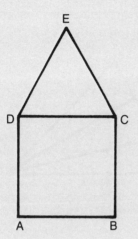

Fig. 29.70

14) In Fig. 29.71 two straight lines bisect each other at X. Therefore:

a △AXC ≡ △DXB   **b** △ABD ≡ △ABC
c △ADX = △CXB   **d** ∠CAX = ∠XDB

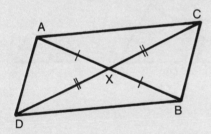

Fig. 29.71

15) The triangles shown in Fig. 29.72 are:

a congruent   **b** similar
c isosceles   **d** none of these

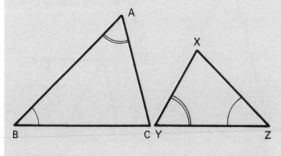

Fig. 29.72

16) If the triangles ABC and XYZ shown in Fig. 29.72 are similar then

a $\dfrac{AC}{XY} = \dfrac{XZ}{BC}$ **b** $\dfrac{AC}{XY} = \dfrac{BC}{XZ}$

c $\dfrac{BC}{AB} = \dfrac{YZ}{XZ}$ **d** $\dfrac{BC}{AB} = \dfrac{XZ}{YZ}$

17) In Fig. 29.73 if $\dfrac{AB}{XY} = \dfrac{AC}{XZ}$ and

∠B = ∠Y then:

a $\dfrac{AB}{XY} = \dfrac{BC}{YZ}$ **b** ∠A = ∠X

c ∠C = ∠Z

d none of the foregoing are necessarily true.

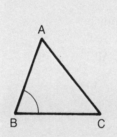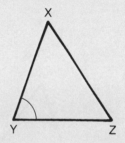

Fig. 29.73

18) In Fig. 29.74, ∠A = ∠X and ∠B = ∠Y. Hence XY =

a $6\frac{7}{8}$ cm   **b** $7\frac{1}{2}$ cm   **c** 8 cm   **d** 15 cm

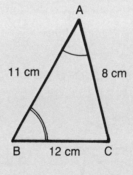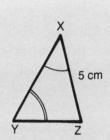

Fig. 29.74

19) In Fig. 29.75, PS = 2SQ. Hence $\dfrac{ST}{QR}$ is equal to:

a $\dfrac{1}{2}$ **b** $\dfrac{2}{3}$ **c** $\dfrac{3}{2}$ **d** $\dfrac{2}{1}$

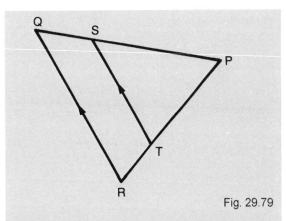

Fig. 29.79

20) In Fig. 29.76, XY is parallel to BC and AB is parallel to YZ. Hence

a $\angle B = \angle Z$

b $\triangle$s ABC and YZC are similar

c $\dfrac{YZ}{ZC} = \dfrac{AC}{BC}$ **d** $\dfrac{ZC}{AC} = \dfrac{YZ}{AB}$

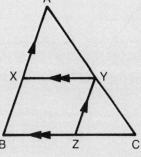

Fig. 29.76

21) In Fig. 29.77, AB is parallel to DC and AB = 3 cm and DC = 5 cm. Hence $\dfrac{XD}{XB}$ is equal to:

a $\dfrac{3}{5}$ **b** $\dfrac{5}{8}$ **c** $\dfrac{5}{3}$ **d** none of these

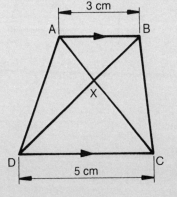

Fig. 29.77

22) In Fig. 29.78, AD = DE = EB. Hence

a $\triangle$s ADC and CEB are equal in area.

b $\triangle$BCD has twice the area of $\triangle$ADC.

c $\triangle$ABC has three times the area of $\triangle$ACD.

d none of the foregoing is correct.

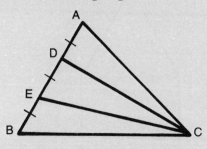

Fig. 29.78

23) In Fig. 29.79, $\triangle$s ABC and DEF are similar triangles. If the area of $\triangle$ABC is $20\,\text{cm}^2$ then the area of $\triangle$DEF is:

a $5\,\text{cm}^2$ **b** $8\,\text{cm}^2$ **c** $10\,\text{cm}^2$

d none of these

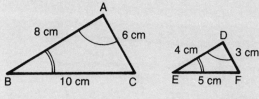

Fig. 29.79

24) In Fig. 29.80, if the area of $\triangle$XYZ is $10\,\text{cm}^2$ then the area of $\triangle$ABC is:

a impossible to find from the given information

b $40\,\text{cm}^2$ **c** $80\,\text{cm}^2$ **d** $160\,\text{cm}^2$

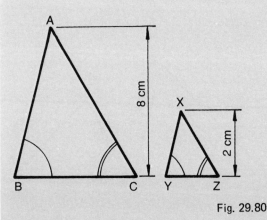

Fig. 29.80

25) In Fig. 29.81, $\angle A = \angle X$ and
$\angle B = \angle Y$. $\triangle ABC$ has an area of $81\,\mathrm{cm}^2$ and
$\triangle XYZ$ has an area of $4\,\mathrm{cm}^2$. If $AB = 4\,\mathrm{cm}$
then XY is equal to:

a $\frac{4}{9}$ cm   **b** $\frac{8}{9}$ cm   **c** $\frac{9}{8}$ cm   **d** $\frac{9}{4}$ cm

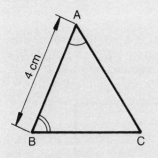
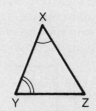

Fig. 29.81

26) In Fig. 29.82, $\dfrac{AX}{XB} = \dfrac{2}{1}$. The area of
$\triangle ABC$ is $18\,\mathrm{cm}^2$. Hence the area of XYCB
is:

a $6\,\mathrm{cm}^2$ **b** $8\,\mathrm{cm}^2$ **c** $9\,\mathrm{cm}^2$ **d** $10\,\mathrm{cm}^2$

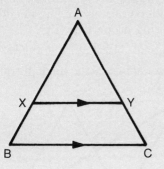

Fig. 29.82

27) In $\triangle ABC$ (Fig. 29.83):
a $a^2 = b^2 + c^2$ **b** $b^2 = a^2 + c^2$
c $c^2 = a^2 + b^2$

d none of the foregoing is true.

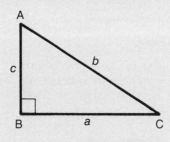

Fig. 29.83

28) In a triangle ABC, $AB = 3\,\mathrm{cm}$,
$BC = 4\,\mathrm{cm}$ and $AC = 5\,\mathrm{cm}$. Hence:
a $\angle A = 90°$ **b** $\angle B = 90°$ **c** $\angle C = 90°$

29) In $\triangle ABC$, $\angle B = 90°$, $BC = 5\,\mathrm{cm}$,
$AB = 12\,\mathrm{cm}$. Hence AC is equal to:

a $10.91\,\mathrm{cm}$ **b** $13.00\,\mathrm{cm}$
c $34.50\,\mathrm{cm}$ **d** $41.11\,\mathrm{cm}$

30) In $\triangle ABC$, $\angle A = 90°$, $BC = 7.8\,\mathrm{cm}$,
$AC = 6.3\,\mathrm{cm}$. Hence AB is equal to:

a $14.53\,\mathrm{cm}$ **b** $10.26\,\mathrm{cm}$
c $4.60\,\mathrm{cm}$ **d** $3.25\,\mathrm{cm}$

CHAPTER 29 SUMMARY

Points to remember

(i) Congruent figures have the same shape and size.
(ii) Similar figures have the same shape.
(iii) A right-angled triangle has the measure of one of its angles equal to $90°$.
(iv) If in a triangle ABC the angle B is a right angle, $AC^2 = AB^2 + BC^2$.
(v) An isosceles triangle has two sides equal. The angles opposite the equal sides are equal.
(vi) An equilateral triangle has all its sides equal and each angle measures $60°$.

(vii) A line segment from a vertex of a triangle and perpendicular to the opposite side is called an altitude.
(viii) If two triangles are similar, their corresponding angles are equal and their corresponding sides are proportional.
(ix) If two triangles are similar, the ratio of their areas is equal to the ratio of the squares of corresponding sides.

Chapter 30 **Quadrilaterals and Polygons**

QUADRILATERAL

A quadrilateral is any four-sided figure (Fig. 30.1). Since it can be split up into two triangles the sum of its angles is 360°.

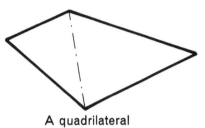

A quadrilateral

Fig. 30.1

PARALLELOGRAM

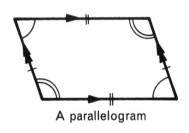

A parallelogram

Fig. 30.2

A parallelogram (Fig. 30.2) has both pairs of opposite sides parallel. It has the following properties:

(1) The sides which are opposite to each other are equal in length.

(2) The angles which are opposite to each other are equal.

(3) The diagonals bisect each other.

(4) The diagonals bisect the parallelogram so that two congruent triangles are formed.

RECTANGLE

A rectangle (Fig. 30.3) is a parallelogram with each of its angles equal to 90°. A rectangle has all the properties of a parallelogram but, in addition, the diagonals are equal in length.

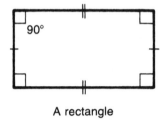

A rectangle

Fig. 30.3

RHOMBUS

A rhombus is a parallelogram with all its sides equal in length (Fig. 30.4). It has all the properties of a parallelogram but, in addition, it has the following properties:

(1) The diagonals bisect at right angles.

(2) The diagonal bisects the angle through which it passes.

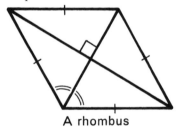

A rhombus

Fig. 30.4

SQUARE

A square (Fig. 30.5) is a rectangle with all its sides equal in length. It has all the properties of a parallelogram, rectangle and rhombus.

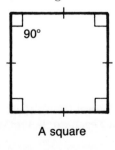

A square

Fig. 30.5

TRAPEZIUM

A trapezium (Fig. 30.6) is a quadrilateral with one pair of sides parallel.

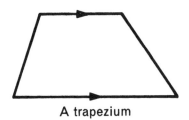

A trapezium

Fig. 30.6

EXAMPLE 1

(1) X, P, Q, Y are points in order on a straight line and XP = QY. The parallelogram PQRS is drawn such that ∠PQR = 130° and QR = QY. The lines XS and YR are produced to meet at Z. Calculate ∠XZY.

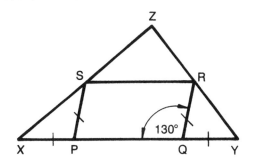

Fig. 30.7

Referring to Fig. 30.7:
Since ∠PQR = 130°
then ∠PSR = 130° (PQRS is a parallelogram)
and ∠SPQ = ∠SRQ = 50°.
Hence ∠XPS = 130° and ∠RQY = 50°.
△ RQY is isosceles (since QR = QY)

∴   ∠QRY = ∠RYQ = 65°

△ SXP is isosceles (since XP = SP)

∴   ∠SXP = ∠PSX = 25°

In △ZXY

∠XZY = 180° − ∠SXP − ∠RYQ

= 180° − 65° − 25° = 90°

(2) A rhombus ABCD and an equilateral triangle ABX lie on opposite sides of AB. If ∠BCD = 82°, calculate ∠ADX and ∠BDX.

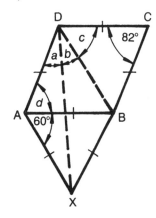

Fig. 30.8

Referring to Fig. 30.8:
    $d = 82°$ (opp. angles of a rhombus are equal)

∠XAB = 60°   (angle of an equilateral triangle ABX)

△ DAX is isosceles since AD = AX

∠DAX = 82° + 60° = 142°

∴ $a = \frac{1}{2}(180° − 142°) = 19°$

△ CDB is isosceles since CD = CB

∴ $c = \frac{1}{2}(180° − 82°) = 49°$

In the rhombus ABCD

∠D = 180° − 82° = 98°

$a + b + c = 98°$

$b = 98° − a − c = 98° − 19° − 49° = 30°$

∴

$a = ∠ADX = 19°$ and $b = ∠XDB = 30°$

Exercise 147 – *Questions 1–11 type B, remainder C*

1) Calculate the angle x in Fig. 30.9.

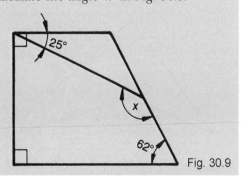

Fig. 30.9

2) Find the angle *x* in Fig. 30.10.

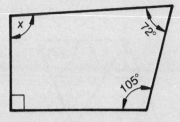

Fig. 30.10

3) In Fig. 30.11, ABCD is a parallelogram. Calculate the angles *x* and *y*.

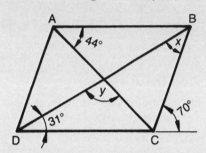

Fig. 30.11

4) A quadrilateral has one and only one pair of sides parallel. It is therefore a:

a rhombus   **b** parallelogram
c rectangle   **d** trapezium

5) A quadrilateral has diagonals which bisect at right angles. It must therefore be a

a rhombus   **b** trapezium
c rectangle   **d** parallelogram

6) In Fig. 30.12, *x* is equal to:

a $a + b + c$ **b** $360° - (a + b + c)$
c $a + b + c + 180°$ **d** $360° - a + b + c$

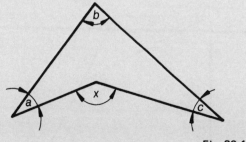

Fig. 30.12

7) In Fig. 30.13, *y* is equal to:
a 40°   **b** 70°   **c** 80°   **d** 100°

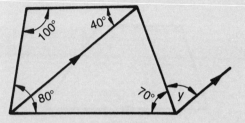

Fig. 30.13

8) In Fig. 30.14, find *p*.

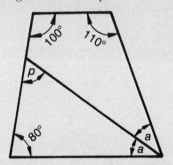

Fig. 30.14

9) In a quadrilateral one angle is equal to 60°. The other three angles are equal. What is the size of the equal angles?

10) Fig. 30.15 shows a rhombus. Are △s ABE and DEC congruent? Does ∠DAC equal ∠DCA? Is the angle DAB bisected by AC?

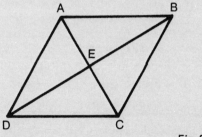

Fig. 30.15

11) ABCD is a quadrilateral in which ∠A = 86°, ∠C = 110° and ∠D = 40°. The bisector of angle ABC cuts the side AD at E. Find ∠AEB.

12) In the quadrilateral ABCD, $\angle DAB = 60°$ and the other three angles are equal. The line CE is drawn parallel to BA to meet AD at E. Calculate the angles ABC and ECD.

13) PQRS is a square. T is a point on the diagonal PR such that PT = PQ. The line through T perpendicular to PR cuts QR at X. Prove that QX = XT = TR.

14) The diagonals of a rhombus are 12 cm and 9 cm long. Calculate the length of the sides of the rhombus.

15) The diagonals of a quadrilateral XYZW intersect at O. Given that OX = OW and OY = OZ prove that

(a) XY = ZW;
(b) YZ is parallel to XW.

16) ABCD is a parallelogram. Parallel lines BE and DF meet the diagonal AC at E and F respectively. Prove that:

(a) AE = FC;
(b) BEDF is a parallelogram.

POLYGONS

Any plane closed figure bounded by straight lines is called a polygon.

(1) A *convex* polygon (Fig. 30.16) has no interior angle greater than 180°.

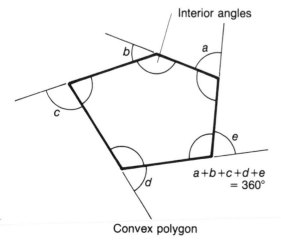

Convex polygon

Fig. 30.16

(2) A *re-entrant* polygon (Fig. 30.17) has at least one interior angle greater than 180°.

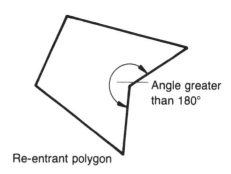

Angle greater than 180°

Re-entrant polygon

Fig. 30.17

(3) A *regular* polygon has all of its sides and all of its angles equal.

(4) A *pentagon* is a polygon with 5 sides.

(5) A *hexagon* is a polygon with 6 sides.

(6) An *octagon* is a polygon with 8 sides.

In a convex polygon having n sides the sum of the interior angles is $(2n - 4)$ right angles. The sum of the exterior angles is 360°, no matter how many sides the polygon has. Note that these statements apply to all polygons not just regular polygons.

EXAMPLE 2

(1) Each interior angle of a regular polygon is 140°. How many sides has it?

Let the polygon have n sides.

The sum of the interior angles is then $140n°$. But the sum of the interior angles is also $(2n - 4)$ right angles or $90(2n - 4)°$.

$$\therefore \qquad 90(2n - 4) = 140n$$

$$180n - 360 = 140n$$

$$40n = 360$$

$$n = 9$$

Hence the polygon has 9 sides.

(2) In a regular polygon, each interior angle is greater by $140°$ than each exterior angle. How many sides has the polygon?

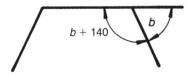

Fig. 30.18

In Fig. 30.18 let b be the exterior angle of a polygon having n sides. Then

$$\text{interior angle} = b + 140$$

Also since the sum of the exterior and interior angles $= 180°$.

$$b + b + 140 = 180 \qquad \therefore \quad 2b = 40$$

$$\therefore \quad b = 20$$

$$\therefore \quad \text{exterior angle} = 20°.$$

But sum of exterior angles $= 360°$.

$$\therefore \quad \text{number of exterior angles} = \frac{360}{20}$$

$$\therefore \quad \text{number of sides} = 18$$

Hence the polygon has 18 sides.

Exercise 148 – *Questions 1–4 type B, remainder C*

1) Find the sum of the interior angles in degrees of a convex polygon with:

(a) 5   (b) 8   (c) 10   (d) 12 sides

2) If the polygons in Question 1 are all regular find the size of the interior angle of each.

3) A hexagon has interior angles of $100°$, $110°$, $120°$ and $128°$. If the remaining two angles are equal, what is their size?

4) Each interior angle of a regular polygon is $150°$. How many sides has it?

5) ABCDE is a regular pentagon and ABX is an equilateral triangle drawn outside the pentagon. Calculate $\angle$AEX.

6) In a regular polygon each interior angle is greater by $150°$ than each exterior angle. Calculate the number of sides of the polygon.

7) A polygon has n sides. Two of its angles are right angles and each of the remaining angles is $144°$. Calculate n.

8) In a pentagon ABCDE, $\angle$A $= 120°$, $\angle$B $= 138°$ and $\angle$D $= \angle$E. The sides AB, DC when produced meet at right angles. Calculate $\angle$BCD and $\angle$AED.

9) In a regular pentagon ABCDE, the lines AD and BE intersect at P. Calculate the angles $\angle$BAD and $\angle$APE.

10) Calculate the exterior angle of a regular polygon in which the interior angle is four times the exterior angle. Hence find the number of sides in the polygon.

11) Each exterior angle of a regular polygon of n sides exceeds by $6°$ each exterior angle of a regular polygon of $2n$ sides. Find an equation for n and solve it.

12) Calculate the number of sides of a regular polygon in which the exterior angle is one-fifth of the interior angle.

AREA OF A PARALLELOGRAM

(1) *The area of a parallelogram is the product of the base and altitude.* Thus in Fig. 30.19:

$$\text{Area of parallelogram ABCD} = \text{CD} \times \text{EF}$$

$$= \text{BC} \times \text{GH}$$

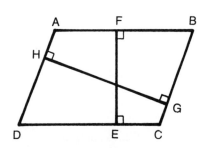

Fig. 30.19

(2) *Parallelograms having equal bases and equal altitudes are equal in area.* Thus in Fig. 30.20:

Area parallelogram ABCD

= area parallelogram CDEF

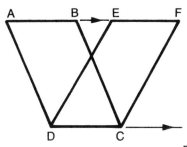

Fig. **30.20**

(3) It follows that:

    (a) Parallelograms which have equal areas and equal bases must have equal altitudes.

    (b) Parallelograms which have equal areas and equal altitudes must have equal bases.

(4) *The area of a triangle is half the area of a parallelogram drawn on the same base and between the same parallels.* Thus in Fig. 30.21:

Area $\triangle$ ABC = $\frac{1}{2}$ area of parallelogram ABED

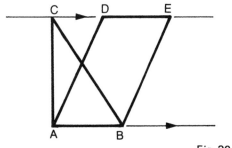

Fig. **30.21**

AREA OF A TRAPEZIUM

A *trapezium* is a quadrilateral which has one pair of sides parallel (Fig. 30.22). Its area is easily found by dividing it up into two triangles as shown in the diagram.

Area $\triangle$ ABC = $\frac{1}{2}ah$

Area $\triangle$ ACD = $\frac{1}{2}bh$

Area of trapezium ABCD = $\frac{1}{2}ah + \frac{1}{2}bh$

= $\frac{1}{2}h(a+b)$

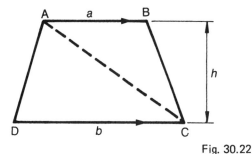

Fig. **30.22**

Hence the area of a trapezium is half the product of the sum of the parallel sides and the distance between them.

EXAMPLE 3

(1) Find the area of the parallelogram ABCD (Fig. 30.23).

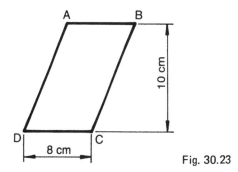

Fig. **30.23**

Area of parallelogram ABCD

= base $\times$ altitude

= $8 \times 10 = 80 \, \text{cm}^2$

(2) In the trapezium PQRS (Fig. 30.24) the parallel sides PQ and SR are both perpendicular to QR. If PQ = 16 cm, PS = 17 cm and RS = 8 cm, calculate the area of the trapezium.

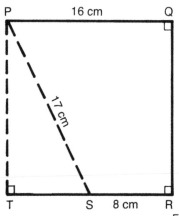

Fig. **30.24**

In Fig. 30.24 draw the lines PT and TS as shown.

In △PST, TS = 8 cm and PS = 17 cm. Using Pythagoras,

$$PT^2 = PS^2 - TS^2 = 17^2 - 8^2 = 225$$

$$PT = \sqrt{225} = 15 \text{ cm}$$

Area of trapezium

$$PQRS = \frac{1}{2} \times 15 \times (16 + 8)$$

$$= \frac{1}{2} \times 15 \times 24$$

$$= 180 \text{ cm}^2$$

(3) Two parallelograms ABCD and ABEF are as shown in Fig. 30.25. Prove that:

(a) DCEF is a parallelogram;
(b) area ABCD = area ABEF − area DCEF

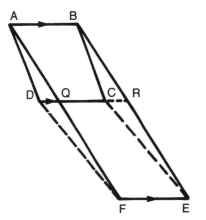

Fig. 30.25

(a) Since ABCD and ABEF are both parallelograms

$$AB = CD = EF$$

and AB, CD and EF are all parallel to each other. Hence DCEF is a parallelogram because the two opposite sides CD and EF are equal and parallel.

(b) Draw CR as shown in Fig. 30.25. Parallelograms ABCD and ABRQ are equal in area since they have the same base AB and the same altitude. Similarly DCEF and QRFE are equal in area.

$$\text{Area ABEF} = \text{area ABRQ} + \text{area QREF}$$

$$= \text{area ABCD} + \text{area DCEF}$$

$$\text{Area ABCD} = \text{area ABEF} - \text{area DCEF}$$

Exercise 149 – *Questions 1 type A, 2–6 type B, remainder C*

1) What is the area of a parallelogram whose base is 7 cm long and whose vertical height is 4 cm?

2) A parallelogram ABCD has AB = 12 cm and BC = 10 cm. ∠ABC = 45°. Calculate the area of ABCD.

3) The area of a parallelogram is 80 cm². If the base is 12 cm long what is its altitude?

4) Fig. 30.26 shows a trapezium. Find x.

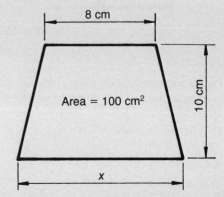

Fig. 30.26

5) E is the mid-point of the side AB of the parallelogram ABCD whose area is 80 cm². Find the area of △DEC.

6) In the rhombus PQRS the side PQ = 17 cm and the diagonal PR = 16 cm. Calculate the area of the rhombus.

7) WXYZ is a parallelogram. A line through W meets ZY at T and XY produced at U. Prove that △s WZT and UYT are similar. If $\frac{ZT}{TY} = \frac{3}{2}$ and the area of WXYZ is 20 cm², calculate:

(a) the area of the trapezium WXYT;
(b) the area of △UYT.

8) The area of a rhombus is 16 cm² and the length of one of its diagonals is 6 cm. Calculate the length of the other diagonal.

9) A point P is taken on the side CD of the parallelogram ABCD and CD is produced to Q making DQ = CP. A line through Q parallel to AD meets BP produced at S. AD is produced to meet BS at R. Prove that ARSQ is a parallelogram and that its area is equal to the area of ABCD.

10) In the parallelogram ABCD the side AB is produced to X so that BX = AB. The line DX cuts BC at E. Prove that:

(a) DBXC is a parallelogram;
(b) Area AED = twice area CEX.

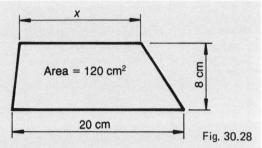

Fig. 30.28

SELF-TEST 30

State the letter (or letters) corresponding to the correct answer (or answers).

1) In Fig. 30.27, x is equal to:

a 190°   **b** 110°   **c** 70°   **d** 60°

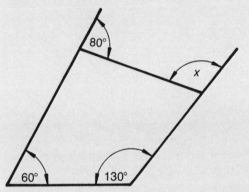

Fig. 30.27

2) A polygon has all its interior angles less than 180°. Hence it is definitely a:

a convex polygon   **b** regular polygon
c re-entrant polygon   **d** quadrilateral

3) A regular polygon has each interior angle equal to 108°. It therefore has:

a 4 sides   **b** 5 sides
c 6 sides   **d** 7 sides

4) A regular polygon has each exterior angle equal to 40°. It therefore has:

a 7 sides   **b** 8 sides
c 9 sides   **d** 10 sides

5) A regular polygon has each interior angle greater by 60° than each exterior angle. It therefore has:

a 4 sides   **b** 6 sides
c 7 sides   **d** 8 sides

6) Fig. 30.28 shows a trapezium. The side marked x is equal to:

a 15 cm   **b** 10 cm   **c** 5 cm   **d** 0.75 cm

7) In Fig. 30.29, ABCD and ABEF are parallelograms which have equal areas. It *must* be true that:

a AF = AD   **b** ∠D = ∠F
c AG = AH   **d** ∠C = ∠E

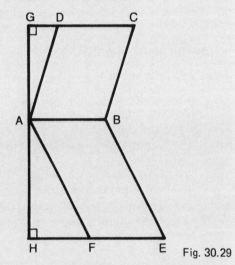

Fig. 30.29

8) In Fig. 30.30, ABCD is a parallelogram and CF = EF. Hence:

a BC = BE   **b** AD = AE
c Area ABCD = area AFE
d Area ABCD = 2 × area ABE

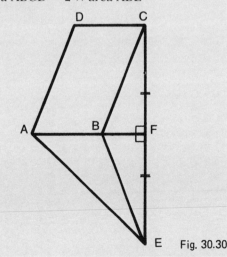

Fig. 30.30

9) In Fig. 30.31, ABCD is a trapezium.
Hence:

a $\angle ADB = 40°$ **b** $\angle ADB = 70°$
c $\angle ADC = 90°$ **d** $\angle ADC = 120°$

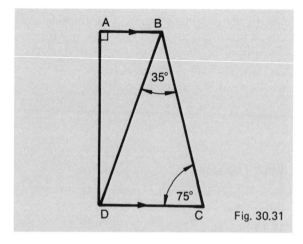

Fig. 30.31

CHAPTER 30 SUMMARY

Points to remember

(i) A parallelogram is a quadrilateral with opposite angles equal, opposite sides equal and parallel.

(ii) The diagonals of a parallelogram bisect each other.

(iii) A trapezium is a quadrilateral with only one pair of parallel sides.

(iv) The area of a trapezium is the product of the sum of the parallel sides and half the distance between them.

(v) The sum of the exterior angles of a convex polygon is 360°.

(vi) The sum of the interior angles of a convex polygon with n sides is $90(2n - 4)°$.

(vii) A regular polygon has all its sides equal and all its angles equal.

(viii) A rhombus is a parallelogram with all its sides equal. The diagonals of a rhombus bisect each other at right angles.

(ix) The area of a quadrilateral is half the product of the diagonals and the sine of the angle between them.

Chapter 31 **The Circle**

Fig. 31.1 shows the main components of a circle.

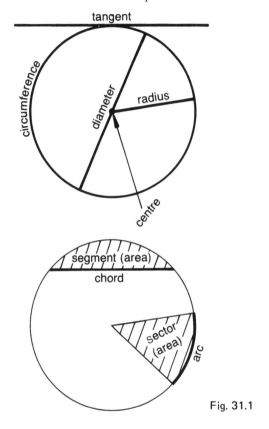

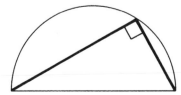

Fig. 31.1

ANGLES IN CIRCLES

The angle which an arc of a circle subtends at the centre is twice the angle which the arc subtends at the circumference.

Thus in Fig. 31.2,

$$\angle AOB = 2 \times \angle APB$$

If a triangle is inscribed in a semicircle the angle opposite the diameter is a right angle (Fig. 31.3).

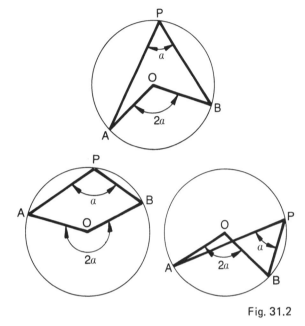

Fig. 31.2

This theorem follows from the fact that *the angle subtended by an arc at the centre is twice the angle subtended by the arc at the circumference.*

Thus in Fig. 31.4:

Angle subtended at the centre by the arc $AB = 180°$.

Hence the angle subtended at the circumference = $90°$.

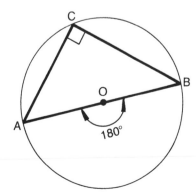

Fig. 31.3

Fig. 31.4

EXAMPLE 1

In Fig. 31.5, O is the centre of the circle. If ∠AOB = 60°, find ∠ACB.

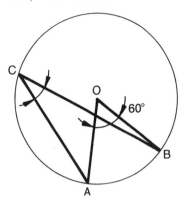

Fig. 31.5

Since ∠AOB is the angle subtended by the arc AB at the centre O and ∠ACB is the angle subtended by AB at the circumference:

$$∠AOB = 2 × ∠ACB$$

Since $∠AOB = 60°$

$$∠ACB = 30°$$

EXAMPLE 2

In Fig. 31.6, find the length of the diameter BC.

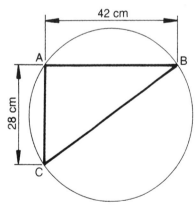

Fig. 31.6

Since BC is a diameter, the angle A is the angle in a semi-circle and hence it is a right angle.

In △ABC, by Pythagoras,

$$BC^2 = 28^2 + 42^2 = 784 + 1764 = 2548$$

$$BC = \sqrt{2548} = 50.48$$

Hence the length of the diameter BC is 50.48 cm.

The chord AB (Fig. 31.7) divides the circle into two arcs. ABP is called the *major* arc and ABQ the *minor* arc. The areas ABP and ABQ are called *segments*.

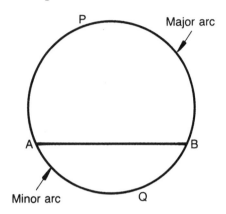

Fig. 31.7

The angles ARB and ASB (Fig. 31.8) are called angles in the segment APB. The angle ATB is called an angle in the segment ABQ.

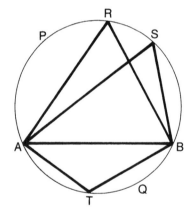

Fig. 31.8

Angles in the same segment of a circle are equal. Thus in Fig. 31.9, ∠APB = ∠AQB since they are angles in the same segment ABQP.

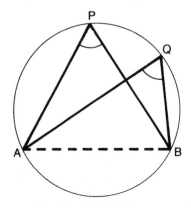

Fig. 31.9

The converse is useful when proving that
4 points are concyclic. Thus in Fig. 31.10, if
∠Z = ∠Y, then the points W, X, Y and Z are
concyclic (i.e. on the circumference of a circle).

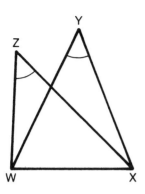

Fig. **31.10**

EXAMPLE 3
Find the angles x and y shown in Fig. 31.11.

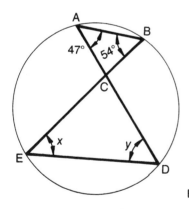

Fig. **31.11**

The angles DEC and BAC are in the same
segment. Hence

$$\angle DEC = \angle BAC$$

$$\therefore \qquad x = 47°$$

The angles ABC and EDC are in the same
segment. Hence

$$\angle EDC = \angle ABC$$

$$\therefore \qquad y = 54°$$

Exercise 150 – *All type B*

1) In Fig. 31.12, if ∠AOB = 76°, find
∠ACB.

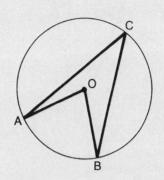

Fig. **31.12**

2) In Fig. 31.13, ABC is an equilateral
triangle inscribed in a circle whose centre
is O. Find ∠BOC.

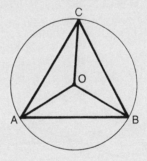

Fig. **31.13**

3) ABC is an isosceles triangle inscribed in a
circle whose centre is O, with AC = CB
(Fig. 31.14). If ∠AOB = 76°, find ∠ABC.

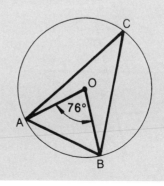

Fig. **31.14**

4) In Fig. 31.15, determine the angle x.

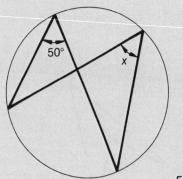

Fig. **31.15**

5) In Fig. 31.16, find the angles x and y.

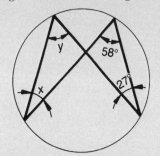

Fig. **31.16**

6) In Fig. 31.17, AB is a diameter. Find AC.

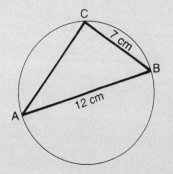

Fig. **31.17**

7) In Fig. 31.18, find each of the angles marked a and b.

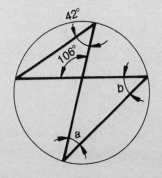

Fig. **31.18**

8) In Fig. 31.19, calculate the diameter of the circle.

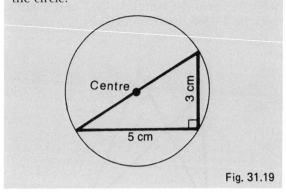

Fig. **31.19**

TANGENT PROPERTIES OF A CIRCLE

A tangent is a line which just touches a circle at one point only (Fig. 31.20). This point is called the point of tangency.

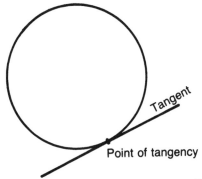

Fig. 31.20

A tangent to a circle is at right angles to a radius drawn from the point of tangency (Fig. 31.21).

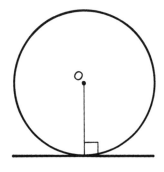

Fig. 31.21

If from a point outside a circle, tangents are drawn to the circle, then the two tangents are equal in length. They also make equal angles with the chord joining the points of tangency (Fig. 31.22). It follows that the line drawn from the point where the tangents meet to the centre of the circle bisects the angle between the two tangents.

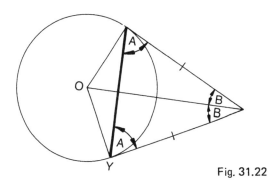

Fig. 31.22

The angle between a tangent and a chord drawn from the point of tangency equals one-half of the angle at the centre subtended by the chord.

Thus in Fig. 31.23, $\angle B = \frac{1}{2} \angle A$.

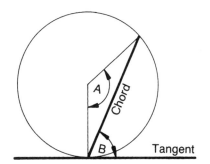

Fig. 31.23

If two circles touch internally or externally then the line which passes through their centres, also passes through the point of tangency (Fig. 31.24).

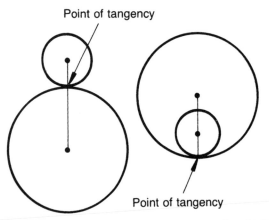

Point of tangency

Point of tangency

Fig. 31.24

A line (Fig. 31.25) which cuts a circle at two points is called a *secant*.

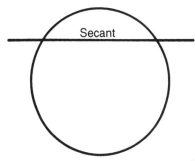

Secant

Fig. 31.25

If from a point outside a circle two lines are drawn, one a secant and the other a tangent to the circle, then the square on the tangent is equal to the rectangle contained by the whole secant and that part of it which lies outside the circle.

Thus in Fig. 31.26, $CT^2 = AC \cdot BC$.

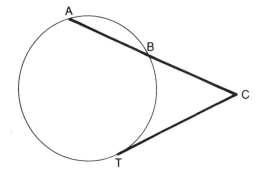

Fig. 31.26

EXAMPLE 4

In Fig. 31.27, calculate the distance x.

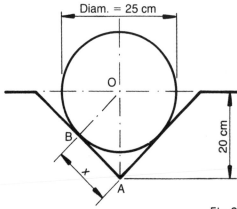

Diam. = 25 cm

20 cm

Fig. 31.27

In triangle OAB,

$$\angle OAB = 90°$$

(angle between a radius and a tangent)

$$OB = 12.5\,cm$$

(OB is a radius and equals $\frac{1}{2}$ of $25 = 12.5\,cm$)

Hence, by Pythagoras,

$$AB^2 = OA^2 - OB^2$$

$$x^2 = 20^2 - 12.5^2$$

$$= 400 - 156.25 = 243.75$$

$$x = \sqrt{243.75} = 15.61\,cm$$

EXAMPLE 5

Three circles are arranged as shown in Fig. 31.28. Find the distance h.

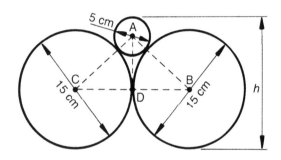

Fig. 31.28

Because the circles are tangential to each other,

$$AC = 7.5 + 2.5 = 10\,cm$$

$$AB = 7.5 + 2.5 = 10\,cm$$

$$BC = 7.5 + 7.5 = 15\,cm$$

Triangle ABC is therefore isosceles. Therefore

$$CD = \frac{1}{2} \times 15 = 7.5$$

In ACD, by Pythagoras,

$$AD^2 = AC^2 - CD^2$$

$$= 10^2 - 7.5^2$$

$$= 100 - 56.25 = 43.75$$

$$AD = \sqrt{43.75} = 6.61\,cm$$

$$h = 7.5 + 6.61 + 2.5 = 16.61\,cm$$

EXAMPLE 6

Find the angle a in Fig. 31.29. What is the size of angle b?

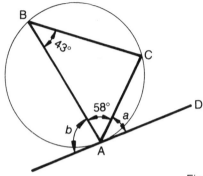

Fig. 31.29

$$\angle ABC = \angle CAD$$

(angle in the alternate segment to $\angle CAD$)

$$a = 43°$$

$$b = 180° - 58° - 43° = 79°$$

Note that the angle $b = \angle ACB$, because this angle is in the alternate segment to b.

EXAMPLE 7

In Fig. 31.30, find the angles a and b.

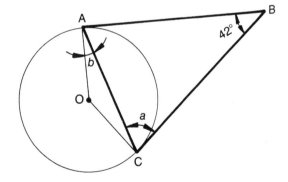

Fig. 31.30

The two tangents AB and BC meet at B and hence

$$AB = BC$$

Therefore $\triangle ABC$ is isosceles and

$$\angle BAC = \angle BCA$$

$$\angle BCA = \frac{1}{2} \times (180° - 42°) = 69°$$

$$a = 69°$$

Since OA is a radius and AB is a tangent

$$\angle OAB = 90°$$

$$b = 90° - a = 90° - 69° = 21°$$

EXAMPLE 8

In Fig. 31.31, the length of the tangent is 8 cm and the length BC is 6 cm. Find the length of the secant AC.

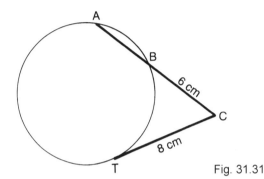

Fig. 31.31

Since the secant AC and the tangent CT meet at C,

$$AC \times BC = CT^2$$

$$AC \times 6 = 8^2$$

$$AC = \frac{64}{6} = 10\tfrac{2}{3} \text{ cm}$$

Exercise 151 – *All type C*

1) Figure 31.32 shows two circles which are just touching. Find x by using Pythagoras' theorem.

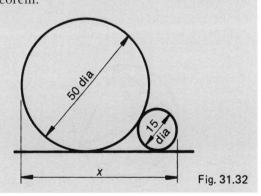

Fig. 31.32

2) In Fig. 31.33 apply Pythagoras' theorem and hence find h.

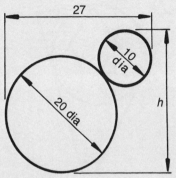

Fig. 31.33

3) In Fig. 31.34, find h.

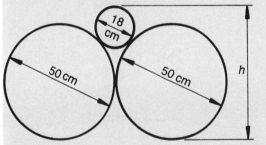

Fig. 31.34

4) In Fig. 31.35, find the dimension x.

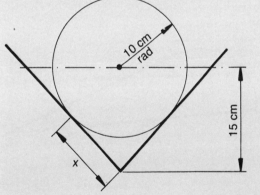

Fig. 31.35

5) In Fig. 31.36 find the angles a and b.

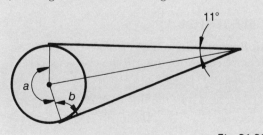

Fig. 31.36

6) In Fig. 31.37, find the angles *a*, *b* and *c*.

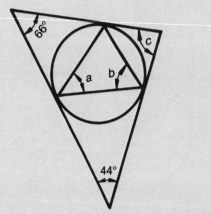

Fig. 31.37

7) In Fig. 31.38 find the length of the secant AC.

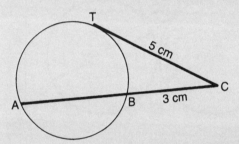

Fig. 31.38

8) In Fig. 31.39 find the length of the chord AB.

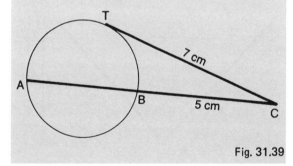

Fig. 31.39

SELF-TEST 31

In the following questions state the letter (or letters) corresponding to the correct answer (or answers).

1) In Fig. 31.40 the line AB is called a:

a secant   **b** chord

c diameter   **d** tangent

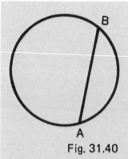

Fig. 31.40

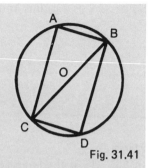

Fig. 31.41

2) In Fig. 31.41, O is the centre of the circle and AB = CD. It is necessarily true that:

a ABDC is a parallelogram

b ABDC is a rhombus

c ABDC is a rectangle

d ABDC is a square

3) In Fig. 31.42 it is true that:

a $\angle A = \angle D$ **b** $\angle A = \angle B$

c $\angle B = \angle D$ **d** $\angle D = \angle F$

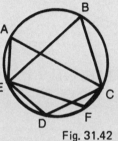

Fig. 31.42

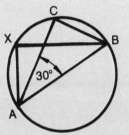

Fig. 31.43

4) A regular five-sided figure is inscribed in a circle. The angle subtended at the circumference by the figure is:

a 36°   **b** 54°   **c** 72°   **d** 108°

5) In Fig. 31.43, AB is a diameter of the circle and $\angle CBX = \angle ABX$. Hence $\angle CAX$ is equal to:

a 15°   **b** 30°   **c** 45°   **d** 60°

6) In Fig. 31.44, OB = OC. Hence it is necessarily true that:

a ABCD is a parallelogram   **c** ABCD is a trapezium

b ABCD is a rectangle   **d** ABCD is a rhombus

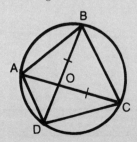

Fig. 31.44

7) In Fig. 31.45, AD and BD are tangents to the circle whose centre is O. If ∠ADB = 40° then ∠ACB is:

a 140°   **b** 70°   **c** 55°   **d** 35°

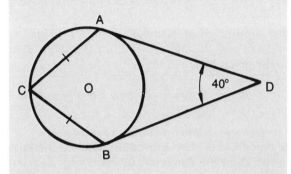

Fig. 31.45

8) In Fig. 31.46, the length of BC is:

a $4\frac{1}{2}$ cm   **b** $5\frac{1}{3}$ cm   **c** 14 cm   **d** 18 cm

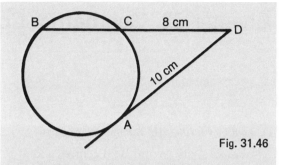

Fig. 31.46

9) In Fig. 31.47, AP is a tangent to the circle. ∠ADC is equal to:

a 70°   **b** 78°   **c** 102°   **d** 110°

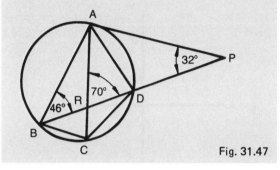

Fig. 31.47

CHAPTER 31 SUMMARY

Points to remember

(i)   A segment is a portion in the plane of a circle, bounded by a chord and an arc cut off by that chord.

(ii) A sector is the portion in the plane of a circle bounded by an arc and the radii joining the end points of that arc to the centre of the circle.

(iii) The perpendicular bisector of a chord of a circle passes through the centre.

(iv) The line joining the centre of a circle to the midpoint of a chord is perpendicular to the chord.

(v)   The angle at the centre of a circle is twice the angle on the circle subtended by the same arc.

(vi) Angles on the circle and standing on the same arc are equal.

(vii) The angle inscribed in a semicircle is a right angle.

(viii) A tangent to a circle meets a radius drawn to the point of contact of the tangent at right angles.

(ix) Tangents to a circle from a point outside the circle are equal.

Chapter 32 **Geometric Constructions**

(1) *To divide a line AB into two equal parts.*

Construction: With A and B as centres and a radius greater than $\frac{1}{2}$AB, draw circular arcs which intersect at X and Y (Fig. 32.1). Join XY. The line XY divides AB into two equal parts and it is also perpendicular to AB.

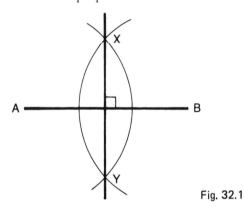

Fig. 32.1

(2) *To draw a perpendicular from a given point A on a straight line.*

Construction: With centre A and any radius draw a circle to cut the straight line at points P and Q (Fig. 32.2). With centres P and Q and a radius greater than AP (or AQ) draw circular

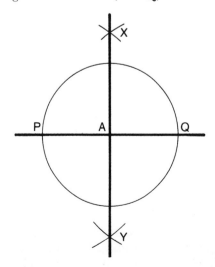

Fig. 32.2

arcs to intersect at X and Y. Join XY. This line will pass through A and it is perpendicular to the given line.

(3) *To draw a perpendicular from a point A at the end of a line* (Fig. 32.3).

Construction: From any point O outside the line and radius OA draw a circle to cut the line at B. Draw the diameter BC and join AC. AC is perpendicular to the straight line (because the angle in a semi-circle is 90°).

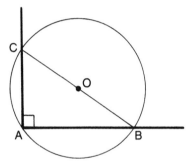

Fig. 32.3

(4) *To draw the perpendicular to a line AB from a given point P which is not on the line.*

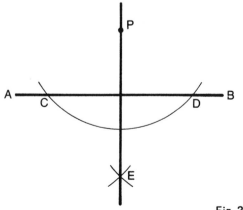

Fig. 32.4

Construction: With P as centre draw a circular arc to cut AB at points C and D. With C and D as centres and a radius greater than $\frac{1}{2}$CD, draw circular arcs to intersect at E. Join PE. The line PE is the required perpendicular (Fig. 32.4).

(5) *To construct an angle of 60°.*

Construction: Draw a line AB. With A as centre and any radius draw a circular arc to cut AB at D. With D as centre and the *same* radius draw a second arc to cut the first arc at C. Join AC. The angle CAD is then 60° (Fig. 32.5).

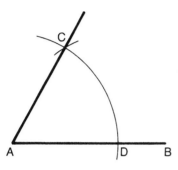

Fig. 32.5

(6) *To bisect a given angle ∠BAC.*

Construction: With centre A and any radius draw an arc to cut AB at D and AC at E. With centres D and E and a radius greater than $\frac{1}{2}$DE draw arcs to intersect at F. Join AF, then AF bisects ∠BAC (Fig. 32.6). Note that by bisecting an angle of 60°, an angle of 30° is obtained. An angle of 45° is obtained by bisecting a right angle.

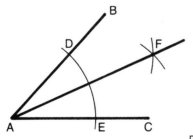

Fig. 32.6

(7) *To construct an angle equal to a given angle BAC.*

Construction: With centre A and any radius draw an arc to cut AB at D and AC at E. Draw the line XY. With centre X and the same radius draw an arc to cut XY at W. With centre W and radius equal to DE draw an arc to cut the first arc at V. Join VX, then ∠VXW = ∠BAC (Fig. 32.7).

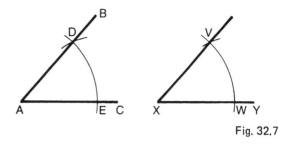

Fig. 32.7

(8) *Through a point P to draw a line parallel to a given line AB.*

Construction: Mark off any two points X and Y on AB. With centre P and radius XY draw an arc. With centre Y and radius XP draw a second arc to cut the first arc at Q. Join PQ, then PQ is parallel to AB (Fig. 32.8).

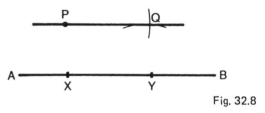

Fig. 32.8

(9) *To divide a straight line AB into a number of equal parts.*

Construction: Suppose that AB has to be divided into four equal parts. Draw AC at any angle to AB. Set off on AC, four equal parts AP, PQ, QR, RS of any convenient length. Join SB. Draw RV, QW and PX each parallel to SB. Then AX = XW = WV = VB (Fig. 32.9).

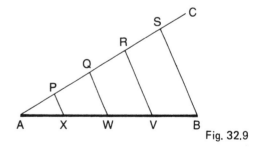

Fig. 32.9

(10) *To draw the circumscribed circle of a given triangle ABC.*

Construction: Construct the perpendicular bisectors of the sides AB and AC (using construction 1) so that they intersect at O. With centre O and radius AO draw a circle which is the required circumscribed circle (Fig. 32.10).

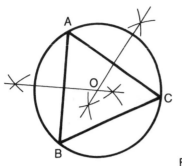

Fig. 32.10

(11) *To draw the inscribed circle of a given triangle ABC.*

Construction: Construct the internal bisectors of ∠B and ∠C (using construction 6) to intersect at O. Construct a perpendicular from O to one of the sides. This is the radius. With centre O draw the inscribed circle of the triangle ABC (Fig. 32.11).

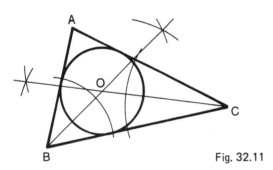

Fig. 32.11

(12) *To draw a triangle whose area is equal to that of a given quadrilateral ABCD.*

Construction: Join BD and draw CE parallel to BD to meet AB produced at E. Then ADE is a triangle whose area is equal to that of the quadrilateral ABCD (Fig. 32.12).

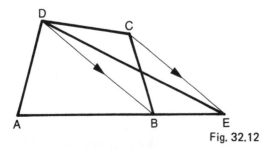

Fig. 32.12

Proof: As DBE and CDB are equal in area. Add to each of these triangles the area ADB.

(13) *To draw a square whose area is equal to that of a given rectangle ABCD.*

Construction: Produce AB to E so that BC is equal to BE. Draw a circle with AE as diameter to meet BC (or BC produced) at F. Then BF is a side of the required square (Fig. 32.13).

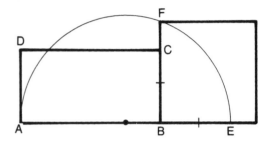

Fig. 32.13

(14) *To draw a tangent to a circle at a given point P on the circumference of the circle.*

Construction: O is the centre of the given circle. Join OP. Using construction 3 draw the line PT which is perpendicular to OP. PT is the required tangent, since at the point of tangency, a tangent is perpendicular to a radius (Fig. 32.14).

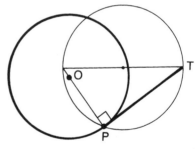

Fig. 32.14

(15) *To draw the segment of a circle so that it contains a given angle θ.*

Construction: Draw the lines AB and AX so that ∠BAX = θ. From A draw AM perpendicular to AX. Draw the perpendicular bisector of AB to meet AM at O. With centre O and radius OA draw the circular arc which terminates at A and B. This is the required segment (Fig. 32.15).

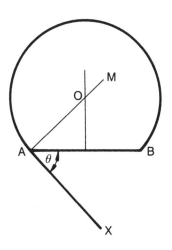

Fig. 32.15

(16) *To construct a triangle given the lengths of each of the three sides.*

Construction: Suppose $a = 6$ cm, $b = 3$ cm and $c = 4$ cm. Draw   BC $= 6$ cm. With centre B and radius 4 cm draw a circular arc. With centre C and radius 3 cm draw a circular arc to cut the first arc at A. Join AB and AC. Then ABC is the required triangle (Fig. 32.16).

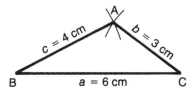

Fig. 32.16

(17) *To construct a triangle given two sides and the included angle between the two sides.*

Construction: Suppose $b = 5$ cm   and $c = 6$ cm   and $\angle A = 60°$. Draw AB $= 6$ cm   and draw AX such that $\angle$ BAX $= 60°$. Along AX mark off AC $= 5$ cm. Then ABC is the required triangle (Fig. 32.17).

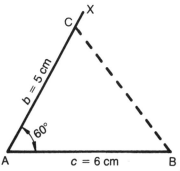

Fig. 32.17

(18) *To construct a triangle (or triangles) given the lengths of two of the sides and an angle which is not the included angle between the two given sides.*

(a) *Construction:* Suppose $a = 5$ cm, $b = 6$ cm   and $\angle B = 60°$. Draw BC $= 5$ cm   and draw BX such that $\angle$ CBX $= 60°$. With centre C and radius of 6 cm describe a circular arc to cut BX at A. Join CA then ABC is the required triangle ABC (Fig. 32.18).

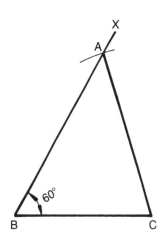

Fig. 32.18

(b) Suppose that $a = 5$ cm, $b = 4.5$ cm and $\angle B = 60°$. The construction is the same as before but the circular arc drawn with C as centre now cuts BX at two points A and A_1. This means that there are two triangles which meet the given conditions, i.e. $\triangle$s ABC and A_1BC (Fig. 32.19). For this reason this case is often called the *ambiguous case*.

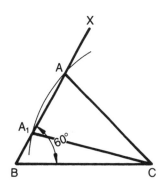

Fig. 32.19

(19) *To construct a common tangent to two given circles.*

Construction: The two given circles have centres X and Y and radii *x* and *y* respectively (Fig. 32.20). With centre X draw a circle whose radius is (*x* − *y*). With diameter XY draw an arc to cut the previously drawn circle at M. Join XM and produce to P at the circumference of the circle. Draw YQ parallel to XP, Q being at the circumference of the circle. Join PQ which is the required tangent.

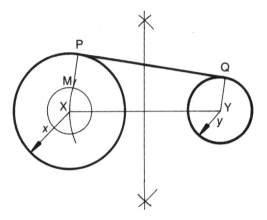

Fig. 32.20

(20) *To construct a pair of tangents from an external point to a given circle* (Fig. 32.21).

Construction: It is required to draw a pair of tangents from the point P to the circle centre O. Join OP. With OP as diameter draw a circle to cut the given circle at points A and B. Join PA and PB which are the required pair of tangents.

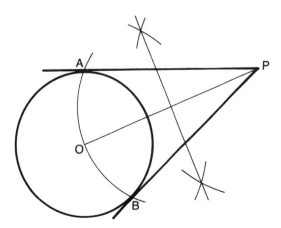

Fig. 32.21

Exercise 152 – *All type B*

1) Construct a triangle ABC with AB = 5 cm, AC = 4 cm and ∠CAB = 45°.

2) Construct the point P inside the triangle ABC in Question 1, so that it is equi-distant from the three sides of the triangle.

3) Draw the line AB 4.6 cm long and construct the isosceles triangle ABC with AC = 7.2 cm. Hence construct the rhombus ABCD.

4) Draw the line AB = 8 cm. At A construct an angle of 60° and at B an angle of 45°. Hence complete the triangle ABC.

5) Construct an angle of 60°. Bisect this angle and so obtain an angle of 30°.

6) Draw a line AB = 8 cm. Construct the perpendicular bisector of AB to cut AB at E. Mark off EC = 3 cm and ED = 3 cm. Join A and C, C and B, B and D and D and A to form the quadrilateral ABCD. Name the quadrilateral ABCD.

7) Construct an angle of 60° and hence construct a regular hexagon.

8) Draw a line AB = 10 cm. At A construct a right angle and hence construct a rectangle having dimensions 10 cm by 5 cm.

9) Draw WX = 5 cm. At W construct an angle of 60°. Along the inclined arm of this angle mark off WZ = 4 cm. Hence complete a drawing of the parallelogram WXYZ.

10) Construct a rectangle ABCD in which AB = 5.8 cm and the diagonal AC = 7.4 cm.

11) Construct a trapezium AXBC in which BX is parallel to AC and ∠CAX = 60°. Measure the distance AX.

12) Construct an equilateral triangle having sides 5 cm long.

13) Construct △ABC with AB = 8 cm, BC = 6 cm and AC = 11.2 cm.

14) Construct the inscribed circle of △ABC (question 13).

15) Construct △ABC in which AB = 8 cm, AC = 7 cm and ∠CAB = 45°. Construct the circumcircle of this triangle.

16) Draw a line AB = 9 cm and divide it into 7 equal parts.

17) Draw the line XY = 7 cm. Mark off PX = 3 cm. Erect a perpendicular through P. Mark off PZ = 5 cm, Z being above XY. Hence complete the triangle XYZ.

18) Draw the rectangle ABCD with AB = 6 cm and AD = 4 cm. Construct a square whose area is equal to that of the rectangle ABCD. Measure the side of your square.

19) Draw two circles whose centres are 8 cm apart and whose diameters are 6 cm and 8 cm. Draw the common tangent to these circles.

20) Draw a circle, centre O, whose radius is 4 cm. Mark off any point P so that OP = 8 cm. Construct a pair of tangents from P to the circle.

CHAPTER 32 SUMMARY

Points to remember

(i)   A unique triangle may be constructed given any one of the following combinations
   (a) Three sides.
   (b) Two sides and the angle between them.
   (c) Two sides and the angle opposite one of them if the given angle is opposite the longer of the two sides.
   (d) One side and two angles.

(ii) If three angles are given, only the shape is determined.

Chapter 33 Loci

A *locus* is a set of positions traced out by a point which moves according to some law. For instance the locus of a point which moves so that it is always 3 cm from a given fixed point is a circle whose radius is 3 cm. It often helps if we mark off a few points according to the given law. By doing this we may gain some idea of what the locus will be. Sometimes three or four points will be sufficient but sometimes ten or more points may be required before the locus can be recognised.

EXAMPLE 1

Given a straight line AB of length 6 cm, find the locus of a point P so that ∠APB is always a right angle.

By drawing a number of points $P_1, P_2, \ldots$, etc. so that ∠AP_1B, ∠AP_2B ... etc. (Fig. 33.1) are all right angles it appears that the locus is a circle with AB as a diameter. We now try to prove that this is so.

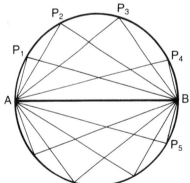

Fig. 33.1

Since the angle in a semi-circle is a right angle, all angles subtended by the diameter AB at the circumference of the circle will be right angles. Hence the locus of P is a circle with AB as diameter.

Exercise 153 – *All type B*

1) Find the locus of a point P which is always 5 cm from a fixed straight line of infinite length.

2) Find the locus of a point P which moves so that it is always 3 cm from a given straight line AB which is 8 cm long.

3) XYZ is a triangle whose base XY is fixed. If XY = 5 cm and the area of △XYZ = 10 cm² find the locus of Z.

4) Given a square of 10 cm side, find all the points which are 8 cm from two of the vertices. How many points are there?

5) Find all the points which are 5 cm from each of two intersecting straight lines inclined at an angle of 45°. How many points are there?

STANDARD LOCI

The following standard loci should be remembered.

(1) The locus of a point equi-distant from two given points A and B is the perpendicular bisector of AB (Fig. 33.2).

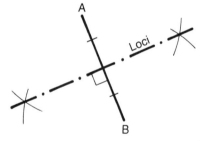

Fig. 33.2

(2) The locus of a point equi-distant from the arms of an angle is the bisector of the angle (Fig. 33.3).

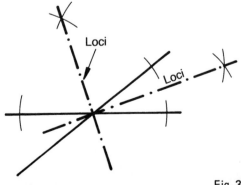

Fig. 33.3

INTERSECTING LOCI

Frequently two pieces of information are given about the position of a point. Each piece of information should then be dealt with separately, since any attempt to comply with the two conditions at the same time will lead to a trial and error method which is not acceptable. Each piece of information will partially locate the point and the intersection of the two loci will determine the required position of the point.

EXAMPLE 2

A point P lies 3 cm from a given straight line and it is also equi-distant from two fixed points not on the line and not perpendicular to it. Find the two possible positions of P.

Condition 1. The point P lies 3 cm from the given straight line (AB in Fig. 33.4). To meet this condition draw two straight lines X_1Y_1 and X_2Y_2 parallel to AB and on either side of it.

Condition 2. P is equi-distant from the two fixed points (R and S in Fig. 33.4). To meet this condition we draw the perpendicular bisector of RS (since △ RSP must be isosceles).

The intersections of the two loci give the required position of the point P. These are the points P_1 and P_2 in Fig. 33.4.

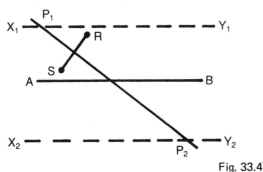

Fig. 33.4

Exercise 154

1) Find the locus of the centre P of a circle of constant radius 3 cm which passes through a fixed point A.

2) Find the locus of the centre, Q, of a circle of constant radius 2 cm which touches externally a fixed circle, centre B and radius 4 cm.

3) Find the locus of the centre of a variable circle which passes through two fixed points A and B.

4) AB is a fixed line of length 8 cm and P is a variable point. The distance of P from the middle point of AB is 5 cm and the distance of P from AB is 4 cm. Construct a point P so that both of these conditions are satisfied. State the number of possible positions of P.

5) X is a point inside a circle, centre C, and Q is the mid-point of a chord which passes through X. Determine the locus of Q as the chord varies. If CX is 5 cm and the radius of the circle is 8 cm construct the locus of Q accurately and hence construct a chord which passes through X and has its mid-point 3 cm from C.

6) XY is a fixed line of given length. State the locus of a point P which moves so that the size of ∠XPY is constant and sketch the locus.

7) AB is a fixed line of 4 cm and R is a point such that the area of △ ABR is 5 cm². S is the mid-point of AR. State the locus of R and the locus of S.

8) T is a fixed point outside a fixed circle whose centre is O. A variable line through T meets the circle at X and Y. Show that the locus of the mid-point of XY is an arc of the circle on OT as diameter.

9) Chords of a circle, centre C, are drawn through a fixed point A within the circle. Show that the mid-points of all these chords lie on a circle and state the position of the centre of the circle.

10) Draw a circle centre O and radius 4 cm. Construct the locus of the mid-points of all chords of this circle which are 6.5 cm long.

CHAPTER 33 SUMMARY

Points to remember

(i)   The locus is the path of a set of points obeying some law.

e.g. The locus of points in a plane the same distance from a fixed point is a circle.

How to Answer Examination Questions 4

1) (a) In Fig. E4.1, ABC is an equilateral triangle and AE, EC and CD are equal in length. Angle ACE = 50° and BCD is a straight line. Find the size of the angle AED.

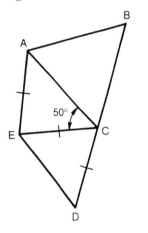

Fig. E4.1

(b) In Fig. E4.2, O is the centre of the circle and PQT is a straight line. Calculate the size of the angle marked y.

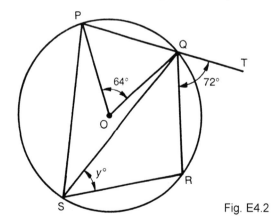

Fig. E4.2

(a) Since ACE is an isosceles triangle,

$$\angle AEC = 180° - 2 \times 50° = 80°$$

Since ABC is an equilateral triangle,

$$\angle BCA = 60°$$

$$\angle ECD = 180° - 50° - 60° = 70°$$

Since CED is an isosceles triangle,

$$\angle CED = \tfrac{1}{2}(180° - 70°) = 55°$$

$$\angle AED = \angle AEC + \angle CED = 80° + 55°$$

$$= 135°$$

(b) Since the angle at the centre is twice the angle at the circumference,

$$\angle PSQ = \tfrac{1}{2}\angle POQ = \tfrac{1}{2} \times 64° = 32°$$

Since PQRS is a cyclic quadrilateral,

$$\angle PSR = \angle TQR = 72°$$

$$y = \angle PSR - \angle PSQ = 72° - 32°$$

$$= 40°$$

2) (a) Chords AB and CD of a circle intersect inside the circle at point X. Given that AX = 4 cm, XB = 8 cm and CX = 5 cm, calculate the length of CD.

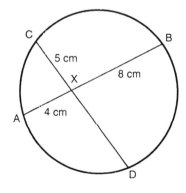

Fig. E4.3

(b) In Fig. E4.4, ABC is a triangle right-angled at A and AD is perpendicular to BC. AB is 6 cm and AC is 8 cm. Determine:
(i) The area of the triangle ABC.
(ii) The length of BC.
(iii) The length of AD.
(iv) The length of BD.

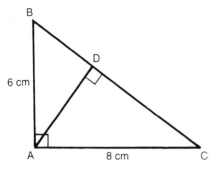

Fig. E4.4

(a) Referring to Fig. E4.3,

$$AX \times XB = CX \times XD$$

$$4 \times 8 = 5 \times XD$$

$$XD = \frac{32}{5} = 6.4\,\text{cm}$$

$$CD = CX + XD = 5 + 6.4$$

$$= 11.4\,\text{cm}$$

(b) (i) Area of $\triangle ABC = \frac{1}{2} \times 6 \times 8 = 24\,\text{cm}^2$

(ii) By Pythagoras' Theorem,

$$BC^2 = AB^2 + AC^2$$

$$= 6^2 + 8^2 = 36 + 64 = 100$$

$$BC = \sqrt{100} = 10\,\text{cm}$$

Alternatively,

Since the given sides are 2×3 and 2×4, the hypotenuse is $2 \times 5 = 10\,\text{cm}$, because a right-angled triangle may have sides of 3, 4 and 5 units.

(iii) Area of $\triangle ABC = \frac{1}{2} \times BC \times AD$

$$= \frac{1}{2} \times 10 \times AD$$

$$= 5AD$$

$$\therefore \quad 5AD = 24$$

$$AD = 4.8\,\text{cm}$$

(iv) In $\triangle ABD$, by Pythagoras' Theorem,

$$BD^2 = AB^2 - AD^2$$

$$= 6^2 - 4.8^2$$

$$= 12.96$$

$$BD = \sqrt{12.96} = 3.6\,\text{cm}$$

3) (a) In Fig. E4.5, ABCD is a rhombus whose diagonals intersect at O. If $x = 29°$, find y.

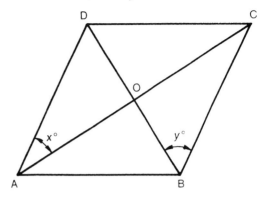

Fig. E4.5

(b) In Fig. E4.6, $\angle DBC = \angle BAD$ and ADC is a straight line.
(i) State which two triangles are similar.
(ii) If $AB = 7\,\text{cm}$, $BC = 6\,\text{cm}$ and $DC = 4\,\text{cm}$, calculate the lengths of BD and AC.

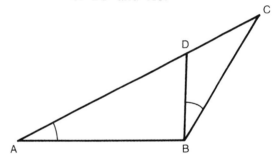

Fig. E4.6

(a) In a rhombus the diagonals intersect at right angles and hence $\angle COB = 90°$.

Also $\angle OCB = x° = 29°$.

Therefore in $\triangle COB$,

$$y + 90° + 29° = 180°$$

$$y = 61°$$

(b) (i) In triangles ABC and BDC,

$$\angle DBC = \angle BAD = a \quad \text{(given)}$$

$$\angle ACB \text{ is common} = b$$

$$\angle ABD = \angle BDC = 180° - (a + b)$$

$$= c$$

Therefore, triangles ABC and BDC are equi-angular and hence similar.

(ii) $\dfrac{BD}{AB} = \dfrac{CD}{BC}$

$$BD = \dfrac{CD \times AB}{BC} = \dfrac{4 \times 7}{6} = 4\tfrac{2}{3}\ cm$$

$$\dfrac{AC}{BC} = \dfrac{AB}{BD}$$

$$AC = \dfrac{BC \times AB}{BD} = \dfrac{6 \times 7}{4.67} = 9\ cm$$

4) (a) In Fig. E4.7, BD is the diameter of the circle and AEF is a straight line which is parallel to BD. Given that angles BAC and CAE are $45°$ and $65°$ respectively,
(i)   Find the size of angle BDC.
(ii) Prove that BC = CD.
(iii) Find the size of angle DEF.

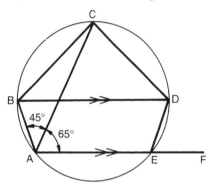

Fig. E4.7

(b) Calculate the number of sides of a regular polygon in which the exterior angle is one-third of the interior angle.

(a) (i)   The angles BAC and BDC are subtended by the chord BC and hence these two angles are equal. Hence,

$$\angle BDC = 45°$$

(ii) Since BD is a diameter, $\angle BCD$ is the angle in a semi-circle.

Hence, $\angle BCD = 90°$

In triangle BCD,

$$\angle CBD = 180° - 90° - 45°$$

$$= 45°$$

$\angle BDC$ is also $45°$ so triangle BCD is isosceles.

Hence,   BC = CD.

(iii) In the cyclic quadrilateral ABDE, since the lines BD and AE are parallel,

$$\angle ABD = 180° - (45° + 65°) = 70°$$

$$\angle DEF = \angle ABD = 70°$$

(b) Let number of sides be n, then,

$$\text{Size of exterior angle} = \dfrac{360}{n}$$

$$\text{Size of interior angle} = 180 - \dfrac{360}{n}$$

Hence,

$$\dfrac{360}{n} = \dfrac{1}{3}\left(180 - \dfrac{360}{n}\right)$$

$$\dfrac{360}{n} = 60 - \dfrac{120}{n}$$

$$360 = 60n - 120$$

$$60n = 480$$

$$n = 8$$

5) (a) In Fig. E4.8, find the size of the angles x, y and z.

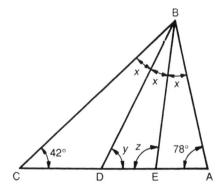

Fig. E4.8

(b) In Fig. E4.9, DE is parallel to BC.
(i) Find the length of BC.
(ii) If the area of the triangle ADE is $8\ cm^2$, determine the area of the quadrilateral BDEC.

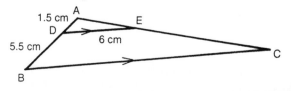

Fig. E4.9

(a) $\angle ABC = 180° - (42° + 78°) = 60°$

$x = \frac{1}{3} \times 60° = 20°$

$y = 42° + 20° = 62°$

$z = 180° - (62° + 20°) = 98°$

(b) (i) Since triangles ADE and ABC are similar,

$$\frac{BC}{DE} = \frac{AB}{AD}$$

$$BC = \frac{DE \times AB}{AD} = \frac{6 \times 7}{1.5} = 28\,cm$$

(ii)

$$\frac{\text{Area of } \triangle ABC}{\text{Area of } \triangle ADE} = \frac{28^2}{6^2}$$

$$\text{Area of } \triangle ABC = \frac{28^2 \times 8}{6^2} = 174.2\,cm^2$$

$$\text{Area of BDEC} = 174.2 - 8 = 166.2\,cm^2$$

EXAMINATION TYPE QUESTIONS 4

This exercise is divided into two sections A and B. The questions in Section A are intended to be done very quickly, but those in Section B should take about 20 minutes each to complete. All the questions are of the type found in CXC examination papers.

Section A

1) (a) The diagram (Fig. E4.10) shows two sides of a quadrilateral ABCD which is symmetrical about the point O. Complete the quadrilateral.

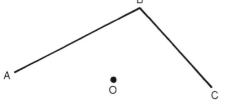

Fig. E4.10

(b) In the triangle PQR (Fig. E4.11), the lengths of PQ and QR are 20 cm and 21 cm respectively and the angle Q is a right angle. Calculate:
(i) The area of the triangle.
(ii) The length of PR.

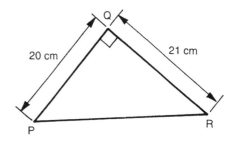

Fig. E4.11

2) (a) ABCDEF is a regular six-sided figure and ABXY is a square in the same plane. Calculate the size of the obtuse angle CXY (Fig. E4.12).

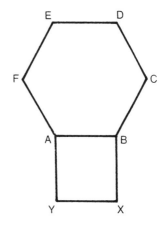

Fig. E4.12

(b) Calculate the size of each interior angle of a regular fifteen-sided polygon.
(c) The diagram (Fig. E4.13) shows a regular pentagon. Sketch the diagram and show, by using dotted lines, all the lines of symmetry.

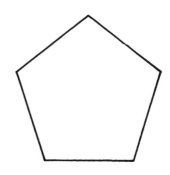

Fig. E4.13

3) (a) In Fig. E4.14, O is the centre of the circle. Find x.

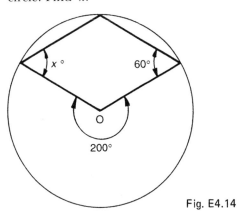

Fig. E4.14

(b) The angles of a triangle are in the ratio $2:3:4$. Calculate the sizes of the three angles.

(c) Copy Fig. E4.15 and draw all the lines of symmetry.

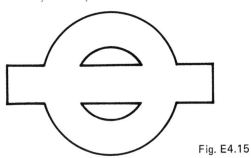

Fig. E4.15

4) (a) The straight lines AB, CD and EF are parallel (Fig. E4.16). Given that angle $EKG = 47°$ and that the straight line LHG is at right angles to GK, calculate the size of the angle marked x in the diagram.

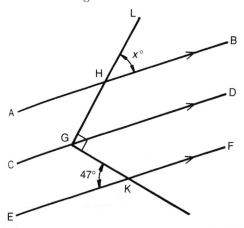

Fig. E4.16

(b) In Fig. E4.17, calculate:
(i) The value of x.
(ii) The size of the angle BDC.

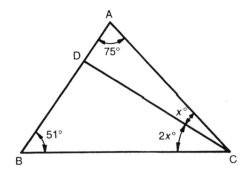

Fig. E4.17

5) (a) Draw a triangle ABC with $AB = 12.0\,cm$, $BC = 11.5\,cm$ and $\angle B = 45°$. Without using a protractor, construct a circle of radius $4\,cm$ which just touches AB and AC.

(b) In Fig. E4.18, PT is a tangent at T to the circle. $AB = AT$ and $\angle BTP = 34°$. Calculate the size of $\angle ABT$.

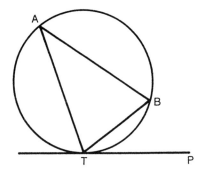

Fig. E4.18

Section B

6) (a) Fig. E4.19 shows a circle, centre C, drawn through the vertices B and D of the rhombus ABCD. The side AD is produced to meet the circle again at E and the lines EB and CD intersect at H. If the angle $DAB = x°$, calculate, in terms of x, the sizes of the angles BCD, CDE, BED and DHB.

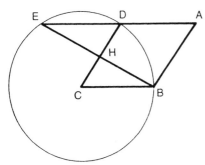

Fig. E4.19

(b) Use rule and compasses only:
  (i) To construct a rectangle XYZW in which XW = 6 cm and the diagonal YW = 13 cm.
  (ii) To find the length of the side of the square which has an area equal to that of the rectangle XYZW. Measure and state this length.

(b) Given that AD = 15 cm, DE = 25 cm and the bisector of the angle EDC meets EC at Y, calculate:
  (i) The ratio of the areas of the triangles CHB and DHE.
  (ii) The ratio of the areas of the triangles ADB and EDB.

7) (a) In a circle two chords AXB and CXD meet at a point X. Given that AX = 5 cm, CX = 9 cm, AC = 7 cm and BX = 7.2 cm, calculate:
  (i) The length of DX.
  (ii) The ratio of the area of the triangle AXC to the area of the triangle BXD.

8) In a triangle ABC, the side AB = 21 cm. Points D and E are taken on AB and AC respectively such that AD = 7 cm, AE = 6 cm, DE = 8 cm and DE is parallel to BC. Calculate:
(a) The length of BC.
(b) The ratio of the area of the triangle AED to the area of the trapezium BDEC.

A point P is taken on AE such that DP bisects the angle ADE and DP produced meets the line through A, parallel to BC, at Q. Calculate:
(c) The length of EP.
(d) The length of AQ.
(e) The ratio of the area of triangle DPE to the area of the triangle PAD.

Chapter 34 **Trigonometry**

THE NOTATION FOR A RIGHT-ANGLED TRIANGLE

The sides of a right-angled triangle are given special names. In Fig. 34.1 the side AB lies opposite the right angle and it is called the *hypotenuse*. The side BC lies opposite to the angle A and it is called the side opposite to A. The side AC is called the side adjacent to A.

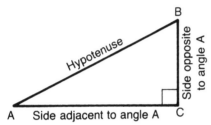

Fig. 34.1

When we consider the angle B (Fig. 34.2) the side AB is still the hypotenuse but AC is now the side opposite to B and BC is the side adjacent to B.

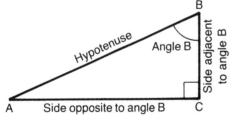

Fig. 34.2

THE TRIGONOMETRICAL RATIOS

Consider any angle θ which is bounded by the lines OA and OB as shown in Fig. 34.3. Take any point P on the boundary line OB. From P draw line PM perpendicular to OA to meet it at the point M. Then,

the ratio $\dfrac{\text{MP}}{\text{OP}}$ is called the sine of $\angle$AOB

the ratio $\dfrac{\text{OM}}{\text{OP}}$ is called the cosine of $\angle$AOB and

the ratio $\dfrac{\text{MP}}{\text{OM}}$ is called the tangent of $\angle$AOB

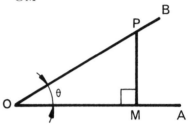

Fig. 34.3

THE SINE OF AN ANGLE

The abbreviation 'sin' is usually used for sine. In any right-angled triangle (Fig. 34.4),

$$\text{the sine of an angle} = \frac{\text{side opposite the angle}}{\text{hypotenuse}}$$

$$\sin A = \frac{BC}{AC}$$

$$\sin C = \frac{AB}{AC}$$

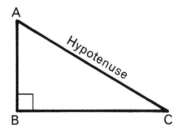

Fig. 34.4

EXAMPLE 1

Find by drawing a suitable triangle the value of sin 30°.

Draw the lines AX and AY which intersect at A so that the angle $\angle$YAX $= 30°$ as shown in Fig. 34.5. Along AY measure off AC equal to 1 unit (say 10 cm) and from C draw CB perpendicular to AX. Measure CB which will be found to be 0.5 units (5 cm in this case).

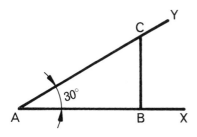

Fig. **34.5**

READING THE TABLE OF SINES OF ANGLES

(1) *To find* sin 12°. The sine of an angle with an exact number of degrees is shown in the column headed 0. Thus sin 12° = 0.208.

(2) *To find* sin 12.6°. The value will be found under the column headed .6. Thus sin 12.6° = 0.218.

Therefore $\sin 30° = \dfrac{5}{10} = 0.5$

Although it is possible to find the sines of angles by drawing this is inconvenient and not very accurate. Tables of sines have been calculated which allow us to find the sine of any angle. Part of this table is reproduced below.

DECIMALS OF A DEGREE

The trigonometrical tables used have been worked in degrees and decimals of a degree, e.g. 31.6° and 48.9°.

To convert an angle given in degrees and minutes we simply divide the minutes by 60, since 60 minutes = 1 degree.

Thus $38°36' = 38\dfrac{36}{60}° = 38.6°$

$32°54' = 32\dfrac{54}{60}° = 32.9°$

EXAMPLE 2
(1) Find the length of AB in Fig. 34.6.

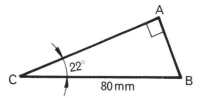

Fig. **34.6**

AB is the side opposite ∠ACB. BC is the hypotenuse since it is opposite the right angle.

Therefore

$$\frac{AB}{BC} = \sin 22°$$

$$AB = BC \times \sin 22° = 80 \times 0.375$$

$$= 30.0\,\text{mm}$$

NATURAL SINES

Degrees	.0	.1	.2	.3	.4	.5	.6	.7	.8	.9
0	0.000	002	003	005	007	009	010	012	014	016
1	.017	019	021	023	024	026	028	030	031	033
2	.035	037	038	040	042	044	045	047	049	051
3	.052	054	056	058	059	061	063	065	066	068
4	.070	071	073	075	077	078	080	082	084	085
5	0.087	089	091	092	094	096	098	099	101	103
6	.105	106	108	110	111	113	115	117	118	120
7	.122	124	125	127	129	131	132	134	136	137
8	.139	141	143	144	146	148	150	151	153	155
9	.156	158	160	162	163	165	167	168	170	172
10	0.174	175	177	179	181	182	184	186	187	189
11	.191	193	194	196	198	199	201	203	204	206
12	.208	210	211	213	215	216	218	220	222	223
13	.225	227	228	230	232	233	235	237	239	240
14	.242	244	245	247	249	250	252	254	255	257
15	0.259	261	262	264	266	267	269	271	272	274
16	.276	277	279	281	282	284	286	287	289	291
17	.292	294	296	297	299	301	302	304	306	307
18	.309	311	312	314	316	317	319	321	322	324
19	.326	327	329	331	332	334	335	337	339	340

(2) Find the length of AB in Fig. 34.7.

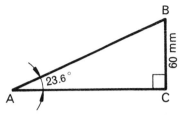

Fig. 34.7

BC is the side opposite to ∠BAC and AB is the hypotenuse.

Therefore

$$\frac{BC}{AB} = \sin 23.6°$$

$$AB = \frac{BC}{\sin 23.6°} = \frac{60}{0.400}$$

$$= 150 \text{ mm}$$

(3) Find the angles CAB and ABC in △ABC which is shown in Fig. 34.8.

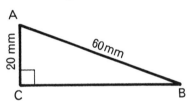

Fig. 34.8

$$\sin B = \frac{AC}{AB} = \frac{20}{60} = 0.333$$

From the sine tables

$$∠B = 19.5°$$

$$∠A = 90° - 19.5° = 70.5°$$

Exercise 155 – *All type A*

1) Find, by drawing, the sines of the following angles:
(a) 30°   (b) 45°   (c) 68°

2) Find, by drawing, the angles whose sines are:
(a) $\frac{1}{3}$ (b) $\frac{3}{4}$ (c) 0.72

3) Use the tables to write down the values of:
(a) sin 12°   (b) sin 18.2°
(c) sin 74.7°   (d) sin 7.4°
(e) sin 87.6°   (f) sin 0.2°

4) Use the tables to write down the angles whose sines are:
(a) 0.156   (b) 0.913   (c) 0.988
(d) 0.080   (e) 0.981   (f) 0.740
(g) 0.051   (h) 0.271

5) Find the lengths of the sides marked x in Fig. 34.9, the triangles being right angled.

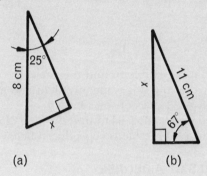

(a)   (b)

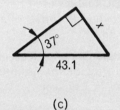

(c)

Fig. 34.9

6) Find the angles marked θ in Fig. 34.10, the triangles being right angled.

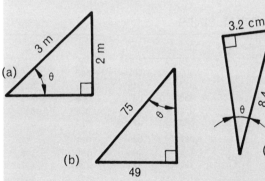

(a)

(b)

(c)

Fig. 34.10

7) In △ABC, ∠C = 90°, ∠B = 23.3° and AC = 11.2 cm. Find AB.

8) In △ABC, ∠B = 90°, ∠A = 67.5° and AC = 0.86 m. Find BC.

9) An equilateral triangle has an altitude of 18.7 cm. Find the length of the equal sides.

10) Find the altitude of an isosceles triangle whose vertex angle is 38° and whose equal sides are 7.9 m long.

11) The equal sides of an isosceles triangle are each 27 cm long and the altitude is 19 cm. Find the angles of the triangle.

THE COSINE OF AN ANGLE

In any right-angled triangle (Fig. 34.11):

the cosine of an angle

$$= \frac{\text{side adjacent to the angle}}{\text{hypotenuse}}$$

$$\cos A = \frac{AB}{AC}$$

$$\cos C = \frac{BC}{AC}$$

The abbreviation 'cos' is usually used for cosine.

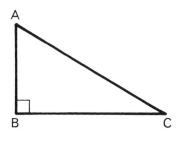

Fig. 34.11

The cosine of an angle may be found by drawing, the construction being similar to that used for the sine of an angle. However, tables of cosines are available and these are used in a similar way to the table of sines.

EXAMPLE 3

(1) Find the length of the side BC in Fig. 34.12.

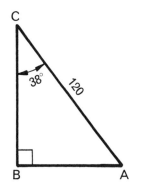

Fig. 34.12

BC is the side adjacent to ∠BCA and AC is the hypotenuse.

Therefore

$$\frac{BC}{AC} = \cos 38°$$

$$BC = AC \times \cos 38° = 120 \times 0.788$$

$$= 94.6 \, \text{mm}$$

(2) Find the length of the side AC in Fig. 34.13.

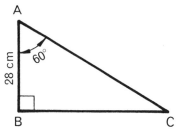

Fig. 34.13

AB is the side adjacent to ∠BAC and AC is the hypotenuse.

Therefore

$$\frac{AB}{AC} = \cos 60°$$

$$AC = \frac{AB}{\cos 60°} = \frac{28}{0.500} = 56 \, \text{cm}$$

(3) Find the angle θ shown in Fig. 34.14.

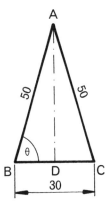

Fig. 34.14

Since △ABC is isosceles the perpendicular AD bisects the base BC and hence BD = 15 mm.

$$\cos \theta = \frac{BD}{AB} = \frac{15}{50} = 0.3$$

$$\theta = 72.5°$$

Exercise 156 – *All type A*

1) Use the tables to write down the values of:

(a) cos 15°   (b) cos 24.3°
(c) cos 78.4°   (d) cos 0.2°
(e) cos 73.3°   (f) cos 39.9°

2) Use the tables to write down the angles whose cosines are:

(a) 0.914   (b) 0.342   (c) 0.967
(d) 0.429   (e) 0.958   (f) 0.009
(g) 0.261   (h) 0.471

3) Find the lengths of the sides marked *x* in Fig. 34.15, the triangles being right-angled.

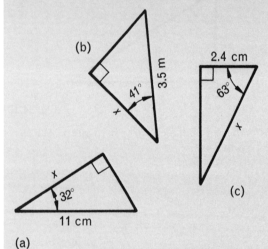

(a)

Fig. 34.15

4) Find the angles marked θ in Fig. 34.16, the triangles being right-angled.

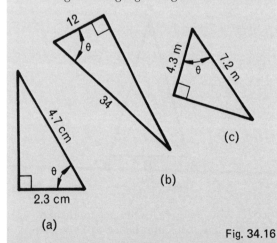

(a)

Fig. 34.16

5) An isosceles triangle has a base of 3.4 cm and the equal sides are each 4.2 cm long. Find the angles of the triangle and also its altitude.

6) In △ABC, ∠C = 90°, ∠B = 33.4° and BC = 2.4 cm. Find AB.

7) In △ABC, ∠B = 90°, ∠A = 62.8° and AC = 4.3 cm. Find AB.

8) In Fig. 34.17, calculate ∠BAC and the length BC.

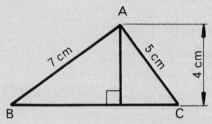

Fig. 34.17

9) In Fig. 34.18 calculate BD, AD, AC and BC.

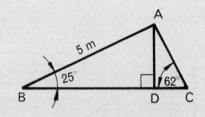

Fig. 34.18

THE TANGENT OF AN ANGLE

In any right-angled triangle (Fig. 34.19),

the tangent of an angle

$$= \frac{\text{side opposite to the angle}}{\text{side adjacent to the angle}}$$

$$\tan A = \frac{BC}{AB}$$

$$\tan C = \frac{AB}{BC}$$

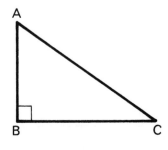

Fig. 34.19

The abbreviation 'tan' is usually used for tangent. From the table of tangents the tangents of angles from $0°$ to $90°$ can be read directly. For example:

$$\tan 37° = 0.754$$

and
$$\tan 62.5° = 1.921$$

EXAMPLE 4

(1) Find the length of the side AB in Fig. 34.20.

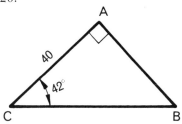

Fig. 34.20

AB is the side opposite $\angle C$ and AC is the side adjacent to $\angle C$. Hence

$$\frac{AB}{AC} = \tan \angle C$$

$$\frac{AB}{AC} = \tan 42°$$

$$AB = AC \times \tan 42° = 40 \times 0.900$$

$$= 36.0 \, mm$$

(2) Find the length of the side BC in Fig. 34.21.

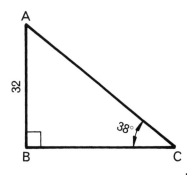

Fig. 34.21

There are two ways of solving this problem.

(a) $\dfrac{AB}{BC} = \tan 38°$ or $BC = \dfrac{AB}{\tan 38°}$

Therefore $BC = \dfrac{32}{0.781} = 41.0 \, mm$

(b) Since $\angle C = 38°$

$$\angle A = 90° - 38° = 52°$$

Now
$$\frac{BC}{AB} = \tan A \quad or \quad BC = AB \times \tan A$$

$$BC = 32 \times 1.280 = 41.0 \, mm$$

Both methods produce the same answer but method (b) is better because it is quicker and more convenient to multiply than divide. Whenever possible the ratio should be arranged so that the quantity to be found is the numerator of the ratio.

Exercise 157 – *All type A*

1) Use tables to write down the values of:
(a) $\tan 18°$ (b) $\tan 32.4°$
(c) $\tan 53.7°$ (d) $\tan 39.5°$
(e) $\tan 11.3°$ (f) $\tan 69.4°$

2) Use tables to write down the angles whose tangents are:
(a) 0.445   (b) 3.271   (c) 0.077
(d) 0.398   (e) 0.356   (f) 0.827
(g) 1.929   (h) 0.016

3) Find the lengths of the sides marked y in Fig. 34.22, the triangles being right-angled.

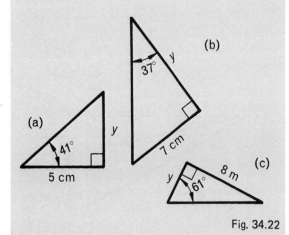

Fig. 34.22

4) Find the angles marked α in Fig. 34.23, the triangles being right-angled.

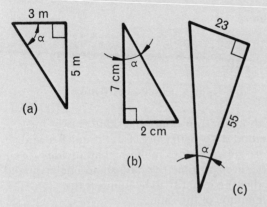

(a)

(b)

(c)

Fig. 34.23

5) An isosceles triangle has a base 10 cm long and the two equal angles are each 57°. Calculate the altitude of the triangle.

6) In $\triangle ABC$, $\angle B = 90°$, $\angle C = 49°$ and $AB = 3.2$ cm. Find BC.

7) In $\triangle ABC$, $\angle A = 12.4°$, $\angle B = 90°$ and $BC = 7.31$ cm. Find AB.

8) Calculate the distance x in Fig. 34.24.

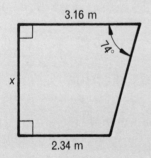

Fig. 34.24

9) Calculate the distance d in Fig. 34.25.

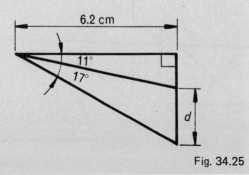

Fig. 34.25

LOGARITHMS OF THE TRIGONOMETRICAL RATIOS

Tables are used to find the log of a trig ratio in the same way as to find the ratio itself.

EXAMPLE 5

(1) Find the value of $28.3 \times \sin 39.3°$.

	number	log
	28.3	1.452
	sin 39.3°	$\bar{1}.802$
Answer =	17.9	1.254

(2) Find the angle A given that

$$\cos\angle A = \frac{20.2}{29.8}$$

	number	log
	20.2	1.305
	29.8	1.474
cos A		$\bar{1}.831$

The angle A is found directly from the log cos table:

$$\angle A = 47.4°$$

(3) If $b = \dfrac{c \sin \angle B}{\sin \angle C}$ find b when $c = 19.3$, $\angle B = 61°$ and $\angle C = 22.1°$.

	number	log
	19.3	1.286
	sin 61°	$\bar{1}.942$
		1.228
	sin 22.1°	$\bar{1}.575$
Answer =	45.0	1.653

Exercise 158 – *Questions 1 and 2 type A, remainder B*

1) From the tables find the following:

(a) log sin 28.6°   (b) log sin 74.4°

(c) log cos 8.1°   (d) log cos 24.3°

(e) log tan 44.5°   (f) log tan 7.1°

2) From the tables find the following:

(a) If log cos $\angle$A = $\bar{1}.735$ find $\angle$A.
(b) If log sin $\angle$A = $\bar{1}.581$ find $\angle$A.
(c) If log tan $\angle$B = 0.575 find $\angle$B.
(d) If log sin ϕ = $\bar{1}.307$ find ϕ.
(e) If log cos θ = $\bar{1}.235$ find θ.
(f) If log tan a = 1.554 find a.

3) By using logs find the following:

(a) If $\cos \angle A = \dfrac{19.3}{27.6}$ find $\angle$A.

(b) If $\sin \angle B = \dfrac{11.2}{35.4}$ find $\angle$B.

(c) If $\tan \angle \theta = \dfrac{28.1}{17.6}$ find θ.

4) If $a = \dfrac{b \sin \angle A}{\sin \angle B}$, find, by using logs, the

value of a when $b = 8.16$ cm,
$\angle$A = 43.5° and $\angle$B = 37.2°

5) If $\cos A = \dfrac{b^2 + c^2 - a^2}{2bc}$, find, by using

logs, the value of $\angle$A when $b = 11.2$ cm,
$c = 9.16$ cm and $a = 8.23$ cm.

6) If $\sin \angle C = \dfrac{c \sin \angle B}{b}$ find, by using logs,

the value of C when $c = 0.323$,
$\angle$B = 29.1° and $b = 0.517$.

7) If $b^2 = a^2 + c^2 - 2ac \cos \angle B$ find the
value of b when $a = 11.3$ cm, $c = 8.26$ cm
and B = 29.4°.

The values of trigonometrical ratios may also
be read directly from your calculator.

†TRIGONOMETRICAL RATIOS FOR 30°, 60° AND 45°

Ratios for 30° and 60°

Fig. 34.26 shows an equilateral triangle ABC
with each of the sides equal to 2 units. From
C draw the perpendicular CD which bisects
the base AB and also bisects $\angle$C.
In $\triangle$ACD,

$$CD^2 = AC^2 - AD^2 = 2^2 - 1^2 = 3$$

therefore

$$CD = \sqrt{3}$$

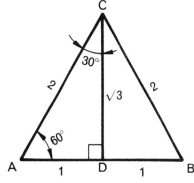

Fig. 34.26

Since all the angles of $\triangle$ABC are 60° and
$\angle$ACD = 30°,

$$\sin 60° = \frac{\sqrt{3}}{2}$$

$$\tan 60° = \frac{\sqrt{3}}{1} = \sqrt{3}$$

$$\cos 60° = \frac{1}{2}$$

$$\sin 30° = \frac{1}{2}$$

$$\tan 30° = \frac{1}{\sqrt{3}} = \frac{\sqrt{3}}{3}$$

$$\cos 30° = \frac{\sqrt{3}}{2}$$

Ratios for 45°

Fig. 34.27 shows a right-angled isosceles
triangle ABC with the equal sides each 1 unit
in length. The equal angles are each 45°. Now

$$AC^2 = AB^2 + BC^2 = 1^2 + 1^2 = 2$$

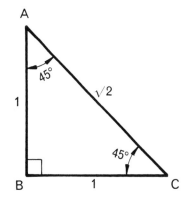

Fig. 34.27

therefore

$$AC = \sqrt{2}$$

$$\sin 45° = \frac{1}{\sqrt{2}} = \frac{\sqrt{2}}{2}$$

$$\cos 45° = \frac{1}{\sqrt{2}} = \frac{\sqrt{2}}{2}$$

$$\tan 45° = \frac{1}{1} = 1$$

†GIVEN ONE RATIO TO FIND THE OTHERS

The method is shown in the following example.

EXAMPLE 6

If $\cos \angle A = 0.7$, find, without using tables, the values of $\sin \angle A$ and $\tan \angle A$.

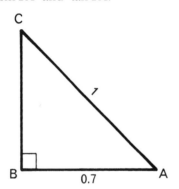

Fig. 34.28

In Fig. 34.28 if we make $AB = 0.7$ units and $AC = 1$ unit, then

$$\cos \angle A = \frac{0.7}{1} = 0.7$$

By Pythagoras' theorem,

$$BC^2 = AC^2 - AB^2 = 1^2 - 0.7^2 = 0.51$$

$$BC = \sqrt{0.51} = 0.7141$$

$$\sin \angle A = \frac{BC}{AC} = \frac{0.714}{1} = 0.714$$

$$\tan \angle A = \frac{BC}{AB} = \frac{0.714}{0.7} = 1.020$$

COMPLEMENTARY ANGLES

Complementary angles are angles whose sum is $90°$.

Consider the triangle ABC shown in Fig. 34.29.

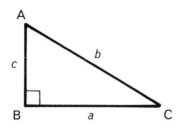

Fig. 34.29

$$\sin A = \frac{a}{b} \qquad \cos C = \frac{a}{b}$$

Hence,

$$\sin A = \cos C = \cos(90° - A)$$

Similarly,

$$\cos A = \sin(90° - A)$$

Therefore, *the sine of an angle is equal to the cosine of its complementary angle and vice versa.*

$$\sin 26° = \cos 64° = 0.438$$

$$\cos 70° = \sin 20° = 0.342$$

*THE SQUARES OF THE TRIGONOMETRICAL RATIOS

The square of $\sin A$ is usually written as $\sin^2 A$. Thus

$$\sin^2 A = (\sin A)^2$$

and similarly for the remaining trigonometrical ratios. That is,

$$\cos^2 A = (\cos A)^2$$

and

$$\tan^2 A = (\tan A)^2$$

EXAMPLE 7

(1) Find the value of $\cos^2 37°$.

$$\cos 37° = 0.799$$

$$\cos^2 37° = (0.799)^2 = 0.638$$

(2) Find the value of $\tan^2 60° + \sin^2 60°$.

$$\tan 60° = \sqrt{3} \qquad \therefore \tan^2 60° = 3$$

$$\sin 60° = \frac{\sqrt{3}}{2} \qquad \therefore \sin^2 60° = \frac{3}{4}$$

$$\tan^2 60° + \sin^2 60° = 3 + \frac{3}{4} = 3\frac{3}{4}$$

It is sometimes useful to remember that

$$\sin^2 A + \cos^2 A = 1$$

which may easily be proved by considering a right-angled triangle (Fig. 34.30).

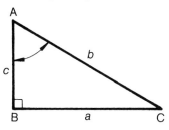

Fig. 34.30

$$\sin A = \frac{a}{b} \qquad \sin^2 A = \frac{a^2}{b^2}$$

$$\cos A = \frac{c}{b} \qquad \cos^2 A = \frac{c^2}{b^2}$$

$$\sin^2 A + \cos^2 A = \frac{a^2}{b^2} + \frac{c^2}{b^2} = \frac{a^2 + c^2}{b^2}$$

But, by Pythagoras

$$a^2 + c^2 = b^2$$

$$\therefore \qquad \sin^2 A + \cos^2 A = \frac{b^2}{b^2} = 1$$

EXAMPLE 8

The angle A is acute and
$5\sin^2 A - 2 = \cos^2 A$. Find the angle A.

Since $\qquad \sin^2 A + \cos^2 A = 1$

$$\cos^2 A = 1 - \sin^2 A$$

$$\therefore \qquad 5\sin^2 A - 2 = 1 - \sin^2 A$$

$$6\sin^2 A - 3 = 0$$

$$6\sin^2 A = 3$$

$$\sin^2 A = 0.5$$

$$\sin A = \pm\sqrt{0.5} = \pm 0.707$$

Since A is acute $\sin A$ must be positive.

Hence $\qquad \sin A = 0.707$

$$A = 45°$$

Another useful relationship is

$$\frac{\sin A}{\cos A} = \tan A$$

which may be proved by considering the right-angled triangle ABC shown in Fig. 34.30.

$$\sin A = \frac{a}{b} \qquad \cos A = \frac{c}{b}$$

$$\frac{\sin A}{\cos A} = \frac{a}{b} \div \frac{c}{b} = \frac{a}{b} \times \frac{b}{c} = \frac{a}{c}$$

But $\qquad \tan A = \frac{a}{c}$

$$\therefore \qquad \frac{\sin A}{\cos A} = \tan A$$

EXAMPLE 9

(1) If $\sin A = 0.643$ and $\cos A = 0.766$ find $\tan A$.

$$\tan A = \frac{0.643}{0.766} = 0.839$$

(2) If $\cos A = 0.342$ and $\tan A = 2.747$, what is the value of $\sin A$?

$$\sin A = \cos A \times \tan A$$

$$= 0.342 \times 2.747 = 0.939$$

Exercise 159 – *Questions 1–10 type B, remainder C*

† **1)** If $\sin A = 0.317$ find the values of $\cos A$ and $\tan A$ without using tables.

† **2)** If $\tan A = \frac{3}{4}$, find the values of $\sin A$ and $\cos A$ without using tables.

† **3)** If $\cos A = \frac{12}{13}$, find without using tables the values of $\sin A$ and $\tan A$.

† **4)** Show that $\cos 60° + \cos 30° = \frac{1 + \sqrt{3}}{2}$.

† **5)** Show that $\sin 60° + \cos 30° = \sqrt{3}$.

† **6)** Show that
$$\cos 45° + \sin 60° + \sin 30° = \frac{\sqrt{2} + \sqrt{3} + 1}{2}.$$

† **7)** Given that $\sin 48° = 0.743$ find the values of $\cos 42°$, without using tables.

8) If $\cos 63° = 0.454$, what is the value of $\sin 27°$?

* **9)** (a) Find the value of $\cos^2 30°$.
(b) Find the value of $\tan^2 30°$.
(c) Find the value of $\sin^2 60°$.

***10)** Evaluate
(a) $\cos^2 41°$ (b) $\sin^2 27°$ (c) $\tan^2 58°$

286 Trigonometry

*11) If the angle A is acute and $2\sin^2 A - \frac{1}{3} = \cos^2 A$ find A.

*12) If the angle θ is acute and $\cos^2\theta + \frac{1}{8} = \sin^2\theta$ find θ.

*13) If $\sin A = 0.985$ and $\cos A = 0.174$, find $\tan A$ without using trigonometry tables.

*14) If $\sin A = 0.899$ and $\tan A = 2.050$, find $\cos A$ without using trigonometry tables.

ANGLE OF ELEVATION

If you look upwards at an object, say the top of a tree, the angle formed between the horizontal and your line of sight is called the *angle of elevation* (Fig. 34.31). It is the angle through which the line of your sight has been elevated.

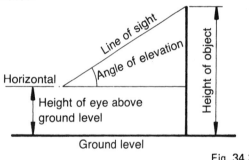

Fig. 34.31

EXAMPLE 10

To find the height of a tower a surveyor sets up his theodolite 100 m from the base of the tower. He finds that the angle of elevation to the top of the tower is 30°. If the instrument is 1.5 m from the ground, what is the height of the tower?

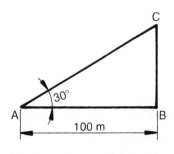

Fig. 34.32

In Fig. 34.32,

$$\frac{BC}{AB} = \tan 30°$$
$$BC = AB \times \tan 30°$$
$$= 100 \times 0.577 = 57.7$$

Hence, height of tower
$$= 57.7 + 1.5 = 59.2\,m$$

ALTITUDE OF THE SUN

The altitude of the sun is simply the angle of elevation of the sun (Fig. 34.33).

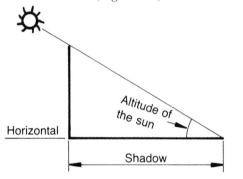

Fig. 34.33

EXAMPLE 11

A flagpole is 15 m high. What length of shadow will it cast when the altitude of the sun is 57°?

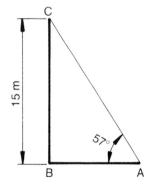

Fig. 34.34

Looking at Fig. 34.34 we have,
$$\triangle ACB = 90° - 57° = 33°$$
$$\frac{AB}{BC} = \tan \angle ACB$$
$$AB = BC \times \tan \angle ACB$$
$$= 15 \times \tan 33° = 9.74$$

Hence the flagpole will cast a shadow 9.74 m long.

ANGLE OF DEPRESSION

If you look downwards at an object, the angle formed between the horizontal and your line of sight is called the angle of depression (Fig. 34.55). It is therefore the angle through which the line of sight is depressed from the horizontal. Note that both the angle of elevation and the angle of depression are measured from the horizontal.

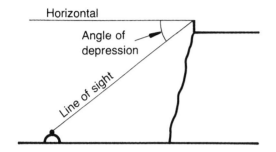

Fig. 34.35

EXAMPLE 12

A person standing on top of a cliff 50 m high is in line with two buoys whose angles of depression are 18° and 20°. Calculate the distance between the buoys.

The problem is illustrated in Fig. 34.36 where the buoys are C and D and the observer is A.

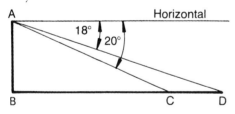

Fig. 34.36

In $\triangle$ BAC,   BAC $= 90° - 20° = 70°$

$$\frac{BC}{AB} = \tan \angle BAC$$

$$BC = AB \times \tan \angle BAC$$

$$= 50 \times \tan 70° = 137.4 \text{ m}$$

In $\triangle$ ABD, $\angle$ BAD $= 90° - 18° = 72°$

$$\frac{BD}{AB} = \tan \angle BAD$$

$$BD = AB \times \tan \angle BAD$$

$$= 50 \times \tan 72° = 153.9 \text{ m}$$

The distance between the buoys

$$= BD - BC = 153.9 - 137.4 = 16.5 \text{ m}$$

Exercise 160 – *Questions 1–8 type B, remainder C*

1) From a point, the angle of elevation of a tower is 30°. If the tower is 20 m distant from the point, what is the height of the tower?

2) A man 1.8 m tall observes the angle of elevation of a tree to be 26°. If he is standing 16 m from the tree, find the height of the tree.

3) A man 1.5 m tall is 15 m away from a tower 20 m high. What is the angle of elevation of the top of the tower from his eyes?

4) A man, lying down on top of a cliff 40 m high observes the angle of depression of a buoy to be 20°. If he is in line with the buoy, calculate the distance between the buoy and the foot of the cliff (which may be assumed to be vertical).

5) A tree is 20 m tall. When the altitude of the sun is 62°, what length of shadow will it cast?

6) A flagpole casts a shadow 18 m long when the altitude of the sun is 54°. What is the height of the flagpole?

7) A man standing on top of a mountain 1200 m high observes the angle of depression of a steeple to be 43°. How far is the steeple from the mountain?

8) In Fig. 34.37, a vertical cliff is 40 m high and is observed from a boat which is 50 m from the foot of the cliff. Calculate the angle of elevation of the top of the cliff from the boat.

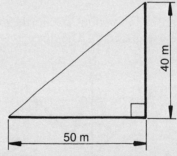

Fig. 34.37

9) A man standing 20 m away from a tower observes the angles of elevation to the top and bottom of a flag-staff standing on the tower as 62° and 60° respectively. Calculate the height of the flagstaff.

10) A surveyor stands 100 m from the base of a tower on which an aerial stands. He measures the angles of elevation to the top and bottom of the aerial as 58° and 56°. Find the height of the aerial.

11) Figure 34.38 shows a tower TR and an observer at O. From O which is 100 m from the base R of tower TR the angle of elevation of the top of the tower is found to be 35°.

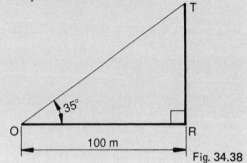

Fig. 34.38

(a) Calculate the height of the tower TR, to 3 significant figures.

(b) The observer walks forward towards the tower until the angle of elevation of the top T is 45°. How far does he walk forward?

(c) Find the distance of the observer from the base of the tower when the angle of elevation of the top is 65°. Give your answer to 3 significant figures.

12) A man standing on top of a cliff 80 m high is in line with two buoys whose angles of depression are 17° and 21°. Calculate the distance between the buoys.

BEARINGS

The four cardinal directions are north, south, east and west (Fig. 34.39). The directions NE,

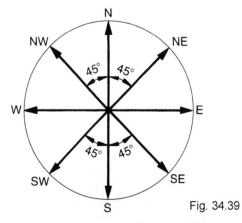

Fig. 34.39

NW, SE and SW are frequently used and are as shown in Fig. 34.39.

However, bearings are usually measured from north in a clockwise direction, N being taken as 0°. Three figures are always stated, for example 005° is written instead of 5° and 035° instead of 35° and so on. east will be 090°, south 180° and west 270°. Some typical bearings are shown in Fig. 34.40.

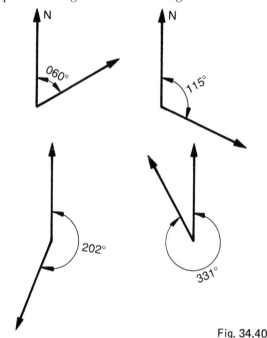

Fig. 34.40

EXAMPLE 13

(1) B is a point due east of a point A on the coast. C is another point on the coast and is 6 km due south of A. The distance BC is 7 km. Calculate the bearing of C from B.

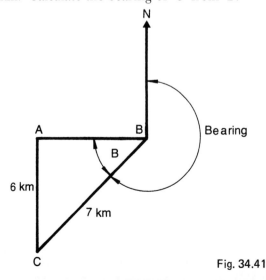

Fig. 34.41

Referring to Fig. 34.41,

$$\sin \angle B = \frac{AC}{BC} = \frac{6}{7} = 0.857$$

$$\angle B = 59°$$

The bearing of C from B

$$= 270° - 59° = 211°.$$

(2) B is 5 km due north of P and C is 2 km due east of P. A ship started from C and steamed in a direction 030°. Calculate the distance the ship had to go before it was due east of B. Find also the distance it is then from B.

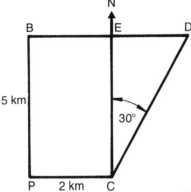

Fig. 34.42

Referring to Fig. 34.42, the ship will be due east of B when it has sailed the distance CD. The bearing N30°E makes the angle $\angle ECD$ equal to 30°. In $\triangle CED$, EC = 5 km and $\angle ECD = 30°$. Hence

$$\frac{EC}{CD} = \cos 30°$$

$$CD = \frac{EC}{\cos 30°} = \frac{5}{\cos 30°} = 5.77 \text{ km}$$

Hence the ship had to sail 5.77 km to become due east of B.

$$\frac{ED}{CD} = \sin 30°$$

$$ED = CD \times \sin 30° = 5.77 \times 0.500$$

$$= 2.885 \text{ km}$$

$$BD = BE + ED = 2 + 2.885 = 4.885 \text{ km}$$

Hence the ship will be 4.885 km due east of B.

(3) A boat sails 8 km from a port P on a bearing of 070°. It then sails 5 km on a bearing of 040°. Calculate the distance that the boat is from P and also its bearing from P.

The details of the journey are shown in Fig. 34.43. The problem is to find the distance PB and the angle BPN.

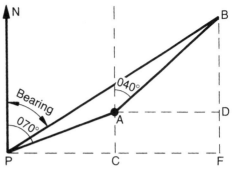

Fig. 34.43

Draw the triangles PAC and ABD as shown in the diagram.

In $\triangle PAC$, AP = 8 km and $\angle APC = 20°$.

$$\frac{PC}{AP} = \cos \angle APC$$

$$PC = AP \times \cos \angle APC = 8 \times \cos 20°$$

$$= 7.518 \text{ km}$$

$$\frac{AC}{AP} = \sin \angle APC$$

$$AC = AP \times \sin \angle APC = 8 \times \sin 20°$$

$$= 2.736 \text{ km}$$

In $\triangle ABD$, AD = 5 km and $\angle BAD = 50°$

$$\frac{AD}{AB} = \cos \angle BAD$$

$$AD = AB \times \cos \angle BAD = 5 \times \cos 50°$$

$$= 3.214 \text{ km}$$

$$\frac{BD}{AB} = \sin \angle BAD$$

$$BD = AB \times \sin BAD = 5 \times \sin 50°$$

$$= 3.830 \text{ km}$$

In $\triangle PBF$,

$$PF = PC + AD = 7.518 + 3.214$$

$$= 10.732 \text{ km}$$

$$BF = AC + BD = 2.736 + 3.830$$

$$= 6.566 \text{ km}$$

Using Pythagoras' theorem,

$$PB^2 = PF^2 + BF^2 = 10.732^2 + 6.566^2$$

$$= 115.2 + 43.1 = 158.3$$

The distance from P is

$$PB = \sqrt{158.3} = 12.58\,\text{km}$$

$$\tan \angle BPF = \frac{BF}{PF} = \frac{6.566}{10.732}$$

$$\angle BPF = 31.5°$$

The bearing from P is

$$90° - 31.5° = 58.5°$$

Exercise 161 – *All type B*

1) A ship sets out from a point A and sails due north to a point B, a distance of 120 km. It then sails due east to a point C. If the bearing of C from A is 037° calculate:

(a) the distance BC;
(b) the distance AC.

2) A boat leaves a harbour A on a course of 120° and it sails 50 km in this direction until it reaches a point B. How far is B east of A? What distance south of A is B?

3) X is a point due west of a point P. Y is a point due south of P. If the distances PX and PY are 10 km and 15 km respectively, calculate the bearing of X from Y.

4) B is 10 km north of P and C is 5 km due west of P. A ship starts from C and sails in a direction of 330°. Calculate the distance the ship has to sail before it is due west of B and find also the distance it is then from B.

5) A fishing boat places a float on the sea at A, 50 metres due north of a buoy B. A second boat places a float at C, whose bearing from A is 150°. A taut net connecting the floats at A and C is 80 metres long. Calculate the distance BC and the bearing of C from B.

6) An aircraft starts to fly from A to B a distance of 140 km, B being due north of A. The aircraft flies on course 018° for a distance of 80 km. Calculate how far the aircraft is then from the line AB and in what direction it should then fly to reach B.

7) X and Y are two lighthouses, Y being 20 km due east of X. From a ship due south of X, the bearing of Y was 055°. Find:

(a) the distance of the ship from Y;
(b) the distance of the ship from X.

8) An aircraft flies 50 km from an aerodrome A on a bearing of 065° and then flies 80 km

on a bearing of 040°. Find the distance of the aircraft from A and also its bearing from A.

9) A boat sails 10 km from a harbour H on a bearing of 150°. It then sails 15 km on a bearing of 020°. How far is the boat from H? What is its bearing from H?

10) Three towns A, B and C lie on a straight road running east from A. B is 6 km from A and C is 22 km from A. Another town D lies to the north of this road and it lies 10 km from both B and C. Calculate the distance of D from A and the bearing of D from A.

SELF-TEST 34

1) In Fig. 34.44, sin x is equal to:

a $\frac{h}{p}$ b $\frac{h}{m}$ c $\frac{m}{p}$ d $\frac{p}{h}$

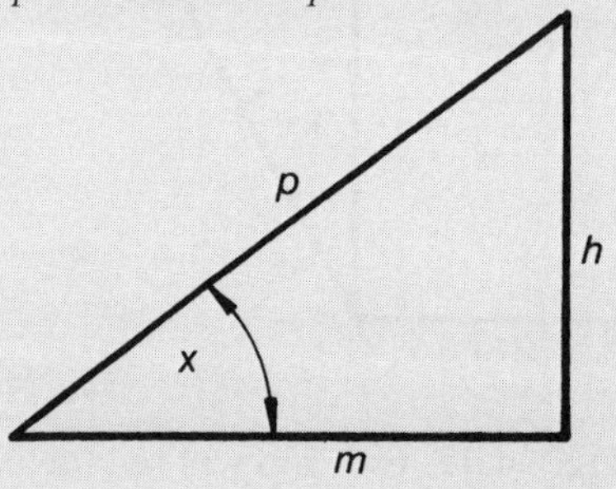

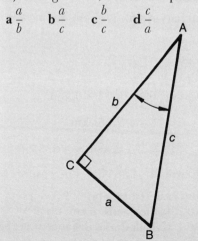

Fig. 34.44

2) In Fig. 34.44, cos x is equal to:

a $\frac{h}{p}$ b $\frac{h}{m}$ c $\frac{m}{p}$ d $\frac{p}{h}$

3) In Fig. 34.44, tan x is equal to:

a $\frac{h}{p}$ b $\frac{h}{m}$ c $\frac{m}{p}$ d $\frac{p}{h}$

4) In Fig. 34.45, sin A is equal to:

a $\frac{a}{b}$ b $\frac{a}{c}$ c $\frac{b}{c}$ d $\frac{c}{a}$

Fig. 34.45

5) In Fig. 34.46, $\tan x$ is equal to:

a $\dfrac{q}{p}$ **b** $\dfrac{q}{r}$ **c** $\dfrac{p}{q}$ **d** $\dfrac{r}{q}$

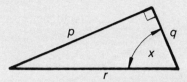

Fig. 34.46

6) In Fig. 34.47, $\cos y$ is equal to:

a $\dfrac{s}{t}$ **b** $\dfrac{r}{s}$ **c** $\dfrac{s}{r}$ **d** $\dfrac{t}{s}$

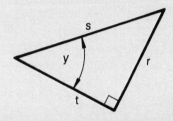

Fig. 34.47

7) The expression for the length AB (Fig. 34.48) is:

a $40 \tan 50°$ **b** $40 \sin 50°$

c $\dfrac{40}{\tan 50°}$ **d** $\dfrac{40}{\sin 50°}$

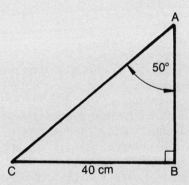

Fig. 34.48

8) The expression for the length AC (Fig. 34.48) is:

a $40 \sin 50°$ **b** $40 \cos 50°$

c $\dfrac{40}{\sin 50°}$ **d** $\dfrac{40}{\cos 50°}$

9) In Fig. 34.49, the expression for the side RN is:

a $(2 \sin 30° + 3 \sin 60°) \, \text{cm}$

b $(2 \sin 30° + 3 \cos 60°) \, \text{cm}$

c $(2 \cos 30° + 3 \cos 60°) \, \text{cm}$

d $(2 \cos 30° + 3 \sin 60°) \, \text{cm}$

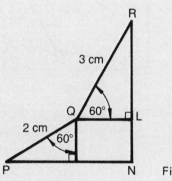

Fig. 34.49

10) In Fig. 34.50, an expression for the length AD is:

a $\dfrac{16\sqrt{3}}{3}$ **b** $8\sqrt{3}$

c $16\sqrt{3}$ **d** $\dfrac{40\sqrt{3}}{3}$

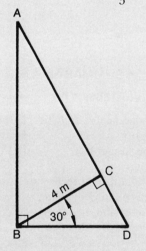

Fig. 34.50

11) In Fig. 34.51, an expression for the angle θ is:

a $\tan \theta = \dfrac{30 - 10\sqrt{3}}{40}$

b $\tan \theta = \dfrac{40}{30 - 10\sqrt{3}}$

c $\tan\theta = \dfrac{20}{50 - 10\sqrt{3}}$

d $\tan\theta = \dfrac{50 - 10\sqrt{3}}{20}$

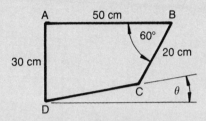

Fig. 34.51

12) The area of the parallelogram PQRS (Fig. 34.52) is:

a $30\sin 70° \text{ cm}^2$ **b** $30\cos 70° \text{ cm}^2$

c $60\sin 70° \text{ cm}^2$ **d** $60\cos 70° \text{ cm}^2$

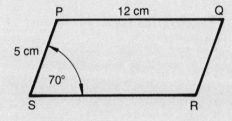

Fig. 34.52

13) In Fig. 34.53, PT and PQ are tangents to the circle whose radius is 2 cm. Hence ∠TPQ is:

a 30°   **b** 45°   **c** 60°   **d** 90°

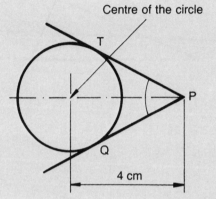

Centre of the circle

Fig. 34.53

14) A man standing on top of a cliff 80 m high is in line with two buoys whose angles of depression are 15° and 20°. The distance between the two buoys is given by the expression:

a $80(\tan 20° - \tan 15°)$

b $80(\tan 75° - \tan 70°)$

c $80\tan 5°$

d $\dfrac{80}{\tan 20° - \tan 15°}$

CHAPTER 34 SUMMARY

Points to remember

(i)   If A is an acute angle in a right-angled triangle

    (a) the tangent of ∠A, written $\tan A$ = length of side opposite A / length of side adjacent to A. $\tan A$ may have any numerical value.

    (b) the cosine of ∠A, written $\cos A$ = length of side adjacent to A / length of hypoteneuse. The value of $\cos A$ cannot be less than -1 or greater than 1.

    (c) the sine of ∠A, written $\sin A$ = length of side opposite A / length of hypotenuse. The value of $\sin A$ cannot be less than -1 or greater than 1.

(ii) $\sin A = \cos(90 - A)$ [A is measured in degrees]

(iii) $\sin^2 A + \cos^2 A = 1$

(iv) $\sin A/\cos A = \tan A$.

(v)   The angle of elevation of a point on an object from a given point on a lower level, is the angle formed by the horizontal line through the given point and the line joining the two points.

(vi)   The angle of depression of a point on an object from a given point on a higher level, is the angle formed by the horizontal line through the given point and the line joining the two points.

(vii)   The bearing of an object from a given point is the angle, measured clockwise, formed by the north line through a given point and the line joining the point and the object.

Chapter 35 The Sine and Cosine Rules

TRIGONOMETRICAL RATIOS BETWEEN 0° AND 360°

In Chapter 34 the definitions for the sine, cosine and tangent of an angle between $0°$ and $90°$ were given. In this chapter we show how to deal with angles between $0°$ and $360°$.

In Fig. 35.1, the axes XOX' and YOY' have been drawn at right angles to each other to form the four quadrants. In each of these four quadrants we make use of the sign convention used when drawing graphs.

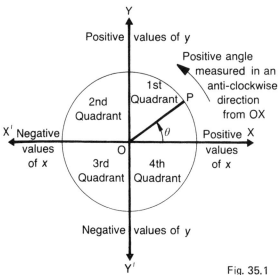

Fig. 35.1

Now an angle, if positive, is always measured in an anti-clockwise direction from OX and an angle is formed by rotating a line (such as OP) in an anti-clockwise direction. It is convenient to make the length of OP equal to 1 unit.

In the first quadrant (Fig. 35.2(a))

$$\sin \theta_1 = \frac{P_1 M_1}{OP_1} = P_1 M_1$$

$$= y \text{ coordinate of } P_1$$

$$\cos \theta_1 = \frac{OM_1}{OP_1} = OM_1$$

$$= x \text{ coordinate of } P_1$$

$$\tan \theta_1 = \frac{P_1 M_1}{OM_1} = \frac{y \text{ coordinate of P}}{x \text{ coordinate of P}}$$

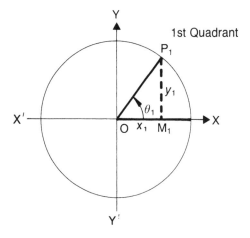

Fig. 35.2(a)

Hence in the *first quadrant* all the trigonometrical ratios are *positive*.

In the second quadrant (Fig. 35.2(b))

$$\sin \theta_2 = \frac{P_2 M_2}{OP_2} = P_2 M_2$$

$$= y \text{ coordinate of } P_2$$

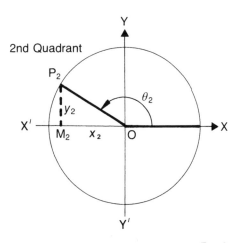

Fig. 35.2(b)

The y coordinate of P_2 is positive and hence in the second quadrant the sine of an angle is positive.

$$\cos\theta_2 = \frac{OM_2}{OP_2} = OM_2$$

$$= x \text{ coordinate of } P_2$$

The x coordinate of P_2 is negative and hence in the second quadrant the cosine of an angle is negative.

$$\tan\theta_2 = \frac{P_2M_2}{OM_2} = \frac{y \text{ coordinate of } P_2}{x \text{ coordinate of } P_2}$$

But the y coordinate of P_2 is positive and the x coordinate of P_2 is negative, hence the tangent of an angle in the second quadrant is negative.

The trigonometrical tables usually give values of the trigonometrical ratios for angles between $0°$ and $90°$. In order to use these tables for angles greater than $90°$ we make use of the triangle OP_2M_2, where we see that

$$P_2M_2 = OP_2 \sin(180 - \theta_2)$$

$$= \sin(180 - \theta_2)$$

But

$$P_2M_2 = \sin\theta_2$$

$$\therefore \quad \sin\theta_2 = \sin(180 - \theta_2)$$

Also

$$OM_2 = -OP_2 \cos(180 - \theta_2)$$

$$= -\cos(180 - \theta_2)$$

$$\therefore \quad \cos\theta_2 = -\cos(180 - \theta_2)$$

Similarly

$$\tan\theta_2 = -\tan(180 - \theta_2)$$

In the third quadrant (Fig. 35.2(c)) by similar considerations

$$\sin\theta_3 = -\sin(\theta_3 - 180°)$$

$$\cos\theta_3 = -\cos(\theta_3 - 180°)$$

$$\tan\theta_3 = \tan(\theta_3 - 180°)$$

In the fourth quadrant (Fig. 25.2(c)),

$$\sin\theta_4 = -\sin(360° - \theta_4)$$

$$\cos\theta_4 = \cos(360° - \theta_4)$$

$$\tan\theta_4 = -\tan(360° - \theta_4)$$

The results are summarised in Fig. 35.3.

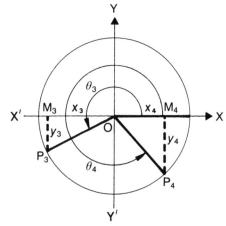

3rd and 4th Quadrants   Fig. 35.2(c)

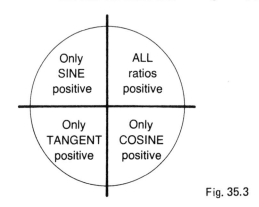

Fig. 35.3

EXAMPLE 1

Find the values of $\sin 158°$, $\cos 158°$ and $\tan 158°$. Referring to Fig. 35.4,

$$\sin 158° = \frac{MP}{OP} = \sin\angle POM$$

$$= \sin(180° - 158°)$$

$$= \sin 22° = 0.375$$

$$\cos 158° = \frac{OM}{OP} = -\cos\angle POM$$

$$= -\cos(180° - 158°)$$

$$= -\cos 22° = -0.927$$

$$\tan 158° = \frac{MP}{OM} = -\tan\angle POM$$

$$= -\tan(180° - 158°)$$

$$= -\tan 22° = -0.404$$

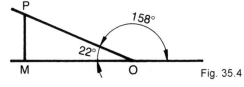

Fig. 35.4

The table below may be used for angles in any quadrant.

Quadrant	Angle	$\sin\theta =$	$\cos\theta =$	$\tan\theta =$
First	$0°-90°$	$\sin\theta$	$\cos\theta$	$\tan\theta$
Second	$90°-180°$	$\sin(180°-\theta)$	$-\cos(180°-\theta)$	$-\tan(180°-\theta)$
Third	$180°-270°$	$-\sin(\theta-180°)$	$-\cos(\theta-180°)$	$\tan(\theta-180°)$
Fourth	$270°-360°$	$-\sin(360°-\theta)$	$\cos(360°-\theta)$	$-\tan(360°-\theta)$

EXAMPLE 2

(1) Find the sine and cosine of the following angles:

(a) $171°$ (b) $216°$ (c) $289°$.

(a) $\sin 171° = \sin(180° - 171°) = \sin 9°$

$= 0.156$

$\cos 171° = -\cos(180° - 171°)$

$= -\cos 9° = -0.988$

(b) $\sin 216° = -\sin(216° - 180°)$

$= -\sin 36° = -0.588$

$\cos 216° = -\cos 36° = -0.809$

(c) $\sin 289° = -\sin(360° - 289°)$

$= -\sin 71° = -0.946$

$\cos 289° = \cos(360° - 289°)$

$= \cos 71° = 0.326.$

(2) Find all the angles between $0°$ and $180°$:

(a) whose sine is 0.468,
(b) whose cosine is −0.357.

(a) The angles whose sines are 0.468 occur in the first and second quadrants.

In the first quadrant:

$$\sin\theta = 0.468$$

$$\theta = 27.8°$$

In the second quadrant:

$$\theta = 180° - 27.8°$$

$$= 152.2° \quad \text{(see Fig. 35.5)}$$

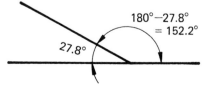

$180°-27.8°$
$= 152.2°$

$27.8°$

Fig. 35.5

(b) The angle whose cosine is -0.357 occurs in the second quadrant (i.e. the angle is between $90°$ and $180°$).

If $\cos\theta = 0.357$

$\theta = 69.1°$

In the second quadrant:

$$\theta = 180° - 69.1°$$

$$\theta = 110.9° \quad \text{(see Fig. 35.6)}$$

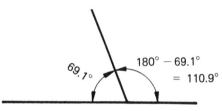

$69.1°$

$180° - 69.1°$
$= 110.9°$

Fig. 35.6

(3) If $\sin A = \dfrac{3}{5}$ find the values of $\cos A$.

As shown in Fig. 35.7, the angle A may be in the first or second quadrants. In the first quadrant, by Pythagoras,

$$OM_1{}^2 = OP_1{}^2 - P_1 M_1{}^2 = 5^2 - 3^2 = 16$$

$$\therefore \quad OM_1 = 4$$

$$\cos A = \frac{OM_1}{OP_1} = \frac{4}{5}$$

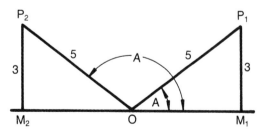

P_2 P_1

5 A 5

3 3

A

M_2 O M_1

Fig. 35.7

In the second quadrant

$$OM_2 = -4$$

$$\cos A = \frac{OM_2}{M_2 P_2} = -\frac{4}{5}$$

†SINE, COSINE AND TANGENT CURVES

The Sine Curve

Using the tables to find values of angles between 0° and 90°, and also the methods previously explained for angles 90° to 360° we can draw up a table of values as shown. Intervals of 30° have been chosen to illustrate this but more angles may be taken to obtain a more accurate graph.

θ	0	30	60	90
$y = \sin\theta$	0	0.500	0.866	1.000

θ		120	150	180
$y = \sin\theta$		0.866	0.500	0

θ		210	240	270
$y = \sin\theta$		−0.500	−0.866	−1.000

θ		300	330	360
$y = \sin\theta$		−0.866	−0.500	0

These values are plotted as shown in Fig. 35.8.

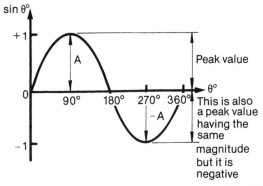

Fig. 35.8

The following features should be noted:

(a) In the first quadrant as θ increases from 0° to 90°, $\sin\theta$ increases from 0 to 1.

(b) In the second quadrant as θ increases from 90° to 180°, $\sin\theta$ decreases from 1 to 0.

(c) In the third quadrant as θ increases from 180° to 270°, $\sin\theta$ decreases from 0 to −1.

(d) In the fourth quadrant as θ increases from 270° to 360°, $\sin\theta$ increases from −1 to 0.

The Cosine Curve

By a similar method the cosine curve may be constructed and it will be found to be as shown in Fig. 35.9.

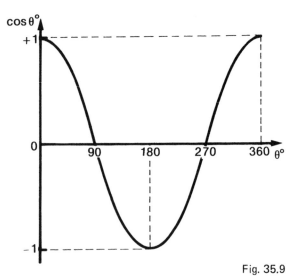

Fig. 35.9

Note that:

(a) In the first quadrant as θ increases from 0° to 90°, $\cos\theta$ decreases from 1 to 0.

(b) In the second quadrant as θ increases from 90° to 180°, $\cos\theta$ decreases from 0 to −1.

(c) In the third quadrant as θ increases from 180° to 270°, $\cos\theta$ increases from −1 to 0.

(d) In the fourth quadrant as θ increases from 270° to 360°, $\cos\theta$ increases from 0 to 1.

The Tangent Curve

Using the methods as described for the sine and cosine curves the tangent curve may be obtained, and is shown in Fig. 35.10.

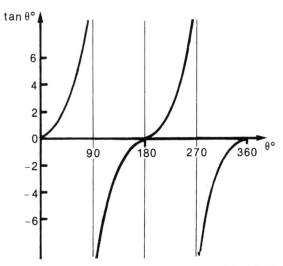

Fig. 35.10

Note that:

(a) In the first quadrant as θ increases from $0°$ to $90°$, $\tan\theta$ increases from 0 to infinity.

(b) In the second quadrant as θ increases from $90°$ to $180°$, $\tan\theta$ increases from minus infinity to 0.

(c) In the third quadrant as θ increases from $180°$ to $270°$ $\tan\theta$ increases from 0 to infinity.

(d) In the fourth quadrant as θ increases from $270°$ to $360°$ $\tan\theta$ increases from minus infinity to 0.

†**Exercise 162** – *All type C*

1) Copy and complete the following table.

θ	$\sin\theta$	$\cos\theta$	$\tan\theta$
108°			
163°			
207°			
320°			
134°			
168°			
225°			
286°			
300°			
95°			

2) If $\sin A = \dfrac{a\sin B}{b}$, find the values of A between $0°$ and $180°$ when $a = 7.26\,\text{cm}$, $b = 9.15\,\text{cm}$ and $B = 18.48°$.

3) If $\cos C = \dfrac{a^2 + b^2 - c^2}{2ab}$, find the values of C between $0°$ and $180°$ when $a = 1.26\,\text{m}$, $b = 1.41\,\text{m}$ and $c = 2.13\,\text{m}$.

4) Copy and complete the following table.

Trigonometrical ratio	Angle in			
	1st quadrant	2nd quadrant	3rd quadrant	4th quadrant
$\sin\theta = 0.515$				
$\sin\theta = 0.216$				
$\sin\theta = -0.407$				
$\cos\theta = 0.881$				
$\cos\theta = -0.760$				
$\cos\theta = -0.082$				
$\tan\theta = 1.600$				
$\tan\theta = 0.813$				
$\tan\theta = -0.231$				

5) Use tables to find the angles x and y between $0°$ and $360°$ where $\sin x = 0.569$ and $\cos y = 0.877$.

6) If $\sin A = \dfrac{12}{13}$ find, without using tables or a calculator, the values of $\tan A$ and $\cos A$, A being acute.

7) Evaluate $\sin A \cos B - \sin B \cos A$ given that $\sin A = \dfrac{3}{5}$ and $\tan B = \dfrac{4}{3}$. A and B are both acute angles.

8) The angle A is acute and $\tan A = \dfrac{15}{8}$. Without using tables or a calculator, find the value of $\sin(180° - A)$. If $B = 90° - A$ find the value of $\tan B$.

9) The angle A is acute and $\cos A = \dfrac{60}{61}$. Without using trigonometry tables or a calculator, find the value of $\tan A$.

†**THE STANDARD NOTATION FOR A TRIANGLE**

In $\triangle ABC$ (Fig. 35.11) the angles are denoted by the capital letters as shown in the diagram. The

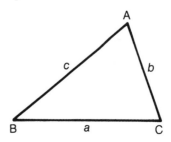

Fig. 35.11

side a lies opposite the angle A, the side b opposite the angle B and the side c opposite the angle C. This is the standard notation for a triangle.

†THE SOLUTION OF TRIANGLES

We now deal with triangles which are not right-angled. Every triangle consists of six elements – three sides and three angles.

To solve a triangle, we must have three elements. These may be:
(1) Two sides and the included angle.
(2) One side and any two angles.
(3) Two sides and an angle opposite one of these sides.
(4) Three sides.

The sine rule or cosine rule may then be used to find the missing elements, i.e. to 'solve' the triangle.

†THE SINE RULE

The sine rule may be used when we are given:

(1) One side and any two angles.

(2) Two sides and an angle opposite to one of the sides.

Using the notation of Fig. 35.12

$$\frac{a}{\sin A} = \frac{b}{\sin B} = \frac{c}{\sin C}$$

This formula is proved below for both acute-angled and obtuse-angled triangles.

(1) When △ABC is acute-angled (Fig. 35.12).

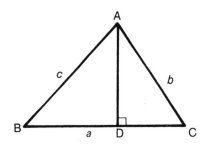

Fig. 35.12

In △ABD, $AD = c \sin B$

In △ADC, $AD = b \sin C$

∴ $b \sin C = c \sin B$

or

$$\frac{b}{\sin B} = \frac{c}{\sin C}$$

Similarly, by drawing the perpendicular from B to AC,

$$\frac{a}{\sin A} = \frac{c}{\sin C}$$

∴

$$\frac{a}{\sin A} = \frac{b}{\sin B} = \frac{c}{\sin C}$$

(2) When △ABC is obtuse-angled (Fig. 35.13).

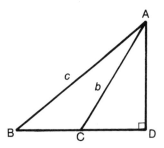

Fig. 35.13

In △ACD,

$$AD = b \sin(180° - C) = b \sin C$$

In △ABD,

$$AD = c \sin B$$

∴ $b \sin C = c \sin B$

$$\frac{b}{\sin B} = \frac{c}{\sin C}$$

As before,

$$\frac{a}{\sin A} = \frac{b}{\sin B} = \frac{c}{\sin C}$$

EXAMPLE 3

Solve △ABC given that A = 42°, C = 72° and $b = 61.8$ mm.

The triangle should be drawn for reference as shown in Fig. 35.14 but there is no need to draw it to scale.

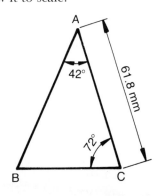

Fig. 35.14

Since

$$A + B + C = 180°$$

$$B = 180° - 42° - 72° = 66°$$

The sine rule states

$$\frac{a}{\sin A} = \frac{b}{\sin B}$$

$$a = \frac{b \sin A}{\sin B}$$

$$= \frac{61.8 \times \sin 42°}{\sin 66°}$$

$$= 45.3 \text{ mm}$$

number	log
61.8	1.791
sin 42°	$\bar{1}$.826
	1.617
sin 66°	$\bar{1}$.961
45.3	1.656

Also,

$$\frac{c}{\sin C} = \frac{b}{\sin B}$$

$$c = \frac{b \sin C}{\sin B}$$

$$= \frac{61.8 \times \sin 72°}{\sin 66°}$$

$$= 64.34 \text{ mm}$$

number	log
61.8	1.791
sin 72°	$\bar{1}$.978
	1.769
sin 66°	$\bar{1}$.961
64.34	1.808

The complete solution is:

$$\angle B = 66°, \quad a = 45.3 \text{ mm}$$

$$c = 64.3 \text{ mm}$$

A rough check on sine rule calculations may be made by remembering that in any triangle the longest side lies opposite to the largest angle and the shortest side lies opposite to the smallest angle. Thus in the previous example:

$$\text{smallest angle} = 42° = A;$$

$$\text{shortest side} = a = 45.3 \text{ mm}$$

$$\text{largest angle} = 72° = C;$$

$$\text{longest side} = c = 64.3 \text{ mm}$$

USE OF THE SINE RULE TO FIND THE DIAMETER OF THE CIRCUMSCRIBING CIRCLE OF A TRIANGLE

Using the notation of Fig. 35.15

$$\frac{a}{\sin A} = \frac{b}{\sin B} = \frac{c}{\sin C} = D$$

where D = diameter of circumcircle.

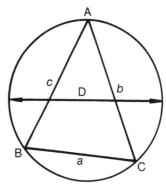

Fig. **35.15**

EXAMPLE 4

In $\triangle ABC$, $B = 41°$, $b = 112 \text{ mm}$ and $a = 87.6 \text{ mm}$. Find the diameter of the circumscribing circle. Referring to Fig. 35.16

$$D = \frac{b}{\sin B} = \frac{112}{\sin 41°} = 171 \text{ mm}$$

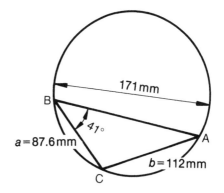

Fig. **35.16**

Exercise 163 – *Questions 1–13 type C, remainder B*

Solve the following triangles ABC by using the sine rule, given:

1) $A = 75°$ $\qquad B = 34°$ $\qquad a = 10.2 \text{ cm}$

2) $C = 61°$ $\qquad B = 71°$ $\qquad b = 91 \text{ mm}$

3) $A = 19°$ $\qquad C = 105°$ $\qquad c = 11.1 \text{ m}$

4) $A = 116°$ $C = 18°$ $a = 17\,\text{cm}$

5) $A = 36°$ $B = 77°$ $b = 2.5\,\text{m}$

6) $A = 49.2°$ $B = 67.3°$ $c = 11.2\,\text{mm}$

7) $A = 17.3°$ $C = 27.1°$ $b = 22.2\,\text{m}$

8) $A = 77.1°$ $C = 21.1°$ $a = 9.79\,\text{m}$

9) $B = 115.1°$ $C = 11.3°$ $c = 516\,\text{mm}$

10) $a = 7\,\text{m}$ $c = 11\,\text{m}$ $C = 22.1°$

11) $b = 15.1\,\text{cm}$ $c = 11.6\,\text{cm}$ $B = 85.2°$

12) $a = 23\,\text{cm}$ $c = 18.2\,\text{cm}$ $A = 49.3°$

13) $a = 9.21\,\text{cm}$ $b = 7.15\,\text{cm}$ $A = 105.1°$

Find the diameter of the circumscribing circle of the following triangles ABC given:

14) $A = 75°$ $B = 48°$ $a = 21\,\text{cm}$

15) $C = 100°$ $B = 50°$ $b = 90\,\text{mm}$

16) $A = 20°$ $C = 102°$ $c = 11\,\text{cm}$

17) $A = 70°$ $C = 35°$ $a = 8.5\,\text{cm}$

18) $a = 16\,\text{cm}$ $b = 14\,\text{cm}$ $B = 40°$

†THE COSINE RULE

This rule is used when we are given:

either (1) two sides of a triangle and the angle between them

or   (2) three sides of a triangle.

In all other cases the sine rule is used. The cosine rule states:

either $a^2 = b^2 + c^2 - 2bc \cos A$

or $b^2 = a^2 + c^2 - 2ac \cos B$

or $c^2 = a^2 + b^2 - 2ab \cos C$

When using the cosine rule remember that if an angle is greater than $90°$ its cosine is negative.

EXAMPLE 5

(1) Solve $\triangle$ ABC if $a = 70\,\text{mm}$, $b = 40\,\text{mm}$ and $C = 64°$.

Referring to Fig. 35.17, to find the side c we use:

$$c^2 = a^2 + b^2 - 2ab \cos C$$

$$= 70^2 + 40^2 - 2 \times 70 \times 40 \times \cos 64°$$

$$= 4050$$

$$c = \sqrt{4050} = 63.6\,\text{mm}$$

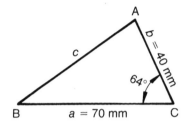

Fig. 35.17

We now use the sine rule to find the angle A:

$$\frac{a}{\sin A} = \frac{c}{\sin C}$$

$$\sin A = \frac{a \sin C}{c} = \frac{70 \times \sin 64°}{63.6}$$

$$A = 81.6°$$

$$B = 180° - 81.6° - 64° = 34.4°$$

The complete solution is

$$A = 81.6°, \quad B = 34.4°$$

and $c = 63.6\,\text{mm}$

(2) Find the side b in $\triangle$ ABC if $a = 160\,\text{mm}$, $c = 200\,\text{mm}$ and $B = 124.2°$.

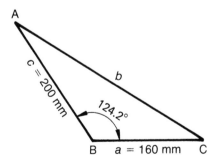

Fig. 35.18

Referring to Fig. 35.18, to find the side b we use:

$$b^2 = a^2 + c^2 - 2ac \cos B$$

$$= 160^2 + 200^2 - 2 \times 160$$

$$\times 200 \times \cos 124.2°$$

Now $\cos 124.2°$

$$= -\cos(180° - 124.2°)$$

$$= -\cos 55.8° = -0.562$$

$\therefore$

$b^2 = 160^2 + 200^2 - 2 \times 160$

$\qquad \times 200 \times (-0.562)$

$\quad = 160^2 + 200^2 + 2 \times 160 \times 200 \times 0.562$

$b = 319 \, \text{mm}$

Exercise 164 – *All type C*

Solve the following triangles ABC using the cosine rule, given:

1) $a = 9 \, \text{cm}$ $b = 11 \, \text{cm}$ $C = 60°$

2) $b = 10 \, \text{cm}$ $c = 14 \, \text{cm}$ $A = 56°$

3) $a = 8.16 \, \text{cm}$ $c = 7.14 \, \text{m}$ $B = 37° \, 18'$

4) $a = 5 \, \text{m}$ $b = 8 \, \text{m}$ $c = 7 \, \text{m}$

5) $a = 312 \, \text{mm}$ $b = 527 \, \text{mm}$ $c = 700 \, \text{mm}$

6) $a = 7.91 \, \text{cm}$ $b = 4.31 \, \text{cm}$ $c = 11.1 \, \text{cm}$

7) $a = 12 \, \text{cm}$ $b = 9 \, \text{cm}$ $C = 118°$

8) $b = 8 \, \text{cm}$ $c = 12 \, \text{cm}$ $A = 132°$

†AREA OF A TRIANGLE

In Chapter 21, two formulae for the area of a triangle were used. They are:

(1) Given the base and altitude of the triangle (Fig. 35.19)

$$\text{Area} = \tfrac{1}{2} \times \text{base} \times \text{altitude}$$

or $\qquad A = \tfrac{1}{2}bh$

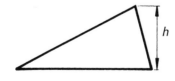

Fig. 35.19

(2) Given the three sides of the triangle (Fig. 35.20)

$$A = \sqrt{s(s-a)(s-b)(s-c)}$$

where

$$s = \tfrac{1}{2}(a+b+c)$$

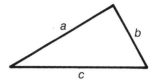

Fig. 35.20

However a third formula can be used to find the area of a triangle when we are given two sides of the triangle and the angle included between these sides. Referring to Fig. 35.21

$$A = \tfrac{1}{2}ab \sin C$$

$$A = \tfrac{1}{2}ac \sin B$$

$$A = \tfrac{1}{2}bc \sin A$$

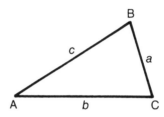

Fig. 35.21

EXAMPLE 6

Find the area of the triangle shown in Fig. 35.22.

$$A = \tfrac{1}{2}ac \sin B$$

$$= \tfrac{1}{2} \times 4 \times 3 \times \sin 30° = 3 \, \text{cm}^2$$

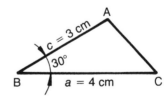

Fig. 35.22

EXAMPLE 7

Find the area of the obtuse-angled triangle shown in Fig. 35.23.

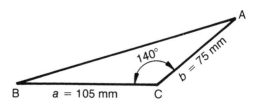

Fig. 35.23

$A = \frac{1}{2}ab\sin C$

$\quad = \frac{1}{2} \times 105 \times 75 \times \sin 140°$

We find the value of $\sin 140°$ by the method used earlier in this chapter.

$\sin 140° = \sin(180° - 140°)$

$\quad = \sin 40° = 0.643$

$A = \frac{1}{2} \times 105 \times 75 \times 0.643$

$\quad = 2430\,\text{mm}^2$

AREA OF A SEGMENT OF A CIRCLE

The area of the segment of the circle shown in Fig. 35.24 may be found by finding the area of the sector OADB and subtracting the area of △AOB from it. Thus

Area of segment

= area of sector OADB − area △AOB

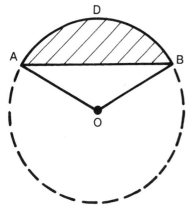

Fig. 35.24

EXAMPLE 8

Find the area of the segment of the circle shown in Fig. 35.25.

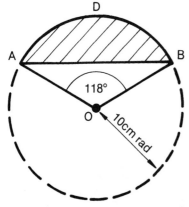

Fig. 35.25

Area of sector OADB $= \dfrac{\pi \times 10^2 \times 118}{360}$

$\quad = 103\,\text{cm}^2$

Area of △AOB $= \frac{1}{2} \times 10 \times 10 \times \sin 118°$

$\quad = 44\,\text{cm}^2$

Area of segment $= 103 - 44 = 59\,\text{cm}^2$

Exercise 165 – *All type C*

In this exercise any of the three formulae given above may be needed.

1) Obtain the area of a triangle whose sides are 39.3 cm and 41.5 cm if the angle between them is 41.5°.

2) Find the area of the figure shown in Fig. 35.26.

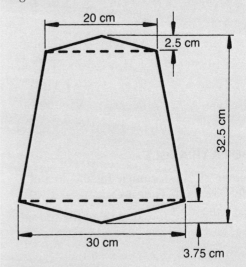

Fig. 35.26

3) Calculate the area of a triangle ABC if:

(a) $a = 4\,\text{cm}$, $b = 5\,\text{cm}$ and $C = 49°$.

(b) $a = 3\,\text{cm}$, $c = 6\,\text{cm}$ and $B = 63.7°$.

4) Find the areas of the quadrilaterals shown in Fig. 35.27.

5) Find the areas of the following triangles:

(a) $a = 5\,\text{cm}$, $b = 7\,\text{cm}$ and $\angle C = 105°$.

(b) $b = 7.3\,\text{cm}$, $c = 12.2\,\text{cm}$ and $\angle A = 135°$.

(c) $a = 9.6\,\text{cm}$, $c = 11.2\,\text{cm}$ and $\angle B = 163°$.

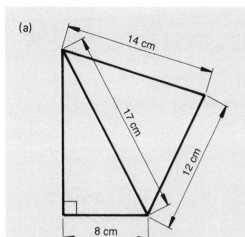

(a)

(b)

(c)

Fig. 35.27

6) Find the area of the parallelogram shown in Fig. 41.28.

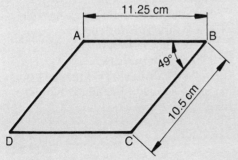

Fig. 35.28

7) Find the area of the trapezium shown in Fig. 35.29.

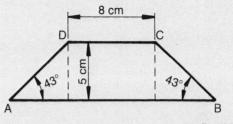

Fig. 35.29

8) Find the area of a regular octagon which has sides 2 cm long.

SELF-TEST 35

1) cos 120° is equal to:

a $-\dfrac{\sqrt{3}}{2}$ b $-\dfrac{1}{2}$ c $+\dfrac{1}{2}$ d $+\dfrac{\sqrt{3}}{2}$

2) sin 150° is equal to:

a $-\dfrac{\sqrt{3}}{2}$ b $-\dfrac{1}{2}$ c $+\dfrac{1}{2}$ d $+\dfrac{\sqrt{3}}{2}$

3) tan 120° is equal to:

a $-\sqrt{3}$ b $-\dfrac{\sqrt{3}}{3}$ c $+\dfrac{\sqrt{3}}{3}$ d $+\sqrt{3}$

4) sin 240° is equal to:

a $-\dfrac{\sqrt{3}}{2}$ b $-\dfrac{1}{2}$ c $+\dfrac{1}{2}$ d $+\dfrac{\sqrt{3}}{2}$

5) cos 210° is equal to:

a $-\dfrac{\sqrt{3}}{2}$ b $-\dfrac{1}{2}$ c $+\dfrac{1}{2}$ d $+\dfrac{\sqrt{3}}{3}$

6) tan 240° is equal to:

a $-\sqrt{3}$ b $-\dfrac{\sqrt{3}}{3}$ c $+\dfrac{\sqrt{3}}{3}$ d $+\sqrt{3}$

7) sin 300° is equal to:

a $-\dfrac{\sqrt{3}}{2}$ b $-\dfrac{1}{2}$ c $+\dfrac{1}{2}$ d $+\dfrac{\sqrt{3}}{2}$

8) cos 300° is equal to:

a $-\dfrac{\sqrt{3}}{2}$ b $-\dfrac{1}{2}$ c $+\dfrac{1}{2}$ d $+\dfrac{\sqrt{3}}{2}$

9) tan 330° is equal to:

a $-\sqrt{3}$ b $-\dfrac{\sqrt{3}}{3}$ c $+\dfrac{\sqrt{3}}{3}$ d $+\sqrt{3}$

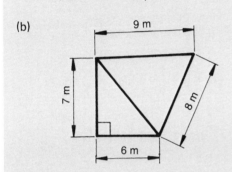

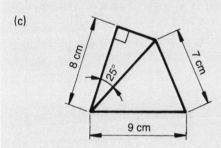

10) In Fig. 35.30, given $\angle A$ and sides a and b, the angle B is given by the expression:

a $b^2 = a^2 + c^2 - 2ac \cos B$

b $\cos B = \dfrac{a^2 + c^2 - b^2}{-2ac}$

c $\dfrac{a}{\sin A} = \dfrac{b}{\sin B}$ **d** $\dfrac{a}{b \sin A}$

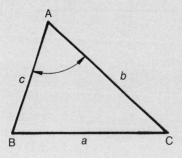

Fig. 35.30

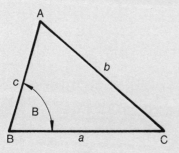

Fig. 35.31

11) In Fig. 35.31, given $\angle B$ and sides a and c, the side b is given by the expression:

a $b^2 = a^2 + c^2 - 2ac \cos B$

b $b^2 = a^2 + c^2 + 2ac \cos B$

c $b = \dfrac{a \sin B}{\sin A}$ **d** $b = \dfrac{\sin A}{a \sin B}$

12) If $\sin A = \dfrac{5}{13}$ then $\cos A$ is equal to:

a $-\dfrac{12}{13}$ **b** $-\dfrac{5}{12}$ **c** $\dfrac{5}{12}$ **d** $\dfrac{12}{13}$

13) If $\tan A = \dfrac{3}{4}$ then $\cos A$ is equal to:

a $-\dfrac{4}{5}$ **b** $-\dfrac{3}{5}$ **c** $\dfrac{3}{5}$ **d** $\dfrac{4}{5}$

14) If $\cos A = -\dfrac{11}{61}$ then $\sin {\rm A}$ is equal to:

a $-\dfrac{60}{61}$ **b** $-\dfrac{11}{60}$ **c** $\dfrac{11}{60}$ **d** $\dfrac{60}{61}$

15) If $\tan A = -\dfrac{12}{5}$ then $\cos A$ is equal to:

a $-\dfrac{12}{13}$ **b** $-\dfrac{5}{13}$ **c** $\dfrac{5}{13}$ **d** $\dfrac{12}{13}$

CHAPTER 35 SUMMARY

Points to remember

(i) Sine rule: in triangle ABC:
$a/\sin A = b/\sin B = c/\sin C$.

(ii) Cosine rule: in triangle ABC:
$a^2 = b^2 + c^2 - 2bc \cos A$,
$b^2 = c^2 + a^2 - 2ca \cos B$, and
$c^2 = a^2 + b^2 - 2ab \cos C$.
Hints for solution of triangles.
(a) Given one side and two angles:
Use angle sum, sine rule twice.
Use cosine rule to check.
(b) Given three sides:
Use cosine rule three times.
Use angle sum to check.

(c) Given two sides and the included angle:
Use cosine rule, sine rule twice.
Use angle sum for check.
(d) Given two sides and a non-included angle:
Use sine rule, angle sum, sine rule.
Use cosine rule for check.
There may be two, one, or no solutions in this case.

(iii) Area of a quadrilateral $= \frac{1}{2}$ product of diagonals $\times$ sine of the angle between them.

Chapter 36 Solid Trigonometry

*THE PLANE

A plane is a surface such as the top of a table or the cover of a book.

*THE ANGLE BETWEEN A LINE AND A PLANE

In Fig. 36.1 the line PA intersects the plane WXYZ at A. To find the angle between PA and the plane draw PL which is perpendicular to the plane and join AL. The angle between PA and the plane is ∠PAL.

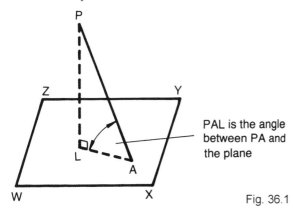

PAL is the angle between PA and the plane

Fig. 36.1

*THE ANGLE BETWEEN TWO PLANES

Two planes which are not parallel intersect in a straight line. Examples of this are the floor and a wall of a room and two walls of a room. To find the angle between two planes draw a line in each plane which is perpendicular to the common line of intersection. The angle between the two lines is the same as the angle between the two planes.

Three planes usually intersect at a point as, for instance, two walls and the floor of a room.

Problems with solid figures are solved by choosing suitable right-angled triangles in different planes. It is essential to make a clear three-dimensional drawing in order to find these triangles. The examples which follow show the methods that should be adopted.

EXAMPLE 1

Figure 36.2 shows a cuboid. Calculate the length of the diagonal AG.

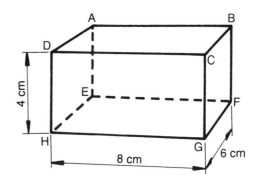

Fig. 36.2

Figure 36.3 shows that in order to find AG we must use the right-angled triangle AGE. GE is the diagonal of the base rectangle.

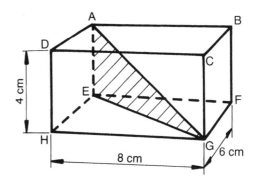

Fig. 36.3

In $\triangle EFG$, $EF = 8\,cm$, $GF = 6\,cm$ and $\angle EFG = 90°$.

Using Pythagoras' theorem,

$$EG^2 = EF^2 + GF^2 = 8^2 + 6^2$$

$$= 64 + 36 = 100$$

$$EG = \sqrt{100} = 10\,cm$$

In $\triangle AGE$, $AE = 4\,cm$, $EG = 10\,cm$ and $\angle AEG = 90°$.

Using Pythagoras' theorem,

$$AG^2 = AE^2 + EG^2 = 4^2 + 10^2$$

$$= 16 + 100 = 116$$

$$AG = \sqrt{116} = 10.8 \, cm$$

EXAMPLE 2

Figure 36.4 shows a triangular prism with the face YDC inclined as shown. Find the angle that this sloping face YDC makes with the base.

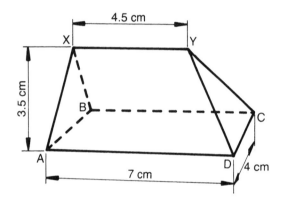

Fig. 36.4

As shown in Fig. 36.5, if we use △YEF, then the required angle is YFE. In △YEF,

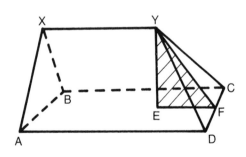

Fig. 36.5

$$EF = 7 - 4.5 = 2.5 \, cm$$

$$YE = 3.5 \, cm$$

$$\tan \angle YFE = \frac{YE}{EF} = \frac{3.5}{2.5}$$

$$\angle YFE = 54.5°$$

Hence the angle that the sloping face YDC makes with the base is 54.5°.

EXAMPLE 3

Figure 36.6 shows a pyramid with a square base. The base has sides 6 cm long and the edges of the pyramid, VA, VB, VC and VD are each 10 cm long. Find the altitude of the pyramid.

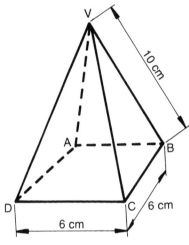

Fig. 36.6

The right-angled triangle VBE (Fig. 36.7) allows the altitude VE to be found, but first we must find BE from the right-angled triangle BEF.

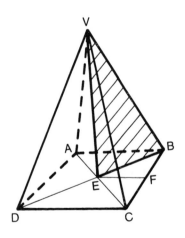

Fig. 36.7

In △BEF, BF = EF = 3 cm and ∠BFE = 90°.

Using Pythagoras' theorem,

$$BE^2 = BF^2 + EF^2 = 3^2 + 3^2 = 9 + 9 = 18$$

In △VBE, BE = 4.24 cm, VB = 10 cm and ∠VEB = 90°.

Using Pythagoras' theorem,

$$VE^2 = VB^2 - BE^2 = 10^2 - 18$$

$$= 100 - 18 = 82$$

$$VE = \sqrt{82} = 9.06\,cm$$

Hence the altitude of the pyramid is 9.06 cm.

*Exercise 166 – *All type C*

1) Figure 36.8 shows a cuboid.
(a) Sketch the rectangle EFGH.
(b) Calculate the diagonal FH of rectangle EFGH.
(c) Sketch the rectangle FHDB adding known dimensions.
(d) Calculate the diagonal BH of rectangle FHDB.

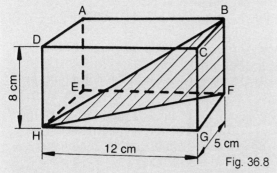

Fig. 36.8

2) Figure 36.9 shows a pyramid on a square base of side 8 cm. The altitude of the pyramid is 12 cm.

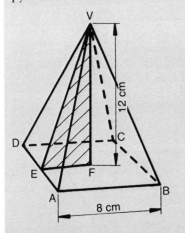

Fig. 36.9

(a) Calculate EF.
(b) Draw the triangle VEF adding known dimensions.
(c) Find the angle VEF.
(d) Calculate the slant height VE.

(e) Calculate the area of △VAD.
(f) Calculate the complete surface area of the pyramid.

3) Figure 36.10 shows a pyramid on a rectangular base. Calculate the length VA.

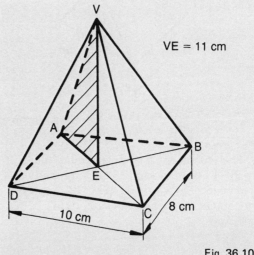

VE = 11 cm

Fig. 36.10

4) Figure 36.11 shows a pyramid on a square base with VA = VB = VC = VD = 5 cm. Calculate the altitude of the pyramid.

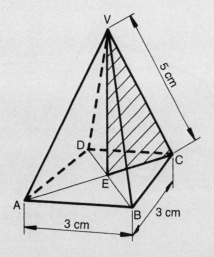

Fig. 36.11

5) Figure 36.12 shows a wooden wedge. The end faces ADF and EBC are isosceles triangles, and ABCD, ABEF and CDFE are rectangles. Find the length EA and the angle *q*.

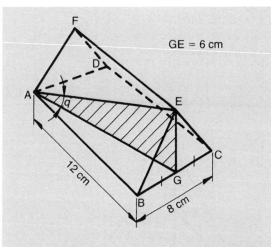

GE = 6 cm

12 cm

8 cm

Fig. 36.12

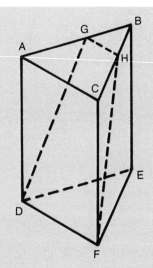

Fig. 36.14

6) The base of the triangular wedge shown in Fig. 36.13 is a rectangle 8 cm long and 6 cm wide. The vertical faces ABC and PQR are equilateral triangles of side 6 cm. Calculate:

(a) the angle between the diagonals PB and PC;
(b) the angle between the plane PBC and the base;
(c) the angle between the diagonal PC and the base.

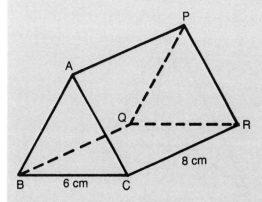

P

A

Q

R

8 cm

B   6 cm   C

Fig. 36.13

7) Figure 36.14 represents a wooden block in the shape of a triangular prism in which the edges AD, BE and CF are equal and vertical and the base DEF is horizontal. AB = BC = DE = EF = 14 cm and $\angle ABC = \angle DEF = 40°$. The points G and H are on the edges AB and BC respectively. BG = BH = 4 cm and DG = FH = 20 cm.

Calculate:

(a) the length of BE;
(b) the angle between FH and the base DEF;
(c) the angle between the plane GHFD and the base DEF;
(d) the distance between the mid-points of GH and DF.

8) Figure 36.15 shows a shed with a slanting roof ABCD. The rectangular base ABEF rests on level ground and the shed has three vertical sides. Calculate:

(a) the angle of inclination of the roof to the ground;
(b) the volume of the shed in cubic metres.

9) The base of a pyramid consists of a regular hexagon ABCDEF of side 4 cm. The vertex of the pyramid is V and VA = VB = VC = VD = VE = VF = 7 cm. Sketch a general view of the solid. Indicate on your diagram the angles p and q described below and calculate the size of these angles:

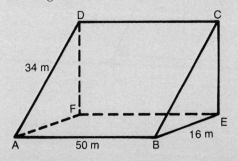

D   C

34 m

F

E

16 m

A   50 m   B

Fig. 36.15

(a) the angle p between VA and the base;
(b) the angle q between the face VCD and the base.

10) In Fig. 36.16, ABCD represents part of a hillside. A line of greatest slope AB is inclined at 36° to the horizontal AE and runs due north from A. The line AC bears 050° (N 50° E) and C is 2500 m east of B. The lines BE and CF are vertical. Calculate:

(a) the height of C above A;
(b) the angle between AB and AC.

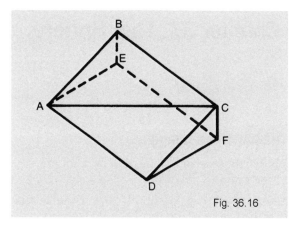

Fig. 36.16

CHAPTER 36 SUMMARY

Points to remember

(i) Three points not in the same line determine a plane.
(ii) A straight line is said to be perpendicular to a plane if it is perpendicular to every line in the plane.
(iii) In drawing three-dimensional figures: lines that cannot be seen in the actual object should be drawn as dotted lines in the figure. Lines nearer the observer should be made darker than lines farther away.
(iv) When figures are complicated, it is helpful to redraw the important parts in their correct proportion as if they were in the plane of the paper.

Chapter 37 **The Sphere, Latitude and Longitude**

†THE EARTH AS A SPHERE

The earth is usually assumed to be a sphere whose radius is 6370 km.

A circle on the surface of the earth whose centre is at the centre of the earth is called a *great circle*. The shortest distance between any two places on the earth's surface is the minor arc of the great circle passing through them. The semi-circles whose end points are N and S are called *meridians*.

†LATITUDE AND LONGITUDE

Any point on the earth's surface can be fixed by using two angles, but we must fix two reference planes at right angles to each other. The two reference planes which are used are:

(1) The equatorial plane, which is a plane through the earth's centre at right angles to the polar axis NS. The intersection of this plane with the earth's surface is called the *equator*.

(2) A plane at right angles to the equatorial plane containing the polar axis NS and also Greenwich. This plane is a meridian plane and its intersection with the earth's surface is called the *Greenwich meridian*.

The *latitude* of the point P (Fig. 37.1) is the angle POQ marked θ in the diagram. It is measured from 0° to 90°N or S of the equator. A circle on the surface of the earth whose centre is not the centre of the earth is called a *small circle*. Small circles whose centres lie on the polar axis NS are *circles of latitude*.

The *longitude* of the point P is the angle POP_1 or QOQ_1 marked ϕ in Fig. 37.1. It is measured east or west of the Greenwich meridian from 0° to 180° each way. The angle ϕ which denotes the longitude is rather like the angle of a slice of an orange. It should be noted that all meridian circles are great circles but all great circles are not meridian circles. For instance, the equator is a great circle but it is not a meridian circle because it does not contain the poles N and S.

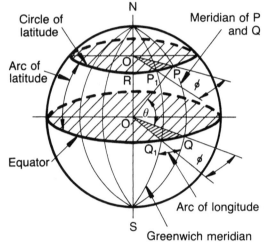

Fig. 37.1

All points with the *same* longitude lie on the same meridian circle. All points with the same latitude lie on the same circle of latitude. Thus in Fig. 37.1 the points P and R have the same latitude.

EXAMPLE 1

(1) Two places A and B have the same longitude. A has latitude 30°N and B has latitude 15°S. Find the distance between them along their meridian.

This problem reduces to finding the length of the arc AB (Fig. 37.2).

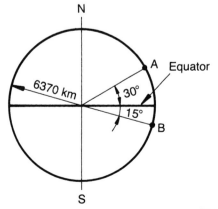

Fig. 37.2

Length of arc $AB = 2\pi \times 6370 \times \dfrac{45°}{360°}$ km

$$= 5005 \text{ km}$$

Therefore distance between the places A and B is 5005 km.

(2) Two places P and Q are on the equator. P has longitude 20°W and Q has longitude 40°E. What is the distance between them?

This problem reduces to finding the length of the arc PQ (Fig. 37.3).

Length of arc $PQ = 2\pi \times 6370 \times \dfrac{60}{360}$ km

$$= 6673 \text{ km}$$

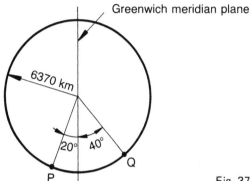

Fig. 37.3

†CIRCLES OF LATITUDE

When two places have the same latitude but different longitudes, to find the distance between them we must first find the radius of the circle of latitude.

Referring to Fig. 37.4, O is the centre of the earth and θ is the latitude. The radius of this circle of latitude is AB and

$$AB = R\cos\theta$$

where R is the radius of the earth.

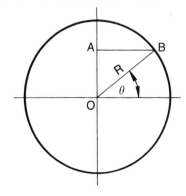

Fig. 37.4

EXAMPLE 2

(1) Find the distance along the parallel of latitude between two places which have the latitude 30°N and which differ in longitude by 60°.

If r (Fig. 37.5) is the radius of the circle of latitude then

$$r = R\cos\theta = 6370 \times \cos 30° \text{ km} = 5516 \text{ km}$$

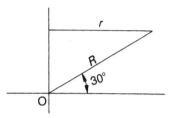

Fig. 37.5

If, in Fig. 37.6, A and B represent the two places then the problem boils down to finding the length of the arc AB.

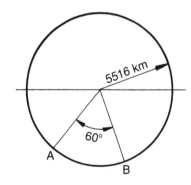

Fig. 37.6

Length of arc $AB = 2\pi \times 5516 \times \dfrac{60}{360}$ km

$$= 5777 \text{ km}$$

Therefore distance along the parallel of latitude between the two places is 5777 km.

(2) P and Q are both in latitude 50°N and the distance between them, measured along the parallel of latitude, is 2000 km. The longitude of P is 16.8°W and Q is situated west of P. Calculate the longitude of Q.

The first step is to find the radius of the circle of latitude. Thus,

$$r = R\cos 50° = 6370 \times \cos 50° \text{ km} = 4095 \text{ km}$$

The problem now boils down to finding the angle ϕ (Fig. 37.7).

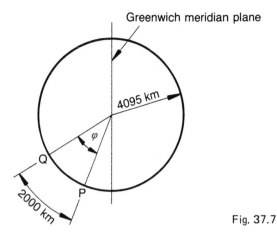

Fig. 37.7

$$2000 = 2\pi \times 4095 \times \frac{\phi}{360}$$

$$\therefore \qquad \phi = \frac{2000 \times 360}{2\pi \times 4095} = 28°$$

The longitude of Q is

$$28° + 16.8° = 44.8°W$$

†**Exercise 167** – *All type B*

(Take the radius of the earth as 6370 km.)

1) The latitudes of two places A and B are 43°N and 12°S and they both lie on the same meridian. Find the distance between them measured along the meridian.

2) The latitudes of two places P and Q are 17°S and 35°S and they both lie on the same meridian. Find the distance between them measured along the meridian.

3) The latitudes of two places are 30.9°N and 9.1°S and they both lie on the same meridian. Find the distance between them measured along the meridian.

4) Find the radius of the circle of latitude 30°S.

5) Find the distance along the parallel of latitude between two places both having a latitude of 60°N which differ in longitude by 40°.

6) The position of Leningrad is Lat. 60°N, Long. 34°E.
(a) Calculate the distance from Leningrad to the north Pole.
(b) Calculate the longitude of the point P that you will reach if you travel this distance due east from Leningrad.

7) A classroom globe has a radius of 22.5 cm. Calculate, in centimetres, the distance, measured along their line of latitude, between two cities both in latitude 50.5°N and in longitudes 5°E and 13.5°E.

8) A ship steamed 500 km due E from A (latitude 20°N, longitude 40°W) to B and then 300 km due N from B to C. Calculate the latitude and longitude of C to the nearest minute.

9) A ship sails due south from a port in latitude 24°S, longitude 46.3°W to a point in latitude 38°S. Find the distance that the ship has travelled. The ship now turns and travels the same distance due east along the line of latitude 38°S. Calculate the new longitude.

10) (a) The distance measured along a parallel of latitude, between two points of longitude 24°W and 28°W respectively is 300 km. Calculate the latitude of either point.
(b) Calculate the great circle distance of Vladivostock (43.2°N, 132°E) from the equator.

CHAPTER 37 SUMMARY

Points to remember

(i)   A great circle is a section made by a plane passing through the centre of the sphere. E.g. the equator is a great circle of the earth.

(ii) Small circles on the surface of the earth parallel to the equator are called **parallels of latitude**.

(iii) The prime meridian is half of a great circle through the north and south Poles and Greenwich, England.

(iv) The angular distance of a point east or west of the prime meridian is called the longitude of the point.

(v)   The angular distance north or south of the equator is called the latitude of the point.

1) Fig. E5.1 shows a roof window ABCD hinged along AD and supported in the open position by a rod EC, as shown in the diagram.

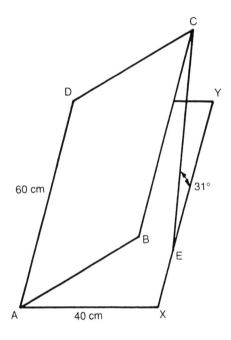

Fig. E5.1

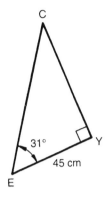

Fig. E5.1a

AXYD shows the position of the window when closed. Given that AD = 60 cm, CD = 40 cm, EX = 15 cm and EC makes an angle of 31° with XY, calculate:
(a) The length CY.
(b) The length EC.
(c) The angle through which the window has been opened.

(a) $EY = (60 - 15)\,cm = 45\,cm$

CY is perpendicular to EY

$\therefore$ $\triangle CEY$ is right-angled at Y.

$$\tan 31° = \frac{CY}{EY} = \frac{CY}{45}$$

$\therefore$ $CY = 45 \tan 31° = 27.0\,cm$

(b) Since $\angle CYE = 90°$

$$EC^2 = EY^2 + YC^2$$
$$= 45^2 + 27^2 = 2754$$

$\therefore$ $EC = \sqrt{2754} = 52.5\,cm$

(c) The angle between the two planes ABCD and AXYD $= \angle BAX$

In $\triangle ABX$, $AB = AX = 40\,cm$
$$BX = CY = 27\,cm$$

Draw AL perpendicular to BX.

$\therefore$ $BL = \frac{1}{2}BX$ (since AB = AX)
$$= 13.5\,cm$$

$$\sin \angle BAL = \frac{BL}{AB} = \frac{13.5}{40} = 0.3375$$

$\therefore$ $\angle BAL = 19.7°$
$\therefore$ $\angle BAX = 39.4°$

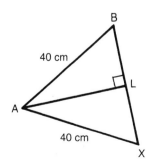

Fig. E5.1b

2) (a) Two points on the same meridian of longitude have latitudes differing by 60°. Calculate the distance between them, measured along the meridian, in kilometres, taking the radius of the earth as 6400 km and π as 3.14.

(b) Points on the circle of latitude $x°N$ are just visible from a satellite H km above the North Pole, where

$$\sin x = \frac{6400}{H + 6400}.$$

(i) Find the latitude when $H = 1600$.

(ii) Find the height of the satellite when $\sin x = 0.9$.

(a) Let the distance between the 2 places be s

$$\therefore \qquad s = 2\pi R \frac{60}{360}$$

where R = radius of the earth.

$$\therefore \qquad s = 2 \times 3.14 \times 6400 \times \frac{60}{360}$$

$$= 6699 \text{ km}$$

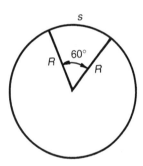

Fig. E5.2

(b) (i) $\sin x = \dfrac{6400}{H + 6400}$

$$= \frac{6400}{1600 + 6400} = \frac{6400}{8000} = \frac{64}{80}$$

$$= 0.8$$

$$\therefore \quad x = 53.1°$$

$$\therefore \quad \text{Latitude} = 53.1°N$$

(ii) When $\sin x = 0.9$

$$0.9 = \frac{6400}{H + 6400}$$

$$\therefore \quad 0.9(H + 6400) = 6400$$

$$\therefore \quad 0.9H + 5760 = 6400$$

$$\therefore \quad 0.9H = 6400 - 5760$$

$$= 640$$

$$\therefore \qquad H = \frac{640}{0.9} = 711$$

$$\therefore \quad \text{Height of satellite} = 711 \text{ km}$$

3) In Fig. E5.3, O is the centre of the earth, N and S are the North and South Poles. A, B and C are the centres of the circles of latitude through K, L and M.

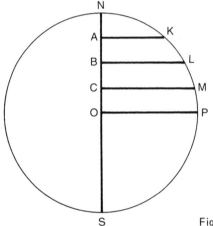

Fig. E5.3

It is given that $NA = AB = BC = CO = \frac{1}{4}R$, where R is the radius of the earth.

(a) If the latitude of K is $x°N$, prove that $\sin x = \frac{3}{4}$, and hence find this latitude.

(b) Calculate the latitude of L.

(c) Given that K, L, M all lie on the same meridian, calculate the distance KL in kilometres if $R = 6400$ km and $\pi = 3.14$.

(a) From K draw KX perpendicular to OP.

$$\sin x = \frac{KX}{OK} = \frac{AO}{R} = \frac{\frac{3}{4}R}{R}$$

$$= \frac{3}{4}.$$

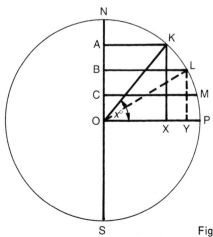

Fig. E5.3a

(b) Latitude of $L = \angle LOP$

$$\sin \angle LOP = \frac{LY}{OL} = \frac{BO}{R} = \frac{\frac{1}{2}R}{R}$$

$$= \frac{1}{2}.$$

$\therefore \quad \angle LOP = 30°$

$\therefore \quad$ Latitude of $L = 30°N$.

(c) $\angle KOL = \angle KOP - \angle LOP = x - \angle LOP$

But $\sin x = \frac{3}{4}$ $\quad \therefore \quad x = 48.6°$

$\angle KOL = 48.6° - 30° = 18.6°$.

$$KL = 2\pi R \frac{18.6}{360} = 2 \times 3.14 \times 6400 \times \frac{18.6}{360}$$

$$= 2076.6 \, km$$

EXAMINATION TYPE QUESTIONS 5

This exercise is divided into two sections A and B. The questions in Section A are intended to be done very quickly, but those in Section B should take about 20 minutes each to compete. All the questions are of the type found in CXC examination papers.

Section A

1)

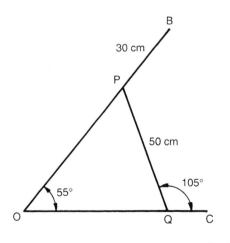

Fig. E5.4

Fig. E5.4 shows a bar OB, hinged at O and supported by a rod PQ. Given that $\angle BOC = 55°$, $\angle PQC = 105°$, $PQ = 50 \, cm$ and $PB = 30 \, cm$, calculate, to the nearest cm:
(a) QB
(b) OB.

2) An airport A is $585 \, km$ due west of a town T and V is a village $270 \, km$ from T on a bearing $030°$. An aeroplane flies on a straight course from A on a bearing $\theta°$, where $\theta < 90°$, and passes $45 \, km$ due south of V. Calculate:
(a) The distance of V east of T.
(b) The angle θ.
(c) How far the aeroplane had travelled from A before it was due north of T.

3) OPQR is a horizontal rectangular plot of land with length $OP = 72 \, m$. A vertical pole TX of height $24 \, m$ stands with its foot X on RQ. If the angle $OPX = 50°$ and the angle $POX = 40°$, calculate:
(a) The lengths of PX and PQ.
(b) The angle of elevation from P of T.

4) X and Y are two points $3 \, m$ apart on a horizontal ceiling. A rod PQ is hung from X and Y by two strings XP and YQ with the strings and rod in the same vertical plane. If $XP = 1.5 \, m$, $YQ = 2.4 \, m$, $\angle YXP = \angle XYQ = 75.8°$, calculate:
(a) The inclination of PQ to the horizontal.
(b) The length of PQ.

If YQ is shortened to $1.5 \, m$ so that PQ rests horizontally, calculate the new inclinations of the strings to the horizontal.

Section B

5)

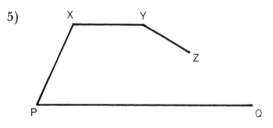

Fig. E5.5

In Fig. E5.5, P and Q represent two lighthouses on an island, P being $24 \, km$ due west of Q. A ship is observed at a point X, $10 \, km$ from P on a bearing $030°$. It sails $8 \, km$ due east from X until it reaches Y and then changes course until it reaches Z, the bearing of Z from P and Q being $070°$ and $320°$ respectively. Calculate:
(a) The shortest distance of X from PQ.
(b) The distance of Y from P.
(c) The distance of Z from Q.

6) ABCD is a piece of cardboard in which
$\angle B = \angle D = 90°$, AB = AD = 50 cm and
$\angle DAC = \angle BAC = 32°$. Calculate:
(a) The length of the perpendicular from D to AC.
(b) DC.

The cardboard is folded along the line AC so that the planes ACD and ACB are at right angles. Calculate $\angle DCB$ in this new position.

7) The line $\dfrac{x}{3} + \dfrac{y}{4} = 1$ cuts the x-axis at
L and the y-axis at M. Find:
(a) The coordinates of L and M.
(b) The equation of the line through L perpendicular to LM.

8) P is the point $(5, 0)$ and Q is the point $(0, 12)$. Calculate the length of PQ.
With the origin at the centre of your graph paper and using 1 cm to represent 1 unit on each axis, draw the line segment PQ.
Under a clockwise rotation of $90°$ about the origin O, the point P is mapped onto A and Q is mapped onto B. Draw the line segment AB.
Produce QP to cut BA at the point S. Write down $\cos \angle PBS$ as a fraction and hence calculate the length SB.

9) In a triangle LMN, LN = 12.0 cm, $\angle LMN = 80°$, $\angle MLN = 30°$. Calculate:
(a) The length of LM.
(b) The area of the triangle LMN.

Chapter 38 **Sets**

COLLECTIONS

A set is a word for a collection of objects, numbers, ideas, etc. Some sets have special names such as a *pack* of cards, a *fleet* of ships, a *pride* of lions and so on. However many sets do not have special names because the objects in the set are seldom considered collectively, for example the objects in a girl's handbag.

ELEMENTS

The different objects, numbers, etc. which form a set are called the *members* or elements of the set, just as the people who belong to a club are called members of the club.

The elements of a set may be specified in two ways:

(a) by listing the elements,
(b) by description.

Some examples are:

Listing	Description
{2, 4, 6, 8, 10}	the set of even numbers between 1 and 11
{a, e, i, o, u}	the set of vowels in the alphabet

The elements making up the set are enclosed in curly brackets or braces { }. The braces stand for the words 'the set of' or 'the set'. Braces can also be used with descriptions. Thus the second set above could be written

$$\{\text{vowels in the alphabet}\}$$

NAMING SETS

When a set is to be used more than once a capital letter is used to denote it. Thus we might write

$$A = \{1, 3, 5, 7, 9, 11\}$$

Now consider

$$B = \{ \text{ all the even numbers} \}$$

It is not possible to list all of the elements of B and so we write

$$B = \{2, 4, 6, 8, \ldots\}$$

where the dots mean and so on.

Exercise 168 – *All type A*

Write down the members of the following sets:
1) $A = \{\text{odd numbers from 5 to 15 inclusive}\}$
2) $X = \{\text{days of the week beginning with T}\}$
3) $B = \{\text{even numbers less than 12}\}$
4) $P = \{\text{prime numbers less than 25}\}$
5) $Q = \{\text{multiples of 3 up to 33}\}$

Name each of the following sets:
6) $A = \{5, 10, 15, 20, 25\}$
7) $B = \{\text{brothers, sisters, mother, father}\}$
8) $C = \{3, 5, 7, 11, 13, 17\}$

TYPES OF SETS

A set in which all of the elements can be listed is called a *finite* set. Thus the set of coins which a collector possesses is a finite set and so is the set of even numbers between 0 and 50.

In some cases it is impossible to list all the members of a set. Such sets are called *infinite* sets. Thus the set of natural numbers is an infinite set. If $A = \{1, 2, 3, 4, \ldots\}$ then A is an infinite set because no matter which is the last number we write, we can always go one larger.

The number of elements in a set A is denoted by $n(A)$. Thus if $A = \{2, 4, 6, 8, 10\}$, $n(A) = 5$ because there are 5 elements in the set A.

A set containing no elements is called a *null* set. It is represented by { } or by Ø (the Danish letter oe). The set of whole numbers between 0.5 and 0.9 is null and so is the set of prime numbers between 8 and 11.

Exercise 169 – *All type A*

Say which of the following sets are finite, infinite or null:

1) $A = \{1, 3, 5, 7, 9, \ldots\}$

2) $B = \{2, 4, 6, 8, 10, 12\}$

3) The set of points on the circumference of a circle.

4) The set of letters in the alphabet.

5) The set of even numbers which can be divided exactly by 3.

6) The set of odd numbers which can be exactly divided by 2.

7) The set of planets in the solar system.

8) The set of people that have swam the Atlantic Ocean.

9) If $A = \{a, b, c, d\}$ what is $n(A)$?

10) $B = \{2, 4, 6, 8, 10, 12, 14, 16, 18, 20\}$. Write down the value of $n(B)$.

Exercise 170 – *All type A*

In the following sets one of the elements is incorrect. Rewrite the set correctly and state, using set notation, the element which is not a member of the corrected set.

1) $P = \{2, 4, 7, 8, 10\}$

2) $Q = \{1, 4, 9, 18, 25, 36\}$

3) $R = \{17, 14, 11, 9, 5, 2\}$

4) $S = \{a, b, c, \phi, e, f\}$

5) $T = \{5, 9, 11, 13, 17, 19, 23, 29\}$

State which of the following statements are true:

6) $7 \in \{\text{prime factors of } 63\}$

7) Cod $\in \{\text{fish}\}$

8) $24 \notin \{\text{multiples of } 5\}$

9) hexagon $\in \{\text{quadrilaterals}\}$

10) octagon $\notin \{\text{polygons}\}$

MEMBERSHIP OF A SET

The symbol $\in$ means 'is a member of'. Thus if

$$A = \{3, 5, 7, 9\}$$

the fact that 5 is a member of A is written $5 \in A$.

The symbol $\notin$ means 'is not a member of'. Because 4 is not a member of A we write $4 \notin A$.

EXAMPLE 1

In the set $P = \{1, 6, 11, 17, 21, 26\}$ the sequence of numbers should be such that the difference between successive ones is 5, but one of the elements is incorrect. Rewrite the set correctly and, using set notation, state which element is not a member of the connected set.

The corrected set is

$$P = \{1, 6, 11, 16, 21, 26\}$$

In the corrected set 17, which appeared in the original set, is not a member and we write

$$17 \notin P$$

SUBSETS

Four groups of people belonging to a youth club are taking part in different activities. The first group is listening to records, the second is playing table tennis, the third is preparing for a concert and the fourth group is listening to a talk.

All the people in the four groups are contained in the set of members of the youth club but each of the groups form a set in their own right. Each of the groups forms a subset of the set of members of the youth club. A subset can be the set of all the members of the club because the leader of the club might want to talk to all the members of the club as well as to each individual group. The leader may choose not to talk to any of the groups and hence the null set is also a subset of the set of members of the club.

$\{1, 3, 5\}$ is a subset of $\{1, 3, 5, 7, 9\}$ because each of the three elements of $\{1, 3, 5\}$ is also an element of $\{1, 3, 5, 7, 9\}$. To indicate that one set is a subset of another we use the symbol $\subset$, which means 'is contained in'. Thus $\{3\} \subset \{1, 3, 5\}$ and $\{1, 3, 5\} \subset \{1, 3, 5, 7, 9\}$. These two statements could written

$$\{3\} \subset \{1, 3, 5\} \subset \{1, 3, 5, 7, 9\}$$

Out of the set $\{7, 8, 9\}$ we can select either 0 elements, 1 element, 2 elements or 3 elements as follows:

(a) $\{\ \}$ (b) $\{7\}$ (c) $\{8\}$
(d) $\{9\}$ (e) $\{7, 8\}$ (f) $\{7, 9\}$
(g) $\{8, 9\}$ (h) $\{7, 8, 9\}$

The two extremes, the null set and the original set, are regarded as subsets of the original set as pointed out above. Thus every set is a subset of itself and the null set is a subset of every set. The sets numbered (b) to (g) inclusive are called *proper* subsets.

The symbol $\subset$ can be used the other way round. Thus if $C = \{2, 4, 6, 8\}$ and $D = \{4, 6\}$ we can write $C \supset D$, i.e. C contains D.

RELATIONS BETWEEN NUMBER SYSTEMS

Counting numbers or **natural numbers** are the numbers $1, 2, 3, 4, \ldots$.

Whole numbers includes natural numbers and also zero. Note that 0 is not a natural number.

Integers are whole numbers but they include negative numbers. Some examples are -27, $-3, 0, 5, 42$.

Rational numbers are numbers which can be expressed as a fraction whose numerator is an integer and whose denominator is a nonzero integer. Thus if Q represents the set of rational numbers

$$Q = \{\text{numbers which can be expressed as } \frac{a}{b}$$
$$\text{when } a \text{ and } b \text{ are integers and } b \neq 0\}$$

Zero is a rational number because it can be the numerator of a fraction whose denominator is not zero. Thus $\frac{0}{3}$ and $\frac{0}{8}$ are rational numbers having a value of 0.

Types of rational numbers

(1) All integers. For example, 8 can be expressed as $\frac{8}{1}$.

(2) Fractions whose denominators do not equal 0. Thus $\frac{2}{3}$ and $\frac{3}{4}$ are rational numbers as are $\frac{-3}{5}$ and $\frac{2}{-3}$.

(3) Decimals which have a limited number of decimal places. Thus 3.28 is rational because it can be expressed as $\frac{328}{1000}$.

(4) Recurring decimals such as $0.\dot{3}$ and $0.\dot{2}7\dot{2}$ because they represent the fractions $\frac{1}{3}$ and $\frac{2}{11}$.

Irrational numbers cannot be expressed as the ratio of two integers. Some examples are $\sqrt{2}$ and $\sqrt{6}$.

Real numbers include all the rational and irrational numbers.

If $N = \{\text{natural numbers}\}$, $W = \{\text{whole numbers}\}$, $Z = \{\text{integers}\}$, $Q = \{\text{rational numbers}\}$ and $R = \{\text{real numbers}\}$, then $N \subset W \subset Z \subset Q \subset R$. That is all natural numbers are included in the set of whole numbers which are included in the set of integers which are included in the set of rational numbers which are included in the set of real numbers.

THE NUMBER OF SUBSETS

If there are n members in a set then the number of subsets that can be formed is given by the formula

$$N = 2^n$$

Hence, if there are 4 members in a set, the number of subsets that can be formed is

$$N = 2^4 = 16$$

Exercise 171 – *All type B*

1) $A = \{3, 5, 6, 8, 9, 11, 12, 13, 15\}$.
List the subsets whose members are:

(a) all the odd numbers of A;
(b) all the even numbers of A;
(c) all the prime numbers in A;
(d) all the numbers in A divisible by 2.

2) $B = \{5, 10, 15, 20\}$. Form *all* the subsets of B. How many are there?

3) If $A = \{3, 6, 9, 12, 15\}$, $B = \{3, 6, 7, 12\}$ and $C = \{3, 12\}$, state which of the following statements are correct:

a $A \subset B$ **b** $B \subset A$ **c** $C \subset A$
d $C \subset B$ **e** $C \subset B \subset A$

4) If $A = \{1, 3\}$, $B = \{1, 3, 5, 7\}$ and $C = \{1, 3, 5\}$ is the statement $A \subset B \subset C$ correct? If not write down the correct statement.

5) Write down all the proper subsets of $\{a, b, c, d\}$.

6) Below are given eight sets. Connect appropriate sets by the symbol $\subset$.

(a) {natural numbers between 1 and 24}
(b) {all cutlery}
(c) {all footwear}
(d) {letters of the alphabet}
(e) {boot, shoe}
(f) {a, e, i, o, u}
(g) {2, 4, 6, 8}
(h) {knife, fork, spoon}.

7) A = {all sports}. List:

(a) a subset of A containing three sports played with a ball
(b) a subset of A containing three sports generally played by girls
(c) four sports not played with a ball.

8) If A = {2, 4, 6, 8, 10} say which of the following statements are correct:

a $2 \in A$ **b** $8 \notin A$
c $7 \in A$ **d** $\{6, 8\} \subset A$
e $\{3, 4\} \subset A$ **f** $\{2, 6, 8\} \supset A$
g $A \supset \{4, 6\}$ **h** $A \subset \{3, 8\}$

9) A set has 5 members. How many subsets can be formed from it?

10) If P = {2, 4, 6, 8, 10, 12, 14, 16}, how many subsets can be formed from P?

EQUALITY

The order in which the elements of a set are written does not matter. Thus {1, 3, 5, 7} is the same as {5, 3, 7, 1} and {3, 1, 7, 5}.

Two sets are said to be equal if their elements are identical. Thus if A = {2, 4, 6, 8} and B = {8, 6, 2, 4} then, because the elements in A are the same as those in B, $A = B$.

If two sets are not equal we use the symbol $\neq$ (meaning not equal to). Thus if A = {3, 5, 7, 9} and B = {2, 4, 6, 8} then $A \neq B$.

THE UNIVERSAL SET

Frequently we use sets which are subsets of much larger sets. Thus suppose that in a class in a school we are asked to form sets (a) of those who like playing hockey, (b) of those who wear spectacles and (c) of those who cycle to school. Each of these sets is a subset of {class}. The class in this case is the universal set.

The universal set is represented by the symbol $\mathcal{E}$, an abbreviation for ensemble, which is the French word for set.

If $\mathcal{E}$ = {natural numbers} then if A = {even numbers} and B = {odd numbers} then $A \subset \mathcal{E}$ and $B \subset \mathcal{E}$.

Exercise 172 – *All type B*

1) $\mathcal{E}$ = {letters of the alphabet}. Give the subsets:

(a) of vowels,
(b) of letters after t,
(c) of consonants.

2) $\mathcal{E}$ = {all polygons}. Write down the subset of polygons with less than nine sides.

3) $\mathcal{E}$ = {natural numbers}. Give the subsets of:

(a) prime numbers less than 20,
(b) numbers less than 20 which are multiples of 3,
(c) all the prime factors of 210.

4) $\mathcal{E}$ = {months of the year}. Write down the subsets of:

(a) the winter months,
(b) the autumn months.

5) $\mathcal{E}$ = {squares of natural numbers}. Write down the subset of the squares of the first five natural numbers (i.e. 1, 2, 3, 4, 5).

SET BUILDER NOTATION

Another way of describing a set is to state a condition which is satisfied by the elements of the set and by no other elements. For example, the equation $x^2 - x = 2$ is only satisfied by certain real numbers. It is satisfied when $x = 2$, since $2^2 - 2 = 2$ and when $x = -1$ since $(-1)^2 - (-1) = 2$. It is *not* satisfied by any other real numbers. Hence the set which satisfies the equation $x^2 - x = 2$ is {−1, 2}.

This set may be described as $\{x : x^2 - x = 2\}$ which is read as 'the set x such that $x^2 - x = 2$'. When a set is described in this way we are using set builder notation.

Set builder notation is very useful when we cannot possibly or cannot conveniently list all the members of a set. Thus suppose we are discussing the set P of all the fifth formers in the Caribbean. Then the set of all fifth formers who live in Jamaica is defined by the condition living in Jamaica. We can denote this set as:

$$\{x \in P: x \text{ lives in Jamaica}\}$$

Similarly the set of all fifth formers in the Caribbean who are over 16 years of age may be denoted by:

$$\{x \in P; x \text{ is over 16 years old}\}$$

EXAMPLE 2

Show that

$$\{x: 2 \leqslant x \leqslant 4\} \subset \{x: 1 \leqslant x \leqslant 7\}.$$

$$\{x: 1 \leqslant x \leqslant 7\} = \{x: 1, 2, 3, 4, 5, 6, 7\}$$

and

$$\{x: 2 \leqslant x \leqslant 4\} = \{2, 3, 4\}$$

Hence

$$\{x: 2 \leqslant x \leqslant 4\} \subset \{x: 1 \leqslant x \leqslant 7\}$$

VENN DIAGRAMS

Sets and set problems may be represented by diagrams called Venn diagrams, after mathematician Joseph Venn who lived in the nineteenth century and who first represented sets diagrammatically.

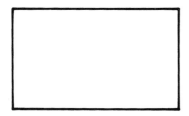

Fig. 38.1

A universal set is represented by a rectangle (Fig. 38.1). If the universal set is $\mathcal{E} = \{\text{class}\}$ then all the children in the class would be represented by all the points inside the rectangle or on its perimeter. All the children in the class who cycled to school would be a subset to the universal set. If we use the letter C to represent this subset, then a circle drawn within the rectangle shows that C is a subset of $\mathcal{E}$ or $C \subset \mathcal{E}$ (Fig. 38.2).

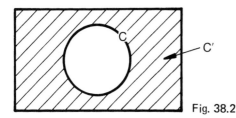

Fig. 38.2

COMPLEMENT

The shaded part of the rectangle in Fig. 38.2 is called the *complement* of the set C and is written C'. It represents all the children in the class who do not cycle to school.

EXAMPLE 3

The universal set is $\mathcal{E} = \{1, 2, 3, 4, 5, 6\}$. If $A = \{1, 3, 5\}$ find the complement of A.

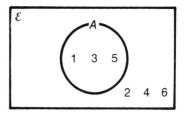

Fig. 38.3

The Venn diagram is shown in Fig. 38.3. The subset A is represented by the circle which contains the numbers 1, 3 and 5 which are the elements of A. The numbers outside the circle, 2, 4 and 6, form the complement of A and hence $A' = \{2, 4, 6\}$.

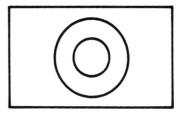

Fig. 38.4

Subsets of a given set are represented by a circle within a circle as shown in Fig. 38.4. If $\mathcal{E} = \{1, 2, 3, 4, 5, 6, 7, 8\}$ and $A = \{2, 3, 4, 5, 6\}$ then $A \subset \mathcal{E}$. If $B = \{3, 4\}$ then $B \subset A \subset \mathcal{E}$. This is represented as shown in Fig. 38.5.

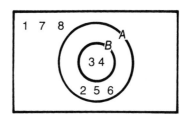

Fig. 38.5

INTERSECTION

The intersection of two sets A and B is the set of elements which are members of both A and B. The shaded portion of Fig. 38.6 represents the intersection of A and B.

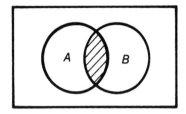

Fig. 38.6

The intersection of A and B is written, in set notation, as $A \cap B$, which is read as 'A intersection B'.

EXAMPLE 4

If $A = \{1, 3, 5, 7, 9\}$ and $B = \{7, 9, 11\}$ find $A \cap B$.

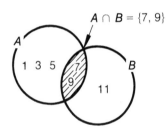

Fig. 38.7

As shown in Fig. 38.7, $A \cap B = \{7, 9\}$. Note that the intersection of A and B is the set which contains all the elements common to both A and B. If there are no common elements in two sets the Venn diagram would look like Fig. 38.8. Thus if $A = \{1, 3, 5, 7\}$ and $B = \{2, 4, 6, 8\}$ then $A \cap B = \emptyset$, $\emptyset$ being the null set. When there is no intersection between two or more sets the sets are said to be *disjoint*. Thus in Fig. 38.8, the sets A and B are disjoint.

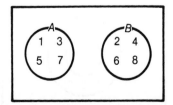

Fig. 38.8

UNION

The union of two sets A and B is all of the elements contained in A or B. Thus if $A = \{3, 4, 5\}$ and $B = \{6, 7, 8\}$ then the union of A and B is $\{3, 4, 5, 6, 7, 8\}$.

If this set is called C then we write $C = A \cup B$, which is read as 'A union B', the symbol $\cup$ standing for 'union'. The Venn diagram (Fig. 38.9) shows $C = A \cup B$, the shaded portion representing C.

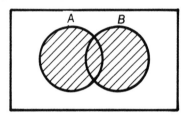

Fig. 38.9

EXAMPLE 5

If $S = \{1, 3, 5, 7\}$ and $R = \{7, 9, 11\}$, write down $S \cup R$.

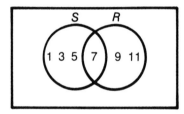

Fig. 38.10

As shown in Fig. 38.10,

$$S \cup R = \{1, 3, 5, 7, 9, 11\}$$

Note that the element 7, which is contained in both S and R, appears only once in the union of S and R.

Exercise 173 – *All type B*

Fig. 38.11 shows the universal set $\mathcal{E}$ and the two subsets A and B. For each of the following write down the answer in the way suggested.

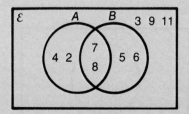

Fig. 38.11

1) Write down all the elements of the universal set. $\mathcal{E} = \{$ $\}$.

2) Write down all the elements of set A.
$A = \{$ $\}$.

3) Write down all the elements of set B.
$B = \{$ $\}$.

4) Write down the complement of A.
$A' = \{$ $\}$.

5) Write down the complement of B.
$B' = \{$ $\}$.

6) Write down $A \cap B$. $A \cap B = \{$ $\}$.

7) Write down $A \cup B$. $A \cup B = \{$ $\}$.

8) Write down the complement of $(A \cup B)$.
$(A \cup B)' = \{$ $\}$.

Link each of the following with one or more of the symbols $\mathcal{E}, \in, \notin, =, \neq, \subset, \supset, \cup$, or $\cap$.

9) 7 $\{2, 4, 6, 8\}$.

10) $\{1, 3, 5, 7\}$ $\{2, 3, 5, 6\}$ $\{3, 5\}$.

11) 8 $\{4, 8, 16, 32\}$.

12) $\{3, 4, 6\}$ $\{6, 3, 4\}$.

13) $\{$rectangles, triangles$\}$ $\{$all plane figures$\}$.

14) $\{1, 3, 5, 7, 9\}$ $\{5, 7\}$.

15) $\{2, 4, 6, 8\}$ $\{3, 5, 7, 9, 11\}$.

16) $\{2, 4\}$ $\{2, 4, 8, 9\}$ $\{1, 2, 4, 8, 9\}$.

17) John $\{$all girl's names$\}$.

18) $\{7, 14, 21, 28\}$ $\{$multiples of 7$\}$.

19) $\{x: 1 \leqslant x \leqslant 7\}$ $\{2, 3, 4, 5, 6, 7\}$.

20) $\{x: 3 \leqslant x \leqslant 5\}$ $\{x: 1 \leqslant x \leqslant 10\}$.

The Venn diagram (Fig. 38.12) shows two sets A and B. Copy and complete:

21) $A = \{$ $\}$.

22) $B = \{$ $\}$.

23) $A \cup B = \{$ $\}$.

24) $A \cap B = \{$ $\}$.

25) A B.

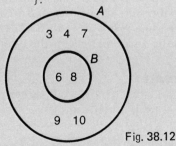

Fig. 38.12

The Venn diagram (Fig. 38.13) shows two sets A and B which are subsets of the universal set $\mathcal{E}$. Copy and complete the following:

26) $\mathcal{E} = \{$ $\}$.

27) $A = \{$ $\}$.

28) $B = \{$ $\}$.

29) $A \cap B = \{$ $\}$.

30) $A \cup B = \{$ $\}$.

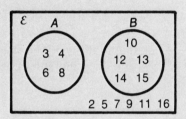

Fig. 38.13

Fig. 38.14 shows a Venn diagram representing the universal set and two subsets. Draw a similar diagram, inserting the elements, to represent each of the following:

31) $\mathcal{E} = \{1, 2, 3, 4, 5, 6, 7, 8, 9, 10\}$,
$A = \{1, 2, 3, 4\}$, $B = \{4, 5, 6, 7, 8\}$.

32) $\mathcal{E} = \{$a, b, c, d, e, f, g, h$\}$, $A = \{$a, b, c, d$\}$,
$A \cap B = \{$c, d$\}$, $A \cup B = \{$a, b, c, d, g, h$\}$.

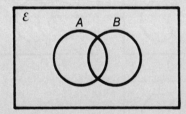

Fig. 38.14

Fig. 38.15 shows three Venn diagrams. Using diagrams similar to these, represent the following:

33) $\mathcal{E} = \{x: 5 \leqslant x \leqslant 12\}$,
$X = \{6, 7, 9, 10, 11\}$, $Y = \{6, 7\}$.

34) $\mathcal{E} = \{x: 3 \leqslant x \leqslant 10\}$, $A = \{4, 5\}$,
$B = \{6, 7\}$.

35) $\mathcal{E} = \{$natural numbers between 1 and 9$\}$,
$P = \{3, 4, 5, 6\}$, $Q = \{5, 6, 7, 8, 9\}$.

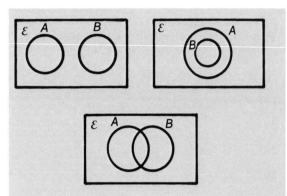

Fig. 38.15

36) Use set notation to describe the shaded portions of the Venn diagrams shown in Fig. 38.16.

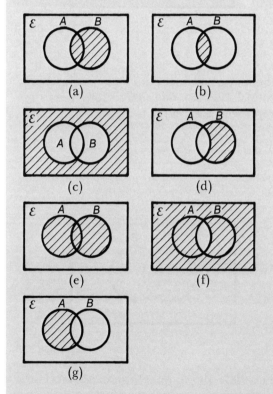

(a)   (b)

(c)   (d)

(e)   (f)

(g)

Fig. 38.16

37) Draw a Venn diagram to represent the following information.

$$\mathcal{E} = \{A, B, C, D, E, F, G, H\}$$
$$X = \{A, B, C, D\}$$
$$Y = \{C, D, E, F, G\}$$

PROBLEMS WITH INTERSECTIONS AND UNIONS

So far we have dealt with the intersection and union of only two sets. It is quite usual for there to be intersections between three or more sets.

In the Venn diagram (Fig. 38.17) the three sets A, B and C intersect. The shaded portion represents $A \cap B \cap C$.

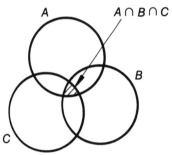

Fig. 38.17

EXAMPLE 6

If $A = \{1, 2, 3, 4, 5\}$, $B = \{2, 3, 5, 6\}$ and $C = \{2, 5, 6, 7\}$, determine:

(a) $A \cap (B \cap C)$,
(b) $(A \cap B) \cap C$.

(a) In problems of this kind always work out the brackets first. Thus:

$$B \cap C = \{2, 5, 6\}$$

Then,

$$A \cap (B \cap C)$$
$$= \{1, 2, 3, 4, 5\} \cap \{2, 5, 6\} = \{2, 5\}$$

(b) Working out the bracket we have,

$$A \cap B = \{2, 3, 5\}$$

Then

$$(A \cap B) \cap C$$
$$= \{2, 3, 5\} \cap \{2, 5, 6, 7\} = \{2, 5\}$$

It will be noticed that the way in which we group A, B and C makes no difference to the final result. That is, $A \cap (B \cap C)$ produces the same result as $(A \cap B) \cap C$. This is known as the *associative law* for the intersection of sets.

EXAMPLE 7

If $A = \{3, 4\}$, $B = \{2, 4, 6, 8\}$ and $C = \{3, 6, 8, 10\}$ find:

(a) $A \cup (B \cup C)$
(b) $(A \cup B) \cup C$.

(a) Again, working out the brackets first we have,

$$B \cup C = \{2, 3, 4, 6, 8, 10\}$$

Then

$$A \cup (B \cup C) = \{3, 4\} \cup \{2, 3, 4, 6, 8, 10\}$$

$$= \{2, 3, 4, 6, 8, 10\}$$

(b) $A \cup B = \{2, 3, 4, 6, 8\}$

$$(A \cup B) \cup C = \{2, 3, 4, 6, 8\} \cup \{3, 6, 8, 10\}$$

$$= \{2, 3, 4, 6, 8, 10\}$$

We see that the associative law is again applicable because we have shown that

$$A \cup (B \cup C) = (A \cup B) \cup C$$

Exercise 174 – *All type B*

If $A = \{2, 3, 5, 7\}$, $B = \{2, 3, 4, 6\}$ and $C = \{2, 5, 6, 7\}$, list the following sets:

1) $A \cap (B \cap C)$

2) $(A \cap B) \cap C$

3) $B \cup (A \cup C)$

4) $A \cup (B \cup C)$

5) $(A \cap B) \cup (B \cap C)$

Given that $\mathcal{E} = \{1, 2, 3, 4, 5, 6, 7, 8, 9\}$, $A = \{2, 3, 4, 5\}$ and $B = \{4, 5, 7, 8\}$ list the following sets:

6) $A \cup (A' \cap B)$

7) $B \cup (A' \cap B)$

8) $A' \cap (A \cap B')$

9) $B' \cup (A \cap B')$

10) $A \cup (A' \cap B')$

THE NUMBER OF ELEMENTS IN A SET

The number of elements in a set A is denoted by $n(A)$. Thus if $A = \{1, 3, 5, 7, 9\}$ then $n(A) = 5$ because there are 5 elements in the set A. We can, if we wish, write $n\{1, 3, 5, 7, 9\} = 5$.

Consider the two sets $A = \{1, 2, 3, 4, 5\}$ and $B = \{3, 5, 7, 9\}$ (see Fig. 38.18).

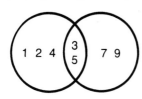

Fig. 38.18

$$A \cup B = \{1, 2, 3, 4, 5, 7, 9\}$$

$$A \cap B = \{3, 5\}$$

$$n(A) = n\{1, 2, 3, 4, 5\} = 5$$

$$n(B) = n\{3, 5, 7, 9\} = 4$$

$$n(A \cap B) = n\{3, 5\} = 2$$

$$n(A \cup B) = n\{1, 2, 3, 4, 5, 7, 9\} = 7$$

The equation connecting the four sets can be seen to be

$$n(A \cup B) = n(A) + (B) - n(A \cap B)$$

It can be shown that this equation applies to any two sets which intersect.

EXAMPLE 8

If $n(A) = 20$, $n(B) = 30$ and $n(A \cup B) = 40$, find $n(A \cap B)$.

Using the equation:

$$n(A \cup B) = n(A) + n(B) - n(A \cap B)$$

we have

$$40 = 20 + 30 - n(A \cap B)$$

$$n(A \cap B) = 20 + 30 - 40 = 10$$

EXAMPLE 9

In a school of 150 pupils, 85 take physics and 115 take mathematics. Each pupil takes at least one of these subjects. How many take both?

Let $\quad\quad\quad\quad P =$ set of physics pupils

$\quad\quad\quad\quad\quad\quad M =$ set of mathematics

and $\quad\quad\quad\quad\quad\quad$ pupils

Then $\quad\quad n(P) = 85 =$ number taking physics

$\quad\quad\quad n(M) = 115 =$ number taking mathematics

$\quad\quad\quad n(P \cup M) = 150 =$ total number of pupils

$\quad\quad\quad n(P \cap M) =$ number taking both mathematics and physics

Using the equation:

$$n(P \cup M) = n(P) + n(M) - n(P \cap M)$$

$$150 = 85 + 115 - n(P \cap M)$$

$$n(P \cap M) = 85 + 115 - 150 = 50$$

Hence 50 pupils take both mathematics and physics.

EXAMPLE 10

The entries on the diagram (Fig. 38.19) show the number of elements in sets A and B. The number of elements in A is equal to the number of elements in B. Find:

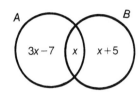

Fig. 38.19

(a) x (b) $n(A)$ (c) $n(B)$
(d) $n(A \cup B)$.

(a) The number of elements in

$$A = n(A) = 3x - 7 + x = 4x - 7$$

The number of elements in

$$B = n(B) = x + 5 + x = 2x + 5$$

We are given that $n(A) = n(B)$.   Hence

$$4x - 7 = 2x + 5$$

$$2x = 12$$

$$x = 6$$

(b) $n(A) = 4x - 7 = 4 \times 6 - 7 = 24 - 7 = 17$

(c) $n(B) = 2x + 5 = 2 \times 6 + 5 = 12 + 5 = 17$

(d) $n(A \cup B) = n(A) + n(B) - n(A \cap B)$

$$= 17 + 17 - 6 = 28$$

†INTERSECTION OF THREE SETS

If three sets A, B and C intersect then it can be shown that

$$n(A \cup B \cup C) = n(A) + n(B) + n(C)$$

$$- n(A \cap B) - n(A \cap C)$$

$$- n(B \cap C) + n(A \cap B \cap C)$$

In Fig. 38.20,

region I + region IV
    represents $n(A \cap B)$

region II + region IV
    represents $n(B \cap C)$

region III + region IV
    represents $n(A \cap C)$

region IV
    represents $n(A \cap B \cap C)$

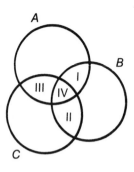

Fig. 38.20

EXAMPLE 11

The entries in Fig. 38.21 show the number of elements in the various regions. Find:

(a) $n(A)$ (b) $n(B)$
(c) $n(C)$ (d) $n(A \cap B)$
(e) $n(A \cap C)$ (f) $n(B \cap C)$
(g) $n(A \cap B \cap C)$ (h) $n(A \cup B \cup C)$

(a) $n(A) = 12 + 8 + 6 + 2 = 28$

(b) $n(B) = 8 + 2 + 13 + 5 = 28$

(c) $n(C) = 18 + 6 + 2 + 5 = 31$

(d) $n(A \cap B) = 8 + 2 = 10$

(e) $n(A \cap C) = 6 + 2 = 8$

(f) $n(B \cap C) = 5 + 2 = 7$

(g) $n(A \cap B \cap C) = 2$

(h) To find $n(A \cup B \cup C)$ we use:

$$n(A \cup B \cup C) = n(A) + n(B) + n(C)$$

$$- n(A \cap B) - n(A \cap C)$$

$$- n(B \cap C) + n(A \cap B \cap C)$$

$$= 28 + 28 + 31 - 10 - 8 - 7 + 2$$

$$= 89 - 25 = 64$$

Alternatively:

$$n(A \cup B \cup C) = 12 + 6 + 2 + 8$$

$$+ 18 + 5 + 13$$

$$= 64$$

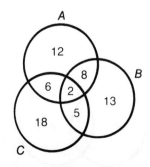

Fig. 38.21

EXAMPLE 12

Out of three recreations, gardening, reading and playing sport, 120 people were invited to state in which they were interested. 60 were interested in gardening, 86 were interested in reading and 64 were interested in playing sport. 32 gardened and read, 38 gardened and played sport and 34 read and played sport. How many were interested in all three activities?

We are given

$$n(G \cup R \cup S) = 120 \quad n(G) = 60$$

$$n(R) = 86 \quad n(S) = 64$$

$$n(G \cap R) = 32 \quad n(G \cap S) = 38$$

and

$$n(R \cap S) = 34.$$

The problem is to find $n(G \cap R \cap S)$. Using the equation,

$$n(G \cup R \cup S) = n(G) + n(R) + n(S)$$
$$- n(G \cap R) - n(G \cap S)$$
$$- n(R \cap S) + n(G \cap R \cap S)$$

$$120 = 60 + 86 + 64 - 32 - 38$$
$$- 34 + n(G \cap R \cap S)$$

$$120 = 106 + n(G \cap R \cap S)$$

$$n(G \cap R \cap S) = 120 - 106 = 14$$

Hence 14 people are interested in all three activities.

Exercise 175 – *All type C*

1) Figure 38.22 shows two intersecting sets A and B. The entries give the number of elements in each region. Find:

(a) $n(A)$ (b) $n(B)$
(c) $n(A \cap B)$ (d) $n(A \cup B)$

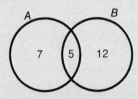

Fig. 38.22

2) The number of elements in sets A and B are shown in Fig. 38.23. Find:

(a) x (b) $n(A)$ (c) $n(B)$
(d) $n(A \cup B)$ if $n(A) = n(B)$

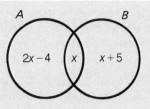

Fig. 38.23

3) 60 candidates in an examination offered history and geography. Every student takes at least one of these subjects and some take two. 55 take history and 45 take geography. How many take both?

4) In a class of 30 pupils, 18 take French and 17 take German. 3 take neither. How many take both French and German?

5) In a group of 25 boys, 18 like Association Football whilst 14 like Rugby Football. How many like both kinds of football?

†**6)** The entries in the diagram (Fig. 38.24) show the number of elements in the various regions. Find:

(a) $n(X)$ (b) $n(Y)$
(c) $n(Z)$ (d) $n(X \cap Y)$
(e) $n(X \cap Z)$ (f) $n(Y \cup Z)$
(g) $n(X \cap Y \cap Z)$ (h) $n(X \cup Y \cup Z)$

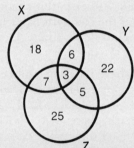

Fig. 38.24

†**7)** Figure 38.25 shows the number of elements in the various regions of a Venn diagram. If $n(A \cup B \cup C) = 150$, find

(a) x (b) $n(A)$ (c) $n(B)$
(d) $n(C)$ (e) $n(A \cap B)$
(f) $n(B \cap C)$ (g) $n(A \cap C)$

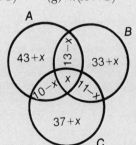

Fig. 38.25

† **8)** Out of 136 students in a school, 60 take French, 100 take chemistry and 48 take physics. If 28 take French and chemistry, 44 take chemistry and physics and 20 take French and physics, how many take all three subjects?

† **9)** In an examination, 60 candidates offered mathematics, 80 offered English and 50 offered physics. If 20 offered maths and English, 15 English and physics, 25 maths and physics and 10 offered all three, how many candidates sat the examination?

†**10)** Of 100 students, 42 take physics, 35 take chemistry and 30 take botany. 20 take none of these subjects. 9 take botany and physics, 10 take botany and chemistry and 11 take physics and chemistry. Find:

(a) the number of students that take all three subjects;
(b) the number that take physics only;
(c) the number that take botany and chemistry only.

CORRESPONDENCE AND EQUIVALENCE

It has been said, earlier in this chapter, that two sets are equal if the elements in each of them are identical. Thus if $A = \{a, e, i, o, u\}$ and $B = \{e, o, u, a, i\}$ then $A = B$.

When two sets have the same number of elements we say that a *one to one correspondence* exists. Thus if $A = \{1, 3, 5, 7, 9\}$ and $B = \{a, e, i, o, u\}$ then $n(A) = n(B) = 5$ and A and B have one to one correspondence. This is often indicated by using a two way arrow, i.e. $A \leftrightharpoons B$, meaning that the members of A can be paired off with the members of B or that the members of B can be paired off with the members of A.

If two sets possess one to one correspondence they are said to be *equivalent*. Thus if $X = \{1, 2, 3, 4, 5, 6\}$ and $Y = \{3, 5, 6, 7, 8, 9\}$ the sets X and Y are equivalent, that is, $X \leftrightharpoons Y$, because $n(X) = n(Y) = 6$. Note that two sets which are equivalent need not be equal.

There are very many examples of equivalent sets. For instance if we have six knives and six forks we can pair each knife with each fork. We have matched up all the members of the set of knives with all the members of the set of forks.

Again, when we count articles we have one to one correspondence, because in every case a number is matched with an article.

Now suppose we have articles packaged so that there are ten articles to a packet. Thus, for every packet there are 10 articles and we say that we have *one to many correspondence*. If we buy oranges at a cost of 40 cents for five oranges we get 5 oranges for 40 cents and we say that we have *many to many correspondence*.

One to many and many to many correspondence is just another way of stating a ratio. Thus 1 to 10 correspondence means the same as the ratio $1:10$ and 5 to 12 correspondence means the same as $5:12$ (see Chapter 5).

Exercise 176 – *All type B*

1) Below are two lots of five sets. Using the two way arrow, write down the sets in lot 1 which are equivalent to those in lot 2.

Lot 1. $A = \{$rectangle, square, rhombus, parallelogram$\}$

$B = \{a, b, c, d, e, f, g\}$

$C = \{$mother, father, sister$\}$

$D = \{1, 3, 5, 7, 9\}$

$E = \{$hammer, chisel, saw$\}$

$W = \{$nail, screw, rule$\}$

Lot 2. $V = \{1, 2, 3, 4, 5, 6, 7\}$

$W = \{a, e, u, o, i\}$

$X = \{$knife, fork, spoon$\}$

$Y = \{$trowel, hoe, fork, spade, stake, mower$\}$

$Z = \{$cylinder, sphere, cuboid, cone$\}$

2) State which of the following statements are true and which are false and if the statement is false, replace the symbol connecting the sets with the correct symbol:

(a) $\{m, n, o, p\} \leftrightharpoons \{2, 4, 6, 9\}$
(b) $\{1, 3, 5\} = \{3, 1, 6\}$
(c) $\{$coal, peat, wood, gas$\}$
$\quad = \{$boy, girl, man, woman$\}$
(d) $\{$screw, nail, nut, bolt, rivet$\}$
$\quad \leftrightharpoons \{1, 2, 3, 4, 5\}$

(e) $\{$lion, tiger, cat, mouse, dog, bear$\}$
$\quad = \{$chair, table, bed, settee$\}$

3) In the following statements write down the type of correspondence which has been used.

(a) 12 eggs for 50 pence.
(b) 25 pins to a packet.

(c) 50 kilograms for $2.
(d) 20 students to a class.
(e) 6 gas rings to a cooker.
(f) 12 months to a year.
(g) 5 items of cutlery to a table place.
(h) 11 players to a team.
(i) 3 pears for 20 pence.
(j) 7 chairs used by 7 people.

†SETS AND LOGICAL CHAINS

The simplest form of logical deduction is the *syllogism* in which two propositions or statements are made and a conclusion is deduced from them. Venn diagrams may be used to deduce a conclusion.

(1) John is a shopkeeper; all shopkeepers are honest. Is John honest?

The Venn diagram (Fig. 38.26) shows that {shopkeepers} are a subset of {honest people}. Since John is a member of {shopkeepers}, John is honest.

If $S = \{shopkeepers\}$
          $H = \{honest\ people\}$
Since $S \subset H$
and $John \in S$
$\Rightarrow$ $John \in H$

where $\Rightarrow$ means 'it imples that'.

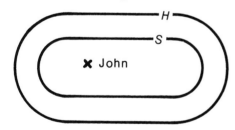

Fig. **38.26**

(2) Modesty is a virtue; good cricketers are modest. Are good cricketers virtuous?

Let $G = \{good\ cricketers\}$
          $M = \{modest\ people\}$
          $V = \{virtuous\ people\}$

The first proposition, modesty is a virtue, can be written
$$M \subset V$$

meaning that all modest people are virtuous people.

The second proposition, good cricketers are modest, can be written
$$G \subset M$$

Hence we have
$$(M \subset V, G \subset M) \Rightarrow G \subset V$$

That is, good cricketers are virtuous. The Venn diagram of Fig. 38.27 shows this in diagrammatic form.

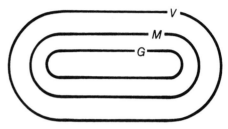

Fig. 38.27

DEDUCTION AND TRUTH

In making logical deductions we must not be concerned with the truth or otherwise of the statements. Consider the following:

(1) All angles greater than $90°$ are reflex. $\theta = 150°$. Hence θ is reflex.

If $A = \{angles\ greater\ than\ 90°\}$
and $R = \{reflex\ angles\}$
then since
$$A \subset R \quad and \quad \theta \in A \Rightarrow \theta \in R.$$

The deduction, that θ is reflex, is logical from the statement that all angles greater than $90°$ are reflex. This statement is false because only angles greater than $180°$ are reflex and hence we correctly made a false deduction.

(2) Paul wears a red shirt. All Trumpton College students wear red shirts.

It is tempting to conclude that Paul is a student at Trumpton as shown in Fig. 38.28(a), where
$$S = \{people\ who\ wear\ red\ shirts\}$$
and $T = \{students\ of\ Trumpton\ College\}$

The other alternative, that Paul does not attend Trumpton College, is shown in Fig. 38.28(b). We cannot say which conclusion is correct and we say that the propositions are inconclusive.

Note that
$$Paul \in S \quad and \quad T \in S \nRightarrow Paul \in T$$

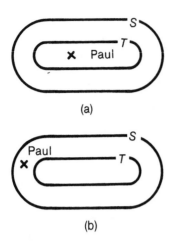

(a)

(b)

Fig. 38.28

That is, a logical chain cannot be formed between Paul and T.

To summarise,

If $\quad x \in B \quad$ and $\quad B \subset A \Rightarrow x \in A$

If $\quad x \in A \quad$ and $\quad B \subset A \nRightarrow x \in B$

Remembering these facts will help to prevent you drawing incorrect conclusions when dealing with logical chains.

SUBSETS AND COMPLEMENTS

Fig. 38.29(a) shows

$$A \subset B \subset \mathcal{E}$$

where $\mathcal{E}$ is the universal set

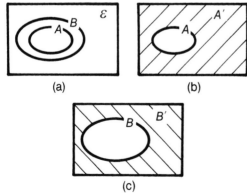

(a)   (b)

(c)

Fig. 38.29

From Figs. 39.29(b) and (c) we see that if

$$A \subset B \Longleftrightarrow B' \subset A'$$

meaning that the two statements $A \subset B$ and $B' \subset A'$ are equivalent.

Consider the propositions: all dealers are rich; no teacher is rich.

If $\quad R = \{\text{rich people}\}, \quad D = \{\text{dealers}\}$

and $\qquad\qquad T = \{\text{teachers}\}$

then the Venn diagram representing the propositions is as shown in Fig. 38.30.

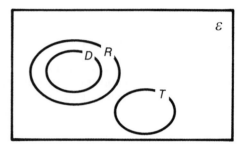

Fig. 38.30

Since $\qquad\quad R = \{\text{rich people}\}$

$\quad R' = \{\text{people who are not rich}\}$

and $\qquad\qquad T \subset R'$

Since

$$D \subset R \Longleftrightarrow R' \subset D' \Longleftrightarrow T \subset R' \subset D'$$

meaning that no teacher is a dealer.

EXAMPLE 13

All athletes train daily; unhappy people are weak; those who train daily are not weak. Form a logical chain and state the conclusions.

Let $\qquad D = \{\text{people who train daily}\}$

$\qquad\quad A = \{\text{athletes}\}$

$\qquad\quad U = \{\text{unhappy people}\}$

$\qquad\quad W = \{\text{weak people}\}$

The four sets are shown in the Venn diagram of Fig. 38.31.

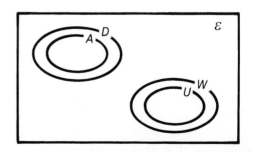

Fig. 38.31

Proposition one gives $A \subset D.$
Proposition two gives $U \subset W \iff W' \subset U'.$
Proposition three gives $D \subset W'.$

The logical chain is

$$A \subset D \subset W' \subset U'$$

We may conclude that:

(a) $A \subset W'$ (athletes are not weak).

(b) $D \subset U'$ (those who train daily are not unhappy).

(c) $A \subset U'$ (athletes are not unhappy).

Conclusion (c) which uses the whole chain is called the *major conclusion*.

Sometimes no conclusion can be reached as shown in Example 14.

INTERSECTING SETS

So far our logical problems have been such that one set was a subset of another or else the two sets were disjoint. However we often have propositions which lead to intersecting sets. For instance, the proposition, 'some girls are pretty' tells us that the sets {girls} and {pretty females} intersect as shown in Fig. 38.32.

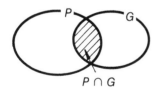

Fig. 38.32

In set notation, if $P = $ {pretty females}   and $G = $ {girls}

$$P \cap G \ \varnothing$$

EXAMPLE 14

In President's Secondary School the students study many subjects including physics, mathematics, history and literature. If a student studies physics, he studies mathematics. A student studies history if and only if he does not study physics. Every student who studies history also studies literature.

Let

$U = $ {students at President's Secondary School}

$H = $ {students who study history}

$L = $ {students who study literature}

$M = $ {students who study mathematics}

$P = $ {students who study physics}

Draw a Venn diagram to illustrate the propositions given above. Then examine each of the following statements and decide if they are true, false or inconclusive:

(a) All physics students study mathematics.

(b) Some history students study mathematics.

(c) Some literature students study history.

(d) Some students study neither physics nor history.

(e) All literature students study history.

The two Venn diagrams shown in Fig. 38.33 are possible illustrations of the propositions given.

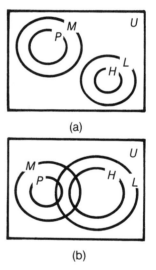

(a)

(b)   Fig. 38.33

(a) $P \subset M.$ Hence all physics students study mathematics.

(b) Inconclusive. Diagram (a) shows $H \cap M = \varnothing$ but diagram (b) shows $H \cap M \neq \varnothing.$

(c) True. All history students study literature, i.e. $H \subset L,$ and provided history is not empty, some literature students must study history.

(d) A student studies history if he does not study physics, i.e. $P' = H.$ Every student belongs to P or $P'.$ Hence the statement is false.

(e) Inconclusive. The statement is only true if $H = L$ and we do not know if this is so.

Exercise 177 – *All type D*

1) Each of the following consists of three statements. Decide whether or not the third statement is a valid conclusion from the other two and draw a Venn diagram to illustrate.

(a) All dogs are black; Bruce is a dog; Bruce is black.
(b) All students like mathematics; Erskin is a student; Erskin likes maths.
(c) Joan is a girl; Joan wears a dress; all girls wear dresses.
(d) The only people who swim well are Grenadians; John swims well; John is a Grenadian.
(e) Paul is industrious; industrious people deserve a medal; Paul deserves a medal.
(f) John likes cricket; all schoolboys like cricket; John is a schoolboy.
(g) All the boys in form II are playing cricket; Peter is in form II; Peter is playing cricket.
(h) Tom is a shopkeeper; all shopkeepers are honest; Tom is honest.

2) In the following state whether the conclusions are correct deductions from the propositions given. Illustrate with Venn diagrams.

(a) All children like ice cream; Hester does not like ice cream. Therefore Hester is not a child.
(b) All university students are hardworking; no hardworking student neglects his studies. Therefore no university student neglects his studies.
(c) All rectangles are parallelograms; a rhombus is not a rectangle. Therefore a rhombus is not a parallelogram.
(d) All Science students take Chemistry; no Literature student takes Science. Therefore no student takes both Chemistry and Literature.
(e) No university lecturers are wealthy; industrialists are wealthy. Therefore no university lecturers are industrialists.

3) In the following questions form a logical chain and state the major conclusion.

(a) Politicians speak too quickly; no teacher speaks too quickly; all speech makers are politicians.
(b) No students at Township Secondary School are illiterate; no literate people want to be unskilled workers; John is a student at Township Secondary School.
(c) All science students are mad; all prefects should cycle; no mad people should cycle.
(d) Fit people are happy; unfit people are not happy; all athletes are fit.

4) Good people (G) are great people (T). Virtuous people (V) are good people. Draw a Venn diagram to represent these statements. Are virtuous people great people?

5) All soldiers are brave; all soldiers are tough. Are all brave men tough?

6) (i) Good losers are always popular.
(ii) Happy men are never lonely.
(iii) Bad losers do not enjoy playing tennis.
(iv) Unhappy men are unpopular.

(a) Draw a Venn diagram to represent the premises given above.
(b) Are all tennis players popular?
(c) Are good losers happy men?
(d) Are men who enjoy playing tennis ever lonely?

7) The following rules apply to a certain club:
(i) When a tie is not worn, a scarf must be worn.
(ii) When a tie and scarf are both worn, a hat must not be worn.
(iii) When a hat is worn or a tie not worn, a scarf must not be worn.

Show that these rules mean:

(a) A tie must be worn on all occasions.
(b) A hat and scarf must never be worn together.

8) Study the following premises:
(i) Abstract thinkers are not practical men.
(ii) Mathematicians always use symbols.
(iii) Non-practical men believe in immortality.
(iv) Non-abstract thinkers do not use symbols.

Now answer the following questions:

(a) Are mathematicians practical men?
(b) Do mathematicians believe in immortality?
(c) Are men who use symbols practical men?

9) In a secondary school, if a student studies chemistry then mathematics is also studied. A student studies literature only if chemistry is not studied. Everyone who studies literature also studies English language. Fig. 38.34 shows two possible Venn diagrams where

$\mathcal{E}$ = {students at the secondary school}

C = {students who study chemistry}

M = {students who study mathematics}

E = {students who study English language}

L = {students who study literature}

Examine the following statements and decide if each is true (T), false (F) or inconclusive (I).

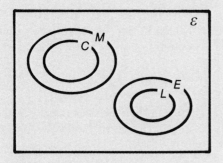

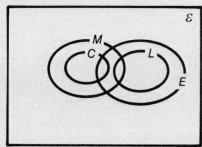

Fig. 38.34

(a) All chemistry students study mathematics.
(b) Some literature students study mathematics.
(c) Some English language students study literature.
(d) Some students study neither chemistry nor literature.
(e) All English language students study literature.

10) Study the following statements:
 (i) Some directors of companies own expensive cars.
 (ii) All directors of companies earn high salaries.
 (iii) All directors are honest.

Now examine the following statements and decide if each is true (T), false (F) or inconclusive (I).

(a) All honest people earn large salaries.
(b) Some honest people own expensive cars.
(c) All people earning large salaries own expensive cars.

11) Some pupils at this school do not play football but all of the pupils play either football or hockey. Some hockey players are also footballers and all hockey players play cricket. Examine these statements and then answer the following questions:

(a) Do all footballers play cricket?
(b) Do some play football only?
(c) Are all hockey players?
(d) Do all play football or cricket?
(e) Do all play hockey or cricket?

SELF-TEST 38

1) Which one of the following pairs of sets is equal?

a {Positive even numbers < 10}{2, 4, 6, 8, 10}

b {Positive prime numbers > 10 and < 20} {11, 13, 17, 19}

c {Positive odd numbers ⩽9}{1, 3, 5, 7}

d {Square numbers < 10}{1, 2, 4, 9}

e {Square numbers > 10 and < 20} {1, 2, 4, 9, 12, 16}

2) $\mathcal{E}$ = {Whole numbers x: $x \geqslant 3$ and < 7}. What is the set of values of x?

a {2, 3, 4, 5, 6, 7}   **b** {3, 4, 5, 6, 7}
c {1, 2, 3, 4, 5, 6}   **d** {3, 4, 5, 6}
e {2, 3, 4, 5, 6}

3) $\mathcal{E}$ = {A pack of playing cards without Jokers}

     R = {aces}

     S = {Picture cards}

     H = {All hearts}

What are the members of $(R \cup S \cup H)$?

a {ace of Hearts, Jack of Hearts, Queen of Hearts, King of Hearts}

b {ace of Hearts, spades, diamonds, clubs; Jack, Queen, King of spades, Hearts, diamonds, clubs; 2, 3, 4, . . . , 10 of Hearts}

c {Queen, King, Jack of spades, Hearts, diamonds, clubs}

d {ace of spades, Hearts, diamonds, clubs; 2, 3, 4, . . . , 10 of Hearts}

4) How many subsets of {v, w, x, y} are there which contain just three elements?

a 2   **b** 3   **c** 4   **d** 5   **e** 6

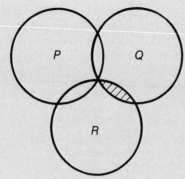

Fig. 38.35

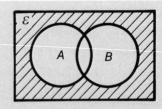

Fig. 38.36

5) If the circles in Fig. 38.35 represent the sets P, Q and R then the shaded area is represented by

a $P \cap Q \cap R$ **b** $P' \cap Q \cap R$
c $P' \cap (Q \cup R)$ **d** $Q \cap R$

6) $n(A \cup B)$ is equal to

a $n(A) + n(B)$ **b** $n(A) - n(B)$
c $n(A) + n(B) + n(A \cap B)$
d $n(A) + n(B) - n(A \cap B)$

7) If $A = \{1, 3, 6, 9, 12, 15\}$, $B = \{3, 6, 7, 12\}$ and $C = \{3, 9\}$ then

a $A \subset B$ **b** $B \subset A$ **c** $C \subset A$ **d** $C \subset B$

8) If the circles in Fig. 38.36 represent the sets A and B then the shaded area represents

a $A \cup B$ **b** $(A \cup B)'$ **c** $A \cap B$ **d** $(A \cap B)'$

9) If $\mathcal{E} = \{1, 2, 3, 4, 5, 6, 7, 8, 9, 10\}$, $A = \{1, 3, 5\}$ and $B = \{1, 2, 4, 6, 8\}$ then $(A \cup B)'$ is equal to

a $\{7, 9, 10\}$ **b** $\varnothing$
c $\{1, 2, 3, 4, 5, 6, 8\}$ **d** $\{1\}$

10) The set of numbers greater than -5 and less than $+3$ can be symbolically represented by

a $\{n: n < -5 \ \& \ n > +3\}$
b $\{n: -5 < n < +3\}$
c $\{n: n > -5 \ \& \ +3 < n\}$
d $\{n: -5 > n > +3\}$

11) Let $U = \{\text{men}\}$, $P = \{\text{male cricketers}\}$ and $Q = \{\text{blind men}\}$. Which of the following is true?

a $P \cup Q = U$ **b** $P' \subset Q$
c $Q' \subset P$ **d** $Q \subset P'$

CHAPTER 38 SUMMARY

Points to remember

(i) Two sets are equal if they have the same members.

(ii) The number of members in a set A is written $n(A)$.

(iii) There are no members in the *empty* set, written ϕ or $\{ \ \}$.

(iv) When there is no end to the number of members in a set, we say that it is an infinite set.

(v) Different groups of members from the same set are called *subsets* of the given set.

(vi) The empty set, and the set itself, are also subsets of the set.

(vii) The members of a given set are also members of a larger set called the *universal set*.
e.g. If $A = \{\text{even numbers}\}$, the universal set U may be $\{\text{whole numbers}\}$.

(viii) When solving set problems, a good way to see how the sets are related is to draw a diagram called a Venn diagram. In a Venn diagram the universal set is usually represented by a rectangle and the other sets by circles.

(ix) The *union* of sets A and B, written $A \cup B$, is the set whose members are in either A or B or both A and B.

(x) The *intersection* of sets A and B, written $A \cap B$, is the set of elements in both A and B.

(xi) The complement of a set A, written A', is the set of elements from the universal which are not in A.

(xii) Given sets A and B,
$n(A \cup B) = n(A) + n(B) - n(A \cap B)$.

Chapter 39 **Number Scales**

THE BINARY SYSTEM

In the ordinary decimal system (sometimes known as the *denary* system) the digits 0 to 9 are used.

Consider the number 5623. It means

$$5 \times 1000 + 6 \times 100 + 2 \times 10 + 3 \times 1$$

Remembering that $10^0 = 1$, we may write

$$5623 = 5 \times 10^3 + 6 \times 10^2 + 2 \times 10^1 + 3 \times 10^0$$

Thus

$$80\,321 = 8 \times 10^4 + 0 \times 10^3 + 3 \times 10^2$$
$$+ 2 \times 10^1 + 1 \times 10^0$$

Now consider the decimal fraction 0.381 3. It means

$$\frac{3}{10} + \frac{8}{100} + \frac{1}{1000} + \frac{3}{10\,000}$$

Therefore,

$$0.3813 = 3 \times 10^{-1} + 8 \times 10^{-2}$$
$$+ 1 \times 10^{-3} + 3 \times 10^{-4}$$

Now consider the number 736.58.

$$736.58 = 7 \times 10^2 + 3 \times 10^1 + 6 \times 10^0$$
$$+ 5 \times 10^{-1} + 8 \times 10^{-2}$$

Note that the decimal point indicates the change from positive powers of 10 to negative powers of 10.

It is perfectly possible to have a number system which works on the powers of any number. The most popular of these systems is the *binary* (bi meaning two) which operates with powers of 2.

It will be noticed in the decimal system that the greatest digit used is 9 which is one less than 10. Thus, in the binary system the greatest digit that can be used is 1 which is one less than 2.

A number written in binary consists only of the digits 0 and 1 and a typical binary number is 1 0 1 0 1 1 1.

The number 1 0 1 0 1 1 1 means:

$$1 \times 2^6 + 0 \times 2^5 + 1 \times 2^4 + 0 \times 2^3 + 1 \times 2^2$$
$$+ 1 \times 2^1 + 1 \times 2^0$$

The number .1 1 0 1 1 means:

$$1 \times 2^{-1} + 1 \times 2^{-2} + 0 \times 2^{-3} + 1 \times 2^{-4} + 1 \times 2^{-5}$$

The number 1 0 1.1 1 means:

$$1 \times 2^2 + 0 \times 2^1 + 1 \times 2^0 + 1 \times 2^{-1} + 1 \times 2^{-2}$$

The *binary point* separates the positive powers of 2 from the negative powers of 2. Numbers containing a binary point are sometimes called *bicimals*.

CONVERSION FROM BINARY TO DECIMAL AND VICE VERSA

There are several ways of converting decimal numbers to binary numbers. A simple method is shown in Example 1.

EXAMPLE 1

(1) Convert 59 to a binary number.

	Remainder	Power of 2	Explanation
59	1	0	$59 \div 2 = 29$ remainder 1
29	1	1	$29 \div 2 = 14$ remainder 1
14	0	2	$14 \div 2 = 7$ remainder 0
7	1	3	$7 \div 2 = 3$ remainder 1
3	1	4	$3 \div 2 = 1$ remainder 1
1	1	5	$1 \div 2 = 0$ remainder 1

Therefore,

$$59 \text{ (decimal)} = 1\ 1\ 1\ 0\ 1\ 1 \text{ (binary)}$$

(2) Convert 0.378 to binary.

0.378	Whole Number	Power of 2	Explanation
0.756	0	2^{-1}	$2 \times 0.378 = 0.756$. Whole number $= 0$
1.512	1	2^{-2}	$2 \times 0.756 = 1.512$. Whole number $= 1$ Remove the whole number 1. Then,
1.024	1	2^{-3}	$2 \times 0.512 = 1.024$. Whole number $= 1$ Remove the whole number 1. Then,
0.048	0	2^{-4}	$2 \times 0.024 = 0.048$. Whole number $= 0$
0.096	0	2^{-5}	$2 \times 0.048 = 0.096$. Whole number $= 0$
0.192	0	2^{-6}	$2 \times 0.096 = 0.192$. Whole number $= 0$
0.384	0	2^{-7}	$2 \times 0.192 = 0.384$. Whole number $= 0$
0.768	0	2^{-8}	$2 \times 0.384 = 0.768$. Whole number $= 0$
1.536	1	2^{-9}	$2 \times 0.768 = 1.536$. Whole number $= 1$ Remove the whole number 1. Then,
1.072	1	2^{-10}	$2 \times 0.536 = 1.072$. Whole number $= 1$
	etc.		

Therefore, $0.378 = .0\,1\,1\,0\,0\,0\,0\,0\,1\,1$ (correct to 10 binary places).

Most decimal fractions do not have an exact equivalent in binary. When converting these all we can do is to work to a specified number of binary places as in the example above. When converting numbers which have a whole number and a decimal part we convert the whole number part as shown in the first example and the decimal part as shown in the second example. Thus,

$$59.378 = 1\,1\,1\,0\,1\,1.0\,1\,1\,0\,0\,0\,0\,0\,1\,1$$

(correct to 10 binary places).

To convert a binary number into its decimal equivalent we make use of a table similar to the one shown below. The table may be extended in either direction as required.

2^6	2^5	2^4	2^3	2^2
64	32	16	8	4

2^1	2^0	2^{-1}	2^{-2}	2^{-3}
2	1	0.5	0.25	0.125

EXAMPLE 2

Convert $1\,1\,0\,1.1\,0\,1$ to decimal.

$$1\,1\,0\,1.1\,0\,1 \text{ (binary)}$$

$$= 1 \times 2^3 + 1 \times 2^2 + 0 \times 2^1 + 1 \times 2^0$$

$$+ 1 \times 2^{-1} + 0 \times 2^{-2} + 1 \times 2^{-3}$$

$$= 8 + 4 + 0 + 1 + 0.5 + 0 + 0.125$$

$$= 13.625 \text{ (decimal)}$$

The binary system is used in computers and other calculating machines. Since only the digits 0 and 1 are used in the system this is equivalent to a two-tier system. For instance, if a device is *off* it represents a 0 – if it is *on* a 1 is represented. Fig. 39.1 shows how the number $1\,0\,1\,1\,0$ can be represented by 5 electric light bulbs.

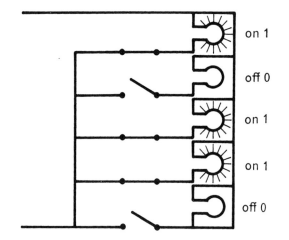

on 1

off 0

on 1

on 1

off 0

Fig. 39.1

ADDITION OF BINARY NUMBERS

When adding binary numbers the following rules apply:

$$1 + 0 = 1$$

$$0 + 1 = 1$$

$$1 + 1 = 1\,0$$

Note that $1 + 1 = 2$ in the decimal system but it is $1\,0$ in binary, i.e. one two and no units.

EXAMPLE 3

(1)
```
            1 1
             1
          1 1    ← numbers carried
        ─────────
        1 0 0
```

(2)
```
        1 0 1 1 1
          1 0 1 1
          1 1 0 1
      1 1 1 1 1 1    ← numbers carried
      ─────────────
      1 0 1 1 1 1
```

(3)
```
        1 1 0 1 0 1
          1 1 1 1 1
      1 1 1 1 1 1    ← numbers carried
      ───────────────
      1 0 1 0 1 0 0
```

SUBTRACTION OF BINARY NUMBERS

In decimal subtraction we 'borrow' and 'pay back' in tens. Similarly, in binary subtraction we 'borrow' and 'pay back' in twos. In Example 4, decimal numbers are used to show the result of 'borrowing' and 'paying back'.

EXAMPLE 4

(1)
```
       2
    1 0̸
      1
    1
    ───
    1
```

(2)
```
        3 2
    1 1̸ 0̸ 1 1
      1̸ 1 0 1
    1 2
    ─────────
    1 1 1 0
```

MULTIPLICATION OF BINARY NUMBERS

The multiplication table in binary is as follows:

$$0 \times 0 = 0 \qquad 0 \times 1 = 0$$

$$1 \times 0 = 0 \qquad 1 \times 1 = 1$$

When multiplying, remember the importance of starting each line of the multiplication under the number we are multiplying by.

EXAMPLE 5

Multiply 1 1 0 1 by 1 0 1.

```
            1 1 0 1
              1 0 1
          ───────────
            1 1 0 1
          0 0 0 0
        1 1 0 1
      1 1 1 1          ← numbers carried
      ───────────────
      1 0 0 0 0 0 1
```

A check may be made by converting into decimal.

1 1 0 1 (binary)   = 13 (decimal)

1 0 1 (binary)   = 5 (decimal)

13×5 (decimal) = 65 (decimal)

$$= 1\,0\,0\,0\,0\,0\,1 \text{ (binary)}$$

Hence the binary product 1 0 0 0 0 0 1 is correct and

$$1\,1\,0\,1 \times 1\,0\,1 = 1\,0\,0\,0\,0\,0\,1$$

DIVISION OF BINARY NUMBERS

Division is really repeated subtraction as shown in Example 6.

EXAMPLE 6

Divide 1 0 0 0 0 0 1 by 1 1 0 1

```
          1 1 0 1 ) 1 0 0 0 0 0 1 ( 1 0 1
                    1 1 0 1
                    ───────
                        1 1 0 1
                        1 1 0 1
                        ───────
                        . . . .
```

$1\,1\,0\,1 \times 1 = 1\,1\,0\,1$.   Place 1 in the answer. $1\,0\,0\,0\,0 - 1\,1\,0\,1 = 1\,1$.   Bring down next figure which is 0. 1 1 0 1 will not go into 1 1 0 so place 0 in answer and bring down the next figure, which is 1. 1 1 0 1 goes into 1 1 0 1 exactly. 1. Hence the answer is 1 0 1.

A check can be made by converting the binary numbers into decimal. Thus
1 1 0 1 (binary) = 13 (decimal)   and
1 0 0 0 0 0 1 (binary) = 65 (decimal).
$65 \div 13 = 5$ (decimal) = 1 0 1 (binary).   Hence

$$1\,0\,0\,0\,0\,0\,1 \div 1\,1\,0\,1 = 1\,0\,1$$

OPERATIONS WITH BICIMALS

EXAMPLE 7

Multiply   1 0 1.1 by 1 1.1.
First disregard the binary point and multiply 1 0 1 1 by 1 1 1.

```
                1 0 1 1
                  1 1 1
                ─────────
                1 0 1 1
              1 0 1 1
            1 0 1 1
            ───────────
            1 0 0 1 1 0 1
```

Now count up the number of digits following the binary point in each number, i.e. $1 + 1 = 2$. In the answer to the multiplication (the product), count this total number of digits from the right and insert the binary point. The product then becomes $1\,0\,0\,1\,1.0\,1$.

To check the product, convert each of the original numbers to decimal. Thus

$$1\,0\,1.1 = 5\tfrac{1}{2} \quad \text{and} \quad 1\,1.1 = 3\tfrac{1}{2}$$

$$5\tfrac{1}{2} \times 3\tfrac{1}{2} = 19\tfrac{1}{4} = 1\,0\,0\,1\,1.0\,1$$

Hence

$$1\,0\,1.1 \times 1\,1.1 = 1\,0\,0\,1\,1.0\,1$$

EXAMPLE 8

Divide $1\,0\,1.1$ by $1\,1$ giving the answer to 4 places after the binary point.

```
        1 1 ) 1 0 1.1 ( 1.1 1 0 1
              1 1
              ─────
              1 0 1
              1 1
              ─────
                1 0 0
                1 1
                ─────
                  1 0 0
                  1 1
                  ─────
                    1
```

The first line $1\,1 \times 1 = 1\,1$.
$1\,0\,1 - 1\,1 = 1\,0$. Bring down 1. Since this figure lies behind the binary point insert a point in the answer.
$1\,0\,1 - 1\,1 = 1\,0$. Since all the figures in the dividend have been used up bring down a zero. $1\,1$ will not go into $1\,0$ so place a zero in the answer and bring down a second zero. Now divide $1\,1$ into $1\,0\,0$. It goes 1 remainder 1. We now have the answer to 4 places after the binary point.
$1\,0\,1 \div 1\,1 = 1.1\,1\,0\,1$ correct to 4 figures after the binary point.

Exercise 178 – *Questions 1–5 type A, 6–8 type B, remainder C*

1) Convert to binary:

(a) 23   (b) 42   (c) 61   (d) 57

2) Convert to denary:

(a) $1\,0\,1\,1\,0$ (b) $1\,1\,1\,0\,0\,1$
(c) $1\,0\,1\,1\,0\,1\,0$ (d) $1\,1\,0\,1\,1\,1$

3) Convert to denary:

(a) $0.1\,1\,0\,1$ (b) $0.0\,1\,1\,1$
(c) $0.0\,0\,1\,1$

4) Convert to binary:

(a) $\dfrac{3}{8}$ (b) $\dfrac{5}{16}$ (c) $\dfrac{7}{8}$

5) Convert to binary, giving the answer to 7 places after the binary point:

(a) 0.169   (b) 18.467   (c) 108.710

6) Add the following binary numbers:

(a) $1\,0\,1\,1 + 1\,1$
(b) $1\,1\,0\,1\,1 + 1\,0\,1\,1$
(c) $1\,0\,1\,1\,1 + 1\,1\,0\,1\,0 + 1\,1\,1$
(d) $1\,0\,1\,1\,0\,1 + 1\,0\,1\,0 + 1\,0\,1\,1\,0\,1$
(e) $0.1\,1\,0\,1 + 0.0\,1\,1\,0$
(f) $0.1\,1\,0\,0\,1 + 0.1\,1\,0\,1\,1$
(g) $1\,1.1\,1\,0\,1 + 1\,1\,1.1\,0\,0\,1 + 1.1\,1\,0\,0$
(h) $1\,0\,1.1\,1 + 1\,1\,1.1\,0 + 1\,0\,0.1\,1$

7) Subtract the following binary numbers:

(a) $1\,1.1 - 1\,0$
(b) $1\,0\,1\,1 - 1\,1\,1$
(c) $1\,1.0\,1 - 1.0\,1$
(d) $1\,1.0\,1\,1 - 1.1\,0\,1$
(e) $1\,0\,1.1\,1\,0 - 1\,1.1\,0\,1$

8) Multiply together the following binary numbers:

(a) $1\,1 \times 1\,0$
(b) $1\,0\,1 \times 1\,1\,1$
(c) $1\,0\,1\,1 \times 1\,0\,1\,0$
(d) $1\,1\,0\,1\,1 \times 1\,1\,0\,1$
(e) $1\,1\,0\,1\,0 \times 1\,0\,1\,1$

9) Divide the following binary numbers:

(a) $1\,0\,0\,1 \div 1\,1$
(b) $1\,1\,0\,0 \div 1\,1$
(c) $1\,0\,0\,1\,0\,1\,1 \div 1\,1\,1\,1$
(d) $1\,1\,0\,0\,1\,0\,0 \div 1\,0\,1\,0$
(e) $1\,0\,1\,0\,1\,1\,1\,1 \div 1\,1\,0\,1\,1$

10) Find the values of the following giving your answer in binary:

(a) $1\,1\,0\,1.1 \times 1.1\,1$
(b) $1\,0\,1.0\,1 \times 1\,1.1\,0\,1$
(c) $1\,0\,1\,0.1 \div 1\,0\,1$ giving the answer to 4 figures after the binary point.
(d) $1\,1\,1\,1.0\,1 \div 1\,1\,0\,1$ giving the answer to 5 figures after the binary point.

OTHER NUMBER SCALES

In the scale of 5, powers of 5 are used. Only the digits 0, 1, 2, 3 and 4 are available because the greatest digit used must be one less than 5. If you are told that the number 3 4 1 2 is in the scale of 5 it means that the number is *based* upon powers of 5. To show that this is so we write 3412_5. The suffix 5 indicates that the number scale of 5 is being used. The number scale is usually called the *base*. We say that the number 3412_5 is to the base 5. Similarly 463_8 is a number to the base 8.

$$3412_5 = 3 \times 5^3 + 4 \times 5^2 + 1 \times 5^1 + 2 \times 5^0$$

$$= 3 \times 125 + 4 \times 25 + 1 \times 5 + 2 \times 1$$

$$= 482_{10}$$

$$463_8 = 4 \times 8^2 + 6 \times 8^1 + 3 \times 8^0$$

$$= 4 \times 64 + 6 \times 8 + 3 \times 1 = 307_{10}$$

In a number system in base 3 we have

$$1 + 0 = 1, \quad 1 + 1 = 2, \quad 1 + 2 = 0 \text{ carry } 1$$

EXAMPLE 9

(1) Find $212_3 + 121_3$.

$$
\begin{array}{r}
212 \\
121 \\
\hline
1110 \\
\end{array}
\qquad 212_3 + 121_3 = 1110_3
$$

(2) Find $1220_3 + 2212_3 + 111_3$.

$$
\begin{array}{r}
1220 \\
2212 \\
111 \\
\hline
12\,020 \\
\end{array}
\qquad 1220_3 + 2212_3 + 111_3 = 12\,020_3
$$

Similar considerations apply to any other number system.

The addition table for the base 6 is shown below.

+	0	1	2	3	4	5
0	0	1	2	3	4	5
1	1	2	3	4	5	10
2	2	3	4	5	10	11
3	3	4	5	10	11	12
4	4	5	10	11	12	13
5	5	10	11	12	13	14

Note that $1 + 5 = 6$ in the decimal system but it is 10 in the base 6, i.e. one six and no

units. Similarly, $4 + 5 = 13$ in the base 6, i.e. one six and three units.

EXAMPLE 10

Find $52_6 + 35_6$.

$$
\begin{array}{r}
52 \\
35 \\
\hline
131 \\
\end{array}
$$

$$\therefore \qquad 52_6 + 35_6 = 131_6$$

EXAMPLE 11

Find $637_8 + 56_8$.

$$
\begin{array}{r}
637 \\
56 \\
\hline
715 \\
\end{array}
\qquad 637_8 + 56_8 = 715_8
$$

Subtraction is done similarly.

EXAMPLE 12

Find $62_8 - 37_8$.

$$
\begin{array}{r}
62 \\
37 \\
\hline
23 \\
\end{array}
\qquad 62_8 - 37_8 = 23_8
$$

CONVERSION FROM ONE BASE TO ANOTHER

It is difficult to change directly from one base to another without going through 10 first because the calculation would have to be done in a strange system. A simple method of converting a number in base 10 to a number in any other base is shown in Example 13.

EXAMPLE 13

(1) Convert 413_{10} into its equivalent in base 8.

	Remainder	Power of 8	Explanation
413			
51	5	8^0	$413 \div 8 = 51$ remainder 5
6	3	8^1	$51 \div 8 = 6$ remainder 3
0	6	8^2	$6 \div 8 = 1$ remainder 6

Hence $413_{10} = 635_8$.

(2) Express $(101_8 - 101_2)$ as a number in base eight.

$$101_2 = (1 \times 2^2 + 0 \times 2^1 + 1 \times 2^0)_{10} = 5_{10}$$

$$5_{10} = 5_8$$

$$\therefore \qquad (101_8 - 101_2) = 101_8 - 5_8 = 74_8$$

Exercise 179 – *Questions 1–3 type B, remainder C*

1) Perform the following additions:

(a) $12_3 + 22_3$
(b) $201_3 + 212_3$
(c) $2222_3 + 1212_3$
(d) $413_5 + 324_5$
(e) $315_6 + 24_6 + 52_6$
(f) $31_4 + 303_4 + 213_4$
(g) $36_8 + 44_8 + 57_8$
(h) $514_6 + 325_6 + 14_6 + 3_6$

2) Perform the following subtractions:

(a) $212_3 - 112_3$
(b) $32_4 - 23_4$
(c) $2122_3 - 1022_3$
(d) $311_4 - 232_4$
(e) $5321_8 - 677_8$
(f) $403_5 - 214_5$

3) Convert the following numbers to decimal:

(a) 325_6 (b) 2120_3 (c) 342_6
(d) 625_7 (e) 2323_4

4) (a) Express $325_{10} + 325_8$ as a number in base 8.
(b) Express $212_3 - 110_2$ as a number in base 3.
(c) Express $222_8 - 222_3$ as a number in base 3.
(d) Express $111_8 + 111_2$ as a number in base 8.

SELF-TEST 39

1) Which of the following is the largest number?

a 1111_2 **b** 21_3 **c** 113_4 **d** 12_5
e 11_6

2) What is the base of the following addition sum?

$$324$$
$$135$$
$$\overline{503}$$

a 2   **b** 3   **c** 4   **d** 5   **e** 6

3) 24_5 is equivalent to:

a 40_3 **b** 112_3 **c** 11000_2
d 120_{10} **e** 31_4

4) Evaluate $2002_3 - 202_3$.

a 100_3 **b** 101_3 **c** 1100_3
d 1010_3 **e** 1001_3

5) Evaluate $1001_2 \times 101_2$.

a 100111_2 **b** 111001_2
c 101101_2 **d** 11001_2
e 111010_2

6) Evaluate $1010_2 \div 101_2$.

a 101_2 **b** 100_2 **c** 11_2
d 10_2 **e** 1_2

7) What is 1204_5 in base ten?

a 179   **b** 895   **c** 1434
d 2408   **e** 14 304

8) The denary (base 10) number 37, written in binary (base 2) is:

a 100011   **b** 100111
c 100001   **d** 110001
e 100101

9) If both numbers are in binary the average of 1011 and 111 is:

a 1000   **b** 10010   **c** 1001
d 10001   **e** 10000

10) When the binary numbers 101 and 11 are multiplied together the answer is:

a 1001   **b** 1010   **c** 1011
d 1110   **e** 1111

11) Which of the binary numbers below represent the denary number 52?

a 100110   **b** 111110
c 110111   **d** 110100
e 110110

CHAPTER 39 SUMMARY

Points to remember

(i) Decimal numbers are numbers based on ten, e.g. $468 = 4 \times 10^2 + 6 \times 10 + 8$

(ii) Binary numbers are numbers based on two, e.g. $101 = 1 \times 2^2 + 0 \times 2^1 + 1$.

Numbers may be written in any base.

Chapter 40 **Matrices**

When a large amount of numerical data has to be used it is often convenient to arrange the numbers in the form of a matrix.

Suppose that a nurseryman offers collections of fruit trees in three separate collections. The table below shows the name of each collection and the number of each type of tree included in it.

Collection	Apple	Pear	Plum	Cherry
A	6	2	1	1
B	3	2	2	1
C	3	1	1	0

After a time the headings and titles could be removed because those concerned with the packing of the collections would know what the various numbers meant. The table could then look like this:

$$\begin{pmatrix} 6 & 2 & 1 & 1 \\ 3 & 2 & 2 & 1 \\ 3 & 1 & 1 & 0 \end{pmatrix}$$

The information has now been arranged in the form of a *matrix*, that is, in the form of an array of numbers.

A matrix is always enclosed in curved brackets. The above matrix has 3 rows and 4 columns. It is called a matrix of order 3×4. In defining the order of a matrix the number of rows is always stated first and then the number of columns. The matrix shown below is of order 2×5 because it has 2 rows and 5 columns.

$$\begin{pmatrix} 1 & 2 & 5 & 2 & 4 \\ 3 & 0 & 3 & 1 & 2 \end{pmatrix}$$

TYPES OF MATRICES

(1) *Row matrix.* This is a matrix having only one row. Thus $(3 \quad 5)$ is a row matrix.

(2) *Column matrix.* This is a matrix having only one column. Thus $\begin{pmatrix} 1 \\ 6 \end{pmatrix}$ is a column matrix.

(3) *Null matrix.* This is a matrix with all its elements zero. Thus $\begin{pmatrix} 0 & 0 \\ 0 & 0 \end{pmatrix}$ is a null matrix.

(4) *Square matrix.* This is a matrix having the same number of rows and columns. Thus $\begin{pmatrix} 2 & 1 \\ 6 & 3 \end{pmatrix}$ is a square matrix.

(5) *Diagonal matrix.* This is a square matrix in which all the elements are zero except the diagonal elements. Thus $\begin{pmatrix} 2 & 0 \\ 0 & 3 \end{pmatrix}$ is a diagonal matrix. Note that the diagonal in a matrix always runs from upper left to lower right.

(6) *Unit matrix.* This is a diagonal matrix in which the diagonal elements equal 1. A unit matrix is usually denoted by the symbol *I*. Thus:

$$I = \begin{pmatrix} 1 & 0 \\ 0 & 1 \end{pmatrix}$$

ADDITION AND SUBTRACTION OF MATRICES

Two matrices may be added or subtracted provided they are of the *same order*. Addition is done by adding together the corresponding elements of each of the two matrices. Thus

$$\begin{pmatrix} 3 & 5 \\ 6 & 2 \end{pmatrix} + \begin{pmatrix} 4 & 7 \\ 8 & 1 \end{pmatrix} = \begin{pmatrix} 3+4 & 5+7 \\ 6+8 & 2+1 \end{pmatrix}$$

$$= \begin{pmatrix} 7 & 12 \\ 14 & 3 \end{pmatrix}$$

Subtraction is done in a similar fashion except the corresponding elements are subtracted. Thus

$$\begin{pmatrix} 6 & 2 \\ 1 & 8 \end{pmatrix} - \begin{pmatrix} 4 & 3 \\ 7 & 5 \end{pmatrix} = \begin{pmatrix} 6-4 & 2-3 \\ 1-7 & 8-5 \end{pmatrix}$$

$$= \begin{pmatrix} 2 & -1 \\ -6 & 3 \end{pmatrix}$$

MULTIPLICATION OF MATRICES

(1) *Scalar multiplication.* A matrix may be multiplied by a number as follows:

$$3\begin{pmatrix} 2 & 1 \\ 6 & 4 \end{pmatrix} = \begin{pmatrix} 3 \times 2 & 3 \times 1 \\ 3 \times 6 & 3 \times 4 \end{pmatrix} = \begin{pmatrix} 6 & 3 \\ 18 & 12 \end{pmatrix}$$

(2) *General matrix multiplication.* Two matrices can only be multiplied together if the number of columns in the first is equal to the number of rows in the second. The multiplication is done by multiplying a row by a column as shown below.

$$\begin{pmatrix} 2 & 3 \\ 4 & 5 \end{pmatrix} \times \begin{pmatrix} 5 & 2 \\ 3 & 6 \end{pmatrix}$$

$$= \begin{pmatrix} 2 \times 5 + 3 \times 3 & 2 \times 2 + 3 \times 6 \\ 4 \times 5 + 5 \times 3 & 4 \times 2 + 5 \times 6 \end{pmatrix}$$

$$= \begin{pmatrix} 19 & 22 \\ 35 & 38 \end{pmatrix}$$

$$\begin{pmatrix} 3 & 4 \\ 2 & 5 \end{pmatrix} \times \begin{pmatrix} 6 \\ 7 \end{pmatrix}$$

$$= \begin{pmatrix} 3 \times 6 + 4 \times 7 \\ 2 \times 6 + 5 \times 7 \end{pmatrix} = \begin{pmatrix} 46 \\ 47 \end{pmatrix}$$

MATRIX NOTATION

It is usual to denote matrices by capital letters. Thus

$$A = \begin{pmatrix} 3 & 1 \\ 7 & 4 \end{pmatrix} \quad \text{and} \quad B = \begin{pmatrix} 2 \\ 3 \end{pmatrix}$$

Generally speaking matrix products are *non-communative*, that is

$$A \times B \quad \text{does not equal} \quad B \times A$$

If A is of order 4×3 and B is of order 3×2, then AB is of order 4×2.

EXAMPLE 1

(1) Form $C = A + B$ if:

$$A = \begin{pmatrix} 3 & 4 \\ 2 & 1 \end{pmatrix} \quad \text{and} \quad B = \begin{pmatrix} 2 & 3 \\ 4 & 2 \end{pmatrix}$$

$$C = \begin{pmatrix} 3 & 4 \\ 2 & 1 \end{pmatrix} + \begin{pmatrix} 2 & 3 \\ 4 & 2 \end{pmatrix} = \begin{pmatrix} 5 & 7 \\ 6 & 3 \end{pmatrix}$$

(2) Form $Q = RS$ if:

$$R = \begin{pmatrix} 1 & 2 \\ 3 & 4 \end{pmatrix} \quad \text{and} \quad S = \begin{pmatrix} 3 & 1 \\ 5 & 6 \end{pmatrix}$$

$$Q = \begin{pmatrix} 1 & 2 \\ 3 & 4 \end{pmatrix}\begin{pmatrix} 3 & 1 \\ 5 & 6 \end{pmatrix} = \begin{pmatrix} 13 & 13 \\ 29 & 27 \end{pmatrix}$$

Note that just as in ordinary algebra the multiplication sign is omitted in matrix algebra.

(3) Form $M = PQR$ if:

$$P = \begin{pmatrix} 2 & 0 \\ 1 & 0 \end{pmatrix}, \quad Q = \begin{pmatrix} -1 & 0 \\ 0 & 1 \end{pmatrix}$$

and

$$R = \begin{pmatrix} 2 & 1 \\ 3 & 0 \end{pmatrix}$$

$$PQ = \begin{pmatrix} 2 & 0 \\ 1 & 0 \end{pmatrix}\begin{pmatrix} -1 & 0 \\ 0 & 1 \end{pmatrix} = \begin{pmatrix} -2 & 0 \\ -1 & 0 \end{pmatrix}$$

$$M = (PQ)R = \begin{pmatrix} -2 & 0 \\ -1 & 0 \end{pmatrix}\begin{pmatrix} 2 & 1 \\ 3 & 0 \end{pmatrix}$$

$$= \begin{pmatrix} -4 & -2 \\ -2 & -1 \end{pmatrix}$$

EQUALITY OF MATRICES

If two matrices are equal then their corresponding elements are equal. Thus if

$$\begin{pmatrix} a & b \\ c & d \end{pmatrix} = \begin{pmatrix} e & f \\ g & h \end{pmatrix}$$

then $a = e$, $b = f$, $c = g$ and $d = h$.

EXAMPLE 2

Find the values of x and y if

$$\begin{pmatrix} 2 & 1 \\ 3 & 4 \end{pmatrix}\begin{pmatrix} x & 2 \\ 5 & y \end{pmatrix} = \begin{pmatrix} 7 & 10 \\ 23 & 30 \end{pmatrix}$$

$$\begin{pmatrix} 2x + 5 & 4 + y \\ 3x + 20 & 6 + 4y \end{pmatrix} = \begin{pmatrix} 7 & 10 \\ 23 & 30 \end{pmatrix}$$

$$\therefore \qquad 2x + 5 = 7 \quad \text{and} \quad x = 1$$

$$4 + y = 10 \quad \text{and} \quad y = 6$$

(We could have used $3x + 20 = 23$ and $6 + 4y = 30$ if we wished.)

TRANSPOSITION OF MATRICES

When the rows of a matrix are interchanged with its columns the matrix is said to be *transposed*. If the original matrix is A, the transpose is denoted by A^T. Thus

$$A = \begin{pmatrix} 3 & 4 \\ 5 & 6 \end{pmatrix} \qquad A^T = \begin{pmatrix} 3 & 5 \\ 4 & 6 \end{pmatrix}$$

DIAGONALISING A MATRIX

Consider the following matrix products:

(a) $\begin{pmatrix} 3 & 2 \\ 5 & 1 \end{pmatrix} \begin{pmatrix} 1 & -2 \\ -5 & 3 \end{pmatrix} = \begin{pmatrix} -7 & 0 \\ 0 & -7 \end{pmatrix}$

(b) $\begin{pmatrix} -1 & -4 \\ 2 & 6 \end{pmatrix} \begin{pmatrix} 6 & 4 \\ -2 & -1 \end{pmatrix} = \begin{pmatrix} 2 & 0 \\ 0 & 2 \end{pmatrix}$

In each of the above, the final matrix is a diagonal matrix and there is a relationship between the elements of the first matrix and the elements of the second matrix.

In general, if

$$A = \begin{pmatrix} a & b \\ c & d \end{pmatrix} \quad \text{and} \quad B = \begin{pmatrix} d & -b \\ -c & a \end{pmatrix}$$

then AB is a diagonal matrix.

Obtaining a diagonal matrix from a given matrix is very useful when solving a pair of linear simultaneous equations.

EXAMPLE 3

Solve the equations

$$2x - 3y = 7 \qquad [1]$$

$$x + 4y = -2 \qquad [2]$$

We may write these equations in matrix form as

$$\begin{pmatrix} 2 & -3 \\ 1 & 4 \end{pmatrix} \begin{pmatrix} x \\ y \end{pmatrix} = \begin{pmatrix} 7 \\ -2 \end{pmatrix}$$

Pre-multiplying both sides of the equation by $\begin{pmatrix} 4 & 3 \\ -1 & 2 \end{pmatrix}$ we get

$$\begin{pmatrix} 4 & 3 \\ -1 & 2 \end{pmatrix} \begin{pmatrix} 2 & -3 \\ 1 & 4 \end{pmatrix} \begin{pmatrix} x \\ y \end{pmatrix}$$

$$= \begin{pmatrix} 4 & 3 \\ -1 & 2 \end{pmatrix} \begin{pmatrix} 7 \\ -2 \end{pmatrix}$$

$$\begin{pmatrix} 11 & 0 \\ 0 & 11 \end{pmatrix} \begin{pmatrix} x \\ y \end{pmatrix} = \begin{pmatrix} 22 \\ -11 \end{pmatrix}$$

$$\begin{pmatrix} 11x \\ 11y \end{pmatrix} = \begin{pmatrix} 22 \\ -11 \end{pmatrix}$$

$$\therefore \quad 11x = 22 \quad \text{and} \quad x = 2$$

$$11y = -11 \quad \text{and} \quad y = -1$$

INVERTING A MATRIX

If $AB = I$ (I is the unit matrix) then B is called the *inverse or reciprocal* of A. The inverse of A is usually written A^{-1} and hence

$$AA^{-1} = I$$

If

$$A = \begin{pmatrix} a & b \\ c & d \end{pmatrix}$$

$$A^{-1} = \frac{1}{ad - bc} \begin{pmatrix} d & -b \\ -c & a \end{pmatrix}$$

The expression $(ad - bc)$ is known as the *determinant* of the matrix A and is written $\det A$ or $|A|$. If $\det A = 0$, then $\dfrac{1}{0}$ is undefined and the matrix A has no inverse. A matrix which has no inverse is said to be *singular*.

EXAMPLE 4

If $A = \begin{pmatrix} 4 & 1 \\ 2 & 3 \end{pmatrix}$ form A^{-1}

$$A^{-1} = \frac{1}{4 \times 3 - 1 \times 2} \begin{pmatrix} 3 & -1 \\ -2 & 4 \end{pmatrix}$$

$$= \frac{1}{10} \begin{pmatrix} 3 & -1 \\ -2 & 4 \end{pmatrix}$$

$$= \begin{pmatrix} 0.3 & -0.1 \\ -0.2 & 0.4 \end{pmatrix}$$

To check

$$AA^{-1} = \begin{pmatrix} 4 & 1 \\ 2 & 3 \end{pmatrix} \begin{pmatrix} 0.3 & -0.1 \\ -0.2 & 0.4 \end{pmatrix}$$

$$= \begin{pmatrix} 1 & 0 \\ 0 & 1 \end{pmatrix}$$

*SOLUTION OF SIMULTANEOUS EQUATIONS

Consider the two simultaneous equations

$$3x + 2y = 12 \qquad [1]$$

$$4x + 5y = 23 \qquad [2]$$

We may write these equations in matrix form as follows:

$$\begin{pmatrix} 3 & 2 \\ 4 & 5 \end{pmatrix} \begin{pmatrix} x \\ y \end{pmatrix} = \begin{pmatrix} 12 \\ 23 \end{pmatrix}$$

If we let

$$A = \begin{pmatrix} 3 & 2 \\ 4 & 5 \end{pmatrix}, \quad X = \begin{pmatrix} x \\ y \end{pmatrix}, \quad K = \begin{pmatrix} 12 \\ 23 \end{pmatrix}$$

Then $AX = K$

and $X = A^{-1}K$

$$A^{-1} = \frac{1}{3 \times 5 - 2 \times 4} \begin{pmatrix} 5 & -2 \\ -4 & 3 \end{pmatrix}$$

$$= \begin{pmatrix} \frac{5}{7} & -\frac{2}{7} \\ -\frac{4}{7} & \frac{3}{7} \end{pmatrix}$$

$$\begin{pmatrix} x \\ y \end{pmatrix} = \begin{pmatrix} \frac{5}{7} & -\frac{2}{7} \\ -\frac{4}{7} & \frac{3}{7} \end{pmatrix} \begin{pmatrix} 12 \\ 23 \end{pmatrix} = \begin{pmatrix} 2 \\ 3 \end{pmatrix}$$

∴ The solutions are $x = 2$ and $y = 3$.

It can also be shown that given equations
$ax + by = c$ and $lx + my = n$,

$$x = \frac{-\begin{pmatrix} b & c \\ m & n \end{pmatrix}}{\begin{pmatrix} a & b \\ l & m \end{pmatrix}}$$

$$y = \frac{\begin{pmatrix} a & c \\ l & n \end{pmatrix}}{\begin{pmatrix} a & b \\ l & m \end{pmatrix}}$$

Hence, the solution of $3x + 2y = 12$ and
$4x + 5y = 23$ is

$$x = \frac{-\begin{pmatrix} 2 & 12 \\ 5 & 23 \end{pmatrix}}{\begin{pmatrix} 3 & 2 \\ 4 & 5 \end{pmatrix}} = -(46 - 60)/(15 - 8)$$

$$= 14/7 = 2$$

$$y = \frac{\begin{pmatrix} 3 & 12 \\ 4 & 23 \end{pmatrix}}{\begin{pmatrix} 3 & 2 \\ 4 & 5 \end{pmatrix}} = (69 - 48)/7 = 21/7 = 3.$$

Exercise 180 – *Questions 1–3, 6 and 7 type B,
remainder C*

1) Find the values of L and M in the
following matrix addition:

$$\begin{pmatrix} L & 4 \\ -3 & 1 \end{pmatrix} + \begin{pmatrix} 1 & 2 \\ -2 & 4 \end{pmatrix} + \begin{pmatrix} -1 & 2 \\ M & 4 \end{pmatrix}$$
$$= \begin{pmatrix} 3 & 8 \\ -6 & 9 \end{pmatrix}$$

2) If $A = \begin{pmatrix} 4 & 5 \\ 2 & 3 \end{pmatrix}$ find A^2 and $\det A$.

3) If $A = \begin{pmatrix} 3 & 1 \\ 2 & 0 \end{pmatrix}$ and $B = \begin{pmatrix} 4 & -1 \\ 2 & 3 \end{pmatrix}$

calculate the following matrices:
(a) $A + B$ (b) $3A - 2B$ (c) AB
(d) BA (e) $\det A$ (f) $\det B$

4) $P = \begin{pmatrix} 2 & 1 \\ 3 & 1 \end{pmatrix}$ $Q = \begin{pmatrix} 1 & 0 \\ 0 & 1 \end{pmatrix}$

$R = \begin{pmatrix} 0 & 1 \\ 1 & 0 \end{pmatrix}$ $S = \begin{pmatrix} 1 & -2 \\ -6 & 3 \end{pmatrix}$

(a) Find each of the following as a single
matrix: $PQ, RS, PQRS, P^2 - Q^2$.
(b) Find the values of a and b if
$aP + bQ = S$.

5) A and B are two matrices.

If $A = \begin{pmatrix} -2 & 3 \\ 4 & -1 \end{pmatrix}$ find A^2 and then use

your answer to find B, given that $A^2 = A - B$.

6) Find the value of

$$\begin{pmatrix} 2 & 3 & 1 \\ 0 & 1 & 2 \end{pmatrix} \begin{pmatrix} 1 \\ 3 \\ -2 \end{pmatrix}$$

7) If

$$\begin{pmatrix} 2 & 3 \\ 4 & 5 \end{pmatrix} \begin{pmatrix} p & 2 \\ 7 & q \end{pmatrix} = \begin{pmatrix} 31 & 1 \\ 55 & 3 \end{pmatrix}$$

find p and q.

8) If $A = \begin{pmatrix} 2 & -1 \\ 1 & 1 \end{pmatrix}$ and $B = \begin{pmatrix} 1 & 2 \\ 1 & 1 \end{pmatrix}$,

write as a single:
(a) $A + B$ (b) $A \times B$
(c) the multiplicative inverse of B.

9) If matrix $A = \begin{pmatrix} 3 & 1 \\ 2 & 4 \end{pmatrix}$ and

matrix $B = \begin{pmatrix} 4 & 2 \\ 1 & 0 \end{pmatrix}$, calculate

(a) (i) $A + B$ (ii) $3A - 2B$
     (iii) AB
(b) (i) Eastern Airlines have 6 Tridents, 4 VC10s and 2 Jumbo Jets. Western Airlines have 3 Tridents, 6 VC10s and 1 Jumbo Jet. Write this information as a 2 by 3 matrix.
     (ii) Tridents carry 150 passengers, VC10s carry 120 passengers and Jumbo Jets carry 375 passengers. Write this information as a 3 by 1 matrix.
     (iii) Multiply these matrices to find a 2 by 1 matrix.
     (iv) What does the 2 by 1 matrix represent?

10) (a) The scores of five English soccer clubs in the first 12 matches in a certain season are given by the matrix:

	Won	Drawn	Lost
Aston Villa	4	4	4
Birmingham	3	2	7
Derby	6	3	3
Stoke	5	2	5
Wolverhampton	2	4	6

The points awarded for a win, a draw or a lost match are given by the matrix

Won	$\begin{pmatrix} 2 \\ 1 \\ 0 \end{pmatrix}$
Drawn	
Lost	

Calculate a matrix which shows the total number of points scored by each of these clubs, showing clearly the method used.

(b) If $A = \begin{pmatrix} 3 & 1 \\ -2 & 0 \end{pmatrix}$ and $B = \begin{pmatrix} -1 & 3 \\ -4 & 2 \end{pmatrix}$ calculate AB and BA.

(c) Solve the equation

$$\begin{pmatrix} 2 & 5 \\ 1 & 3 \end{pmatrix}\begin{pmatrix} x \\ y \end{pmatrix} = \begin{pmatrix} 3 \\ 1 \end{pmatrix}.$$

11) Solve the following simultaneous equations using matrices:

(a) $x + 3y = 7$ [1]
     $2x + 5y = 12$ [2]
(b) $4x + 3y = 24$ [1]
     $2x + 5y = 26$ [2]
(c) $2x + 7y = 11$ [1]
     $5x + 3y = 13$ [2]

SELF-TEST 40

1) If $X = \begin{pmatrix} -4 & 3 \\ 2 & -1 \end{pmatrix}$ then X^2 equals:

a $\begin{pmatrix} 22 & -15 \\ -10 & 7 \end{pmatrix}$ b $\begin{pmatrix} 16 & 9 \\ 4 & 1 \end{pmatrix}$

c $\begin{pmatrix} -8 & 6 \\ 4 & -2 \end{pmatrix}$ d $\begin{pmatrix} -16 & 9 \\ 4 & -1 \end{pmatrix}$

e $\begin{pmatrix} 22 & -10 \\ -15 & 7 \end{pmatrix}$

2) The inverse under multiplication of the matrix $\begin{pmatrix} 5 & 7 \\ 2 & 3 \end{pmatrix}$ is:

a $\begin{pmatrix} -3 & -7 \\ -2 & -5 \end{pmatrix}$ b $\begin{pmatrix} -5 & 2 \\ 7 & -3 \end{pmatrix}$

c $\begin{pmatrix} 3 & -7 \\ -2 & 5 \end{pmatrix}$ d $\begin{pmatrix} 0 & 0 \\ 0 & 0 \end{pmatrix}$

3) If $M = \begin{pmatrix} 2 & 3 \\ 4 & 5 \end{pmatrix}$ and $N = \begin{pmatrix} 3 & 1 \\ 2 & 2 \end{pmatrix}$

then MN is:

a $\begin{pmatrix} 12 & 8 \\ 22 & 14 \end{pmatrix}$ b $\begin{pmatrix} 10 & 14 \\ 12 & 16 \end{pmatrix}$

c $\begin{pmatrix} 6 & 3 \\ 8 & 10 \end{pmatrix}$ d $\begin{pmatrix} 5 & 4 \\ 6 & 7 \end{pmatrix}$

4) Expressed as a single matrix the operation $\begin{pmatrix} 1 & 0 \\ 3 & 2 \end{pmatrix}$ followed by $\begin{pmatrix} 4 & 1 \\ 1 & 0 \end{pmatrix}$ is:

a $\begin{pmatrix} 5 & 1 \\ 4 & 2 \end{pmatrix}$ b $\begin{pmatrix} 4 & 1 \\ 14 & 3 \end{pmatrix}$

c $\begin{pmatrix} 7 & 2 \\ 1 & 0 \end{pmatrix}$ d $\begin{pmatrix} 4 & 2 \\ 5 & 1 \end{pmatrix}$

5) The inverse of the 2×2 matrix $\begin{pmatrix} 6 & 10 \\ 2 & 4 \end{pmatrix}$ is:

a $\begin{pmatrix} 1 & -2\frac{1}{2} \\ -\frac{1}{2} & 1\frac{1}{2} \end{pmatrix}$ **b** $\begin{pmatrix} -4 & -10 \\ -2 & 6 \end{pmatrix}$

c $\begin{pmatrix} -2 & 6 \\ -10 & 4 \end{pmatrix}$ **d** $\begin{pmatrix} 1 & 2\frac{1}{2} \\ \frac{1}{2} & 1\frac{1}{2} \end{pmatrix}$

6) If $A = \begin{pmatrix} a & b \\ c & d \end{pmatrix}$ then A^{-1} is equal to:

a $\begin{pmatrix} \frac{1}{a} & \frac{1}{b} \\ \frac{1}{c} & \frac{1}{d} \end{pmatrix}$ **b** $\begin{pmatrix} c & d \\ a & b \end{pmatrix}$

c $\dfrac{1}{ad - bc} \begin{pmatrix} b & -d \\ -a & c \end{pmatrix}$

d $\dfrac{1}{ad - bc} \begin{pmatrix} d & -b \\ -c & a \end{pmatrix}$

7) If $A = \begin{pmatrix} 1 \\ 2 \\ 4 \\ 1 \end{pmatrix}$ and $B = \begin{pmatrix} 3 \\ 0 \\ 1 \\ 4 \end{pmatrix}$ then $B - 2A$ is equal to:

a $\begin{pmatrix} 5 \\ 4 \\ 9 \\ 6 \end{pmatrix}$ **b** $\begin{pmatrix} 1 \\ -4 \\ -7 \\ 2 \end{pmatrix}$ **c** $\begin{pmatrix} 0 \\ -5 \\ -5 \\ 1 \end{pmatrix}$

d $\begin{pmatrix} 6 \\ 5 \\ 7 \\ 7 \end{pmatrix}$

8) If $\begin{pmatrix} 2 & x \\ 4 & y \end{pmatrix} \begin{pmatrix} 5 \\ 2 \end{pmatrix} = \begin{pmatrix} 14 \\ 30 \end{pmatrix}$ the values of x and y are

a 5 and 2 **b** 14 and 30
c 2 and 5 **d** 12 and 25

CHAPTER 40 SUMMARY

Points to remember

(i) Given a 2×2 matrix $A = \begin{pmatrix} a & b \\ c & d \end{pmatrix}$ the determinant of A, written $\det A$ or $|A| = ad - bc$.

(ii) The inverse of A, written $A^{-1} = 1/|A| \begin{pmatrix} d & -b \\ -c & a \end{pmatrix}$

(iii) If $|A| = 0$, then the matrix A has no inverse.

(iv) $AA^{-1} = A^{-1}A = I$

(v) The identity matrix $I = \begin{pmatrix} 1 & 0 \\ 0 & 1 \end{pmatrix}$

(vi) The transpose of A, written $A^T = \begin{pmatrix} a & c \\ b & d \end{pmatrix}$.

Chapter 41 **Transformational Geometry**

INTRODUCTION

If we are presented with a geometric figure, there are many things that can be done to it.

Consider the following:

(a) Slide the quadrilateral ABCD to A′B′C′D′ (Fig. 41.1).

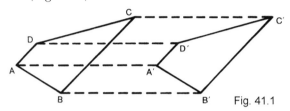

Fig. 41.1

(b) Rotate the triangle ABC to A′B′C′ (Fig. 41.2)

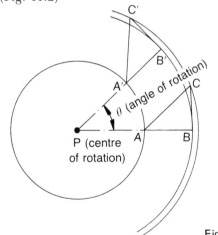

Fig. **41.2**

(c) Change the size of triangle PQR to that of triangle P′Q′R′ (Fig. 41.3)

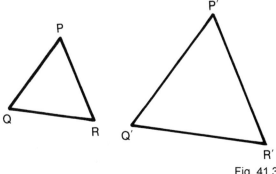

Fig. **41.3**

In each case we say that the original figure has been *transformed*. The operation that was applied is called a *transformation*. The original figure is called the *pre-image* and the transformed figure is called the *image*. For example, in Fig. 41.2, △A′B′C′ is the image of △ABC.

A transformation may be defined as: an operation such that each point in the pre-image has a unique image and each point in the image is the image of exactly one point.

A transformation is often referred to as a *mapping*. A transformation therefore maps a pre-image onto an image.

Fig. 41.1 showed a translation, Fig. 41.2 a rotation and Fig. 41.3 an enlargement. There are other transformations and we shall now consider different types of transformation in detail.

TRANSLATION

In Fig. 41.4, the line AB has taken up a new position A′B′. Every point in AB has moved the same distance in the same direction. AB is said to have been translated to A′B′. It can be seen from the diagram that every point in AB has been moved 1 unit to the right and 3 units upwards. Thus A(1, 2) translates to A′(2, 5) and B(5, 7) translates to B′(6, 10).

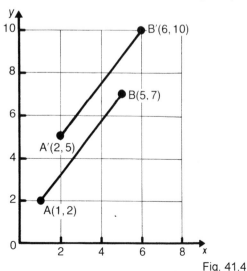

Fig. **41.4**

Similarly in Fig. 41.5, the triangle XYZ has been translated to X′Y′Z′. Every point in XYZ has been moved with a displacement of 5 units to the left and 4 units downwards. The translation which maps the point X(7, 8) to X′(2, 4) also maps Y(7, 6) to Y′(2, 2) and Z(10, 6) to Z′(5, 2). Generally, this transformation maps (x, y) onto $(x - 5, y - 4)$. If this translation is denoted by T_1, we may write

$$T_1: (x, y) \rightarrow (x - 5, y - 4)$$

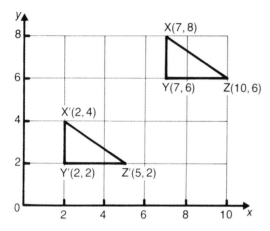

Fig. 41.5

Note that the translation is uniquely defined by the constants -5 and -4, which are added to the coordinates of the given point. We may therefore conveniently describe this translation by the column vector $\begin{pmatrix} -5 \\ -4 \end{pmatrix}$.

Given the column vector that describes a translation we may find the image of any point in the plane under this translation.

EXAMPLE 1

What is the image of $(2, -1)$ under the translation $\begin{pmatrix} 3 \\ -4 \end{pmatrix}$?

The image of $(2, -1)$ is $(2 + 3, -1 - 4) = (5, -5)$.

PROPERTIES OF TRANSLATIONS

If A and B are two points whose images are A′ and B′ respectively, then since AA′ ∥ BB′ and AA′ = BB′ the quadrilateral AA′B′B is a parallelogram as shown in Fig. 41.6.

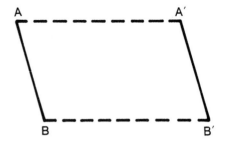

Fig. 41.6

Hence, if two figures are related by a translation then corresponding segments in these figures are equal and parallel. Size and shape do not change under a translation which is, therefore, a *congruency transformation*. This means that if a geometric figure undergoes a translation the image and the pre-image are congruent figures.

Exercise 181

1) The rectangle ABCD is formed by joining the four points A(1, 5), B(5, 5), C(5, 3) and D(1, 3). What is the image of ABCD under the translation $\begin{pmatrix} 3 \\ 2 \end{pmatrix}$?

2) A given translation maps $(4, 7)$ onto $(-2, 1)$. What is the image of $(3, 4)$ under this translation?

3) The triangle ABC is formed by joining the three points A(4, 1), B(6, 1) and C(4, 5). Draw the triangle on graph paper and show its image under the translation $\begin{pmatrix} -2 \\ 2 \end{pmatrix}$.

4) A trapezium ABCD is such that A is the point $(2, 1)$, B is the point $(7, 1)$, C is the point $(6, 3)$ and D is the point $(3, 3)$. If the image of ABCD under the translation $\begin{pmatrix} -5 \\ -2 \end{pmatrix}$ is A′B′C′D′, find the coordinates of A′, B′, C′ and D′.

REFLECTION

The idea of a reflection is a familiar one. If a girl looks into the mirror she sees a reflection of herself. A reflection is another transformation and reflections are very useful in studying various properties of geometric figures.

To get an idea how a reflection works in a plane, write a large letter E on a piece of thin paper. Fold the paper over so that the E is covered. Now trace the E on the portion of the paper which was folded over. Unfold the paper and hold it up to the light. You should see a diagram similar to the one shown in Fig. 41.7. The E on the left represents the original E, the dotted line represents the crease formed by folding the paper and the E on the left represents the traced E.

The E on the right is the *reflection image* of the original E in the dotted line.

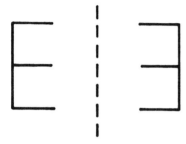

Fig. 41.7

Figures 41.8 and 41.9 show a point A and a point A′ formed by folding along the line shown and tracing as before. In each figure, A′ is called the image of A in the line *l*. If we

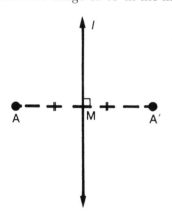

Fig. 41.8

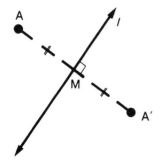

Fig. 41.9

draw AA′ and let it meet *l* in M then AM = MA′ and *l* is perpendicular to AA′. If the point A lies on *l* then A and A′ will be the same point.

A reflection image of a point is therefore defined as follows:

If a point A is not on a line l, the reflection image of A in l is the point A′ such that l is the perpendicular bisector of AA′.

It follows that if A′ is the image of A, then A is the image of A′. The line *l* is called the *line of reflection*.

EXAMPLE 2

In Fig. 41.10, find the image of A in the reflecting line *l*.

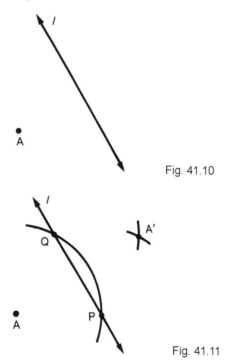

Fig. 41.10

Fig. 41.11

The construction is shown in Fig. 41.11. With centre A and any convenient radius, draw an arc to cut the line *l* at the points P and Q. With centre P and then Q, draw two arcs to intersect at A′. A′ is then the image of A in the line *l*.

REFLECTING A LINE

To reflect the line AB in *l* (Fig. 41.12), we reflect each point in AB. This is an impossible task since AB contains an infinite number of

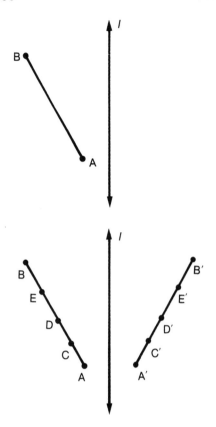

Fig. 41.12

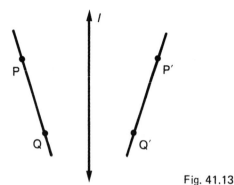

Fig. 41.13

points. However, we can reflect a few points such as A, B, C, D and E and obtain their images A′, B′, C′, D′ and E′ respectively. These images all lie on the straight line A′B′. Hence we say that

Reflections preserve collinearity.

This simply means that the reflection image of a straight line is a straight line. The reflection image of a straight line may therefore be found by reflecting any two points on the line and joining them with a straight line.

Thus in Fig. 41.13, the image of PQ in l is P′Q′ where P′ and Q′ are the images of P and Q in l.

It follows that if C is any point on AB and lying between A and B, then C′, the image of C, lies between A′ and B′. This property is called betweeness and we say that

Reflections preserve betweeness.

If in Fig. 41.13 we measure the lengths of the lines PQ and P′Q′ we would find that they were the same length. That is, PQ = P′Q′.

This is always the case with reflections and we say

Reflections preserve distance.

REFLECTING POLYGONS

All we need to do to reflect a polygon is to reflect its sides.

EXAMPLE 3
Reflect the triangle ABC in the line l (Fig. 41.14).

To obtain the reflection we reflect the points A, B and C and join their images A′, B′ and C′ as shown in the diagram.

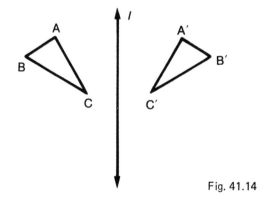

Fig. 41.14

If we measure the angles between corresponding sides in the pre-image and the image we see that they are equal. Hence we say

Reflections preserve angle measure.

ORIENTATION AND REFLECTION

If, in Fig. 41.14, a pencil point is placed at A and moved round the triangle towards B and then to C and back to A, the pencil point would have moved in a *counterclockwise* direction. If we repeat the action for the triangle A'B'C' the pencil point moves in a *clockwise* direction. We say that the points A, B, C, in that order are *counterclockwise oriented* whilst the points A', B', C', in that order are *clockwise oriented*.

If the points in a figure are oriented in one direction, then the corresponding image points, after reflection, are oriented in the opposite direction. We say that

Reflection reverses orientation.

SYMMETRIC FIGURES

Many of the figures found in elementary geometry are symmetrical. Let us see what this means.

B   D   C   Fig. 41.15

Consider the isosceles triangle ABC (Fig. 41.15) in which $AB = AC$ and AD is perpendicular to BC. We see that

the image of A in AD is A

the image of B in AD is C

the image of C in AD is B

Therefore, the image of $\triangle ABC$ in AD is $\triangle ACB$. We say that $\triangle ABC$ is reflection symmetric over AD.

Definition: A figure is reflection symmetric over a line l if and only if it coincides with its reflection image in l. The line l is called a line of symmetry of the figure.

or

A figure has *line symmetry* if it can be folded along a line and the two halves match. The folded line is a *line of symmetry*.

If we denote reflection in a line l by M_1, then if the image of A in l is A' we may write

$$M_l(A) = A'$$

We can deduce many of the properties of polygons using a knowledge of symmetry.

EXAMPLE 4

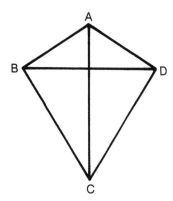

Fig. 41.16

The symmetry of the kite ABCD (Fig. 41.16) about AC is the basis for the following deductions:

(a) AC is the perpendicular bisector of BD.

(b) AC bisects the angles BAD and BCD.

(c) Triangles ABC and ADC are congruent.

Properties of symmetry may also be used to make deductions about the circle.

EXAMPLE 5

The circle is symmetrical about any diameter. Since the diameter is a line of symmetry of the circle, any chord perpendicular to the diameter is bisected by it.

The line perpendicular to the diameter at its end point is a tangent to the circle.

SUMMARY OF THE PROPERTIES OF REFLECTIONS

(a) Every point has exactly one reflection image.

(b) Reflections preserve collinearity, betweeness, distance and angle measure.

CONGRUENCE

In Fig. 41.17, $\triangle ABC$ is reflected in the line l to give the image $A'B'C'$.

The image $A'B'C'$ is then reflected in the line m, where m and l are parallel, to give the final image $A''B''C''$.

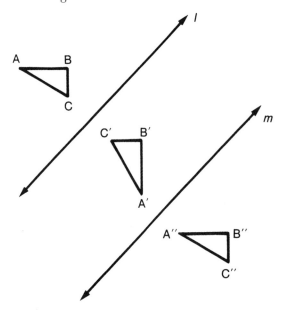

Fig. 41.17

Triangles ABC and $A''B''C''$ are alike in every respect. In fact, $A''B''C''$ could have been obtained by translating one triangle into the other. This suggests that a translation can be affected by two reflections. This is indeed the case and we say that: a translation T is a composite of two reflections. We write

$$T = M_m \circ M_l$$

Congruence may now be defined as follows: *Two figures L and M are congruent if and only if there is a composite of reflections mapping L onto M.*

Thus in Fig. 41.17 the triangles ABC and $A''B''C''$ are congruent.

Exercise 182 – *All type B*

1) The image of A is P, of B is Q and of C is R. Name the image of $\triangle ABC$.

2) Is it possible for a figure to have no lines of symmetry? Give an example.

3) How many lines of symmetry does an equilateral triangle have?

4) How many lines of symmetry does a square have? Draw a square and indicate on it the lines of symmetry.

5) State the coordinates of $(3, -4)$ after reflection in:
(a) the x-axis,   (b) the y-axis,
(c) the line $x = 2$,   (d) the line $y = -1$,
(e) the line $y = x$.

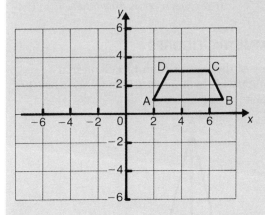

Fig. 41.18

6) Fig. 41.18 shows the trapezium $ABCD$. Copy the diagram and show the reflection of this figure in:
(a) the x-axis,   (b) the y-axis and
(c) the line $y = x$.

7) The triangle ABC is formed by joining the three points $A(3, 2)$, $B(5, 2)$ and $C(3, 6)$.

(a) Draw the triangle on graph paper.
(b) Reflect this triangle in the x-axis showing the result on your graph paper and state the coordinates of the image of the points A, B and C.
(c) Reflect the triangle in the y-axis and show the result on your diagram. Write down the coordinates of the image of the points A, B and C after this transformation.

ROTATION

The composite of two reflections over parallel lines is a translation. We now consider the case in which the lines intersect.

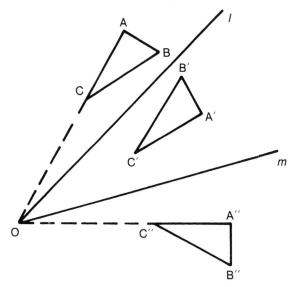

Fig. 41.19

FINDING THE CENTRE OF ROTATION

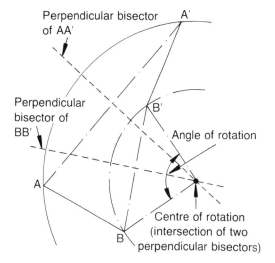

Fig. 41.20

In Fig. 41.19, △A″B″C″ is the image of △ABC after a composite of two reflections in the intersecting lines *l* and *m*. Since the orientations of triangles ABC and A″B″C″ are both clockwise the resulting transformation is not a reflection. Further, since the lines *l* and *m* are not parallel, the transformation is not a translation.

If we examine the directions of CA and C″A″ we see that the change from CA to C″A″ is similar to the change in direction of the minute hand of a clock in moving from 2 to 3, i.e. a clockwise rotation of about 30°. There are similar changes in the directions from AB to A″B″ and from CB to C″B″.

Hence the transformation is called a *rotation*.

Definition: A transformation R *is a rotation if and only if* R *is the composite of two reflections* M₁ *and* Mₘ *where the lines* l *and* m *are not parallel.*

In Fig. 41.19, O coincides with its image when reflected in *l* and again when reflected in *m*. The point O is called the *centre of rotation*.

It can be shown by actual measurement that ∠COC″ = ∠BOB″ = ∠AOA″. If these three angles equal θ°, then we say that △ABC has been rotated through an angle of θ° in a clockwise direction. The angle θ is called the *magnitude* of the rotation and clockwise is the *direction* of the rotation. We may write

$$R_\theta = M_m \circ M_l$$

In Fig. 41.20 the line AB has been transformed into A′B′. To find the centre of rotation first join AA′ and BB′ then construct the perpendicular bisectors of AA′ and BB′. The point of intersection of the two perpendicular bisectors is the centre of rotation.

If θ = 180°, the rotation is called a *half turn*.

EXAMPLE 6

In Fig. 41.21, △ABC has been rotated, about O, through 180° in a clockwise direction to give the image A′B′C′.

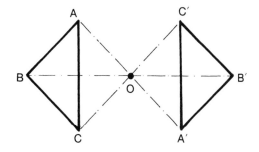

Fig. 41.21

AA′, BB′ and CC′ meet at O which is the mid-point of AA′, BB′ and CC′. To find the image of a point such as A, under a half turn (i.e. a rotation of 180°) we simply draw the line segment AA′ with O as the mid-point.

Note the similarity between this method and that used to find the image of a point on reflection in a line. A rotation of $180°$ is sometimes called a *point reflection* or *reflection in a point*. Hence, in Fig. 41.21, A' is the image of A under reflection in the point O.

ROTATIONAL SYMMETRY

In Fig. 41.22(a), if the rectangle ABCD is cut out and rotated about O (by sticking a pin through O) it will occupy the position shown in Fig. 41.22(b). If the lettering is removed, there will be no change in the two rectangles.

The rectangle ABCD is said to have *rotational symmetry*.

Definition: A figure has rotational symmetry if it coincides with its image by rotation about a point.

or

A figure has *rotational symmetry* if it can be turned about a point through an angle less than $360°$ so that it matches the original figure.

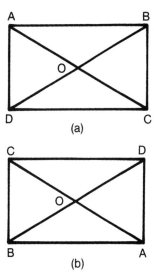

(a)

(b)   Fig. 41.22

The rectangle ABCD shown in Fig. 41.22 has only two positions that are the same under rotation in the plane. We say, therefore, that the rectangle has *rotational symmetry of order 2* in the plane.

Similarly, we can show that an equilateral triangle has rotational symmetry of order 3 whilst a square has rotational symmetry of order 4.

Definition: The order of rotational symmetry of a figure is the number of ways in which rotational symmetry can be preserved.

PROPERTIES OF ROTATIONS

(a) Lengths of line segments, measures of angles and orientation remain unchanged (i.e. invariant) under a rotation.

(b) The centre of rotation remains invariant under all rotations about that centre.

(c) The distance of any point from the centre of rotation remains invariant.

(d) Under a rotation geometric figures are left invariant in shape and size, i.e. a rotation is a congruency transformation which is often called an *isometry*.

Exercise 183 – *All type B*

1) What is the image of the point $(2, 3)$ under an anticlockwise rotation of $90°$ about the origin?

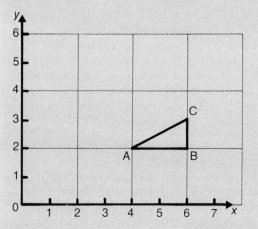

Fig. 41.23

2) Using the origin as the centre of rotation, draw the image of the triangle ABC shown in Fig. 41.23 after it has been given a rotation of $60°$ clockwise. Write down the coordinates of the images of the points A, B and C.

3) Triangle ABC has vertices $A(2, 3)$, $B(4, 4)$ and $C(3, 5)$. Plot these points on graph paper and join them to form the triangle. Show the image of $\triangle ABC$ after it has been given a rotation of $90°$ about the point $(1, 5)$ anticlockwise.

4) The line AB with end points $A(2, 2)$ and $B(4, 2)$ is transformed into $A'B'$ by a rotation such that A' is the point $(8, 4)$ and B' is the point $(8, 2)$. Find, by drawing, the coordinates of the centre of rotation and write down the magnitude and direction of the rotation.

Fig. 41.24

5) Fig. 41.24 shows a square, a rhombus, an isosceles trapezium, an equilateral triangle, an isosceles triangle and a hexagon. Copy the diagrams and on each draw all the axes of symmetry and state the number of axes of symmetry that each figure possesses. Determine also the order of rotational symmetry, if any, for each of the figures.

6) Plot the points given below on graph paper and then join them up in alphabetical order. State which of the shapes has line symmetry and state the number of axes of symmetry. Write down also the order of rotational symmetry.

(a) $A(2, 5)$, $B(4, 12)$ and $C(6, 10)$
(b) $A(4, 5)$, $B(6, 5)$, $C(6, 10)$ and $D(4, 10)$
(c) $A(4, 5)$, $B(6, 5)$, $C(6, 10)$ and $D(4, 12)$
(d) $A(4, 10)$, $B(8, 10)$, $C(10, 15)$ and $D(6, 15)$
(e) $A(4, 3)$, $B(6, 10)$ and $D(3, 3)$
(f) $A(2, 2)$, $B(6, 5)$, $C(6, 15)$ and $D(2, 15)$
(g) $A(0, 10)$, $B(5, 5)$, $C(10, 5)$, $D(15, 10)$,
$\quad$ $E(15, 15)$, $F(10, 20)$, $G(5, 20)$ and $H(0, 15)$.
(h) $A(0, 5)$, $B(5, 0)$, $C(0, -5)$ and $D(-5, 0)$
(i) $A(0, 2)$, $B(2, 3)$, $C(6, 3)$, $D(6, 1)$ and $E(2, 1)$

Fig. 41.25

7) Fig. 41.25 shows some letters. For each write down the order of rotational symmetry and on a neat sketch show the point of symmetry, if any.

SIZE TRANSFORMATIONS

So far we have studied transformations in which the pre-image and the image of a figure have the same shape and size.

Consider now the case of viewing a triangle through a magnifying glass. The original triangle and the image formed in the magnifying glass will have the same shape (i.e. corresponding angles will be equal) but the sides of the image will be longer. This transformation is therefore different from those studied earlier in that the sizes of the pre-image and the image are different.

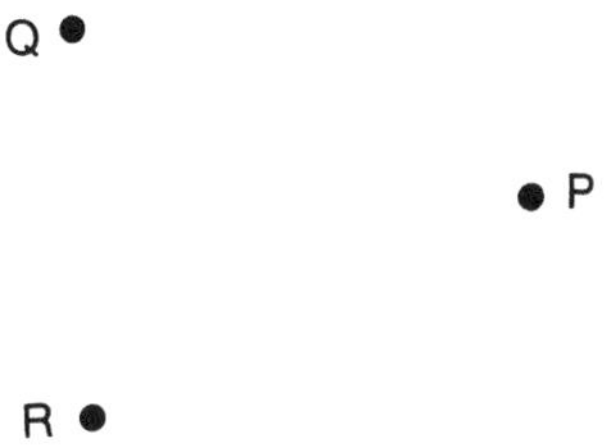

Q •

$\qquad$ • P

R •

Fig. 41.26

Let us now take the three points P, Q and R (Fig. 41.26). Suppose $PR = 6$ units and $QR = 2$ units. Then,

$$\frac{PR}{QR} = \frac{6}{2} = 3$$

The distance from P to R is three times that from Q to R. Also the distance of R from Q is $\frac{1}{3}$ the distance from R to P. We have compared the distances of two points P and Q from a third point R. It must be noted that there is an unlimited number of points that are three times as far from R as is Q.

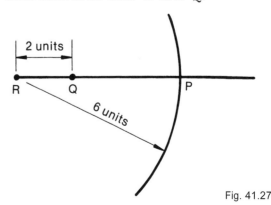

Fig. 41.27

If, on the other hand, we consider a portion of the line RQ as shown in Fig. 41.27 we notice that a circle with centre R and radius 3 units intersects RQ at exactly one point, P. Thus there is only one point on this portion of RQ that is three times as far from R as is Q.

To define a transformation all we need to know is how the image of each point is determined. If we denote the portion of the line RQ shown in Fig. 41.27 by $\overrightarrow{RQ}$ then the transformation described above may be defined as follows:

P is the image of Q if P is a point on $\overrightarrow{RQ}$ such that the distance of P from R is three times the distance of Q from R.

A general definition of this type of transformation, denoted by E, may be written as:

Given a point O and a real number k, *then* A' *is the image of the point A, under the transformation E if A' lies on $\overrightarrow{OA}$ and* $OA' = kOA$.

E is said to be the size transformation with magnitude k and centre O. When k is greater than 1 $(k > 1)$ the transformation is called an *enlargement*. If k is less than 1 $(k < 1)$ the transformation is called a *contraction* or a *reduction*.

The image of a geometric figure consists of the points which make up the figure.

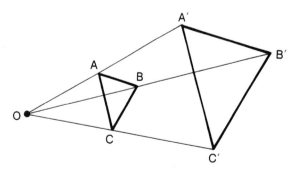

Fig. 41.28

Fig. 41.28 shows a triangle ABC and its image $A'B'C'$ under a size transformation with centre O and magnitude 2, i.e.

$$\frac{OA'}{OA} = \frac{OB'}{OB} = \frac{OC'}{OC} = \frac{2}{1}$$

EXAMPLE 8

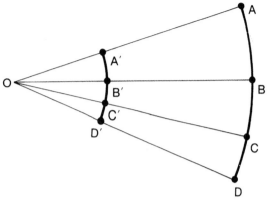

Fig. 41.29

In Fig. 41.29, the arc ABCD is transformed by a size transformation of magnitude $\frac{1}{3}$ and centre O to produce an image $A'B'C'D'$. Note that

$$\frac{OA'}{OA} = \frac{OB'}{OB} = \frac{OC'}{OC} = \frac{OD'}{OD} = \frac{1}{3}$$

Some examples of size transformations in the physical world are:

(a) A car and its scale model
(b) A photograph and its enlargement.

Two geometric figures are *similar* if one can be transformed into another by an enlargement, contraction, translation or rotation.

PROPERTIES OF SIZE TRANSFORMATIONS

(a) Angles between corresponding line segments are invariant.
(b) The image of a line, not passing through the centre of the enlargement, is a parallel line not passing through the centre of the enlargement.
(c) A line through the centre of the enlargement is invariant.
(d) Lengths of all line segments are magnified or diminished in the ratio $k : 1$, where k is the magnification factor.
(e) The shape of a geometric figure is invariant but lengths are not invariant.
(f) An enlargement or a contraction is not a congruency transformation but it is a similarity transformation.

From the above properties of size transformations the following familiar statements may be deduced:

(a) In similar figures corresponding angles have the same measure.

(b) In similar figures corresponding sides are proportional.

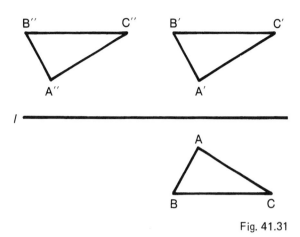

Exercise 184 – *All type B*

1) A circle has a centre O and a radius of 5 cm. What is its image under a size transformation with centre O and magnitude 3?

2) E is an enlargement of magnitude 10. If $E(\triangle ABC) = \triangle A'B'C'$ and $BC = 15\,cm$ find $B'C'$.

3) In Fig. 41.30, CD is mapped onto AB by a contraction. Find the magnitude of the contraction and then find the length OB.

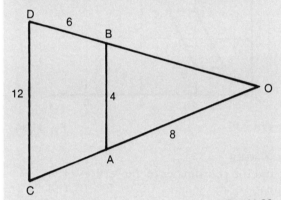

Fig. 41.30

4) Draw on graph paper the triangle ABC where $A(1,2)$, $B(3,4)$ and $C(2,6)$ are the vertices. Draw the image of ABC if it is enlarged by a size transformation of magnitude 2, centre at the origin.

5) The triangle $A(2,1)$, $B(4,2)$ and $C(3,3)$ is transformed into $A'(7,6)$, $B'(11,8)$ and $C'(9,10)$. Draw, on graph paper, the pre-image and the image of the triangle. Hence find the magnitude of the enlargement and the centre of the transformation.

†GLIDE REFLECTIONS

In Fig. 41.31, the triangle ABC is reflected in the line l to triangle A'B'C' followed by translation to triangle A"B"C". The composite of these two transformations is called a *glide reflection*. A good example of an object and its glide reflection image is successive footprints.

Fig. 41.31

Definition: If r_m is a reflection in a line m and T a transformation parallel to m, then $G = T \circ r_m$ is a *glide reflection*.

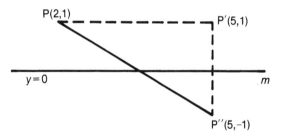

Fig. 41.32

In Fig. 41.32, the point $P(2,1)$ is translated to $P'(5,1)$ and then reflected in the line $y = 0$ to $P''(5,-1)$. P'' is the image of P under a glide reflection.

PROPERTIES OF GLIDE REFLECTIONS

(a) A glide reflection, G, is completely defined by giving the reflecting line and the magnitude and direction of the translation.

(b) If $G = T_0 r_m$ and $G(P) = P'$, then the mid-point of PP' lies on m (Fig. 41.32).

(c) Under a glide transformation the object and its image are congruent.

(d) Under a glide transformation the object and its image have opposite orientation.

Of the transformations studied so far, only translation and rotation preserve orientation. If, therefore, two congruent triangles have opposite orientations there is either a reflection or a glide reflection which maps one onto the other.

†SHEAR

A shear may be defined as a transformation which changes the shape of a figure but preserves its area.

If a pack of cards is stacked so as to form a rectangular prism and the short edges are pushed so that the face containing them remains flat but slopes, the original rectangular face has been *sheared* into a parallelogram.

Under a shear a point moves in one direction parallel to the line of the shear.

In Fig. 41.33, AB is the line of shear or the line of zero movement. On a coordinate system, the simplest situation arises when the x-axis is the line of zero movement and the shear is parallel to it. In this case the movement of a point $P(x, y)$ is a fixed multiple of the y-coordinate. That is, the image of $P(x, y)$ is $P'(x + ky, y)$, where k is a constant.

Note that shear is neither a congruency nor a similarity transformation.

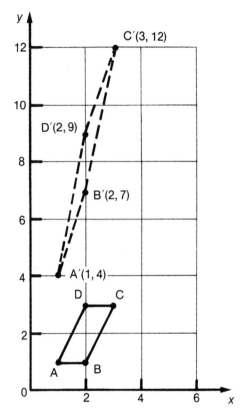

Fig. 41.34

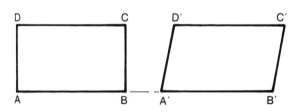

Fig. 41.33

EXAMPLE 8

Find the coordinates of the vertices of the image of the parallelogram $A(1, 1)$, $B(2, 1)$, $C(3, 3)$ and $D(2, 3)$ under the shear given by $(x, y) \rightarrow (x, 3x + y)$.

If the image is $A'B'C'D'$ then

$\quad A'$ is the point $(1, 3 \times 1 + 1)$ or $(1, 4)$

$\quad B'$ is the point $(2, 3 \times 2 + 1)$ or $(2, 7)$

$\quad C'$ is the point $(3, 3 \times 3 + 3)$ or $(3, 12)$

$\quad D'$ is the point $(2, 3 \times 2 + 3)$ or $(2, 9)$

The parallelogram and its image are shown in Fig. 41.34.

EXAMPLE 9

Find the coordinates of the vertices of the image of the square $A(2, 0)$, $B(4, 0)$, $C(4, 2)$ and $D(2, 2)$ under the shear given by $(x, y) \rightarrow (x + 2y, y)$.

If the image is $A'B'C'D'$ then

$\quad A'$ is the point $(2, 0)$, $\ B'$ is the point $(4, 0)$, C' is the point $(8, 2)$, and D' is the point $(6, 2)$.

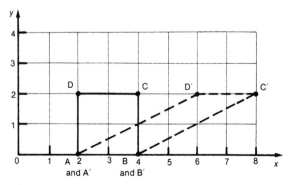

Fig. 41.35

The transformation is shown in Fig. 41.35 and we see that A and A' and B and B' coincide.

PROPERTIES OF A SHEAR TRANSFORMATION

(a) A shear preserves collinearity and betweeness.
(b) A shear preserves distance between two points on lines parallel to the line of zero movement.
(c) A shear preserves area.
(d) A shear does not, in general, preserve angle measure or distance.

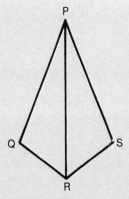

Fig. 41.36

Exercise 185 – *All type C*

1) Find the coordinates of the vertices of triangle $A'B'C'$, the image of triangle ABC, under the shear given by $(x,y) \to (x, 2x + y)$. A is the point $(1,0)$, B is the point $(3,4)$ and C is the point $(2,-1)$.

2) In a shear the line $y = 0$ is invariant and the point $(1,1)$ is mapped onto $(3,1)$. Find the image of the points $(2,0)$ and $(3,2)$.

3) In a shear the line $x = 0$ is invariant. The line $y = 0$ is mapped onto the line $y = x$. Find the images of the points $(0,1)$ and $(1,1)$.

4) Find the coordinates of the vertices of $A'B'C'D'$, the image of the square $ABCD$ under the shear given by $(x,y) \to (x + 3y, y)$. A is the point $(1,3)$, B is the point $(3,3)$, C is the point $(3,5)$ and D is the point $(1,5)$.

5) The line AB with end points $A(1,1)$ and $B(2,3)$ is given a glide reflection. The line is first given a translation $\binom{2}{4}$ followed by a reflection in the line $y = 0$. Find the coordinates of A' and B', the images of A and B under this transformation.

6) A point P is transformed under a glide reflection to P'. If P is the point $(3,2)$ and P' the point $(1,5)$ find the equation of the reflecting line, the translation being $\binom{0}{3}$.

SELF-TEST 41

1) The point $P(3,1)$ is reflected in the x-axis $(y = 0)$. What are the coordinates of the image of P?

a $(3,-1)$ **b** $(-3,1)$ **c** $(-3,-1)$
d $(-1,-3)$ **e** $(-1,3)$

2) Triangle PQR (Fig. 41.36) is reflected in the line PR. Which one of the following statements is *false*?

a The image of P is P
b QS bisects angle PQR
c QR and its image intersect on the line PR
d QS is perpendicular to the line PR

3) Triangle PQR is rotated through $90°$ about P in an anticlockwise direction. The transformation maps P onto P', Q onto Q' and R onto R'. Which one of the following is true?

a $Q = Q'$ **b** $RQ \perp R'Q'$
c $Q'P' \parallel QP$ **d** $RP \perp R'Q'$

4) T is a transformation which maps triangle LMN onto triangle $L'M'N'$ such that $L(-4,2) \to L'(-2,4)$, $M(-2,5) \to M'(-5,2)$ and $N(-2,2) \to N'(-2,2)$. T is a:

a rotation of $+90°$ about N
b reflection in the line $y = x$
c rotation through $-90°$ about N
d reflection in the line $y = -x$

5) Which one of the four figures in Fig. 41.37 possesses rotational symmetry of order 2?

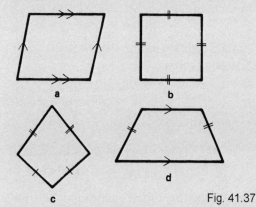

Fig. 41.37

6) If PQRS is any rectangle such that
PQ ≠ QR then PQRS has two of the
following properties:
  (i) Rotational symmetry of order 2.
  (ii) Rotational symmetry of order greater
       than 2.
  (iii) No axes of bilateral symmetry.
  (iv) Two axes of bilateral symmetry.
  (v) Four axes of bilateral symmetry.
Which are the properties?

a (ii) and (v)   **b** (i) and (iii)
c (i) and (iv)   **d** (ii) and (iv)

7) Which one of these statements is never true?

a A reflection followed by a reflection is
   equivalent to a rotation.
b A reflection followed by a reflection is
   equivalent to a translation.

c A translation followed by a rotation is
   equivalent to a rotation.
d A reflection followed by a translation is
   equivalent to a translation.

8) T is the transformation which enlarges
triangle XYZ. Which one of the following
statements is true?

a angle XYZ = angle X'Y'Z'   **b** XY = X'Y'
c $\triangle$XYZ $\equiv$ $\triangle$X'Y'Z'   **d** YZ = Y'Z'

9) Which one of the following statements is
false?

a Translation preserves orientation.
b A glide reflection preserves orientation.
c A shear preserves area.
d A size transformation preserves shape.

CHAPTER 41 SUMMARY

Points to remember

(i)   A transformation is a change or
      movement of a two-dimensional figure.
      E.g. slides, turns, etc.
(ii) In some transformations the size and
      shape of the figure is unchanged. These
      are called *isometries*.
(iii) A *translation* is a movement of a figure
      along a straight line for a certain
      distance without turning the figure
      during the move.
(iv) A reflection is a transformation in which
      the object and its image are the same
      distance from the reflecting line.
(v)   The reflecting line bisects the line

segment joining a point and its image at
right angles.
(vi) A rotation is a circular movement about
      a point.
(vii) A rotation may be in a clockwise or anti-
      clockwise direction.
(viii) A *glide reflection* is a reflection in a line
      m followed by a translation parallel
      to *m*.
(ix) A *shear* is a transformation of points in a
      plane in which one line remains fixed,
      and all other points move parallel to the
      line by an amount proportional to their
      distances from the line.

Chapter 42 **Vectors**

A vector is a quantity which has both magnitude and direction. A velocity of 30 km/h due west is a vector quantity and so is a force of 80 newtons acting downwards.

Representing Vector Quantities

If Susan walks 8 metres due east, how can we represent this vector quantity in a diagram? We first choose a suitable scale to represent the information. In Fig. 42.1 a scale of 1 cm = 1 m has been chosen. We then draw a line 8 cm long to represent 8 m in an easterly direction. An arrow is placed on the line to make it clear that Susan walked to the east (and not to the west).

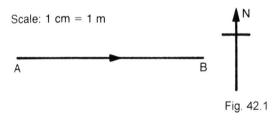

Scale: 1 cm = 1 m

Fig. 42.1

When we want to refer to a vector several times we need a shorthand way of doing this. The usual way is to name the end points of the vector. The vector described by Susan would have started at A and ended at B. If we now want to refer to the vector we write $\overrightarrow{AB}$, which means 'the vector from A to B'.

Draw the following vectors using a convenient scale for each. Label each vector correctly.

1) $\overrightarrow{AB}$ 5 m due north

2) $\overrightarrow{XY}$ 8 km due south

3) $\overrightarrow{PQ}$ 7 km due west

4) $\overrightarrow{MN}$ 10 m due east

5) $\overrightarrow{RS}$ 6 m south-east

In Fig. 42.2, A, B and C are three points marked out in a field. A man walks from A to B (i.e. he describes $\overrightarrow{AB}$) and then walks from B to C (i.e. he describes $\overrightarrow{BC}$). Instead, the man could have walked from A to C, thus describing the vector $\overrightarrow{AC}$.

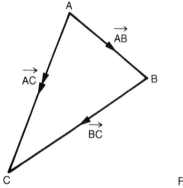

Fig. 42.2

Now going from A to C direct has the same result as going from A to C via B. We therefore call $\overrightarrow{AC}$ the *resultant* of the vectors $\overrightarrow{AB}$ and $\overrightarrow{BC}$. Note that the arrows on the vectors $\overrightarrow{AB}$ and $\overrightarrow{BC}$ follow nose to tail. The resultant $\overrightarrow{AC}$ is marked with a double arrow.

The resultant of any two vectors is equal to the length and direction of the line needed to complete the triangle. This is called the triangle law.

EXAMPLE 1

Two vectors act as shown in Fig. 42.3. Find the resultant of these two vectors.

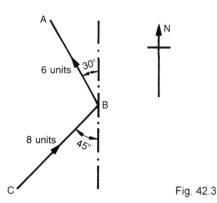

Fig. 42.3

The vector triangle is drawn to scale in Fig. 42.4. The resultant is $\overrightarrow{CA}$. The length of $\overrightarrow{CA}$, written $|\overrightarrow{CA}|$, is 11.2 units. To state its direction we measure the angle ACX which is found to be 31°.

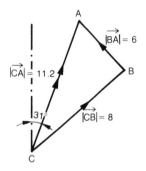

Fig. 42.4

Exercise 187 – *All type B*

Find the resultant (in magnitude and direction) of the pairs of vectors shown in Fig. 42.5.

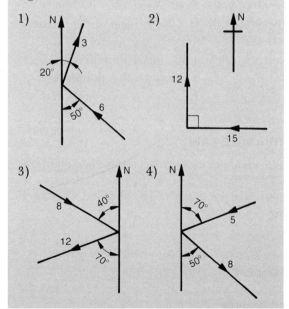

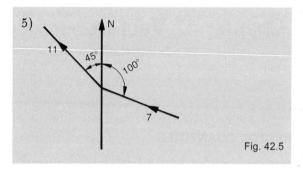

Fig. 42.5

†EQUAL VECTORS

Two vectors are equal if they have the *same magnitude* and the same direction. Hence in Fig. 42.6, the vector AB is equal to the vector CD, because the length of AB is equal to that of CD and AB is parallel to CD.

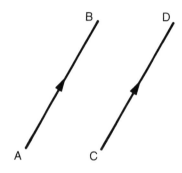

Fig. 42.6

†INVERSE VECTORS

In Fig. 42.7, the vector $\overrightarrow{BA}$ has the same magnitude as $\overrightarrow{AB}$ but its direction is reversed. Hence $\overrightarrow{BA} = -\overrightarrow{AB}$. $\overrightarrow{BA}$ is said to be the inverse of $\overrightarrow{AB}$.

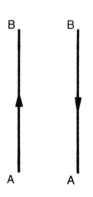

Fig. 42.7

THE SUM OF TWO VECTORS

In Fig. 42.8 the arrows on the vectors $\overrightarrow{AB}$ and $\overrightarrow{BC}$ follow nose to tail. Hence we say that $\overrightarrow{AC}$ is the resultant of these two vectors and we write:

$$\overrightarrow{AB} + \overrightarrow{BC} = \overrightarrow{AC}$$

The resultant vector $\overrightarrow{AC}$ is the sum of the two vectors $\overrightarrow{AB}$ and $\overrightarrow{BC}$.

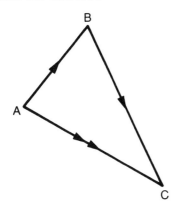

Fig. 42.8

EXAMPLE 2

ABCD is a parallelogram (Fig. 42.9). $\overrightarrow{AB} = \mathbf{x}$ and $\overrightarrow{BC} = \mathbf{y}$.

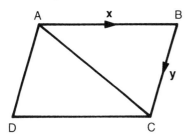

Fig. 42.9

(a) Express $\overrightarrow{DC}$ in terms of $\mathbf{x}$.

(b) Express $\overrightarrow{AD}$ in terms of $\mathbf{y}$.

(c) Express $\overrightarrow{AC}$ in terms of $\mathbf{x}$ and $\mathbf{y}$.

(a) $\overrightarrow{DC}$ is equal to $\overrightarrow{AB}$ because they have the same magnitude and AB and DC are parallel. Hence $\overrightarrow{DC} = \mathbf{x}$.

(b) For the same reasons, $\overrightarrow{AD} = \overrightarrow{BC}$ and hence $\overrightarrow{AD} = \mathbf{y}$.

(c) AC is the resultant of AB and BC because the arrows on AB and AC follow nose to tail. Hence:

$$\overrightarrow{AC} = \overrightarrow{AB} + \overrightarrow{BC} = \mathbf{x} + \mathbf{y}$$

More than two vectors may be added together. The resultant of the four vectors shown in Fig. 42.10 is found by drawing the vector diagram as shown. Thus:

$$\mathbf{a} + \mathbf{b} + \mathbf{c} + \mathbf{d} = \mathbf{r}$$

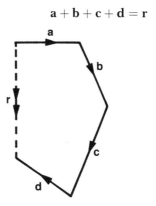

Fig. 42.10

The addition of vectors is commutative. That is, it does not matter in which order the vectors are added. In Fig. 42.11 in (a) $\mathbf{a}$ has been added to $\mathbf{b}$ whilst in (b) $\mathbf{b}$ has been added to $\mathbf{a}$. In each case the resultant is the same.

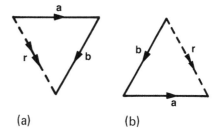

(a)   (b)

Fig. 42.11

†SUBTRACTION OF VECTORS

To subtract a vector we add its inverse. Hence

$$\overrightarrow{AC} - \overrightarrow{BC} = \overrightarrow{AC} + \overrightarrow{CB} = \overrightarrow{AB}$$

as shown in Fig. 42.12.

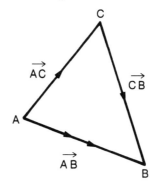

Fig. 42.12

†MULTIPLYING BY A SCALAR

If a vector $\overrightarrow{AB}$ is 5 m due north, then the vector $3\overrightarrow{AB}$ is 15 m due north. In general, if k is any number, the vector $k\overrightarrow{AB}$ is a vector in the same direction as $\overrightarrow{AB}$ whose length is k times the length of $\overrightarrow{AB}$.

EXAMPLE 3

C is the mid-point of AD (Fig. 42.13) and $AC = \mathbf{a}$. Express DA in terms of $\mathbf{a}$.

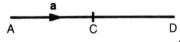

Fig. 42.13

$$\overrightarrow{AD} = \overrightarrow{AC} + \overrightarrow{CD} = \mathbf{a} + \mathbf{a} = 2\mathbf{a}$$

Since $\overrightarrow{DA}$ is the inverse of $\overrightarrow{AD}$,

$$\overrightarrow{DA} = -2\mathbf{a}$$

†DISTRIBUTIVE LAW FOR VECTORS

From our previous work

$$3\mathbf{a} = \mathbf{a} + \mathbf{a} + \mathbf{a}$$

$$\therefore \quad 3(\mathbf{a} + \mathbf{b}) = (\mathbf{a} + \mathbf{b}) + (\mathbf{a} + \mathbf{b}) + (\mathbf{a} + \mathbf{b})$$

$$= \mathbf{a} + \mathbf{b} + \mathbf{a} + \mathbf{b} + \mathbf{a} + \mathbf{b}$$

$$= (\mathbf{a} + \mathbf{a} + \mathbf{a}) + (\mathbf{b} + \mathbf{b} + \mathbf{b})$$

$$= 3\mathbf{a} + 3\mathbf{b}$$

Similarly it can be shown that, if k is a scalar,

$$k(\mathbf{a} + \mathbf{b}) = k\mathbf{a} + k\mathbf{b}$$

This is the distributive law for vectors.

EXAMPLE 4

In Fig. 42.14, $\overrightarrow{PX} = \mathbf{a}$ and $\overrightarrow{XQ} = \mathbf{b}$. $\overrightarrow{YP} = 2\mathbf{a}$ and $\overrightarrow{QZ} = 2\mathbf{b}$. Find YZ in terms of $\mathbf{a}$ and $\mathbf{b}$ and show that PQ and YZ are parallel.

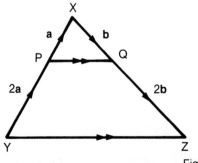

Fig. 42.14

Referring to Fig. 42.14, we see that

$$\overrightarrow{PQ} = \mathbf{a} + \mathbf{b}$$

$$\overrightarrow{YZ} = \overrightarrow{YX} + \overrightarrow{XZ} = (2\mathbf{a} + \mathbf{a}) + (2\mathbf{b} + \mathbf{b})$$

$$= 3\mathbf{a} + 3\mathbf{b} = 3(\mathbf{a} + \mathbf{b})$$

Hence $\overrightarrow{YZ}$ is 3 times the magnitude of $\overrightarrow{PQ}$. Since $\overrightarrow{PQ} = (\mathbf{a} + \mathbf{b})$ and $\overrightarrow{YZ} = 3(\mathbf{a} + \mathbf{b})$, $\overrightarrow{PQ}$ and $\overrightarrow{YZ}$ must be in the same direction; i.e. they are parallel to each other.

EXAMPLE 5

In Fig. 42.15, M is the mid-point of RS. $PQ = \mathbf{a}$, $QR = \mathbf{b}$ and $MR = \mathbf{c}$. Express each of the following in terms of $\mathbf{a}$, $\mathbf{b}$ and $\mathbf{c}$.

(a) $\overrightarrow{SR}$ (b) $\overrightarrow{PR}$ (c) $\overrightarrow{QM}$ (d) $\overrightarrow{PM}$

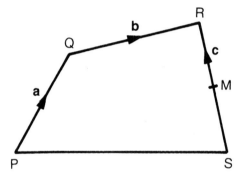

Fig. 42.15

(a) In Fig. 42.16(a),

$$\overrightarrow{SR} = 2\overrightarrow{MR} = 2\mathbf{c}$$

(b) In $\triangle PQR$ (Fig. 42.16(b)), PR is the resultant of PQ and QR. Hence:

$$\overrightarrow{PR} = \overrightarrow{PQ} + \overrightarrow{QR} = \mathbf{a} + \mathbf{b}$$

(c) In $\triangle QRM$ (Fig. 42.16(c)), QR is the resultant of QM and RM. Hence:

$$\overrightarrow{QR} = \overrightarrow{QM} + \overrightarrow{MR}$$

$$\overrightarrow{QM} = \overrightarrow{QR} - \overrightarrow{MR} = \mathbf{b} - \mathbf{c}$$

(d) In $\triangle PRM$ (Fig. 42.16(d)), PR is the resultant of PM and MR. Hence:

$$\overrightarrow{PR} = \overrightarrow{PM} + \overrightarrow{MR}$$

$$\overrightarrow{PM} = \overrightarrow{PR} - \overrightarrow{MR} = \mathbf{a} + \mathbf{b} - \mathbf{c}$$

(a)

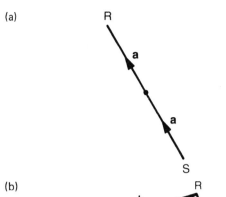

(b)

(c)

(d)

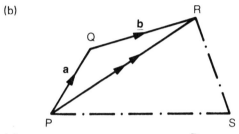

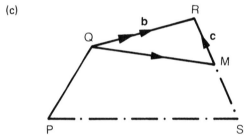

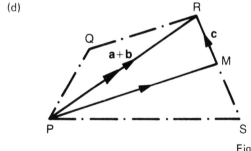

Fig. 42.16

Exercise 188 – *All type C*

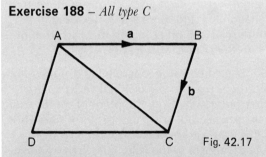

Fig. 42.17

1) In Fig. 42.17, ABCD is a parallelogram. AB = **a** and BC = **b**. Express in terms of **a** and **b**:

(a) $\overrightarrow{AD}$ (b) $\overrightarrow{CD}$ (c) $\overrightarrow{AC}$.

2) In Fig. 42.18, NP = 2MN. If MN = **a**, express in terms of **a**:

(a) $\overrightarrow{NP}$ (b) $\overrightarrow{PM}$.

Fig. 42.18

3) In Fig. 42.19, XYZ is an isosceles triangle. W is the mid-point of XZ. If $\overrightarrow{XY}$ = **a** and $\overrightarrow{YZ}$ = **b**, express in terms of **a** and **b**:

(a) $\overrightarrow{XZ}$ (b) $\overrightarrow{ZW}$ (c) $\overrightarrow{YW}$.

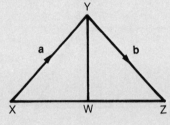

Fig. 42.19

4) In Fig. 42.20, ABC is a triangle in which AC = **a**, BC = **b** and AD = **c**. D is the mid-point of AB. Express in terms of **a**, **b** and **c**:

(a) $\overrightarrow{DB}$ (b) $\overrightarrow{BA}$ (c) $\overrightarrow{CD}$.

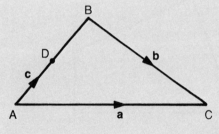

Fig. 42.20

5) In Fig. 42.21, D and E are the mid-points of AB and AC respectively. AD = **a** and AE = **b**. Express in terms of **a** and **b**:

(a) $\overrightarrow{ED}$ (b) $\overrightarrow{DE}$ (c) $\overrightarrow{BD}$

(d) $\overrightarrow{AB}$ (e) $\overrightarrow{CE}$ (f) $\overrightarrow{AC}$.

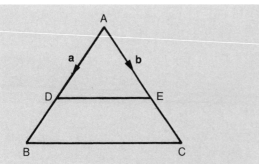

Fig. 42.21

6) In Fig. 42.22, AB is parallel to DC and DC = 2AB. If $\overrightarrow{DA} = \mathbf{a}$ and $\overrightarrow{AB} = \mathbf{b}$, express in terms of **a** and **b**:

(a) $\overrightarrow{DB}$ (b) $\overrightarrow{DC}$ (c) $\overrightarrow{BC}$.

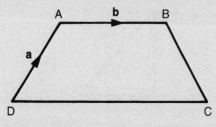

Fig. 42.22

7) In Fig. 42.23, ST = 2TP. If $\overrightarrow{TP} = \mathbf{a}$, $\overrightarrow{PQ} = \mathbf{b}$ and $\overrightarrow{QR} = \mathbf{c}$, express in terms of **a**, **b** and **c**:

(a) $\overrightarrow{RT}$ (b) $\overrightarrow{ST}$ (c) $\overrightarrow{SR}$.

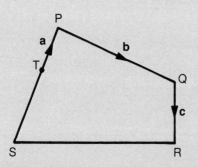

Fig. 42.23

8) In Fig. 42.24, ABCDEF is a regular hexagon. If AF = **a**, AB = **b** and BC = **c**, express each of the following in terms of **a**, **b** and **c**:

(a) $\overrightarrow{DC}$ (b) $\overrightarrow{DE}$ (c) $\overrightarrow{FE}$

(d) $\overrightarrow{FC}$ (e) $\overrightarrow{AE}$ (f) $\overrightarrow{AD}$.

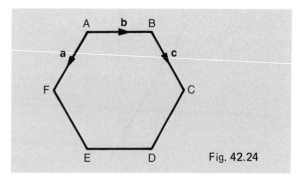

Fig. 42.24

†THE PARALLELOGRAM OF VECTORS

Two vectors may be added by drawing a parallelogram of vectors. This is an alternative method to the triangle of vectors so far used. The method is shown in Example 6.

EXAMPLE 6

Draw the parallelogram of vectors for the two vectors shown in Fig. 42.25(a) and hence find their resultant in magnitude and direction.

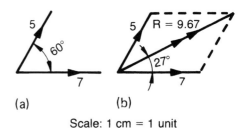

Scale: 1 cm = 1 unit

Fig. 42.25

The two vectors are drawn to scale with the angle between them accurately made by using a protractor. The parallelogram is then completed as shown by the dotted lines in diagram (b). The diagonal drawn from the point where the two original vectors meet gives the resultant vector, in magnitude and direction. On scaling, it is found to be 9.6 units acting in a direction of 27° to the 7 unit vector.

Note that when using a parallelogram of vectors both the arrows on the original vectors must either point away from the point of intersection of the two vectors or they must point towards it. In Fig. 42.26(a) the arrows on the two vectors do not conform to the rule. One arrow points towards A whilst the other points away from A. However, the horizontal vector remains unchanged if we draw it as shown in diagram (b), i.e. with its arrow pointing away from A. Alternatively, the parallelogram may be drawn as shown in diagram (c) with both arrows pointing towards A. Note that if both arrows point away from A (diagram (b)) then the arrows on the resultant also point away from A. If both arrows point towards A, then the resultant vector also points towards A.

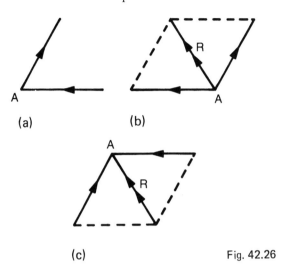

(a)   (b)

(c)   Fig. 42.26

Exercise 189 – *All type B*

By drawing a parallelogram of vectors find the resultant vector in each of the cases shown in Fig. 42.27.

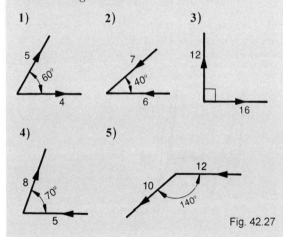

1)   2)   3)

4)   5)

Fig. 42.27

†APPLICATION OF VECTORS TO GEOMETRY

It will be recalled that the vectors $\mathbf{a}$ and $k\mathbf{a}$, where k is a scalar, are parallel, and also that $k(\mathbf{a} + \mathbf{b}) = k\mathbf{a} + k\mathbf{b}$.

These two facts are useful in solving certain geometric problems.

EXAMPLE 7

(1) ABCD is a parallelogram. DN and BM are perpendicular to the diagonal AC. Show that BM = DN.

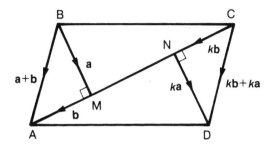

Fig. 42.28

BM and DN are parallel since they both lie at $90°$ to AC. Let $\overrightarrow{BM} = \mathbf{a}$ and $\overrightarrow{ND} = k\mathbf{a}$ (Fig. 42.28).

Also, AM and NC lie in the same straight line. Let $\overrightarrow{MA} = \mathbf{b}$ and $\overrightarrow{CN} = k\mathbf{b}$.

$$\overrightarrow{BA} = \overrightarrow{BM} + \overrightarrow{MA} = \mathbf{a} + \mathbf{b}$$

$$\overrightarrow{CD} = \overrightarrow{CN} + \overrightarrow{ND} = k\mathbf{b} + k\mathbf{a} = k(\mathbf{a} + \mathbf{b})$$

Since $\overrightarrow{BA} = \overrightarrow{CD}$

$$\mathbf{a} + \mathbf{b} = k(\mathbf{a} + \mathbf{b})$$

$\therefore$ $$k = 1$$

$\therefore$ $$\mathbf{a} = k\mathbf{a}$$

Hence $$BM = DN$$

(2) In $\triangle ABC$, D is a point on AB such that BD = 2AD and E is a point in AC such that CE = 2AE. Show that DE is parallel to BC and that BC = 3DE.

The conditions are shown in Fig. 42.29.

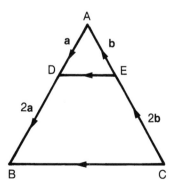

Fig. 42.29

Let $\overrightarrow{AD} = \mathbf{a}$, then $\overrightarrow{DB} = 2\mathbf{a}$.

Let $\overrightarrow{EA} = \mathbf{b}$, then $\overrightarrow{CE} = 2\mathbf{b}$.

Referring to Fig. 42.29, we see that

$$\overrightarrow{ED} = \mathbf{b} + \mathbf{a}$$

$$\overrightarrow{CB} = (\mathbf{b} + 2\mathbf{b}) + (\mathbf{a} + 2\mathbf{a})$$

$$= 3\mathbf{b} + 3\mathbf{a} = 3(\mathbf{b} + \mathbf{a})$$

Hence DE is parallel to BC and BC = 3DE.

Exercise 190 – *All type C*

The following questions should be solved by using vectors.

1) In $\triangle PQR$ (Fig. 42.30), the line ST is drawn parallel to QR so that PS = 3SQ. Prove that PT = 3TR.

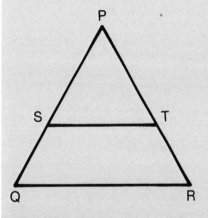

Fig. 42.30

2) In the parallelogram ABCD, the point P is taken on the side AB such that AP = 2PB. The lines BD and PC intersect at O. Show that OC = 3PO.

3) In $\triangle ABC$, the point P is the mid-point of AB. A line through P parallel to BC meets AC at Q. Prove that $PQ = \frac{1}{2}BC$.

4) In Fig. 42.31, ABCD is a parallelogram. Q is the mid-point of CD. Show that 2AQ = AD + AC = 2AD + AB.

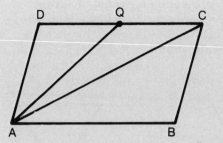

Fig. 42.31

5) AB is parallel to DC and AB = DC. Prove that BC is parallel to AD and that BC = AD.

6) In Fig. 42.32, D is the mid-point of BC and $AG = \frac{2}{3}AD$. Prove that 2BD + BA = 3BG.

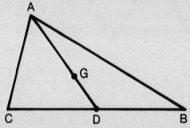

Fig. 42.32

7) In $\triangle ABC$, P is the mid-point of AB and Q is the mid-point of AC. Show that BC is parallel to PQ and that BC = 2PQ.

8) Two parallelograms ABCD and ABEF are shown in Fig. 42.33. Prove that DCEF is a parallelogram.

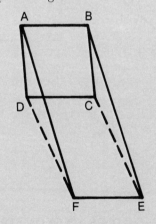

Fig. 42.33

CHAPTER 42 SUMMARY

Points to remember

(i)   A vector quantity has both magnitude and direction.

(ii)   A vector quantity may be represented by a directed line segment.

(iii) The vectors $\overrightarrow{AB}$ and $\overrightarrow{BA}$ are equal in length, but are in opposite directions. Hence $\overrightarrow{AB} = -\overrightarrow{BA}$.

(iv) If $\overrightarrow{AB} = \mathbf{a}$, and $\overrightarrow{PQ} = k\mathbf{a}$, then $\overrightarrow{PQ}$ is parallel to $\overrightarrow{AB}$, and k times as long.

(v)   If $\overrightarrow{AB} = k\overrightarrow{BC}$, then points A, B and C are in a straight line (collinear).

(vi) $\overrightarrow{AB} + \overrightarrow{BC} = \overrightarrow{AC}$.

(vii) $\overrightarrow{AC} - \overrightarrow{BC} = \overrightarrow{AC} + \overrightarrow{CB} = \overrightarrow{AB}$.

Chapter 43 **Applications of Vectors**

VECTOR QUANTITIES

As stated in Chapter 42, a *vector* is a quantity which possesses both magnitude (or size) and direction. Some examples of vector quantities are:

(1) A displacement from one point to another, e.g. 15 m due east.

(2) A velocity in a given direction, e.g. 8 m/s due north.

(3) A force acting in a given direction, e.g. 20 newtons acting downwards.

VELOCITY VECTORS

Velocity is speed in a given direction. Hence velocity is a vector quantity. Common examples of velocity vectors are the flight of aeroplanes and the motion of a boat through water.

COURSE AND AIRSPEED

The direction in which an aircraft is heading (i.e. pointing) is called its *course*. It is the angle between the longitudinal axis of the aircraft and the direction of north (Fig. 43.1).

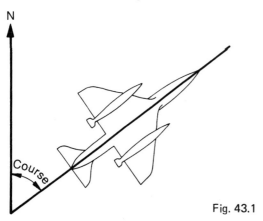

Fig. 43.1

The course is usually given in the three digit notation, e.g. 036° or 205°. The airspeed is the speed of the aircraft in still air and the airspeed at which an aircraft is flying may be read directly from the airspeed indicator which is an instrument mounted in the cockpit. The course is measured by means of the aircraft's compass and hence airspeed and course form a vector quantity.

TRACK AND GROUNDSPEED

The track is the direction which the aircraft follows relative to the ground. If the sun is immediately overhead the track is the path of the aircraft's shadow over the ground. When a pilot wishes to fly from aerodrome A to aerodrome B, his track would be the straight line joining A and B. The groundspeed is the speed of the aircraft relative to the ground and it is affected by the direction and speed of the wind. It is the groundspeed which determines the time that a flight will take. Groundspeed and track form a vector quantity just as did airspeed and course.

WIND DIRECTION AND SPEED

The direction of the wind is always given as the direction from which the wind is blowing. The arrow on the wind vector always points in the direction to which the wind blows. Thus a wind of 40 km/h blowing from 060° will be represented as shown in Fig. 43.2.

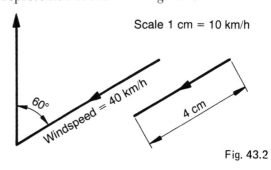

Fig. 43.2

DRIFT

The wind always tries to blow an aircraft off course, that is, it causes *drift*. The drift is the angle between the course and the track (Fig. 43.3). If there is no wind there is no drift and the airspeed and groundspeed are identical as are the course and the track.

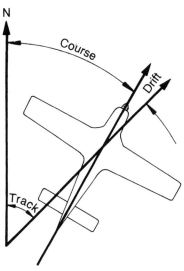

Fig. 43.3

THE TRIANGLE OF VELOCITIES

When an aeroplane is flying it has two velocities as follows:

(1) its velocity through the air due to the engine,

(2) the velocity due to the wind.

These two velocities combine to give a resultant velocity which is the groundspeed.

In order to determine this resultant velocity we draw a triangle of velocities similar to the one shown in Fig. 43.4. In drawing this triangle note that *the arrows on the airspeed and windspeed vectors follow nose to tail.*

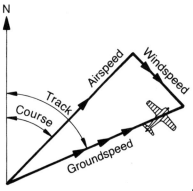

Fig. 43.4

Case 1: Given airspeed and course, windspeed and direction and to find groundspeed and track.

EXAMPLE 1

An aircraft whose airspeed is 400 km/h flies on a course of 050°. If the wind blows at 50 km/h from 310° find the track and groundspeed.

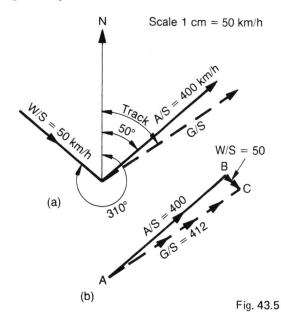

Fig. 43.5

(a) Draw diagram (a) in Fig. 43.5 which shows the directions of the airspeed (A/S) and the windspeed (W/S). On this diagram only the angles are drawn accurately.

(b) To draw the velocity triangle first choose a suitable scale to represent the velocities. In Fig. 45.10 (b) a scale of 1 cm = 50 km/h has been chosen. Using set-squares draw AB parallel to the A/S and 8 cm long to represent 400 km/h. From B draw a line parallel to the W/S 1 cm long to give the point C. Join AC. AC represents the groundspeed (G/S) in magnitude and direction. Scale off AC which is found to be 8.24 cm representing 412 km/h. To find the direction of AC (i.e. the track) draw a line parallel to AC onto diagram (a) as shown. Using a protractor the track is found to be 57°.

Case 2: Given airspeed and course, groundspeed and track to find windspeed and direction.

EXAMPLE 2

The course and airspeed of an aircraft are 060° and 500 km/h whilst its track and groundspeed are 070° and 520 km/h. Find the speed and direction of the wind.

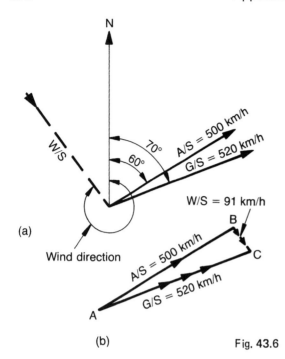

(a)

Wind direction

(b)

Fig. 43.6

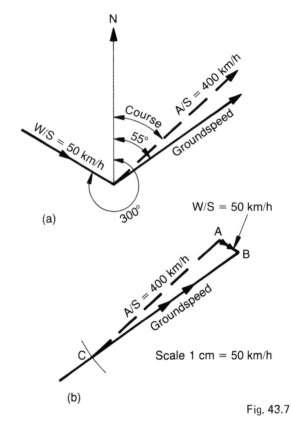

(a)

W/S = 50 km/h

Scale 1 cm = 50 km/h

(b)

Fig. 43.7

(a) Draw diagram (a) in Fig. 43.6 which shows the directions of the airspeed (A/S) and the groundspeed (G/S). On this diagram only the angles are drawn accurately.

(b) To draw the velocity triangle shown in diagram (b) a scale of 1 cm = 50 km/h has been chosen. Using set-squares draw AB, 10 cm long, parallel to A/S and then draw AC, 10.4 cm long, parallel to G/S. Join BC. BC represents the windspeed and scaling BC the windspeed is found to be 91 km/h. To find the wind direction draw a line parallel to BC on diagram (a) as shown. By using a protractor the wind direction is found to be 322° (that is, the wind blows from 322°).

Case 3: Given airspeed, track, windspeed and wind direction to find the course and groundspeed.

Since a navigator knows his airspeed and the track required and also the windspeed and direction this is the case usually met with in practice.

EXAMPLE 3

An aircraft has an airspeed of 400 km/h and its track is 055°. The speed of the wind is 50 km/h blowing from 300°. Find the course and groundspeed.

On diagram (a) in Fig. 43.7 we can draw the wind direction and also the track of the aircraft.

(a) Choosing a scale of 1 cm = 50 km/h we draw AB = 1 cm to represent the windspeed (diagram (b)). From B draw a line parallel to G/S. The length of this line is not known as yet. With compasses set at 8 cm (to represent the A/S of 400 km/h) and centre A draw an arc to cut the G/S line at C. BC represents the G/S and by scaling, the G/S = 419. Drawing a line parallel to AC on diagram (a) the course is found to be 048.5°.

Exercise 191 – *All type C*

Find the track and groundspeed in each of the following:

1) Course 270°, airspeed 300 km/h; wind 135°, 60 km/h.

2) Course 090°, airspeed 500 km/h; wind 010°, 50 km/h.

3) Course 150°, airspeed 400 km/h; wind 070°, 50 km/h.

4) Course 310°, airspeed 350 km/h; wind 110°, 40 km/h.

5) Course 020°, airspeed 300 km/h; wind 320°, 80 km/h.

Find the wind velocity for each of the following:

6) Course 050°, airspeed 280 km/h; track 060°, groundspeed 300 km/h.

7) Course 160°, airspeed 350 km/h; track 180°, groundspeed 330 km/h.

8) Course 210°, airspeed 420 km/h; track 190°, groundspeed 410 km/h.

9) Course 300°, airspeed 450 km/h; track 320°, groundspeed 435 km/h.

10) Course 060°, airspeed 250 km/h; track 040°, groundspeed 260 km/h.

Find the course and groundspeed for each of the following:

11) Track 090°, airspeed 300 km/h; wind 060°, 50 km/h.

12) Track 150°, airspeed 400 km/h; wind 040°, 30 km/h.

13) Track 210°, airspeed 350 km/h; wind 100°, 50 km/h.

14) Track 300°, airspeed 250 km/h; wind 120°, 45 km/h.

15) Track 010°, airspeed 300 km/h; wind 330°, 60 km/h.

THE TRIANGLE OF VELOCITIES APPLIED TO BOATS

The motion of a boat through water is very similar to the flight of an aeroplane through air. The corresponding terms are: for wind velocity read *current velocity*; for airspeed read *the speed of the boat through the water* (i.e. *waterspeed*); for groundspeed and track read *resultant speed* and the *direction of motion of the boat.*

EXAMPLE 4

P is the point on the bank of a river 240 m wide flowing at 2 m/s. R is directly opposite P. A boat travels through the water at 8 m/s.

(a) If the boat starts from P and heads directly across the stream how far downstream from R will it reach the bank?

(b) Calculate the speed relative to the banks with which a direct crossing from P to R will be made.

(a) The triangle of velocities is shown in Fig. 43.8 from which $\theta = 14°$.

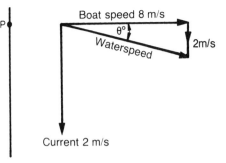

Fig. **43.8**

Referring to Fig. 43.9, it will be seen that distance downstream from R is

$$240 \tan 14° = 60 \, \text{m}.$$

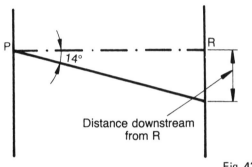

Fig. **43.9**

(b) The problem here is to find the waterspeed. From the triangle of velocities (Fig. 43.10)

$$\text{Waterspeed} = \sqrt{8^2 - 2^2} = \sqrt{60} = 7.75 \, \text{m/s}$$

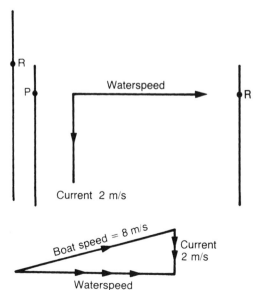

Fig. **43.10**

Exercise 192 – *All type C*

1) A boat which has a speed of 10 km/h is to be steered across a river in which there is a steady current of 5 km/h flowing parallel to the banks. If the river is 800 m wide and the boat is to cross at right angles to the bank find the direction in which it should be steered (relative to the bank).

2) A stream flows at 8 km/h. A motor boat can travel at 20 km/h in still water. What angle must the boat make with the direction of the flow of the stream to reach a point directly across the stream?

3) The speed of a boat in still water is 12 km/h. The navigator wishes to travel due east from A to B (Fig. 43.11) in a current which he estimates to be of velocity 5 km/h in a direction 140°. Unknown to the navigator when he sails the actual velocity of the current is 4 km/h in a direction 140°. By drawing show the actual path of the boat and find the speed of the boat and the bearing of its path.

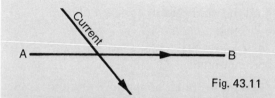

Fig. 43.11

4) A man crosses a river flowing at 2 m/s by means of a rowing boat which he can propel through still water at 5 m/s. Q is the point on the far bank directly opposite his starting point P. By accurate drawing find:
(a) at what angle to PQ he must head the boat in order to land at Q;
(b) how far downstream from Q he will land if the river is 240 m wide and he heads the boat slightly upstream at 15° to PQ.

5) A river flows at 6 km/h due south between parallel banks.
(a) A motor boat whose speed in still water is 9 km/h leaves a point on one bank and steers a course due east. Find by scale drawing the actual path of the boat and state the bearing.
(b) A second motor boat, whose speed in still water is also 9 km/h, leaves a point on one bank and sets a course so as to travel due east. Find, by a second scale drawing, the course set by the boat.

CHAPTER 43 SUMMARY

Points to remember

(i) *Velocity* and *force* are examples of vectors. The velocity of an object is defined by its speed and its direction. Similarly force has magnitude and it is exerted in a specified direction.

(ii) Velocity and force may be represented by lines of given magnitude and in stated directions.

Chapter 44 **Vectors, Matrices and Transformations**

VECTORS REPRESENTED AS MATRICES

The point P (Fig. 44.1) has the rectangular coordinates $x = 4$ and $y = 3$, usually written $(4, 3)$ for brevity. The position vector corresponding to OP is written $\overrightarrow{OP}$. The magnitude of the vector is represented by the length OP, and the direction of the vector by the direction of the arrow.

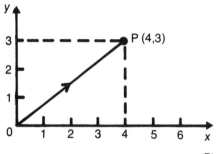

Fig. 44.1

The column matrix $\begin{pmatrix} 4 \\ 3 \end{pmatrix}$ can be thought of as a position vector representing the carriage from the origin to the point P whose coordinates are $(4, 3)$.

In general if the coordinates of P are (x, y) the position vector corresponding to $\overrightarrow{OP}$ is $\begin{pmatrix} x \\ y \end{pmatrix}$. The magnitude (or modulus) of $\overrightarrow{OP}$ is the distance from O to P and is found by using Pythagoras. In the example of Fig. 44.1 the magnitude of $\overrightarrow{OP}$ is $\sqrt{4^2 + 3^2} = 5$.

ADDITION OF VECTORS

Two vectors may be added by drawing a parallelogram of vectors (Fig. 44.2). If OA represents the vector P and OB the vector Q then $P + Q$ is represented by the vector OC, where OC is the diagonal of the parallelogram OACB.

We may write $\overrightarrow{OA} + \overrightarrow{OB} = \overrightarrow{OC}$ or $P + Q = R$.

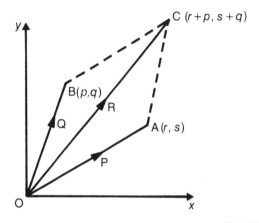

Fig. 44.2

In Fig. 44.2, $P = \begin{pmatrix} r \\ s \end{pmatrix}$, $Q = \begin{pmatrix} p \\ q \end{pmatrix}$ and hence

$$R = P + Q = \begin{pmatrix} r \\ s \end{pmatrix} + \begin{pmatrix} p \\ q \end{pmatrix} = \begin{pmatrix} r+p \\ s+q \end{pmatrix}$$

EXAMPLE 1

If $U = \begin{pmatrix} 2 \\ 1 \end{pmatrix}$ and $V = \begin{pmatrix} 1 \\ 3 \end{pmatrix}$ find $R = U + V$ and determine the magnitude of R. What is the direction of R?

$$R = \begin{pmatrix} 2 \\ 1 \end{pmatrix} + \begin{pmatrix} 1 \\ 3 \end{pmatrix} = \begin{pmatrix} 3 \\ 4 \end{pmatrix}$$

Since the coordinates of point P (Fig. 44.3) are $(3, 4)$ the length of OP is

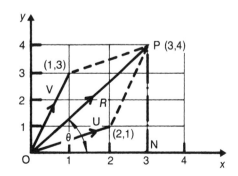

Fig. 44.3

$\sqrt{3^2 + 4^2} = 5$. Hence the magnitude of R is 5.

$$\tan \theta = \frac{PN}{ON} = \frac{4}{3}$$

$$\therefore \qquad \theta = 53.13°$$

Exercise 193 – *All type B*

1) Find the modulus of each of the following vectors and state its direction:

(a) $\begin{pmatrix} 3 \\ 1 \end{pmatrix}$ (b) $\begin{pmatrix} 5 \\ 7 \end{pmatrix}$ (c) $\begin{pmatrix} 3 \\ 8 \end{pmatrix}$

2) If $U = \begin{pmatrix} 1 \\ 4 \end{pmatrix}$ and $V = \begin{pmatrix} 3 \\ 2 \end{pmatrix}$ find

$R = U + V$. State the magnitude of R and its direciton.

3) If $P = \begin{pmatrix} 2 \\ 6 \end{pmatrix}$ and $Q = \begin{pmatrix} 4 \\ 2 \end{pmatrix}$ find

$R = P + Q$. State the magnitude of R and its direction.

4) $R = M + N$. If $R = \begin{pmatrix} 7 \\ 6 \end{pmatrix}$ and

$N = \begin{pmatrix} 2 \\ 4 \end{pmatrix}$ find M. Calculate the

magnitude of M and determine its direction.

TRANSFORMATIONS AND MATRICES

Transformations and matrices are closely related. Most of the transformations which were studied in Chapter 41 may be described by using matrices.

REFLECTION

Let us associate the column matrix $\begin{pmatrix} x \\ y \end{pmatrix}$ with the point (x, y).

We have seen that the reflection of (x, y) over the x-axis is $(x, -y)$ (Fig. 44.4). Now the matrix multiplication gives us

$$\begin{pmatrix} 1 & 0 \\ 0 & -1 \end{pmatrix} \begin{pmatrix} x \\ y \end{pmatrix} = \begin{pmatrix} x \\ -y \end{pmatrix}$$

Hence the matrix $\begin{pmatrix} 1 & 0 \\ 0 & -1 \end{pmatrix}$ can be

associated with the transformation M_{Ox} (i.e. the reflection over Ox).

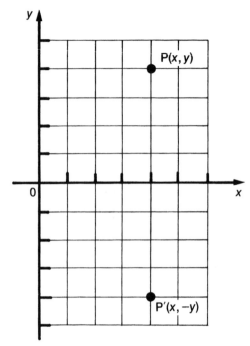

Fig. 44.4

Similarly it can be shown that reflection over

Oy can be described by the matrix $\begin{pmatrix} -1 & 0 \\ 0 & 1 \end{pmatrix}$

and reflections over $y = x$ and $y = -x$

can be described by the matrices $\begin{pmatrix} 0 & 1 \\ 1 & 0 \end{pmatrix}$

and $\begin{pmatrix} 0 & -1 \\ -1 & 0 \end{pmatrix}$ respectively.

OBTAINING A MATRIX TO DESCRIBE A PARTICULAR TRANSFORMATION

Suppose we want to obtain the matrix for reflection in the line $y = x$ (Fig. 44.5). Using graph paper we can draw the line $y = x$ (Fig. 44.5). Choosing two or three points we can construct their reflections in the line $y = x$. For example, if we choose the two points $(3, 2)$ and $(2, 1)$ we find that:

Image of $(3, 2)$ is $(2, 3)$

Image of $(2, 1)$ is $(1, 2)$

From this pattern we may conjecture that the reflection of any point (r, s) in $y = x$ is (s, r).

We therefore need to find a matrix $\begin{pmatrix} a & b \\ c & d \end{pmatrix}$

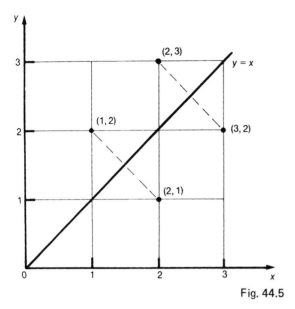

Fig. 44.5

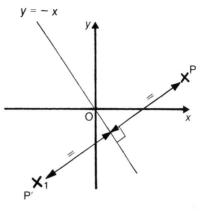

Fig. 44.6

such that

$$\begin{pmatrix} a & b \\ c & d \end{pmatrix}\begin{pmatrix} r \\ s \end{pmatrix} = \begin{pmatrix} s \\ r \end{pmatrix}$$

We obtain this matrix by choosing special values for r and s.

If we choose $(1, 0)$ and $(0, 1)$ then

$$\begin{pmatrix} a & b \\ c & d \end{pmatrix}\begin{pmatrix} 1 \\ 0 \end{pmatrix} = \begin{pmatrix} 0 \\ 1 \end{pmatrix}, \qquad \begin{pmatrix} a \\ c \end{pmatrix} = \begin{pmatrix} 0 \\ 1 \end{pmatrix}$$

and $a = 0$ and $c = 1$

and

$$\begin{pmatrix} a & b \\ c & d \end{pmatrix}\begin{pmatrix} 0 \\ 1 \end{pmatrix} = \begin{pmatrix} 1 \\ 0 \end{pmatrix}, \qquad \begin{pmatrix} b \\ d \end{pmatrix} = \begin{pmatrix} 1 \\ 0 \end{pmatrix}$$

and $b = 1$ and $d = 0$

Hence the transformations matrix is $\begin{pmatrix} 0 & 1 \\ 1 & 0 \end{pmatrix}$.

Note that in choosing two points to obtain the transformation matrix we can, in fact, choose any two points we like. We only choose the points $(1, 0)$ and $(0, 1)$ because these values make the work easier.

REFLECTION IN THE LINE $y = -x$

In Fig. 44.6, the point P has been reflected so that its image is P'. The line $y = -x$ is the perpendicular bisector of PP'.

The matrix $\begin{pmatrix} 0 & -1 \\ -1 & 0 \end{pmatrix}$ will transform the

point P into its reflection in the line $y = -x$.

Generally, reflection in the line
$ax + by + c = 0$ is given by

$$\begin{pmatrix} x' \\ y' \end{pmatrix} = \frac{1}{a^2 + b^2}\begin{pmatrix} b^2 - a^2 & -2ab \\ -2ab & a^2 - b^2 \end{pmatrix}\begin{pmatrix} x \\ y \end{pmatrix}$$

$$-\frac{1}{a^2 + b^2}\begin{pmatrix} 2a & 0 \\ 2b & 0 \end{pmatrix}\begin{pmatrix} c \\ 1 \end{pmatrix}$$

EXAMPLE 2

If a point P has the coordinates $(3, 2)$ find its reflection (a) in the x-axis, (b) in the y-axis, (c) in the line $y = -x$, (d) in the line $y = x$.

(a) To find the coordinates of the image of P, the position vector $\begin{pmatrix} 3 \\ 2 \end{pmatrix}$ is premultiplied by the

matrix $\begin{pmatrix} 1 & 0 \\ 0 & -1 \end{pmatrix}$. Thus:

$$\begin{pmatrix} 1 & 0 \\ 0 & -1 \end{pmatrix}\begin{pmatrix} 3 \\ 2 \end{pmatrix} = \begin{pmatrix} 3 \\ -2 \end{pmatrix}$$

Hence the point P is transformed to the point $(3, -2)$.

(b) The coordinates of the image of P are found by the matrix multiplication:

$$\begin{pmatrix} -1 & 0 \\ 0 & 1 \end{pmatrix}\begin{pmatrix} 3 \\ 2 \end{pmatrix} = \begin{pmatrix} -3 \\ 2 \end{pmatrix}$$

Here the point P has the image $P'(-3, 2)$.

(c) The following matrix product gives the coordinates of the image of P:

$$\begin{pmatrix} 0 & -1 \\ -1 & 0 \end{pmatrix}\begin{pmatrix} 3 \\ 2 \end{pmatrix} = \begin{pmatrix} -2 \\ -3 \end{pmatrix}$$

Hence the coordinates of the image of P in the origin are $(-3, -2)$.

(d) The coordinates of the image of P are found by obtaining the following matrix product:

$$\begin{pmatrix} 0 & 1 \\ 1 & 0 \end{pmatrix} \begin{pmatrix} 3 \\ 2 \end{pmatrix} = \begin{pmatrix} 2 \\ 3 \end{pmatrix}$$

Hence the point P has the image P′(2, 3).

ISOMETRICS

These are transformations which preserve all lengths. Hence in an *isometric* transformation shape, size, area and angles are unaltered. Translation and reflection are examples of isometric transformations.

OTHER TRANSFORMATIONS

If a position vector is premultiplied by a 2 × 2 matrix it is transformed into another column matrix.

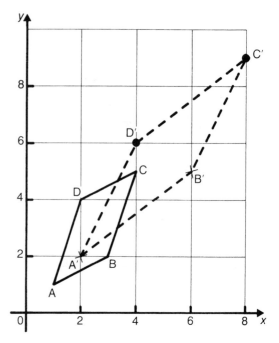

Fig. 44.7

EXAMPLE 3

A parallelogram has the coordinate matrix

$$\begin{array}{cccc} A & B & C & D \end{array}$$
$$\begin{pmatrix} 1 & 3 & 4 & 2 \\ 1 & 2 & 5 & 4 \end{pmatrix}$$

i.e. (1, 1), (3, 2), (4, 5) and (2, 4) are the coordinates of the points A, B, C and D respectively.

It is transformed into A′B′C′D′ by the matrix $\begin{pmatrix} 2 & 0 \\ 1 & 1 \end{pmatrix}$. Find the coordinate matrix for A′B′C′D′.

$$\begin{pmatrix} 2 & 0 \\ 1 & 1 \end{pmatrix} \begin{array}{cccc} A & B & C & D \\ \begin{pmatrix} 1 & 3 & 4 & 2 \\ 1 & 2 & 5 & 4 \end{pmatrix} \end{array}$$

$$= \begin{array}{cccc} A' & B' & C' & D' \\ \begin{pmatrix} 2 & 6 & 8 & 4 \\ 2 & 5 & 9 & 6 \end{pmatrix} \end{array}$$

The transformed parallelogram A′B′C′D′ and the original parallelogram ABCD are shown in Fig. 44.7. Note that A′B′C′D′ is larger than ABCD and hence the transformation is not isometric.

DOUBLE TRANSFORMATIONS

A double transformation is one transformation (e.g. a reflection) followed by a second transformation (e.g. a translation). A double transformation may be made into a single operation by multiplying the two matrices, which describe the transformations, together. We premultiply the matrix describing the first transformation by the matrix describing the second transformation.

EXAMPLE 4

A rectangle ABCD has the coordinate matrix

$$\begin{array}{cccc} A & B & C & D \end{array}$$
$$\begin{pmatrix} 2 & 6 & 6 & 2 \\ 1 & 1 & 3 & 3 \end{pmatrix}$$

It is given a double transformation under $\begin{pmatrix} 1 & 3 \\ 0 & 1 \end{pmatrix}$ followed by $\begin{pmatrix} 1 & 0 \\ 4 & 1 \end{pmatrix}$. Find the coordinate matrix for the image of ABCD.

The single matrix which will give the double transformation is:

$$M = \begin{pmatrix} 1 & 0 \\ 4 & 1 \end{pmatrix} \begin{pmatrix} 1 & 3 \\ 0 & 1 \end{pmatrix} = \begin{pmatrix} 1 & 3 \\ 4 & 13 \end{pmatrix}$$

If $A'B'C'D'$ is the image of ABCD, its coordinate matrix is found by premultiplying the coordinate matrix for ABCD by M. Thus:

$$\begin{array}{cccc} & A & B & C & D \end{array}$$
$$\begin{pmatrix} 1 & 3 \\ 4 & 13 \end{pmatrix} \begin{pmatrix} 2 & 6 & 6 & 2 \\ 1 & 1 & 3 & 3 \end{pmatrix}$$

$$\begin{array}{cccc} & A' & B' & C' & D' \end{array}$$
$$= \begin{pmatrix} 5 & 9 & 15 & 11 \\ 21 & 37 & 63 & 47 \end{pmatrix}$$

GLIDE REFLECTION

This transformation is produced by a translation followed by a reflection.

EXAMPLE 5

The point $P(2,4)$ is given a glide reflection. After translation under $\begin{pmatrix} 4 \\ 0 \end{pmatrix}$ it is reflected in the x-axis. Determine the coordinates of the image of P. The translation is:

$$\begin{pmatrix} 2 \\ 4 \end{pmatrix} + \begin{pmatrix} 4 \\ 0 \end{pmatrix} = \begin{pmatrix} 6 \\ 4 \end{pmatrix}$$

The reflection is:

$$\begin{pmatrix} 1 & 0 \\ 0 & -1 \end{pmatrix} \begin{pmatrix} 6 \\ 4 \end{pmatrix} = \begin{pmatrix} 6 \\ -4 \end{pmatrix}$$

As shown in Fig. 44.8, the coordinates of the image of P are $(6, -4)$.

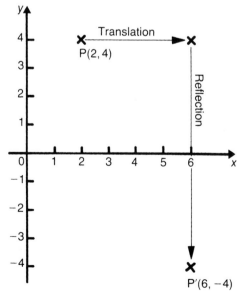

Fig. 44.8

ROTATION

In Fig. 44.9 the point P has been given an anticlockwise rotation of $30°$ about the origin.

It can be shown that the matrix

$\begin{pmatrix} \cos\alpha & -\sin\alpha \\ \sin\alpha & \cos\alpha \end{pmatrix}$ will rotate the point $\begin{pmatrix} x \\ y \end{pmatrix}$ through the angle α counterclockwise about the origin.

A rotation through the angle α about (h,k) is given by

$$\begin{pmatrix} x' \\ y' \end{pmatrix} = \begin{pmatrix} \cos\alpha & -\sin\alpha \\ \sin\alpha & \cos\alpha \end{pmatrix} \begin{pmatrix} x \\ y \end{pmatrix}$$
$$+ \begin{pmatrix} 1-\cos\alpha & \sin\alpha \\ -\sin\alpha & 1-\cos\alpha \end{pmatrix} \begin{pmatrix} h \\ k \end{pmatrix}$$

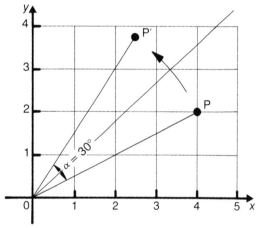

Fig. 44.9

EXAMPLE 6

A point P has the coordinates $(3,4)$. Find its new coordinates if it is rotated through $30°$ counterclockwise about the origin.

The new coordinates are found by premultiplying the position vector $\begin{pmatrix} 3 \\ 4 \end{pmatrix}$ by the matrix

$$\begin{pmatrix} \cos 30° & -\sin 30° \\ \sin 30° & \cos 30° \end{pmatrix} = \begin{pmatrix} 0.866 & -0.5 \\ 0.5 & 0.866 \end{pmatrix}$$

Thus

$$\begin{pmatrix} 0.866 & -0.5 \\ 0.5 & 0.866 \end{pmatrix} \begin{pmatrix} 3 \\ 4 \end{pmatrix} = \begin{pmatrix} 0.598 \\ 4.964 \end{pmatrix}$$

EXAMPLE 7

The point $P(2, 4)$ is rotated $\frac{1}{4}$ of a turn about the origin. Find the coordinates of P', the image of P.

Since $\frac{1}{4}$ turn $= 90°$, the coordinates of P' are found by premultiplying the position vector $\begin{pmatrix} 2 \\ 4 \end{pmatrix}$ by the matrix

$$\begin{pmatrix} \cos 90° & -\sin 90° \\ \sin 90° & \cos 90° \end{pmatrix} = \begin{pmatrix} 0 & -1 \\ 1 & 0 \end{pmatrix}$$

$$\begin{pmatrix} 0 & -1 \\ 1 & 0 \end{pmatrix}\begin{pmatrix} 2 \\ 4 \end{pmatrix} = \begin{pmatrix} -4 \\ 2 \end{pmatrix}$$

Hence the image is $P'(-4, 2)$.

INVERSE TRANSFORMATIONS

The inverse of a transformation puts a point (or a figure) back to its original position. Suppose that a point P is given a transformation described by a matrix A so that its image is P'. The transformation of P' back to P is described by the matrix A^{-1}, i.e. the inverse of the matrix A.

EXAMPLE 8

The image of a rectangle is $A'(8, 12)$, $B'(12, 16)$, $C'(24, 13)$, $D'(17, 27)$. The matrix $\begin{pmatrix} 2 & 3 \\ 2 & 5 \end{pmatrix}$ effects the transformation of ABCD onto $A'B'C'D'$. Find the coordinate matrix of ABCD.

$$\begin{pmatrix} 2 & 3 \\ 2 & 5 \end{pmatrix}^{-1} = \frac{1}{4}\begin{pmatrix} 5 & -3 \\ -2 & 2 \end{pmatrix}$$

$$= \begin{pmatrix} 1.25 & -0.75 \\ -0.5 & 0.5 \end{pmatrix}$$

Hence,

$$\begin{pmatrix} 1.25 & -0.75 \\ -0.5 & 0.5 \end{pmatrix}\begin{array}{c}A'B'C'D'\\\begin{pmatrix} 8 & 12 & 24 & 17 \\ 12 & 16 & 13 & 27 \end{pmatrix}\end{array}$$

$$= \begin{array}{c}ABCD\\\begin{pmatrix} 1 & 3 & 3 & 1 \\ 2 & 2 & 5 & 5 \end{pmatrix}\end{array}$$

Exercise 194 – All type C

1) The vertices of the square ABCD are respectively $(0, 1)$, $(2, 1)$, $(2, 3)$ and $(0, 3)$. Obtain the coordinate matrix for the image of ABCD after each of the following reflections:
(a) Reflection in the x-axis.
(b) Reflection in the y-axis.
(c) Reflection in the origin.
(d) Reflection in the line $y = x$.
(e) If the square ABCD is translated by the vector $\begin{pmatrix} 1 \\ 3 \end{pmatrix}$ write down the coordinate matrix for the transformation.

2) Triangle $A'B'C'$ is the image of triangle ABC after translation by the vector $\begin{pmatrix} -3 \\ 2 \end{pmatrix}$. A', B' and C' have the coordinates $(5, 3)$, $(3, 1)$ and $(4, 2)$ respectively. Give the coordinates of A, B and C before translation.

3) Write down the coordinates of the following points under the translation $\begin{pmatrix} -2 \\ 4 \end{pmatrix}$.
(a) $(1, 3)$ (b) $(2, 1)$ (c) $(-4, -3)$
(d) $(-2, 5)$ (e) $(7, 0)$

4) The vertices of a triangle ABC have the following coordinates: $(2, 1)$, $(5, 1)$ and $(5, 4)$. Find the coordinates of the images of A, B and C under the translation $\begin{pmatrix} -3 \\ -7 \end{pmatrix}$. On graph paper show the original triangle ABC and its transformation.

5) A plane figure has the coordinate matrix:

$$\begin{array}{c}ABCDE\\\begin{pmatrix} 1 & 3 & 4 & 2 & 0 \\ -2 & 0 & 2 & 4 & 5 \end{pmatrix}\end{array}$$

Obtain the coordinate matrix of the figure after the following transformations:
(a) Translation under $\begin{pmatrix} -1 \\ -2 \end{pmatrix}$.
(b) Reflection in the x-axis.
(c) Reflection in the y-axis.
(d) Reflection in the origin.
(e) Reflection in the line $y = x$.

6) Map the points shown in the following coordinate matrix:

$$\begin{matrix} \text{A} & \text{B} & \text{C} & \text{D} \\ \begin{pmatrix} 1 & 3 & 6 & 4 \\ 2 & 3 & 5 & 0 \end{pmatrix} \end{matrix}$$

Join them up to give the figure ABCD. Rotate ABCD through $50°$ anticlockwise about the origin to give the image of ABCD. Mark the image $A'B'C'D'$ and write down the coordinate matrix for this image.

7) The vertices of the square WXYZ are respectively $(1, 2)$, $(3, 2)$, $(3, 4)$ and $(1, 4)$. It is given a rotation of $40°$ about the origin. Find the coordinates of the vertices of the transposed figure.

8) The triangle ABC whose vertices are the points $(1, 3)$, $(3, 5)$ and $(2, 7)$ respectively is given a glide reflection. After translation under $\begin{pmatrix} 0 \\ 3 \end{pmatrix}$ it is reflected in the y-axis. Determine the coordinate matrix for the image of ABC.

9) The point $P(-3, -1)$ is given a transformation under $\begin{pmatrix} 3 & 1 \\ 3 & 2 \end{pmatrix}$ followed by a second transformation under $\begin{pmatrix} 2 & 1 \\ 4 & 2 \end{pmatrix}$.

(a) Find the single matrix which will accomplish the double transformation.
(b) Determine the coordinates of the image of P under these transformations.

10) The triangle ABC with vertices $(10, 10)$, $(20, 15)$ and $(15, 20)$ respectively is given a transformation under $\begin{pmatrix} 1 & 4 \\ 0 & 1 \end{pmatrix}$ followed by a reflection in the x-axis.

(a) Determine the single matrix which will give the double transformation.
(b) Find the coordinate matrix for the image of ABC under these transformations.

11) The point $P(2, 6)$ is given an anticlockwise rotation of $45°$ about the origin followed by a translation under $\begin{pmatrix} -4 \\ -5 \end{pmatrix}$. Find by an accurate drawing the coordinates of the image of P.

12) The square $A(2, 1)$, $B(4, 1)$, $C(4, 3)$, $D(2, 3)$ is given a rotation (anticlockwise) of $\frac{1}{4}$ turn followed by a translation under $\begin{pmatrix} -1 \\ -5 \end{pmatrix}$. Draw the transformed figure and state the coordinates of its vertices.

13) If A denotes the translation $\begin{pmatrix} 3 \\ 2 \end{pmatrix}$ and B denotes the translation $\begin{pmatrix} 1 \\ -1 \end{pmatrix}$, write down the coordinates of the points onto which $(2, 1)$ is mapped under the following transformations:

(a) AB (b) BA (c) B^2
(d) A^{-1} (e) B^{-1} (f) ABA
(g) BAB

14) Let T be the transformation described by the matrix $\begin{pmatrix} 2 & 1 \\ 1 & 1 \end{pmatrix}$. After transformation under this matrix the image of $\triangle ABC$ is $A'(8, 5)$, $B'(11, 6)$, $C'(11, 7)$. Find the coordinates of the points A, B and C.

SIMILARITIES

Similarities are transformations which multiply all lengths by a scale factor. If the scale factor is greater than 1, the transformation is called an *enlargement*. If the scale factor is less than 1, the transformation is said to be a *reduction*. With both reductions and enlargements, angles are preserved and hence the transformed figures are similar to the original figures (see Chapter 29).

In Fig. 44.10, the points $A(3, 2)$, $B(8, 2)$, $C(8, 3)$ and $D(3, 3)$ have been plotted. The points have been joined to give the rectangle ABCD. In order to form the rectangle $A'B'C'D'$, each of the points (x, y) have been mapped onto (x', y') by the mapping:

$$(x, y) \rightarrow (2x, 2y)$$

Thus, $A(3, 2) \rightarrow A'(6, 4)$

and $B(8, 2) \rightarrow B'(16, 4)$ etc.

As can be seen from the diagram, the image $A'B'C'D'$ is twice the size of ABCD. That is, ABCD has been enlarged by a factor of 2. The same result could have been obtained by

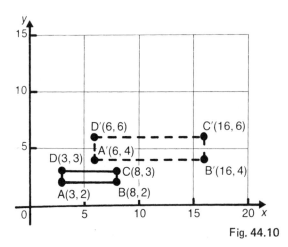

Fig. 44.10

multiplying the coordinate matrix of ABCD by the scalar 2. Thus,

$$2\begin{pmatrix} A & B & C & D \\ 3 & 8 & 8 & 3 \\ 2 & 2 & 3 & 3 \end{pmatrix} = \begin{pmatrix} A' & B' & C' & D' \\ 6 & 16 & 16 & 6 \\ 4 & 4 & 6 & 6 \end{pmatrix}$$

The same enlargement would be produced by premultiplying the coordinate matrix of ABCD by the 2×2 matrix $\begin{pmatrix} 2 & 0 \\ 0 & 2 \end{pmatrix}$. Thus:

$$\begin{pmatrix} 2 & 0 \\ 0 & 2 \end{pmatrix} \begin{pmatrix} A & B & C & D \\ 3 & 8 & 8 & 3 \\ 2 & 2 & 3 & 3 \end{pmatrix}$$

$$= \begin{pmatrix} A' & B' & C' & D' \\ 6 & 16 & 16 & 6 \\ 4 & 4 & 6 & 6 \end{pmatrix}$$

If an enlargement or reduction of $n : 1$ is required then the coordinate matrix of the figure is premultiplied by the 2×2 matrix $\begin{pmatrix} n & 0 \\ 0 & n \end{pmatrix}$.

An enlargement with a scale factor n and centre O can be constructed by drawing lines from O (the origin) through the points A, B and C (Fig. 44.11) and marking off $OA' = n \times OA$, $OB' = n \times OB$ and $OC' = n \times OC$. When a figure is enlarged in this way the enlarged figure ($A'B'C'$ in the diagram) is similar to the original figure ABC and corresponding lines are parallel.

The centre of an enlargement or reduction need not be at the origin. Consider the triangle ABC formed by A(2, 1), B(4, 2), C(3, 3) in Fig. 44.12.

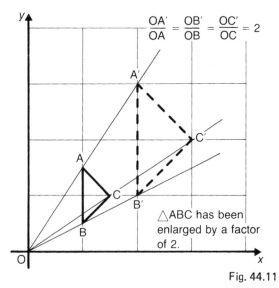

$$\frac{OA'}{OA} = \frac{OB'}{OB} = \frac{OC'}{OC} = 2$$

△ABC has been enlarged by a factor of 2.

Fig. 44.11

It is transformed onto A'(7, 6), B'(11, 8), C'(9, 10) by means of an enlargement, centre the origin, and a translation. The centre of enlargement, S, is found by joining AA', BB' and CC' and producing them to intersect at a single point. This point is the centre of enlargement.

From the diagram we see that the centre of enlargement is S(−3, −4).

The centre of enlargement can be found by solving a matrix equation of the type:

$$\begin{pmatrix} n & 0 \\ 0 & n \end{pmatrix} \begin{pmatrix} x \\ y \end{pmatrix} + \begin{pmatrix} h \\ k \end{pmatrix} = \begin{pmatrix} x \\ y \end{pmatrix}$$

where n is the enlargement factor, x and y are the coordinates of the centre of rotation and $\begin{pmatrix} h \\ k \end{pmatrix}$ is a vector describing a translation.

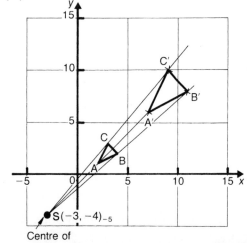

S(−3, −4)

Centre of enlargement

Fig. 44.12

An enlargement or reduction with scale factor n and centre (h, k) is given by

$$\begin{pmatrix} x' \\ y' \end{pmatrix} = \begin{pmatrix} n & 0 \\ 0 & n \end{pmatrix} \begin{pmatrix} x \\ y \end{pmatrix} + \begin{pmatrix} 1-n & 0 \\ 0 & 1-n \end{pmatrix} \begin{pmatrix} h \\ k \end{pmatrix}$$

EXAMPLE 9

The rectangle $A(2, 1), B(4, 1), C(4, 4), D(2, 4)$ is mapped onto $A''B''C''D''$ by the enlargement

$$\begin{pmatrix} x \\ y \end{pmatrix} \rightarrow \begin{pmatrix} 4 & 0 \\ 0 & 4 \end{pmatrix} \begin{pmatrix} x \\ y \end{pmatrix} + \begin{pmatrix} 6 \\ 9 \end{pmatrix}$$

(a) Find the coordinates of the centre of enlargement.
(b) On a diagram show the transformation and the centre of enlargement.

To find the coordinates of the centre of enlargement we solve the matrix equation:

$$\begin{pmatrix} 4 & 0 \\ 0 & 4 \end{pmatrix} \begin{pmatrix} x \\ y \end{pmatrix} + \begin{pmatrix} 6 \\ 9 \end{pmatrix} = \begin{pmatrix} x \\ y \end{pmatrix}$$

$$\begin{pmatrix} 4x \\ 4y \end{pmatrix} + \begin{pmatrix} 6 \\ 9 \end{pmatrix} = \begin{pmatrix} x \\ y \end{pmatrix}$$

$$\begin{pmatrix} 4x + 6 \\ 4y + 9 \end{pmatrix} = \begin{pmatrix} x \\ y \end{pmatrix}$$

$4x + 6 = x \quad 3x = -6 \quad$ and $\quad x = -2$

$4y + 9 = y \quad 3y = -9 \quad$ and $\quad y = -3$

The coordinates of the centre of enlargement are therefore $(-2, -3)$.

The enlargement gives the image:

$$\begin{matrix} & A & B & C & D \\ \begin{pmatrix} 4 & 0 \\ 0 & 4 \end{pmatrix} & \begin{pmatrix} 2 & 4 & 4 & 2 \\ 1 & 1 & 4 & 4 \end{pmatrix} \end{matrix}$$

$$= \begin{matrix} A' & B' & C' & D' \\ \begin{pmatrix} 8 & 16 & 16 & 8 \\ 4 & 4 & 16 & 16 \end{pmatrix} \end{matrix}$$

The translation gives the image:

$$\begin{matrix} A'' & B'' & C'' & D'' \\ \begin{pmatrix} 14 & 22 & 22 & 14 \\ 13 & 13 & 25 & 25 \end{pmatrix} \end{matrix}$$

The transformation and the centre of enlargement are shown in Fig. 44.13.

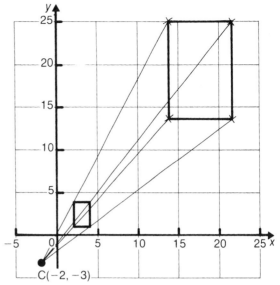

Fig. **44.13**

STRETCH

A *one-way stretch* is an enlargement in one direction only. Thus in Fig. 44.14 ABCD has been mapped onto $AB'C'D$ by a one-way stretch of scale factor 2. The scale factor gives the ratio

$$\frac{\text{area } AB'C'D}{\text{area } ABCD}$$

Thus in the diagram area $AB'C'D$ is twice area ABCD.

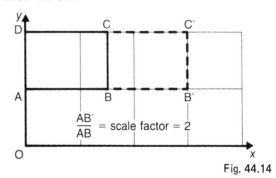

Fig. **44.14**

A one-way stretch is described by the matrix

$$\begin{pmatrix} K & 0 \\ 0 & 1 \end{pmatrix}$$

where K is the scale factor and the y-axis is the invariant line.

If the x-axis is the invariant line then a one-way stretch is described by

$$\begin{pmatrix} 1 & 0 \\ 0 & K \end{pmatrix}$$

EXAMPLE 10

Find the image of the rectangle A(2, 3), B(2, 0), C(3, 0), D(3, 3) under the transformation given by the matrix $\begin{pmatrix} 1 & 0 \\ 0 & 2 \end{pmatrix}$.

$$\begin{pmatrix} 1 & 0 \\ 0 & 2 \end{pmatrix} \begin{matrix} A & B & C & D \\ \begin{pmatrix} 2 & 2 & 3 & 3 \\ 3 & 0 & 0 & 3 \end{pmatrix} \end{matrix}$$

$$= \begin{matrix} A' & B & C & D' \\ \begin{pmatrix} 2 & 2 & 3 & 3 \\ 6 & 0 & 0 & 6 \end{pmatrix} \end{matrix}$$

As shown in Fig. 44.15, the transformation is a one-way stretch with a scale factor of 2, the x-axis being the invariant line.

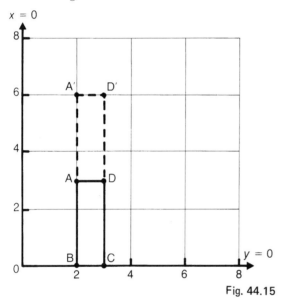

Fig. 44.15

When two one-way stretches are combined at right angles the result is a *two-way stretch*. There are two scale factors, one in each direction, and the origin is the invariant point. A two-way stretch is described by the matrix

$$\begin{pmatrix} H & 0 \\ 0 & K \end{pmatrix}$$

where H and K are the two scale factors. Note that if H or K is equal to 1 the stretch is one way. If $H = K$ the stretch is an enlargement with a scale factor of K and centre $(0, 0)$.

EXAMPLE 11

Find the image of the rectangle O(0, 0), A(2, 0), B(2, 1) and C(0, 1) under the transformation given by the matrix $\begin{pmatrix} 2 & 0 \\ 0 & 3 \end{pmatrix}$.

$$\begin{pmatrix} 2 & 0 \\ 0 & 3 \end{pmatrix} \begin{matrix} O & A & B & C \\ \begin{pmatrix} 0 & 2 & 2 & 0 \\ 0 & 0 & 1 & 1 \end{pmatrix} \end{matrix}$$

$$= \begin{matrix} O & A' & B' & C' \\ \begin{pmatrix} 0 & 4 & 4 & 0 \\ 0 & 0 & 3 & 3 \end{pmatrix} \end{matrix}$$

As can be seen from Fig. 44.16, the transformation is a two-way stretch with a scale factor of 3 parallel to the y-axis and a scale factor of 2 parallel to the x-axis. The origin is the invariant point.

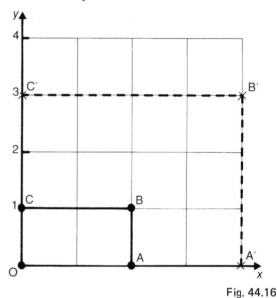

Fig. 44.16

SHEARING

Recall that a shear is a transformation which maps parallel lines onto parallel lines. Thus in Fig. 44.17 a shear transforms the rectangle

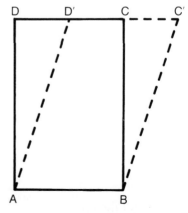

Fig. 44.17

ABCD into the parallelogram ABC′D′. Note that the line AB is invariant (i.e. it does not alter) and that all other points have to move parallel to this invariant line. One of the important features of this transformation is that area is preserved although shape is not.

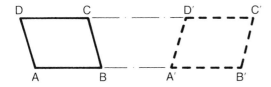

Fig. 44.18

In Fig. 44.17, the invariant line AB coincided with one side of the rectangle ABCD. However this need not be the case. Thus in Fig. 44.18, MN is the invariant line which maps ABCD onto A′B′C′D′.

A matrix that describes a shear, keeping each point of $y = 0$ fixed is of the type:

$$\begin{pmatrix} 1 & K \\ 0 & 1 \end{pmatrix}$$

The element K in the matrix gives the amount of translation of the points C and D in Fig. 44.19. The transformation of ABCD into ABC′D′ is obtained as follows:

$$\begin{pmatrix} 1 & 2 \\ 0 & 1 \end{pmatrix} \overset{\text{A B C D}}{\begin{pmatrix} 1 & 2 & 2 & 1 \\ 0 & 0 & 1 & 1 \end{pmatrix}}$$

$$= \overset{\text{A B C′ D′}}{\begin{pmatrix} 1 & 2 & 4 & 3 \\ 0 & 0 & 1 & 1 \end{pmatrix}}$$

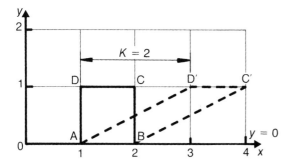

Fig. 44.19

Similarly, the matrix

$$\begin{pmatrix} 1 & 0 \\ K & 1 \end{pmatrix}$$

describes the shear which keeps each point of $x = 0$ fixed.

Exercise 195 – *All type C*

1) Draw on graph paper the triangle A(2, 3), B(4, 1), C(4, 4). Draw the image of △ABC if it is enlarged by a scale factor of 3, centre at the origin.

2) Draw on graph paper the triangle A(1, 1), B(3, 1), C(3, 2). Then draw its image under the transformations whose matrices are:

(a) $\begin{pmatrix} 2 & 0 \\ 0 & 2 \end{pmatrix}$ (b) $\begin{pmatrix} \frac{1}{2} & 0 \\ 0 & \frac{1}{2} \end{pmatrix} + \begin{pmatrix} 2 \\ 1 \end{pmatrix}$

(c) $\begin{pmatrix} -2 & 0 \\ 0 & -2 \end{pmatrix}$

For each transformation find the centre of enlargement.

3) The rectangle A(2, 2), B(4, 2), C(4, 3), D(2, 3) is mapped onto A′B′C′D′ by the enlargement

$$\begin{pmatrix} x \\ y \end{pmatrix} \rightarrow \begin{pmatrix} 3 & 0 \\ 0 & 3 \end{pmatrix}\begin{pmatrix} x \\ y \end{pmatrix} + \begin{pmatrix} 3 \\ 5 \end{pmatrix}$$

Find the coordinates of the centre of enlargement.

4) Apply the shear described by the matrix $\begin{pmatrix} 1 & 3 \\ 0 & 1 \end{pmatrix}$ to the following figures. Illustrate the transformations on separate diagrams.

(a) The square with vertices (0, 0), (2, 0), (2, 2) and (0, 2).
(b) The rectangle with vertices (−2, 0), (1, 0), (1, 2) and (−2, 2).
(c) The parallelogram with vertices (5, 2), (8, 2), (7, 4) and (4, 4).
(d) The trapezium with vertices (2, 1), (6, 1), (6, 3) and (3, 3).

5) Find the image of the rectangle W(2, 4), X(2, 0), Y(4, 0), Z(4, 4) under the transformations given by the following matrices:

(a) $\begin{pmatrix} 2 & 0 \\ 0 & 1 \end{pmatrix}$ (b) $\begin{pmatrix} -3 & 0 \\ 0 & 1 \end{pmatrix}$

(c) $\begin{pmatrix} 1 & 0 \\ 0 & 1\frac{1}{2} \end{pmatrix}$ (d) $\begin{pmatrix} 1 & 0 \\ 0 & -\frac{1}{2} \end{pmatrix}$

6) Find the image of the rectangle $A(0, 0)$, $B(2, 0)$, $C(2, 1)$, $D(0, 1)$ under the transformations given by the following matrices:

(a) $\begin{pmatrix} 2 & 0 \\ 0 & 3 \end{pmatrix}$ (b) $\begin{pmatrix} \frac{1}{2} & 0 \\ 0 & \frac{1}{2} \end{pmatrix} + \begin{pmatrix} 2 \\ 1 \end{pmatrix}$

(c) $\begin{pmatrix} \frac{1}{2} & 0 \\ 0 & 4 \end{pmatrix}$ (d) $\begin{pmatrix} 1\frac{1}{2} & 0 \\ 0 & -1\frac{1}{2} \end{pmatrix}$

SELF-TEST 44

1) The matrix $\begin{pmatrix} 3 & 0 \\ 0 & 1 \end{pmatrix}$ will produce:

a an enlargement   **b** a rotation
c a reflection   **d** a one-way stretch

2) The matrix $\begin{pmatrix} 1 & 0 \\ 0 & -1 \end{pmatrix}$ will produce:

a a rotation through $90°$ clockwise
b a rotation through $90°$ anticlockwise
c a reflection in the line $x = 0$
d a reflection in the line $y = 0$

3) $U = \begin{pmatrix} x \\ y \end{pmatrix}$ and $V = \begin{pmatrix} a \\ b \end{pmatrix}$. If $R = U + V$ then the magnitude of R is:

a $\sqrt{x^2 + y^2}$ **b** $\sqrt{a^2 + b^2}$
c $\sqrt{(x+a)^2 + (y+b)^2}$
d $\sqrt{(x+a) + (y+b)}$

4) A point is given a double transformation under $\begin{pmatrix} 1 & 0 \\ 3 & 2 \end{pmatrix}$ followed by $\begin{pmatrix} 4 & 1 \\ 1 & 0 \end{pmatrix}$. Find the single matrix which will affect the transformation.

a $\begin{pmatrix} 5 & 1 \\ 4 & 2 \end{pmatrix}$ **b** $\begin{pmatrix} 4 & 1 \\ 14 & 3 \end{pmatrix}$ **c** $\begin{pmatrix} 7 & 2 \\ 1 & 0 \end{pmatrix}$
d $\begin{pmatrix} 4 & 2 \\ 5 & 1 \end{pmatrix}$

5) The matrix which will produce a reflection in the line $y = x$ is:

a $\begin{pmatrix} 1 & 0 \\ 0 & -1 \end{pmatrix}$ **b** $\begin{pmatrix} -1 & 0 \\ 0 & 1 \end{pmatrix}$
c $\begin{pmatrix} -1 & 0 \\ 0 & -1 \end{pmatrix}$ **d** $\begin{pmatrix} 0 & 1 \\ 1 & 0 \end{pmatrix}$

6) A triangle ABC is mapped onto $A'B'C'$ by the enlargement $\begin{pmatrix} x \\ y \end{pmatrix} \rightarrow \begin{pmatrix} 5 & 0 \\ 0 & 5 \end{pmatrix}\begin{pmatrix} x \\ y \end{pmatrix} + \begin{pmatrix} 4 \\ 6 \end{pmatrix}$.
What are the coordinates of the centre of the enlargement?

a $(-1, -1.5)$ **b** $(-1.5, -1)$
c $(20, 30)$ **d** $(30, 20)$

7) The matrix $\begin{pmatrix} 3 & 0 \\ 0 & 1 \end{pmatrix}$ describes one of the following:

a a one-way stretch with the x-axis as the invariant line
b a one-way stretch with the y-axis as the invariant line
c a shear which keeps each point of $y = 0$ fixed
d a shear which keeps each point of $x = 0$ fixed.

8) The matrix $\begin{pmatrix} 3 & 0 \\ 0 & 4 \end{pmatrix}$ describes one of the following:

a an enlargement with a scale factor of 3
b an enlargement with a scale factor of 4
c a two-way stretch with the origin as the invariant point
d an enlargement with centre at the point $(3, 4)$.

CHAPTER 44 SUMMARY

Points to remember

Matrices for some special transformations.

(i)   Anticlockwise rotation through $\angle\theta$

$$\begin{pmatrix} \cos\theta & -\sin\theta \\ \sin\theta & \cos\theta \end{pmatrix}$$

(ii)   Enlargement with scale factor k

$$\begin{pmatrix} k & 0 \\ 0 & k \end{pmatrix}$$

(iii)   Reflection in the y-axis.

$$\begin{pmatrix} -1 & 0 \\ 0 & 1 \end{pmatrix}$$

(iv)   Reflection in the x-axis.

$$\begin{pmatrix} 1 & 0 \\ 0 & -1 \end{pmatrix}$$

(v)   Reflection in the origin.

$$\begin{pmatrix} -1 & 0 \\ 0 & -1 \end{pmatrix}$$

(vi)   Shear with points on Ox fixed.

$$\begin{pmatrix} 1 & k \\ 0 & 1 \end{pmatrix}$$

(vii)   Shear with points on Oy fixed.

$$\begin{pmatrix} 1 & 0 \\ k & 1 \end{pmatrix}$$

How to Answer Examination Questions 6

1) Find the coordinates of the image of $(3,1)$ under an anticlockwise rotation of $90°$ with centre:
(a) $(0,0)$
(b) $(1,2)$.

The image (x', y') of (x, y) under an anticlockwise rotation θ with centre (h, k) is given by

$$\begin{pmatrix} x' \\ y' \end{pmatrix} = \begin{pmatrix} \cos\theta & -\sin\theta \\ \sin\theta & \cos\theta \end{pmatrix} \begin{pmatrix} x \\ y \end{pmatrix}$$
$$+ \begin{pmatrix} 1-\cos\theta & \sin\theta \\ -\sin\theta & 1-\cos\theta \end{pmatrix} \begin{pmatrix} h \\ k \end{pmatrix}$$

$$\therefore \quad x' = x\cos\theta - y\sin\theta + h(1-\cos\theta) + k\sin\theta$$
$$y' = x\sin\theta + y\cos\theta + k(1-\cos\theta) - h\sin\theta$$

(a) To find the image of $(3,1)$ under an anticlockwise rotation of $90°$ about $(0,0)$ we put $x = 3,\ y = 1,\ \theta = 90,\ h = 0,\ k = 0$.

Then $x' = 3\cos 90° - 1\sin 90° + 0 = -1$
$ y' = 3\cos 90° + 1\cos 90° + 0 = 3$

$\therefore$ Image of $(3,1)$ is $(-1,3)$.

(b) Similarly, the image of $(3,1)$ under a rotation of $90°$ with centre $(1,2)$ is given by

$$x' = -1 + 1(1-\cos 90°) + 2\sin 90°$$
$$= -1 + 1 + 2 = 2$$
$$y' = 3\sin 90° + 1\cos 90° + 2(1-\cos 90°)$$
$$- 1\sin 90°$$
$$= 3 + 2 - 1 = 4$$

$\therefore$ Image of $(3,1)$ is $(2,4)$.

2) The vertices O, P, Q, R of the rectangle OPQR are $(0,0)$, $(3,0)$, $(3,2)$ and $(0,2)$ respectively.
OPQR is mapped onto OPQ_1R_1 by a shear such that R_1 is the point $(1,2)$. Find the coordinates of Q_1.
OPQ_1R_1 is mapped onto $OP_1Q_2R_2$ by an enlargement centre O and scale factor $2\frac{1}{2}$.

Find the coordinates of Q_2 and calculate the area of the parallelogram $OP_1Q_2R_2$.

$R(0,2)$ is mapped onto $R_1(1,2)$ under a shear
$\therefore$ Point R moves in a direction parallel to OX.
 OX is the line of shear
$\therefore$ Image of (x,y) is $(x + ky, y)$
$\therefore$ Image of $(0,2)$ is $(0 + 2k, 2) = (1,2)$
$$2k = 1$$
$$\therefore \qquad k = \tfrac{1}{2}$$

Image of $(3,2) = (3 + \tfrac{1}{2} \times 2, 2) = (4,2)$.
$\therefore\ Q_1$ is $(4,2)$

Enlargement of (x,y) with scale factor k is (kx, ky).

Enlargement Q_2 of $Q_1(4,2)$ with scale factor $2\frac{1}{2} = (\tfrac{5}{2} \times 4, \tfrac{5}{2} \times 2) = (10,5)$.

Area of $OPQ_1R_1 = OP \times OR = 3 \times 2 = 6$ square units

Area of $OP_1Q_2R_2 = (2\tfrac{1}{2})^2$. Area of OPQ_1R_1

Area of $OP_1Q_2R_2 = (\tfrac{5}{2})^2 \times 6 = \tfrac{25}{4} \times 6 = \tfrac{75}{2}$
$$= 37.5 \text{ square units}$$

3) In the triangle OPQ, R is the mid-point of OP and S is the mid-point of PQ.
Given that $\overrightarrow{OQ} = 2\mathbf{q}$ and $\overrightarrow{OP} = 2\mathbf{p}$, write down $\overrightarrow{QP}$, $\overrightarrow{OS}$ and $\overrightarrow{QR}$ in terms of $\mathbf{p}$ and $\mathbf{q}$, giving your answers in their simplest form.
Hence prove that $\overrightarrow{RS} = \tfrac{1}{2}\overrightarrow{OQ}$.

In triangle OPQ:
$$\overrightarrow{OP} = \overrightarrow{OQ} + \overrightarrow{QP}$$

$$\therefore \qquad \overrightarrow{OP} - \overrightarrow{OQ} = \overrightarrow{QP}$$

$$2\mathbf{p} - 2\mathbf{q} = \overrightarrow{QP}$$

$$\overrightarrow{QS} = \tfrac{1}{2}\overrightarrow{QP} \text{ (S is mid-point of QP)}$$
$$= \tfrac{1}{2}(2\mathbf{p} - 2\mathbf{q})$$
$$= \mathbf{p} - \mathbf{q}$$

From triangle OSQ,

$$\overrightarrow{OS} = \overrightarrow{OQ} + \overrightarrow{QS} = 2\mathbf{q} + \mathbf{p} - \mathbf{q} = \mathbf{q} + \mathbf{p}$$

From triangle ORQ,

$$\overrightarrow{QR} = \overrightarrow{QO} + \overrightarrow{OR} = -\overrightarrow{OQ} + \overrightarrow{OR}$$

$$= -2\mathbf{q} + \mathbf{p} = \mathbf{p} - 2\mathbf{q}$$

$$\overrightarrow{PS} = \tfrac{1}{2}\overrightarrow{PQ} = \tfrac{1}{2}(2\mathbf{q} - 2\mathbf{p}) = \mathbf{q} - \mathbf{p}$$

$$\overrightarrow{RS} = \overrightarrow{RP} + \overrightarrow{PS} = \mathbf{p} + \mathbf{q} - \mathbf{p} = \mathbf{q} = \tfrac{1}{2}\overrightarrow{OQ}$$

4) In a velocity triangle drawn to show the flight of an aircraft, the wind speed is represented in direction and magnitude by the vector **w**, the airspeed and course by the vector **a** and the ground speed and track by the vector **g**. Write down the vector equation connecting **w**, **a** and **g**.
In the particular case in which **w** and **a** are at right angles to each other and $|\mathbf{w}| = |\mathbf{a}|$, calculate the ratio $|\mathbf{a}| : |\mathbf{g}|$. Note: $|\mathbf{a}|$ denotes 'the length of the vector **a**'.

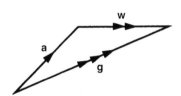

Fig. E6.1

$$\mathbf{g} = \mathbf{a} + \mathbf{w}$$

Since **a** and **w** are perpendicular,

$$|\mathbf{a}|^2 + |\mathbf{w}|^2 = |\mathbf{g}|^2$$

$$\therefore \quad 2|\mathbf{a}|^2 = |\mathbf{g}|^2 \quad (\text{since } |\mathbf{a}| = |\mathbf{w}|)$$

$$\sqrt{2}\,|\mathbf{a}| = |\mathbf{g}|$$

$$\therefore \quad \frac{|\mathbf{a}|}{|\mathbf{g}|} = \frac{1}{\sqrt{2}}$$

$$|\mathbf{a}| : |\mathbf{g}| = 1 : \sqrt{2}$$

EXAMINATION TYPE QUESTIONS 6

This exercise is divided into two sections A and B. The questions in Section A are intended to be done very quickly, but those in Section B should take about 20 minutes each to complete. All the questions are of the type found in CXC examination papers.

Section A

1) (a) Given a universal set $\mathcal{U}$ and two sets P and Q such that $P \cup Q = \mathcal{U}$ and $P \cap Q = \varnothing$, simplify:
  (i) $P \cup Q'$ (ii) $P \cap Q'$.
 (b) The universal set is the set of the positive integers less than or equal to a given integer N. Sets A, B and C are defined as follows:

$$A = \{x : x \text{ is a multiple of } 2\}$$

$$B = \{x : x \text{ is a multiple of } 5\}$$

$$C = \{x : x \text{ is a multiple of } 7\}.$$

Define, in the same form, the sets:
(i) $A \cap B$ (ii) $A \cap B \cap C$.
Given that $n(A \cap B) = 8$, write down the largest and smallest possible values of N, and state the value of $n(A \cap B \cap C)$.

2) P, Q, R, S are mid-points of the sides of the square ABCD. PR and QS intersect at O. The square PQRS can be mapped onto the square ABCD by a transformation T followed by an enlargement centre O.
(a) Describe T clearly and state the scale factor of the enlargement.
(b) Given that the area of PQRS $= 8.5\,\text{cm}^2$, calculate the area of ABCD.

3) A and B are fixed points in a given plane and P is a variable point in the plane. Describe completely the locus of P in each of the following cases:
(a) $\angle$PAB is always $90°$.
(b) $\angle$APB is always $90°$.
(c) PA = PB.

4) An aeroplane with an airspeed of $208\,\text{km/h}$ sets a course of $010°$. The wind is blowing at $64\,\text{km/h}$ from bearing $325°$.
Find by accurate scale drawing the track and ground speed of the aeroplane.
(All lines in the diagram must be clearly marked with an arrow. Use a scale of $1\,\text{cm}$ to $20\,\text{km/h}$.)
With the same wind blowing, another aeroplane with an airspeed of $144\,\text{km/h}$ has to travel from A to B. The bearing of B from A is $253°$.

Find by accurate drawing the course to be set.

Section B

5) (a) Under a certain transformation, the image (x', y') of a point (x, y) is given by

$$\begin{pmatrix} x' \\ y' \end{pmatrix} = \begin{pmatrix} 3 & 1 \\ -1 & 1 \end{pmatrix} \begin{pmatrix} x \\ y \end{pmatrix} + \begin{pmatrix} 2 \\ 6 \end{pmatrix}$$

   (i) Find the coordinates of P, the image of $(0, 0)$.
   (ii) Find the coordinates of Q, the image of $(3, 2)$.
   (iii) Given that the image of the point (a, b) is the point $(0, 0)$, write down two equations, each containing a and b. Hence find the values of a and b.

   (b) Find the value of x for which the matrix

$$\begin{pmatrix} x+4 & 0 \\ 0 & 3 \end{pmatrix}$$

   (i) is singular.
   (ii) represents an enlargement. State the scale factor of this enlargement.

6) A ship sets sail due south from a port in latitude $24°S$ and longitude $46°20'W$, to a point in latitude $38°S$. Taking π to be 3.14 and the radius of the earth to be $6336\,km$, calculate the distance travelled by the ship. If the ship now turns and travels the same distance due east along a line of latitude $38°S$, calculate its new longitude.

7) Fig. E6.2 represents a river with parallel banks PQ and RS with the current flowing at $3\,km/h$ parallel to the banks. The stretch is divided into 8 squares as shown in the diagram.

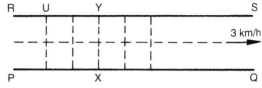

Fig. E6.2

   (a) A boat which has a speed of $6\,km/h$ in still water, starts at X and sails towards Y. If the river is $2\,km$ wide, calculate the distance from Y, on the bank RS, at which the boat will arrive.
   (b) A second boat, whose speed in still water is $v\,km/h$, starts from X and heads towards the point U. If this boat reaches the opposite bank at Y, calculate the value of v, giving your answer in the form $a\sqrt{b}$, where a and b are whole numbers.

8) (a) If $\overrightarrow{OA} = \begin{pmatrix} -2 \\ 3 \end{pmatrix}$, $\overrightarrow{OB} = \begin{pmatrix} 2 \\ 5 \end{pmatrix}$, find $\overrightarrow{AB}$.

   (b) The diagonals of a rectangle OPQR intersect at S. If $\overrightarrow{OP} = \mathbf{p}$ and $\overrightarrow{OR} = \mathbf{r}$, express in terms of $\mathbf{p}$ and/or $\mathbf{r}$:
   (i) $\overrightarrow{QR}$ (ii) $\overrightarrow{PS}$
   If $|\mathbf{p}| = 5$, and $|\mathbf{r}| = 12$, calculate $\angle QOP$ giving your answer to the nearest degree.

Chapter 45 **Statistics**

INTRODUCTION

Statistics is the name given to the science of collecting and analysing facts. In almost all scientific and business publications, in newspapers and in Government reports these facts are presented by means of tables and diagrams. The most commonly used diagrams and charts are discussed below.

THE PROPORTIONATE BAR CHART

The proportionate bar chart (Fig. 45.1) relies on heights (or areas) to convey the proportions of a whole. The bar should be of the same width throughout its length or height. This diagram is accurate, quick and easy to construct and it can show quite a large number of components without confusion. Although Fig. 45.1 shows the bar drawn vertically it may also be drawn horizontally if desired.

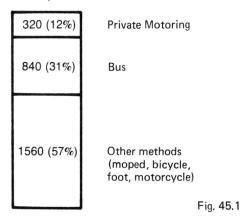

Fig. 45.1

EXAMPLE 1

Draw a proportionate bar chart for the figures below which show the way people travel to work in the Bridgetown area.

Type of transport	Numbers using
Other methods	1560
Bus	840
Private motoring	320

The easiest way is to draw the chart on graph paper. However, if plain paper is used, the lengths of the component parts must be calculated and then drawn accurately using a rule (Fig. 45.1).

Total number $= 1560 + 840 + 320 = 2720$

Suppose that the total height of the diagram is to be 6 cm. Then

1560 travellers are represented by

$$\frac{1560}{2720} \times 6 = 3.44 \text{ cm}$$

840 travellers are represented by

$$\frac{840}{2720} \times 6 = 1.85 \text{ cm}$$

320 travellers are represented by

$$\frac{320}{2720} \times 6 = 0.71 \text{ cm}$$

Alternatively, the proportions can be expressed as percentages which are calculated as shown below.

Type of transport	Percentage of travellers using
Other methods	$\frac{1560}{2720} \times 100 = 57\%$
Bus	$\frac{840}{2720} \times 100 = 31\%$
Private motoring	$\frac{320}{2720} \times 100 = 12\%$

SIMPLE BAR CHARTS

In these charts the information is represented by a series of bars all of the same width. The height or the length of each bar represents the magnitude of the figures. The bars may be drawn vertically or horizontally as shown in Figs. 45.2 and 45.3 which present the information given in Example 1.

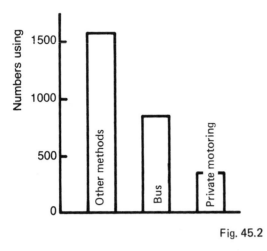

Fig. 45.2

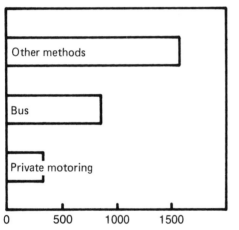

Fig. 45.3

CHRONOLOGICAL BAR CHARTS

This type of chart compares quantities over periods of time. It is very similar to the vertical bar chart and its construction is basically the same as a graph.

EXAMPLE 2

The information below gives the number of colour television sets sold in a region during the period 1990–95.

Year	Number of sets sold (thousands)
1990	77.2
1991	84.0
1992	91.3
1993	114.6
1994	130.9
1995	142.5

Draw a chronological bar chart to represent this information.

When drawing a chronological bar chart, time is always marked off along the horizontal axis. The chart is drawn in Fig. 45.4 and it clearly shows how the sales of TV sets have increased over the period illustrated.

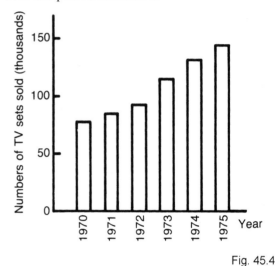

Fig. 45.4

PIE CHART

A pie chart displays the proportions of a whole as sector angles or sector areas, the circle as a whole representing the component parts.

EXAMPLE 3

Represent the information given in Example 1 in the form of a pie chart.

The first step is to calculate the sector angles. Remembering that a circle contains $360°$ the sector angles are calculated as shown below:

Type of transport	Sector angle (°)
Other methods	$\dfrac{1560}{2720} \times 360 = 206°$
Bus	$\dfrac{840}{2720} \times 360 = 111°$
Private motoring	$\dfrac{320}{2720} \times 360 = 43°$

Using a protractor the pie chart (Fig. 45.5) can now be drawn. If desired percentages can be displayed on the diagram.

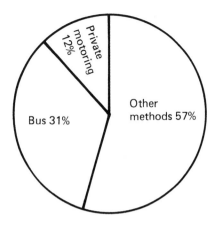

Fig. 45.5

Pie charts are very useful when component parts of a whole are to be represented. Up to eight component parts can be accommodated but above this number the chart loses its effectiveness.

Exercise 196 – *All type A*

1) In Fig. 45.6, find the values of *x* and *y*.

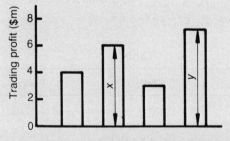

Fig. 45.6

2) Draw a proportionate bar chart for the information below which relates to expenditure per head on transport. In each case find the percentage expenditure and show it on your diagram.

Type of transport	Expenditure ($)
Private motoring	$1.10
Rail	$2.75
Other public transport	$3.15
Total	$7.00

3) The table below shows the number of people employed on various kinds of work in a factory.

Type of personnel	Number employed
Unskilled workers	45
Craftsmen	25
Draughtsmen	5
Clerical staff	10
Total	85

(a) Draw a vertical bar chart to represent this information.
(b) Draw a simple horizontal bar chart to show this data.
(c) Draw a pie chart, showing percentages, for this information.

4) The information below gives details of the temperature range used when forging various metals. Draw a horizontal bar chart to represent these data.

Metal	Temperature (°C)
Carbon steel	770–1300
Wrought iron	860–1340
Brass	600– 800
Copper	500–1000

5) The figures below give the World population (in millions of people) from 1750 to 1950. Draw a chronological bar chart to represent this information.

Year	Population
1750	728
1800	906
1850	1171
1900	1608
1950	2504

6) The information in the following table gives the production of fruit on a certain farm during six successive years. Draw a chronological bar chart to represent this information.

Year	Fruit production (tonnes)
1	395
2	410
3	495
4	560
5	420
6	515

7) The data below give the area of the various continents of the world.

Continent	Area (millions of square miles)
Africa	30.3
Asia	26.9
Europe	4.9
N. America	24.3
S. America	17.9
Oceania	22.8
U.S.S.R.	20.5

Draw a pie chart to depict this information.

8) Figure 45.7 is a pie chart which shows the total sales of a Departmental Store for one week. Find the correct size of each sector angle. (The diagram is NOT drawn to scale.)

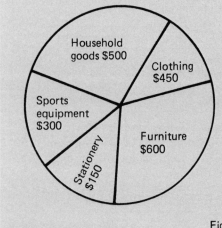

Fig. 45.7

RAW DATA

Raw data are collected information which is not organised numerically, that is, it is not arranged in any sort of order.

Consider the marks of 50 students obtained in a test:

  4 3 5 4 3 5 5 4 3 6 5 4 5 3 4 4 5 5 7

  4 3 4 3 4 5 4 3 6 1 3 6 3 2 6 6 3 5 2

  7 5 7 1 7 6 5 8 6 4 3 5

This is an example of raw data and we see that they are not organised into any sort of order.

FREQUENCY DISTRIBUTIONS

One way of organising raw data into order is to arrange them in the form of a frequency distribution. The number of students obtaining 3 marks is found, the number obtaining 4 marks is found, and so on. A tally chart is the best way of doing this.

On examining the raw data we see that the lowest mark is 1 and the greatest is 8. The marks from 1 to 8 inclusive are written in column 1 of the tally chart. We now take each figure in the raw data, just as it comes, and for each figure we place a tally mark opposite the appropriate mark.

The fifth tally mark for each number is usually made in an oblique direction thereby tying the tally marks into bundles of five.

When the tally marks are complete they are counted and the numerical value recorded in the column headed Frequency. Hence the frequency is the number of times each mark occurs. From the tally chart below it will be seen that the mark 1 occurs twice (a frequency of 2), the mark 5 occurs twelve times (a frequency of 12) and so on.

Table 1

Mark	Tally	Frequency
1	1 1	2
2	1 1	2
3	1111 1111 1	11
4	1111 1111 1	11
5	1111 1111 11	12
6	1111 11	7
7	1 1 1 1	4
8	1	1
	Total	50

†GROUPED DISTRIBUTIONS

When dealing with a large amount of numerical data it is useful to group the numbers into classes or categories. We can then find the number of items belonging to each class, thus obtaining a class frequency.

EXAMPLE 4

The following gives the heights of 100 men in centimetres:

```
153 162 168 154 151 168 162 153 161
167 157 154 165 156 163 165 160 171
170 173 164 158 163 155 167 162 168
153 161 166 163 162 163 163 163 164
165 163 162 162 163 161 162 162 158
162 167 158 169 168 168 156 160 158
169 156 158 157 168 163 164 162 164
163 162 161 169 164 161 156 167 168
167 159 164 171 168 165 159 165 168
159 162 165 168 154 163 162 157 150
165 169 164 163 163 163 169 160 164
167
```

Draw up a tally chart for the classes 150–154, 155–159, 160–164, 165–169 and 170–174.

The tally chart is shown in table 2.

Table 2

Class (cm)	Tally	Frequency
150–154	~~1111~~ 1 1 1	8
155–159	~~1111~~ ~~1111~~ ~~1111~~ 1	16
160–164	~~1111~~ ~~1111~~ ~~1111~~ ~~1111~~ ~~1111~~ ~~1111~~ ~~1111~~ ~~1111~~ 1 1 1	43
165–169	~~1111~~ ~~1111~~ ~~1111~~ ~~1111~~ ~~1111~~ 1 1 1 1	29
170–174	1 1 1 1	4
	Total	100

The main advantage of grouping is that it produces a clear overall picture of the distribution. However too many groups destroy the pattern of the distribution whilst too few will destroy much of the detail contained in the raw data. Depending upon the amount of raw data, the number of classes is usually between 5 and 20.

†CLASS INTERVALS

In Table 2, the first class is 150–154. These figures give the class interval. For the second class the class interval is 155–159. The end numbers 155 and 159 are called the *class limits* for the second class, 155 being the lower limit and 159 the upper limit.

†CLASS BOUNDARIES

In Table 2, the heights have been recorded to the nearest centimetre. The class interval 155–159 theoretically includes all the heights between 154.5 cm and 159.5 cm. These numbers are called the lower and upper class boundaries respectively.

For any frequency distribution the class boundaries may be found by adding the upper limit of one class to the lower limit of the next class and dividing the sum by two.

EXAMPLE 5

The figures below show part of a frequency distribution. State the lower and upper class boundaries for the second class.

Lifetime of electric bulbs

Lifetime (hours)	Frequency
400–449	22
450–499	38
500–549	62

For the second class:

lower class boundary
$$= \frac{449 + 450}{2} = 449.5 \text{ hours}$$

upper class boundary
$$= \frac{499 + 500}{2} = 499.5 \text{ hours}$$

†WIDTH OF A CLASS INTERVAL

The width of a class interval is the difference between the lower and upper class boundaries. That is

width of class interval
= upper class boundary
– lower class boundary

For Example 4,

width of second class interval
= 499.5 – 449.5 = 50 hours

(A common mistake is to take the class width as being the difference between the upper and lower class limits giving, in Example 4, 499–450 = 49 hours, which is incorrect.)

DISCRETE AND CONTINUOUS VARIABLES

A variable which can take any value between two given values is called a *continuous variable*. Thus the height of an individual, which can be 158 cm, 164.2 cm or 177.832 cm depending upon the accuracy of measurement, is a continuous variable.

A variable which can only have certain values is called a *discrete variable*. Thus the number of children in a family can only take whole number values such as 0, 1, 2, 3, etc. It cannot be $2\frac{1}{2}$, $3\frac{1}{4}$, etc., and it is therefore a discrete variable. Note that the values of a discrete variable need not be whole numbers. The sizes of shoes is a discrete variable but these can be $4\frac{1}{2}$, 5, $5\frac{1}{2}$, 6, etc.

THE HISTOGRAM

The *histogram* is a diagram which is used to represent a frequency distribution. It consists of a set of rectangles whose *areas* represent the frequencies of the various classes. If all the classes have the same width then all the rectangles will be the same width and the frequencies are then represented by the heights of the rectangles. Figure 45.8 shows the histogram for the frequency distribution of Table 1.

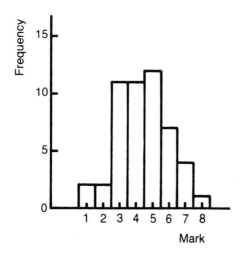

Fig. 45.8

†HISTOGRAM FOR A GROUPED DISTRIBUTION

A histogram for a grouped distribution may be drawn by using the mid-points of the class

intervals as the centres of the rectangles. The histogram for the distribution of Table 2 is shown in Fig. 45.9. Note that the extremes of the base of each rectangle represent the lower and upper class boundaries.

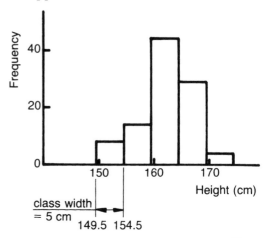

Fig. 45.9

DISCRETE DISTRIBUTIONS

The histogram shown in Fig. 45.9 represents a distribution in which the variable is continuous. The data in Example 5 are discrete and we shall see how a discrete distribution is represented.

EXAMPLE 6

Five coins were tossed 100 times and after each toss the number of heads was recorded. The table below gives the number of tosses during which 0, 1, 2, 3, 4 and 5 heads were obtained. Represent these data in a suitable diagram.

Number of heads	Number of tosses (frequency)
0	4
1	15
2	34
3	29
4	16
5	2
Total	100

Since the data are discrete (there cannot be 2.3 or 3.6 heads) Fig. 45.10 seems the most natural diagram to use. This diagram is in the form of a vertical bar chart in which the bars have zero width. Figure 45.11 shows the same data represented as a histogram. Note that the area under the diagram gives the total frequency of

100 which is as it should be. Discrete data are often represented as a histogram as was done in Fig. 45.8, despite the fact that in doing this we are treating the data as though they were continuous.

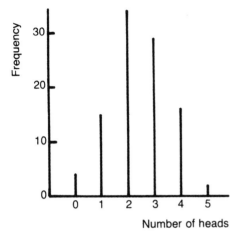

Fig. 45.10

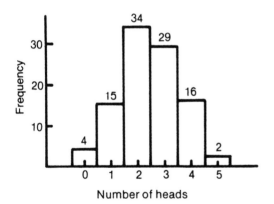

Fig. 45.11

THE FREQUENCY POLYGON

The frequency polygon is a second way of representing a frequency distribution. It is drawn by connecting the mid-points of the tops of the rectangles in a histogram by straight lines as shown in Example 6.

EXAMPLE 7

Draw a frequency polygon for the information given below which relates to the ages of people working in a factory:

Age (years)	15–19	20–24	25–29	30–34	35–39
Frequency	5	23	58	104	141

Age (years)	40–44	45–49	50–54	55–59
Frequency	98	43	19	6

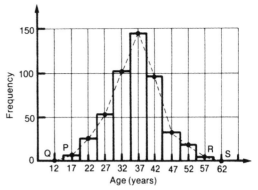

Fig. 45.12

The frequency polygon is drawn in Fig. 45.12. It is usual to add the extensions PQ and RS to the next lower and next higher class mid-points at the ends of the diagram. When this is done the area of the frequency polygon is equal to the area of the histogram.

FREQUENCY CURVES

Collected data may be considered as a sample which has been taken from a large population. Very many observations are possible in this population. Hence, for continuous data, we can choose very small class intervals and still have a reasonable number of observations falling in each class. The rectangles making up the histogram then become very small in width and the frequency polygon, to all intents, becomes a curve which is called a *frequency curve*.

TYPES OF FREQUENCY CURVE

The various types of frequency curves which occur in practice are shown in Fig. 45.13.

(a) The symmetrical or bell shaped curve is usually called the *normal curve*. It occurs when the data are obtained by taking measurements, e.g. the heights of individuals in a human population or the intelligence quotient of individuals.

(b) Moderately skewed distributions occur when a small sample is taken from a population which would give a symmetrical distribution. For instance, if a sample of 50 men is measured for height the distribution will, almost certainly, be skewed. However, many positively skewed distributions occur in their own right. Some examples are: the number of children per family, the age at which women marry, etc. Negatively skewed distributions occur very rarely.

(c) J type distributions occur, for instance, in examining the lifetime of electronic devices, in looking at the parking times of vehicles in a street, etc. The reverse J type curve is very similar to a growth curve whilst the J type is a decay curve such as might be obtained when examining the life of a nuclear fuel which becomes less radio-active with time.

(d) The U type distribution occurs when a minimum value is being sought. Such a distribution might occur when looking at the number of passengers carried at various times of the day by public transport (i.e. buses, trains, etc.). During the morning rush-hour the buses are packed with people travelling to work and school. Later in the day demand falls off but increases again as the evening rush-hour approaches.

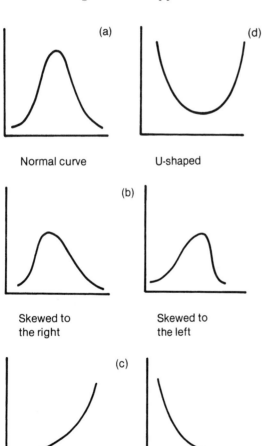

(a) Normal curve

(d) U-shaped

(b) Skewed to the right

Skewed to the left

(c) Reverse J-shaped

J-shaped

Fig. 45.13

Exercise 197 – *All type B*

1) The following marks were obtained by 50 students during a test:

5 4 6 5 4 6 6 5 4 7 6 5 6 4 5 5 6 6 8 5 4 2
8 6 8 3 6 4 7 7 3 4 7 4 1 7 4 5 6 4 5 8 7 6
9 7 5 4 6 2

Draw up a frequency distribution by means of a tally chart and hence draw a histogram.

2) The following is a record of the percentage marks obtained by 100 students in an examination:

45 93 35 56 16 50 63 30 86 65 57 39 44
75 25 45 74 93 84 25 77 28 54 50 12 85
55 34 50 57 55 48 78 15 27 79 68 26 66
80 91 62 67 52 50 75 96 36 83 20 45 71
63 51 40 46 61 62 67 57 53 45 51 40 46
31 54 67 66 52 49 54 55 52 56 59 38 52
43 55 51 47 54 56 56 42 53 40 51 58 52
27 56 42 86 50 31 61 33 36

Draw up a tally chart for the classes 0–9, 10–19, 20–29, . . . , 90–99 and hence form a frequency distribution.

3) Draw a histogram of the following data which gives the earnings of part-time employees.

Wage $	Frequency
12–15	2
16–19	5
17–20	8
21–23	6
24–27	2

4) Draw a histogram for the data shown below:

Mass (kg)	Frequency
0–4	50
5–9	64
10–14	43
15–19	26
20–24	17

5) The diameters of machined parts are:

Diameter (mm)	Frequency
14.96–14.98	3
14.99–15.01	8
15.02–15.04	12

Write down:

(a) The upper and lower class boundaries for the second class.
(b) The class width of the classes in the table.
(c) The class interval for the first class.

6) Classify each of the following as continuous or discrete variables:

(a) The diameters of ball bearings.
(b) The number of shirts sold per day.
(c) The mass of packets of chemical.
(d) The number of bunches of anthuriums packed by a grower.
(e) The daily temperature.
(f) The lifetime of electric light bulbs.
(g) The number of telephone calls made per day by a person.

7) An industrial organisation gives an aptitude test to all applicants for employment. The results of 150 people taking the test were:

Score (out of 10)	Frequency
1	6
2	12
3	15
4	21
5	35
6	24
7	20
8	10
9	6
10	1

Draw a histogram of this information.

8) The lengths of 100 pieces of wood were measured with the following results:

Length (cm)	Frequency
29.5	2
29.6	4
29.7	11
29.8	18
29.9	31
30.0	22
30.1	8
30.2	3
30.3	1

Draw a histogram of this information.

9) Draw a frequency polygon to represent the lengths of the pieces of wood in Question 8.

10) Fig. 45.14 shows a frequency polygon. Draw the corresponding histogram.

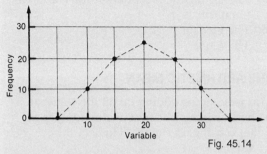

Fig. 45.14

11) (a) What form of distribution is shown by the frequency curve of Fig. 45.15?
(b) Name two populations which have this distribution.

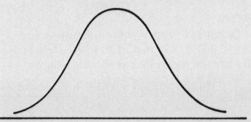

Fig. 45.15

12) In a survey of orders received, a furniture store obtained the following distribution.

Value of orders ($)	Number of orders
100 and up to 200	169
200 and up to 300	176
300 and up to 400	75
400 and up to 500	32
500 and up to 600	8

(a) Draw a histogram to represent this information.
(b) Sketch, on the same diagram, the frequency polygon.
(c) Draw a frequency curve to represent this distribution.

STATISTICAL AVERAGES

We have seen that a mass of raw data does not mean very much until it is arranged into a frequency distribution or until it is represented as a histogram.

A second way of making the data more understandable is to try and find a single value which will represent all the values in a distribution. This single representative value is called an average.

In statistics several kinds of average are used. The more important are:

(a) The arithmetic mean, often referred to as the mean.
(b) The median.
(c) The mode.

THE ARITHMETIC MEAN

This is found by adding up all the values in a set and dividing this sum by the number of values making up the set. That is,

arithmetic mean

$$= \frac{\text{sum of all the values}}{\text{the number of values}}$$

EXAMPLE 8

The heights of 5 men were measured as follows: 177.8, 175.3, 174.8, 179.1, 176.5 cm. Calculate the mean height of the 5 men.

$$\text{Mean} = \frac{177.8 + 175.3 + 174.8 + 179.1 + 176.5}{5}$$

$$= \frac{883.5}{5} = 176.7 \text{ cm}$$

Note that the unit of the mean is the same as the unit used for each of the quantities in the set.

THE MEAN OF A FREQUENCY DISTRIBUTION

When finding the mean of a frequency distribution we must take into account the frequencies as well as the measured observations.

EXAMPLE 9

Five packets of chemical have a mass of 20.01 grammes, 3 have a mass of 19.98 grams and 2 have a mass of 20.03 grams. What is the mean mass of the packet?

Mass of 5 packets @ 20.01 grams $=$ 100.05
Mass of 3 packets @ 19.98 grams $=$ 59.94
Mass of 2 packets @ 20.03 grams $=$ 40.06

Total mass of 10 packets $=$ 200.05

Mean mass

$$= \frac{\text{total mass}}{10} = \frac{200.05}{10}$$

$$= 20.005 \text{ grams}$$

This example gives the clue whereby we may find the mean of a frequency distribution.

EXAMPLE 10

Each of 200 similar engine components are measured correct to the nearest millimetre and recorded as follows:

Length (mm)	Frequency
198	8
199	30
200	132
201	24
202	6

Calculate the mean length of the 200 components.

$$\text{Mean length} = [(198 \times 8) + (199 \times 30)$$
$$+ (200 \times 132) + (201 \times 24)$$
$$+ (202 \times 6)] \div 200$$
$$= 199.95 \text{ mm}$$

The calculation is often set out in tabular form as shown below. This method reduces the risk of making errors when performing the calculation.

Length (mm)	Frequency	Length × frequency
198	8	1584
199	30	5970
200	132	26400
201	24	4824
202	6	1212
Total	200	39990

$$\text{mean} = \frac{\text{total of (length} \times \text{frequency)}}{\text{total frequency}}$$

$$= \frac{39\,990}{200} = 199.95 \text{ mm}$$

If $x_1, x_2, x_3, \ldots, x_n$ are measured observations which have frequencies $f_1, f_2, f_3, \ldots, f_n$ then the mean of the distribution is

$$\bar{x} = \frac{x_1 f_1 + x_2 f_2 + x_3 f_3 + \ldots + x_n f_n}{f_1 + f_2 + f_3 + \ldots + f_n}$$

$$= \frac{\sum xf}{\sum f}$$

The symbol $\sum$ means 'sum of' and hence $\sum xf$ tells us to multiply together corresponding values of x and f and add the products together.

EXAMPLE 11

Find the mean of the frequency distribution shown in the following table.

Mark x	Frequency f	xf
1	2	2
2	2	4
3	11	33
4	11	44
5	12	60
6	7	42
7	4	28
8	1	8
	50	221

We have $\sum xf = 221$ and $\sum f = 50$.

$$\therefore \quad \bar{x} = \frac{221}{50} = 4.42$$

The mean mark is 4.42.

†THE MEAN OF A GROUPED DISTRIBUTION

The mean of a grouped distribution may be found by taking the values of x as the class mid-points.

EXAMPLE 12

Calculate the mean of the grouped distribution shown in Table 2 (page 395).

Class (cm)	Class mid-point x	Frequency f	xf
150–154	152	8	1 216
155–159	157	16	2 512
160–164	162	43	6 966
165–169	167	29	4 843
170–174	172	4	688
		100	16 225

We have $\sum xf = 16\,225$ and $\sum f = 100$.

$$\therefore \quad \bar{x} = \frac{16\,225}{100} = 162.25$$

The mean height of the men is 162.25 cm.

THE CODED METHOD OF CALCULATING THE MEAN

The calculation of the mean may be greatly speeded up by using a unit method which is often called a coded method. The first step is to choose any value in the x column as the assumed mean. This assumed mean is then used as a datum to determine the coded values, which are values of x in terms of the units above and below the assumed mean.

The coded values for the data of Example 12 might be as follows:

Assumed mean   162 cm,   unit size $= 5$ cm

x	152	157	162	167	172
x_c	-2	-1	0	$+1$	$+2$

The coded value for $x = 152$ is $x_c = -2$ because this value of 152 is 2 units less than the assumed mean of 162. It is very important to assign to the coded value a plus or a minus sign depending on whether the value of x is greater or less than the assumed mean.

Although any value of x may be chosen as the assumed mean, the arithmetic in calculating the mean will be simpler if the middle value of x is chosen. The unit size of 5 cm was chosen because each value of x is 5 cm greater than the preceding value.

The coded values for the data of Example 12 may now be calculated using coded values as follows:

Class (cm)	Class mid-point x	Coded value x_c	Frequency f	$x_c f$
150–154	152	-2	8	-16
155–159	157	-1	16	-16
160–164	162	0	43	0
165–169	167	$+1$	29	$+29$
170–174	172	$+2$	4	$+8$
			100	$+5$

Coded value of the mean

$$= \bar{x}_c = \frac{\sum x_c f}{\sum f} = \frac{+5}{100} = +0.05$$

This value of $\bar{x}_c$ indicates that the mean of the distribution is 0.05 units greater than the assumed mean. Hence

$$\text{mean} = \text{assumed mean} + \bar{x}_c \times \text{unit size}$$
$$= 162 + 0.05 \times 5$$
$$= 162 + 0.25$$
$$= 162.25$$

As before, the mean height of the men is
162.25 cm.

THE MEDIAN

If a set of values is arranged in ascending (or
descending) order of size the median is the
value which lies half-way along the series. Thus
the median of 3, 4, 4, 5, 6, 8, 8, 9, 10 is 6
because there are four numbers below this value
and four numbers above it.

When there are an even number of values in the
set the median is found by taking the mean of
the middle two values. Thus the median of 3, 3,
5, 7, 9, 10, 13, 15 is $\dfrac{7+9}{2} = 8$.

The median of a discrete frequency distribution
may be found by setting out the scores in
numerical order and finding the middle value.

EXAMPLE 13

The table below shows the distribution of
numbers obtained when a die is thrown 30
times. Determine the median.

Number obtained	1	2	3	4	5	6
Frequency	2	7	5	7	3	6

The total frequency is 30. Hence the median
must lie between the 15th and 16th items in
the distribution. We now look at the values of
the 15th and 16th items. These are both 4
and hence the median is 4.

It is unnecessary to write down all the values in
numerical order to find the median but if we do
this we obtain:

1, 1, 2, 2, 2, 2, 2, 2, 2, 3, 3, 3, 3, 3, 4, 4,

4, 4, 4, 4, 4, 5, 5, 5, 6, 6, 6, 6, 6, 6

Looking at this set of values we see that the two
middle values are 4 and hence the median is 4.

†CUMULATIVE FREQUENCY DISTRIBUTIONS

To find the median of a continuous distribution
we need to draw a cumulative frequency
distribution. The way in which it is obtained is
shown in Example 14.

EXAMPLE 14

Obtain a cumulative frequency distribution for
the information given in Table 2, which is
repeated below.

Height (cm)	150–154	155–159	160–164
Frequency	8	16	43

Height (cm)	165–169	170–174
Frequency	29	4

The class boundaries are 149.5 to 154.5, 154.5
to 159.5, 159.5 to 164.5, 164.5 to 169.5 and
169.5 to 174.5. In obtaining the cumulative
frequency distribution the lower boundary limit
for each class is normally used.

Height (cm)	Cumulative frequency
less than 149.5	0
less than 154.5	8
less than 159.5	8 + 16 = 24
less than 164.5	24 + 43 = 67
less than 169.5	67 + 29 = 96
less than 174.5	96 + 4 = 100

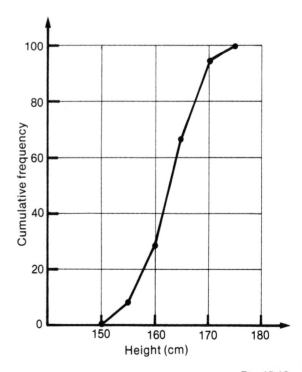

Fig. 45.16

The distribution may be represented by a
cumulative frequency polygon (Fig. 45.16) or by
a cumulative frequency curve (Fig. 45.17).

The cumulative frequency curve is often called an *ogive* after the architectural term for this shape.

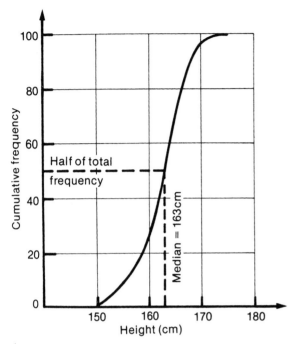

Fig. 45.17

The median of the distribution is obtained from the cumulative frequency curve by finding the value of the variable corresponding to half the total frequency. Thus in Fig. 45.17, the median value is 163 cm which corresponds to a cumulative frequency of 50 (i.e. half the total frequency of 100).

The cumulative frequency curve may also be used to find the proportion (or percentage) of the sample which lies above or below a given value of the variable.

EXAMPLE 15

In Example 14 find, by using the ogive, the number of men with a height:

(a) less than 157 cm,
(b) between 155 and 165 cm,
(c) greater than 162 cm.

The ogive is shown again in Fig. 45.18. From the diagram we see:

(a) The cumulative frequency corresponding to a height of 157 cm is 14. Hence 14 men have a height less than 157 cm.

(b) The cumulative frequencies corresponding to heights of 155 cm and 165 cm are 9 and 70 respectively. Hence the number of men with heights between 155 cm and 165 cm is 70 − 9 = 61.

(c) The cumulative frequency corresponding to a height of 162 cm is 42. Hence the number of men with a height greater than 162 cm is 100 − 42 = 58.

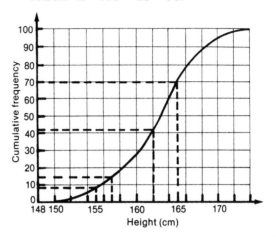

Fig. 45.18

THE MODE

The mode of a set of values is the value which occurs most frequently. That is, it is the most common value. Thus the mode of 2, 3, 3, 4, 4, 4, 5, 6, 6, 7 is 4 because this number occurs three times, which is more than any of the other numbers in the set.

Sometimes, in a set of numbers, no mode exists, as for the set 2, 4, 7, 8, 9, 11 in which each number occurs once. It is possible for there to be more than one mode. The set 2, 3, 3, 3, 4, 4, 5, 6, 6, 6, 7, 8 has two modes 3 and 6, because each of these numbers occurs three times which is more than any of the other numbers.

A set of values which has two modes is called *bimodal*. If the set has only one mode it is said to be *unimodal* but if there are more than two modes the set is called *multimodal*.

THE MODE OF A FREQUENCY DISTRIBUTION

To find the mode of a frequency distribution we draw a histogram and hence a frequency curve. The mode is then the value of the variable

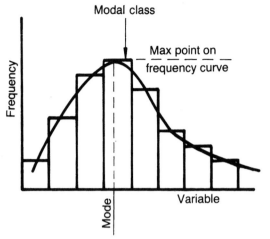

Fig. 45.19

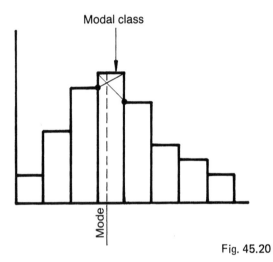

Fig. 45.20

corresponding to the maximum point on the curve (Fig. 45.19). The mode can also be obtained directly from the histogram as shown in Fig. 45.20.

EXAMPLE 16
The heights of a group of boys are measured to the nearest centimetre with the following results:

Height (cm)	157	158	159	160	161	162
Frequency	20	36	44	46	39	30

Height (cm)	163	164	165	166	167
Frequency	22	17	10	4	2

Find the mode of distribution.

By constructing the histogram (Fig. 45.21) the mode is found to be 159.7. It is worthwhile noting that the modal class is 159.5 to 160.5 cm.

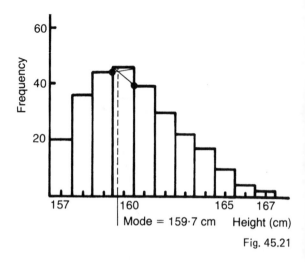

Mode = 159·7 cm   Height (cm)

Fig. 45.21

COMPARISON OF STATISTICAL AVERAGES

The mean

Advantages
(a) Is the best known average.
(b) Can be calculated exactly.
(c) Makes use of all the data.
(d) Can be used in further statistical work.

Disadvantages
(a) Is greatly affected by extreme values.
(b) When the data are discrete can give an impossible value (19.168 runs per innings.)
(c) Cannot be obtained graphically.

The median

Advantages
(a) Is not affected by extreme values.
(b) Can be obtained even if some of the values in the distribution are unknown.
(c) It can represent an actual value in the data.

Disadvantages
(a) For a grouped distribution its value can only be obtained from the ogive.
(b) When only a few observations are available the median may not be characteristic of the group.
(c) Cannot be used in further statistical calculations.

The mode

Advantages
(a) Is not affected by extreme values.
(b) It is easy to obtain from a histogram.
(c) To determine its value only values near to the modal class are required.

Disadvantages
(a) There may be more than one mode.
(b) When the data is grouped its value cannot be determined exactly.
(c) Cannot be used in further statistical calculations.

WHICH AVERAGE TO USE

The *mean* is the most familiar kind of average and it is extensively used in business, sales data, income, expenditure, rates of pay, etc. It is easy to understand but in some circumstances it is definitely misleading. For instance, if the hourly wages of five office workers are $3.04, $3.28, $3.76, $9.20 and $3.52 the mean wage is $4.56. But this value is greatly affected by the extreme value of $9.20. Hence the mean wage gives a false impression of the wages paid in this office.

The *median* is not affected by extreme values and it will give a better indication of the wages paid in the office discussed above (the median wage is $3.52). For distributions which have a frequency curve that is very skew, the median is usually the best average to use.

The *mode* is used when the commonest value of a distribution is required. For instance, a clothing manufacturer will not be particularly interested in the mean length of men's legs because, almost certainly, it will not represent a stock size in trousers. It may in fact be some point between stock sizes and in such cases the mode is probably the best average to use. However, which average is used will depend upon a particular set of circumstances.

RELATION BETWEEN THE MEAN, MEDIAN AND MODE

When the frequency curve representing a distribution, is symmetrical the mean, median and mode all have the same value (Fig. 45.22).

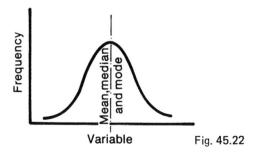

Fig. 45.22

However when the frequency curve is skewed they will have different values (Fig. 45.23).

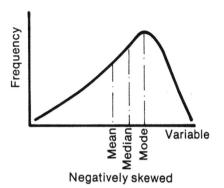

Negatively skewed

Fig. 45.23

†QUARTILES

We have seen that the median divides a set of values into two equal parts. Using similar methods we can divide a set of quantities into four equal parts. The values which so divide the set are called *quartiles*. They are often denoted by the symbols Q_1, Q_2 and Q_3, Q_1 being the first or lower quartile, Q_2 the second quartile and Q_3 the third or upper quartile. Note that the value of Q_2 is equal to the median.

EXAMPLE 17

In an experiment in a biology laboratory, the masses of 100 leaves were found. The distribution of masses is shown in the following table.

Mass (grams)	Frequency
0–4	1
5–9	2
10–14	15
15–19	21
20–24	26
25–29	28
30–34	4
35–39	2
40–44	1

Draw a cumulative frequency curve and from it determine the values of the first, second and third quartiles.

The cumulative frequency distribution is as follows:

Mass (grams)	Cumulative frequency
less than 4.5	1
less than 9.5	3
less than 14.5	18
less than 19.5	39
less than 24.5	65
less than 29.5	93
less than 34.5	97
less than 39.5	99
less than 44.5	100

The cumulative frequency curve is shown in Fig. 45.24.

The first quartile is the value of the variable corresponding to one-quarter of the total frequency, i.e. $\frac{1}{4}$ of $100 = 25$. Its value, from the diagram, is 16.2 grams.

The second quartile is the value of the variable corresponding to two-fourths (i.e. one-half) of the total frequency, i.e. $\frac{1}{2}$ of $100 = 50$. Its value, from the ogive, is 22.0 grams.

The third quartile is the value of the variable corresponding to three-quarters of the total frequency, i.e. $\frac{3}{4}$ of $100 = 75$. Its value, from the ogive, is 26.5 grams.

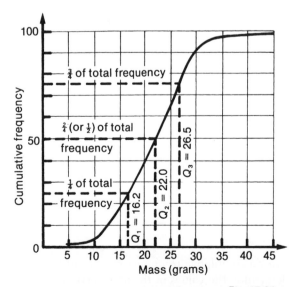

Fig. 45.24

Exercise 198 – *Questions 1–3, 9–11 and 18–20 type A, remainder B*

1) Find the mean of $23, \$27, \$30, \$28$ and 32.

2) The heights of some men are as follows: 172, 170, 181, 175, 179 and 173 cm. Calculate the mean height of the men.

3) Five people earn $42 per week, 3 earn $38 per week and 2 earn $44 per week. What is the mean wage for the 10 people?

4) Calculate the mean length from the following table:

Length (mm)	Frequency
198	1
199	4
200	17
201	2
202	1

5) Calculate the mean height of 50 people from the table below:

Height (cm)	Frequency
160	1
161	5
162	10
163	16
164	10
165	6
166	2

6) The diameters of 200 ball bearings were measured with the results shown below:

Diameter (mm)	Frequency
5.94–5.96	8
5.97–5.99	37
6.00–6.02	90
6.03–6.05	52
6.06–6.08	13

Using the class mid-points and coded values, calculate the mean diameter of the ball bearings.

7) The table below shows the amount of pocket money received by a sample of 10-year-old children.

Pocket money (cents)	Frequency
10–19	5
20–29	7
30–39	18
40–49	26
50–59	14
60–69	10
70–79	10
80–89	6
90–99	4

Using the class mid-points, calculate the mean amount of pocket money received by the children.

8) A school decided that all its 900 pupils should sit an intelligence test. The following results were obtained.

Range of mark	Frequency
0–9	5
10–19	33
20–29	82
30–39	148
40–49	270
50–59	215
60–69	87
70–79	44
80–89	12
90–99	4

Calculate the mean value of these results.

9) Find the median of the numbers 5, 3, 8, 6, 4, 2, 8.

10) Find the median of the numbers 2, 4, 6, 5, 3, 1, 8, 9.

11) The marks of a student in five examinations were: 54, 63, 49, 78 and 57. What is his median mark?

12) The figures below are measurements of the noise level (in dBA units) at 36 discotheques.

93   90 98   88 103 92 89   82 86
87   91 89   85   95 86 86   94 85
103   92 88 102   99 85 98 100 95
98 105 86 100   92 96 91   87 88

(a) Display these data in the form of a grouped frequency table using intervals 81–85, 86–90, etc.
(b) Draw a cumulative frequency polygon for your grouped distribution.
(c) From this frequency polygon estimate the number of discotheques at which the noise level exceeds 94 dBa units.

13) For the distribution of Question 8:
(a) Construct a cumulative frequency table.
(b) Plot a cumulative frequency curve (suitable scales are: 2 cm for 10 marks horizontally and 2 cm for 100 pupils vertically).
(c) Estimate how many pupils score:
   (i) less than 16 marks,
   (ii) more than 65 marks,
(d) From the ogive obtain the median mark and the lower and upper quartiles.

14) For the data of Question 6, draw a cumulative frequency curve and from it estimate the number of ball bearings with a diameter:
(a) less than 5.98 mm,
(b) between 6.00 mm and 6.05 mm,
(c) greater than 6.07 mm.

15) Sketch the frequency curve corresponding to the cumulative frequency curve shown in Fig. 45.25.

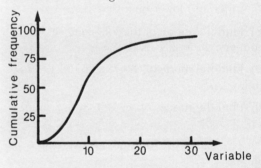

Fig. 45.25

16) (a) Draw a sketch graph of:
   (i) a normal distribution curve,
   (ii) a positively skewed distribution curve.
   In each case indicate on your diagram the estimated position of the mean of the distribution.
(b) Fifteen pupils are asked to estimate the length, to the nearest 2 cm, of their teacher's table. The estimates, arranged in descending order, were as follows:
   148, 146, 144, 142, 140, 140, 138, 138, 138, 136, 136, 134, 132, 132, 128.
   Find the median and the upper and lower quartiles.

17) The table below shows the frequency distribution of the 'life' of 200 electric light bulbs, which were tested by the firm making them.

Life (hours)	Number of bulbs
301–400	7
401–500	23
501–600	28
601–700	36
701–800	37
801–900	28
901–1000	22
1001–1100	16
1101–1200	3

(a) State:
    (i) the class interval size,
    (ii) the modal class.
(b) Using a scale of 1 cm to represent 100 hours and also 10 light bulbs, construct a cumulative frequency curve.
(c) Use the graph to estimate the median life of the electric light bulbs.
(d) From the graph obtain the values of the upper and lower quartiles.

18) Find the mode of the following set of numbers: 3, 5, 2, 7, 5, 8, 2, 7.

19) Find the mode of 38.7, 29.6, 32.1, 35.8, 43.2.

20) Find the modes of 8, 4, 9, 3, 5, 3, 8, 5, 3, 8, 9, 5, 6, 7.

21) The marks of 100 students were as follows:

Mark	Frequency
1	2
2	8
3	20
4	32
5	18
6	9
7	6
8	3
9	2

Obtain the median mark.

22) Find the mode of the distribution of Question 4.

23) Find the mode of the distribution of Question 5.

MEASURES OF DISPERSION

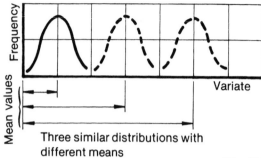

Three similar distributions with different means

Fig. 45.26

A statistical average gives some idea of the position of a distribution (Fig. 45.26). Hence statistical averages are often called *measures of location*. We now need a measure which will define the spread or dispersion of the data. The measures commonly used are:

(a) the range,
(b) the quartile deviation (often called the semi-interquartile range),
(c) the standard deviation.

THE RANGE

The range is the difference between the largest and smallest observations in a sample. That is

Range

    = largest observation – smallest observation

EXAMPLE 18

The wages paid in an office are $57.00, $62.00, $84.00, $68.40 and $80.00 per week. Find the range of the wages.

    Lowest wage = $57.00
    Highest wage = $84.00
Range of wage = $84.00 – $57.00 = $27.00

EXAMPLE 19

32 children were asked to estimate the length of a metal rod to the nearest centimetre. The table below shows the results obtained.

Estimated length (cm)	Frequency
35	1
36	3
37	4
38	8
39	6
40	5
41	3
42	2

What is the range of these estimates?

Lower boundary limit of the first class

$= 34.5 \, \text{cm}$

Upper boundary limit of the last class

$= 42.5 \, \text{cm}$

Range $= 42.5 \, \text{cm} - 34.5 \, \text{cm} = 8 \, \text{cm}$

The range gives some idea of the spread of a distribution but it depends solely upon the extreme values of the observations. It gives no information about the way in which the distribution is spread and hence it is seldom used as a measure of dispersion for a frequency distribution. However, with small samples, the range is very effective as a measure of dispersion.

QUARTILE DEVIATION

The quartile deviation, sometimes called the semi-interquartile range, is found by using the formula

Quartile deviation $= \frac{1}{2}(Q_3 - Q_1)$

where Q_3 = the upper quartile and Q_1 = the lower quartile.

EXAMPLE 20

An examination of the wages paid by a certain firm showed that the upper quartile was $64 per week whilst the lower quartile was $48 per week. Find the semi-interquartile range.

We are given $Q_3 = \$64$ and $Q_1 = \$48$. Hence

Semi-interquartile range $= \frac{1}{2}(\$64 - \$48) = \$8$

The quartile deviation has the advantage that it ignores extreme values in the distribution. However, the measure only covers that half of the distribution centred upon the median and hence it does not show the dispersion of the distribution as a whole. A small value of the quartile deviation shows that the data has only a small spread between the quartiles. The quartile deviation is used extensively as a measure of dispersion in business and educational statistics.

*THE STANDARD DEVIATION

This is the most important of the measures of dispersion. It is usually represented by the symbol σ (Greek letter sigma) and it may be

calculated by using either of the formulae shown below, n being the number of values.

$$\sigma = \sqrt{\frac{\Sigma(x - \bar{x})^2}{n}} \quad \text{or} \quad \sigma = \sqrt{\frac{\Sigma x^2}{n} - (\bar{x})^2}$$

EXAMPLE 21

Find the standard deviation of the numbers 2, 4, 7, 8 and 9.

(a) Using the formula $\sigma = \sqrt{\dfrac{\Sigma(x - \bar{x})^2}{n}}$

$$\bar{x} = \frac{2 + 4 + 7 + 8 + 9}{5} = 6$$

x	$x - \bar{x}$	$(x - \bar{x})^2$
2	-4	16
4	-2	4
7	1	1
8	2	4
9	3	9
		34

$$\sigma = \sqrt{\frac{34}{5}} = \sqrt{6.8} = 2.61$$

(b) Using the formula $\sigma = \sqrt{\dfrac{\Sigma x^2}{n} - (\bar{x})^2}$

x	x^2
2	4
4	16
7	49
8	64
9	81
	214

$$\sigma = \sqrt{\frac{214}{5} - 6^2} = \sqrt{42.8 - 36} = \sqrt{6.8}$$

$$= 2.61$$

THE STANDARD DEVIATION OF A FREQUENCY DISTRIBUTION

The standard deviation of a frequency distribution is best calculated by using a coded method and an assumed mean. When this method is used the coded value of the standard deviation is calculated from the formula below, f being the frequency appropriate to x_c.

$$\sigma_c = \sqrt{\frac{\Sigma f x_c^2}{n} - (\bar{x}_c)^2}$$

The standard deviation of the distribution is then found by using

$$\sigma = \sigma_c \times \text{unit size}$$

EXAMPLE 22

The table below shows the distribution of maximum loads, in tonnes, supported by certain cables. Calculate the mean and standard deviation for this distribution.

Max. load (tonnes)	Number of cables
8.3–8.5	2
8.6–8.8	8
8.9–9.1	14
9.2–9.4	6
9.5–9.7	1

Assumed mean = 9.0 tonnes,

unit size = 0.3 tonnes

Class	Class mid-point x	Coded value x_c	Frequency f	fx_c	fx_c^2
8.3–8.5	8.4	−2	2	−4	8
8.6–8.8	8.7	−1	8	−8	8
8.9–9.1	9.0	0	14	0	0
9.2–9.4	9.3	1	6	6	6
9.5–9.7	9.6	2	1	2	4
			31	−4	26

$$\bar{x}_c = \frac{-4}{31} = -0.13$$

$$\bar{x} = 9.0 + (-0.13) \times 0.3 = 9.0 - 0.039$$

$$= 8.961 \text{ tonnes}$$

$$\sigma_c = \sqrt{\frac{26}{31} - (-0.13)^2}$$

$$= \sqrt{0.839 - 0.017} = \sqrt{0.822} = 0.907$$

$$\sigma = 0.907 \times 0.3 = 0.272 \text{ tonnes}$$

A rough check on the standard deviation may be obtained by dividing the range of the data by 6. Thus

$$\text{Rough check for } \sigma = \frac{9.75 - 8.25}{6} = \frac{1.5}{6}$$

$$= 0.25 \text{ tonnes}$$

This compares fairly well with the calculated value of 0.272 tonnes and we now know that the calculated value of σ is of the correct order, i.e. it is not wildly out. Strictly speaking this rough check only applies to symmetrical distributions but it may be taken to apply to moderately skewed distributions.

The standard deviation is the most important measure of dispersion. Every value in the distribution is used in its calculation. It is expressed in the same units as the original data and the mean, which is always associated with it. The larger the spread of the original data the larger will be the value of the standard deviation.

The standard deviation is extensively used in more advanced statistical work. It has the disadvantages that it is more difficult to calculate than the other measures of dispersion and it gives undue weight to the extreme values because the deviations from the mean are squared.

When a set of values is increased (or decreased) by a constant amount the value of the mean is increased (or decreased) by this constant amount. The value of the standard deviation remains unaltered because the spread of the data has not altered.

When a set of values is multiplied by a constant amount the values of both the original mean and the original standard deviation are multiplied by this constant amount.

EXAMPLE 23

(a) Find the mean and standard deviation for the set of numbers: 2, 4, 8 and 10.
(b) If each number is increased by 2, find the new mean and standard deviation.
(c) If each of the original numbers is doubled find the new mean and standard deviation.

(a) $$\bar{x} = \frac{2 + 4 + 8 + 10}{4} = 6$$

$$\sigma_c = \sqrt{\frac{2^2 + 4^2 + 8^2 + 10^2}{4} - 6^2} = \sqrt{10}$$

(b) When each number is increased by 2, they become 4, 6, 10 and 12. The new mean, $\bar{x}_N$, is given by

$$\bar{x}_N = \frac{4 + 6 + 10 + 12}{4} = 8$$

Hence when each of the numbers is increased by 2, the mean of the set of numbers is also increased by 2.

$$\sigma_c = \sqrt{\frac{4^2 + 6^2 + 10^2 + 12^2}{4} - 8^2} = \sqrt{10}$$

Hence the standard deviation of the set of numbers remains the same when each number of the set is increased by 2.

(c) When each number is doubled they become 4, 8, 16 and 20. The mean of this set is

$$\bar{x} = \frac{4 + 8 + 16 + 20}{4} = 12 = 2 \times 6$$

The standard deviation of the doubled set of numbers is

$$\sigma_c = \sqrt{\frac{4^2 + 8^2 + 16^2 + 20^2}{4} - 12^2}$$

$$= \sqrt{40} = \sqrt{4 \times 10} = 2 \times \sqrt{10}$$

Hence, when a set of numbers is doubled, their mean and standard deviation are both doubled.

*ANALYSIS OF STATISTICAL DATA

If a frequency curve is symmetrical then the area under the curve is divided into certain proportions as follows:

68% of all the items in the distribution lie within 1 standard deviation on either side of the mean.

95% of all the items in the distribution lie within 2 standard deviations on either side of the mean.

Practically 100% of all the items in the distribution lie within 3 standard deviations on either side of the mean (see Fig. 45.27).

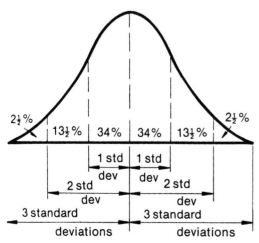

Fig. 45.27

Hence all that is needed to obtain a picture of the frequency curve is the values of the mean and the standard deviation and the number of items making up the distribution.

EXAMPLE 24

As a result of a household survey on food expenditure on 400 items the mean expenditure was found to be $40 with a standard deviation of $6. Sketch a frequency curve to represent the distribution.

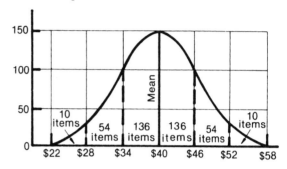

Fig. 45.28

(a) Draw a horizontal axis and mark off $40 in its centre.

(b) Erect a vertical at this $ mark and label this the mean.

(c) Mark off three standard deviations on either side of the mean as shown in Fig. 45.28 and label them in dollars. To the left of the mean the values will be:

1 standard deviation $= \$40 - \$6 = \$34$

2 standard deviations $= \$40 - \$12 = \$28$

3 standard deviations $= \$40 - \$18 = \$22$

To the right of the mean the values will be $46, $52 and $58 representing 1, 2 and 3 standard deviations respectively.

(d) Calculate the number of items belonging to each of the six divisions making up the frequency curve. Thus

between the mean and $46 there will be

34% of 400 = 136 items

between $46 and $52 there will be

$13\frac{1}{2}$% of 400 = 54 items

between $52 and $58 there will be

$2\frac{1}{2}$% of 400 = 10 items

and similarly to the left of the mean.

The curve may now be sketched by marking off the heights of the curve at the mid-point of each division. These heights are simply made equal to the number of items in the division. Note that the scale on the left of Fig. 45.28 is not a frequency scale; it is used only to obtain the relative heights of the curve. With a little practice the frequency curve may be sketched without the necessity of marking its heights.

*SKEWED DISTRIBUTIONS

The skewness of a distribution may be calculated by using the formula

$$\text{Coefficient of skewness}$$
$$= \frac{(\text{mean} - \text{mode})}{\text{standard deviation}}$$

Since, for a symmetrical distribution, the mean and the mode have the same value, the coefficient of skewness will be zero for this type of distribution. For a positively skewed distribution, the mean and median are always larger than the mode. Hence for a positively skewed distribution the coefficient is always positive. For a negatively skewed distribution the mean and median are always smaller than the mode (see Fig. 45.23). Hence for a negatively skewed distribution the coefficient is always negative. A highly skewed distribution will have a value for the coefficient of about ± 1 but values up to ± 3 are theoretically possible.

In industrial and economic statistics it is useful to know, for instance, that distribution of incomes is skewed and to what extent. The age distribution of workers in a factory will also be skewed. If the distributions of age and incomes are compared some interesting questions might be answered. For instance, do the older workers earn less than the more energetic younger workers or does experience make up for loss of speed and agility?

EXAMPLE 25

The analysis of 40 personal loans advanced by a finance company showed that the mean amount lent was $2218, the modal amount lent was $1908 with a standard deviation of $1292. Calculate the coefficient of skewness and comment upon its value.

$$\text{Coefficient of skewness}$$
$$= \frac{(2218 - 1908)}{1292} = +0.24$$

The frequency curve has quite a high degree of positive skewness.

SAMPLING

In statistics we are often called upon to make decisions about populations by taking a sample from the population. The samples which are taken must be representative of the population as a whole. These representative samples may be obtained by *random sampling* in which every item of a population has an equal chance of being chosen in the sample. One way of doing this is to give each item in the population a number and conduct a raffle. A second way is to use a table of random numbers, part of which is shown below.

Random Numbers

```
50632  25496  95652  24657  73557  76152
50020  24819  52984  76168  07136  40876
79971  54195  25708  51817  36732  72484
```

EXAMPLE 26

An auditor wishes to choose 8 accounts randomly from a set of 80 numbered accounts (numbered 00, 01, 02, . . . , 79). Use a table of random numbers to obtain the numbers of the 8 accounts which will constitute the sample.

In using a table of random numbers we do not usually start at line 1 and column 1. Instead it is usual to begin at some arbitrary point in the table.

In the above table let us begin in row 2, column 3, that is at the number 52984. We now read the numbers in pairs working along the lines. Thus the first number is 52. The second number is 98 and does not count since our accounts are numbered from 00 to 79. We therefore ignore the number 98 and carry on. The 8 random numbers are 52, (98), 47, 61, 68, 07, 13, 64 and 08.

If a repetition of numbers is obtained these repeated numbers are also ignored.

THE SAMPLE SIZE

The sample size required depends upon many factors such as the degree of certainty required and the amount of error that can be tolerated in the population characteristic being studied. The sample size required does not depend upon the size of the population. Usually a sample of about 100 items will give a satisfactory result.

EXAMPLE 27

A sample of 100 sacks of flour was weighed and the mean weight was found to be 55.3 kg. A lorry is to be loaded with 800 such sacks. Estimate the load on the lorry.

We can say that the mean weight of all the sacks of flour is 55.3 kg, and hence

$$\text{Load carried by the lorry}$$
$$= 800 \times 55.3 = 44\,240 \text{ kg}$$

CLUSTER SAMPLING

This method is used where the size of the population is unknown as would be the case with plants, animals and fish. The people conducting the survey go to small areas which are randomly selected and count every item fitting the given description.

EXAMPLE 28

A biology student took a photograph of a small district from which it was hoped to estimate the number of a species of plant in that district. Each cross in Fig. 45.29 represents the location of the plant being studied. Using a cluster sampling method, estimate the number of plants in the district.

First we divide up the area in Fig. 45.29 into a number of equal squares (we have chosen 16).

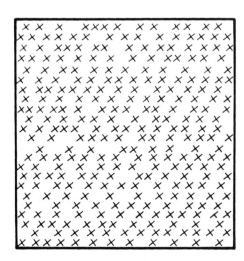

Fig. 45.29

We note that there are approximately 20 crosses per square so we randomly choose 5 of these squares by using a table of random numbers.

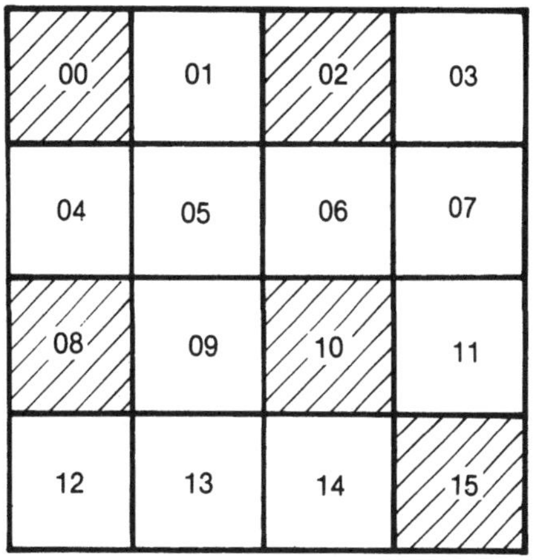

Fig. 45.30

The five squares chosen by this method are shown in Fig. 45.30. The number of crosses in each of these squares is counted and found to be 16, 20, 17, 26 and 19 respectively, giving a mean number of crosses per square as 19.6.

Hence the estimated number of crosses in the diagram is $19.6 \times 16 = 314$. Hence it is estimated that there are 314 plants of the type being studied.

Exercise 199 – *Questions 1–5 type B, remainder C*

1) The wages of five office workers are $59.00, $55.60, $64.80, $98.40 and $74.80. Determine the range of these wages.

2) The largest of 50 measurements is 29.88 cm. If the range is 0.12 cm, find the smallest measurement.

3) Draw an ogive for the following frequency distribution and hence find the upper and lower quartiles. Then calculate the value of the quartile deviation.

Family income ($ per annum)	Number of families
1000 and up to 1500	2
1500 and up to 2000	12
2000 and up to 3000	78
3000 and up to 4000	121
4000 and up to 6000	60

4) Find the standard deviation of the numbers 2, 3, 6, 1, 5 and 7.

5) Find the mean and standard deviation of the numbers 3.1, 2.4, 3.9, 4.5 and 2.1.

6) Calculate the mean and standard deviation for the data given in the table below:

Length (cm)	Frequency
19.1	1
19.2	3
19.3	7
19.4	12
19.5	6
19.6	1

7) The examination marks obtained by 100 candidates are distributed as follows:

Mark	Number of candidates
0–19	8
20–29	7
30–39	14
40–49	23
50–59	26
60–69	12
70–79	6
80–89	4

Make use of an assumed mean to estimate the mean and standard deviation.

8) The table below shows the age distribution of a sample of the female population of a certain territory. Estimate the mean and standard deviation.

Age (years)	Frequency
0–14	33
15–29	29
30–44	23
45–59	26
60–74	24

9) As a result of a survey on expenditure on furniture in 200 households the mean expenditure per annum was found to be $248 with a standard deviation of $25. Sketch a frequency curve to represent this distribution.

10) 120 students were weighed. Their mean weight was found to be 57 kg with a standard deviation of 5 kg. Sketch a frequency curve to represent this distribution.

11) The wages of the employees of a small firm have a mean of $68, a median of $65 and a standard deviation of $9.95. Calculate the value of the coefficient of skewness and comment upon its value.

12) The heights of 100 men were measured. Their mean height was found to be 172 cm with a standard deviation of 5 cm. If the median height was 170 cm, calculate the value of the coefficient of skewness. Sketch the frequency curve indicating clearly the direction of the skewness.

13) In a store room there are bundles of pencils each containing different numbers of pencils. A random sample of 8 bundles gave the following numbers of pencils: 28, 32, 41, 27, 33, 42, 39 and 30. If there are 150 bundles in all, estimate the total number of pencils in stock.

14) A supermarket buys 80 lambs. 5 of these are chosen at random and weighed after dressing with the following results: 16, 15.8, 17.3, 15.4 and 15.5 kg. Estimate the total weight of the 80 dressed lambs.

15) The table below is part of a table of random numbers.

64937 03355 95863 20790 65304 55189
00745 65253 11822 15804 15630 64759
51135 98527 62586 41889 25439 88036
24034 67283 09448 56301 57683 30277
94623 85418 68829 06652 41982 49159
21631 91157

An accountant wishes to examine 12 invoices from a set of 100 invoices numbered 00 to 99. Use the above table of random numbers to obtain the 12 invoices which will constitute the sample.

16) An area is divided up into 25 equal squares. A sample of 6 of these squares is to constitute a sample. Use the table of random numbers given in Question 15 to obtain the 6 squares and show these in a diagram.

17) In order to obtain the total number of boats in a harbour (Fig. 45.31) the area is to be divided up into 5 km squares. 5 of these squares are to constitute a sample. By using the table of random numbers given in Question 15, decide which squares are to constitute the sample and hence estimate the number of boats in the harbour.

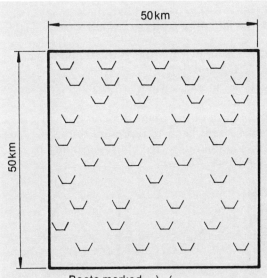

Boats marked ⌄

Fig. 45.31

18) A student of marine biology took a photograph (Fig. 45.32) of a set of cockles on a beach just before they buried themselves in the sand. Divide up the area of the photograph into a suitable number of squares and take a sample of these squares using the table of random numbers given in Question 15. Count up the number of cockles in each square of your sample and hence estimate the mean number of cockles per square. Hence estimate the total number of cockles on the beach.

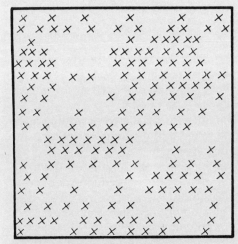

Position of cockles marked ×

Fig. 45.32

SELF-TEST 45

1) A pie chart is drawn to represent the following information:

Ingredient	Amount (grams)
Flour	280
Fruit	70
Eggs	20
Butter	30
Sugar	100

The sector angle used to represent fruit is:

a 5°   **b** 50°   **c** 70°   **d** 100°

2) The size of a farm is 120 hectares. It is cropped with fruit, vegetables, sugar cane and bananas. If the number of hectares used for each is shown in a pie diagram and the sector angle representing vegetables is 60°, then the number of hectares used for this crop is

a 20   **b** 30   **c** 60   **d** 90

3) The range of a distribution is:

a the smallest observation
b the largest observation
c another name for the standard deviation.
d the difference between the largest observation and the smallest observation

4) Consider the numbers 13, 18, 12, 11, 13, 19, 11, 16 and 11. The number 13 is the:

a mean   **b** median   **c** mode   **d** range

5) The mean of four numbers is 14. Three of the numbers are 4, 10 and 16. What is the fourth number?

a 10   **b** 26   **c** 30   **d** 36

6) The median of the values 4, 12, 6, 6, 8, 14 and 20 is:

a 6   **b** 8   **c** 10   **d** 70

7) The diameters of some ball bearings are measured to the nearest 0.01 mm. The measurements are grouped into classes. What is the width of the class interval 18.02–18.04 mm?

a 0.01 mm   **b** 0.02 mm   **c** 0.03 mm
d 0.04 mm

8) The information below relates to the mass (in grams) of packets of chemical.

Mass (grams)	Frequency
20	1
21	2
22	4
23	5
24	4
25	1

The mean of this distribution is:

a 0.7 g   **b** 22.3 g   **c** 22.7 g   **d** 23 g

9) In Question 8 the mode is:

a 22 g   **b** $22\frac{2}{3}$ g   **c** 23 g   **d** 24 g

10) Which of the following is a measure of dispersion?

a median   **b** range   **c** frequency
d mode

11) The weights of some children were analysed with the following results:

Weight (kg)	Frequency
24–28	5
28–32	12
32–36	10
36–40	3

The standard deviation is:

a 0.87 kg   **b** 3.49 kg   **c** 16 kg   **d** 17 kg

12) Which one of the following is a discrete variable?

a the temperature of a room
b the number of spectators at a cricket match
c the quantity of liquid in a flask
d the length of a piece of wood

13) The upper quartile of the numbers 2, 5, 3, 7, 4, 4 and 6 is:

a 3   **b** 4   **c** 4.5   **d** 6

14) Which of the frequency curves shown in Fig. 45.33 is likely to represent the distribution of the age of bridegrooms at marriage?

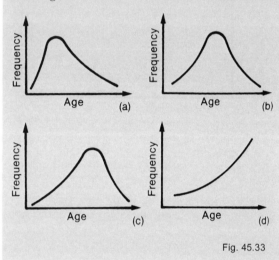

Fig. 45.33

CHAPTER 45 SUMMARY

Points to remember

(i) A bar chart shows data as rectangles or bars. The bars should be the same width and evenly spaced across the page.

(ii) A pie chart is a circle divided up like portions of a pie. The size of the angle of each portion is proportional to the percentage of the whole occupied by the portion.

(iii) A table showing the number of times (the frequency) each value occurs is known as a frequency distribution.

(iv) The *range* of the data is the difference between the smallest and largest values.

(v) A bar chart representing a frequency distribution, and drawn with the bars touching, is known as a *histogram*.

(vi) When the set of data is large, the values are grouped in classes, and the resulting table is called a *grouped frequency distribution*.

(vii) A single value taken to represent a set of values is called an *average*.

(viii) Three main averages are *the mean, the mode* and *the median*.

(ix) The mean is calculated by adding all the values and dividing by the total number of values.

(x) The median is the middle value when the values are arranged in order of magnitude.

(xi) The mode is the value that occurs most often.

(xii) *The lower quartile or first quartile* is that value which a quarter of the values are less than.

(xiii) The *upper quartile* or *third quartile* is that value which a quarter of the values are greater than.

(xiv) The *interquartile range = upper quartile − lower quartile*.

Chapter 46 **Probability**

EQUIPROBABLE EVENTS AND FAVOURABLE OUTCOMES

When a fair die is rolled each of the six faces has an equal *probability* of landing uppermost.

Similarly in a well-shuffled pack of 52 cards there is an equal probability of drawing one particular card, say the 2 of clubs or the Queen of Hearts. We call drawing the Queen of Hearts (or the 2 of clubs or any other card) an *event*, and we can say that drawing the 2 of clubs and the Queen of Hearts are *equiprobable events*.

Suppose we wanted to work out the probability of drawing a Queen from the pack. If we succeed in drawing a Queen we call this a *favourable outcome*. Now there are 4 equiprobable events which can produce the favourable outcome – if we draw a Queen of Hearts, a Queen of spades, a Queen of clubs or a Queen of diamonds. This means that we have 4 chances out of 52 of drawing a Queen and the probability is $\frac{4}{52}$ or $\frac{1}{13}$. So we can define the probability of a favourable outcome as follows

Probability of favourable outcome

$$= \frac{\text{number of equiprobable events which produce a favourable outcome}}{\text{the total number of equiprobable events}}$$

The examples below should make this clearer.

EXAMPLE 1

(1) To find the probability (Pr) of obtaining a head in a single toss of a fair coin we note that there are 2 equiprobable outcomes (i.e. the coin can come down heads or tails), 1 of which is favourable. Hence

$$\text{Pr (heads)} = \frac{1}{2}$$

(2) To find the probability of drawing an ace from a deck of 52 playing cards we note that there are 4 aces in the pack. Hence there are 52 equiprobable outcomes, 4 of which are

favourable. Hence

$$\text{Pr (ace)} = \frac{4}{52} = \frac{1}{13}$$

(3) To find the probability of drawing a diamond from a deck of 52 playing cards we note that there are 52 equiprobable outcomes of which 13 are favourable. Hence

$$\text{Pr (diamond)} = \frac{13}{52} = \frac{1}{4}$$

EXAMPLE 2

20 discs are marked with the numbers 1 to 20 inclusive. They are placed in a box and one disc is drawn from it. What is the probability that the number on the disc will be a multiple of 5?

Any of the numbers 5, 10, 15 and 20 is a multiple of 5. Hence there are 20 equiprobable outcomes 4 of which are favourable. Hence

$$\text{Pr (multiple of 5)} = \frac{4}{20} = \frac{1}{5}$$

NON-EQUIPROBABLE EVENTS

When 3 coins are thrown the possible outcomes, all equiprobable, are

HHH   HHT   HTT   HTH
THH   TTH   THT   TTT

The probability of one head showing is

$$\text{Pr (1 head)} = \frac{3}{8}$$

because there are 8 equiprobable outcomes 3 of which are favourable (i.e. HTT, TTH and THT).

If we list the possible outcomes as

0 heads, 1 head, 2 heads and 3 heads

we note that

$$\text{Pr (0 heads)} = \tfrac{1}{8}$$

$$\text{Pr (1 head)} = \tfrac{3}{8}$$

$$\text{Pr (2 heads)} = \tfrac{3}{8}$$

$$\text{Pr (3 heads)} = \tfrac{1}{8}$$

Hence the outcomes of 0 heads, 1 head, 2 heads and 3 heads are *not* equiprobable events. It is therefore *incorrect* to state that Pr (1 head) $= \frac{1}{4}$ on the basis of 1 favourable outcome from 4 equiprobable outcomes.

USE OF SET NOTATION

Suppose a person writes down a whole number greater than 2 but less than 12. The universal set of all possible outcomes is

$$\mathcal{E} = \{x: 2 < x < 12\}$$

$$= \{3, 4, 5, 6, 7, 8, 9, 10, 11\}$$

The sub-set of all odd numbers in the universal set is

$$A = \{3, 5, 7, 9, 11\}$$

The probability that the person writes down an odd number is

$$\text{Pr (odd number)} = \frac{n(A)}{n(\mathcal{E})} = \frac{5}{9}$$

The Venn diagram is shown in Fig. 46.1.

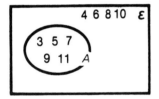

Fig. 46.1

PROBABILITY SCALE

When an event is absolutely certain to happen we say that the probability of it happening is 1. Thus the probability that one day each of us will die is 1.

When an event can never happen we say that the probability of it happening is 0. Thus the probability that one of us can jump a height of 5 metres unaided is 0.

All probabilities must, therefore, have a value between 0 and 1. They may be expressed as a fraction or a decimal. Thus

$$\text{Pr (head)} = \frac{1}{2} = 0.5$$

The probability of obtaining a 3 in a single roll of a die is

$$\text{Pr (3)} = \frac{1}{6} = 0.167$$

Probabilities may be expressed on a probability scale (Fig. 46.2).

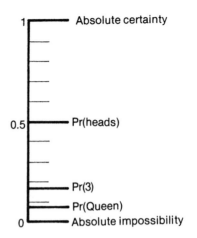

Fig. 46.2

TOTAL PROBABILITY

If we toss a coin it will come down heads or tails. That is

$$\text{Pr (head)} = \frac{1}{2} \quad \text{and} \quad \text{Pr (tails)} = \frac{1}{2}$$

The total probability, that is the probability covering all possible events is $\frac{1}{2} + \frac{1}{2} = 1$. Another way of saying this is

$$\text{Pr (favourable outcomes)}$$

$$+ \text{Pr (unfavourable outcomes)} = 1$$

Thus if the probability of getting an ace is $\frac{1}{13}$, the probability of not getting an ace is $1 - \frac{1}{13} = \frac{12}{13}$.

Fig. 46.3

In set notation (see Fig. 46.3), we have

$$\text{Pr }(A) + \text{Pr }(A') = 1$$

EXAMPLE 3

A box contains 5 blue balls, 2 red balls, 4 yellow balls and 9 black balls. A ball is drawn at random from the box. Calculate the probability that it will be:

(a) a red ball,   (b) not a red ball.

If $\quad \mathcal{E} = \{\text{all the balls in the box}\}$

$\qquad n(\mathcal{E}) = 20$

If $\quad A = \{\text{all the red balls in the box}\}$

$\qquad n(A) = 2$

(a) $\quad$ Pr (red ball) $= \dfrac{n(A)}{n(\mathcal{E})} = \dfrac{2}{20} = 0.1$

(b) $\quad$ Pr (not a red ball) $= 1 - 0.1 = 0.9$

EXPERIMENTAL PROBABILITY

Although it is possible to calculate many probabilities in the ways shown above, in a great many cases we have to rely on an experiment in order to establish the probability of an event happening. To find the probability of a particular outcome we use

$$\text{Probability} = \dfrac{\text{number of 'successful' trials}}{\text{total number of trials conducted}}$$

EXAMPLE 4

100 ball bearings are examined and 4 are found to be not round. If a ball bearing is chosen at random from the 100, calculate the probability of it being not round.

In this case a 'successful' trial is one in which a not round ball bearing is found. The total number of trials conducted is 100.

$\therefore \qquad$ Pr (not round) $= \dfrac{4}{100} = 0.04$

EXAMPLE 5

A survey was carried out by some students who recorded the first digit of the registration number of some cars which passed their school gate. The results obtained were as follows:

Digit	1	2	3	4	5	6	7	8	9
Frequency	38	27	27	22	22	34	20	7	3

Determine:

(a) the probability that the first digit is a 5,

(b) the probability that the first digit is 6 or higher.

Total number of trials conducted

$\quad = 38 + 27 + 27 + 22 + 22 + 34 + 20 + 7 + 3$

$\quad = 200$

(a) Number of trials in which the first digit was $5 = 22$.

$$\text{Pr (5)} = \dfrac{22}{200} = 0.11$$

(b) Number of trials in which the first digit was 6 or higher

$$= 34 + 20 + 7 + 3 = 64$$

$$\text{Pr (6 or higher)} = \dfrac{64}{200} = 0.32$$

Exercise 200 – *All type A*

1) A die is rolled. Calculate the probability of:

(a) a four,
(b) a number less than four,
(c) a two or a three,
(d) an odd number.

2) 40 discs marked with the numbers 1 to 40 are placed in a box and one disc is drawn from it. Determine the probability that the number on the disc will be:

(a) a multiple of 5,
(b) odd,
(c) more than 7,
(d) less than 4.

3) A card is drawn from a deck of 52 playing cards. Find the probability that it will be:

(a) the Queen of spades,
(b) a King,
(c) a picture card (i.e. an ace, King, Queen or Jack),
(d) the Jack of Hearts or the ace of clubs.

4) A letter is chosen from the word FLAGSTAFF. Find the probability that it will be:

(a) L $\qquad$ (b) A $\qquad$ (c) F

5) A bag contains 3 red balls, 4 blue, 6 black and 7 white. One ball is drawn from the bag. Calculate the probability that it will be:

(a) blue,
(b) red or black,
(c) not white.

6) Two dice are thrown together and their scores added. Determine the probability that the sum will be:

(a) 7   (b) less than 6,   (c) more than 8.

7) 30 boys were measured for height. 3 were under 1.50 m. If one boy is selected at random, calculate the probability that he will be under 1.50 m in height.

8) 100 girls were weighed with the results given on the histogram shown in Fig. 46.4. Calculate:

(a) the probability of selecting a girl with a weight of 41 kg,
(b) the probability of selecting a girl with a weight of 43 kg or greater.

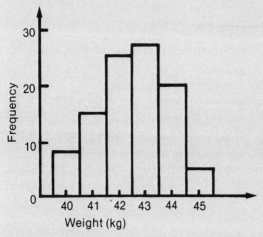

Fig. 46.4

9) During a certain period of the year the number of blooms on each of a number of hibiscus bushes was recorded as follows:

Number of blooms	5	6	7	8	9	10	11	12
Frequency	15	19	24	26	23	18	15	10

Calculate the probability of finding a hibiscus bush with:
(a) less than 7 blooms, (b) exactly 9 blooms, (c) 10 or more blooms.

10) In a test the pupils of a group scored the following marks (out of 10).

Mark	1	2	3	4	5	6	7	8	9	10
Frequency	1	4	5	7	8	8	7	6	3	1

Calculate the probability of selecting a pupil who had:

(a) a mark of 3 or less,   (b) a mark of 6,
(c) a mark of 8 or higher.

*PERMUTATIONS

We have seen that the probability value is based upon the ratio of the number of equally probable favourable outcomes to the number of possible outcomes. With simple problems the number of outcomes can be counted directly.

For more complex problems, however, permutations and combinations are required to determine the number of possible outcomes. Consider the three letters *A*, *B* and *C*. If we select groups of two letters at a time there are six possible arrangements or *permutations* which are:

$$AB, AC, BC, BA, CA \text{ and } CB$$

To permute or permutate is to change the order of things; each possible arrangement is called a permutation. In a permutation the order of the things is important.

In the above permutations *AB* is *not* the same as *BA* nor is *BC* the same as *CB*.

The permutation of *n* objects, taken *n* at a time is

Permutation of *n* objects

$$= n! = n \times (n-1) \times (n-2) \times \ldots \times 2 \times 1$$

$n!$ is called factorial *n*. Hence

factorial $4 = 4! = 4 \times 3 \times 2 \times 1 = 24$

factorial $7 = 7! = 7 \times 6 \times 5 \times 4 \times 3 \times 2 \times 1$

$$= 5040$$

EXAMPLE 6

Three members of a club committee have volunteered to serve as president, secretary and treasurer. In how many ways can the three volunteers take the positions.

Permutations of the three offices

$$= 3! = 3 \times 2 \times 1 = 6$$

The result can be illustrated by a diagram (Fig. 46.5) where the three volunteers are called A, B and C.

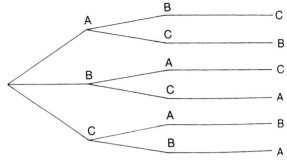

Fig. 46.5

Usually we are concerned about the number of permutations of a sub-group of the set of things. The number of permutations of n things taken r at a time, r being less than n is

$$_nP_r = \frac{n!}{(n-r)!}$$

$$= n \times (n-1) \times (n-2) \times \ldots \times (n-r+1)$$

$$_5P_4 = 5 \times (5-1) \times (5-2) \times (5-3)$$

$$= 5 \times 4 \times 3 \times 2 = 120$$

EXAMPLE 7

There are nine horses in a race. How many ways are there of nominating the first three horses?

The number of ways is the number of permutations of 9 things taken 3 at a time. That is

$$_9P_3 = 9 \times 8 \times 7 = 504$$

*PERMUTATIONS OF THINGS WHICH ARE NOT ALL DIFFERENT

The number of permutations of n things consisting of groups in which n_1 are all alike, n_2 are all alike, etc., such that $n = n_1 + n_2 + \ldots$ is

$$\frac{n!}{n_1!n_2!\ldots}$$

EXAMPLE 8

Determine the number of permutations of the word STATISTICS.

There is 1 A, 1 C, 2 I's, 3 S's and 3 T's. Hence

Number of permutations

$$= \frac{10!}{1! \times 1! \times 2! \times 3! \times 3!} = 50\,400$$

*COMBINATIONS

In a permutation the order of the things is important. In a combination the order is unimportant. Thus abc is a combination of the three letters a, b and c. It is regarded as being the same as bca or cab. Note that a combination of three letters taken three at a time gives three permutations.

The number of combinations of n things taken r at a time is

$$_nC_r = \frac{n!}{r! \times (n-r)!}$$

$$= \frac{n \times (n-1) \times (n-2) \times \ldots \times (n-r+1)}{r!}$$

$$_6C_3 = \frac{6!}{3! \times 3!} = \frac{6 \times 5 \times 4 \times 3 \times 2 \times 1}{3 \times 2 \times 1 \times 3 \times 2 \times 1}$$

$$= \frac{6 \times 5 \times 4}{3 \times 2 \times 1} = 20$$

Note that the value of r gives the number of factors on the top and bottom lines.

$$_7C_2 = \frac{7 \times 6}{2 \times 1} = 21$$

It can be shown that

$$_nC_r = {_nC_{(n-r)}}$$

The use of this relationship may save considerable labour in computation.

$$_{20}C_{16} = {_{20}C_4} = \frac{20 \times 19 \times 18 \times 17}{4 \times 3 \times 2 \times 1} = 4845$$

EXAMPLE 9

In how many ways can a hockey team consisting of 11 players be chosen from a squad of 14 players?

11 players can be selected from 14 players in $_{14}C_{11}$ combinations

$$_{14}C_{11} = {_{14}C_3} = \frac{14 \times 13 \times 12}{3 \times 2 \times 1} = 364$$

Hence the team can be selected in 364 different ways.

EXAMPLE 10

Out of 5 mathematics teachers and 7 English teachers a committee consisting of 2 mathematics teachers and 3 English teachers is to be formed. In how many ways can this be done if any of the mathematics teachers and any of the English teachers can be chosen?

2 mathematics teachers out of 5 can be chosen in $_2C_5$ different ways.

3 English teachers out of 7 English teachers can be chosen in $_2C_5$ different ways.

Now each combination of mathematics teachers can be combined with each combination of English teachers. Hence

Total number of possible selections

$$= {_5C_2} \times {_7C_3}$$

$$= \frac{5 \times 4}{2 \times 1} \times \frac{7 \times 6 \times 5}{3 \times 2 \times 1}$$

$$= 10 \times 35 = 350$$

*PROBABILITY, PERMUTATIONS AND COMBINATIONS

It was mentioned earlier in this chapter that the methods of permutations and combinations provide a basis for determining the possible number of outcomes in comparatively complex situations. Assuming that all events are equiprobable we can determine the probability of an event occurring by finding the number of combinations of favourable outcomes as compared with the number of outcomes that are possible.

EXAMPLE 11

Consider the word OMNIBUS. 4 letters are chosen at random from the word. What is the probability that they will be MNIB in that order?

Number of favourable outcomes = 1

Total number of equiprobable outcomes

$$= {_7P_4} = 7 \times 6 \times 5 \times 4 = 840$$

Pr (choosing MNIB) $= \dfrac{1}{840} = 0.001\,19$

EXAMPLE 12

A committee consists of 14 students of which 5 are physics students and 9 are geography students. A sub-committee is to be formed by randomly choosing 5 students. What is the probability that it will consist of 2 physics students and 3 geography students?

2 physics students out of 5 can be chosen in $_5C_2$ different ways.

3 geography students out of 9 can be chosen in $_9C_3$ different ways.

The number of favourable outcomes

$$= {_5C_2} \times {_9C_3}$$

$$= \frac{5 \times 4}{2 \times 1} \times \frac{9 \times 8 \times 7}{3 \times 2 \times 1}$$

$$= 10 \times 84 = 840$$

Total number of equiprobable outcomes

$$= {_{14}C_5}$$

$$= \frac{14 \times 13 \times 12 \times 11 \times 10}{5 \times 4 \times 3 \times 2 \times 1}$$

$$= 2002$$

Pr (2 physics and 3 geography students)

$$= \frac{840}{2002} = 0.42$$

Exercise 201 – All type C

1) From a pack of 52 playing cards the ace, King, Queen, Jack and Ten of clubs are taken. In how many ways can 4 of these cards be placed in a row from left to right?

2) Evaluate: (a) $_5P_2$ (b) $_7P_5$ (c) $_{12}P_4$.

3) How many numbers each containing four digits can be made from the digits 1, 2, 3, 4, 5, 6, 7 and 8 if none of the digits is to be used more than once?

4) How many different arrangements can be made by taking 5 of the letters of the word HORSEMAN, the order of the letters being important?

5) In how many ways can 7 books be distributed to 3 readers when each reader can have any of the books?

6) Find the number of different ways of arranging the letters of the word CASSOCK.

7) How many different arrangements can be made of the word ENSEMBLE by using all of its letters?

8) In how many different ways can 5 A's, 2 B's, 1 C, 1 D and 3 E's be arranged?

9) How many four letter arrangements can be made from the word HOUSEHOLD?

10) Evaluate: (a) $_5C_3$ (b) $_{33}C_{28}$.

11) How many combinations of 4 letters can be made from the word PLACES?

12) In how many ways can a cricket team of 11 players be chosen from a squad of 13 players?

13) 11 people are to travel in two cars. The larger will carry 6 people. In how many ways can the party be split up?

14) A mixed hockey team is to be chosen from a squad of 9 men and 8 women. If the team is to consist of 6 men and 5 women find in how many ways the team can be selected.

15) A gardening firm offers 6 varieties of red flowers and 4 varieties of yellow flowers. A gardener places an order for 5 different varieties. What is the probability that he will receive 3 red varieties and 2 yellow varieties?

16) From the word FLAGS three letters are chosen at random. What is the probability that they will be LAG in that order?

17) Out of 5 mathematics students and 8 physics students a committee consisting of 3 mathematicians and 4 physicists is to be formed. In how many ways can this be done if two particular mathematicians must not be on the committee?

18) Five cards are drawn from a pack of 52 playing cards. Find the probability that:

(a) 4 are Kings
(b) 3 are aces and 2 are Kings.

19) Three cards are drawn from a pack of 52 playing cards. Calculate the probability that they will:

(a) be all of the one suit,
(b) be of different suits.

20) A department in a firm consists of five engineers and nine technicians. A group of four is to be formed from the 14 individuals. If these are randomly assigned what is the probability that the group will include:

(a) three engineers, (b) no engineers,
(c) no technicians.

*MUTUALLY EXCLUSIVE EVENTS

If two events are such that they cannot happen together then they are said to be *mutually*

exclusive. For instance, suppose we wish to know the probability of a 3 or a 4 occurring in a single roll of a fair die. In a single roll either a 3 or a 4 can occur but not both. Hence the events of throwing a 3 or a 4 are mutually exclusive events. Similarly it is impossible to cut a jack and a king in a single cut of a deck of playing cards. Hence these two events are mutually exclusive.

Mutually exclusive events can be represented by the Venn diagram shown in Fig. 46.6. The shaded area gives the probability of one of the events happening. We see that

$$\text{Pr } (A \text{ or } B) = \text{Pr } (A \cup B) = \text{Pr } (A) + \text{Pr } (B)$$

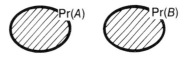

Fig. 46.6

EXAMPLE 13

A die with faces numbered 1 to 6 is rolled once. What is the probability of obtaining either a 3 or a 4?

Let the probability of obtaining a 3 be

$$\text{Pr } (A) = \frac{1}{6}$$

and the probability of obtaining a 4 be

$$\text{Pr } (B) = \frac{1}{6}$$

The probability of obtaining either a 3 or a 4 is

$$\text{Pr } (A \text{ or } B) = \text{Pr } (A) + \text{Pr } (B) = \frac{1}{6} + \frac{1}{6} = \frac{1}{3}$$

The rule for mutually exclusive events, often called the addition law of probability, may be extended to any number of events. If $E_1, E_2, \ldots, E_n$ are mutually exclusive events then the probability of *one* of the events happening is

$$\text{Pr } (E_1 \text{ or } E_2 \ldots \text{ or } E_n)$$
$$= \text{Pr } (E_1) + \text{Pr } (E_2) + \ldots + \text{Pr } (E_n)$$

EXAMPLE 14

Determine the probability of drawing an ace, a Jack or the King of spades from a deck of 52 playing cards.

Let the probability of drawing an ace be

$$\text{Pr } (E_1) = \frac{4}{52}$$

Let the probability of drawing a Jack be

$$\text{Pr } (E_2) = \frac{4}{52}$$

Let the probability of drawing the King of spades be

$$\text{Pr } (E_3) = \frac{1}{52}$$

The probability of drawing an ace, a Jack or the King of spades is

$$\text{Pr } (E_1 \text{ or } E_2 \text{ or } E_3)$$

$$= \text{Pr } (E_1) + \text{Pr } (E_2) + \text{Pr } (E_3)$$

$$= \frac{4}{52} + \frac{4}{52} + \frac{1}{52}$$

$$= \frac{9}{52} = 0.173$$

*NON-MUTUALLY EXCLUSIVE EVENTS

If a pack of playing cards is cut once the events of drawing a Jack and drawing a diamond are not mutually exclusive events since it is possible to draw the Jack of diamonds. The Venn diagram (Fig. 46.7) represents non-mutually exclusive events. The shaded region gives the probability that either the event A or the event B or both A and B will occur

$$\text{Pr } (A \text{ or } B \text{ or both})$$

$$= \text{Pr } (A) + \text{Pr } (B) - \text{Pr } (A \cap B)$$

$$= \text{Pr } (A) + \text{Pr } (B) - \text{Pr } (A) \times \text{Pr } (B)$$

Pr(A and B)

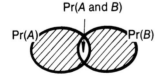

Fig. 46.7

EXAMPLE 15

If E_1 is the event of drawing a Jack and E_2 is the event of drawing a diamond from a deck of 52 playing cards, find the probability of drawing a Jack or a diamond or the Jack of diamonds.

$$\text{Pr } (E_1 \text{ or } E_2 \text{ or both})$$

$$= \text{Pr } (E_1) + \text{Pr } (E_2) - \text{Pr } (E_1) \times \text{Pr } (E_2)$$

$$= \frac{4}{52} + \frac{13}{52} - \frac{4}{52} \times \frac{13}{52}$$

$$= \frac{16}{52} = \frac{4}{13} = 0.308$$

The case of three non-mutually exclusive events is shown in Fig. 46.7.

$$\text{Pr } (E_1 \text{ or } E_2 \text{ or } E_3)$$

$$= \text{Pr } (E_1) + \text{Pr } (E_2) + \text{Pr } (E_3) - \text{Pr } (E_1)$$

$$\times \text{Pr } (E_2) - \text{Pr } (E_1) \times \text{Pr } (E_3) - \text{Pr } (E_2)$$

$$\times \text{Pr } (E_3) + \text{Pr } (E_1) \times \text{Pr } (E_2) \times \text{Pr } (E_3)$$

This formula is rather cumbersome and an easier formula to use is given below.

Let $\text{Pr } (\overline{E}_1)$

= the probability of event E_1 not occurring

$$= 1 - \text{Pr } (E_1)$$

$$\text{Pr } (\overline{E}_2)$$

= the probability of event E_2 not occurring

$$= 1 - \text{Pr } (E_2)$$

and $\text{Pr } (\overline{E}_3)$

= the probability of event E_3 not occurring

$$= 1 - \text{Pr } (E_3)$$

then $\text{Pr } (E_1 \text{ or } E_2 \text{ or } E_3)$

$$= 1 - \text{Pr } (\overline{E}_1) \times \text{Pr } (\overline{E}_2) \times \text{Pr } (\overline{E}_3)$$

EXAMPLE 16

Three people A, B and C set out to solve a crossword puzzle. Based upon their past performances in solving this type of puzzle, the probability that A will solve it is $\text{Pr } (A) = \frac{2}{3}$, the probability that B will solve it is $\text{Pr } (B) = \frac{3}{4}$ and the probability that C will solve it is $\text{Pr } (C) = \frac{4}{5}$. Determine the probability that the puzzle will be solved.

The events of solving the puzzle are non-mutually exclusive events since any one of the three people may solve it, any two of them may solve it or all three may solve it. Now

$$\Pr(\bar{A}) = 1 - \frac{2}{3} = \frac{1}{3}; \quad \Pr(\bar{B}) = 1 - \frac{3}{4} = \frac{1}{4};$$

$$\Pr(\bar{C}) = 1 - \frac{4}{5} = \frac{1}{5}$$

Hence $\Pr(A \text{ or } B \text{ or } C)$

$$= 1 - \frac{1}{3} \times \frac{1}{4} \times \frac{1}{5} = \frac{59}{60} = 0.983$$

*INDEPENDENT EVENTS

An independent event is one which has no effect upon subsequent events. If a die is rolled twice what happens on the first roll does not affect what happens on the second roll. Hence the two rolls of the die are independent events. Similarly the events of tossing a coin and then drawing a card from a pack of playing cards are independent events because the way in which the coin lands has no effect on the draw from the pack of cards.

In Fig. 46.7, the unshaded region represents the probability of *both* the events A and B occurring. Thus

$$\Pr(A \text{ and } B) = \Pr(A \cap B) = \Pr(A) \times \Pr(B)$$

EXAMPLE 17
A fair coin is tossed and then a card is drawn from a deck of 52 playing cards. Determine the probability that a head and an ace will result.

The events of tossing a head and drawing an ace are independent events.

Let E_1 be the event of tossing a head, then

$$\Pr(E_1) = \frac{1}{2}$$

Let E_2 be the event of drawing an ace, then

$$\Pr(E_2) = \frac{4}{52} = \frac{1}{13}$$

The probability of both E_1 and E_2 occurring is

$$\Pr(E_1 \text{ and } E_2) = \Pr(E_1) \times \Pr(E_2)$$

$$= \frac{1}{2} \times \frac{1}{13} = \frac{1}{26} = 0.038$$

The rule for independent events, often called the multiplication law of probability, can be extended to cover any number of independent events. Thus

$$\Pr(E_1 \text{ and } E_2 \text{ and } \ldots E_n)$$

$$= \Pr(E_1) \times \Pr(E_2) \times \ldots \times \Pr(E_n)$$

*DEPENDENT EVENTS

Consider a bag containing 3 red balls and 2 blue balls. A ball is drawn at random from the bag and not replaced. The probability that the ball is red is

$$\Pr(\text{red}) = \frac{3}{5}$$

Now let us choose a second ball. The probability that this is also red is

$$\Pr(\text{red}) = \frac{2}{4} = \frac{1}{2}$$

Hence the probability of drawing two red balls is

$$\Pr(\text{red and red}) = \frac{3}{5} \times \frac{1}{2} = \frac{3}{10} = 0.3$$

The events of drawing one red ball and not replacing it followed by drawing a second red ball are dependent events because the probability of the second event depends upon what happened during the first draw.

Therefore two events are said to be dependent when the occurrence (or non-occurrence) of the first event does affect the probability of the occurrence of the second event.

EXAMPLE 18
A bag contains 5 white balls, 3 black balls and 2 green balls. A ball is chosen at random from the bag and not replaced. In three draws find the probability of obtaining white, black and green in that order.

Let $\Pr(E_1)$

$$= \text{probability of drawing a white ball} = \frac{5}{10}$$

$$\Pr(E_2)$$

$$= \text{probability of drawing a black ball} = \frac{3}{9}$$

$$\Pr(E_3)$$

$$= \text{probability of drawing a green ball} = \frac{2}{8}$$

$\Pr(E_1 \text{ and } E_2 \text{ and } E_3)$

$$= \Pr(E_1) \times \Pr(E_2) \times \Pr(E_3)$$

$$= \frac{5}{10} \times \frac{3}{9} \times \frac{2}{8} = \frac{1}{24} = 0.042$$

When two events are dependent, the probability that E_2 occurs given that E_1 has occurred is denoted by $\text{Pr}\,(E_2/E_1)$. $\text{Pr}\,(E_2/E_1)$ is called a *conditional* probability. The Venn diagram (Fig. 46.8) illustrates conditional probability.

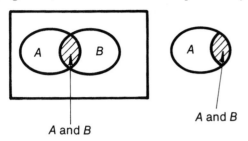

A and B

Fig. 46.8

Suppose we wish to find the probability of B occurring given that A has occurred then the original Venn diagram is reduced to the smaller diagram on the right. From this we conclude that

$$\text{Pr}\,(B/A) = \frac{\text{Pr}\,(A \text{ and } B)}{\text{Pr}\,(A)}$$

EXAMPLE 19

100 individuals applied for a post as a computer programmer. 30 had previous programming experience (P), 40 had a recognised qualification as a computer programmer (Q) and 20 had both a qualification and experience.

(a) Draw a Venn diagram to illustrate the problem.
(b) Determine the conditional probability that an applicant, chosen at random, has a qualification given that he also has experience.

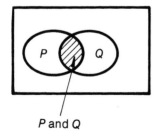

P and Q

Fig. 46.9

(a) The Venn diagram is shown in Fig. 46.9.

(b) The probability of a randomly selected applicant having experience is

$$\text{Pr}\,(P) = \frac{30}{100} = 0.3$$

The probability of the applicant having experience and a qualification is

$$\text{Pr}\,(P \text{ and } Q) = \frac{20}{100} = 0.2$$

The probability that the applicant has a qualification given that he has experience is

$$\text{Pr}\,(Q/P) = \frac{\text{Pr}\,(P \text{ and } Q)}{\text{Pr}\,(P)} = \frac{0.2}{0.3} = 0.67$$

*THE PROBABILITY TREE

A tree diagram is a useful way of illustrating the possible events associated with repeated trials.

EXAMPLE 20
A coin is tossed three times. Draw a tree diagram to illustrate the various possibilities and their associated probabilities.

On the first toss the coin can show either a head or a tail. The probability of a head is $\frac{1}{2}$ and the probability of a tail is also $\frac{1}{2}$. Showing possible heads by a full line and possible tails by a dotted line we may draw Fig. 46.10(a).

On the second toss, for each of the branches in Fig. 46.10(a) we may obtain either a head or a tail. Hence for each of the branches in diagram (a) we draw two more branches as shown in diagram (b). Diagram (b) tells us that the probability of a head occurring in both tosses is

$$\text{Pr}\,(H \text{ and } H) = \text{Pr}\,(H) \times \text{Pr}\,(H)$$
$$= \frac{1}{2} \times \frac{1}{2} = \frac{1}{4}$$

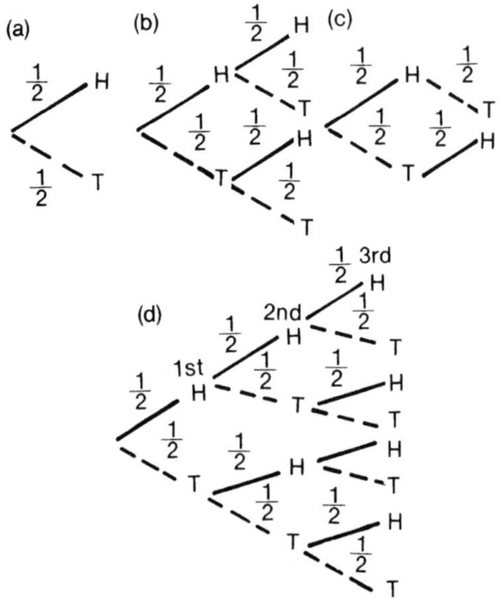

Fig. 46.10

One head may be obtained in one of two ways as shown in diagram (c).

$$\text{Pr (one head)}$$

$$= \text{Pr (H and T or T and H)}$$

$$= \text{Pr (H and T)} + \text{Pr (T and H)}$$

$$= \text{Pr (H)} \times \text{Pr (T)} + \text{Pr (T)} \times \text{Pr (H)}$$

$$= \frac{1}{2} \times \frac{1}{2} + \frac{1}{2} \times \frac{1}{2} = \frac{1}{4} + \frac{1}{4} = \frac{1}{2}$$

Carrying on in the same way the tree diagram for three tosses is shown in diagram (d).

All the possibilities that can occur are shown in Fig. 46.11. The various probabilities associated with these possibilities are as follows:

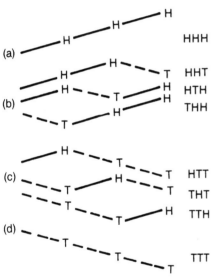

Fig. 46.11

(a) Pr (H and H and H)

$$= \text{Pr (H)} \times \text{Pr (H)} \times \text{Pr (H)} = \frac{1}{2} \times \frac{1}{2} \times \frac{1}{2} = \frac{1}{8}$$

(b) Pr (two heads)

$$= \text{Pr (H and H and T or H and T and H or T and H and H)}$$

$$= \text{Pr (H)} \times \text{Pr (H)} \times \text{Pr (T)} + \text{Pr (H)} \times \text{Pr (T)}$$
$$\times \text{Pr (H)} + \text{Pr (T)} \times \text{Pr (H)} \times \text{Pr (H)}$$

$$= \frac{1}{2} \times \frac{1}{2} \times \frac{1}{2} + \frac{1}{2} \times \frac{1}{2} \times \frac{1}{2} + \frac{1}{2} \times \frac{1}{2} \times \frac{1}{2} = \frac{3}{8}$$

(c) Pr (one head)

$$= \text{Pr (H and T and T or T and H and T or T and T and H)}$$

$$= \text{Pr (H)} \times \text{Pr (T)} \times \text{Pr (T)} + \text{Pr (T)} \times \text{Pr (H)}$$
$$\times \text{Pr (T)} + \text{Pr (T)} \times \text{Pr (T)} \times \text{Pr (H)}$$

$$= \frac{1}{2} \times \frac{1}{2} \times \frac{1}{2} + \frac{1}{2} \times \frac{1}{2} \times \frac{1}{2} + \frac{1}{2} \times \frac{1}{2} \times \frac{1}{2} = \frac{3}{8}$$

(d) Pr (no heads)

$$= \text{Pr (T and T and T)}$$

$$= \text{Pr (T)} \times \text{Pr (T)} \times \text{Pr (T)}$$

$$= \frac{1}{2} \times \frac{1}{2} \times \frac{1}{2} = \frac{1}{8}$$

Note that the total probability covering all possible events is

$$\frac{1}{8} + \frac{3}{8} + \frac{3}{8} + \frac{1}{8} = 1.$$

EXAMPLE 21

A box contains 4 black and 6 red balls. A ball is drawn at random from the box and not replaced. A second ball is then drawn. Determine the probabilities of the following:

(a) red then red being drawn,
(b) black then red being drawn,
(c) red then black being drawn,
(d) black then black being drawn,
(e) one red ball being drawn.

The probability tree is shown in Fig. 46.12.

(a) Pr (red and red) $= \dfrac{6}{10} \times \dfrac{5}{9} = \dfrac{1}{3} = 0.333$

(b) Pr (black and red) $= \dfrac{4}{10} \times \dfrac{6}{9} = \dfrac{4}{15} = 0.267$

(c) Pr (red and black) $= \dfrac{6}{10} \times \dfrac{4}{9} = \dfrac{4}{15} = 0.267$

(d) Pr (black and black) $= \dfrac{4}{10} \times \dfrac{3}{9} = \dfrac{2}{15}$

$$= 0.133$$

(e) Pr (one red)

$$= \text{Pr (red and black or black and red)}$$

$$= \frac{4}{15} + \frac{4}{15} = \frac{8}{15} = 0.533$$

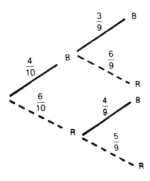

Fig. 46.12

Exercise 202 – *All type C*

1) A card is cut from a pack of 52 playing cards. Determine the probability that it will be an ace or the King of Hearts.

2) A coin is tossed and a die is rolled. Calculate the probabilities of:

(a) a tail and a five,
(b) a head and an even number.

3) A box contains 8 red counters and 12 white ones. A counter is drawn from the box and then replaced. A second counter is then drawn. Determine the probabilities that:

(a) both counters will be red,
(b) both counters will be white,
(c) one counter will be white and the other red.

4) A bag contains 3 red balls and 2 green balls. A ball is drawn and it is not replaced. A second ball is then drawn. Calculate the probabilities of:

(a) two red balls being chosen,
(b) two green balls being chosen,
(c) a red ball followed by a green ball being chosen.
(d) one red ball being chosen.

5) Six cards marked A, B, C, D, E and F are shuffled and two cards are drawn without replacement. What is the probability that the cards will be B and D but not necessarily in that order?

6) For the cards of Question 5, find the probability that one card will be a vowel and the other will be a consonant, if the cards are replaced after drawing.

7) A box contains 3 red and 4 black balls. Draw a probability tree to show the probabilities of drawing one ball, then a second and then a third without replacement. Then answer the following questions:

(a) What is the probability of drawing red, black, red in that order?
(b) What are the chances of drawing red, red, black in that order?
(c) What is the probability of drawing black, red, black in that order?
(d) Determine the probability of drawing one red ball in the three draws.
(e) What is the probability of drawing two red balls in the three draws?

8) Nine cards are numbered 1 to 9 inclusive. If cards are drawn one at a time at random and they are not replaced, find the probability that the result will be an odd card, even, even, odd, odd, even, odd and even.

9) The probability of one even happening is $\frac{3}{5}$ and the probability of a second event happening is $\frac{2}{3}$. Calculate the probability of:

(a) both events occurring,
(b) one or both of the events occurring.

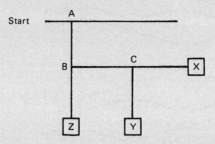

Fig. 46.13

10) A, B and C (Fig. 46.13) are points in a model railway system. The probability of going straight on at each point is 0.6. Find the probability that a model train will end up at:

(a) X   (b) Y   (c) Z

11) Two people work independently at solving a particular problem. The probabilities that each will solve it are $\frac{3}{4}$ and $\frac{4}{5}$ respectively. Calculate the probability that the problem will be solved by one or other or both of the participants.

12) Five designers work independently at solving a design problem. The respective probabilities of each solving it are $\frac{1}{4}$, $\frac{1}{3}$, $\frac{1}{2}$, $\frac{3}{4}$ and $\frac{5}{6}$. Calculate the probability that the problem will be solved.

13) Customers to a shop were quizzed about their ages. The results are shown in the table below.

	Male	Female
Under 30	30%	25%
30 and over	40%	5%

Use this table to calculate the following probabilities:

(a) If one customer is chosen at random what is the probability that the customer will be male?

(b) What is the probability that a randomly chosen customer will be under 30 given that the customer is female?

14) Of 150 students, 50 are currently studying statistics and 40 are studying accountancy. 15 students are enrolled in both subjects. Calculate the probability that a randomly chosen student will be enrolled in either statistics or accountancy.

15) A firm had 200 applicants for jobs during a particular year. 80 of them had some prior experience and 60 had a professional qualification. 40 had both prior experience and a professional qualification.

(a) Draw a Venn diagram to portray these events.

(b) Calculate the probability that one applicant chosen at random had either prior experience or a professional qualification or both.

(c) What is the probability that a randomly chosen applicant had either prior experience or a professional qualification but not both?

(d) Find the conditional probability that a randomly chosen applicant had a professional qualification given that the applicant had prior experience.

16) Two separate divisions of a company are pump manufacture and engine manufacture. The probability that the pump manufacturing division will have a profit margin of 20% this year is estimated at 0.40. The probability that the engine manufacturing division will have a profit margin of 20% during the same period is

0.30. The probability that both divisions will have a profit margin of at least 20% is 0.10. Find the probability that the pump division will have at least a 20% profit margin given that the engine division achieved this profit margin.

17) Three cards are chosen at random from a deck of 52 playing cards without replacement. What is the probability that the three cards are aces?

18) If in Question 17 the cards are replaced and shuffled after each draw, what now is the probability of drawing three aces?

SELF-TEST 46

1) A card is drawn at random from a deck of 52 playing cards. What is the probability that it is a Queen?

a $\frac{1}{52}$ **b** $\frac{1}{13}$ **c** $\frac{1}{8}$ **d** $\frac{1}{4}$

2) Contained in a bag are two black balls and one white ball. Two of the three are chosen at random. What is the probability that they will both be black?

a $\frac{1}{6}$ **b** $\frac{2}{9}$ **c** $\frac{1}{3}$ **d** $\frac{2}{3}$

3) m is the probability of a certain event occurring and n is the probability of a second event occurring. If the two events are independent then the probability of both events occurring is:

a $m+n$ **b** $1-(m+n)$ **c** mn
d $1-mn$

4) The following figures are supposed to give the probabilities of certain events occurring. One of the figures is incorrect. Which one?

a 0   **b** 1   **c** −0.5   **d** 0.6

5) If p is a probability then one of the following is necessarily true. Which?

a p is negative   **b** p is positive
c p is greater than 1
d p lies between 0.5 and 1

6) A biased die with faces numbered 1 to 6 is rolled once. The figures below give the probabilities of obtaining each of the numbers on the die after a single roll. What is the probability of obtaining a 3 or a 4?

Face	1	2	3	4	5	6
Probability	0.2	0.15	0.15	0.25	0.1	0.15

a 0.0375   **b** 0.40   **c** 0.60   **d** 0.9625

7) Three people A, B and C set out to try and solve a numerical puzzle. From past experience it is thought that the probability of A solving it is $\frac{1}{2}$, of B solving it is $\frac{1}{4}$ and of C solving it is $\frac{1}{3}$. What is the probability that the puzzle will be solved?

a 0.025   **b** 0.05   **c** 0.75   **d** 0.95

8) A bag contains 4 white balls, 2 black balls and 5 green balls. A ball is drawn at random from the bag and not replaced. What is the probability of obtaining black, green and white in that order?

a $\frac{40}{1331}$ **b** $\frac{4}{99}$ **c** $\frac{25}{98}$ **d** 1

CHAPTER 46 SUMMARY

Points to remember

(i) A *sample space* is the set of all possible outcomes of an experiment.

(ii) A subset of the sample space is called *an event*.

(iii) If an event A occurs r times in n trials of an experiment, the probability of A occurring, $P(A), = r/n$.

(iv) If E = the set of equally likely outcomes of an experiment, S is an event from E, then $P(S) = n(S)/n(E)$.

(v) $0 \le P(S) \le 1$.

(vi) A certainty has a probability equal to 1.

(vii) If two events cannot occur at the same time, they are said to be mutually exclusive.

(viii) If A and B are mutually exclusive events, $P(A \text{ or } B) = P(A) + P(B)$.

(ix) If the occurrence of A has no effect on the occurrence of B, A and B are said to be independent.

(x) If A and B are independent, $P(A \text{ and } B) = P(A) \cdot P(B)$.

(xi) $P(A) + P(\text{not } A) = 1$.

(xii) If events A and B are not mutually exclusive, $P(A \text{ or } B) = P(A) + P(B) - P(A \text{ and } B)$.

How to Answer Examination Questions 7

Scores	0–9	10–19	20–29	30–39	40–49	50–59
No. of students	1	2	4	7	16	20

Scores	60–69	70–79	80–89	90–99
No. of students	14	8	6	2

1) The above table shows the scores obtained by 80 students on a regular Mathematics test. Draw an ogive for the distribution of scores. Use the ogive to find:
(a) the median score
(b) the quartiles
(c) the number of students who obtained 50% or more.

Scores	Cumulative frequency
less than 9.5	1
less than 19.5	3
less than 29.5	7
less than 39.5	14
less than 49.5	30
less than 59.5	50
less than 69.5	64
less than 79.5	72
less than 89.5	78
less than 99.5	80

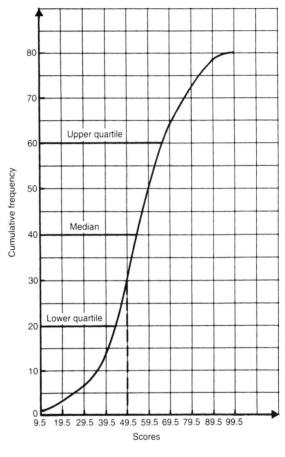

Fig. E7.1

From Fig. E7.1
(a) Median = 55.
(b) Lower quartile = 45.
   Upper quartile = 67.
(c) Number of students who obtained 50% or more = 50.

2) (a) A coin is tossed five times. What is the probability of five successive heads?
  (b) Five coins are tossed simultaneously. Calculate the probability of there being at least one head and at least one tail.
  (c) Calculate the probability of a '3' turning up at least once in two tosses of a fair die.

(a) Probability of a head in one toss $= \frac{1}{2}$

Since tosses are independent,

Probability of 5 heads $= \frac{1}{2} \times \frac{1}{2} \times \frac{1}{2} \times \frac{1}{2} \times \frac{1}{2}$

$= \left(\frac{1}{2}\right)^5 = \frac{1}{32}$

(b) Probability of at least one head and at least one tail

$= 1 -$ Probability of 5 heads

$-$ Probability of 5 tails

$= 1 - \frac{1}{32} - \frac{1}{32} = \frac{15}{16}$

(c) Let E_1 = event of '3' on 1st toss and
E_2 = event of '3' on 2nd toss.

$E_1 + E_2$ = event of '3' on 1st toss or '3' on 2nd toss or both

= event that at least one '3' turns up

$Pr(E_1 + E_2) = Pr(E_1) + Pr(E_2) - Pr(E_1 E_2)$

$= \frac{1}{6} + \frac{1}{6} - \frac{1}{6} \times \frac{1}{6} = \frac{11}{36}$

3) A box contains 6 red balls, 4 white balls and 5 blue balls. If 3 balls are drawn successively from the box, find the probability that they are drawn in the order red, white and blue if each ball is (a) replaced, (b) not replaced.

Let   R = event 'red' on 1st draw

        W = event 'white' on 2nd draw

        B = event 'blue' on 3rd draw.

(a) Since each ball is replaced, then R, W and B are independent.

$Pr(RWB) = Pr(R) \times Pr(W) \times Pr(B)$

$= \frac{6}{6+4+5} \times \frac{4}{6+4+5}$

$\times \frac{5}{6+4+5}$

$= \frac{6}{15} \times \frac{4}{15} \times \frac{5}{15} = \frac{8}{225}$

(b) Since each ball is not replaced, then R, W and B are dependent.

$Pr(RWB) = \frac{6}{6+4+5} \times \frac{4}{5+4+5}$

$\times \frac{5}{5+3+5}$

$= \frac{6}{15} \times \frac{4}{14} \times \frac{5}{13} = \frac{4}{91}$

EXAMINATION TYPE QUESTIONS 7

This exercise is divided into two sections A and B. The questions in Section A are intended to be done very quickly, but those in Section B should take about 20 minutes each to complete. All the questions are of the type found in CXC examination papers.

Section A

Wages	Number of employees
$150.00–£159.99	8
$160.00–$169.99	10
$170.00–$179.99	16
$180.00–$189.99	14
$190.00–$199.99	10
$200.00–$209.99	5
$210.00–$219.99	2

1) The above table shows a frequency distribution of the weekly wages in dollars of 65 employees at the ABC factory. Construct an ogive for this distribution. Use your graph to estimate:
(a) the median wage.
(b) the upper quartile.
(c) the interquartile range of the distribution.

2) The mean annual salary paid to all workers in a company was $50 000. The mean annual salary paid to the male and female employees was $52 000 and $42 000 respectively. Determine the percentages of male and female employees in the company.

3) On a fourth year examination to 150 students, the mean score in English was 78 with standard deviation 8.0, and in maths the mean was 73 with standard deviation 7.6. A student scored 75 in English and 71 in maths. Use this information to determine in which subject the student had the relative higher standing, giving reasons for your answer.

4) (a) If the probability that Lara will score 100 runs in the next test match is 0.6 and the probability that Hooper will score 100 is 0.4, what is the probability that they will each score 100 in the next test match?
(b) A box contains 4 white balls and 3 black balls. A ball is drawn from the box, and without replacing it, a second ball is then drawn. What is the probability that both balls drawn are black?

5) A bag contains 4 balls, one marked with the letter L, one with the letter E and two with the letter S. The balls are drawn at random from the bag, one at a time, without replacement. In each of the following cases calculate the probability that:
(a) The first two balls to be drawn out will each have the letter S marked on them.

(b) The second ball to be drawn will have the letter E marked on it.

(c) The order in which the balls are drawn will spell out the word LESS.

Section B

6) Fig. E7.2 shows a circular disc whose centre is O, with an arrow marked on its surface. An ordinary die is thrown and if 1 is shown, the disc is rotated clockwise through 90°, otherwise it is not moved. If the game is started with the arrow pointing to P as shown, write down as a fraction the probability that the arrow is pointing:

(a) To P after 1 throw.

(b) To R after 2 throws.

(c) To Q after 2 throws.

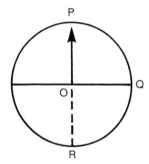

Fig. E7.2

7) A man can obtain scores of 1, 2, 3, 4, 5 or 6 by throwing an ordinary die. After 50 throws he obtains the scores shown in the following table.

Score	1	2	3	4	5	6
No. of times	13	7	7	8	9	6

Calculate his mean score and the standard deviation.

8) Given $A = \{4, 5, 6\}$, $B = \{7, 8, 9\}$, if $x \in A$ and $y \in B$, calculate the probability that:

(a) xy is odd.

(b) xy is even.

9) In Fig. E7.3 the numbers of elements are shown in the sets P, Q and R. Also the universal set $\mathcal{E} = P \cup Q \cup R$.

(a) State the value of $n(Q \cup R)'$.

(b) If $x \in (P \cup Q) \cap R$, find the probability that $x \in P$.

(c) If $n(R) = n(P)$, find the two values of k.

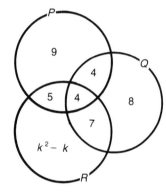

Fig. E7.3

Specimen Exams

Paper 01 – Specimen test 1

1. The universal set is $U = \{1,2,3,4,5,6,7,8,9\}$ and the set $A = \{1,3,5,7,9\}$. The complement of A is

    A $\{1,3,5,7,9\}$ **B** $\{1,2,3,4,5,6,7,8,9\}$ **C** $\{2,4,6,8\}$ **D** $\{\ \}$

2. Which of the following pairs of sets are equal?

    I $\{a,b,c,d\}$ and $\{w,x,y,z\}$
    II $\{1\}$ and $\emptyset$
    III $\{1,2,3,4\}$ and $\{2,4,1,3\}$
    A I only   **B** II only   **C** III only   **D** I, II and III

3. If $P \subset Q$ and $Q \subset P$, which of the following must be true?

    I $P = \emptyset$ II $P = Q$ III $P = Q'$
    A I only   **B** II only   **C** III only   **D** II and III only

4. The number of subsets of $\{a, b, c\}$ including the set itself and the null set is

    A 9   **B** 8   **C** 6   **D** 3

5. If $(x,y) \in \{(1,2), (2,4), (3,6)\}$ then y in terms of x is written

    A $y = 2^x$ **B** $y = 2x$ **C** $y = \frac{x}{2}$ **D** $y = x^2$

6. If $f(x) = 3x + 4$, then $f(x + y) =$

    A $x + y + 4$ **B** $x + 3y + 4$ **C** $3x + 3y + 4$ **D** $3x + y + 4$

7. If $f:(x) \rightarrow x^2 - 5x + 3$, then $f(4) - f(3)$ is

    A -4 **B** 2   **C** 1   **D** -1

8. If $f:x \rightarrow x^2 - 1$, on the domain $\{-2, -1, 0,1,2\}$, the range of the relation is

    A $\{3,0,-1\}$ **B** $\{3,1,0\}$ **C** $\{-3,0,-1\}$ **D** $\{-3,-1,0,1,3\}$

9. The graph of $y = 1/x$ is symmetrical about

    A the x-axis only   **B** the y-axis only
    C both coordinate axes   **D** neither coordinate axis

10. Given $F(x) = (3x + 2)/(x - 4)$, what is $F^{-1}(x)$?

    A $(x - 4)/(3x + 2)$ **B** $(4x + 2)/(x - 3)$ **C** $(2 - 3x)/(4 - x)$ **D** $(2x + 6)/(x - 4)$

11. $\left(1\frac{2}{3}\right)^2$ is equal to

    A $2\frac{7}{9}$ **B** $2\frac{4}{9}$ **C** $\frac{4}{6}$ **D** $1\frac{4}{9}$

12. $\dfrac{10^2 - 5^2}{10^2 + 5^2}$ is equal to

    A $\frac{3}{5}$ **B** $\frac{2}{5}$ **C** $\frac{1}{3}$ **D** $\frac{1}{5}$

13. The number 0.030 905 correct to three significant figures is

    A 0.030   **B** 0.0309   **C** 0.031   **D** 0.3090

14. The L.C.M. of 3, 4 and 6 is

    A 12   **B** 13   **C** 24   **D** 72

15. Which of the following statements are true?

    I π may be written as a recurring decimal.
    II $\sqrt{13}$ is an irrational number.
    III $\frac{1}{6}$ is an integer
    IV 0.7 may be written as a rational number.
    A I and II only   **B** I and III only   **C** II and IV only   **D** III and IV only

16. What are the next two numbers in the sequence 45, 42, 37, 30?

    A 21 and 12   **B** 21 and 11   **C** 21 and 10   **D** 21 and 9

17. The value of 0.2^3 is

    A 0.008   **B** 0.006   **C** 0.6   **D** 0.8

18. The length of a rectangle is 10 centimetres more than its width. If the perimeter is 140 centimetres, then its length in centimetres is

    A 14   **B** 30   **C** 40   **D** 65

19. What is the area of the triangle PQR if $\angle$ PQR $= 90°$, PQ $= 6$ centimetres and QR $= 8$ centimetres?

    A 10 cm   **B** 14 cm   **C** 24 cm   **D** 30 cm

20. The perimeter of a rectangle is 70 centimetres. If the ratio of the width to the length is $2 : 5$, then the width in centimetres is

    A 10   **B** 14   **C** 20   **D** 28

21. The length of the arc that subtends an angle of $60°$ at the centre of a circle of radius 12 centimetres is

    A 2π cm   **B** 4π cm   **C** $\dfrac{72\pi}{5}$ cm   **D** 24π cm

22. The area of a trapezium is 50 square centimetres and its height is 5 cm. Given that the length of parallel sides are 4 centimetres and x centimetres, then $x =$

    A 20   **B** 16   **C** 12.5   **D** 10

23. The base of a prism is a triangle whose sides are of length 6 centimetres, 8 centimetres and 10 centimetres. If the height of the prism is 30 centimetres, its volume is

    A 240 cm^3 **B** 480 cm^3 **C** 720 cm^3 **D** 1440 cm^3

24. A regular hexagon is inscribed in a circle of radius 7 centimetres. How much longer is the circumference of the circle than the perimeter of the hexagon? (Take $\pi = 22/7$)

    A 2 cm　　**B** 4 cm　　**C** 14 cm　　**D** 20 cm

25. A cylindrical container of diameter 10 centimetres holds 0.1 litres. What is the area of its curved surface in square centimetres?

    A 10　　**B** 30　　**C** 40　　**D** 100

26. A dealer bought 40 articles at a total cost of $20.00. He sold them at 64 cents each. What was his percentage profit?

    A 15　　**B** 28　　**C** 45　　**D** 50

27. "$4500 cash" or "one half down and 12 monthly payments of $220"
    The above sales card was marked on a used car. What is the difference in cost between the two plans?

    A $220　　**B** $390　　**C** $2250　　**D** $2640

28. A sum of $800 amounted to $815 after 9 months at simple interest. What rate of interest per annum was earned?

    A $\frac{5}{2}4$ %　　**B** $1\frac{2}{3}$%　　**C** $2\frac{1}{2}$ %　　**D** 6%

29. X, Y and Z share a sum of money in the ratio $5:6:9$. If Z receives $24 more than X, how much money was shared?

    A $120　　**B** $160　　**C** $216　　**D** $480

30. On the street oranges are sold at 100 for $25.00 and in the supermarket at 3 for $1.00. What is the ratio of the street price to the supermarket price?

    A $1:4$　　**B** $1:3$　　**C** $5:6$　　**D** $3:4$

31. By selling a car for $1500 a dealer experienced a 25 per cent loss. What was his buying price?

    A $2000　　**B** $1875　　**C** $1750　　**D** $1525

32. A bookseller buys a book for $9.00. His advertised selling price is 20 per cent higher, but he allows schools a discount of 10 per cent. What is the selling price to schools?

    A $9.10　　**B** $9.30　　**C** $9.72　　**D** $9.90

33. In April a supermarket owner bought 1 tonne of potatoes for $60.00. In December he bought $\frac{3}{5}$ of a tonne for $60.00. What was the percentage increase in price from April to December?

    A $33\frac{1}{3}$%　　**B** 40%　　**C** 60%　　**D** $66\frac{2}{3}$%

34. Which of the following *cannot* be the probability of an event occurring?

    A $\frac{1}{2}$　　**B** 0.7　　**C** 1　　**D** 2

35.

Radius (mm)	Frequency
14–15	8
16–17	11
18–19	14

The table above shows a frequency distribution for the radii of ball bearings. What is the class width?

    A 1 mm　　**B** 2 mm　　**C** 3 mm　　**D** 5 mm

36. The mean of ten numbers is 36. If one of the numbers is 18, what is the mean of the other nine?

   A 18   **B** 27   **C** 38   **D** 54

37. A bag contains 4 white balls, 3 red balls and 2 green balls. If on each of 3 draws, a ball is drawn from the bag and not replaced, the probability of obtaining a white, a red and a green in that order is

   A $\frac{1}{21}$ **B** $\frac{1}{8}$ **C** $\frac{1}{3}$ **D** $\frac{3}{8}$

38. If the probability of a child getting measles is 0.13, how many children out of 1200 may be expected to get measles?

   A 100   **B** 120   **C** 130   **D** 156

39. What is the 1st quartile for the scores: 2, 6, 8, 3, 10, 5, 6, 9?

   A 7   **B** 6   **C** 4   **D** 2

40. 3x dollars and y cents may be expressed in cents as

   A $(3x + y)$ cents   **B** $(3x + 3y)$ cents   **C** $(300x + 100y)$ cents   **D** $(300x + y)$ cents

41. If $x = 5$ and $y = -3$, then $x^2 - y^3 =$

   A -2 **B** 16   **C** 34   **D** 52

42. If Mary is x years old and John is twice as old as she, John's age next year will be

   A $(x + 1)$ years   **B** $(x + 2)$ years   **C** $(2x + 1)$ years   **D** $(2x + 2)$ years

43. If $12x - 5 = 3x + 7$, then $x =$

   A $\frac{4}{3}$ **B** $\frac{2}{9}$ **C** $\frac{2}{15}$ **D** $-\frac{2}{15}$

44. If $a * b = a(a - b)$, then $2 * 4 =$

   A -4 **B** -2 **C** 4   **D** 8

45. If $5x = 1$, then $x =$

   A -1 **B** 0   **C** $\frac{1}{5}$ **D** 1

46. The tension in an elastic string is directly proportional to its extension.
   If the extension is 10 centimetres when the tension is 15 kilograms,
   what is the tension when the extension is 12 centimetres?

   A 22.5 kg   **B** 18 kg   **C** 12.5 kg   **D** 8 kg

47. If $x = \sqrt{y}$ and $y = \sqrt{n}$, then x expressed in terms of n is

   A $\sqrt{n}$ **B** $\sqrt[3]{n}$ **C** n **D** $\sqrt[4]{n}$

48. If $3^2 \times 3^x = 3^{16}$, then $x =$

   A 4   **B** 8   **C** 14   **D** 24

49. What is the size of an exterior angle of a regular octagon?

   A $36°$ **B** $45°$ **C** $54°$ **D** $60°$

50. If two parallel lines are cut by a third straight line, which of the following are True?

    I   alternate angles are supplementary
    II   corresponding angles are equal
    III   co-interior angles are supplementary
    IV   vertically opposite angles are complementary

    A I and II only   **B** II and III only   **C** III and IV only   **D** I and IV only

51. What is the gradient of the line $y = 2x - 1$?

    A -1 **B** $\frac{1}{2}$ **C** 1 **D** 2

52. In the figure below A_1, B_1, C_1 are images of A, B, C, respectively. The transformation is

    A a reflection   **B** an enlargement   **C** a translation   **D** a shear

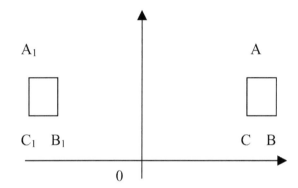

53. Under an enlargement centre $(0,0)$ and scale factor 2, the image of $(-1,3)$ is

    A $(\frac{1}{2}, -\frac{3}{2})$ **B** $(2, -6)$ **C** $(-3, 1)$ **D** $(1,1)$

54. Under the translation T, the image of $(2,3)$ is $(4,7)$. What is the image of $(-4,2)$ under T?

    A $(-2,5)$ **B** $(-2,6)$ **C** $(0,9)$ **D** $(-6,-2)$

55. Which of the following figures has (have) only rotational symmetry?

    I   isosceles triangle
    II   kite
    III   isosceles trapezium
    IV   parallelogram

    A I only   **B** I and III only   **C** II and IV only   **D** IV only

56. Two equal non-intersecting circles are drawn. How many lines of symmetry (mirror lines) does the figure have?

    A 0   **B** 1   **C** 2   **D** 3

57. The vertices P, Q of a triangle PQR are fixed 4 centimetres apart. If the triangle is right-angled, and of area 4 cm^2, then the number of possible triangles in a given plane through PQ is

    A 2   **B** 4   **C** 6   **D** 8

58. Which of the following equations will describe a line parallel to the x-axis?

   I $x = 5$ II $y = 5$ III $x = y + 5$ IV $y = x + 5$

   A I only   **B** II only   **C** I and III only   **D** II and IV only

59. P is a rectangle and Q is a parallelogram. If the sides of P are equal to the sides of Q, which of the following must be true?

   I   perimeter of P = perimeter of Q
   II   area of P = area of Q
   III   area of P > area of Q

   A I and II only   **B** I and III only   **C** II only   **D** III only

60. The length of a rectangle is three times its width. If the distance around it is 16 units, the width is

   A 2 units   **B** 4 units   **C** 8 units   **D** 12 units

END OF TEST

Paper 01 – Specimen test 2

Instructions to candidates
Answer ALL questions in Section 1, and any TWO in Section II

SECTION I

All working must be clearly shown

1. (a) Express 125.0476
      (i)   correct to 3 decimal places
      (ii) correct to 4 significant figures
      (iii) in standard form (scientific notation) .

                                        (3 marks)

  (b) Find the smallest number which can be divided exactly by 8, 12 and 15. Give reasons for your answer.   **(3 marks)**

  (c) A stove is bought on hire purchase for a deposit of \$150 and 24 monthly payments of \$45 each.
      Calculate the total hire purchase price of the stove.   **(4 marks)**

                                                 Total 10 marks

2. (a) Simplify $(64x^{-6})^{2/3}$.   **(2 marks)**

  (b) Factorise completely
      (i) $6x^2 + 2x - 28$
      (ii) $x^2 - 2x$.   **(3 marks)**

  (c) Simplify
$$(6x^2 + 2x - 28)/(x^2 - 2x)$$
                                          (2 marks)

  (d) Given that $f = uv/(u + v)$, express u in terms of v and f.   **(4 marks)**

                                                 Total 11 marks

3. (a) In a small school there are 52 pupils who take one or more of the subjects Music, Information Technology (IT), and Art. 10 pupils study all three subjects, 12 study Music and IT only, 4 study Music and Art only, and 8 study IT and Art only. An equal number of students study Music, IT and Art only.

    (i)   Draw a Venn diagram to show the above information, showing clearly the number in each region.   **(3 marks)**

    (ii) Find the total number of students studying Music.   **(3 marks)**

(b) Using ruler and compasses only, construct the triangle PQR in which PQ $= 6$ cm, $\angle$QPR $= 45°$, $\angle$PQR $= 60°$. Measure the lengths PR and QR, giving your answers in cm, correct to 1 decimal place.   **(6 marks)**

Total 12 marks

4. (a) Given that $f(x) = (x + 3)/(2x - 4)$

    (i)   find $f(5)$
    (ii) find the value of x for which $f(x) = 1$.   **(5 marks)**

(b) (i)   Write down the value of the x-coordinate of a point on the y-axis.
    (ii) Write down the value of the y-coordinate of a point on the x-axis.   **(3 marks)**

(c) The line $2x + 3y = 12$ cuts the x-axis at H and the y-axis at K. Find

    (i)   the coordinates of H.
    (ii) the coordinates of K.
    (iii) the gradient of HK.   **(4 marks)**

Total 12 marks

5. An open glass jar of internal radius 4 cm contains water to a depth of 10.75 cm.

    (i)   Calculate the surface area of the glass which is wet.
        [Leave your answer in terms of π.]   **(5 marks)**

    (ii) When a steel ball is dropped into the jar and completely covered, the water rises a further 4.25 cm. Calculate the radius of the ball, giving your answer correct to 1 decimal place (take $\pi = 3.14$).   **(7 marks)**

Total 12 marks

6. (a) In the right-angled triangle DEF the hypotenuse DF $= 13$ cm, and DE $= 5$ cm. Calculate the area of the triangle.   **(4 marks)**

(b) The side AP of the triangle PAQ is produced to the point B, and AQ produced to C. Given that PB $= 30$ cm, PQ $= 50$ cm, $\angle$PAQ $= 58°$, $\angle$PQC $= 110°$; calculate

    (i)   AB   (ii) QB.   **(7 marks)**

Total 11 marks

7. (a) The vector $\overrightarrow{AB} = \begin{pmatrix} 6 \\ 8 \end{pmatrix}$

Write down

    (i)   the unit vector parallel to $\overrightarrow{AB}$
    (ii) the vector of length 5 units which is parallel to $\overrightarrow{AB}$.   **(6 marks)**

(b) The point Q (7,6) is the image of the point P (7,2) under a reflection in the line $y = k$.
  (i) On the graph paper provided plot the points P and Q, and draw the line $y = k$.
  (ii) What is the value of k?
  (iii) Under a transformation T, the image of Q is Q_1 $(-7, 2)$, and the image of P is P_1 $(-7, 6)$.
      Plot and label the points P_1 and Q_1.
      Describe *fully* the transformation T. **(6 marks)**

Total 12 marks

8. (a)

Amount of money ($)	10	15	15	30	35	50
No. of pupils	2	6	8	3	10	1

  The above table shows the amount of money in the pockets of 30 pupils in a class.
  (i) Write down the mode of this distribution.
  (ii) Find the median.
  (iii) Calculate the mean. **(5 marks)**

(b) Two six-sided dice are rolled.
  (i) How many different pairs of scores are possible?
  (ii) What is the probability of a total of 12 on one throw?
  (iii) What is the probability of two odd numbers on a throw? **(5 marks)**

Total 10 marks

SECTION II

Answer two questions in this section

RELATIONS, FUNCTIONS AND GRAPHS

9. (a) Solve the simultaneous equations
  $x - y = 3$
  $xy + 10x + y = 150.$
  (6 marks)

(b) Draw up a table of values for the function
  $F: x \rightarrow 2x^2 + x - 1$, for $-2 \leqslant x \leqslant 1.5$, taking values of x at intervals of 0.5.
  Using a scale of 2 cm to represent 1 unit on both axes, draw the graph of the function.

  With the same scale and axes draw the graph of $g: x \rightarrow \frac{1}{2}(x + 1)$.

  Use your graphs to find
  (i) the solution of the equation $4x^2 + x - 3 = 0$.
  (ii) the range of values of x for which $\frac{1}{2}(x + 1)$ is greater than $2x^2 + x - 1$. **(9 marks)**

Total 15 marks

10. (a) A "small farmer" keeps sheep and goats. These animals cost him $250 each, and he has only $2500 to spend. He decides that he will purchase at least one of each.

  (i) Using x to represent the number of sheep, and y to represent the number of goats, write down THREE inequalities (excluding $x \geqslant 0$ and $y \geqslant 0$), to represent the above conditions.

(ii) If on the average, there are 2 lambs for each sheep and 1 kid for each goat, and he has space for only 11 young, write down an inequality to represent these conditions.

(iii) Using a scale of 1 cm to represent 1 animal on each axis, draw a graph to represent the inequalities in (i) and (ii) above.

(iv) Shade the UNWANTED region which satisfies the above inequalities.

(9 marks)

(b) The kids are sold for $150 each, and the lambs at $100 each.

(i) Write an expression to represent his income from selling these animals.

(ii) Use your graph in (a) to find the numbers of lambs and kids he should keep to maximize his profit. What is this maximum profit? **(6 marks)**

Total 15 marks

TRIGONOMETRY AND GEOMETRY

11. (a)

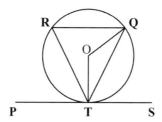

In the diagram above, PTS is a tangent to the circle centre O. The chord RQ is parallel to PTS, and $\angle QTS = 72°$.

(i) Calculate, giving reasons for your answer, the size of the angle TOQ , and the angle RTQ.

(ii) Show that RT = QT. **(7 marks)**

(b) WXYZ is a parallelogram with the point T on ZY such that XT = 3 cm, TY = 2 cm, and the area of WXYZ = 20 cm^2 . WT and XY are produced to meet at U.

(i) What is the area of the triangle WZT? Give reasons for your answer.

(ii) Write down the value of the ratio: area of triangle TYU / area of triangle TZW . Hence, calculate the area of the triangle TYU. **(8 marks)**

12. (a) Given that sin α = 4/5, express as a fraction the value of

(i) cos α

(ii) tan α. **(5 marks)**

(b) Three towns P, Q and R lie on a straight road running east from P. Q is 6 km from P, and R is 22 km from P.

Another town S, 14 km from R, lies to the north of this road, and $\angle QSR = 82°$.

Calculate,

(i) the size of the angle SQR

(ii) the size of the angle SRQ

(iii) the distance SP

(iv) the bearing of S from P. **(10 marks)**

Total 15 marks

VECTORS and MATRICES

13. (a) Find the value of x if the vectors represented by $\begin{pmatrix} x \\ 5 \end{pmatrix}$ and $\begin{pmatrix} 12 \\ 15 \end{pmatrix}$ are parallel.

     (2 marks)

   (b) Calculate the length and direction, relative to the positive x-axis, of the vector $\begin{pmatrix} 3 \\ 4 \end{pmatrix}$

     (3 marks)

   (c) The diagonals of a quadrilateral PQRS intersect at O. Given that $\overrightarrow{SO} = \overrightarrow{OQ} = \mathbf{a}$, and $\overrightarrow{RO} = \overrightarrow{OP} = \mathbf{b}$,
       (i)   Express, in terms of $\mathbf{a}$ and $\mathbf{b}$, $\overrightarrow{PQ}$ and $\overrightarrow{SR}$.
       (ii) What is the relation between $\overrightarrow{PQ}$ and $\overrightarrow{SR}$?   **(4 marks)**

   (d) The sides OA and OB of a triangle OAB are produced to M and N respectively, such that $\overrightarrow{OM} = 3\overrightarrow{OA}$ and $\overrightarrow{ON} = 2\overrightarrow{OB}$.
       P is a point on MN such that $\overrightarrow{MN} = 4\overrightarrow{MP}$. A and T are points on OM such that $\angle OAB = \angle OTN = 90°$. Given that $\overrightarrow{OA} = \mathbf{a}$, $\overrightarrow{OB} = \mathbf{b}$, express in terms of $\mathbf{a}$ and $\mathbf{b}$,
       (i) $\overrightarrow{MN}$ (ii) $\overrightarrow{MP}$ (iii) $\overrightarrow{BP}$ **(6 marks)**

     Total 15 marks

14. (a) (i)   Find the equation of the line of reflection in which the point $(-1,4)$ is mapped onto $(5,4)$.
       (ii) Find the coordinates of the centre of rotation through $180°$ in which the point $(12, 0)$ is mapped onto $(0,4)$.   **(6 marks)**

   (b) Under a transformation S, the image (x', y') of a point (x, y) is given by
   $$\begin{pmatrix} x' \\ y' \end{pmatrix} = \begin{pmatrix} 1 & 3 \\ -2 & -5 \end{pmatrix}\begin{pmatrix} x \\ y \end{pmatrix} - \begin{pmatrix} 2 \\ 4 \end{pmatrix}$$

       (i)   Find the coordinates of the image of $(1,3)$ under S.

       (ii) Determine the inverse of $\begin{pmatrix} 1 & 3 \\ -2 & -5 \end{pmatrix}$

       (iii) Calculate the coordinates of the point whose image is $(1,2)$ under S.

     (9 marks)

     Total 15 marks

END OF PAPER

Paper 02 – Specimen test 1

1. If $X = \{5,13,23,15\}$, which of the following is not a subset of X?
   A $\{5, 13\}$ **B** $\{5, 10\}$ **C** $\{23, 15\}$ **D** $\{5, 13, 23, 15\}$

2. $P = \{1,3,2\}$, $Q = \{3, 7, 6\}$, $R = \{1,4,5\}$, $S = P \cap Q \cap R$.
   What is $n(S)$?
   A 9   **B** 7   **C** 2   **D** 0

Questions 3 and 4 refer to the information below.

The universal set, $U = \{$positive integers which are less than 15$\}$
$Y = \{$multiples of 5$\}$
$X = \{$even integers$\}$
$Z = \{$multiples of 3$\}$

3. $X \cap Y =$

     A $\{\ \}$ **B** $\{2,10\}$ **C** $\{10\}$ **D** $\{5,10,15\}$

4. $Y \cap Z =$

     A $\{3,5\}$ **B** $\{15\}$ **C** $\{\ \}$ **D** $\{3,5,6,10\}$

5.

Year	1920	1940	1960
Population	1000	2000	4000

The above table shows the population of a town at twenty-year periods from 1920 to 1960. If the increase continues at the same rate, the population in 1980 should be

     A 5000   **B** 6000   **C** 8000   **D** 10 000

Questions 6–8 refer to the following statement:
The property tax t varies directly as the assessed valuation, v, where k is the constant of the variation.

6. Which of the following statements represents the above information?

     A $t = 1/v + k$ **B** $t = k/v$ **C** $t = v + k$ **D** $t = kv$

7. Which of the following statements must be true?

     I   As t increases, v increases
     II   As t increases, v decreases
     III   As v increases, t decreases
     IV   As v increases, t increases

     A I only   **B** II only   **C** II and III only   **D** I and IV only

8. Given that $k = 0.10$, $v = \$8000$, what is t?

     A $\$40$ **B** 80   **C** 400   **D** $\$800$

9. Given $F: x \rightarrow 2x - 5$ and $G: x \rightarrow 3x + 1$, then $FG: x \rightarrow$

     A $(2x - 5)(3x + 1)$ **B** $(5x - 4)$ **C** $(6x - 14)$ **D** $(6x - 3)$

10. What is the minimum value of $3x^2 - 8x + 5$?

     A -5 **B** $-\frac{1}{3}$ **C** 1   **D** $\frac{5}{3}$

11. During an epidemic $\frac{2}{5}$ of the people in a certain place died and 600 were left. How many people died?

     A 240   **B** 360   **C** 400   **D** 900

12. When \$48 is divided into the ratio $5:7$ the smaller share is

   A \$12   **B** \$14   **C** \$20   **D** \$24

13. In standard form $(3.5 \times 10^3) \times (6 \times 10^{-2})$ is equal to

   A 2.1×10^2 **B** 21×10^1 **C** 2.1×10^5 **D** 21×10^{-5}

14. The average attendance of a class for 5 days is 34. If the attendance for 4 days was 36, 37, 38 and 34, what was the attendance on the fifth day?

   A 25   **B** 29   **C** 34   **D** 36

15. Given that 1 Pound = US\$1.98, then US\$33 is equivalent to

   A £6.53   **B** £16.67   **C** £33.98   **D** £65.34

16. In a division problem a pupil divided by 26 instead of 39 and got an answer 201. What was the correct answer?

   A 266   **B** 240   **C** 136   **D** 134

17. The H.C.F. of 16 and 20 is

   A 2   **B** 4   **C** 80   **D** 320

18. If x and y are whole numbers greater than 1, and $x^y = 25$, then $y^x =$

   A 4   **B** 10   **C** 25   **D** 32

19. {multiples of 4} $\cap$ {multiples of 6} is equal to

   A $\{4, 6\}$ **B** $\{4,6,8,12,16,18, \ldots\}$ **C** $\{12,24\}$ **D** $\{12,24,36, \ldots\}$

20.
$$1 + 3 = 4$$
$$1 + 3 + 5 = 9$$
$$1 + 3 + 5 + 7 = 16$$

   Using the pattern above, what is the sum of the first 20 odd numbers?

   A 200   **B** 210   **C** 400   **D** 420

21. How many 1 centimetre cubes would be needed to form a cube of side 3 centimetres?

   A 3   **B** 9   **C** 18   **D** 27

22. A man starts a journey of 360 kilometres at 0800 hours and reaches his destination at 1200 hours. What is his average speed for the journey in kilometres per hour?

   A 90   **B** 60   **C** 45   **D** 30

23. What is the area of the sector of angle $72°$ cut from a circle of radius 6 centimetres?

   A 6π cm^2 **B** $36\pi/5$ cm^2 **C** $72\pi/5$ cm^2 **D** 72π cm^2

24. The ratio of the volumes of two cylinders of equal heights is $4:9$. What is the ratio of their curved surface areas?

   A $16:81$ **B** $8:27$ **C** $4:9$ **D** $2:3$

25. In a right-angled triangle the lengths of the hypotenuse and one side are given as 7 centimetres and 2 centimetres respectively, to the nearest centimetre. What is the minimum length of the third side?

    A $3\sqrt{5}$ cm   **B** 6 cm   **C** 3 cm   **D** $\sqrt{5}$ cm

26. Two cars X and Y are 6 kilometres apart on a straight stretch of road. If they travel towards each other at speeds of 40 and 50 kilometres per hour respectively, after how many minutes will they meet?

    A 4   **B** 8   **C** 15   **D** 36

27. A flywheel of diameter 28 centimetres rotates at 1000 revolutions per minute. What is the speed, in kilometres per hour, of a point on the circumference?

    A 52.8   **B** 33.6   **C** 16.8   **D** it cannot be determined from the data

28. A customer was allowed $12\frac{1}{2}$ per cent discount off the regular price of a television set. If the discount amounted to $110, the original price of the set was

    A $1375   **B** $1100   **C** $880   **D** $770

29. An increase of 10% gave workers a salary of $550. What salary will an increase of 20% give?

    A $1100   **B** $825   **C** $600   **D** $560

30. A tax of $1500 is due on January 1. A penalty for non-payment is 1 per cent per month or fraction of a month. If this tax is not paid until April 17, what penalty should be paid?

    A $5   **B** $15   **C** $45   **D** $60

31. Electricity rates are 25 cents per unit. If a consumer pays $63.00 after being allowed 10 per cent for prompt payment, how many units were used?

    A 220   **B** 280   **C** 375   **D** 425

32. If by selling a shirt for $22.80 a profit of 20 per cent is made, how much did the shirt cost?

    A $18.24   **B** $19.00   **C** $20.40   **D** $21.00

33. The value of a bicycle depreciates by 10 per cent of its value each year. If the price was $500 when new, what will be its value at the end of 2 years?

    A $490   **B** $480   **C** $405   **D** $400

34. A woman's basic pay for a 40 hour week is $160.00. Overtime is paid for at time and a quarter. In a certain week she worked overtime and her total wage was $200. How many hours overtime did she work?

    A 5   **B** 8   **C** 9   **D** 10

35. The rateable value of a house is $450. If the rates are 80 cents in the dollar, the rates payable are

    A $270   **B** $360   **C** $370   **D** $430

36.

Score	0 1 2 3 4 5 6 7 8 9 10
Frequency	0 3 2 6 4 5 2 3 2 5 6

What is the modal score in the distribution above?

    A 10   **B** 8   **C** 5   **D** 4

37. If a fair coin is tossed and then a card drawn from a pack of 52 playing cards, what is the probability of a tail and a queen resulting?

A $\frac{2}{53}$ **B** $\frac{1}{26}$ **C** $\frac{1}{2}$ **D** $\frac{15}{26}$

38. Two dice are thrown together and their scores added. What is the probability it will be 10?

A $\frac{1}{12}$ **B** $\frac{1}{10}$ **C** $\frac{1}{4}$ **D** $\frac{1}{2}$

39. A coin is tossed twice and comes down heads each time. If the coin is tossed a third time, what is the probability that it will come down heads again?

A 1   **B** $\frac{1}{2}$ **C** $\frac{1}{4}$ **D** $\frac{1}{8}$

40. Given $P(X) = \frac{1}{3}$, $P(Y) = 15$, and $P(X \cap Y) = \frac{2}{15}$, then $P(X \cup Y) =$

A $\frac{10}{15}$ **B** $\frac{8}{16}$ **C** $\frac{6}{15}$ **D** $\frac{5}{15}$

41. $(2x^2)^4$ expressed in the form ax^n is

A $8x^6$ **B** $8x^8$ **C** $16x^6$ **D** $16x^8$

42. $2/x + 3/2x$ expressed as a single fraction is

A $\dfrac{5}{3x}$ **B** $\dfrac{7}{2x}$ **C** $\dfrac{5}{2x^2}$ **D** $\dfrac{7}{2x^2}$

43. If $x^2 - 5x + a = 0$ when $x = 3$, what is the value of a?

A 6   **B** 5   **C** 4   **D** -3

44. If x is a real number, for what set of values is $-x + 1 < 0$?

A $\{x : x < 1\}$ **B** $\{x : x < -1\}$ **C** $\{x : x > 1\}$ **D** $\{x : x > -1\}$

45. If $\dfrac{1}{f} = \dfrac{1}{v} + \dfrac{1}{u}$, then in terms of f and v, $u =$

A $f - v$ **B** $\dfrac{fv}{v + f}$ **C** $v - f$ **D** $fv/(v - f)$

46. Which pair (x, y) satisfies $2x - y = 11$ and $x + y = 4$?

A (1, 3)   **B** (6, 2)   **C** (5, 1)   **D** (7, 3)

47. The solution set of $x^2 + 3x - 10 = 0$ is $\{2, p\}$. What is the value of p?

A -8 **B** -5 **C** 1   **D** $1\frac{1}{2}$

48. A regular polygon has each of its interior angles equal to $162°$. How many sides does the polygon have?

A 8   **B** 10   **C** 20   **D** 24

49. If $\sin A = \dfrac{3}{5}$, then cos A is equal to

A $\frac{2}{5}$ **B** $\frac{3}{4}$ **C** $\frac{4}{5}$ **D** $\frac{5}{3}$

50. The line $3x + y + 1 = 0$ is perpendicular to the line whose equation is

   A $y = x + 3$ **B** $y = -x + 3$ **C** $3x + y = -1$ **D** $3y - x = 1$

51. Under reflection in the line $y = 1$, the image of (2,5) is

   A (2,3)   **B** (2,4)   **C** (3,5)   **D** (4,5)

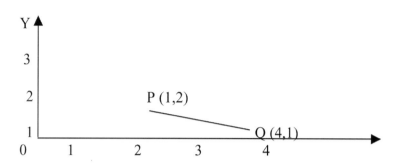

52. Under a translation T, shown in the figure above, the image of P is Q. T may be described by the vector

   A $\begin{pmatrix} 1 \\ 3 \end{pmatrix}$ **B** $\begin{pmatrix} 1 \\ 3 \end{pmatrix}$ **C** $\begin{pmatrix} 3 \\ -1 \end{pmatrix}$ **D** $\begin{pmatrix} 1 \\ -3 \end{pmatrix}$

Questions 53–55 below consist of four lettered headings followed by a list of numbered phrases. For each numbered phrase, select one heading which is most closely related to it. Each heading may be used once, more than once or not at all.

   A square   **B** kite   **C** rhombus   **D** trapezium

53. A quadrilateral with four lines of symmetry and rotational symmetry of order 4.

54. A quadrilateral whose unequal diagonals bisect each other.

55. A quadrilateral with only one pair of parallel sides.

56. A line AB is rotated through $180°$ about a point 0 not in AB. If $A'B'$ is the image of AB, then $ABA'B'$ is a

   A kite   **B** parallelogram   **C** trapezium   **D** square

57. Two places on latitude $60°$N have longitudes $15°$W and $45°$E respectively. Given that the radius of the earth is R kilometres, what is the distance between the two places, in terms of π?

   A $\pi R/12$ **B** $\pi R/6$ **C** $\pi R/2$ **D** πR

58. Given **i** and **j** are unit vectors along the coordinate axes Ox and Oy respectively, what is the length of the vector $5\mathbf{i} - 12\mathbf{j}$?

   A 7   **B** 13   **C** 14   **D** 17

59. Given $\overrightarrow{LM} = 4\mathbf{p} + l\mathbf{q}$, $\overrightarrow{RS} = (l+1)\mathbf{p} + \frac{1}{2}\mathbf{q}$ and $\overrightarrow{LM} = 2\overrightarrow{RS}$ what is the value of l ?

   A 1   **B** 2   **C** 3   **D** 4

60. Given a quadrilateral PQRS in which $\overrightarrow{PQ} = \mathbf{p}$, $\overrightarrow{QR} = \mathbf{q}$, $\overrightarrow{SR} = \mathbf{r}$ and $\overrightarrow{PS} = 2\mathbf{q}$, what type of quadrilateral is PQRS?

   A square   **B** parallelogram   **C** trapezium   **D** rhombus

END OF TEST

Paper 02 – Specimen test 2

Instructions to Candidates.
Answer ALL questions in Section I, and any TWO in Section II

SECTION I

All working must be clearly shown.

1. (a) Given that $p = 4$, and $q = -2$, calculate the value of $3p^2q + q^3$. **(3 marks)**

   (b) Simplify $(3x + y)(2x - 3y)$ **(3 marks)**

   (c) Express as a single fraction in its lowest terms
   $(3x + 5)/(x^2 + 2x - 3) - 2/(x - 1)$ **(5 marks)**

   Total 11 marks

2. (a) After spending one-tenth of my income on rent, and two-thirds of the remainder on other expenses, I have \$660 left. Calculate my income. **(6 marks)**

   (b) An article in a store is marked at a price of \$132 which includes a tax of \$12. Express the tax as a percentage of the price before the tax was added. **(3 marks)**

   Total 9 marks

3. (a) Given the following information:
   $U = \{1,2,3, \ldots ,100\}$
   $A = \{12,24,36, \ldots , 96\}$
   $B = \{24,48,72,96\}$
   $C = \{36,72\}$.

   (i) Draw a Venn diagram to show the above data.
   (ii) State the value of $n(A)$. **(6 marks)**

   (b) One side of a rectangle is d cm long. The other side is 4 cm shorter. The side of a square is 8 cm shorter than the longer side of the rectangle.
   The area of the rectangle is 32 cm^2 more than the area of the square.

   (i) Use the above information to write an equation in d, and solve it.
   (ii) Calculate the area of the square. **(6 marks)**

   Total 12 marks

4. (a) Three identical cylinders of a tractor engine have a total capacity of 2.25 litres.
   Given that the internal diameter of each cylinder is 9.80 cm, calculate in cm correct to 3 significant figures, the internal length of a cylinder. **(5 marks)**

   (b) B is a point at sea, due east of a point A on the coast. Another point C on the coast is 12 km due south of A. The distance BC = 14 km. Calculate

   (i) the distance AB.
   (ii) the bearing of C from B.
   (iii) the shortest distance from A of a boat sailing in the direction CB. **(7 marks)**

   Total 12 marks

5. Without using set square or protractor, construct
    (i)   the triangle ABC in which BC = 7.5 cm, AB = 5.4 cm, $\angle ABC = 60°$;
    (ii)   the point D on BC between B and C which is equidistant from AB and AC. Measure and
           state the distance of D from AB.   **Total 11 marks**

6. (a)   On graph paper using 1 cm to represent 1 unit, draw diagrams to show the vectors

    (i) $p = \begin{pmatrix} -3 \\ 4 \end{pmatrix}$ (ii) $q = \begin{pmatrix} 4 \\ 2 \end{pmatrix}$ (iii) $p+q$.   **(4 marks)**

    (b)   (i)   If the point $(-2,3)$ is mapped onto the point $(6,3)$ under reflection in the line $x = k$, find
                 the value of k.
          (ii)   Write down the coordinates of the image of $(-3,1)$ under a clockwise rotation of $90°$
                 about the origin.
          (iii) Under a rotation of $180°$ about the point (p,q), the point $(8,0)$ is mapped onto $(0, 10)$.
                 Find the value of p and q.
          (iv)   Two lines $2x - 3y = r$, and $x + 4y = s$ intersect at the point $(5,1)$. Find the values of r and
                 of s.

                                                                         (8 marks)

                                                                         Total 12 marks

7. (a)   Given that $p > 0$, $q > 0$, and that

$$\begin{pmatrix} p & p \\ q & q \end{pmatrix}\begin{pmatrix} p & q \\ p & q \end{pmatrix} = \begin{pmatrix} 8 & r \\ r & 2 \end{pmatrix}$$

    find the values of p, q and r.

    (b)   The line $x/3 + y/4 = 1$ cuts the x-axis at H and the y-axis at K. Find the coordinates of H
          and of K.   **(3 marks)**

    (c)   L is the point $(5,0)$ and M is the point $(0,12)$. Calculate the length LM.   **(3 marks)**
                                                                         Total 10 marks

8. The table below shows the data collected in a survey of 120 houses in a parish. The number of
   occupants in each house ranges from 0 to 10 and the frequencies with which these occurred are
   shown.

No. of occupants	0	1	2	3	4	5	6	7	8	9	10
No. of houses	2	9	12	18	28	25	14	5	4	2	1

    (i)   Show the data on a pie chart.
    (ii)   State the mode.
    (iii) If one of the houses is chosen at random, what is the probability that it is not empty?
                                                                         (11 marks)

SECTION II

RELATIONS, FUNCTIONS AND GRAPHS

9. (a)   If $f(x) = 2^x$, calculate
    (i) $f(2)$, $f(1)$, $f(0)$, $f(-1)$, $f(-2)$.
    (ii) Using 1 cm to represent 1 unit on the x-axis and 2 cm to represent 1 unit on the y-axis,
          use the values in (i) to draw a graph of $f(x) = 2^x$.
    (iii) Use your graph to find the value of x, for which $2^x = 6$.   **(8 marks)**

(b)   The distance, s centimetres, that a particle moves from a fixed point is the sum of two terms, one of which varies as the time, t seconds, and the other as the square of the time. If the particle moves 48 cm in the first 2 sec and 90 cm in the first 3 sec, find how far it moves in the fourth second.   **(7 marks)**

Total 15 marks

10. (a)   Solve the following simultaneous equations:

$2x - y = 9,$ and $x^2 + 2y^2 = 54$ **(8 marks)**

(b)   Given that $f(x) = (8x - 5)/(3x - 4)$, find two values of x for which $f(x) = 5x$.   **(7 marks)**

Total 15 marks

GEOMETRY AND TRIGONOMETRY

11. (a)   S and T are points in latitude $60°$N, and their longitudes differ by $70°$. Given that the radius of the earth, $R = 6370$ km,

   (i)   Calculate the radius of the circle of latitude containing S and T.
   (ii)   If M is the midpoint of the straight line ST going through the earth, calculate the distance SM.
   (iii)   If C is the centre of the earth, calculate, in degrees, $\angle$SCM.   **(8 marks)**

(b)   The diagonals AC and BD of a cyclic quadrilateral ABCD cut at O. Given that $\angle$DAC $= x°$, $\angle$CAB $= 2x°$, $\angle$AOB $= 72°$, and $\angle$ABD $= 2 \angle$BDC, find, giving reasons for your answers

   (i) $\angle$BDC, in terms of x;
   (ii) $\angle$ABD, in terms of x;
   (iii)   the value of x.   **(7 marks)**

Total 15 marks

12. (a)   ABC is an isosceles triangle with AB = AC. The base BC is 24 cm long and the area is 108 cm^2. Calculate

   (i)   the length of the perpendicular from A to BC.
   (ii)   the magnitude of the angle BAC, in degrees.   **(9 marks)**

(b)   In a triangle XYZ, the angle XYZ $= 53°$, the angle YZX $= 80°$, and XY $= 8.7$ cm. Calculate the length of YZ.   **(6 marks)**

Total 15 marks

VECTORS AND MATRICES

13. (a)   ABCD is a parallelogram. The side AB is produced to F so that BF = AB, and DF cuts BC at E. Given that $\overrightarrow{AB} = 2\mathbf{u}$ and $\overrightarrow{AD} = 4\mathbf{v}$, express, in terms of $\mathbf{u}$ and $\mathbf{v}$,

   (i)   **BD**   (ii)   **DF**   (iii)   **FC**.   **(7 marks)**

(b)   (i)   Given that $\overrightarrow{OA} = \begin{pmatrix} 1 \\ 4 \end{pmatrix}$ $\overrightarrow{OB} = \begin{pmatrix} 6 \\ -8 \end{pmatrix}$ write $\overrightarrow{AB}$ as a column vector, and find its length.

   (ii)   If $\overrightarrow{OC} = \begin{pmatrix} 4 \\ 6 \end{pmatrix}$,   and $\overrightarrow{CD} = \overrightarrow{AB}$, write $\overrightarrow{OD}$ as a column vector.   **(8 marks)**

Total 15 marks

14. (a) Given that R is a $90°$ clockwise rotation about the origin and E is the enlargement, centre (0,0) and scale factor 4, find the coordinates of the image of a point P with coordinates $(2, -3)$ under the transformation (i) RE   (ii) ER   **(6 marks)**

(b) The image (x_1, y_1) of a point (x, y) under a transformation is given by

$$\begin{pmatrix} X_1 \\ Y_1 \end{pmatrix} = \begin{pmatrix} 1 & 2 \\ -2 & -3 \end{pmatrix} \begin{pmatrix} x \\ y \end{pmatrix} + \begin{pmatrix} 1 \\ 4 \end{pmatrix}$$

(i) Find the coordinates of the image of (2,1) under this transformation.

(ii) Find the inverse of $\begin{pmatrix} 1 & 2 \\ -2 & -3 \end{pmatrix}$

(iii) Given that the image of (h, k) under this transformation is $(4, 2)$, find (h, k).

                                                                        (9 marks)

                                                                  Total 15 marks

END OF PAPER

Answers

ANSWERS TO CHAPTER 1

Exercise 1

1) 13   2) 10   3) 57   4) 7   5) 35
6) 15   7) 45   8) 74   9) 13   10) 20
11) 5   12) 10   13) 7   14) 7   15) 14
16) 21   17) 17   18) 13
19) (a) 689   (b) 282   (c) 600   (d) 1900
20) (a) 8000 (b) 2000   (c) 0   (d) 0   (e) 0
    (f) 20   (g) 8   (h) 30   (i) 14   (j) 9
    (k) Meaningless   (l) 0   (m) 50   (n) 14

Exercise 2

1) (a) 1, 2, 3, 4, 6, 8, 12, 24   (b) 1, 2, 4, 7, 8, 14, 28, 56
    (c) 1, 2, 3, 6, 7, 14, 21, 42
2) 2, 3, 4, 6, 12, 6, 12, 18 and 24
3) 12, 15, 18, 21, 24, 27, 30, 33, 36 and 39
4) (a) $2 \times 2 \times 2 \times 3$ (b) $2 \times 2 \times 3 \times 3$ (c) $2 \times 2 \times 2 \times 7$
    (d) $2 \times 2 \times 3 \times 11$
5) 23, 29
6) (a) 24 (b) 60   (c) 12   (d) 24   (e) 40
    (f) 100 (g) 160   (h) 120   (i) 420   (j) 5040
7) (a) 32 (b) 81   (c) 125   (d) 36   (e) 512
8) (a) 4   (b) 12   (c) 5   (d) 13   (e) 6
    (f) 14

Exercise 3

1) 192, 768   2) 13, 16   3) 29, 35   4) 6, 2   5) 48, 96

Self-test 1

1) **a**   2) **c**   3) **b**   4) **b**   5) **c**
6) **d**   7) **d**   8) **c**   9) **d**   10) **a**
11) **d**   12) **b**   13) **c**   14) **b**

ANSWERS TO CHAPTER 2

Exercise 4

1) $\frac{21}{28}$ 2) $\frac{12}{20}$ 3) $\frac{25}{30}$ 4) $\frac{7}{63}$ 5) $\frac{8}{12}$
6) $\frac{4}{24}$ 7) $\frac{24}{64}$ 8) $\frac{25}{35}$

Exercise 5

1) $\frac{1}{2}$ 2) $\frac{3}{5}$ 3) $\frac{1}{8}$ 4) $\frac{3}{5}$ 5) $\frac{7}{8}$
6) $\frac{3}{4}$ 7) $\frac{5}{7}$ 8) $\frac{18}{35}$ 9) $\frac{2}{3}$ 10) $\frac{2}{3}$

Exercise 6

1) $3\frac{1}{2}$ 2) $2\frac{1}{4}$ 3) $2\frac{1}{5}$ 4) $1\frac{1}{11}$ 5) $2\frac{5}{8}$
6) $\frac{19}{8}$ 7) $\frac{51}{10}$ 8) $\frac{26}{3}$ 9) $\frac{127}{20}$ 10) $\frac{31}{7}$

Exercise 7

1) 40   2) 12   3) 48   4) 12   5) 24
6) 50   7) 160   8) 200   9) 420   10) 2520

Exercise 8

1) $\frac{1}{2}, \frac{7}{12}, \frac{2}{3}, \frac{5}{6}$ 2) $\frac{3}{4}, \frac{6}{7}, \frac{7}{8}, \frac{9}{10}$ 3) $\frac{11}{20}, \frac{3}{5}, \frac{7}{10}, \frac{13}{16}$
4) $\frac{3}{5}, \frac{5}{8}, \frac{13}{20}, \frac{3}{4}$ 5) $\frac{9}{14}, \frac{11}{16}, \frac{7}{10}, \frac{3}{4}$ 6) $\frac{3}{8}, \frac{2}{5}, \frac{5}{9}, \frac{4}{7}$

Exercise 9

1) $\frac{5}{6}$ 2) $1\frac{3}{10}$ 3) $1\frac{1}{8}$ 4) $\frac{11}{20}$ 5) $2\frac{1}{8}$
6) $1\frac{47}{120}$ 7) $4\frac{15}{16}$ 8) $14\frac{4}{15}$ 9) $13\frac{23}{56}$ 10) $10\frac{2}{3}$
11) $11\frac{5}{16}$ 12) $10\frac{13}{15}$

Exercise 10

1) $\frac{1}{6}$ 2) $\frac{2}{15}$ 3) $\frac{1}{6}$ 4) $\frac{1}{2}$ 5) $\frac{1}{24}$
6) $\frac{7}{8}$ 7) $2\frac{2}{7}$ 8) $1\frac{1}{5}$ 9) $2\frac{19}{40}$ 10) $\frac{51}{160}$
11) $\frac{41}{80}$

Exercise 11

1) $1\frac{3}{8}$ 2) $\frac{7}{20}$ 3) $6\frac{7}{8}$ 4) $\frac{2}{3}$ 5) $8\frac{13}{80}$
6) $12\frac{9}{40}$ 7) $2\frac{21}{80}$ 8) $8\frac{23}{32}$ 9) $5\frac{31}{40}$ 10) $3\frac{31}{100}$

Exercise 12

1) $\frac{8}{15}$ 2) $\frac{15}{28}$ 3) $\frac{10}{27}$ 4) $1\frac{19}{36}$ 5) $4\frac{9}{10}$
6) $6\frac{2}{3}$ 7) $1\frac{32}{45}$ 8) $2\frac{53}{56}$

Exercise 13

1) $1\frac{1}{3}$ 2) 4   3) $\frac{7}{16}$ 4) $1\frac{1}{2}$ 5) $\frac{1}{24}$
6) 4   7) $6\frac{3}{4}$ 8) $8\frac{1}{4}$ 9) 12   10) 100
11) 3   12) 2

Exercise 14

1) $\frac{3}{5}$ 2) 8   3) $1\frac{1}{3}$ 4) $1\frac{1}{2}$ 5) $\frac{2}{3}$
6) $\frac{25}{26}$ 7) $1\frac{1}{5}$ 8) $3\frac{5}{6}$

Exercise 15

1) $3\frac{13}{14}$ 2) $\frac{1}{4} \div (\frac{1}{8} \times \frac{2}{5})$ 3) $3\frac{7}{81}$ 4) $\frac{5}{6}$ 5) $\frac{2}{3}$
6) $2\frac{1}{2}$ 7) $1\frac{2}{5}$ 8) $\frac{31}{60}$ 9) $\frac{1}{6}$ 10) $\frac{3}{25}$

Self-test 2

1) **a**   2) **c, d**   3) **b**   4) **c**   5) **d**
6) **d**   7) **d**   8) **c**   9) **c**   10) **a**
11) **a**   12) **c**   13) **a**   14) **b**   15) **d**

ANSWERS TO CHAPTER 3

Exercise 16

1) 0.7   2) 0.37   3) 0.589   4) 0.009   5) 0.03
6) 0.017   7) 8.06   8) 24.0209 9) 50.008 10) $\frac{2}{10}$
11) $4\frac{6}{10}$ 12) $3\frac{58}{100}$ 13) $437\frac{25}{100}$ 14) $\frac{4}{1000}$ 15) $\frac{36}{1000}$
16) $400\frac{29}{1000}$ 17) $\frac{1}{1000}$ 18) $\frac{389}{10\,000}$

Exercise 17

1) 3   2) 11.5   3) 24.040   4) 58.616   5) 54.852
6) 4.12   7) 15.616   8) 0.339   9) 0.812   10) 5.4109

Exercise 18

1) 41, 410, 4100   2) 24.2, 242, 2420
3) 0.46, 4.6, 46   4) 3.5, 35, 350
5) 1.486, 14.86, 148.6   6) 0.01753, 0.1753, 1.753
7) 48.53   8) 9
9) 1700.6   10) 5639.6

Exercise 19

1) 0.36, 0.036, 0.0036   2) 6.4198, 0.64198, 0.064198
3) 0.007, 0.0007, 0.00007   4) 51.04, 5.104, 0.5104
5) 0.0352, 0.00352, 0.000352   6) 0.054   7) 0.00205
8) 0.004   9) 0.0000086   10) 0.0627428

Exercise 20

1) 743.0266   2) 0.951534   3) 0.2888
4) 7.41125   5) 0.001376

Exercise 21

1) 1.33   2) 0.016   3) 189.74   4) 4.1066   5) 43.2

Exercise 22

1) (a) 24.8658   (b) 24.87   (c) 25
2) (a) 0.008357   (b) 0.00836   (c) 0.0084
3) (a) 4.9785   (b) 4.98   (c) 5
4) 22
5) 35.60
6) (a) 28 388 000   (b) 28 000 000
7) (a) 4.1498   (b) 4.150   (c) 4.15
8) 9.20
9) (a) 361   (b) 36   (c) 70   (d) 76.2
10) (a) 2.4 ± 0.05 (b) 3.16 ± 0.005 (c) 18.432 ± 0.0005
11) (a) 20 ± 4.2 (b) 0.3 ± 0.04 (c) 3.84 ± 0.20
     (d) 4.40 ± 0.02

Exercise 23

(These answers, being 'rough checks' are not the only possible ones.)

1) $200 \times 0.005 = 1$ 2) $30 \times 0.3 = 9$
3) $0.7 \times 0.1 \times 2 = 0.14$ 4) $80 \div 20 = 4$
5) $0.06 \div 0.003 = 20$ 6) $30 \times 30 \times 0.03 = 27$
7) $\dfrac{0.7 \times 0.006}{0.03} = 0.14$ 8) $\dfrac{30 \times 30}{10 \times 3} = 30$

Exercise 24

1) 0.25   2) 0.75   3) 0.375   4) 0.6875   5) 0.5
6) 0.6667   7) 0.6563   8) 0.4531   9) 1.8333   10) 2.4375
11) 0.333   12) 0.778   13) 0.133   14) 0.189   15) 0.356
16) 0.232   17) 0.525   18) 0.384   19) 0.328   20) 0.567

Exercise 25

1) $\frac{1}{5}$ 2) $\frac{9}{20}$ 3) $\frac{5}{16}$ 4) $2\frac{11}{20}$ 5) $\frac{3}{400}$
6) $2\frac{1}{8}$ 7) 0.00010   8) 0.001875

Exercise 26

1) 0.12   2) 4   3) 8   4) 8   5) 61
6) 500   7) 30   8) 23   9) 4784   10) 2277
11) 18 382   12) 27 081

Self-test 3

1) c   2) b   3) d   4) a   5) b
6) d   7) c   8) d   9) d   10) b

11) c   12) c   13) b   14) b   15) b
16) d

ANSWERS TO CHAPTER 4

Exercise 27

1) 68 c, 4 c, 63 c, 7 c
2) 216 c, 359 c, 1768 c
3) $0.35, $0.78, $0.06, $0.03
4) $2.46, $9.83, $265.32
5) (a) $10.06   (b) $215.58   (c) $5.41   (d) $2.35
    (e) $1.99
6) (a) $2.24   (b) $7.93   (c) $68.62   (d) $0.78
    (e) $2.09

Exercise 28

1) $1.80   2) $5.95   3) $16.77   4) $168.72
5) 13 c   6) 21 c   7) $1.31   8) $2.17
9) $6.21   10) $17.28   11) $223.56   12) $181.44

Exercise 29

1) $118.80   2) $227.80   3) $5.07
4) $464   5) $40.57   6) $811.76
7) $197.06   8) £11.78
9) (a) $746.27   (b) $7777.22   (c) $257.62

Self-test 4

1) a   2) d   3) c   4) b   5) d   6) b
7) b   8)(a) c (b) d   9) d

ANSWERS TO CHAPTER 5

Exercise 30

1) $\frac{8}{3}$ 2) $\frac{2}{3}$ 3) $\frac{3}{1}$ 4) $\frac{3}{5}$ 5) $\frac{2}{3}$
6) $\frac{3}{20}$ 7) $\frac{25}{4}$ 8) 150 m   9) $192   10) $\frac{6}{1}$

Exercise 31

1) $500, $300   2) $64, $16
3) $50, $40, $30   4) $280
5) 15 kg, 22.5 kg, 37.5 kg   6) 84 mm, 294 mm, 462 mm
7) $6258, $4470   8) $3.60

Exercise 32

1) $14.40   2) $31.80   3) $0.88, $48.40   4) $15.00
5) 33.2 litres   6) $18\frac{1}{3}$, $36\frac{2}{3}$, 2 egg yolks, 40 g, 1 tablespoon
7) $1440   8) 7 hours

Exercise 33

1) $13\frac{1}{2}$ days   2) $3\frac{1}{3}$ days   3) 160 rev/min   4) 6   5) 20

Self-test 5

1) b   2) d   3) b   4) (a) c (b) d   5) b
6) b   7) d   8) d

ANSWERS TO CHAPTER 6

Exercise 34

1) 70%   2) 55%   3) 36%   4) 80%   5) 62%
6) 25%   7) 24%   8) 95%

Exercise 35

1) 70% 2) 73% 3) 68% 4) 81.3% 5) 92.7%
6) 33.3% 7) 81.9% 8) 2%

Exercise 36

1) 0.32 2) 0.78 3) 0.06 4) 0.24 5) 0.315
6) 0.482 7) 0.025 8) 0.0125 9) 0.0395 10) 0.201

Exercise 37

1) (a) 10 (b) 24 (c) 6 (d) 2.4
(e) 21.3 (f) 2.52
2) (a) 12.5% (b) 20% (c) 16% (d) 16.3%
(e) 45.5%
3) 60%, 27 4) 115 cm 5) 88.7 cm
6) (a) $7.20 (b) $13.20 (c) $187.50
7) (a) 2.08% bad (b) 3.08% absent
(c) 87.8% eat lunch at school
8) 15 200 9) 150 kg 10) 600

Exercise 38

1) 25% 2) (a) 20% (b) $16\frac{2}{3}\%$
3) (a) $13\frac{1}{3}\%$ (b) 9.95%
4) 10.7% 5) 20% 6) $33\frac{1}{3}\%$
7) 12.5% 8) 17.6%

Exercise 39

1) $50.40 2) $342 3) 18 c 4) $85.00 5) $2120.40
6) 20% 7) (a) $225 (b) $12\frac{1}{2}\%$

Exercise 40

1) (a) $6.00 (b) $4.35
2) (a) $16.00 (b) 56 c
3) $12.00
4) (a) $3.40 (b) $59.20
5) $64.00 6) $2.85 7) $3.00
8) $20.00 9) $5000 10) $48 600

Self-test 6

1) d 2) c 3) d 4) c 5) c
6) b 7) c 8) c 9) d 10) c
11) b 12) (a) a (b) d (c) b
13) c 14) b 15) c

ANSWERS TO CHAPTER 7

Exercise 41

1) 22.24 mm 2) $12\frac{1}{8}$ kg 3) 64 c 4) $1.782
5) 97.6 6) 2000 7) 14 years 6 months
8) $2.74 9) 40 10) 76 11) 63

Exercise 42

1) 75 km/h 2) 4 hours 3) 350 km 4) 26 km/h
5) 75 km/h 6) 80 km/h 7) 5 hours 8) 38.4 km/h

Self-test 7

1) b 2) c 3) b 4) c 5) d
6) b 7) b 8) c 9) c 10) d

ANSWERS TO CHAPTER 8

Exercise 43

1) $201.16 2) $134.55 3) $173.16 4) $165.60
5) $3.36 6) $4.50 7) $2.40 8) $2.76

Exercise 44

1) $201.96 2) $216.00 3) $243.66
4) $6.50 5) 6 hours 6) 12 hours

Exercise 45

1) $13 2) $265.50 3) $221.25 4) $592.50

Exercise 46

1) $337.50 2) $565 3) $964 4) $624 5) $423

Exercise 47

1) $63.00 2) $120 3) 90 c in the $
4) 31 c in the $ 5) $1161 000 6) 9 c in the $
7) $6 800 000 8) 55 c in the $ 9) $39 100
10) 2.9 c in the $

Exercise 48

1) $72 2) $800 3) $1320 4) $4690 5) $3673
6) $330 7) $100 8) $102

Exercise 49

1) $74.25 2) $215.04 3) $206.25
4) 12% 5) $239.58 6) $1634.40; $194.40
7) $10.09 8) $116.67 9) 26.7%
10) 38.4%

Exercise 50

1) $52 2) 420 kWh 3) 12 c
4) $55.10 5) $49.32

Self-test 8

1) c 2) b 3) c 4) b 5) d
6) b 7) c 8) b 9) d

ANSWERS TO CHAPTER 9

Exercise 51

1) $126 2) $20 3) 4 years
4) 5 months 5) $2\frac{1}{2}$ years 6) 7%
7) 9% 8) $320 9) $180 at $3\frac{1}{2}\%$, 30 c
10) $66 11) $14.56
12) (a) $189 (b) $275 (c) $3200
(d) $10 010 (e) $1701

Exercise 52

1) $117.33 2) $331.22 3) $2566.11
4) $9461.47 5) $2503.65 6) $432; $541.68
7) $2765.44 8) $3013 9) $175.35
10) $342.50 11) $1572.50 12) $9471
13) $1230.30 14) $6655.58 15) $3269.40
16) $5261.51 17) $2440.38 18) $4026.53

Self-test 9

1) b 2) a 3) c 4) a 5) c

6) **b**   7) **b**   8) **a**   9) **b**   10) **c**
11) **b**   12) **c**

ANSWERS TO CHAPTER 10

Exercise 53

1) (a) $1256   (b) $351   (c) $165.20
2) (a) $174.60   (b) $364.50   (c) $573.30
3) (a) $24   (b) $81   (c) $637.50
4) (a) $22.50   (b) $125   (c) $96
5) (a) 10.8%   (b) 2.35%   (c) 6.12%
6) $80; $10\frac{2}{3}$%   7) $738; $63; 8.54%
8) 32 c   9) $1125   10) 4.4%
11) 46.4%   12) $11 800

Exercise 54

1) (a) $400   (b) $362.32   (c) $583.33
2) (a) $28   (b) $60   (c) $20
3) $681.82; $40.91; 6.82%
4) $240   5) 300   6) $218.18

Self-test 10

1) **c**   2) **c**   3) **b**   4) **a**   5) **c**
6) **a**   7) **c**

ANSWERS TO CHAPTER 11

Exercise 55

1) 2.25   2) 4.41   3) 74.0   4) 9.92
5) 59.0   6) 27.4   7) 18.1   8) 62.6
9) 64.2   10) 75.69   11) 529   12) 1650
13) 9 550 000   14) 12 500   15) 9620
16) 0.000 361   17) 0.531   18) 0.000 0177   19) 0.0801
20) 0.000 000 334   21) 9.86
22) (a) 25   (b) 16   (c) 0.0156   (d) 0.0036

Exercise 56

1) 10   2) 15   3) 49   4) 24   5) 120
6) 30   7) 336   8) 2520

Exercise 57

1) $\frac{2}{3}$ 2) $\frac{3}{4}$ 3) $\frac{5}{7}$ 4) $\frac{2}{3}$ 5) $\frac{2}{10}$
6) $\frac{2}{3}$ 7) $\frac{5}{8}$ 8) $\frac{5}{7}$ 9) $\frac{4}{5}$ 10) $\frac{1}{6}$
11) 13   12) 12   13) 3   14) 9   15) 6

Exercise 58

1) 1.84   2) 2.86   3) 2.29   4) 3.04   5) 2.65
6) 1.73   7) 5.92   8) 9.44   9) 7.29   10) 9.10
11) 8.90   12) 7.08   13) 30.0   14) 26.9   15) 84.5
16) 298   17) 62.8   18) 29 000   19) 0.392   20) 0.0411
21) 0.198   22) 0.0280   23) 0.444

Exercise 59

1) 1.311   2) 1.960   3) 2.934   4) 3.551   5) 8.730
6) 9.508

Exercise 60

1) 0.294   2) 0.122   3) 0.190   4) 0.108
5) 0.143   6) 0.0286   7) 0.0112   8) 0.0188
9) 0.001 11   10) 0.000 140   11) 6.54   12) 592
13) 25.4   14) 1280   15) 508

Exercise 61

1) 0.004 33   2) 53.3   3) 0.000 160   4) 0.345
5) 0.231   6) 7.47   7) 0.001 03   8) 0.005 20
9) 5.80   10) 9.79   11) 0.223   12) 0.347
13) 13.7   14) 0.0654   15) 0.273 67

Self-test 11

1) **d**   2) **a**   3) **b**   4) **b**   5) **a**
6) **b**   7) **c**   8) **b**   9) **b**   10) **a**
11) **c**   12) **b**   13) **c**   14) **c**   15) **a**
16) **b**   17) **a**   18) **b**   19) **c**   20) **c**

ANSWERS TO EXAMINATION TYPE QUESTIONS 1

1) (a) 441   (b) 57.6 km/h   (c) 11811
2) (a) 27.3 m   (b) $8   (c) 24%
3) (a) $13   (b) (i) 0.0495   (ii) 0.049
4) (a) 18.75%; $1690   (b) $65.25
    (c) $480; 24%
5) (a) $216   (b) $4\frac{1}{2}$ hours   (c) $5.12
6) (a) 45 km/h   (b) 7   (c) 1100
7) (a) 24 seconds   (b) $178
    (c) $1.35
8) (a) $\frac{1}{16}$ (b) $17.50   (c) 39 km/h
9) (a) 64 km/h   (b) 12.40 p.m.   (c) 16 km
    (d) 82 km/h; 8 min
10) $96; $124.80; $19.20; 13%; 60%
11) $4600;   (a) $6700; $7725; $8575
   (b) 45.7%; $19 500
12) (a) $2222   (b) $3700   (c) $5525

ANSWERS TO CHAPTER 12

Exercise 62

1) +15   2) −12   3) −32   4) +14   5) −24
6) +26   7) −18   8) +23

Exercise 63

1) −5   2) −9   3) +5   4) +5   5) −1
6) 0   7) −4   8) +7

Exercise 64

1) +2   2) +3   3) +14   4) +4   5) +1
6) −5   7) −5   8) +16

Exercise 65

1) −42   2) −42   3) +42   4) +42   5) −48
6) +4   7) +120   8) +9

Exercise 66

1) −3   2) −3   3) +3   4) +3   5) −2
6) −1   7) +2   8) −1   9) −2   10) +12
11) $−1\frac{1}{3}$ 12) −2   13) −12   14) −3

Exercise 67

1) 5 and 198   2) −9
3) Rational: 1.57, $\frac{1}{4}$, −5.625, $\sqrt{9}$, 6.76 and $−3\frac{1}{2}$
   Irrational: $\sqrt{15}$
4) 9.5782, −7.38, $\sqrt{8}$ and $7\frac{2}{3}$

Exercise 68

1) 13, 16
2) 29, 35
3) $-6, -8$
4) 3, 5
5) $\frac{1}{108}, \frac{1}{324}$
6) 64, 81
7) 2, -2
8) 2.0736, 2.488 32
9) 0.1875, $-0.093\,75$
10) $-1.4641, 1.610\,51$

Self-test 12

1) d
2) a
3) d
4) d
5) b
6) c
7) c
8) c

ANSWERS TO CHAPTER 13

Exercise 69

1) $7x$
2) $4x - 3$
3) $5x + y$
4) $\dfrac{x + y}{z}$
5) $\frac{1}{2}x$ or $\dfrac{x}{2}$
6) $8xyz$
7) $\dfrac{xy}{z}$
8) $3x - 4y$

Exercise 70

1) 9
2) 3
3) 3
4) 18
5) 45
6) 6
7) 45
8) 30
9) 23
10) 38
11) 33
12) 33
13) 28
14) 7
15) $\frac{3}{4}$
16) 5
17) 5
18) $7\frac{7}{10}$

Exercise 71

1) 4
2) 81
3) 54
4) 32
5) 1152
6) 74
7) 20
8) 3024
9) 3
10) $18\frac{26}{27}$

Exercise 72

1) $18x$
2) $2x$
3) $-3x$
4) $-6x$
5) $-5x$
6) $5x$
7) $-5a$
8) $12m$
9) $5b^2$
10) ab
11) $14xy$
12) $-3x$
13) $-6x^2$
14) $7x - 3y + 6z$
15) $9a^2b - 3ab^3 + 4a^2b^2 + 11b^4$
16) $1.2x^3 + 0.3x^2 + 6.2x - 2.8$
17) $9pq - 0.1qr$
18) $-0.4a^2b^2 - 1.2a^3 - 5.5b^3$
19) $10xy$
20) $12ab$
21) $12m$
22) $4pq$
23) $-xy$
24) $6ab$
25) $-24mn$
26) $-12ab$
27) $24pqr$
28) $60abcd$
29) $2x$
30) $-\dfrac{4a}{7b}$
31) $\dfrac{5a}{8b}$
32) $\dfrac{a}{b}$
33) $\dfrac{2a}{b}$
34) $2b$
35) $3xy$
36) $-2ab$
37) $2ab$
38) $\dfrac{7ab}{3}$
39) a^2
40) $-b^2$
41) $-m^2$
42) p^2
43) $6a^2$
44) $5x^2$
45) $-15q^2$
46) $-9m^2$
47) $9pq^2$
48) $-24m^2n^4$
49) $-21a^3b$
50) $10q^4r^6$
51) $30mnp$
52) $-75a^3b^2$
53) $-5m^5n^4$

Exercise 73

1) $3x + 12$
2) $2a + 2b$
3) $9x + 6y$
4) $\dfrac{x}{2} - \dfrac{1}{2}$
5) $10p - 15q$
6) $7a - 21m$
7) $-a - b$
8) $-a + 2b$
9) $-3p + 3q$
10) $-7m + 6$
11) $-4x - 12$
12) $-4x + 10$
13) $-20 + 15x$
14) $2k^2 - 10k$
15) $-9xy - 12y$
16) $ap - aq - ar$
17) $4abxy - 4acxy + 4dxy$
18) $3x^4 - 6x^3y + 3x^2y^2$
19) $-14P^3 + 7P^2 - 7P$
20) $2m - 6m^2 + 4mn$
21) $5x + 11$
22) $14 - 2a$
23) $x + 7$
24) $16 - 17x$
25) $7x - 11y$
26) $\dfrac{7y}{6} - \dfrac{3}{2}$
27) $-8a - 11b + 11c$
28) $7x - 2x^2$
29) $3a - 9b$
30) $-x^3 + 18x^2 - 9x - 15$

Exercise 74

1) 7
2) -4
3) $\frac{1}{2}$
4) 25
5) 12
6) 4
7) 12
8) 1
9) 14 884
10) 19

Self-test 13

1) T
2) T
3) F
4) T
5) T
6) F
7) T
8) T
9) T
10) F
11) T
12) T
13) T
14) F
15) F
16) T
17) F
18) T
19) T
20) F
21) T
22) T
23) T
24) T
25) F
26) F
27) T
28) F
29) F
30) T
31) T
32) F
33) T
34) T
35) F
36) T
37) F
38) F

ANSWERS TO CHAPTER 14

Exercise 75

1) $4(x + y)$
2) $5(x - 2)$
3) $2x(2 - 3y)$
4) $m(x - y)$
5) $5(a - 2b + 3c)$
6) $3y(1 - 3y)$
7) $ab(b^2 - 1)$
8) $3x(x - 2)$
9) $7(a - 2b)$
10) $9a(4a - 1)$

Exercise 76

1) p^2q
2) ab^2
3) $3mn$
4) b
5) $3xyz$
6) $xy(xy - a + by)$
7) $5x(x^2 - 2xy + 3y^2)$
8) $3xy(3x^2 - 2xy + y^4)$
9) $\dfrac{1}{3}\left(x - \dfrac{y}{2} + \dfrac{z}{3}\right)$
10) $I_0(1 + \alpha t)$
11) $a(2a - 3b)$ or $(2a - b)(a - b)$
12) $x(x^2 - x + 7)$
13) $\dfrac{m^2}{pn}\left(1 - \dfrac{m}{n} + \dfrac{m^2}{pn}\right)$
14) $\dfrac{xy}{a}\left(\dfrac{x}{2} - \dfrac{2y}{5a} + \dfrac{y^2}{a^2}\right)$
15) $\dfrac{l^2m}{5}\left(\dfrac{m}{3} - \dfrac{1}{4} + \dfrac{lm}{2}\right)$
16) $\dfrac{a^2}{2x^3}\left(a - \dfrac{b}{2x} - \dfrac{c}{3}\right)$

Exercise 77

1) $x^2 + 4x + 3$
2) $2x^2 + 11x + 15$
3) $10x^2 + 16x - 8$
4) $a^2 - 3a - 18$
5) $6x^2 - 13x - 5$
6) $x^2 - 5x + 6$
7) $8x^2 - 14x + 3$
8) $x^2 - 1$
9) $4x^2 - 9$
10) $2x^2 - 3x - 20$

Exercise 78

1) $(x + y)(a + b)$
2) $(p - q)(m + n)$
3) $(ac + d)^2$
4) $(2p + q)(r - 2s)$

5) $2(a - b)(2x + 3y)$ 6) $(x^2 + y^2)(ab - cd)$
7) $(mn - pq)(3x - 1)$ 8) $(k^2l - mn)(l - 1)$

Exercise 79

1) $(x - 2)(x - 3)$ 2) $(x + 4)(x + 2)$
3) $(x - 2)(x - 5)$ 4) $(x - 5)(x - 6)$
5) $(x + 1)(x - 2)$ 6) $(x + 3)(x - 5)$
7) $(x - 2)(x + 4)$ 8) $(x + 4)(x - 3)$
9) $(2x - 5)(x - 1)$ 10) $(2x + 3)(x + 5)$
11) $(3x - 2)(x + 1)$ 12) $(x + 2)(3x - 14)$
13) $(2x + 1)(x - 3)$ 14) $(5x - 3)(2x + 5)$
15) $(3x - 7)(2x + 5)$

Exercise 80

1) $(x + 1)^2$ 2) $(x - 1)^2$
3) $(x + 2)^2$ 4) $(3x + 1)^2$
5) $(5x - 2)^2$ 6) $(x - 2)^2$
7) $(2x + 1)(2x - 1)$ 8) $(a + b)(a - b)$
9) $(1 + x)(1 - x)$ 10) $(11x + 8)(11x - 8)$
11) $x - 3$ 12) $x - 7$
13) $2x + 5$ 14) $5x - 3$
15) $x + 1$ 16) $x - 1$
17) $3p - 5$

Self-test 14

1) T 2) F 3) T 4) T 5) F
6) T 7) T 8) F 9) F 10) T
11) F 12) T 13) F 14) T 15) T
16) F 17) T 18) F 19) T 20) T
21) T 22) F 23) T 24) T 25) T
26) T 27) F 28) T 29) T 30) T

ANSWERS TO CHAPTER 15

Exercise 81

1) $\dfrac{b}{c}$ 2) $\dfrac{9s^2}{2t}$ 3) $\dfrac{8acz}{3y^3}$ 4) $\dfrac{9qs}{pr}$ 5) $\dfrac{21b^2}{10ac}$

Exercise 82

1) $\frac{3}{5}$ 2) $\frac{5}{6}$ 3) $\dfrac{16(a + 2b)}{9(a + b)}$

4) $\frac{3}{2}$ 5) $\dfrac{1}{x + 2y}$ 6) $\dfrac{5x}{4(x + 4)}$

7) $a - b$ 8) $\dfrac{1}{3a - 2b}$ 9) $\dfrac{1}{4x + 5}$

10) $\dfrac{1}{2x - 3}$ 11) $\dfrac{1}{x + 3}$ 12) $a + b$

13) $a(a - 3x)$ 14) $2x - y$

Exercise 83

1) $\dfrac{47x}{60}$ 2) $\dfrac{a}{36}$ 3) $\dfrac{1}{2q}$

4) $\dfrac{32}{15y}$ 5) $\dfrac{9q - 10p}{15pq}$ 6) $\dfrac{9x^2 - 5y^2}{6xy}$

7) $\dfrac{15xz - 4y}{5z}$ 8) $\dfrac{40 - 11x}{40}$ 9) $\dfrac{19m - n}{7}$

10) $\dfrac{a + 11b}{4}$ 11) $\dfrac{8n - 3m}{3}$ 12) $\dfrac{5x - 2}{20}$

13) $\dfrac{x - 14}{12}$ 14) $\dfrac{13x - 21}{30}$

Exercise 84

1) $12x$ 2) $6xy$
3) $12ab$ 4) abc
5) $36m^2n^2p^2q$ 6) $10a^2b^4$
7) $(m - n)^2$ 8) $(x + 1)(x + 3)^2$
9) $x^2 - 1$ 10) $9a^2 - b^2$

11) $\dfrac{1}{x - 5}$ 12) $\dfrac{4x + 3}{(2x + 1)(2x - 1)}$

13) $\dfrac{3}{x - 3}$ 14) $\dfrac{3}{x(x + 5)}$

15) $-\dfrac{2x}{x^2 - 9}$ 16) $\dfrac{2x^2 + 4xy - 3x + 3y}{(x + y)^2(x - y)}$

Self-test 15

1) a 2) a, c 3) b 4) a, d 5) c
6) b 7) d 8) d 9) b 10) c
11) c 12) a

ANSWERS TO CHAPTER 16

Exercise 85

1) $x = 5$ 2) $t < 7$ 3) $q = 2$
4) $x > 20$ 5) $q = -3$ 6) $x = 3$
7) $y = 6$ 8) $m < 12$ 9) $x = 2$
10) $x > 3$ 11) $p = 4$ 12) $x > -2$
13) $x = -1$ 14) $x = 4$ 15) $x = 2$
16) $x = 6$ 17) $m = 2$ 18) $x > -8$
19) $d = 6$ 20) $x = 5$ 21) $x = 3$

22) $m \geqslant 5$ 23) $x \geqslant -\dfrac{29}{5}$ 24) $x = 2$

25) $x \leqslant \dfrac{45}{8}$ 26) $x = -2$ 27) $x = -15$

28) $x = \dfrac{50}{47}$ 29) $m \geqslant -\dfrac{3}{2}$ 30) $x = \dfrac{15}{28}$

31) $m = 1$ 32) $x = \dfrac{5}{2}$ 33) $t > 6$

34) $x = \dfrac{21}{5}$ 35) $y \geqslant -70$ 36) $x = \dfrac{5}{3}$

37) $x = 13$ 38) $x = -10$ 39) $m = \dfrac{25}{26}$

40) $y = \dfrac{9}{7}$

Exercise 86

1) $(x - 5)$ years 2) $(3a + 8b)$ cents
3) $(5x + y + z)$ hours 4) $2(l + b)$ mm
5) A has $(a - x)$, B has $(b + x)$ 6) $(120 + x)$ minutes

7) $\$\left(Y + \dfrac{nx}{100}\right)$ 8) $\$\dfrac{nx}{100m}$

9) $6a + 4b + c$ 10) $\$(Mx + Ny + P)$

Exercise 87

1) 15
2) 10 at 5c and 5 at 8c
3) 30 metres
4) 7
5) 5
6) 15, 16, 17
7) A gets \$118 and B gets \$262
8) 5
9) 16, 12, 18 cm
10) 20°, 50° and 110°

Self-test 16

1) T	2) F	3) T	4) T	5) F
6) F	7) F	8) F	9) T	10) T
11) T	12) T	13) F	14) F	15) F
16) T	17) F	18) F	19) T	20) F
21) T	22) F	23) F	24) F	25) F
26) c	27) c	28) a	29) d	30) b
31) c	32) d	33) b	34) d	35) d
36) b	37) c	38) c		

ANSWERS TO CHAPTER 17

Exercise 88

1) 17	2) 160	3) 18.9	4) 252	5) 0.2
6) 400	7) 21	8) 180	9) 1875	10) 6

Exercise 89

1) $\frac{1}{2}$ or 0.5	2) 5	3) 3	4) 4	5) 100
6) 8.59	7) 2.55	8) 6		

Exercise 90

1) $\frac{c}{\pi}$ 2) $\frac{S}{\pi n}$ 3) $\frac{c}{P}$

4) $\frac{A}{\pi r}$ 5) $\frac{v^2}{2g}$ 6) $\frac{I}{PT}$

7) $\frac{a}{x}$ 8) $\frac{E}{I}$ 9) ax

10) $\frac{PV}{R}$ 11) $\frac{0.866}{d}$ 12) $\frac{ST}{S}$

13) $\frac{33\,000H}{PAN}$ 14) $\frac{4V}{\pi d^3}$ 15) $p + 14.7$

16) $\frac{v-u}{a}$ 17) $\frac{n-p}{c}$ 18) $\frac{y-b}{a}$

19) $5(y-17)$ 20) $\frac{H-S}{L}$ 21) $\frac{b-a}{c}$

22) $\frac{B-D}{1.28}$ 23) $\frac{R(V-2)}{V}$ 24) $C(R+r)$

25) $S/\pi r - r$ 26) $\frac{H}{wS} + t$ 27) $2pC + n$

28) $D - \frac{TL}{12}$ 29) $\frac{Vr}{V-2}$ 30) $\frac{SF}{S-P}$

31) $\frac{V^2}{2g}$ 32) $\frac{w^2}{k^2}$ 33) $\frac{t^2 g}{4\pi^2}$

34) $\frac{4\pi^2 W}{gt^2}$ 35) $\frac{Pr}{V^2 + gr}$ 36) $\frac{Z^2 y}{1 - Z^2}$

37) $\frac{2-k}{k-3}$ 38) $\frac{3-5a}{4a}$ 39) $\frac{2ka}{aV^2 + 2k}$

40) $\frac{2S - dn(n-l)}{2n}$ 41) $\frac{c^2 + 4h^2}{8h}$ 42) $\frac{xD}{x+h}$

43) $\frac{p(D^2 + d^2)}{D^2 - d^2}$

Self-test 17

1) b	2) d	3) c	4) c	5) d
6) b	7) d	8) a	9) b	10) c
11) c	12) b	13) c	14) a	15) d
16) c	17) d	18) c	19) b	20) d

ANSWERS TO CHAPTER 18

Exercise 91

1) $x = 1, y = 2$ 2) $x = 4, y = 5$ 3) $x = 4, y = 1$
4) $x = 7, y = 3$ 5) $x = \frac{1}{2}, y = \frac{3}{4}$ 6) $x = 3, y = 2$
7) $x = 4, y = 3$ 8) $x = 3, y = 4$ 9) $x = 1\frac{1}{2}, y = 1$
10) $x = -1, y = -2$ 11) $x = 6, y = 3$ 12) $x = 2, y = -1\frac{1}{2}$

Exercise 92

1) 15, 12 2) 16 3) $x = 120, y = 200$
4) copper 9, tin 7 5) $x = 40, y = 75$ 6) 300
7) A is 64, B is 48, $n = 40$
8) 30 c 9) 15, 21 10) 12

Self-test 18

1) a	2) a	3) b	4) d	5) c
6) a	7) a	8) c	9) a, b	10) b
11) b, c	12) b, c			

ANSWERS TO CHAPTER 19

Exercise 93

1) ± 5 2) ± 2.83 3) ± 4
4) ± 4 5) ± 4 6) ± 1.73
7) 2 or 5 8) $\frac{4}{3}$ or -3 9) 0 or -7
10) 0 or $2\frac{1}{2}$ 11) -8 or 4 12) -5 or -4
13) 3 14) -9 or 8 15) $\frac{1}{3}$ or 2
16) $\frac{4}{7}$ or $\frac{3}{2}$ 17) $-\frac{4}{3}$ or $\frac{7}{3}$ 18) 0 or 3
19) 0 or -8 20) $-\frac{1}{2}$ or $\frac{3}{2}$

Exercise 94

1) $(x+2)^2$ 2) $(3x+2)^2$ 3) $(2x-3)^2$
4) $(5x-1)^2$ 5) $(x+2)^2 - 1$ 6) $(x+3)^2 - 11$
7) $(x-4)^2 - 13$ 8) $(x-4)^2 - 18$ 9) $4(x+1)^2 - 3$

10) $3\left(x + \frac{2}{3}\right)^2 - \frac{19}{3}$ 11) $10(x-1)^2 - 1$ 12) $2 - (x-2)^2$

13) $9 - 2(x-1)^2$ 14) $\frac{13}{4} - 4\left(x - \frac{1}{4}\right)^2$

Exercise 95

1) 1.18 or -0.43 2) 1.62 or -0.62 3) 0.57 or -2.91
4) 0.21 or -1.35 5) 1 or -0.2 6) 3.89 or -0.39
7) -3.78 or 0.44 8) -9.18 or 2.18 9) -11 or 6
10) 3.30 or -0.30

Exercise 96

1) $x = 1, y = 2$ or $x = 2, y = 1$
2) $x = -17, y = -20$ or $x = 9, y = 6$
3) $x = 6, y = 3$ or $x = 8.5, y = 0.5$
4) $x = 9, y = 3$ or $x = 4, y = 8$
5) $x = 3.2, y = -0.4$ or $x = 4, y = -2$
6) $x = 2.2, y = 5.4$ or $x = 3, y = 5$
7) $x = 4, y = \frac{1}{2}$ or $x = \frac{1}{3}, y = 6$
8) $x = 1.5, y = -10.5$ or $x = -5, y = -30$

Exercise 97

1) 6 or -7 2) 9 m, 8 m   3) 15 cm
4) 4 m × 1 m   5) 13.35 m   6) 5, 6 and 7
7) 10 cm   8) $\frac{2}{5}$ 9) 8.83 m or 3.17 m
10) $d(d - 2) + (d - 4)^2 = 1.48; d = 11$ cm

Self-test 19

1) d   2) a   3) b   4) c   5) c
6) b   7) b   8) b   9) d   10) a
11) b   12) c, d

ANSWERS TO CHAPTER 20

Exercise 98

1) 3^{14} 2) b^{19} 3) 5^5
4) 2^7 5) 7^6 6) $81x^8 y^{12}$

7) $a^{10} b^{15} c^5$ 8) $\dfrac{5^7 a^{21}}{2^7 b^{14}}$ 9) $\frac{1}{10}, \frac{1}{32}, \frac{1}{81}, \frac{1}{25}$

10) 2, 2, 2   11) $3^4, 3^{12}, 3^{12}$ 12) $x^{\frac{1}{3}}, x^{\frac{3}{5}}, x^{\frac{4}{7}}$
13) 30   14) $1, \frac{1}{5}, 100$ 15) 12
16) $m = 2$ 17) $x = 1$ 18) $x = -12$
19) $p = 3$ 20) $x = 1$

Exercise 99

1) 8×10^3 2) 9.25×10^4 3) 8.93×10^2
4) 5.6×10^6 5) 3.5×10^{-2} 6) 7×10^{-1}
7) 3.65×10^{-4} 8) 7.12×10^{-3}

Exercise 100

1) 0.861   2) 0.913   3) 1.801
4) 2.855   5) 3.260   6) 4.895
7) 1.845   8) 5.246   9) $\bar{1}.250$
10) $\bar{3}.802$ 11) $\bar{2}.838$ 12) $\bar{4}.856$
13) 407   14) 53.7   15) 4.17
16) 1260   17) 0.170   18) 0.0398
19) 0.000 427   20) 0.003 55

Exercise 101

1) 342   2) 560   3) 123
4) 0.0103   5) 6.67   6) 26.4
7) 394   8) 0.005 38   9) 0.134
10) 0.000 189   11) 9040   12) 19 900
13) 0.179   14) 0.000 176   15) 1.59
16) 4.22   17) 92.6   18) 2.60
19) 1.07   20) 0.395   21) 0.947
22) 0.922

Exercise 102

1) 3.44   2) 3.61   3) 8.30
4) 225   5) 1.48   6) 1.21

7) 2.25   8) 3.97   9) 75.0

10) $I = \dfrac{Wl^3}{48Ey}; 37.5$

11) (a) 1000   (b) 3.16   (c) 1.58
12) (a) 1.253   (b) $\frac{2}{3}$ (c) 4.32
       (d) 100   (e) 0.1
13) 1.25   14) 5.62   15) 4.25

Self-test 20

1) b   2) b   3) c   4) c   5) a
6) d   7) b   8) a   9) b   10) c
11) c   12) b   13) c   14) c   15) c
16) b   17) c   18) d   19) d   20) d
21) b   22) b

ANSWERS TO EXAMINATION TYPE QUESTIONS 2

1) (a) (i) $3(x^2 + 4)$ (ii) $3x(x + 4)$
       (iii) $3(x + 3)(x + 1)$
    (b) (i) $x = 0$ or -4 (ii) $x = \pm 2$

2) (a) $x = \dfrac{y - c}{m}$ (b) (i) $y = -8$ (ii) $x = 18$

3) (a) $x = 2, y = -1$
    (b) (i) $x^2 + 2xy + y^2$ (ii) $xy = 6$
4) (a) $x = 1.69$ (b) $x = 6$ or -1
5) (a) $16\frac{1}{32}$ (b) $p = 3$
6) (a) $(x - 3)(x - 1)(2x - 1)$ (b) $(3x + 7)(3x + 1)$
    (c) $3(3 + x)(3 - x)$ (d) $(x - 2)(x - 5)$
7) (a) $(4 - 3x)(3 + 2x)$ (b) $x = 1\frac{1}{3}$ or $-1\frac{1}{2}$

8) (a) $x = \dfrac{y - p}{1 + yp}$ (b) $\dfrac{2}{2x - 3}$

    (c) (i) $1\frac{1}{2}$ (ii) 0.3   (iii) 8

9) (a) $\dfrac{3x - 7}{(x^2 - 1)(x - 1)}$ (b) $x = 32$

    (c) $p = 1, q = -2$
10) $y = -6, x = -7$; $y = 1.75, x = 24$

11) (a) $\dfrac{60}{x}$; $\dfrac{60}{x + 4}$ (b) $x = 12$ or -16 (c) 224

12) (a) $1\frac{1}{11}$ (b) 0.8977

    (c) $\dfrac{5}{(x - 1)(2x + 3)}$ (d) $x = 9.3$ or -0.8

13) (a) $\$(x - 5)$ (b) $\dfrac{3750}{x - 5}$ (c) $\dfrac{4000}{x}$

14) (a) $y = \dfrac{6 - x}{2x + 3}$ (b) $\dfrac{15}{2y + 1}$ (c) $\frac{3}{4}$ or -2

15) (a) (i) 0.778 15   (ii) 0.954 24   (iii) 0.176 09
    (b) $x = 8$

ANSWERS TO CHAPTER 21

Exercise 103

1) (a) 5630   (b) 680   (c) 17 698
    (d) 5.92   (e) 0.68   (f) 6.895
    (g) 0.073   (h) 45.97   (i) 0.798
    (j) 0.005
2) (a) 9.753   (b) 0.259   (c) 0.058
    (d) 0.029 85   (e) 0.790 685

3) (a) 468   (b) 78.2   (c) 516 000
   (d) 389.7   (e) 8.8
4) (a) 1234   (b) 580 000   (c) 258
   (d) 3890   (e) 52
5) (a) 0.53 kg   (b) 35 kg   (c) 2.473 kg
   (d) 597.6 kg
6) (a) 56   (b) 0.096   (c) 8630
   (d) 81   (e) 0.584
7) 18.2 tonnes
8) 19 400 kg

Exercise 104

1) 8 km   2) 15 Mg   3) 3.8 Mm
4) 1.891 Gg   5) 7 mm   6) 1.3 μm
7) 28 g   8) 360 mm   9) 64 mg
10) 3.6 mA   11) 5.3×10^4 m   12) 1.8×10^4 g
13) 3.563×10^6 g   14) 1.876×10^{10} g   15) 7×10^{-2} m
16) 7.8×10^{-2} g   17) 3.58×10^{-10} m   18) 1.82×10^{-5} m
19) 2.706×10^{14} m   20) 2.53×10^{-4} g

Exercise 105

1) 8.8 mm   2) 0.0128 m^2
3) (a) 1200 mm^2 (b) 275   (c) 260   (d) 774   (e) 1050
   (f) 1094 mm^2
4) 22.1 cm^2 5) 13.42 cm^2 6) 9.62 cm^2 7) 143 cm^2
8) 53.7 m^2 9) 28 cm^2 10) 2.12 m   11) 3062 mm^2
12) 15.7 m
13) (a) 11 200 mm^2 (b) 3.02 cm^2
14) (a) 22.0 mm   (b) 86.8 m   (c) 26.4 cm
15) (a) 10.9 mm   (b) 5.900 cm   (c) 62.1 m
16) 6.2 cm^2 17) 3.41 cm   18) 2.592 mm^2 19) 909
20) (a) 1.047 cm   (b) 2.29 cm
21) (a) 119.6°   (b) 10.16°
22) 8.92
23) (a) 4.71 m^2 (b) 5.08 cm^2 (c) 76.2 cm^2
24) 288.6 mm^2
25) (a) 32.145 and 32.155 mm   (b) 3.575 mm and 3.585 mm
   (c) 4.995 and 5.005 mm   (d) 14.195 mm and 14.205 mm
26) 154.9 ± 0.25 cm   27) 600.25 and 650.25 mm^2
28) 79 400 mm^2

Exercise 106

1) 5×10^6 cm^3 2) 8×10^7 mm^3 3) 1.8×10^{10} mm^3
4) 0.83 m^3 5) 8.5×10^{-4} m^3 6) 0.0785 m^3
7) 5 m^3 8) 0.0025 ℓ 9) 827 000 ℓ
10) 8.275 ℓ

Exercise 107

1) 76.2 m   2) 10.6 m
3) 0.008 75 m^2 4) 91.7 mm
5) 2474 m   6) 128 300 mm^3
7) 6.54 cm   8) 1.768×10^6
9) $V = t\left(\dfrac{\pi d^2}{4} - l^2\right)$; 2.46 cm^3
10) (a) 37.14 m^2 (b) 24.57 m^2 (c) 38 300 litres
11) 40 cm   12) (a) 47.19 cm   (b) 4303 cm^2
13) 2.56 cm   14) 55 800 kg
15) 55 mm; 13.5 mm
16) (a) 6877 litres   (b) 15.82 m^2 (c) 5.107 m^2
17) 22.54 cm; $\frac{1}{2}$ 18) 52 kg
20) 3.832 cm; 4.69 cm; 214.1 cm^2
21) $93\frac{1}{3}$ cm^3 22) 35 cm^3; 11.14 m

Exercise 109

1) 8h 51 min   2) 6h 23 min   3) 10h 24 min
4) 3h 54 min   5) 7h 45 min   6) 17h 40 min
7) 6h 37 min   8) 11h 47 min   9) 7h 31 min
10) 12h 6 min

Self-test 21

1) a   2) d   3) c   4) d   5) d
6) d   7) b   8) c   9) b   10) a
11) c   12) b, d   13) d   14) b   15) a
16) d   17) d   18) b   19) a, d   20) a
21) d   22) d   23) a

ANSWERS TO CHAPTER 22

Exercise 112

1) 250–290 m^2
2) (a) 3   (b) 6   (c) 7   (d) 95; 75; 95 m^2
3) (a) 33 m   (b) 7.5 m × 8.5 m   (c) 132 m^2 (d) 132 m^2
4) Lounge: 5 m × 5 m; 25 m^2 Dining room: 3m × 5 m; 15 m^2
   Bedroom 1: 5 m × 5 m; 25 m^2 Bedroom 2: 3 m× 5 m; 15 m^2
   W.C.: 2 m× 2 m; 4 m^2 Bathroom: 3 m × 3 m; 9 m^2
5) 22 m^2 6) 150 m^3

ANSWERS TO CHAPTER 23

Exercise 113

2) 7.5; 3.7   3) 254.5 cm^2 4) 45   5) 2.3 min

Exercise 115

6) $x = 3$ or 4 7) $x = 4$ 8) $x = \pm 3$
9) $x = -5.4$ or 3.7
10) (a) $x = -6.54$ or -0.46 (b) $x = -7.28$ or 0.28
   (c) $x = -6$ or -1
11) (a) $x = -1$ or 0.3 (b) $x = -1.39$ or 0.72
   (c) $x = -1.21$ or 0.55
12) (a) $x = \pm 3$ (b) $x = \pm 2.24$ (c) no real roots

Exercise 116

1) (a) ± 1.15 (b) -0.72 or 1.39 (c) 0 or 2.33
2) -6.16 or 0.16 3) $x = 4$, $y = 1$ 4) $x = 7$, $y = 3$
5) $x = 3$, $y = 2$ 6) -0.54 or 1.40
7) 0.3, 11.25   (a) 0 and 2   (b) 0.84; $2x^2 - 8x = 0$
8) 4, 4.75; 5, 3.85 or 0.65   9) $x^2 - x - 11 = 0$; 3.85
10) 1, -1.75, -2, $\dfrac{x^2}{4} + \dfrac{24}{x} - 12 = \dfrac{x}{3} - 2$, 2.6, 5.4

Self-test 23

1) T   2) T   3) F   4) T   5) T
6) F   7) T   8) T   9) F   10) F
11) T   12) F   13) F   14) T   15) T
16) T   17) F   18) F   19) T   20) T
21) b   22) b   23) b   24) c   25) b

ANSWERS TO CHAPTER 24

Exercise 117

1) Right-angled triangle, 9   2) Rectangle, 30
3) Parallelogram, 24   4) Trapezium, 8
5) Right-angled triangle, $7\frac{1}{2}$

Exercise 118

1) 4.24 2) 3.61 3) 6.40 4) 5.83
5) 4.47 6) (1.5, 5.5) 7) (−2, 6.5) 8) (2.5, 6)

Exercise 119

1) 1, 3 2) −3, 4
3) −5, −2 4) 4, −3
5) $m = 4, c = 13$ 6) $m = 2, c = −2$
7) $m = 2, c = 1$ 8) $m = 3, c = −2$
9) $m = −2, c = −3$ 10) $m = −3, c = 4$
11) $m = 5, c = 7$ 12) $a = 3, b = 4$
13) $a = 5, b = 1$ (both approx.) 14) $a = 0.5, b = 3$ (both approx.)
15) $m = 1.3, c = 20$ 16) $E = 4I$

Exercise 120

1) a 2) b 3) c 4) a 5) c
6) b 7) c

Self-test 24

1) c 2) a 3) a 4) c 5) c
6) d 7) a 8) d 9) c 10) d

ANSWERS TO CHAPTER 25

Exercise 121

1) (a) 3, 10; 5, 14; 7, 18; 9, 22 (b) 3, 18; 5, 30; 7, 42; 9, 54
2) (a) 9 (b) 36 3) (a) 11 (b) $x \to 3x − 1$
4) (a) 2, 0; 3, −2; 4, −4; 5, −6 (b) 2, 4; 3, 8; 4, 16; 5, 32
5) (a) $x \to 4x + 1$ (b) 4, 17; 8, 33
6) 1, 0; 2, 0; 3, 2; 4, 6 7) $x \to 2x$

Exercise 122

1) (a) 4 (b) 2 (c) 44 (d) $\frac{1}{4}$
2) (a) 17 (b) −23 (c) −7
3) (a) 1 (b) 21 (c) 0 (d) 5 (e) 33
4) −1; 53; −1
5) $6\frac{1}{2}; −3\frac{1}{2}$
6) $1\frac{1}{2}; \frac{1}{4}; −3\frac{1}{2}$
7) a, c and d

Exercise 123

1) (a) $y = kx^2$ (b) $U = k\sqrt{V}$
(c) $S = \dfrac{k}{T^3}$ (d) $h = \dfrac{k}{\sqrt[3]{m}}$
2) (a) $\frac{81}{8}$ (b) $1\frac{1}{3}$ (c) $\frac{8}{9}$
3) 4.5 4) 36 5) $\sqrt{2}:1$
7) (b) 1.089 (c) $P = 1.50 \times 1.089^x$
(d) 3.52 million (e) 1.94 million
8) (a)

T	1	2	3	4	5
N	2	4	8	16	25

(b) 6
9) 3 600 000
10) (b) 10% (c) $10 700 (d) 11.5 years

Exercise 124

1) $x \to \dfrac{x}{3}$ 2) $x \to \dfrac{x+3}{2}$ 3) $x \to 2x + 3$
4) $x \to \dfrac{x+15}{6}$ 5) $x \to \dfrac{2x+5}{2-x}$ 6) (a) 0 (b) $\frac{5}{6}$

7) (a) $\frac{10}{3}$ (b) not possible 8) $\frac{5}{2}; \frac{5}{4}$
9) (a) 9 (b) −2 (c) −27 (d) −131 (e) −8
10) $\dfrac{x-9}{15}; \dfrac{x+1}{15}$
11) $f^{-1}(x) = \dfrac{5x+3}{x-1}; x = 13$
12) $f^{-1}(x) = \dfrac{3x+1}{4x-3}; x = \frac{16}{17}$

Exercise 125

1) (a) {2, 4, 8}; {10, 15} (b) {1, 2}; {5, 7, 9}
2) (a) {(2, 2), (2, 5), (2, 7) (5, 2), (5, 5), (5, 7), (7, 2), (7, 5), (7, 7)}
(b) {(3, 3), (3, 8), (8, 3), (8, 8)}
(c) {(2, 3), (2, 8), (5, 3), (5, 8), (7, 3), (7, 8)}
(d) {(3, 2), (3, 5), (3, 7), (8, 2), (8, 5), (8, 7)}
4) (a) 25 (b) 15 (c) 15 (d) 9

ANSWERS TO CHAPTER 26

Exercise 126

1) −5, 19 2) −4, 8 3) 3 4) 5.5 or −6.5
5) −4, 6, 1.25 6) 8

Exercise 127

1) (a) 0.71 per min (b) 1.4 per min 2) −0.078
3) 0.078 g/s
4) (a) 0.09 million per year (b) 0.13 million per year
5) (a) 3.5 (b) 0

Exercise 128

1) $−3\frac{1}{3}$ 2) $13\frac{1}{4}$ 3) 9, −23
4) (a) −2.25 (b) 3.3 or −0.3 (c) 2.4 or −0.4
5) $2\frac{1}{4}$ 6) $\frac{7}{2}, −\frac{1}{2}, +\frac{1}{2}; −1\frac{13}{24}, \frac{5}{6}$
7) 262 8) $7.36 \times 7.36 \times 3.68$
9) $x = \frac{2}{3}, k = \frac{4}{3}$ 10) (a) 625 (b) 38.23×11.77

Exercise 129

1) $x = −1; −4$ 2) $x = 2; 11$ 3) $x = 1; 3$
4) $x = 1; −5$ 5) $x = 1\frac{1}{2}; 4\frac{3}{4}$ 6) $x = −2; 15$

Exercise 130

1) 136 2) 13 3) $5\frac{1}{6}$ 4) $18\frac{2}{3}$ 5) $3\frac{3}{4}$

Exercise 131

1) 60 km/h 2) 5 hours 3) 300 km 4) 50 km/h
5) 36.4 km/h 6) 10.6 km/h 7) 22.1 km/h 8) 150 m/s
9) 24 m/s 10) $\frac{2}{27}$ m/s 11) 70 m/s

Exercise 132

1) (a) 60 m (b) 6 m (c) 80 m (d) 120 m
(e) 300 m
2) (a) acceleration 5 m/s² (b) acceleration $\frac{1}{2}$ m/s²
(c) retardation 1.5 m/s² (d) retardation 2.5 m/s²
3) 150 m
4) (a) 0.2 m/s² (b) 4 m/s (c) 210 m
5) (a) 1 m/s² (b) 3 m/s (c) 5 m/s (d) 250 m
6) (a) 1 m/s² (b) 2 m/s (c) 0.5 m/s (d) 30 m/s
(e) 875 m
7) (b) 2 m/s² (c) 1.6 m/s² (d) 384 m

8) (b) 239 m
9) (b) (i) 2.5 m/s^2 (ii) 10 m/s^2
10) (a) 3.2 m/s^2 (b) 12.4 s   (c) 135 m

Self-test 26

1) **a**   2) **d**   3) **c**   4) **d**   5) **a**
6) **c**   7) **b**   8) **d**   9) **c**   10) **d**
11) **b**   12) **a**   13) **a**   14) **b**   15) **c**
16) **b**   17) **b**   18) **b**

ANSWERS TO CHAPTER 27

Exercise 133

1) $x > 2$ 2) $x > 7$ 3) $x > 2$
4) $x \leqslant 4$ 5) $x \leqslant 3$ 6) $x \leqslant 8$
7) $\{\bar{2}\}$ 8) $\{\ \}$ 9) 4, 5, 6, 7
10) 0, 1, 2, 3, 4, 5, 6, 7

Exercise 134

1) $x \geqslant 2$ or $x \leqslant -4$ 2) $x \geqslant -3$ or $x \leqslant -5$
3) $x \leqslant 3$ and $x \geqslant 2$, i.e. $2 \leqslant x \leqslant 3$
4) $x \geqslant \frac{1}{3}$ or $x \leqslant -2$ 5) $x \geqslant \frac{1}{2}$ and $x \leqslant 4$
6) 20   7) 8   8) 8

Exercise 136

6) $0 < x < 4$

Exercise 137

1) 14   2) 11 and -5
3) 60 boxes of Sure-clean; 20 boxes of Quick-wash; $7.20
4) 24 of P, 8 of Q; $880
5) (a) 15 hectares
    (b) 5 of sugar cane, 4 of sweet potatoes   (c) $56
6) A(0, 1), B(2, 3), C(5, 0); 13
7) 4 van journeys, 4 lorry journeys: $36
8) (b) 28   (c) 19   (d) 7
9) (b) 1 tin of ham, 5 of beef   (c) $5.60
10) 13 (11 type A and 2 type B)

Self-test 27

1) **c**   2) **c**   3) **c**   4) **c**   5) **d**
6) **d**   7) **a**

ANSWERS TO EXAMINATION TYPE QUESTIONS 3

1) (a) 42 860 cm^2 (b) 796 litres
2) 8×10^{-2} mm
3) 10.63 cm
4) 3 m; 112 m^2; 128 m^3
5) $c = 4$ and $m = 1$; $y = 7$
6) $M = LWTD$ 7) 12 cm
8) 4224 g   9) $y = 4$
10) (a) 35   (b) 321.9 m^2
11) (b) $-2.6 \leqslant x \leqslant 2.6$ (c) 2.30 and -1.30
    (d) $-1.30 \leqslant x \leqslant 2.30$
12) (a) $5(x + \frac{4}{5})^2 - \frac{1}{5}$ (b) $-\frac{1}{5}$
    (c) $\frac{49}{12} - 3(x - \frac{5}{6})^2$ (d) $\frac{49}{12}$

13) (a) $(x + 3y)(x - 3y)$; $x = 4$, $y = -\frac{1}{3}$
    (b) $W = \dfrac{kV^2}{L}$
    (c) (i) 0.8   (ii) 57.6 cm   (iii) 220 V
14) 27.7 cm^2
15) (a) 2.8; 4.2   (c) first machine; 5.4 newtons

ANSWERS TO CHAPTER 28

Exercise 138

1) 135°   2) 54°   3) 60°   4) 63°   5) 18°
6) 135°   7) 288°   8) 288°   9) 108°   10) 90°
11) 28° 37′   12) 69° 23′   13) 14° 22′ 34″
14) 62° 48′ 11″   15) 179° 11′ 25″   16) 21° 3′
17) 22° 48′   18) 5° 54′ 50″   19) 36° 58′ 11″

Exercise 139

1) (a) 3.21   (b) 3.13
2) (a) 286° 29′ (b) 99° 7′   (c) 9° 7′
3) (a) 1.45   (b) 3.30   (c) 5.15   (d) 0.091
4) (a) 3.75 cm   (b) 15.7 cm   (c) 23.6
5) (a) 2.4 cm^2 (b) 44.1 cm^2 (c) 52.4 cm^2

Exercise 140

1) 20°   2) 100°   3) 35°
4) 70°, 110°, 110°, 70°
5) 65°   6) 80°   7) **c**
8) **c**   9) 54°   10) 130°
11) 65°   12) 230°, 32°   13) **b, d**

Self-test 28

1) **d**   2) **a**   3) **b**   4) **a**   5) **b**   6) **d**

ANSWERS TO CHAPTER 29

Exercise 141

1) $x = 49°$, $y = 151°$ 2) $x = 77°$, $y = 81°$
3) $x = 63°$, $y = 98°$ 4) $x = 37°$, $y = 127°$
5) $x = 140°$, $y = 60°$ 6) $x = 80°$, $y = 70°$

Exercise 142

1) $a = 10$ cm   2) $b = 22.4$ cm   3) $c = 2.65$ cm
4) (a) 3.87 cm   (b) 4.24 cm   (c) 5.29 cm
5) (a) 7.42 cm   (b) 3.71 cm   (c) 6.54 cm
6) (a) 60°   (b) 40°   (c) 40°
7) (a) $x = 70°$, $y = 40°$, $z = 35°$
    (b) $x = 110°$, $y = 70°$, $z = 70°$

Exercise 143

1) **c**   2) **b, c, d**
3) RQ = 7 cm, SX = 4 cm, ∠SXP = 97°
4) PY = 6 cm   5) BC = 5 cm, ∠BCA = 42°
6) △ADF ≡ △DFE ≡ △FEC ≡ △BED;
    △DGH ≡ △GJE ≡ △HGJ ≡ △HJF

Exercise 144

1) {AFI}; {CK}; {BDM}; {HJ}; {GL}
2) **b**   3) **b, d**   4) **d**

5) **a, c** 6) **b** 7) **a, b**
8) **c** 9) BC = 32 mm 10) EC = $4\frac{1}{2}$ cm, AB = $8\frac{1}{2}$ cm

Exercise 145

1) 72 cm^2 2) 36 cm^2 3) **b** 4) **b** 5) **c**
6) **c**

Exercise 146

2) CA 4) 74° 6) $\frac{3}{4}$
8) $\frac{3}{8}, \frac{3}{8}, \frac{9}{64}$ 9) (a) 5 cm; 4 cm (b) $\frac{4}{25}$
11) 3.2 cm 12) 29° 13) 1.8 cm
15) $\frac{3}{4}$; (a) 9 cm^2 (b) 4 cm^2

Self-test 29

1) **b, c** 2) **b** 3) **d** 4) **d** 5) **b**
6) **b** 7) **d** 8) **b** 9) **c** 10) **a**
11) **c** 12) **a, c** 13) **a** 14) **a, c** 15) **b**
16) **b, d** 17) **d** 18) **a** 19) **b** 20) **a, b**
21) **c** 22) **a, b, c** 23) **a** 24) **d** 25) **b**
26) **d** 27) **b** 28) **b** 29) **b** 30) **c**

ANSWERS TO CHAPTER 30

Exercise 147

1) $x = 143°$ 2) $x = 93°$
3) $x = 39°, y = 105°$ 4) **d**
5) **a** 6) **a**
7) **b** 8) 65°
9) 100° 10) Yes, Yes, Yes
11) 32° 12) 100°; 20°
14) 7.5 cm

Exercise 148

1) (a) 540° (b) 1080° (c) 1440° (d) 1800°
2) (a) 108° (b) 135° (c) 144° (d) 150°
3) 131° 4) 12 5) 6° 6) 24
7) 7 8) 132°, 75° 9) 72°, 108°
10) 36°, 10 11) $n = 30$ 12) 12

Exercise 149

1) 28 cm^2 2) $60\sqrt{2}$ 3) $6\frac{2}{3}$ cm
4) 12 cm 5) 40 cm^2 6) 240 cm^2
7) (a) 14 cm^2 (b) $2\frac{2}{3}$ cm^2 8) $2\frac{2}{3}$ cm

Self-test 30

1) **b** 2) **a** 3) **b** 4) **c** 5) **b**
6) **b** 7) **c** 8) **a, d** 9) **c**

ANSWERS TO CHAPTER 31

Exercise 150

1) 38° 2) 120° 3) 71° 4) 50°
5) $x = 27°, y = 58°$ 6) $\sqrt{95}$ cm
7) $a = 32°, b = 42°$ 8) $\sqrt{34}$ cm

Exercise 151

1) 59.9 2) 24.0 3) 57.0 cm 4) 11.2 cm
5) $a = 202°, b = 90°$ 6) $a = 55°, b = 57°, c = 70°$
7) $8\frac{1}{3}$ cm 8) 4.80 cm

Self-test 31

1) **b** 2) **c** 3) **b, d** 4) **d** 5) **b**
6) **c** 7) **b** 8) **a** 9) **a**

ANSWERS TO EXAMINATION TYPE QUESTIONS 4

1) (a) Parallelogram (b) (i) 210 cm^2 (ii) 29 cm
2) (a) 105° (b) 156°
3) (a) 40° (b) 40°; 60°; 80°
4) (a) 43° (b) (i) 18° (ii) 93°
5) (b) 73°
6) (a) $x°; x°; \frac{1}{2}x°; 1\frac{1}{2}x°$
   (b) (i) 9:25 (ii) 3:5
7) (a) (i) 4 cm (ii) 25:16 (b) (ii) 8.3
8) (a) 24 cm (b) 1:8 (c) $3\frac{1}{2}$ cm
   (d) 7 cm (e) 8:7

ANSWERS TO CHAPTER 34

Exercise 155

1) (a) 0.5 (b) 0.7 (c) 0.9
2) (a) 19.5° (b) 48.6° (c) 46.1°
3) (a) 0.208 (b) 0.312 (c) 0.965
   (d) 0.129 (e) 0.999 (f) 0.003
4) (a) 9° (b) 66° (c) 81.1°
   (d) 4.6° (e) 78.9° (f) 47.7°
   (g) 2.9° (h) 15.7°
5) (a) 3.38 cm (b) 10.1 cm (c) 25.9
6) (a) 41.8° (b) 40.8° (c) 22.4°
7) 28.3 cm 8) 0.795 m 9) 21.6 cm
10) 7.48 m 11) 44.8°, 44.8°, 90.4°

Exercise 156

1) (a) 0.966 (b) 0.911 (c) 0.201
   (d) 1.000 (e) 0.287 (f) 0.767
2) (a) 24° (b) 70° (c) 14.8°
   (d) 64.6° (e) 16.5° (f) 89.5°
   (g) 74.9° (h) 62.0°
3) (a) 9.33 cm (b) 2.64 m (c) 5.29 cm
4) (a) 60.7° (b) 69.3° (c) 53.3°
5) 66.1°, 66.1°, 47.8°, 3.84 cm
6) 2.88 cm (7) 1.97 cm
8) ∠BAC = 92°, BC = 8.74 cm
9) BD = 4.53 m, AD = 2.11 m, AC = 2.39 m, BC = 5.65 m

Exercise 157

1) (a) 0.325 (b) 0.635 (c) 1.361
   (d) 0.824 (e) 0.200 (f) 2.660
2) (a) 24.0° (b) 73.0° (c) 4.4°
   (d) 21.7° (e) 19.6° (f) 39.6°
   (g) 62.6° (h) 0.9°
3) (a) 4.35 cm (b) 9.29 cm (c) 4.43 m
4) (a) 59° (b) 15.9° (c) 22.7°
5) 7.70 cm 6) 2.78 cm 7) 33.3 cm
8) 2.86 m 9) 2.09 cm

Exercise 158

1) (a) $\bar{1}.680$ (b) $\bar{1}.984$ (c) $\bar{1}.996$
   (d) $\bar{1}.960$ (e) $\bar{1}.993$ (f) $\bar{1}.094$
2) (a) 57.0° (b) 22.4° (c) 75.1°
   (d) 11.7° (e) 80.1° (f) 88.4°

3) (a) 45.6° (b) 18.4° (c) 58.0°
4) 9.29 cm 5) 46.2° 6) 17.7°
7) 5.8 cm

Exercise 159

1) 0.948, 0.335 2) $\frac{3}{5}, \frac{4}{5}$
3) $\frac{5}{13}, \frac{5}{12}$ 7) 0.743
8) 0.454 9) (a) $\frac{3}{4}$ (b) $\frac{1}{3}$ (c) $\frac{3}{4}$
10) (a) 0.570 (b) 0.206 (c) 2.561
11) 41.8° 12) 48.6° 13) 5.660 14) 0.439

Exercise 160

1) 11.6 m 2) 9.60 m 3) 51°
4) 110 m 5) 10.6 m 6) 24.8 m
7) 1290 m 8) 38.7° 9) 3.0 m
10) 11.7 m
11) (a) 70.0 m (b) 30 m (c) 32.6 m
12) 53.3 m

Exercise 161

1) (a) 90.4 km (b) 150 km 2) 43.3 km; 25 km
3) 326.3° 4) 11.6 km; 10.8 km
5) 44.4 m, S 64.3° E 6) 24.7 km; 338.8°
7) (a) 24.4 km (b) 14.0 km 8) 127 km; 49.6°
9) 11.5 km; N 61.8° E 10) 15.2 km; 66.8°

Self-test 34

1) a 2) c 3) b 4) b 5) c
6) d 7) c 8) c 9) a 10) a
11) a 12) c 13) c 14) b

ANSWERS TO CHAPTER 35

Exercise 162

1)

θ	$\sin \theta$	$\cos \theta$	$\tan \theta$
108°	0.951	−0.309	−3.08
163°	0.292	−0.956	−0.305
207°	−0.454	−0.891	0.510
320°	−0.643	0.766	−0.839
134°	0.719	−0.695	−1.04
168°	0.208	−0.978	−0.213
225°	−0.707	−0.707	1.000
286°	−0.961	0.276	−3.49
300°	−0.866	0.500	−1.732
95°	0.996	−0.087	−11.4

2) 14.6°, 165.4°
3) 105.7°

1st quadrant	2nd quadrant	3rd quadrant	4th quadrant
4) 31.0°	149.0°		
12.5°	167.5°		
		204.0°	336.0°
28.2°			331.8°
	139.5°	220.5°	
	94.7°	265.3°	
58.0°		238.0°	
39.1°		219.1°	
	167.0°		347.0°

5) $y = 28.7°$ or $= 331.3°$; $x = 34.6°$ or 146.4°
6) $\tan A = \frac{12}{5}$; $\cos A = \frac{5}{13}$
7) $-\frac{7}{25}$ 8) $\frac{15}{17}; \frac{8}{15}$ 9) $\frac{11}{60}$

Exercise 163

1) $C = 71°, b = 5.90$ cm, $c = 9.99$ cm
2) $A = 48°, a = 71.5$ mm, $c = 84.2$ mm
3) $B = 56°, a = 3.74$ m, $b = 9.53$ m
4) $B = 46°, b = 13.6$ cm, $c = 5.85$ cm
5) $C = 67°, a = 1.51$ m, $c = 2.36$ m
6) $C = 63.5°, a = 9.49$ mm, $b = 11.6$ mm
7) $B = 135.6°, a = 9.39$ m, $c = 14.4$ m
8) $B = 81.9°, b = 9.95$ m, $c = 3.61$ m
9) $A = 53.7°, b = 2390$ mm, $a = 2125$ mm
10) $A = 13.9°, B = 144.0°, b = 17.2$ m
11) $C = 50.0°, A = 44.8°, a = 10.7$ cm
12) $C = 36.9°, B = 93.8°, b = 30.3$ cm
13) $B = 48.5°, C = 26.4°, c = 4.24$ cm
14) 21.7 cm 15) 118 mm 16) 11.3 cm
17) 9.05 cm 18) 21.8 cm

Exercise 164

1) $c = 10.2$ cm, $A = 50.2°, B = 69.8°$
2) $a = 11.8$ cm, $B = 44.6°, C = 79.4°$
3) $b = 4.99$ m, $A = 82.6°, C = 60.2°$
4) $A = 38.2°, C = 60.0°, B = 81.8°$
5) $A = 24.7°, B = 44.9°, C = 110.4°$
6) $A = 34.6°, B = 18.4°, C = 127.0°$
7) $c = 18.1$ cm, $A = 34.9°, B = 26.1°$
8) $a = 18.3$ cm, $B = 18.9°, C = 29.1°$

Exercise 165

1) 540 cm² 2) 738 cm²
3) (a) 7.55 cm² (b) 8.07 cm²
4) (a) 143 cm² (b) 53.7 cm² (c) 43.6 cm²
5) (a) 16.9 cm² (b) 31.5 cm² (c) 15.7 cm²
6) 89.2 cm² 7) 66.8 cm² 8) 19.3 cm²

Self-test 35

1) b 2) c 3) a 4) a 5) a
6) d 7) a 8) c 9) b 10) c
11) a 12) a, d 13) a, d 14) a, d 15) b, c

ANSWERS TO CHAPTER 36

Exercise 166

1) (b) 13 cm (d) 15.3 cm
2) (a) 4 cm (c) 71.6° (d) 12.7 cm (e) 50.6 cm²
   (f) 266 cm²
3) 12.7 cm 4) 4.53 cm 5) 14 cm; 25.4°
6) (a) 34.9° (b) 33° (c) 31.3°
7) (a) 17.3 cm (b) 60° (c) 61.5° (d) 19.7 cm
8) (a) 61.9° (b) 12 000 m³
9) (a) 55.2° (b) 58.9°
10) (a) 1520 m (b) 44.0°

ANSWERS TO CHAPTER 37

Exercise 167

1) 6120 km 2) 2000 km 3) 4450 km 4) 5520 km
5) 2220 km 6) (a) 3340 km (b) 94° E
7) 2.12 cm 8) 35.2° W, 22.7° N
9) 1560 km, 28.6° W 10) (a) 47.6° (b) 4800 km

ANSWERS TO EXAMINATION TYPE QUESTIONS 5

1) (a) 73 cm   (b) 89 cm
2) (a) 135 km   (b) 075.3°   (c) 604.8 km
3) (a) 46.3 m; 35.5 m   (b) 27.4°
4) (a) 31.7°   (b) 1.95 m; 69.5°
5) (a) 8.66 km   (b) 15.62 km   (c) 8.74 km
6) (a) 26.5 cm   (b) 31.2 cm; 73.6°
7) (a) (3, 0); (0, 4)   (b) $x/4 - y/3 = 3/4$
8) 13; 12/13; 6.5
9) (a) 11.4 cm   (b) 34.2 cm^2

ANSWERS TO CHAPTER 38

Exercise 168

1) $A = \{5, 7, 9, 11, 13, 15\}$
2) $X = \{$Tuesday, Thursday$\}$
3) $B = \{2, 4, 6, 8, 10\}$
4) $P = \{2, 3, 5, 7, 11, 13, 17, 19, 23\}$
5) $Q = \{3, 6, 9, 12, 15, 18, 21, 24, 27, 30, 33\}$
6) {multiples of 5 less than 30}
7) {family}
8) {prime numbers greater than 2 but less than 18}

Exercise 169

1) infinte   2) finite   3) infinite
4) finite   5) infinite   6) null
7) finite   8) null   9) $n(A) = 4$
10) $n(B) = 10$

Exercise 170

1) $P = \{2, 4, 6, 8, 10\}$, $7 \notin P$
2) $Q = \{1, 4, 9, 16, 25, 36\}$, $18 \notin Q$
3) $R = \{17, 14, 11, 8, 5, 2\}$, $9 \notin R$
4) $S = \{a, b, c, d, e, f\}$, $\emptyset \notin S$
5) $T = \{5, 7, 11, 13, 17, 19, 23, 29\}$, $9 \notin T$
6) True   7) True   8) True
9) False   10) False

Exercise 171

1) (a) $\{3, 5, 9, 11, 13, 15\}$ (b) $\{6, 8, 12\}$
   (c) $\{3, 5, 11, 13\}$ (d) $\{6, 8, 12\}$
2) 16   3) **c** and **d**
4) No. $A \subset C \subset B$
5) $\{a\}, \{b\}, \{c\}, \{d\}, \{a, b\}, \{a, c\}, \{a, d\}, \{b, c\}, \{b, d\}, \{c, d\},$
   $\{a, b, c\}, \{a, c, d\}, \{a, b, d\}, \{b, c, d\}$
6) $g \subset a; h \subset b; e \subset c; f \subset d$
8) **a, d, g**   9) $2^5 = 32$ 10) $2^8 = 256$

Exercise 172

1) (a) $\{a, e, i, o, u\}$ (b) $\{u, v, w, x, y, z\}$
   (c) $\{b, c, d, f, g, h, k, l, m, n, p, q, r, s, t, v, w, x, y, z\}$
2) {triangle, quadrilateral, pentagon, hexagon, heptagon, octagon}
3) (a) $\{2, 3, 5, 7, 11, 13, 17, 19\}$
   (b) $\{3, 6, 9, 12, 15, 18\}$ (c) $\{2, 3, 5, 7\}$
4) (a) {Dec., Jan., Feb.}   (b) {Sept., Oct., Nov.}
5) $\{1, 4, 9, 16, 25\}$

Exercise 173

1) $\{2, 3, 4, 5, 6, 7, 8, 9, 11\}$ 2) $\{2, 4, 7, 8\}$
3) $\{5, 6, 7, 8\}$ 4) $\{3, 5, 6, 9, 11\}$
5) $\{2, 3, 4, 9, 11\}$ 6) $\{7, 8\}$
7) $\{2, 4, 5, 6, 7, 8\}$ 8) $\{3, 9, 11\}$
9) $7 \notin \{2, 4, 6, 8\}$
10) $\{1, 3, 5, 7\} \cap \{2, 3, 5, 6\} = \{3, 5\}$
11) $8 \in \{4, 8, 16, 32\}$ 12) $\{3, 4, 6\} = \{6, 3, 4\}$
13) {rectangles, triangles} $\subset$ {all plane figures}
14) $\{1, 3, 5, 7, 9\} \supset \{5, 7\}$
15) $\{2, 4, 6, 8\} \neq \{3, 5, 7, 9, 11\}$
16) $\{2, 4\} \subset \{2, 4, 8, 9\} \subset \{1, 2, 4, 8, 9\}$
17) John $\notin$ {all girl's names}
18) $\{7, 14, 21, 28\} \subset$ {multiples of 7}
19) $\{x : 1 \leqslant x \leqslant 7\} \supset \{2, 3, 4, 5, 6, 7\}$
20) $\{x : 3 \leqslant x \leqslant 5\} \subset \{x : 1 \leqslant x \leqslant 10\}$
21) $\{3, 4, 6, 7, 8, 9, 10\}$ 22) $\{6, 8\}$
23) $\{3, 4, 6, 7, 8, 9, 10\}$ 24) $\{6, 8\}$
25) $A \supset B$
26) $\{2, 3, 4, 5, 6, 7, 8, 9, 10, 11, 12, 13, 14, 15, 16\}$
27) $A = \{3, 4, 6, 8\}$ 28) $B = \{10, 12, 13, 14, 15\}$
29) $A \cap B = \emptyset$
30) $A \cup B = \{3, 4, 6, 8, 10, 12, 13, 14, 15\}$

31) 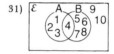   32)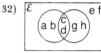

33) 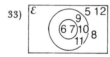   34)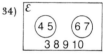

35)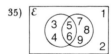

36) (a) B (b) $A \cap B$ (c) $(A \cup B)'$
   (d) $B \cap A'$ (e) $A \cup B$ (f) $A' \cup B'$
   (g) $A \cap B'$

37)

Exercise 174

1) $\{2\}$ 2) $\{2\}$
3) $\{2, 3, 4, 5, 6, 7\}$ 4) $\{2, 3, 4, 5, 6, 7\}$
5) $\{2, 3, 6\}$ 6) $\{2, 3, 4, 5, 7, 8\}$
7) $\{4, 5, 7, 8\}$ 8) $\emptyset$
9) $\{1, 2, 3, 6, 9\}$ 10) $\{1, 2, 3, 4, 5, 6, 9\}$

Exercise 175

1) (a) 12   (b) 17   (c) 5   (d) 24
2) (a) 9   (b) 23   (c) 23   (d) 37
3) 40   4) 8   5) 7
6) (a) 34   (b) 36   (c) 40   (d) 9   (e) 10
   (f) 68   (g) 3   (h) 86
7) (a) 3   (b) 66   (c) 57   (d) 58   (e) 13
   (f) 11   (g) 10

8) 20   9) 140
10) (a) 3   (b) 25   (c) 7

Exercise 176

1) $A = Z$; $B = V$; $C = X$; $D = W$; $E = X$; $W = X$
2) (a) true   (b) false $\{1, 3, 5\} = \{3, 1, 6\}$ (c) true
   (d) true {lion, tiger, cat, mouse, dog, bear} ≠ {chair, table, bed, settee}   (e) false
3) (a) many to many   (b) many to one
   (c) many to many   (d) many to one
   (e) many to one   (f) many to one
   (g) many to one   (h) many to one
   (i) many to many   (j) one to one

Exercise 177

1) (a)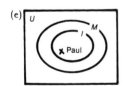
Valid U = Animals,
B = Black animals,
D = Dogs, × = Bruce

(b)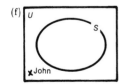
Valid U = Persons who like Maths
S = Students

(c)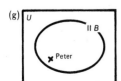
Invalid D = Girls who wear dresses

(d)
Valid S = People who swim well

(e)
Valid I = Industrious people
M = People who deserve medals

(f)
Invalid U = People liking cricket
S = Schoolboys

(g)
Value U = Boys playing cricket

(h)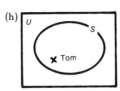
U = Honest people
S = Shopkeeters

2) (a)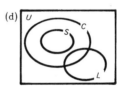
Valid U = People
I = People who like ice-cream
C = Children

(b)
Valid H = Hardworking people
S = University students
N = People who neglect their studies

(c)
Invalid U = Quadrilaterals
P = Parallelograms
R = Rectangles
H = Rhombi

(d)
Invalid U = Students
C = Chemistry students
S = Science students
L = Literature students

(e)
Valid W = Wealthy people
L = University lecturers
I = Industrialists

3) (a) No teacher is a speech maker
   (b) John does not want to be an unskilled worker
   (c) No science student is a prefect
   (d) All athletes are happy

4)
Yes

5) No.

6) (a)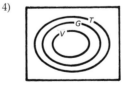
P = Popular people
G = Good losers
T = Tennis players
M = Unhappy men
L = Lonely people

(b) Yes   (c) Yes   (d) No
8) (a) No   (b) Yes   (c) No
9) (a) T   (b) I   (c) T   (d) T   (e) F
10) (a) I   (b) T   (c) F
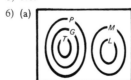

11) (a) No   (b) Yes   (c) No   (d) Yes   (e) No

Self-test 38

1) **b**   2) **d**   3) **b**   4) **c**   5) **a**
6) **d**   7) **c**   8) **b**   9) **a**   10) **b**
11) **d**

ANSWERS TO CHAPTER 39

Exercise 178

1) (a) 10111 (b) 101010
   (c) 111101 (d) 111001
2) (a) 22 (b) 57 (c) 90 (d) 55
3) (a) 0.8125 (b) 0.4375 (c) 0.1875
4) (a) 0.011 (b) 0.0101 (c) 0.111
5) (a) 0.0010101 (b) 10010.0111011
   (c) 1101100.1011010
6) (a) 1110 (b) 100110 (c) 111000
   (d) 1100100 (e) 1.0011 (f) 1.10100
   (g) 1101.0010 (h) 10010.00
7) (a) 1.1 (b) 100 (c) 10
   (d) 1.110 (e) 10.001
8) (a) 110 (b) 100011 (c) 1101110
   (d) 101011111 (e) 100011110
9) (a) 11 (b) 100 (c) 101 (d) 1010 (e) 1101
10) (a) 10111.101 (b) 1011.00001
    (c) 10.0010 (d) 1.00110

Exercise 179

1) (a) 111_3 (b) 1120_3 (c) 11211_3
   (d) 1242_5 (e) 435_6 (f) 1213_4
   (g) 161_8 (h) 1304_6
2) (a) 100_3 (b) 3_4 (c) 1100_3
   (d) 13_4 (e) 4422_8 (f) 134_4
3) (a) 125 (b) 69 (c) 134
   (d) 313 (e) 187
4) (a) 1032_8 (b) 122_3 (c) 11110_3
   (d) 120_8

Self-test 3

1) **c**   2) **e**   3) **b**   4) **c**   5) **c**
6) **d**   7) **a**   8) **e**   9) **c**   10) **e**
11) **d**

ANSWERS TO CHAPTER 40

Exercise 180

1) $L = 3, M = -1$

2) $\begin{pmatrix} 26 & 35 \\ 14 & 19 \end{pmatrix}, 2$

3) (a) $\begin{pmatrix} 7 & 0 \\ 4 & 3 \end{pmatrix}$ (b) $\begin{pmatrix} 1 & 5 \\ 2 & -6 \end{pmatrix}$

   (c) $\begin{pmatrix} 14 & 0 \\ 8 & -2 \end{pmatrix}$ (d) $\begin{pmatrix} 10 & 4 \\ 12 & 2 \end{pmatrix}$ (e) -2 (f) 14

4) (a) $PQ = \begin{pmatrix} 2 & 1 \\ 3 & 1 \end{pmatrix}$,

   $RS = \begin{pmatrix} -6 & 3 \\ 1 & -2 \end{pmatrix}$,

$PQRS = \begin{pmatrix} -11 & 4 \\ -17 & 7 \end{pmatrix}$

$P^2 - Q^2 = \begin{pmatrix} 6 & 3 \\ 9 & 3 \end{pmatrix}$

   (b) $a = -2, b = 5$

5) $A^2 = \begin{pmatrix} 16 & -9 \\ -12 & 13 \end{pmatrix}$

   $B = \begin{pmatrix} -18 & 12 \\ 16 & -14 \end{pmatrix}$

6) $\begin{pmatrix} 9 \\ -1 \end{pmatrix}$

7) $p = 5, q = -1$

8) (a) $\begin{pmatrix} 3 & 1 \\ 2 & 2 \end{pmatrix}$ (b) $\begin{pmatrix} 1 & 3 \\ 2 & 3 \end{pmatrix}$ (c) $\begin{pmatrix} -1 & 2 \\ 1 & -1 \end{pmatrix}$

9) (a) (i) $\begin{pmatrix} 7 & 3 \\ 3 & 4 \end{pmatrix}$ (ii) $\begin{pmatrix} 1 & -1 \\ 4 & 12 \end{pmatrix}$ (iii) $\begin{pmatrix} 13 & 6 \\ 12 & 4 \end{pmatrix}$

   (b) (i) $\begin{pmatrix} 6 & 4 & 2 \\ 3 & 6 & 1 \end{pmatrix}$ (ii) $\begin{pmatrix} 150 \\ 120 \\ 375 \end{pmatrix}$ (iii) $\begin{pmatrix} 2130 \\ 1545 \end{pmatrix}$

   (iv) the number of passengers who travel by eastern Airlines and western Airlines

10) (a) Aston Villa $\begin{pmatrix} 12 \\ 8 \\ 15 \\ 12 \\ 8 \end{pmatrix}$
        Birmingham
        Derby
        Stoke
        Wolverhampton

   (b) $AB = \begin{pmatrix} -7 & 11 \\ 2 & -6 \end{pmatrix}$ $BA = \begin{pmatrix} -9 & -1 \\ -16 & -4 \end{pmatrix}$

   (c) $x = 4, y = -1$

11) (a) $x = 1, y = 2$ (b) $x = 3, y = 4$
    (c) $x = 2, y = 1$

Self-test 40

1) **a**   2) **c**   3) **a**   4) **c**   5) **a**
6) **d**   7) **b**   8) **c**

ANSWERS TO CHAPTER 41

Exercise 181

1) A$'$ (4, 7), B$'$ (8, 7), C$'$ (8, 5), D$'$ (4, 5)
2) $(-3, -2)$
3) A$'$ (2, 3), B$'$ (4, 3), C$'$ (2, 7)
4) A$'$ $(-3, -1)$, B$'$ (2, -1), C$'$ (1, 1), D$'$ $(-2, 1)$

Exercise 182

1) $\triangle$PQR   2) Yes   3) 3   4) 4
5) (a) (3, 4)   (b) $(-3, -4)$ (c) $(1, -4)$
   (d) (3, 2)   (e) $(-4, 3)$
6) (a) A$'$ (2, -1), B$'$ (7, -1), C$'$ (6, -3), D$'$ (3, -3)
   (b) A$'$ $(-1, 1)$, B$'$ $(-7, 1)$, C$'$ $(-6, 3)$, D$'$ $(-3, 3)$
   (c) A$'$ (1, 2), B$'$ (1, 7), C$'$ (3, 6), D$'$ (3, 3)
7) (b) A$'$ (3, -2), B$'$ (5, -2), C$'$ (3, -6)
   (c) A$'$ $(-3, 2)$, B$'$ $(-5, 2)$, C$'$ $(-3, 6)$

Exercise 183

1) $(-3, 2)$

2) A′ $(3.73, -2.46)$, B′ $(4.73, -4.20)$, C′ $(5.60, -3.70)$

3) A′ $(3, 6)$, B′ $(2, 8)$, C′ $(1, 7)$ 4) $(6, 0)$; 90° clockwise

5) Square 4, 4; Rhombus 2, 2; Isosceles trapezium 1, 1;
Equilateral triangles 3, 3; Isosceles triangle 1, 1; Regular
hexagon 3, 6

6)

	(a)	(b)	(c)	(d)	(e)	(f)	(g)	(h)	(i)
Axes of symmetry	–	2	–	–	–	–	4	4	1
Order of rotational symmetry	1	2	1	1	1	1	4	4	1

7) 0, 0, 0, 2, 0, 2, 0, 0, 2

Exercise 184

1) A circle centre 0 of radius 15 cm 2) 45 cm 3) $\frac{1}{3}$, 3

4) A′ $(2, 4)$, B′ $(6, 8)$, C′ $(4, 12)$ 5) 2: 1; $(-3, -4)$

Exercise 185

1) A′ $(1, 2)$, B′ $(3, 10)$, C′ $(2, 3)$

2) $(2, 0)$, $(7, 2)$

3) $(0, 1)$, $(1, 2)$

4) A′ $(10, 3)$, B′ $(12, 3)$, C′ $(18, 5)$, D′ $(16, 5)$

5) A′ $(3, -5)$, B′ $(4, -7)$

6) $x = 2$

Self-test 41

1) **a** 2) **b** 3) **d** 4) **d** 5) **a**

6) **c** 7) **d** 8) **a** 9) **b**

ANSWERS TO CHAPTER 42

Exercise 187

1) 7.0 at 16° to N 2) 19.2 at 51° to N

3) 11.9 at 31° to N 4) 7.0 at 12° to N

5) 17.2 at 58° to N

Exercise 188

1) (a) **b** (b) $-$**a** (c) **a** + **b**

2) (a) 2**a** (b) -3**a**

3) (a) **a** + **b** (b) $-\frac{1}{2}$(**a** + **b**) (c) $\frac{1}{2}$(**b** − **a**)

4) (a) **c** (b) -2**c** (c) $-$**a** + **c** or $-$(**b** + **c**)

5) (a) **a** − **b** (b) **b** − **a** (c) $-$**a**

(d) 2**a** (e) $-$**b** (f) 2**b**

6) (a) **a** + **b** (b) 2**b** (c) **b** − **a**

7) (a) $-$(**a** + **b** + **c**) (b) 2**a** (c) 3**a** + **b** + **c**

8) (a) $-$**a** (b) $-$**b** (c) **c**

(d) 2**b** or **a** + **b** + **c** (e) 2**a** + **b** (f) 2**c** or **b** + **c** − **a**

Exercise 189

1) 7.81 at 33.7° to 4 vector 2) 12.2 at 21.6° to 6 vector

3) 20.0 at 36.9° to 16 vector 4) 7.85 at 73.2° to 5 vector

5) 20.7 at 18.1° to 12 vector

ANSWERS TO CHAPTER 43

Exercise 191

1) 340 km/h; 277° 2) 500 km/h; 095°

3) 400 km/h; 157° 4) 400 km/h; 308°

5) 270 km/h; 035° 6) 50 km/h; 305°

7) 110 km/h; 090° 8) 150 km/h; 286°

9) 155 km/h; 228° 10) 90 km/h; 024°

11) 250 km/h; 081° 12) 410 km/h; 146°

13) 360 km/h; 202° 14) 295 km/h; 300°

15) 240 km/h; 000°

Exercise 192

1) Upstream at 60° 2) 113° 25′

3) 14 km/h; 86.8° 4) (a) 23.6° (b) 35 m

5) (a) 123° 30′ (b) 048°

ANSWERS TO CHAPTER 44

Exercise 193

1) (a) $\sqrt{10} = 3.16$; 18.4° (b) $\sqrt{74} = 8.06$; 54.5°

(c) $\sqrt{73} = 8.54$; 69.5°

2) $R = \begin{pmatrix} 4 \\ 6 \end{pmatrix}$; 7.21 at 56.3°

3) $R = \begin{pmatrix} 6 \\ 8 \end{pmatrix}$; 10 at 53.1°

4) $M = \begin{pmatrix} 5 \\ 2 \end{pmatrix}$; 5.39 at 21.6°

Exercise 194

1) (a) $\begin{array}{cccc} A' & B' & C' & D' \end{array}$ $\begin{pmatrix} 0 & 2 & 2 & 0 \\ -1 & -1 & -3 & -3 \end{pmatrix}$

(b) $\begin{array}{cccc} A' & B' & C' & D' \end{array}$ $\begin{pmatrix} 0 & -2 & -2 & 0 \\ 1 & 1 & 3 & 3 \end{pmatrix}$

(c) $\begin{array}{cccc} A' & B' & C' & D' \end{array}$ $\begin{pmatrix} -1 & -1 & -3 & -3 \\ 0 & -2 & -2 & 0 \end{pmatrix}$

(d) $\begin{array}{cccc} A' & B' & C' & D' \end{array}$ $\begin{pmatrix} 1 & 1 & 3 & 3 \\ 0 & 2 & 2 & 0 \end{pmatrix}$

(e) $\begin{array}{cccc} A' & B' & C' & D' \end{array}$ $\begin{pmatrix} 1 & 3 & 3 & 1 \\ 4 & 4 & 6 & 6 \end{pmatrix}$

2) $\begin{array}{ccc} A & B & C \end{array}$ $\begin{pmatrix} 8 & 6 & 7 \\ 1 & -1 & 0 \end{pmatrix}$

3) (a) $(-1, 7)$ (b) $(0, 5)$ (c) $(-6, 1)$

(d) $(-4, 9)$ (e) $(5, 4)$

4) $\begin{array}{ccc} A' & B' & C' \end{array}$ $\begin{pmatrix} -1 & 2 & 2 \\ -6 & -6 & -3 \end{pmatrix}$

5) (a) $\begin{array}{ccccc} A' & B' & C' & D' & E' \end{array}$ $\begin{pmatrix} 0 & 2 & 3 & 1 & -1 \\ -4 & -2 & 0 & 2 & 3 \end{pmatrix}$

(b) $\begin{array}{ccccc} A' & B' & C' & D' & E' \end{array}$
$$\begin{pmatrix} 1 & 3 & 4 & 2 & 0 \\ 2 & 0 & -2 & -4 & -5 \end{pmatrix}$$

(c) $\begin{array}{ccccc} A' & B' & C' & D' & E' \end{array}$
$$\begin{pmatrix} -1 & -3 & -4 & -2 & 0 \\ -2 & 0 & 2 & 4 & 5 \end{pmatrix}$$

(d) $\begin{array}{ccccc} A' & B' & C' & D' & E' \end{array}$
$$\begin{pmatrix} 2 & 0 & -2 & -4 & -5 \\ -1 & -3 & -4 & -2 & 0 \end{pmatrix}$$

(e) $\begin{array}{ccccc} A' & B' & C' & D' & E' \end{array}$
$$\begin{pmatrix} -2 & 0 & 2 & 4 & 5 \\ 1 & 3 & 4 & 2 & 0 \end{pmatrix}$$

6) $\begin{array}{cccc} A' & B' & C' & D' \end{array}$
$$\begin{pmatrix} -0.889 & -0.370 & 0.027 & 2.571 \\ 2.052 & 4.226 & 7.819 & 3.064 \end{pmatrix}$$

7) $\begin{array}{cccc} W' & X' & Y' & Z' \end{array}$
$$\begin{pmatrix} -0.520 & 1.012 & -0.273 & -1.805 \\ 2.175 & 3.460 & 4.992 & 3.707 \end{pmatrix}$$

8) $\begin{array}{ccc} A' & B' & C' \end{array}$
$$\begin{pmatrix} -1 & -3 & -2 \\ 6 & 8 & 10 \end{pmatrix}$$

9) (a) $\begin{pmatrix} 9 & 4 \\ 18 & 8 \end{pmatrix}$ (b) $(-31, -62)$

10) (a) $\begin{pmatrix} 1 & 4 \\ 0 & -1 \end{pmatrix}$

(b) $\begin{array}{ccc} A' & B' & C' \end{array}$
$$\begin{pmatrix} 50 & 80 & 95 \\ -10 & -15 & -20 \end{pmatrix}$$

11) $(-6.84, 0.68)$

12) $(-2, -3), (-2, -1), (-4, -1), (-4, -3)$

13) (a) $(6, 2)$ (b) $(6, 2)$ (c) $(4, -1)$
     (d) $(-1, -1)$ (e) $(1, 2)$ (f) $(9, 4)$ (g) $(7, 1)$

14) A $(3, 2)$; B $(5, 2)$; C $(4, 3)$

Exercise 195

2) (a) $(0, 0)$ (b) $(4, 2)$ (c) $(0, 0)$

3) $(-\frac{3}{2}, -\frac{5}{2})$

4) (a) $\begin{pmatrix} 0 & 2 & 8 & 6 \\ 0 & 0 & 2 & 2 \end{pmatrix}$ (b) $\begin{pmatrix} -2 & 1 & 7 & 4 \\ 0 & 0 & 2 & 2 \end{pmatrix}$

    (c) $\begin{pmatrix} 11 & 14 & 19 & 16 \\ 2 & 2 & 4 & 4 \end{pmatrix}$ (d) $\begin{pmatrix} 5 & 9 & 15 & 12 \\ 1 & 1 & 3 & 3 \end{pmatrix}$

5) (a) $\begin{pmatrix} 4 & 4 & 8 & 8 \\ 4 & 0 & 0 & 4 \end{pmatrix}$ (b) $\begin{pmatrix} -6 & -6 & -12 & -12 \\ 4 & 0 & 0 & 4 \end{pmatrix}$

    (c) $\begin{pmatrix} 2 & 2 & 4 & 4 \\ 6 & 0 & 0 & 6 \end{pmatrix}$ (d) $\begin{pmatrix} 2 & 2 & 4 & 4 \\ -2 & 0 & 0 & -2 \end{pmatrix}$

6) (a) $\begin{pmatrix} 0 & 4 & 4 & 0 \\ 0 & 0 & 3 & 3 \end{pmatrix}$ (b) $\begin{pmatrix} 0 & -1 & -1 & 0 \\ 0 & 0 & 2 & 2 \end{pmatrix}$

    (c) $\begin{pmatrix} 0 & 1 & 1 & 0 \\ 0 & 0 & 4 & 4 \end{pmatrix}$ (d) $\begin{pmatrix} 0 & 3 & 3 & 0 \\ 0 & 0 & -1\frac{1}{2} & -1\frac{1}{2} \end{pmatrix}$

Self-test 44

1) **d**   2) **d**   3) **c**   4) **c**   5) **d**
6) **a**   7) **b**   8) **c**

ANSWERS TO EXAMINATION TYPE QUESTIONS 6

1) (a) (i) P   (ii) Q$'$
    (b) (i) $\{x: x \text{ is a multiple of } 10\}$
       (ii) $\{x: x \text{ is a multiple of } 70\}$; $80 \leqslant N \leqslant 89$

2) (a) An anticlockwise rotation of $45°$ about O.
      Scale factor $= \sqrt{2}$.
    (b) 17 cm^2

3) (a) Line through A perpendicular to AB
    (b) A circle with diameter AB
    (c) Perpendicular bisector of AB

4) $024° - 027°$; $165 \text{ km/h} - 167 \text{ km/h}$; $277° - 279°$

5) (a) (i) $(2, 6)$ (ii) $(13, 5)$ (iii) $(\frac{3}{2}, -\frac{9}{2})$
    (b) (i) -4 (ii) -1; 3

6) 1548.8 km; $28° \, 34' \text{ W}$

7) (a) 1 km (b) $3\sqrt{2}$

8) (a) $\begin{pmatrix} 4 \\ 2 \end{pmatrix}$

    (b) (i) $-\mathbf{p}$ (ii) $\frac{1}{2}(\mathbf{r} - \mathbf{p})$; $67°$

ANSWERS TO CHAPTER 45

Exercise 196

1) $x = 6, y = 7$
2) Private motoring 15.7%; rail 39.3%; other 45%
3) Unskilled workers 52.9%; craftsmen 29.4%; draughtsmen 5.9%; clerical staff 11.8%
8) Clothing $81°$, furniture $108°$, stationery $27°$, sports equipment $54°$, household goods $90°$

Exercise 197

5) (a) 15.015 and 14.985 mm (b) 0.03 mm
    (c) $14.96 - 14.98 \text{ mm}$
6) Discrete b, d, g

Exercise 198

1) $28   2) 175 cm 3) $41.20
4) 199.92 mm 5) 163.1 cm 6) 6.01375 mm
7) 50.6 cents 8) 46.3 9) 5
10) $4\frac{1}{2}$ 11) 57

12) (a)

$81 - 85$	$86 - 90$	$91 - 95$	$96 - 100$	$101 - 105$
4	12	9	7	4

(b)

Less than	80.5	85.5	90.5	95.5	100.5	105.5
Cum. freq.	0	4	16	25	32	36

(c) 13

13) (a)

Less than	9.5	19.5	29.5	39.5	49.5	59.5
Cum. freq.	5	38	120	268	538	753

	69.5	79.5	89.5	99.5
	840	884	896	900

(c) (i) 20   (ii) 100
(d) $Q_1 = 37$, $Q_2 = 46$, $Q_3 = 57$

14)

Less than	5.965	5.995	6.025	6.055	6.085
Cum. freq.	8	45	135	187	200

  (a) 22   (b) 126   (c) 4

16) (b) 138, 41, 135

17) (a) (i) 100 hours   (ii) 701 – 800 hours

  (b)

Less than	400.5	500.5	600.5	700.5	800.5
Cum. freq.	7	30	58	94	181

Less than	900.5	1000.5	1100.5	1200.5
Cum. freq.	159	181	197	200

  (c) 718 hours   (d) 900 hours and 570 hours

18) 5   19) no mode   20) 3, 5, 8   21) 4

22) 199.95 mm   23) 163 cm

Exercise 199

1) \$42.80   2) 29.76 cm

3) \$2850 and \$4050; \$600   4) 2.16

5) 3.2; 0.899   6) 19.4; 0.109 cm

7) 47.3; 18.0   8) 34.7; 21.6 years

11) 0.904   12) 1.2

13) 5100   14) 1280 kg

17) 40   18) 160

Self-test 45

1) b   2) a   3) d   4) b   5) b

6) b   7) c   8) c   9) c   10) b

11) b   12) b   13) d   14) c

ANSWERS TO CHAPTER 46

Exercise 200

1) (a) $\frac{1}{6}$ (b) $\frac{1}{2}$ (c) $\frac{1}{3}$ (d) $\frac{1}{2}$

2) (a) $\frac{1}{5}$ (b) $\frac{1}{2}$ (c) $\frac{33}{40}$ (d) $\frac{3}{40}$

3) (a) $\frac{1}{52}$ (b) $\frac{1}{13}$ (c) $\frac{4}{13}$ (d) $\frac{1}{26}$

4) (a) $\frac{1}{9}$ (b) $\frac{2}{9}$ (c) $\frac{1}{3}$

5) (a) $\frac{1}{5}$ (b) $\frac{9}{20}$ (c) $\frac{13}{20}$

6) (a) $\frac{1}{6}$ (b) $\frac{5}{18}$ (c) $\frac{5}{18}$

7) $\frac{1}{10}$

8) (a) 0.15   (b) 0.52

9) (a) $\frac{34}{150}$ (b) $\frac{23}{150}$ (c) $\frac{43}{150}$

10) (a) $\frac{1}{5}$ (b) $\frac{4}{25}$ (c) $\frac{1}{5}$

Exercise 201

1) 120   2) (a) 20   (b) 2520   (c) 11 880

3) 70   4) 6720   5) 210   6) 2520

7) 6720   8) 332 640   9) 126

10) (a) 10   (b) 237 336   11) 15   12) 78

13) 462   14) 4704   15) $\frac{10}{21}$ 16) $\frac{1}{60}$

17) 70   18) (a) $\frac{1}{54\,145}$ (b) $\frac{1}{108\,290}$

19) (a) $\frac{22}{425}$ (b) $\frac{1}{425}$

20) (a) $\frac{90}{1001}$ (b) $\frac{18}{143}$ (c) $\frac{5}{1001}$

Exercise 202

1) $\frac{5}{52}$ 2) (a) $\frac{1}{12}$ (b) $\frac{1}{4}$

3) (a) $\frac{4}{25}$ (b) $\frac{9}{25}$ (c) $\frac{12}{25}$

4) (a) $\frac{3}{10}$ (b) $\frac{1}{10}$ (c) $\frac{3}{10}$ (d) $\frac{3}{5}$

5) $\frac{1}{15}$ 6) $\frac{4}{9}$

7) (a) $\frac{4}{35}$ (b) $\frac{4}{35}$ (c) $\frac{6}{35}$ (d) $\frac{18}{35}$

10) (a) 0.096   (b) 0.064   (c) 0.24   11) $\frac{19}{20}$

12) $\frac{95}{96}$

13) (a) $\frac{7}{10}$ (b) $\frac{5}{6}$

14) $\frac{1}{2}$ 15) (b) $\frac{1}{2}$ (c) $\frac{3}{10}$ (d) $\frac{1}{2}$

15) (b) $\frac{1}{2}$ (c) $\frac{3}{10}$ (d) $\frac{1}{2}$ 16) $\frac{1}{3}$

17) $\frac{1}{5525}$ 18) $\frac{1}{35\,152}$

Self-test 46

1) b   2) a   3) c   4) c   5) b

6) b   7) d   8) b

ANSWERS TO EXAMINATION TYPE QUESTIONS 7

1) (a) 179   (b) 190.5   (c) 22

2) 80%; 20%

3) Maths. His score in English is 3 points below class average. This is $\frac{3}{8} = 0.375$ standard deviation.
His score in maths is 2 points below class average. This is $\frac{2}{7.6} = 0.263$ standard deviation.

4) (a) 0.24   (b) $\frac{1}{7}$

5) (a) $\frac{1}{6}$ (b) $\frac{1}{4}$ (c) $\frac{1}{12}$

6) (a) $\frac{5}{6}$ (b) $\frac{1}{36}$ (c) $\frac{5}{18}$

7) 3.22; 3.67

8) (a) $\frac{2}{9}$ (b) $\frac{7}{9}$

9) (a) 9   (b) $\frac{9}{16}$ (c) 3 or -2

ANSWERS TO PAPER 01 – SPECIMEN TEST 2

1. (a) (i) 125.048   (ii) 125.0   (iii) 1.250476×10^2
  (b) 120   (c) \$1230.

2. (a) $16/x^4$
  (b) (i) $2(3x + 7)(x - 2)$ (ii) $x(x - 2)$
  (c) $2(3x + 7)/x$
  (d) $fv/(v - f)$

3. (a) (ii) 32   (b) 4.4

4. (a) (i) $\frac{4}{3}$ (ii) 7
  (b) (i) 0   (ii) 0
  (c) (i) H(6, 0)   (ii) (0, 4)   (iii) $-\frac{2}{3}$.

5. (i) 102π (ii) 3.7

6. (a) 30   (b) (i) 85.4   (ii) 72.4

7. (a) (i) $\binom{3}{3}$ (ii)$\binom{3}{4}$
  (b) (ii) $k = 4$.

8. (a) (i) \$35   (ii) \$25   (iii) \$26.70
  (b) (i) 36   (ii) $\frac{1}{36}$ (iii) $\frac{1}{4}$

9. (a) $x = 9, y = 6$ and $x = -17, y = -20$.
  (b) (i) $-1, 1.3$ (ii) $x = 0.75$

10. (a) (i) $x \geq 1, y \geq 1, x + y \leq 10$.   (ii) $2x + y \leq 11$.
  (b) (i) $200x + 150y$ (ii) 1 sheep and 9 goats   \$1550.

11. (a) (i) $\angle$TOQ $= 144°$, $\angle$RTQ $= 36°$
  (b) (i) 6   (ii) 2 $\frac{2}{3}$.

12. (a) (i) $\frac{3}{4}$ (ii) $\frac{4}{3}$
  (b) (i) $60°$ (ii) $38°$ (iii) 13.9 cm   (iv) $052.1°$

13. (a) 4   (b) 5; $\tan\theta = \frac{4}{3}$, where θ is the angle formed by the vector and $0x$.
  (c) (i) $\overrightarrow{PQ} = \mathbf{a} - \mathbf{b}$, $\overrightarrow{SR} = \mathbf{a} - \mathbf{b}$ (ii) $\overrightarrow{PQ} = \overrightarrow{SR}$
  (d) (i) $2\mathbf{b} - 3\mathbf{a}$ (ii) $\frac{1}{2}\mathbf{b} - \frac{3}{4}\mathbf{a}$ (iii) $9/4\mathbf{a} - \frac{1}{2}\mathbf{b}$

14. (a) (i) $x = 2$ (ii) (6, 2)
  (b) (i) (8, -21)   (ii) $\begin{pmatrix} -5 & -3 \\ 2 & 1 \end{pmatrix}$ (iii) $(-33, 12)$.

ANSWERS TO PAPER 02 – SPECIMEN TEST 2

1. (a) -104 (b) $6x^2 - 7xy - 3y^2$ (c) $1/(x + 3)$.

2. (a) 2200   (b) 10%

Answers

3. (a) 8   (b) (i) 10   (ii) 4
4. (a) 9.95   (b) (i) 7.21   (ii) $210°$ (iii) 6.18
5. (ii) 4.7 cm
6. (b) (i) $k = 4$ (ii) $(-1, 3)$
   (iii) $p = 4, q = 5$ (iv) $r = 7, s = 9$
7. (a) $p = 2, q = 1, r = 4$
   (b) H is $(3, 0)$, K is $(0, 4)$ (c) 13
8. (ii) Mode = 4;   (iii) 59/60
9. (a) (i) 4; 2; 1; $\frac{1}{2}$; $\frac{1}{4}$.   (iii) 2.6   (b) 54 cm
10. (a) $x = 2, y = -5; x = 6, y = 3$ (b) 1/5, 5/3

11. (a) (i) 3185 km   (ii) 1826.8 km   (iii) $16.7°$
    (b) (i) $2x$ (ii) $4x$ (iii) 18
12. (a) (i) 9 cm   (ii) $106.2°$ (b) 6.46 cm
13. (a) (i) $-2\mathbf{u} + 4\mathbf{v}$ (ii) $-4\mathbf{v} + 4\mathbf{u}$ (iii) $4\mathbf{v} - 2\mathbf{u}$
    (b) (i) $\begin{pmatrix} 5 \\ -12 \end{pmatrix}$ (ii) $\begin{pmatrix} 9 \\ -6 \end{pmatrix}$
14. (a) (i) $(-12, -8)$ (ii) $(-12, 8)$
    (b) (i) $(5, -3)$ (ii) $\begin{pmatrix} -3 & -2 \\ 2 & 1 \end{pmatrix}$ (iii) $(-5, 4)$.

Index

Acceleration 197
Acute angle 222
Acute-angled triangle 226
Addition of algebraic terms 72
   of binary numbers 336
   of currency 23
   of decimals 14
   of directed numbers 66
   of fractions 8
   of matrices 341
   of vectors 337, 363
   of whole numbers 1
Addition law of probability 423
Additive identity 2
Air speed 370
Algebra, basic 71
Algebraic fractions 82
Analysis of statistical data 411
Angles and straight lines 219
   between a line and a plane 305
   between two planes 305
   in circles 253
   of depression 287
   of elevation 286
   in triangles 227
Angular measurement 219
Anti-logarithms 116
Area of plane figures 128
   of parallelogram 248
   of segment of a circle 302
   of trapezium 249
   of triangle 249, 301
   under a curve 193
   units of 127
Arithmetic mean 400
   operations 1
Associative law for sets 324
   for addition and multiplication 1
Average 36
   speed 37, 177
   statistical 399
Axes of reference 153

Bank loans 44
Bar chart 391
Base of a number system 335
Basic algebra 71
Bearings 288
Bicimals 335

Binary systems 335
Binomial expression 78
Brackets, use of 74

Cancelling with fractions 10
Capacity 132
Cartesian product 184
Characteristic of logarithm 116
Checks for calculations 18
Chord of a circle 253
Chronological bar chart 392
Circle 253
   mensuration of 128
   sector of 253
   segment of 253
   of latitude 311
Circumference of a circle 128, 253
Class boundaries 395
   intervals 395
Clock 139
Cluster sampling 413
Closure 2
Collections for sets 318
Column matrix 341
Combinations 421
Commission 40
Commutative law 1
Complementary angles 222
Complement of a set 321, 330
Completing the square 107
Composite function 183
Compound interest 49
Cone, frustum of 134
   volume of 134
Congruence 362
Congruent triangles 230
Construction of simple equations 92
Constructions, geometric 262
Continuous variables 396
Conversion from binary to decimal 339
   from one base to another 339
Coordinate geometry 165
Coordinates, rectangular 153, 165
Correspondence of sets 328
Cosine curve 296
   of an angle 279
   rule 300
Counting numbers 319
Course 370

Cumulative frequency distribution	402
Currency	23
Current, velocity of	373
Cylinder, volume of	134
Decimal places	15
point	12
system	14
to fraction conversion	18
of a degree	277
Deduction and truth	329
Degrees in angular measurement	220
Denominator of a fraction	5
Dependent events	425
Depression, angle of	287
Denary system	335
Depreciation	50
Diagonal matrix	341
Diagonalising a matrix	343
Difference	1
Directed numbers	66
Direct proportion	27
Direct variation	179
Discrete distributions	396
variables	396
Discount	32
Disjoint sets	322
Dispersion, measures of	408
Distance-time graphs	195
Distributive law	1
for vectors	364
Division by zero	1
of algebraic terms	72
of binary numbers	337
of currency	21
of decimal numbers	16
of directed numbers	68
of fractions	11
of whole numbers	1
Domain	173
Double transformations	378
Drift	370
Earth as a sphere	310
Element of a set	317
Electricity bills	45
Elevation, angle of	286
Enlargement	381
Equal vectors	362
Equality of matrices	342
of sets	320
Equation from formula	95
logarithmic	119
of a straight line	166
quadratic	106
simple	88
simultaneous	101, 343

Equator	310
Equilateral triangle	226
Equi-probable events	417
Equivalence of sets	328
Errors in measurement	129
Evaluating formulae	95
Experimental data on graphs	168
Experimental probability	419
Factorising, algebraic	77
Factors of numbers	3
Favourable outcomes	418
Finite sets	317
Foreign exchange	25
Formulae	95
Fractional indices	114
Fractions, algebraic	82
arithmetic	6
to decimal conversion	19
Frequency curves	397
distributions	394
Frustum of cone	134
Functions	173
Geometric constructions	262
Glide reflection	357
Graphical solution of equations	158
Graphs, plotting of	153
of linear equations	166
of linear inequalities	206
Gradient of curve	187
Great Circle	310
Groundspeed	370
Grouped distributions	394
Hexagon	247
Highest common factor	3, 77
Hire purchase	43
Histogram	396
Horizontal bar chart	392
Imaginary numbers	69
Improper fractions	6
Income tax	42
Independent events	425
Indices, laws of	114
Inequalities	204
Inequations	88, 205
Infinite sets	318
Integers	69, 319
Interest, compound	49
simple	47
Intersecting graphs	159
loci	268
Intersection of sets	322
Irrational numbers	68, 317

Inverse function 181
  proportion 28
  of a matrix 343
  variation 180
  vectors 362
  transformation 380
Investment 53
Isometrics 378
Isometrics projection 146
Isosceles triangle 229

J-shaped frequency curve 398

Latitude 310
Laws of indices 114
Length of a line 165
Length, unit of 125
Linear equations 166
  programming 208
Line symmetry 351
Litre 132
Loci 268
Logarithms 115
Logarithmic equations 119
Logical chains and sets 329
Longitude 310
Loss 31
Lowest common denominator 8
Lowest common multiple 3, 8, 84
Lowest terms of a fraction 5

Making algebraic expressions 91
Mantissa 116
Mapping 173
Mass, unit of 125
Matrices 342
Matrix notation 342
Maximum and minimum 192
Mean, arithmetic 400
Measures of dispersion 408
Median 402
Membership of a set 318
Mensuration 125
Meridian 310
Metric system 125
Mid-point of a line 166
Mixed numbers 6
Mode 403
Modulus of a vector 375
Multiples 3
Multiplication, inverse 10
Multiplication law of probability 425
Multiplication of algebraic terms 72
  binary numbers 337
  currency 21
  decimals 13
  directed numbers 68

fractions 10
  matrices 342
  vectors by a scalar 364
  whole numbers 1
Multiplicative identity 2
Multiplicative property of zero 2
Mutually exclusive events 423

Natural growth, law of 177
Natural numbers 69, 319
Negative indices 114
  numbers 66
Nets of solids 137
Non-mutually exclusive events 424
Normal curve 398, 411
Notation for a triangle 228, 276, 297
Null matrix 341
Null set 317
Number in standard form 115
Number of elements in a set 325
  of subsets 319
Number scales 336
Numerator of fraction 5

Oblique projection 148
Obtuse angle 222
Obtuse-angled triangle 226
Octagon 247
Operations with bicimals 337
  fractions 11
  numbers 1, 75
Orientation and reflection 350
Orthographic projection 142
Overtime 39

Parabola 157
Parallelogram 244
  area of 128, 248
  of vectors 366
Parallel lines 170
Payment by the hour 39
Pentagon 247
Percentage change 30
Percentages 30
Permutations 420
Perpendicular lines 170
Pie chart 392
Plane, the 305
Plans of houses and buildings 150
Positive numbers 67
Polygons 244
Powers of quantities 72
  of numbers 3
Prime factors 3
  numbers 3
Probability 417
  scale 418
  tree 426

Product	1
Product of two binomial expressions	78
Profit	31
Proper fractions	6
subsets	319
Proportional parts	26
Pyramid, mensuration of	134
Pythagoras' theorem	228
Quadratic equations	106
expressions	79, 192
formula	108
functions, graphs of	156
inequations	205
Quadrilaterals	244
Quartile deviation	409
Quartiles	405
Quotient	1
Radian measure	220
Random numbers	412
Range	173, 408
Range of a computation	18
Rates	41
Ratio	27
Rates of change	189
Rational numbers	69, 319
Raw data	394
Ready reckoners	21
Real numbers	69, 319
Reciprocal	11
Reciprocal function	177
Reciprocal of numbers	59
Rectangle	244
area of	128
Rectangular coordinates	165
Recurring decimals	18
Reductions	381
Reflection	376, 348
Reflex angle	222
Relations	173
Resultant vectors	361
Rhombus	244
Right angle	222
Right-angled triangle	226
Rotational symmetry	354
transformation	352
Rough checks for calculations	17
Row matrix	341
Salaries	41
Sales tax	42
Sampling	412
Scalene triangle	226
Scales on graphs	153
Secant of a circle	257
Sector of a circle	128, 253
Segment of a circle	253
Semi-interquartile	408
Sequence of arithmetic operations	2
Sequence of numbers	4, 70
Sets	317
and logical chains	329
Set builder notation	320
Shares	53
Shearing transformation	358, 384
Short cuts in calculations	21
SI units	126
Significant figures	17
Similarities	381
Similar triangles	233
Simple equations	88
graphs of	155
Simple interest	47
Simultaneous equations	101, 343
graphs of	160
Sine curve	296
rule	298
Sine of an angle	276
Size transformation	355
Skewed distributions	412
frequency curves	397
Small circle	310
Solid trigonometry	305
Solution of triangles	298
Speed, average	195
Sphere, mensuration of	134
Square	244
Square matrix	341
Squares of numbers	56
trigonometrical ratios	284
Square roots of numbers	56
Standard deviation	409
Standard form of numbers	115
Standard loci	268
notation for a triangle	209, 297
Statistics	391
Stock	54
Straight line, equation of	166
Stretch	383
Substitution in formulae	71
Subsets	318, 330
Subtraction of binary numbers	337
of decimals	13
of directed numbers	67
of fractions	9
of matrices	341
of vectors	363
of whole numbers	1
Sum	1
Sum of two vectors	363
Supplementary angles	222
Symbols, use of	71
Symmetric figures	351

Tangent curve	296
of an angle	280
properties of a circle	256
to a circle	256
Tetrahedron	133
Total probability	418
Track	370
Transformational geometry	347
Transformations and matrices	375
Translation	347
Transposition of formulae	96
matrices	342
Trapezium	245
area of	249
mensuration of	128
Trapezoidal rule	194
Triangle, area of	128, 301
law of vectors	361
of velocities	371
Trigonometrical ratios	293
Turning points	190
Types of fractions	6
matrices	341
numbers	69
sets	317
triangles	226

Union of sets	322
Unit matrix	341
Units of area	127
capacity	132
volume	132
Universal set	320
U-shaped frequency curve	398
Variation	179
Vectors	361
represented as matrices	375
Velocity-time graphs	197
Velocity vectors	370
Venn diagrams	321
Vertical bar chart	391
Volume, units of	132
Wages	35
Waterspeed	373
Whole numbers, definition of	69
Width of class interval	395
Wind speed	370
Zero index	114